PHILOSOPHICAL QUESTIONS

PHILOSOPHICAL QUESTIONS

READINGS AND INTERACTIVE GUIDES

James Fieser

University of Tennessee at Martin

Norman Lillegard

University of Tennessee at Martin

New York • Oxford
OXFORD UNIVERSITY PRESS
2005

Oxford University Press

Oxford   New York
Auckland   Bangkok   Buenos Aires   Cape Town   Chennai
Dar es Salaam   Delhi   Hong Kong   Istanbul   Karachi   Kolkata
Kuala Lumpur   Madrid   Melbourne   Mexico City   Mumbai
Nairobi   São Paulo   Shanghai   Taipei   Tokyo   Toronto

Published by Oxford University Press, Inc.
198 Madison Avenue, New York, New York 10016
www.oup.com

Library of Congress Cataloging-in-Publication Data

Philosophical questions : readings and interactive guides / edited by James Fieser, Norman Lillegard.
    p. cm.
  Includes bibliographical references and index.
  ISBN 0-19-513983-6 (alk. paper)
   1. Philosophy--Introductions.   I. Fieser, James.   II. Lillegard, Norman, 1938-

  BD21.P4675 2004
  100--dc22

                                                                        2004045575

Text design by Cathleen Elliott

Printing number: 9 8 7 6 5 4 3 2 1

Printed in the United States of America
on acid-free paper

CONTENTS

3 HUMAN NATURE AND THE SELF   116

4 SOULS, MINDS, BODIES, AND MACHINES   222

6 · ETHICS   422

PREFACE FOR
THE INSTRUCTOR

Primary philosophical writings are inherently difficult, and philosophy instructors commonly experience problems with introductory courses that use these as the main required reading. Many students will not read the material at all, and even those who do will typically not gain much from their efforts. So, few students come to class with the kind of focused questions that can facilitate good discussions. The interactive approach of this book addresses these problems and offers a way of engaging readers in primary philosophical sources. It has two distinctive features. First, throughout this book, questions are interspersed which prompt the reader to reflect on the material presented. Second, the material itself—selected from the writings of influential philosophers, past and present—is broken into manageable segments, and commented on by the authors of this book. The text, then, is an interactive dialogue between classic philosophers, the authors, and the reader.

All the primary selections are presented in short and manageable sections with organizational headings and subheadings added. Some of the Greek texts are newly translated or have newly revised translations that appear here for the first time. Other translated material is corrected and adapted for clarity. The writings of Hobbes, Locke, Berkeley, Hume, Reid, and Mill present a special problem because of their dated English. In these texts, spelling and punctuation are modernized, parentheses are introduced when appropriate, longer sentences are divided when possible, and bracketed words are added for clarification. The commentaries provide a gloss on difficult passages, explain archaic or technical terminology, and expand upon allusions to unfamiliar literature and arguments.

Flexibility and variety have been built into this text. Each chapter contains some relatively easy selections, so that an instructor who wants to survey many issues could use only the easier selections and skip the more difficult material. However, some instructors might want to explore certain issues in greater depth. Some of the more difficult selections can be used by instructors who want to pursue particular topics, especially in the philosophy of mind and epistemology. Although the readings in some cases are fairly advanced, they have been interspersed with explanatory material that should, along with the instructor's tutoring, make these selections intelligible to students in introductory courses. There are, moreover, enough selections from Eastern, Anglo-American, and Continental philosophy to enable various emphases.

This text is not designed for students to write answers in the book itself, but, instead, to record their responses on a separate piece of paper or in an essay booklet that can then be evaluated by teachers, secretaries, or student assistants. This is of particular benefit for classes with large enrollments since it adds a systematic written component to a course's requirements. Answers to study questions could also be submitted electronically. The questions were designed with several possibilities in mind. First, instructors might assign all or only some of the questions in the book. Second, some of the questions are designed merely to determine that the material has indeed been read, and with at least minimal comprehension. Third, some of the questions require more than minimal comprehension, and some are intended to provide an impetus to independent philosophical reflection. Some instructors will want to stress these questions and omit others. These questions can also help students to focus in a way that enlivens class discussion. Fourth, questions can be assigned with the specific intention of provoking class discussion. Students can be advised ahead of time that they will be asked to comment on certain questions in class. Fifth, instructors often have difficulty knowing which parts of a text are most challenging. Students can be encouraged to bring up difficulties they are having with any question. As a result, instructors will often find that topics need further explanation which they may have thought obvious or already sufficiently covered. A Companion Website and an Instructor's Manual with Test Questions accompany the book.

Other features of this book are explained for the students in Chapter 1. With the interactive approach of this book, readers will hopefully be encouraged to reflect on their own, to imagine new possibilities, and to challenge assured truths.

PHILOSOPHICAL QUESTIONS

INTRODUCING THE BOOK

A. PHILOSOPHICAL QUESTIONS AND WONDER

Aristotle remarked that philosophy begins with wonder. The world is "wonderful" in more than one way. Why are things as they are? Why is there anything at all? Both children and adults wonder about and question many things. Indeed, children may have more capacity for wonder than do many adults. To the extent that philosophy involves wonder, it is a mistake to think that it is a subject suitable only for adults. It's true that there are no youthful philosophical prodigies comparable to what we sometimes find in math or music. It's also true that there are parts of philosophy that are technical and beyond the ability of children. Nevertheless, adults might learn something from the fresh way in which children raise questions and wonder how certain things might be. We can gain some insights into the sort of thing that philosophy is by recounting some conversations between children and a seasoned philosopher. We will see that many of the problems that have always preoccupied philosophers are problems that can give rise to perplexity in both children and adults and are at the center of much that is important to all people.

The philosopher Gareth Matthews has spent a good deal of time in philosophical discussions with children. In his book *Dialogues with Children* he recounts a conversation with a group of 8- to 11-year-olds about the possibility that plants have feelings. At first sight, that may seem nothing more than "childish," not worthy of the attention of a thoughtful adult. The children are themselves initially reluctant to ascribe feelings to plants. Yet as they reflect further, some wonder if there might not be something to the idea that plants can feel. One child gives examples of what appear to be "sensitivity"—such as Venus flytraps that seem to sense and respond to the presence of flies by closing shut on them. Another child advances the notion that plants might communicate with each other in some way.

The children also wonder whether plants could be happy or unhappy. This then leads to a general question about what sorts of beings could be happy. Could an ant, for example, be happy? Darwin cited with approval a contemporary who seemed to think that ants play and have fun with each other, like puppies or children! Matthews asks "[W]hy is it important, in determining whether something can be happy, to find out if it can talk?" The children felt that language could reveal moods. But perhaps, they suggested, moods could be revealed in other ways. One child said "In a sort of way a plant shows that it is happy by blooming." The children then discussed how gestures also express moods and feelings. It is clear that we sometimes discern someone's mood by noticing gestures or posture. But is there some important difference between the "gestures" of plants—such as blooming, wilting, turning to the sun— and the gestures of humans—slouching, holding one's head, dancing? There seems to be a world of difference. But if plants can feel, perhaps the difference is not so great. Can they feel? Some of the children suggested that plants are more like machines. The Venus flytrap is like a spring that is activated by touch, one child suggests. Another insists that for anything to have feelings it must have a brain, and plants don't have brains. After reflecting on these remarks, Matthews devised a story in which Aunt Gertie attributes happiness to her flowers while they are flourishing and blooming in the sun. The children enjoy the story, but one of them still feels that plants could not feel happy since they lack minds. He does not equate having a mind with having a brain, however, and many philosophers would run to his defense on that point.

This brief review of an hour-long discussion between an adult philosopher and some children exhibits patterns of thought and imagination that are rich and philosophically suggestive. As adults, we might begin to wonder with the children about just how to describe the differences between plants and ourselves or between ourselves and other animals, or even between ourselves and robots or other machines. Surely plants do not have anything we would want to call a brain. But does that show they could not have feelings? Does an insect have feelings? Does a frog? If a frog's brain is mostly removed, could it still have feelings? And, what sorts of feelings would be involved in happiness? The children laughed at the suggestion that happiness is itself some simple feeling, like the feeling of warmth from the stove that heated their meeting room. There is indeed something comical in that suggestion. Aristotle held that happiness is a state of flourishing, of doing ones best, and that is an idea that seems intuitively plausible. But transferring this idea to a plant, as Aunt Gertie did in the story, may seem fanciful to some. It is not just silly, however. We might say that a happy plant is one that is doing well, realizing its full potential as a plant.

The moral of the story is this. Philosophy is something even children can do to the extent that it involves imagination and mental flexibility. It also requires an ability to see connections, to see how one type of philosophical question leads naturally to others. It can be fun, a kind of play, as we see in the conversations with children. At the same time, it involves matters of the utmost importance for all of us, such as the nature of happiness and the nature of the mind or soul.

The discussion we've been looking at focuses on one rather specific issue—the feelings of plants. Philosophy deals with a large range of issues, but they are all driven by the same sense of wonder that the children expressed in their conversation with Matthews. Some of the main questions that contemporary philosophers puzzle over are these: What justifies religious belief? What, if anything, is unique about humans? What is the relation between the human mind and the body? What is knowledge, and under what conditions might we have it? What makes an action right or wrong? What justifies the existence of governments? These are some of the philosophical questions that we will puzzle over in the forthcoming chapters. They are still "wonderful" questions. Anyone who feels no pull from any of them has lost the sense of wonder.

B. FEATURES OF THIS BOOK

The chapters of this book explore six key subject areas of philosophy by interspersing selections from prominent philosophers past and present with introductory comments and study questions. Some features of the book deserve special mentioning.

FIRST REACTIONS AND QUESTIONS TO DISCUSS

Each chapter and section in this book begins with some general questions on the philosophical issues at hand. The purpose of these questions is not to quiz readers on the subject matter. Instead the questions aim to provoke wonder, puzzlement, and discussion on the topic—the kind of puzzling that philosophers themselves have engaged in as they explored and proposed theories on a topic. These are the kind of questions that go beyond the philosophy classrooms and the selections from the philosophers themselves. They are, in fact, questions that continually arise in everyday life, though often only in a crude form. In fact, many of the sections in the text begin with illustrations from daily life, the sorts of things that we read in newspapers or journals, or the things that we learn about from TV reports.

EXPLANATORY COMMENTS

Philosophers over the past 2500 years have written for particular audiences. The intellectual and cultural worlds of ancient Greece or China, for example, differ in important ways from the cultural worlds of today. Consequently, we may sometimes be confused by an argument or claim or way of speaking that would have been clearer to readers of the time. The study guides include explanatory sections inserted into the primary texts that are designed to help you with these problems.

ASK YOURSELF

Throughout the readings in this book, you will find questions interspersed with the primary texts in boxes designated *Ask Yourself*. These will enable you to better work through what is admittedly sometimes difficult reading. Philosophical discussions can become quite complex. The study guide questions and comments will help to keep you on your toes as the complexity increases.

THINKING LOGICALLY

Every now and then, you will find *Thinking Logically* boxes in the text that discuss particular arguments that you may need to understand in order to appreciate the answers to the philosophical questions being discussed in a given selection. Below you will find a general discussion of logic that you will need to be familiar with if you want to make good use of the logic boxes.

CAN OF WORMS

If you have ever reached into a can of worms and tried to pull out just one worm, you know it is almost impossible if there are very many of them. They get tangled up with one another so that when you pull you get the whole pile—or the worm breaks! Similarly, if you pull on one philosophical question, you tend to get many more tangled up with it. The above discussion with the children illustrates this "can of worms" phenomenon. When the children questioned whether plants could feel, it forced them to think about our usual assumption that only something with a mind could feel. For in some way plants might seem to feel, yet it seems implausible to suppose they have minds. More specifically, it raises a question about the nature of the mind and body. Immediately we see that the children are considering questions about knowledge in general when trying to figure this out. How could we *know* that a plant feels? The children believed further that only things with feelings could be happy—and the nature of happiness has figured into discussions of ethics for thousands of years. Here you have the can of worms, one issue tangled up with another. At the end of each section of a chapter, there will be a box entitled *Can of Worms*. These explore how questions in one section of the chapter relate to issues dealt with in other sections or in other chapters.

SUMMARIES

At the close of each section and chapter there are summaries of the part in question. These should prove helpful for review purposes. But it might also be very useful to look over these summaries *before* studying a section, in order to get a sense of the general topics in that section.

GLOSSARY

A glossary of key terms appears at the close of this book. Like other disciplines, philosophy has some technical and semi-technical terms, and most of them will be briefly defined in the glossary.

C. A LITTLE LOGIC

Philosophers come to their views through intuitions, scientific findings, personal self-examination, and many other sources. But one thing that stands out in the majority of philosophical writings is *argument*. It is important to understand what "argument" in this context does *not* mean. It does not mean the thing that happens when two or more people disagree and start shouting at each other. In philosophy an argument is simply a set of statements, where some are offered as *support* for others. "Arguments" in this sense are things that we are constantly thinking up in our "discussions with ourselves," or when we want to explore any issue, as well as when we have a disagreement with someone else. Consider this example, which we will call "Argument A":

1. Parking lot 1 is generally full by noon.
2. It is now noon.
3. Parking lot 1 is now full.

In this set of statements, 1 and 2 are offered as *reasons* for asserting, or believing, 3. Logicians commonly refer to the reasons, such as 1 and 2, as *premises,* and that which they support, 3, as a *conclusion.* The whole set, 1–3, is called an *argument.* We could, alternatively, say that 1 and 2 are an argument for 3. Or we might say that 1 and 2 are the *reasons* for 3, or for believing 3. We can see from this example that we all use arguments constantly and that they are one of the main ways we arrive at our beliefs. That is, we normally have *reasons* for believing what we do believe, even when we do not spell them out.

ASK YOURSELF

1. Give your own example of an argument, in the strict sense just explained, and label the premises and conclusion.

Here is another argument, called "Argument B":

1'. Parking lot 1 is now full.
2'. It is a waste of time trying to find a parking space in lots that are full.
3'. It is a waste of time trying to find a parking space in parking lot 1.

Obviously, 1' is the same is 3 in the previous argument. What that shows is that a conclusion from one argument can serve as a premise in a further argument. And the conclusion of that further argument can function as a premise in a further argument, and so forth.

DEDUCTIVE ARGUMENTS AND INDUCTIVE ARGUMENTS

There is an important difference between argument A and argument B. In A, if the premises are true, then *probably* the conclusion is true also. It is of course possible that there is a parking space available in parking lot 1 even at noon, though *generally* that would not be the case. So, the premises do not give conclusive reasons for believing the conclusion. But they do give support for the conclusion. The premises could be true and the conclusion false. But *probably* the conclusion is true, given that the premises are true. Argument B is different. If the premises are true—that is, really true, not just maybe true—the conclusion will *have* to be true. Think about it. Is there any way the conclusion of argument B could be false if the premises are definitely true? If it is not immediately obvious that there is no way, a little thought should show you that in fact it is impossible for both premises to be true and the conclusion false.

Argument A is an *inductive* argument, and it is in fact an inductively *strong* argument because the premises offer strong support for the conclusion. Argument B is a *deductive* argument and is in fact a *valid* deductive argument. A valid deductive argument is one in which, *if* the premises are true, the conclusion *must* be true. Of course, if not all the premises *are* true, then it still might be the case that the conclusion is false, even though the argument is valid. Suppose however that all the premises *are* true. Then argument B is not only valid, it is *sound*. So, an argument is sound if and only if it is deductively valid *and* has all true premises. Sound arguments are the strongest kind of arguments there can be. The logician's uses of the words "valid," "deduction," and "sound" do not always correspond with the uses of non-logicians. For example, Sherlock Holmes often claims to be *deducing* a conclusion, when in fact his argument is inductive, rather than deductively valid. That is, he collects evidence that strongly supports a conclusion or makes it highly probable, but not absolutely certain. Most philosophers follow the logician's use, and they would say that Sherlock has only "induced" his conclusions, or arrived at them inductively.

ASK YOURSELF

2. Define: premise; argument; inductive argument; valid deductive argument; sound argument.

3. Classify each of the following arguments as either deductively valid, inductively strong, or sound (check the definitions):

   1. You cannot *know* A (A is some statement, such as "it is raining") unless A is true.
   2. A is false.
   3. So, you do not know A.

   1. Usually democracies work better than other forms of government.
   2. The United States is a democracy, and Cuba is not.
   3. The form of government in the United States will work better than Cuba's does.

4. Try to cook up an example of your own of each of the following (check the definitions first): (a) an inductive argument, (b) a valid deductive argument, (c) a sound argument.

It is important for our living and thinking that our arguments be good ones. That does not mean they must all be deductively valid or sound. But it does mean that we should always look for the best possible arguments for any conclusions we want to hold to or defend. Philosophical writings are good places to look for good arguments—although there are certainly some bad ones there too.

Philosophy consists to a very large degree of the construction of arguments, both inductive and deductive, and criticism of those arguments, or defense of them against criticism, by using further arguments or in other ways. However, philosophers do not always fully spell out their arguments. Neither do the rest of us. How many of us, while driving to school, would actually spell out arguments A and B as we drive past parking lot 1 and head for parking lot 2 or some more remote lot? Nonetheless those arguments are behind what we do. All of us reason, all of us have reasons for what we do and believe, even though it may seem that sometimes we may do something "for no reason." Argument pervades everyone's life.

The next few sections provide some examples of ways in which arguments can be evaluated and critiqued.

REFUTATION BY COUNTEREXAMPLE

Philosophers are generally more inclined than most people to spell out their arguments, and more inclined to criticize the arguments of others. Moreover, they have developed techniques for criticizing arguments and some of those techniques or strategies have labels. You will become familiar with some of those techniques and learn some of the labels in the Thinking Logically boxes inserted in the following readings. Here is one technique, called "refutation by counterexample." Counterexamples to a given argument are arguments that have the same *form* as the given argument, but that have an obviously false conclusion even though the premises are true. Consider the following argument.

1. If all preemptive wars are unjust, then the war in Iraq is unjust.
2. The war in Iraq is unjust.
3. Therefore, all preemptive wars are unjust.

It might well be that 3 is true. It might also be that 1 and 2 are true. But this is still a bad argument, since the conclusion does not *follow* from the premises. Here is a counterexample with the same form as the preceding argument:

1′. If Rams fans are clever, then James (who is a Rams fan) is clever.
2′. James is clever.
3′. All Rams fans are clever.

I hope you will agree that 3′ is pretty obviously false. Surely there must be Rams fans who are not the least bit clever. Many may be downright dull. Nonetheless, 1′ and 2′ could be true. Certainly, *if* all Rams fans are clever (but maybe not all are), then James, the Rams fan, is clever. So 1′ could be true; 2′ could be also. James might even be one of the few clever Rams fans. But 3′ is, well, silly. In any case, it certainly does not follow from 1′ and 2′. Likewise, certainly 3 does not follow from 1 and 2. And 3 may not be silly, the way 3′ is. But nonetheless it just does not *follow* from 1 and 2. The counterexample ought to make that clear. So if you want to argue for 3, you need to look for a better argument.

ASK YOURSELF

5. See if you can critique the following argument by producing a counterexample in which the conclusion is obviously false, even though the premises are true:

1. If all events have causes, then the rotation of the earth has a cause.
2. The rotation of the earth does have a cause.
3. Therefore, all events have causes.

Note: This argument has the following form:

1. If A, then B.
2. B
3. Therefore A.

You can get a counterexample by replacing A and B with statements such that 1 and 2 are true, but 3 is obviously false. That would show that the conclusion does not follow from the premises in the argument above *or in any other argument that has that same form.* Even if a conclusion fails to follow from the premises, this itself does not show that the conclusion is false. It is true that all events have causes.

Here is a more complex, and controversial, refutation by counterexample. Consider the following argument, which we will label "Pro-Life."

1. A being that is now *potentially* an innocent human person has the same rights as an innocent human person.
2. This fetus is now potentially an innocent human person.
3. An innocent human person has the right to not be killed.
4. Therefore, this fetus has a right to not be killed.

ASK YOURSELF

6. Do you think "Pro-Life" is inductive, or is it deductively valid? Explain.

Someone might criticize "Pro Life" by producing a *counterexample,* which we will label "Pro-Choice":

1'. A being that is now potentially a president of the United States has the same rights as the president of the United States.
2'. This fetus is now potentially president of the United States.
3'. The president of the United States has a right to give orders to the armed forces.
4'. Therefore, this fetus has a right to give orders to the armed forces.

It looks like "Pro-Choice" has the same logical *form* as "Pro-Life". But the conclusion of Pro-Choice is obviously false, whereas the conclusion of "Pro-Life" is not *obviously* false. Where did things go wrong? The person who advances "Pro-Choice" will claim that something went wrong with premise 1. "Pro-Life" seems to rely on the idea that if something is potentially X, then it has the same rights as X. If "Pro-Life" were *fully spelled out* it would include that claim as a premise. But it is clearly not *generally* the case that if some X potentially has R (e.g., has certain rights), then it must actually have R now. The counterexample makes that fact clear. The role of the missing premise is perhaps even clearer in "Pro choice." There is a technical term for arguments that are not fully spelled out. They are called "enthymemes." We often get clearer about the actual force or value of an argument when we succeed in making all the premises explicit.

Refutations by counterexample are common in philosophy. They need to be looked at carefully. Certainly "Pro-Choice" does not conclusively refute "Pro-Life." It might be that "Pro-Life" only depends upon the claim that in this specific case, the fact that A (a fetus) is potentially X entails that it is X now. Someone who advances "Pro-Life" does not necessarily hold that it is *generally* true that whatever is potentially X has the same rights as X. However, once the counterexample is produced, the pro-life advocate should realize that she needs to give some special reason for believing that in the case of the fetus it has the rights now that it has potentially.

7. Suppose that you are using "Pro-Life" in a discussion and are confronted with "Pro-Choice" as a counterexample. Would you feel that you had to respond by giving some *special* reason for thinking that in the case of the fetus, it should have the same rights *now* as it has potentially? Explain.

CONFUSING NECESSARY AND SUFFICIENT CONDITIONS

Here is a further technique for criticizing or appraising arguments and the sets of beliefs upon which they depend. Generally, if A is necessary for B, then we state this as "if B, then A." If A is sufficient for B, then we state this as "if A, then B." If A is both necessary and sufficient for B, then we can state that as "A if and only if B." Consider the following:

1. If there is a fire (A), then oxygen is present (B).

This tells us that there being a fire is sufficient for there being oxygen present (If A, then B). Whenever there is a fire, there is oxygen. However, it does not tell us that there being a fire is necessary for there being oxygen present. It does not tell us that:

2. If there is oxygen present, then there is a fire.

If 2 were true, there would be fires inside our lungs and all over the place. Oxygen is necessary for fire, but not sufficient. So, the following would be a bad argument:

1. If there is a fire here (A), then oxygen is present (B).
2. Oxygen is present (B).
3. Therefore, there is a fire here (A).

Although the point is simple, it is easy to get confused about this distinction.

8. In which of the following is there a confusion of necessary and sufficient conditions. (a) All rich people are Republicans, therefore, if you are a Republican, then you are a rich person. (b) If George is clever, he will not fail the exam, and he is clever, so he will not fail the exam.

9. In the arguments in the previous question, indicate which of the following are necessary conditions and which are sufficient: being rich; being a Republican; being clever; not failing.

The following example is more complex and has to do with how we think about the mind and its relations to the brain. The mistaken reasoning here, which consists in confusing necessary with sufficient conditions, is common, even among otherwise intelligent people.

1. If certain mental events occur, such as a feeling of pain (A), then certain specific brain fibers are firing (B).
2. Therefore, mental events such as pains are nothing more than (or are identical with) processes in the brain. So if a feeling of pain occurs (A), then specific brain fibers are firing (B); *and* if specific brain fibers are firing (B), then a feeling of pain occurs (A).

Many people accept some version of this argument. They shouldn't: 2 certainly does not follow from 1. What is being claimed in 1 is that having certain brain fibers firing is a *necessary condition* for pain (If A, then B). It does not imply that brain fibers firing is *sufficient* for pain (If B, then A). But the conclusion, 2, only looks plausible if having parts of the brain firing is *sufficient* for pain. This argument *confuses necessary with sufficient conditions*. Thus, if parts of the brain firing were sufficient for the mental event of feeling pains, that amounts to the claim that if parts of the brain are firing, pains are occurring. Even that might not be enough to show that having a pain is *identical with* having parts of the brain firing, but it gets us a lot closer to showing it. Anyway, it does *not* amount to the claim that if pains are occurring, then parts of the brain are firing. Someone might mistakenly think it does amount to that when they notice that damage to parts of the brain eliminate pain. Then "if parts of the brain are damaged (not firing), then, no pain" (If not B, then not A). That only shows that undamaged parts of the brain are *necessary* for pain. A lot of other things might be necessary too. For example, consciousness might be necessary, and consciousness might be possible without any brain at all, or it might not depend upon the proper functioning of any particular part of the brain. Perhaps you only get pain when you have specific brain fibers firing *and* the pain fairy is at work. And so forth. At any rate, the truth of 1 does not show that certain brain events are sufficient for pain. Other things might show it, but 1 does not. These issues are discussed further in Chapter 4.

REDUCTION TO ABSURDITY

Someone might believe the following three statements:

Mary likes Bill. Mary does not like anyone John likes. John likes Bill.

You might see the problem right away. You can criticize someone's beliefs by "reducing those beliefs to absurdity." If someone believes a contradiction, they certainly believe an absurdity. Now it follows from the fact that Mary doesn't like anyone John likes, plus the fact that John likes Bill, that Mary does not like Bill. Right? So, the person who believes those three statements in effect believes this: Mary likes Bill, and, it is not the case that Mary likes Bill. Too stupid to be possible, you think? But people sometimes hold inconsistent beliefs simply because they are not paying close attention to how their various beliefs hang together, or fail to hang together. Here is a slightly revised example from Plato's dialogue *Euthyphro*. Socrates discovers that Euthyphro, a young man whom he has been questioning, believes both of the following:

1. Those actions are good that are approved by the Gods (so what they do not approve of is not good).
2. The Gods disagree with one another; they do not all approve of the same things.

From these two claims it follows that a certain act, A, could be both good and not good. Do you see why? Suppose Zeus approves of A. Suppose that Hera does not approve of A. Then A is both good and not good, according to 1. And *that* is a contradiction. Now, contradictions are absurd since no one can coherently believe a contradiction. You cannot assert or coherently believe *both* that Einstein won the 1921 Nobel Prize for physics *and* that it is *not* the case that Einstein won the 1921 Nobel Prize for physics.

Socrates' argument is an example of *reduction to absurdity*. If I can show that a set of beliefs that I or some other person proposes leads to a contradiction, then I have shown that something in that set of beliefs must be given up or revised, or that position abandoned. In the dialogue mentioned, Euthyphro does in fact revise his view on good actions as soon as Socrates shows him that his view leads to a contradiction. There are many attempts, in the history of philosophy, science, and other disciplines, to show that certain positions or beliefs are inconsistent and lead to contradictions. When successful, such attempts almost always lead the person who holds the position or beliefs in question to revise their thinking so as to get rid of the contradiction.

ASK YOURSELF

10. The following set of beliefs could be criticized by a *reduction to absurdity*. Explain exactly how.

    1. Combustion is caused by the release of phlogiston.

    2. Anything weighs less without its phlogiston then with it.

    3. X was "combusted."

    4. X weighed more *after* being combusted than before.

If you have understood the foregoing discussion, then you may see how a claim could be proved by showing that denying it leads to a contradiction. That form of argument is also called *reductio ad absurdum* and is often used in formal logic. For example, the immediately preceding argument could be used to prove 5, "It is not the case that combustion is caused by the release of phologiston" (given the truth of 2–4), since the denial of 5 *is* 1.

OTHER KINDS OF CRITIQUES

The various techniques used by philosophers for constructing and criticizing arguments are used by people generally, but often without a clear awareness of what they are doing or what the pitfalls are. Here are some common ways of criticizing arguments:

    1. We try to show that even if the premises are true, the conclusion does not have to be true (that is, it does not *follow*).

    2. We may claim that even if the premises are true, they do not make the conclusion very *probable*.

    3. We may point out that one or more of the premises is *in fact* not true.

As a variant on #1, we might criticize an argument by claiming that the premises are not even relevant to the conclusion. To illustrate, an enemy of Protestant reformer Martin Luther made this argument: (a) Luther was a filthy monk; therefore (b) Luther's theological views are unworthy of consideration. The argument is bad since the fact that someone doesn't bathe too often is not *relevant to* the claim that their theology also stinks. That is, premise (a) is not relevant to conclusion (b). This is also known as an *ad hominem* argument—literally an argument "to the person."

There are many other ways of attacking or defending arguments, and we will discuss some of them in the Thinking Logically boxes. Some arguments are complex and may elicit several kinds of criticism all at once. The construction and criticism of arguments is central to philosophy; it is what *being logical* actually amounts to, and for the most part philosophers have been quite concerned to be logical.

FURTHER READINGS

Kneale, W. C., and Kneale, M., *The Development of Logic* (Oxford: Oxford University Press, 1962).

Matthews, Gareth, *Philosophy and the Young Child* (Cambridge: Harvard University Press, 1982).

Matthews, Gareth, *The Philosophy of Childhood* (Cambridge: Harvard University Press, 1996).

Porter, Burton F., *The Voice of Reason: Fundamentals of Critical Thinking* (Oxford: Oxford University Press, 2001).

Salmon, Wesley, *Introduction to Logic and Critical Thinking* (Belmont, CA: Wadsworth Publishing Company, 2001).

CHAPTER 2

THE PHILOSOPHY OF RELIGION

**I**n the first half of the seventeenth century, Protestant and Catholic Christians in Europe fought each other almost continuously for nearly 30 years. That conflict, and many others carried on in the name of religion, may have been motivated by nonreligious factors, such as territorial ambitions, but certainly the appalling death and destruction were partly due to religious fervor. Religion still arouses strong passions. Christians of some denominations still squabble with other Christians and still occasionally consign the other side to hell. Things usually get worse when it comes to religions that are completely different from one's own. Intolerance toward "unbelievers" has led to inquisitions and persecutions of Jews by Christians, enslavement of Christians by Muslims, and so forth. In the twenty-first century we have been made starkly aware of the way in which religious belief and conflict can be enlisted in support of terrorism and mass destruction. This dark fact becomes more intelligible when we reflect on the great importance that religious beliefs have for many people. We naturally tend to oppose anything that we perceive as a threat to our most central and deeply held beliefs. Despite this dark side of religion, though, religious belief appears to have been a force for good in many places. The campaign against the slave trade in the nineteenth century originated largely in Christian circles in England. Religious belief played a seminal role in the civil rights movement and opposition to racism in the 1950s and 1960s in the

United States. A great many humanitarian efforts and institutions, such as hospital and aid programs, have been funded by churches, and they have sometimes been led by such exemplary figures as Mother Theresa of Calcutta. Many people sense that life without religion is a dreary and despairing thing. Religion's major impact on society, for both good and bad, along with the intellectual difficulties involved in articulating, clarifying, and maintaining religious ideas, have naturally motivated philosophers to say quite a bit about it.

FIRST REACTIONS

Think about how you feel right now regarding the following questions, noting whether you agree, disagree, or are not sure about the views expressed. Make a note of your answers on a separate piece of question, and hang on to it. We will return to these questions at the end of this chapter. You may discover then that your answers are not the same as they are now.

a. What, if anything, do you think discredits the idea that God exists?

b. Does the widespread presence of evil undermine the commonly held view that God is good?

c. Some people claim that they have had a mystical religious experience in which they felt they were united with God, and not simply in communication with him. Do you think that humans are capable of being in union with God?

d. Can you think of an argument for God's existence and, if so, how successful do you think that argument is?

e. If you accept the theory of evolution, does this mean that God does not exist or that God did not create the world?

f. Do we need to have rational evidence that God exists, or is it better to simply believe on the basis of faith alone?

As we will see in this chapter, some people have sought to discredit religion, perhaps in part because of the bad uses to which religious beliefs have sometimes been put. Hume argued that religious beliefs are irrational and not acceptable, no matter what the benefits of having those beliefs may be. Marx and Nietzsche tried to show that religious beliefs conceal hidden agendas and resentments of a less than admirable sort. On the other hand, there are impressive accounts of religious experiences from different religions around the world, which, it can be argued, provide support for religious belief. Moreover, there is a long tradition of philosophical theology that attempts to prove or make highly plausible some central religious claims—most basically, that God exists. Because debates about religious belief are not obviously things that can be settled by scientific experiments, philosophers have a good deal to say about things such as the rationality of religion, the nature of religious concepts, the relations between reason and faith, and the bearing of religious experience on religious truth claims. These are the issues that we will explore in this chapter.

A. CHALLENGES TO RELIGIOUS BELIEF

Suppose that you do not believe in God, in spite of the best arguments in favor of God's existence. How would you disprove the claims of believers? It wouldn't be enough to simply point out the failures of such theistic proofs, since many believers question their success.

It might not even help to point out inconsistencies in religious belief systems, since some believers feel that basic religious doctrines are inherently paradoxical. Even drawing attention to hypocritical and immoral conduct within religion would show nothing since believers routinely criticize this as well. Disproving religion is in principal an uphill battle since the subject is beyond the scope of scientific scrutiny. If my neighbor claims that there is an elephant behind his garage, I can prove him wrong if I walk behind his garage and don't see any elephant. However, if my neighbor claims that God exists, I can't inspect all the nooks and crannies of the universe to confirm or disconfirm that claim. And even if such an inspection were possible, it wouldn't have any bearing on religious truths since most people don't think of God as a being located on some distant planet. However, there are other ways to challenge the central assumptions of religious belief.

**QUESTIONS
TO DISCUSS**

a. The term "miracle" is used in many different senses. What do you think constitutes a full-fledged miracle?

b. Suppose that you believe that miracles have occurred within your own religious tradition. What would you say about the occurrence of miracles in other religions?

c. Can you think of a way in which religious belief might lull believers into accepting their own oppressed social standing and other injustices?

d. Do you think that the notion of God is doomed to extinction in human society?

1. THE IRRATIONALITY OF BELIEVING IN MIRACLES: DAVID HUME

Several years ago, a book entitled *Like a Mighty Wind* appeared, which triggered quite a controversy. It reported a series of breathtaking miracles that occurred in a remote area of Indonesia, which at the time was experiencing a dramatic Christian revival. There were reports of water being turned into wine, people eating poison and not being harmed, and people walking across a 30-foot-deep river. Most extraordinary was a story about a man being raised from the dead:

> When we arrived there, there were more than a thousand people. That man had been dead for two days and was very stinky. In our tropical country, when you're dead six hours you start to decay. But after two days—oh, I tell you, you couldn't stand within 100 feet of him. . . . We went and stood around this dead person. We began to sing. . . . Then sang a second song, and nothing happened. On the fifth song, nothing happened. But on the sixth song, that man began to move his toes—and the team began to get scared. We have a story in Indonesia, that sometimes when people die they wake up and hug a person by their coffin and then die again. However, we just went ahead and sang. When we sang the seventh and eighth songs, that brother woke up, looked around and smiled. He didn't hug anybody. He just opened his mouth and said, "Jesus has brought me back to life!" [From Mel Tari, *Like a Mighty Wind,* 8]

Stirred by these miracle accounts, several readers of *Like a Mighty Wind* traveled to Indonesia to see what really happened. Some returned saying that it was a hoax, and others returned absolutely convinced that miracles occurred just as reported.

What should we think about these miracle reports? Eighteenth-century Scottish philosopher David Hume (1711–1776) argued that we must simply dismiss stories like these, without even bothering to investigate the sources. The very facts that they report are so

improbable on face value that they should carry no weight for a rational person. Hume's central argument can be summarized in a single sentence: The testimony of uniform natural law outweighs the testimony of any alleged miracle. To explain, imagine a scale with two balancing pans. In the one pan we place the strongest evidence in support of the occurrence of a miracle. In the other we place our lifelong experience of consistent laws of nature. According to Hume, the second pan will always outweigh the first. To understand Hume's argument, it is important to be clear about what Hume is specifically arguing against. Hume is not arguing that miracles are impossible, for, he concedes, there is no logical contradiction in the idea of a miracle. Nor is he arguing that miracles have never occurred, since, after all, they are possible. Finally, Hume is not arguing against first-hand experiences of miracles, such as what I might have personally witnessed if I were in Indonesia at the time of the revival; few of us, in fact, claim to witness miracles directly. Instead, Hume is arguing against *second-hand reports* of miracles, which I might read about in a book such as *Like a Mighty Wind*. In short, Hume is arguing that it is never reasonable to believe second-hand reports concerning miracles.

Levels of Evidence. Hume's argument rests on the nature of sense experience in general. All judgments about sense experience—and not just those involving miracles—are best understood using the metaphor of a weighing scale with two balancing pans, as noted above. We place all of our experiential evidence for a particular contention in one pan, and all of our evidence against that contention in the other pan. We then believe whichever view has the weightier evidence. Hume recognizes that this style of weighing evidence is not always accurate, such as when I predict from past experience that the weather will be warmer next June than it will be next December.

FROM DAVID HUME, *An Enquiry Concerning Human Understanding* (1748), SECTION 10

Though experience be our only guide in reasoning concerning matters of fact; it must be acknowledged, that this guide is not altogether infallible, but in some cases is apt to lead us into errors. One, who in our climate, should expect better weather in any week of June than in one of December, would reason justly, and conformably to experience; but it is certain, that he may happen, in the event, to find himself mistaken. However, we may observe, that, in such a case, he would have no cause to complain of experience; because it commonly informs us beforehand of the uncertainty, by that contrariety of events, which we may learn from a diligent observation. All effects follow not with like certainty from their supposed causes. Some events are found, in all countries and all ages, to have been constantly conjoined together: Others are found to have been more variable, and sometimes to disappoint our expectations; so that, in our reasonings concerning matter of fact, there are all imaginable degrees of assurance, from the highest certainty to the lowest species of moral evidence.

ASK YOURSELF

1. What are the possible levels or degrees of assurance when assessing matters of fact?

Given these differing degrees or levels of assurance, Hume argues that the higher the degree of evidence, the stronger our belief should be.

A wise man, therefore, proportions his belief to the evidence. In such conclusions as are founded on an infallible experience, he expects the event with the last degree of assurance, and regards his past experience as a full *proof* of the future existence of that event. In other cases, he proceeds with more caution: He weighs the opposite experiments: He considers which side is supported by the greater number of experiments: To that side he inclines, with doubt and hesitation; and when at last he fixes his judgement, the evidence exceeds not what we properly call *probability*. All probability, then, supposes an opposition of experiments and observations, where the one side is found to overbalance the other, and to produce a degree of evidence, proportioned to the superiority. A hundred instances or experiments on one side, and fifty on another, afford a doubtful expectation of any event; though a hundred uniform experiments, with only one that is contradictory, reasonably beget a pretty strong degree of assurance. In all cases, we must balance the opposite experiments, where they are opposite, and deduct the smaller number from the greater, in order to know the exact force of the superior evidence.

ASK YOURSELF

2. How should a wise person proportion his belief in a given claim?

3. All judgments about matters of fact (or sensory experience) involve probability. What does probability suppose?

Sensory Evidence from Testimony.   There are several ways of gaining sensory evidence for a particular contention. We may personally conduct scientific experiments, as Hume notes above. We may draw from the ordinary life experiences that we have gained over the years. Perhaps most importantly, we may rely on the testimonies of other people. Testimonies also count as sensory evidence, which we must balance against our other sensory experiences.

To apply these principles to a particular instance; we may observe, that there is no species of reasoning more common, more useful, and even necessary to human life, than that which is derived from the testimony of men, and the reports of eyewitnesses and spectators. This species of reasoning, perhaps, one may deny to be founded on the relation of cause and effect. I shall not dispute about a word. It will be sufficient to observe that our assurance in any argument of this kind is derived from no other principle than our observation of the veracity of human testimony, and of the usual conformity of facts to the reports of witnesses. It being a general maxim, that no objects have any discoverable connection together, and that all the inferences, which we can draw from one to another, are founded merely on our experience of their constant and regular conjunction; it is evident, that we ought not to make an exception to this maxim in favour of human testimony, whose connection with any event seems, in itself, as little necessary as any other. Were not the memory tenacious to a certain degree; had not men commonly an inclination to truth and a principle of probity; were they not sensible to shame, when detected in a falsehood: Were not these, I say, discovered by *experience* to be qualities, inherent in human nature, we should never repose the least confidence in human testimony. A man delirious, or noted for falsehood and villainy, has no manner of authority with us.

ASK YOURSELF

4. What other evidence from experience gives or takes away from the confidence we have in a person's testimony?

Other Factors in Evaluating Testimonies. Before discussing testimonies in favor of miracles in particular, Hume continues listing general factors which weigh in favor of or against someone's testimony.

And as the evidence, derived from witnesses and human testimony, is founded on past experience, so it varies with the experience, and is regarded either as a *proof* or a *probability,* according as the conjunction between any particular kind of report and any kind of object has been found to be constant or variable. There are a number of circumstances to be taken into consideration in all judgments of this kind; and the ultimate standard, by which we determine all disputes, that may arise concerning them, is always derived from experience and observation. Where this experience is not entirely uniform on any side, it is attended with an unavoidable contrariety in our judgments, and with the same opposition and mutual destruction of argument as in every other kind of evidence. We frequently hesitate concerning the reports of others. We balance the opposite circumstances, which cause any doubt or uncertainty; and when we discover a superiority on any side, we incline to it; but still with a diminution of assurance, in proportion to the force of its antagonist.

This contrariety of evidence, in the present case, may be derived from several different causes; from the opposition of contrary testimony; from the character or number of the witnesses; from the manner of their delivering their testimony; or from the union of all these circumstances. We entertain a suspicion concerning any matter of fact, when the witnesses contradict each other; when they are but few, or of a doubtful character; when they have an interest in what they affirm; when they deliver their testimony with hesitation, or on the contrary, with too violent asseverations. There are many other particulars of the same kind, which may diminish or destroy the force of any argument, derived from human testimony.

ASK YOURSELF

5. What are some reasons that we are suspicious of some testimonies?

Hume notes that sometimes a reported event seems so improbable that we wouldn't be persuaded of its truth even if told by the most reliable witness. In such cases, the alleged event is incompatible with what we know about the world in general.

Suppose, for instance, that the fact, which the testimony endeavors to establish, partakes of the extraordinary and the marvelous; in that case, the evidence, resulting from the testimony, admits of a diminution, greater or less, in proportion as the fact is more or less unusual. The reason why we place any credit in witnesses and historians, is not derived from any *connection,* which we perceive *a priori*, between testimony and reality, but because we are accustomed to find a conformity between them. But when the fact attested is such a one as has seldom fallen under our observation, here is a contest of two opposite experiences; of which the one destroys the other, as far as its force goes, and the superior can only operate on the mind by the force, which remains. The very same principle of experience, which gives us a certain degree of assurance in the testimony of witnesses, gives us also, in this case, another degree of assurance against the fact, which they endeavor to establish; from which contradiction there necessarily arises a counterpoize, and mutual destruction of belief and authority.

I should not believe such a story were it told me by Cato; was a proverbial saying in Rome, even during the lifetime of that philosophical patriot. The incredibility of a fact, it was allowed, might invalidate so great an authority.

The Indian prince, who refused to believe the first relations concerning the effects of frost, reasoned justly; and it naturally required very strong testimony to engage his assent to facts, that arose from a state of nature, with which he was unacquainted, and which bore so little analogy to those events, of which he had had constant and uniform experience. Though they were not contrary to his experience, they were not conformable to it.

ASK YOURSELF

6. Consider a prince from India who never personally witnessed frost. According to Hume, would it be reasonable for him to believe the testimony of someone who claimed that water could freeze?

7. Would it be reasonable, on your view? More generally, do you ever have good reasons for believing some testimonies which go beyond your own experience, or even the experience of most people? Give an example, if you can, from the sciences.

In view of the above points about evaluating testimonies in general, Hume turns to evaluating testimonies of miracles.

The Evidence of Nature versus the Testimony of Miracles. Just as testimonies of improbable events (such as alien abductions) are counterbalanced by our general life experiences, this is even more so with testimonies of miracles. The testimony itself counts as evidence for the alleged miracle, but this is outweighed by our life experiences that speak against such a possibility.

But in order to increase the probability against the testimony of witnesses, let us suppose, that the fact, which they affirm, instead of being only marvelous, is really miraculous; and suppose also, that the testimony considered apart and in itself, amounts to an entire proof; in that case, there is proof against proof, of which the strongest must prevail, but still with a diminution of its force, in proportion to that of its antagonist.

A miracle is a violation of the laws of nature; and as a firm and unalterable experience has established these laws, the proof against a miracle, from the very nature of the fact, is as entire as any argument from experience can possibly be imagined. Why is it more than probable, that all men must die; that lead cannot, of itself, remain suspended in the air; that fire consumes wood, and is extinguished by water; unless it be, that these events are found agreeable to the laws of nature, and there is required a violation of these laws, or in other words, a miracle to prevent them? Nothing is esteemed a miracle, if it ever happen in the common course of nature. It is no miracle that a man, seemingly in good health, should die on a sudden: Because such a kind of death, though more unusual than any other, has yet been frequently observed to happen. But it is a miracle, that a dead man should come to life; because that has never been observed in any age or country. There must, therefore, be a uniform experience against every miraculous event, otherwise the event would not merit that appellation. And as a uniform experience amounts to a proof, there is here a direct and full *proof,* from the nature of the fact, against the existence of any miracle; nor can such a proof be destroyed, or the miracle rendered credible, but by an opposite proof, which is superior.

ASK YOURSELF

8. What is Hume's definition of a miracle?

9. Why, according to Hume, does uniform experience constitute evidence against the existence of any miracle?

Definition of a Miracle. Hume recognizes that we must be clear about which type of events qualify as miracles. In the above paragraph he defines a miracle as a violation of a law of nature. This eliminates many events that are commonly called miracles, such as fortunate accidents, or improbable medical recoveries. He discusses possible events that fit the definition of a miracle.

Sometimes an event may not, *in itself,* seem to be contrary to the laws of nature, and yet, if it were real, it might, by reason of some circumstances, be denominated a miracle; because, in *fact,* it is contrary to these laws. Thus if a person, claiming a divine authority, should command a sick person to be well, a healthful man to fall down dead, the clouds to pour rain, the winds to blow, in short, should order many natural events, which immediately follow upon his command; these might justly be esteemed miracles, because they are really, in this case, contrary to the laws of nature. For if any suspicion remain, that the event and command concurred by accident there is no miracle and no transgression of the laws of nature. If this suspicion be removed, there is evidently a miracle, and a transgression of these laws; because nothing can be more contrary to nature than that the voice or command of a man should have such an influence. A miracle may be accurately defined, *a transgression of a law of nature by a particular volition of the Deity, or by the interposition of some invisible agent.* A miracle may either be discoverable by men or not. This alters not its nature and essence. The raising of a house or ship into the air is a visible miracle. The raising of a feather, when the wind wants ever so little of a force requisite for that purpose, is as real a miracle, though not so sensible with regard to us.

ASK YOURSELF

10. Suppose that a divine authority commands some natural event, such as the clouds pouring rain, and that event happens. What aspect of this would involve a violation of a law of nature?

11. Suppose that a feather would start to move without any air current. Even though it violated a law of nature, to an observer it would not appear that way. For Hume, would this still count as a miracle?

So far Hume has been assuming that a miracle testimony is as strong as can be, and the person reporting an alleged miracle has integrity. However, Hume argues, most reports of miracles do not live up to this high standard, which diminishes further the trustworthiness of miracle testimonies. He describes four factors that reduce the credibility of most miracle accounts.

In the foregoing reasoning we have supposed, that the testimony, upon which a miracle is founded, may possibly amount to an entire proof, and that the falsehood of that testimony would be a real prodigy: But it is easy to show, that we have been a great deal too liberal in our concession, and that there never was a miraculous event established on so full an evidence.

Witnesses Lack Integrity. The first factor that reduces the credibility of most miracle testimonies is that the witnesses lack integrity.

For *first,* there is not to be found, in all history, any miracle attested by a sufficient number of men, of such unquestioned good-sense, education, and learning, as to secure us against all delusion in themselves; of such undoubted integrity, as to place them beyond all suspicion of any design to deceive others; of such credit and reputation in the eyes of mankind, as to have a great deal to lose in case of their being detected in any falsehood; and at the same time, attesting facts performed in such a public manner and in so celebrated a part of the world, as to render the detection unavoidable: All which circumstances are requisite to give us a full assurance in the testimony of men.

ASK YOURSELF

12. Which character traits do eyewitnesses of miracles typically lack, according to Hume?

Predisposition to Sensationalize. The second factor that reduces the credibility of most miracle testimonies is that people fall prey to a tendency to sensationalize. We enjoy hearing and telling strange stories, and this encourages others to invent strange stories.

Secondly. We may observe in human nature a principle which, if strictly examined, will be found to diminish extremely the assurance which we might, from human testimony, have in any kind of prodigy. The maxim by which we commonly conduct ourselves in our reasonings is that the objects, of which we have no experience, resemble those of which we have; that what we have found to be most usual is always most probable; and that where there is an opposition of arguments, we ought to give the preference to such as are founded on the greatest number of past observations. But though in proceeding by this rule we readily reject any fact which is unusual and incredible in an ordinary degree; yet in advancing farther, the mind observes not always the same rule; but when anything is affirmed utterly absurd and miraculous, it rather the more readily admits of such a fact, upon account of that very circumstance, which ought to destroy all its authority. The passion of surprise and wonder arising from miracles, being an agreeable emotion, gives a sensible tendency towards the belief of those events from which it is derived. And this goes so far, that even those who cannot enjoy this pleasure immediately, nor can believe those miraculous events, of which they are informed, yet love to partake of the satisfaction at second-hand or by rebound, and place a pride and delight in exciting the admiration of others.

ASK YOURSELF

13. Which emotions surrounding sensational stories make them so enjoyable?

Hume claims that religious leaders capitalize on this tendency to sensationalize and invent such stories for the greater good of their religious cause.

With what greediness are the miraculous accounts of travelers received, their descriptions of sea and land monsters, their relations of wonderful adventures, strange men, and uncouth manners? But if the spirit of religion join itself to the love of wonder, there is an end of common sense; and human testimony, in these circumstances, loses all pretensions to authority. A religionist may be an enthusiast, and imagine he sees what has no reality: He may know his narrative to be false, and yet persevere in it, with the best intentions in the world, for the sake of promoting so holy a cause: Or even where this delusion has not place, vanity, excited by so strong a temptation, operates on him more powerfully than on the rest of mankind in any other circumstances; and self-interest with equal force. His auditors may not have, and commonly have not, sufficient judgment to canvass his evidence: What judgment they have, they renounce by principle, in these sublime and mysterious subjects: Or if they were ever so willing to employ it, passion and a heated imagination disturb the regularity of its operations. Their credulity increases his impudence: And his impudence overpowers their credulity.

ASK YOURSELF

14. According to Hume, what motivates religious leaders to take advantage of our desire to hear sensational stories?

Abound in Barbarous Nations. The third factor which reduces the credibility of most miracle testimonies is that such stories typically originate in "ignorant and barbarous" countries—that is, countries that are culturally and scientifically primitive. This factor is similar to the first mentioned above. However, the first factor targets the integrity of the individual eyewitness, whereas this third factor targets the entire social context from which such stories arise.

Thirdly. It forms a strong presumption against all supernatural and miraculous relations, that they are observed chiefly to abound among ignorant and barbarous nations; or if a civilized people has ever given admission to any of them, that people will be found to have received them from ignorant and barbarous ancestors, who transmitted them with that inviolable sanction and authority, which always attend received opinions. When we peruse the first histories of all nations, we are apt to imagine ourselves transported into some new world; where the whole frame of nature is disjointed, and every element performs its operations in a different manner, from what it does at present. Battles, revolutions, pestilence, famine and death, are never the effect of those natural causes, which we experience. Prodigies, omens, oracles, judgments, quite obscure the few natural events, that are intermingled with them. But as the former grow thinner every page, in proportion as we advance nearer the enlightened ages, we soon learn, that there is nothing mysterious or supernatural in the case, but that all proceeds from the usual propensity of mankind towards the marvelous, and that, though this inclination may at intervals receive a check from sense and learning, it can never be thoroughly extirpated from human nature.

15. In such countries, what are the causes assigned to events such as battles, revolutions, pestilence, famine, and death?

THINKING LOGICALLY

In logic there is a fallacy of reasoning called "*ad hominem* argumentation"—that is, an argument *to the man*. According to this fallacy, the arguer seeks to (a) discredit a contention by insulting the people who hold it or (b) establish a contention by insulting the people who deny it. I would be committing this fallacy if, for example, I stated that "We must reject Bob's view of health care reform since Bob cheats on his wife." Bob's marital infidelity is irrelevant to the question of his views on health care. Sometimes, though, it may indeed be relevant to point out some feature of a person's character. For example, it would not be a fallacy for me to say "We must reject Bob's view of gender roles within marriages since Bob cheats on his wife." Here we may reasonably think that Bob's view about gender roles might be tainted by his womanizing.

16. Hume says some pretty harsh things about reports of miracles: The witnesses lack integrity and the stories originate in ignorant countries. Is any of this *ad hominem* argumentation?

Another logical fallacy is "circular reasoning," which involves assuming the truth of a conclusion in the premise of one's argument. I use circular reasoning, for example, if I say "It is impossible to talk without using words, since words are necessary for talking." The problem here is that my premise (words are necessary for talking) means exactly the same thing as my conclusion (it is impossible to talk without using words). Consider whether Hume might be guilty of circular reasoning. If he claims that witnesses of a miracle lack integrity—without any independent evidence of that fact—then he is in effect saying that we cannot believe witnesses to a miracle because they are not the kind of people to be believed.

17. Is Hume engaged in circular reasoning, or does he offer (or even hint at) any reasons for thinking that witnesses of alleged miracles typically lack integrity?

Miracles Support Rival Religious Systems. The fourth factor that Hume thinks reduces the credibility of miracle testimonies is that miracles are done in the context of a given religious system, particularly to defend that religion. Suppose that there are ten religions, each one doctrinally incompatible with the other nine religions, and each one supported by its own miracles. The credibility of a miracle in any single religious system would be outweighed by the miracles of the nine other religious systems.

I may add as a *fourth* reason, which diminishes the authority of prodigies, that there is no testimony for any, even those which have not been expressly detected, that is not opposed by an infinite number of witnesses; so that not only the miracle destroys the credit of testimony, but the testimony destroys itself. To make this the better understood, let us consider, that, in matters of religion, whatever is different is contrary; and that it is impossible the religions of ancient ROME, of Turkey, of Siam, and of China should, all of them, be established on any solid foundation. Every miracle, therefore, pretended to have been wrought in any of these religions (and all of them abound in miracles), as its direct scope is to establish the particular system to which it is attributed; so has it the same force, though more indirectly, to overthrow every other system. In destroying a rival system, it likewise destroys the credit of those miracles, on which that system was established; so that all the prodigies of different religions are to be regarded as contrary facts, and the evidences of these prodigies, whether weak or strong, as opposite to each other. According to this method of reasoning, when we believe any miracle of Mahomet or his successors, we have for our warrant the testimony of a few barbarous Arabians: And on the other hand, we are to regard the authority of Titus Livius, Plutarch, Tacitus, and, in short, of all the authors and witnesses, Grecian, Chinese, and Roman Catholic, who have related any miracle in their particular religion; I say, we are to regard their testimony in the same light as if they had mentioned that Mahometan miracle, and had in express terms contradicted it, with the same certainty as they have for the miracle they relate. This argument may appear over subtle and refined; but is not in reality different from the reasoning of a judge, who supposes, that the credit of two witnesses, maintaining a crime against any one, is destroyed by the testimony of two others, who affirm him to have been two hundred leagues distant, at the same instant when the crime is said to have been committed.

ASK YOURSELF

18. Suppose that a miracle in Islam is supported by the testimony of a few Muslim believers. Suppose, also, that the ancient Greeks report their own miracles for their own Greek religion. How, according to Hume, should we regard the Greek reports in relation to the initial Muslim report?

Summary. Hume summarizes the key point of his essay. Most testimonies about miracles are unreliable, but even if they were reliable, they should not be believed since they go against the immense evidence we have in favor of constant natural law. His argument can be outlined as follows:

1. The evidence from experience in support of a law of nature is extremely strong.
2. A miracle is a violation of a law of nature.
3. Therefore, the evidence from experience against the occurrence of a miracle is extremely strong.

Upon the whole, then, it appears, that no testimony for any kind of miracle has ever amounted to a probability, much less to a proof; and that, even supposing it amounted to a proof, it would be opposed by another proof; derived from the very nature of the fact, which it would endeavor to establish. It is experience only, which gives authority to human testimony; and it is the same experience, which assures us of the laws of nature. When, therefore, these two kinds of experience are contrary, we have nothing to do but subtract the one from the other, and embrace an opinion, either on one side or the other, with that assurance which arises from the remainder. But according to the principle here explained, this subtraction, with regard to all popular religions, amounts to an entire annihilation; and therefore we may establish it as a maxim, that no human testimony can have such force as to prove a miracle, and make it a just foundation for any such system of religion.

ASK YOURSELF

19. What does Hume believe we should do when comparing two contrary experiences, specifically, experiences of miracles versus experiences of natural law?

20. Suppose, as sometimes happens, that a scientist reports an observation which contradicts what was considered to be a law of nature. According to Hume, should any other scientist pay attention? Should they pay attention only if they can repeat that observation?

Hume continues by arguing that, even if miracles did occur, it would be unreasonable to make them the foundation of religious systems, as is sometimes done in the world's religions.

Miracles in Christianity. In conclusion, Hume observes that theologians typically base the truth of Christianity upon the occurrence of miracles (such as the virgin birth and the resurrection), and in fact in his day such strategies were common. Hume argues instead that Christianity is founded on faith. Thus, he sees his attack on miracles above as an aid to true Christian belief since it undermines any attempt to rationally prove Christianity by appealing to Christian miracles. Hume's concluding comments here are among the most puzzling in his writings. On the surface, Hume appears to endorse a faith-oriented belief in Christianity. However, even Hume's critics in his own day saw his comments as an attempt to conceal his true view, which is that belief in Christianity has no merit whatsoever, whether based on miracles or on faith.

I am the better pleased with the method of reasoning here delivered, as I think it may serve to confound those dangerous friends or disguised enemies to the *Christian Religion,* who have undertaken to defend it by the principles of human reason. Our most holy religion is founded on *Faith,* not on reason; and it is a sure method of exposing it to put it to such a trial as it is, by no means, fitted to endure. To make this more evident, let us examine those miracles, related in scripture; and not to lose ourselves in too wide a field, let us confine ourselves to such as we find in the *Pentateuch,* which we shall examine, according to the principles of these pretended Christians, not as the word or testimony of God himself, but as the production of a mere human writer and historian. Here then we are first to consider a book, presented to us by a barbarous and ignorant people, written in an age when they were still more barbarous, and in all probability long after the facts which it relates, corroborated by no concurring testimony, and resembling those fabulous accounts, which every nation gives of its origin. Upon reading this book, we find it full of prodigies and miracles. It gives an account of a state of the world and of human nature entirely different from the present: Of our fall from that state: Of the age of man, extended to near a thousand years: Of the destruction of the world by a deluge: Of the arbitrary choice of one people, as the favorites of heaven; and that people the countrymen of the author: Of their deliverance from bondage by prodigies the most astonishing imaginable: I desire any one to lay his hand upon his heart, and after a serious consideration declare, whether he thinks that the falsehood of such a book, supported by such a testimony, would be more extraordinary and miraculous than all the miracles it relates; which is, however, necessary to make it be received, according to the measures of probability above established.

ASK YOURSELF

21. How does Hume think that we should evaluate the miracles of the Old Testament (particularly those he describes from the Pentateuch)?

Hume's concluding paragraph is particularly—and intentionally—hazy. He argues that Christianity is intimately linked with miracles. Since a reasonable person should not believe reports of miracles, then an act of God is required to make him believe. In Hume's words, it requires a miracle of faith. According to John Briggs, an eighteenth-century critic of Hume, Hume's real point is that belief in Christianity requires "miraculous stupidity."

What we have said of miracles may be applied, without any variation, to prophecies; and indeed, all prophecies are real miracles, and as such only, can be admitted as proofs of any revelation. If it did not exceed the capacity of human nature to foretell future events, it would be absurd to employ any prophecy as an argument for a divine mission or authority from heaven. So that, upon the whole, we may conclude, that the *Christian Religion* not only was at first attended with miracles, but even at this day cannot be believed by any reasonable person without one. Mere reason is insufficient to convince us of its veracity: And whoever is moved by *Faith* to assent to it, is conscious of a continued miracle in his own person, which subverts all the principles of his understanding, and gives him a determination to believe what is most contrary to custom and experience.

ASK YOURSELF

22. Hume concludes that whoever is moved by faith to believe in the miracles of Christianity is "conscious of a continued miracle in his own person." What does this miracle of Christian faith determine us to believe?

23. Suppose that God exists, and you were in a unique position to know that with undisputable certainty. Would you have a better reason for believing in certain reports of miracles than someone who did not?

24. A common criticism of Hume's view of miracles is that he has a rather narrow notion of the kind of evidence that might support miracle testimony, limiting it mainly to the credibility of the witnesses. According to the believer, though, the entire religious belief system itself constitutes strong evidence in support of at least some miracle claims. For example, the believer contends that religion offers a compelling account of creation, the place of humans in the world, the afterlife, and God's occasional miraculous intervention in the course of events. Should these factor into the evidence-weighing process regarding miracles? Explain.

2. RELIGION AS THE OPIUM OF THE MASSES: KARL MARX

During the nineteenth century, religious skeptics took a unique approach to the critique of religious belief. Rather than trying to prove that religious beliefs were factually false, they instead offered psychological and sociological explanations for how religious convictions arise in the minds of believers and how they function in society. Darwin, for example, argued that the human emotions underlying religious belief evolved over time and contributed to the survival of primitive people. Darwin's explanation does not technically mean that religious beliefs are false. However, it does have a negative impact on religion since Darwin contends that such belief is not the result of a personal spiritual encounter with God. We are in a sense programmed—or even brainwashed—into religious beliefs by purely natural causes. The German philosopher and economist Karl Marx offered his own sociological explanation of religious belief. His views are a direct consequence of his notion that humans are fundamentally economic beings—workers and producers. He thought that once this was understood it would become clear that religion is worse than just false: It is a device used in the service of exploitation.

The Opium of the People. According to Marx, the actual function of religious beliefs in people's lives is to comfort them in their miseries. It functions like a drug or an aspirin. It temporarily takes away the headache of existence.

FROM KARL MARX, *Toward a Critique of Hegel's Philosophy of Right* (1843)

For Germany the criticism of religion has been essentially completed, and criticism of religion is the premise of all criticism. The profane existence of error is compromised when its heavenly *oratio pro aris et focis* [defense of altar and hearth] has been refuted. Man, who has found only the reflection of himself in the fantastic reality of heaven where he sought a supernatural being, will no longer be inclined to find the semblance of himself, only the non-human being, where he seeks and must seek his true reality. The basis of irreligious criticism is: Man makes religion, religion does not make man.

ASK YOURSELF

25. People imagine God as a perfect being. But, according to Marx, where did they get that idea of perfection?

26. Marx simply asserts—rather than argues—that people make religion. Think of one reason in support of Marx's assertion.

And indeed religion is the self-consciousness and self-regard of man who has either not yet found or has already lost himself. But man is not an abstract being squatting outside the world. Man is the world of men, the state, society. This state and this society produce religion, which is an inverted consciousness of the world because they are an inverted world. Religion is the generalized theory of this world, its encyclopaedic compendium, its logic in popular form, its spiritualistic point d'honneur, its enthusiasm, its moral sanction, its solemn complement, its general ground of consolation and justification. It is the fantastic realization of the human essence inasmuch as the human essence possesses no true reality. The struggle against religion is therefore indirectly the struggle against that world whose spiritual aroma is religion.

Religious suffering is the expression of real suffering and at the same time the protest against real suffering. Religion is the sigh of the oppressed creature, the heart of a heartless world, as it is the spirit of spiritless conditions. It is the opium of the people.

The abolition of religion as people's illusory happiness is the demand for their real happiness. The demand to abandon illusions about their condition is a demand to abandon a condition which requires illusions.

ASK YOURSELF

27. What is the "real suffering" which religion expresses and protests against?

28. What, on Marx's view, would bring real, as opposed to illusory, happiness?

The criticism of religion is thus in embryo a criticism of the vale of tears whose halo is religion.

Criticism has plucked imaginary flowers from the chain, not so that man will wear the chain that is without fantasy or consolation but so that he will throw it off and pluck the living flower. The criticism of religion disillusions man so that he thinks, acts, and shapes his reality like a disillusioned man who has come to his senses, so that he revolves around himself and thus around his true sun. Religion is only the illusory sun that revolves around man so long as he does not revolve about himself.

Thus it is the task of history, once the otherworldly truth has disappeared, to establish the truth of this world. The immediate task of philosophy which is in the service of history is to unmask human self-alienation in its unholy forms now that it has been unmasked in its holy form. Thus the criticism of heaven turns into the criticism of the earth, the criticism of religion into the criticism of law, and the criticism of theology into the criticism of Politics.

ASK YOURSELF

29. What does it mean to say that religion involves alienation?

30. What then would be the "unholy form" of alienation?

Marx's Naturalism. Marx simply denies that the sorts of questions which sometimes give rise to religious belief should even be asked.

From Karl Marx, *Economic and Philosophical Manuscripts*

A being only considers himself independent when he stands on his own feet; and he only stands on his own feet when he owes his existence to himself. A man who lives by the grace of another regards himself as a dependent being. But I live completely by the grace of another if I owe him not only the sustenance of my life, but if he has, moreover, created my life, if he is the source of my life; and if it is not of my own creation, my life has necessarily a source of this kind outside it. The Creation is therefore an idea very difficult to dislodge from popular consciousness. The self-mediated being of nature and of man is incomprehensible to it, because it contradicts everything palpable in practical life.

The creation of the earth has received a mighty blow from geogeny—i.e., from the science which presents the formation of the earth, the coming-to-be of the earth, as a process, as self generation. Generatio aequivoca is the only practical refutation of the theory of creation. Now it is certainly easy to say to the single individual what Aristotle has already said. You have been begotten by your father and your mother; therefore in you the mating of two human beings—a species-act of human beings—has produced the human being. You see, therefore, that even physically, man owes his existence to man. Therefore you must not only keep sight of the one aspect—the infinite progression which leads you further to enquire: 'Who begot my father? Who his grandfather?", etc. You must also hold on to the circular movement sensuously perceptible in that progression, by which man repeats himself in procreation, thus always remaining the subject. You will reply, however: I grant you this circular movement; now grant me the progression which drives me ever further until I ask: Who begot thc first man, and nature as a whole?

It seems that Marx is mixed up here about certain arguments for the existence of God. Aristotle, and Aquinas following him, held that the entire series which constitutes the universe itself requires some explanation. That would *not* be an explanation which goes back to the first man (Adam).

I can only answer you: Your question is itself a product of abstraction. Ask yourself how you arrived at that question. Ask yourself whether your question is not posed from a standpoint to which I cannot reply, because it is a perverse one. Ask yourself whether that progression as such exists for a reasonable mind. When you ask about the creation of nature and man, you are abstracting, in so doing, from man and nature. You postulate them as nonexistent, and yet you want me to prove them to you as existing. Now I say to you: Give up your abstraction and you will also give up your question. Or if you want to hold on to your abstraction, then be consistent, and if you think of man and nature as non-existent, then think of yourself as non-existent, for you too are surely nature and man. Don't think, don't ask me, for as soon as you think and ask, your abstraction from the existence of nature and man has no meaning. Or are you such an egoist that you postulate everything as nothing, and yet want yourself to be?

ASK YOURSELF

31. Are there any good arguments in the preceding paragraph? If you think so, state one. If you think not, say what you think is flawed about any argument that is offered.

You can reply: I do not want to postulate the nothingness of nature. I ask you about its genesis, just as I ask the anatomist about the formation of bones, etc. But since for the socialist man the entire so-called history of the world is nothing but the begetting of man through human labor, nothing but the coming-to-be of nature for man, he has the visible, irrefutable proof of his birth through himself, of his process of coming-to-be. Since the real existence of man and nature has become practical, sensuous and perceptible—since man has become for man as the being of nature, and nature for man as the being of man—the question about an alien being, about a being above nature and man—a question which implies the admission of the inessentiality of nature and of man—has become impossible in practice. Atheism, as the denial of this inessentiality, has no longer any meaning, for atheism is a negation of God, and postulates the existence of man through this negation; but socialism as socialism no longer stands in any need of such a mediation. It proceeds from the practically and theoretically sensuous consciousness of man and of nature as the essence. Socialism is man's positive self-consciousness, no longer mediated through the annulment of religion, just as real life is man's positive reality.

ASK YOURSELF

32. According to Marx, belief in a transcendent God implies that nature and humanity are _____?

3. THE DEATH OF GOD: FRIEDRICH NIETZSCHE

German philosopher Friedrich Nietzsche (1844–1900) was a professor of philology at the University of Basel. He resigned at the young age of 34 due to poor health. He wrote extensively as he traveled, but, during the last decade of his life he was afflicted with a mental disorder and remained under the care of his mother and sister. From his earliest writings, Nietzsche revolted against traditional value systems and beliefs, which, he claimed, crushed a person's vitality. The belief in God was one such belief. Like Marx, Nietzsche does not attempt to disprove God's existence, but he tries to show (a) the damage that religious culture has done to society and (b) the difficulties involved in going beyond religion to a "higher" and nobler condition.

The Significance of the End of Religious Belief. Although Nietzsche was an atheist, he nevertheless felt that giving up belief in God would make a difference. But other disbelievers, he thinks, give up religion without fully realizing the consequences. The following parable expresses these ideas.

FROM FRIEDRICH NIETZSCHE, *The Joyful Wisdom* (1882)

Have you ever heard of the madman who on a bright morning lighted a lantern and ran to the market place calling out unceasingly: "I seek God!" I seek God!—As there were many people standing about who did not believe in God, he caused a great deal of amusement. "Why? is he lost? said one. Has he strayed away like a child? said another. Or does he keep himself hidden? Is he afraid of us? Has he taken a sea voyage? Has he emigrated?"—the people cried out laughingly, all in a hubbub. The insane man jumped into their midst and transfixed them with his glances. "Where is God gone?" he called out. "I mean to tell you. We have killed him—you and I. We are all his murderers. But how have we done it? How were we able to drink up the sea? Who gave us the sponge to wipe away the whole horizon? What did we do when we loosened this earth from its sun? Whither does it now move? Whither do we move? Away from all suns? Do we not dash on unceasingly? Backward, sideways, forward, in all directions? Is there still an above and below? Do we not stray, as through infinite nothingness? Does not empty space breathe upon us?

ASK YOURSELF

33. In the above passage, Nietzsche refers to certain modern beliefs which all of us hold. What are they?

Has it not become colder? Does not night come on continually, darker and darker? Shall we not have to light lanterns in the morning? Do we not hear the noise of the gravediggers who are burying God? Do we not smell the divine putrefaction? For even Gods putrefy. God is dead. God remains dead. And we have killed him. How shall we console ourselves, the most murderous of all murderers? "The holiest and the mightiest that the world has hitherto possessed has bled to death under our knife—who will wipe the blood from us? With what water could we cleanse ourselves? What lustrums, what sacred games shall we have to devise? Is not the magnitude of this deed too great for us? Shall we not ourselves have to become Gods, merely to seem worthy of it? There never was a greater event, and on account of it, all who are born after us belong to a higher history than any history hitherto"—Here the madman was silent and looked again at his hearers; they also were silent and looked at him in surprise. At last he threw his lantern on the ground, so that it broke in pieces and was extinguished. "I come too early," he then said, "I am not yet at the right time. This prodigious event is still on its way, and is traveling-it has not yet reached men's ears. Lightning and thunder need time, the light of the stars needs time, deeds need time, even after they are done, to be seen and heard. This deed is as yet further from them than the furthest star and yet they have done it!"—It is further stated that the madman made his way into different churches on the same day, and there intoned his Requiem aeternam deo. When led out and called to account, he always gave the reply: "What are these churches now, if they are not the tombs and monuments of God?"

ASK YOURSELF

34. What does the madman mean when he says he has "come too early"?

The Consequences of the End of Religious Belief. Nietzsche argues that the belief in science which has come to replace religious belief for many people is really itself a hangover from religious and "metaphysical" attitudes.

[I]t is always a metaphysical belief on which our belief in science rests—and that even we knowing ones of today, the godless and anti-metaphysical, still take our fire from the conflagration kindled by a belief a millennium old, the Christian belief, which was also the belief of Plato, that God is truth, that the truth is divine. . . . But what if this itself always becomes more untrustworthy, what if nothing any longer proves itself divine, except it be error, blindness, and falsehood; what if God himself turns out to be our most persistent lie?

Nietzsche seems to suggest that the belief in "truth" is itself outmoded. There is no fixed truth, not even in science. The belief that there is truth is a leftover from belief in God. The two go together. He believes that the consequences of the loss of religion are so radical that it is difficult to imagine them.

The most important of more recent events—that "God is dead," that the belief in the Christian God has become unworthy of belief—already begins to cast its first shadows over Europe. To the few at least whose eye, whose suspecting glance, is strong enough and subtle enough for this drama, some sun seems to have set, some old, profound confidence seems to have changed into doubt: our old world must seem to them daily more darksome, distrustful, strange, and "old." In the main, however, one may say that the event itself is far too great, too remote, too much beyond most people's power of apprehension for one to suppose that so much as the report of it could have reached them; not to speak of many who already knew what had really taken place, and what must all collapse now that this belief had been undermined. This is because so much was built upon it, so much rested on it, and had become one with it: for example, our entire European morality. This lengthy, vast, and uninterrupted process of crumbling, destruction, ruin, and overthrow which is now imminent: who has realized it sufficiently today to have to stand up as the teacher and herald of such a tremendous logic of terror, as the prophet of a period of gloom and eclipse, the like of which has probably never taken place on earth before? . . . Even we, the born riddle-readers, who wait as it were on the mountains posted between today and tomorrow, and engirt by their contradiction, we, the firstlings and premature children of the coming century, into whose sight especially the shadows which must forthwith envelop Europe should already have come—how is it that even we, without genuine sympathy for this period of gloom, contemplate its advent without any personal solicitude or fear?

ASK YOURSELF

35. Nietzsche considers "the death of God" to be a dramatic and fearful event. What, according to Nietzsche, formerly rested upon notions of God and religion?

Religion, Science, Pessimism, and Need. According to Nietzsche, people are reluctant to give up religion because of a certain need to believe, to rely on something. But that same need shows itself in many other forms.

How much faith a person requires in order to flourish—how much "fixed opinion" he requires which he does not wish to have shaken, because he holds himself thereby—is a measure of his power (or more plainly speaking, of his weakness). Most people in old Europe, as it seems to me, still need Christianity at present, and on that account it still finds belief. For such is man: a theological dogma might be refuted to him a thousand times—provided, however, that he had need of it, he would again and again accept it as "true" according to the famous "proof of power" of which the Bible speaks. Some have still need of metaphysics. But also there is the impatient longing for certainty which at present discharges itself in scientific, positivist fashion among large numbers of the people, the longing by all means to get at something stable (while on account of the warmth of the longing the establishing of the certainty is more leisurely and negligently undertaken): even this is still the longing for a hold, a support. In short, the instinct of weakness, which, while not actually creating religions, metaphysics, and convictions of all kinds, nevertheless preserves them. In fact, around all these positivist systems there fume the vapors of a certain pessimistic gloom, something of weariness, fatalism, disillusionment, and fear of new disillusionment—or else manifest animosity, ill-humor, anarchic exasperation, and whatever there is of symptom or masquerade of the feeling of weakness. Even the readiness with which our cleverest contemporaries get lost in wretched corners and alleys, for example, in *Vaterländerei* (so I designate what the French call "chauvinisme" and the Germans "German") [i.e., extreme patriotism], or in petty aesthetic creeds in the manner of Parisian nature (which only brings into prominence and uncovers that aspect of nature which excites simultaneously disgust and astonishment—they like at present to call this aspect *la vérité vraie* [i.e., the true truth]), or in Nihilism in the St. Petersburg style (that is to say, in the belief in unbelief, even to martyrdom for it): this shows always and above all the need of belief, support, backbone, and buttress.

ASK YOURSELF

36. According to Nietzsche, the instinct of _____ preserves religions, metaphysics, and convictions of all kinds.

SUMMING UP THE ISSUE OF CHALLENGES TO RELIGIOUS BELIEF

Skeptical philosophers have challenged religious belief on a variety of grounds. David Hume argued that it is never reasonable to believe second-hand reports concerning miracles. According to Hume, we should assess reports of miracles the way we assess any factual issue: We take the best evidence in favor of a claim and balance it against opposing evidence. The result will be that our experience of uniform natural law will always outweigh the testimony of any alleged miracle, regardless of how strong that testimony is. Although Hume assumes for the sake of argument that a testimony in favor of a miracle might come from a reliable source, he argues that in most cases the testimonies are actually very weak, which makes belief in miracles all the more unreasonable. Several nineteenth-century writers offered sociological explanations of how religious notions arise. Karl Marx argued that religion is a "projection" of what is best in human beings into a fanciful beyond. In that way, people are alienated from themselves and the failure to achieve happiness here and now is rationalized. Religion provides an imaginary solution to suffering and gives downtrodden and exploited people groundless hopes for a better life beyond the grave. Friedrich Nietzsche too believed that God and religion were human inventions, but he felt that civilization has advanced to the point that primitive notions of religion are no longer viable. In essence, God—or the idea of God—is dead, and it is civilization that has killed him. For Nietzsche, this is both a good and a bad thing. It is good to the extent that it gives us a new freedom. It is bad, though, because religion did offer a value system and, without God, we must scramble to find a new set of values.

CAN OF WORMS

Challenges to religious belief often involve questions about the nature of knowledge. Hume's discussion of miracles raises questions about how we assess factual evidence—particularly eyewitness testimony. What counts as strong or weak testimony, and does our experience of nature as consistent and law-like discredit reports of miracles? Marx's view of religion as an opium is connected with his economic and political theories: capitalist business owners strip workers of their humanity, and keep them pacified through religion. For Marx, the solution is the elimination of the capitalist system, possibly through a revolution among workers who will lay claim to a country's economic resources. Nietzsche's view of the death of God raises fundamental questions about morality: If we abandon a system of moral values grounded in religion, what kind of morality are we left with? Until recent centuries, a common presumption was that morality was not even possible without belief in God and an afterlife. Some major ethicists today would disagree, but the challenge remains to articulate what that nonreligious authority is behind moral values.

B. THE PROBLEM OF EVIL

When Allied forces entered Nazi concentration camps at the close of World War II, the scope of Hitler's assault against Europe's Jewish population quickly became apparent. Jews were systematically rounded up from all countries within Nazi reach, herded into death camps, and executed with machine-like precision. The total body count was around six million. The small fraction of the Jewish people that escaped extermination was left without their communities, homes, and families. Many survivors asked a very natural question: How could God permit suffering on this enormous scale? This question was all the more pointed in view of the thousands of innocent children that were among the casualties. Some Jews, unable to reconcile the horrors they experienced with the notion of divine goodness, abandoned their faith entirely.

**QUESTIONS
TO DISCUSS**

a. Many people who experience suffering in their lives raise the following question—if only temporarily: How could God permit such a thing to happen? Can you give an example of this?

b. Can you think of a way to rescue God from the charge that he is responsible for not preventing at least some major cases of suffering?

c. What justification might there be for God to allow the suffering of innocent children, and would that justification be of comfort to the parents of those children?

d. Is there anything that might explain the existence of natural evils, such as diseases and earthquakes, given that the world was created and is sustained by a loving God?

The grandfather of all critiques of religion is the argument from evil: How could an all-good God permit human suffering and other evils? The question arises in virtually all religions, and answers are as varied as the religions themselves. For example, the Zoroastrian religion teaches that there are two main spiritual forces in the universe—one good and the other evil—and all suffering results from the activity of the evil force. The question of human suffering often arises in religious discussions, not so much to undermine the religion itself, but to clarify God's nature and human expectations of God. In the Judeo-Christian tradition, the Old Testament Book of Job is the classic discussion of the problem. In that work, Job is a devoted believer who is suffering from financial, physical, and family disasters. Job and his friends speculate about why God would allow this to happen, and in the end Job resolves the issue by recognizing his insignificance in comparison with God's greatness. Some philosophers, on the other hand, have molded the problem of evil into an argument against the existence of God.

1. GOD AND HUMAN SUFFERING: FYODOR DOSTOEVSKY

Russian writer Fyodor Dostoevsky (1821–1881) explored religious and philosophical problems in the context of his novels, which are widely considered to be among the greatest ever written. In a late novel entitled *The Brothers Karamazov,* one of the brothers, Ivan, who is rebelling against his religious and moral heritage, puts the Christian beliefs of his brother Alyosha to the test by citing examples of terrible evils. Alyosha is a novice, that is, a beginning Christian monk who much admires an older monk, Zossima.

The Cruelty of Religious People. All sorts of evils seem to pose a challenge to religious belief. Ivan points out that believers in God are themselves often evil.

FROM FYODOR DOSTOEVSKY, *The Brothers Karamazov* (1879), 5.4

"Yours must be a fine God, if man created Him in his image and likeness. You asked just now what I was driving at. You see, I am fond of collecting certain facts, and, would you believe, I even copy anecdotes of a certain sort from newspapers and books, and I've already got a fine collection. The Turks, of course, have gone into it, but they are foreigners. I have specimens from home that are even better than the Turks. You know we prefer beating—rods and scourges—that's our national institution. Nailing ears is unthinkable for us, for we are, after all, Europeans. But the rod and the scourge we have always with us and they cannot be taken from us. Abroad now they scarcely do any beating. Manners are more humane, or laws have been passed, so that they don't dare to flog men now. But they make up for it in another way just as national as ours. And so national that it would be practically impossible among us, though I believe we are being inoculated with it, since the religious movement began in our aristocracy. I have a charming pamphlet, translated from the French, describing how, quite recently, five years ago, a murderer, Richard, was executed—a young man, I believe, of three and twenty, who repented and was converted to the Christian faith at the very scaffold. This Richard was an illegitimate child who was given as a child of six by his parents to some shepherds on the Swiss mountains.

"They brought him up to work for them. He grew up like a little wild beast among them. The shepherds taught him nothing, and scarcely fed or clothed him, but sent him out at seven to herd the flock in cold and wet, and no one hesitated or scrupled to treat him so. Quite the contrary, they thought they had every right, for Richard had been given to them as a chattel, and they did not even see the necessity of feeding him. Richard himself describes how in those years, like the Prodigal Son in the Gospel, he longed to eat of the mash given to the pigs, which were fattened for sale. But they wouldn't even give that, and beat him when he stole from the pigs. And that was how he spent all his childhood and his youth, till he grew up and was strong enough to go away and be a thief. The savage began to earn his living as a day labourer in Geneva. He drank what he earned, he lived like a brute, and finished by killing and robbing an old man. He was caught, tried, and condemned to death. They are not sentimentalists there. And in prison he was immediately surrounded by pastors, members of Christian brotherhoods, philanthropic ladies, and the like. They taught him to read and write in prison, and expounded the Gospel to him. They exhorted him, worked upon him, drummed at him incessantly, till at last he solemnly confessed his crime. He was converted. He wrote to the court himself that he was a monster, but that in the end God had vouchsafed him light and shown grace. All Geneva was in excitement The well-bred society of the town rushed to the prison, kissed Richard and embraced him; 'You are our brother, you have found grace.' And Richard does nothing but weep with emotion, 'Yes, I've found grace! All my youth and childhood I was glad of pigs' food, but now even I have found grace. I am dying in the Lord.' 'Yes, Richard, die in the Lord; you have shed blood and must die. Though it's not your fault that you knew not the Lord, when you coveted the pigs' food and were beaten for stealing it (which was very wrong of you, for stealing is forbidden); but you've shed blood and you must die.' And on the last day, Richard, perfectly limp, did nothing but cry and repeat every minute: 'This is my happiest day. I am going to the Lord.' 'Yes,' cry the pastors and the judges and philanthropic ladies. 'This is the happiest day of your life, for you are going to the Lord!' They all walk or drive to the scaffold in procession behind the prison van. At the scaffold they call to Richard: 'Die, brother, die in the Lord, for even thou hast found grace!' And so, covered with his brothers' kisses, Richard is dragged on to the scaffold, and led to the guillotine. And they chopped off his head in brotherly fashion, because he had found grace. Yes, that's characteristic. That pamphlet is translated into Russian by some Russian philanthropists of aristocratic rank and evangelical aspirations, and has been distributed gratis for the enlightenment of the people. The case of Richard is interesting because it's national. Though to us it's absurd to cut off a man's head, because he has become our brother and has found grace, yet we have our own speciality, which is all but worse."

ASK YOURSELF

37. What is Dostoevsky suggesting about religious people in this passage? Do you think he is exaggerating?

Cruelty to Animals. Ivan continues noting that innocent animals suffer terrible cruelties. Why would a good God permit this? How can anyone live in the face of such cruelties?

"Our historical pastime is the direct satisfaction of inflicting pain. There are lines in Nekrassov describing how a peasant lashes a horse on the eyes, 'on its meek eyes,' everyone must have seen it. It's peculiarly Russian. He describes how a feeble little nag has foundered under too heavy a load and cannot move. The peasant beats it, beats it savagely, beats it at last not knowing what he is doing in the intoxication of cruelty, thrashes it mercilessly over and over again. 'However weak you are, you must pull, if you die for it.' The nag strains, and then he begins lashing the poor defenceless creature on its weeping, on its 'meek eyes.' The frantic beast tugs and draws the load, trembling all over, gasping for breath, moving sideways, with a sort of unnatural spasmodic action—it's awful in Nekrassov. But that's only a horse, and God has horses to be beaten. So the Tartars have taught us, and they left us the knout as a remembrance of it."

ASK YOURSELF

38. Could an animal possibly deserve cruel punishment?

More Examples of Terrible Evil. Ivan points out that some of the worst evils in the world are those suffered by innocent children.

"But men, too, can be beaten. A well-educated, cultured gentleman and his wife beat their own child with a birch-rod, a girl of seven. I have an exact account of it. The papa was glad that the birch was covered with twigs. 'It stings more,' said he, and so be began stinging his daughter. I know for a fact there are people who at every blow are worked up to sensuality, to literal sensuality, which increases progressively at every blow they inflict. They beat for a minute, for five minutes, for ten minutes, more often and more savagely. The child screams. At last the child cannot scream, it gasps, 'Daddy daddy!' By some diabolical unseemly chance the case was brought into court. A counsel is engaged. The Russian people have long called a barrister 's conscience for hire.' The counsel protests in his client's defense. 'It's such a simple thing,' he says, 'an everyday domestic event. A father corrects his child. To our shame be it said, it is brought into court.' The jury, convinced by him, give a favorable verdict. The public roars with delight that the torturer is acquitted. Ah, pity I wasn't there! I would have proposed to raise a subscription in his honor! Charming pictures.

"But I've still better things about children. I've collected a great, great deal about Russian children, Alyosha. There was a little girl of five who was hated by her father and mother, 'most worthy and respectable people, of good education and breeding.' You see, I must repeat again, it is a peculiar characteristic of many people, this love of torturing children, and children only. To all other types of humanity these torturers behave mildly and benevolently, like cultivated children, even fond of children themselves in that sense. It's just their defenselessness that tempts the tormentor, just the angelic confidence of the child who has no refuge and no appeal, that sets his vile blood on fire. In every man, of course, a demon lies hidden—the demon of rage, the demon of lustful heat at the screams of the tortured victim, the demon of lawlessness let off the chain, the demon of diseases that follow on vice, gout, kidney disease, and so on.

"This poor child of five was subjected to every possible torture by those cultivated parents. They beat her, thrashed her, kicked her for no reason till her body was one bruise. Then, they went to greater refinements of cruelty—shut her up all night in the cold and frost in a privy, and because she didn't ask to be taken up at night (as though a child of five sleeping its angelic, sound sleep could be trained to wake and ask), they smeared her face and filled her mouth with excrement, and it was her mother, her mother did this. And that mother could sleep, hearing the poor child's groans! Can you understand why a little creature, who can't even understand what's done to her, should beat her little aching heart with her tiny fist in the dark and the cold, and weep her meek unresentful tears to dear, kind God to protect her? Do you understand that, friend and brother, you pious and humble novice? Do you understand why this infamy must be and is permitted? Without it, I am told, man could not have existed on earth, for he could not have known good and evil. Why should he know that diabolical good and evil when it costs so much? Why, the whole world of knowledge is not worth that child's prayer to dear, kind God'! I say nothing of the sufferings of grown-up people, they have eaten the apple, damn them, and the devil take them all! But these little ones! I am making you suffer, Alyosha, you are not yourself. I'll leave off if you like."

"Never mind. I want to suffer too," muttered Alyosha.

ASK YOURSELF

39. Why might someone think that human life requires knowledge of good and evil?

"One picture, only one more, because it's so curious, so characteristic, and I have only just read it in some collection of Russian antiquities. I've forgotten the name. I must look it up. It was in the darkest days of serfdom at the beginning of the century, and long live the Liberator of the People! There was in those days a general of aristocratic connections, the owner of great estates, one of those men—somewhat exceptional, I believe, even then—who, retiring from the service into a life of leisure, are convinced that they've earned absolute power over the lives of their subjects. There were such men then. So our general, settled on his property of two thousand souls, lives in pomp, and domineers over his poor neighbors as though they were dependents and buffoons. He has kennels of hundreds of hounds and nearly a hundred dog-boys—all mounted, and in uniform. One day a serf-boy, a little child of eight, threw a stone in play and hurt the paw of the general's favorite hound. 'Why is my favorite dog lame?' He is told that the boy threw a stone that hurt the dog's paw. 'So you did it.' The general looked the child up and down. 'Take him.' He was taken—taken from his mother and kept shut up all night. Early that morning the general comes out on horseback, with the hounds, his dependents, dog-boys, and huntsmen, all mounted around him in full hunting parade. The servants are summoned for their edification, and in front of them all stands the mother of the child. The child is brought from the lock-up. It's a gloomy, cold, foggy, autumn day, a capital day for hunting. The general orders the child to be undressed; the child is stripped naked. He shivers, numb with terror, not daring to cry. . . . 'Make him run,' commands the general. 'Run! run!' shout the dog-boys. The boy runs. . . . 'At him!' yells the general, and he sets the whole pack of hounds on the child.

"The hounds catch him, and tear him to pieces before his mother's eyes! . . . I believe the general was afterwards declared incapable of administering his estates. Well—what did he deserve? To be shot? To be shot for the satisfaction of our moral feelings? Speak, Alyosha!"

"To be shot," murmured Alyosha, lifting his eyes to Ivan with a pale, twisted smile.

"Bravo!" cried Ivan delighted. "If even you say so . . . You're a pretty monk! So there is a little devil sitting in your heart, Alyosha Karamazov!"

"What I said was absurd, but . . ."

"That's just the point, that 'but'!" cried Ivan. "Let me tell you, novice, that the absurd is only too necessary on earth. The world stands on absurdities, and perhaps nothing would have come to pass in it without them. We know what we know!"

"What do you know?"

"I understand nothing," Ivan went on, as though in delirium. "I don't want to understand anything now. I want to stick to the fact. I made up my mind long ago not to understand. If I try to understand anything, I shall be false to the fact, and I have determined to stick to the fact."

ASK YOURSELF

40. Someone might think they "understand" why there are terrible evils in the world if they have an explanation of it—for example, an explanation in terms of free will. According to Ivan, such explanations may make us false to _____.

"Why are you trying me?" Alyosha cried, with sudden distress. "Will you say what you mean at last?"

"Of course, I will; that's what I've been leading up to. You are dear to me, I don't want to let you go, and I won't give you up to your Zossima."

Ivan for a minute was silent, his face became all at once very sad.

"Listen! I took the case of children only to make my case clearer . . . I must have justice, or I will destroy myself. And not justice in some remote infinite time and space, but here on earth, and that I could see myself. I have believed in it. I want to see it, and if I am dead by then, let me rise again, for if it all happens without me, it will be too unfair. Surely I haven't suffered simply that I, my crimes and my sufferings, may manure the soil of the future harmony for somebody else. I want to see with my own eyes the hind lie down with the lion and the victim rise up and embrace his murderer. I want to be there when everyone suddenly understands what it has all been for. All the religions of the world are built on this longing, and

I am a believer. But then there are the children, and what am I to do about them? That's a question I can't answer. For the hundredth time I repeat, there are numbers of questions, but I've only taken the children, because in their case what I mean is so unanswerably clear. Listen! If all must suffer to pay for the eternal harmony, what have children to do with it, tell me, please? It's beyond all comprehension why they should suffer, and why they should pay for the harmony. Why should they, too, furnish material to enrich the soil for the harmony of the future?"

ASK YOURSELF

41. Ivan's references to a "harmony" refer to a harmony between our experience of unexplained evil and the purposes, the hidden plan, of _____.

"I understand solidarity in sin among men. I understand solidarity in retribution, too; but there can be no such solidarity with children. And if it is really true that they must share responsibility for all their fathers' crimes, such a truth is not of this world and is beyond my comprehension. Some jester will say, perhaps, that the child would have grown up and have sinned, but you see he didn't grow up, he was torn to pieces by the dogs, at eight years old. Oh, Alyosha, I am not blaspheming! I understand, of course, what an upheaval of the universe it will be when everything in heaven and earth blends in one hymn of praise and everything that lives and has lived cries aloud: 'Thou art just, O Lord, for Thy ways are revealed.' When the mother embraces the fiend who threw her child to the dogs, and all three cry aloud with tears, 'Thou art just, O Lord!' then, of course, the crown of knowledge will be reached and all will be made clear. But what pulls me up here is that I can't accept that harmony. And while I am on earth, I make haste to take my own measures. You see, Alyosha, perhaps it really may happen that if I live to that moment, or rise again to see it, I, too, perhaps, may cry aloud with the rest, looking at the mother embracing the child's torturer, 'Thou art just, O Lord!' but I don't want to cry aloud then. While there is still time, I hasten to protect myself, and so I renounce the higher harmony altogether. It's not worth the tears of that one tortured child who beat itself on the breast with its little fist and prayed in its stinking outhouse, with its unexpiated tears to 'dear, kind God'! It's not worth it, because those tears are unatoned for. They must be atoned for, or there can be no harmony. But how? How are you going to atone for them? Is it possible? By their being avenged? But what do I care for avenging them? What do I care for a hell for oppressors? What good can hell do, since those children have already been tortured? And what becomes of harmony, if there is hell?"

ASK YOURSELF

42. Suppose that vengeance is taken on all evil doers. Or suppose that those who do evil suffer for it eternally in hell. Would that take care of the problem of evil? Why, or why not?

"I want to forgive. I want to embrace. I don't want more suffering. And if the sufferings of children go to swell the sum of sufferings which was necessary to pay for truth, then I protest that the truth is not worth such a price. I don't want the mother to embrace the oppressor who threw her son to the dogs! She dare not forgive him! Let her forgive him for herself, if she will, let her forgive the torturer for the immeasurable suffering of her mother's heart. But the sufferings of her tortured child she has no right to forgive; she dare not forgive the torturer, even if the child were to forgive him! And if that is so, if they dare not forgive, what becomes of harmony? Is there in the whole world a being who would have the right to forgive and could forgive? I don't want harmony. From love for humanity I don't want it. I would rather be left with the unavenged suffering. I would rather remain with my unavenged suffering and unsatisfied indignation, even if I were wrong. Besides, too high a price is asked for harmony; it's beyond our means to pay so much to enter on it. And so I hasten to give back my entrance ticket, and if I am an honest man I am bound to give it back as soon as possible. And that I am doing. It's not God that I don't accept, Alyosha, only I most respectfully return him the ticket."

"That's rebellion," murmered Alyosha, looking down.

"Rebellion? I am sorry you call it that," said Ivan earnestly. "One can hardly live in rebellion, and I want to live. Tell me yourself, I challenge your answer. Imagine that you are creating a fabric of human destiny with the object of making men happy in the end, giving them peace and rest at last, but that it was essential and inevitable to torture to death only one tiny creature—that baby beating its breast with its fist, for instance—and to found that edifice on its unavenged tears, would you consent to be the architect?"

"No, I wouldn't consent," said Alyosha softly.

"And can you admit the idea that men for whom you are building it would agree to accept their happiness on the foundation of the unexpiated blood of a little victim? And accepting it would remain happy for ever?"

"No, I can't admit it. Brother," said Alyosha suddenly, with flashing eyes, "you said just now, is there a being in the whole world who would have the right to forgive and could forgive? But there is a Being and He can forgive everything, all and for all, because He gave His innocent blood for all and everything. You have forgotten Him, and on Him is built the edifice, and it is to Him they cry aloud, 'Thou art just, O Lord, for Thy ways are revealed!'"

"Ah! the One without sin and His blood! No, I have not forgotten Him; on the contrary I've been wondering all the time how it was you did not bring Him in before, for usually all arguments on your side put Him in the foreground."

ASK YOURSELF

43. Can you think of any solution to the problem of evil that takes account of the sufferings of animals and children?

2.   THE LOGICAL PROBLEM OF EVIL: JOHN L. MACKIE

One of the more influential recent presentations of the problem of evil is that by John L. Mackie (1917–1981). Many previous discussions of the issue, such as Dostoevsky's, point out problems in reconciling God's existence with the presence of evil in the world. The uniqueness of Mackie's discussion, though, lies in his attempt to show that belief in an all good and all powerful God is *logically inconsistent* with the fact of suffering in the world. The result, for Mackie, is that people who believe in God must at the same time acknowledge that their belief is illogical.

From John L. Mackie, "Evil and Omnipotence" (1955)

The traditional arguments for the existence of God have been fairly thoroughly criticized by philosophers. But the theologian can, if he wishes, accept this criticism. He can admit that no rational proof of God's existence is possible. And he can still retain all that is essential to his position, by holding that God's existence is known in some other, non-rational way. I think, however, that a more telling criticism can be made by way of the traditional problem of evil. Here it can be shown, not that religious beliefs lack rational support, but that they are positively irrational, that the several parts of the essential theological doctrine are inconsistent with one another, so that the theologian can maintain his position as a whole only by a much more extreme rejection of reason than in the former case. He must now be prepared to believe, not merely what cannot be proved, but what can be *disproved* from other beliefs that he also holds.

ASK YOURSELF

44. According to Mackie, the failure of theistic proofs shows that religious belief lacks rational support. What, though, does the problem of evil show about religious belief?

Mackie lays out the basic problem by stating the premises and showing how a contradiction subsequently arises.

In its simplest form the problem is this: God is omnipotent; God is wholly good; and yet evil exists. There seems to be some contradiction between these three propositions, so that if any two of them were true the third would be false. But at the same time all three are essential parts of most theological positions: the theologian, it seems, at once must adhere and *cannot consistently* adhere to all three. (The problem does not arise only for theists, but I shall discuss it in the form in which it presents itself for ordinary theism.)

However, the contradiction does not arise immediately; to show it we need some additional premises, or perhaps some quasi-logical rules connecting the terms "good," "evil," and "omnipotent." These additional principles are that good is opposed to evil, in such a way that a good thing always eliminates evil as far as it can, and that there are no limits to what an omnipotent thing can do. From these it follows that a good omnipotent thing eliminates evil completely, and then the propositions that a good omnipotent thing exists, and that evil exists, are incompatible.

ASK YOURSELF

45. What are the "additional premises" that Mackie supplies in order to generate a contradiction between God and the presence of evil?

Adequate and Inadequate Solutions. According to Mackie, the only real solution to the problem of evil is to abandon one of the key premises, such as that God is all-powerful, or that evil truly exists.

Now once the problem is fully stated it is clear that it can be solved, in the sense that the problem will not arise if one gives up at least one of the propositions that constitute it. If you are prepared to say that God is not wholly good, or not quite omnipotent, or that evil does not exist, or that good is not opposed to the kind of evil that exists, or that there are limits to what an omnipotent thing can do, then the problem of evil will not arise for you.

There are, then, quite a number of adequate solutions of the problem of evil, and some of these have been adopted, or almost adopted, by various thinkers. For example, a few have been prepared to deny God's omnipotence, and rather more have been prepared to keep the term "omnipotence" but severely to restrict its meaning, recording quite a number of things that an omnipotent being cannot do. Some have said that evil is an illusion, perhaps because they held that the whole world of temporal, changing things is an illusion, and that what we call evil belongs only to this world, or perhaps because they held that although temporal things are much as we see them, those that we call evil are not really evil. Some have said that what we call evil is merely the privation of good, that evil in a positive sense, evil that would really be opposed to good, does not exist. Many have agreed with Pope that disorder is harmony not understood, and that partial evil is universal good. Whether any of these views is *true* is, of course, another question. But each of them gives an adequate solution of the problem of evil in the sense that if you accept it this problem does not arise for you, though you may, of course, have *other* problems to face.

ASK YOURSELF

46. What was Alexander Pope's solution to the problem of evil?

Although there are genuine solutions to the problem of evil, Mackie believes that most theologians have bypassed these or at best advocated them in a half-hearted way. The result is that theological literature abounds with fallacious solutions that claim to remove the contradiction without abandoning any of the key premises. Mackie proposes to examine several of these, pointing out their inadequacies.

Whether Good Can Exist Without Evil. A common proposed solution to the problem of evil is that good and evil are connected in such a way that the one cannot exist without the other. For example, imagine that everything in the world was colored red; without any non-red object, we'd never be able to actually perceive the redness of things. By parallel reasoning, without the presence of some evil, we could not perceive goodness in the world around us.

It may be replied that good and evil are necessary counterparts in the same way as any quality and its logical opposite: redness can occur, it is suggested, only if non-redness also occurs. But unless evil is merely the privation of good, they are not logical opposites, and some further argument would be needed to show that they are counterparts in the same way as genuine logical opposites. Let us assume that this could be given. There is still doubt of the correctness of the metaphysical principle that a quality must have a real opposite: I suggest that it is not really impossible that everything should be, say, red, that the truth is merely that if everything were red we should not notice redness, and so we should have no word "red"; we observe and give names to qualities only if they have real opposites. If so, the principle that a term must have an opposite would belong only to our language or to our thought, and would not be an ontological principle, and, correspondingly, the rule that good cannot exist without evil would not state a logical necessity of a sort that God would just have to put up with. God might have made everything good, though *we* should not have noticed it if he had.

In the above, Mackie responds by drawing a distinction between what is ontologically necessary for a particular quality to *actually exist,* and what is epistemologically necessary for us to *recognize* a particular quality. According to Mackie, we need non-red things only to *recognize* red things around us, and not for any red things to *actually exist.*

ASK YOURSELF

47. According to Mackie, if no evil existed in the world, what impact would this have on goodness in the world?

Suppose, though, that evil was ontologically required for goodness to actually exist—rather than required for merely recognizing goodness. How much evil would that take? According to Mackie, not very much.

But, finally, even if we concede that this *is* an ontological principle, it will provide a solution for the problem of evil only if one is prepared to say, "Evil exists, but only just enough evil to serve as the counterpart of good." I doubt whether any theist will accept this. After all, the *ontological* requirement that non-redness should occur would be satisfied even if all the universe, except for a minute speck, were red, and, if there were a corresponding requirement for evil as a counterpart to good, a minute dose of evil would presumably do. But theists are not usually willing to say, in all contexts, that all the evil that occurs is a minute and necessary dose. . . .

ASK YOURSELF

48. Suppose that we needed non-redness in order for redness to actually exist. How much non-redness would we need?

Whether the Universe Is Better with Some Evil in It. Another popular solution to the problem of evil is the suggestion that the universe is, on the whole, better because of the presence of evil. For example, we might say that if there were no poverty, tragedy, or unhappiness, then there would be no opportunity for charity, heroism, and sympathy—which are human qualities that make the world much better than it would be otherwise.

Much more important is a solution . . . that evil may contribute to the goodness of a whole in which it is found, so that the universe as a whole is better as it is, with some evil in it, than it would be if there were no evil. This solution may be developed in either of two ways. It may be supported by an aesthetic analogy, by the fact that contrasts heighten beauty, that in a musical work, for example, there may occur discords which somehow add to the beauty of the work as a whole. Alternatively, it may be worked out in connection with the notion of progress, that the best possible organization of the universe will not be static, but progressive, that the gradual overcoming of evil by good is really a finer thing than would be the eternal unchallenged supremacy of good.

In either case, this solution usually starts from the assumption that the evil whose existence gives rise to the problem of evil is primarily what is called physical evil, that is to say, pain. . . . But let us see exactly what is being done here. Let us call pain and misery "first order evil" or "evil (1)." What contrasts with this, namely, pleasure and happiness, will be called "first order good" or "good (1)." Distinct from this is "second order good" or "good (2)" which somehow emerges in a complex situation in which evil (1) is a necessary component—logically, not merely causally, necessary. (Exactly *how* it emerges does not matter: in the crudest version of this solution good (2) is simply the heightening of happiness by the contrast with misery, in other versions it includes sympathy with suffering, heroism in facing danger, and the gradual decrease of first order evil and increase of first order good.) It is also being assumed that second order good is more important than first order good or evil, in particular that it more than outweighs the first order evil it involves.

Now that is a particularly subtle attempt to solve the problem of evil. It defends God's goodness and omnipotence on the ground that (on a sufficiently long view) this is the best of all logically possible worlds, because it includes the important second order goods, and yet it admits that real evils, namely first order evils, exist. But does it still hold that good and evil are opposed? Not, clearly, in the sense that we set out originally: good does not tend to eliminate evil in general. Instead, we have a modified, a more complex pattern. First order good (e.g. happiness) *contrasts with* first order evil (e.g. misery): these two are opposed in a fairly mechanical way; some second order goods (e.g. benevolence) try to maximize first order good and minimize first order evil; but God's goodness is not this, it is rather the will to maximize *second* order good. We might, therefore, call God's goodness an example of a third order goodness, or good (3). While this account is different from our original one, it might well be held to be an improvement on it, to give a more accurate description of the way in which good is opposed to evil, and to be consistent with the essential theist position.

ASK YOURSELF

49. What is the difference between a first-order, second-order, and third-order good?

Having presented this solution in its strongest form, Mackie continues by pointing out its limitations.

There might, however, be several objections to this solution.

First, some might argue that such qualities as benevolence—and a *fortiori* the third order goodness which promotes benevolence—have a merely derivative value, that they are not higher sorts of good, but merely means to good (1), that is, to happiness, so that it would be absurd for God to keep misery in existence in order to make possible the virtues of benevolence, heroism, etc. The theist who adopts the present solution must, of course, deny this, but he can do so with some plausibility, so I should not press this objection.

Secondly, it follows from this solution that God is not in our sense benevolent or sympathetic: he is not concerned to minimize evil (1), but only to promote good (2); and this might be a disturbing conclusion for some theists.

But, thirdly, the fatal objection is this. Our analysis shows clearly the possibility of the existence of a *second* order evil, an evil (2) contrasting with good (2) as evil (1) contrasts with good (1). This would include malevolence, cruelty, callousness, cowardice, and states in which good (1) is decreasing an evil (1) increasing. And just as good (2) is held to be the important kind of good, the kind that God is concerned to promote, so evil (2) will, by analogy, be the important kind of evil, the kind which God, if he were wholly good and omnipotent, would eliminate. And yet evil (2) plainly exists, and indeed most theists (in other contexts) stress its existence more than that of evil (1). We should, therefore, state the problem of evil in terms of second order evil, and against this form of the problem the present solution is useless. . . .

ASK YOURSELF

50. The principal problem with this solution is that it does not show how goodness counterbalances second-order evils—the kind of evil that a good God should be most concerned to eliminate. What are Mackie's examples of second-order evils?

Whether Evil Is Due to Human Freewill. The final solution that Mackie considers is commonly called the *free will defense:* Evil is the result of free human choice, for which God bears no responsibility. The presumption here is that the world is a better place if it contains people with free wills, even if those people at times choose to do evil.

Perhaps the most important proposed solution of the problem of evil is that evil is not to be ascribed to God at all, but to the independent actions of human beings, supposed to have been endowed by God with freedom of the will. This solution may be combined with the preceding one: first order evil (e.g. pain) may be justified as a logically necessary component in second order good (e.g. sympathy) while second order evil (e.g. cruelty) is not *justified,* but is so ascribed to human beings that God cannot be held responsible for it. This combination evades my third criticism of the preceding solution.

The freewill solution also involves the preceding solution at a higher level. To explain why a wholly good God gave men freewill although it would lead to some important evils, it must be argued that it is better on the whole that men should act freely, and sometimes err, than that they should be innocent automata, acting rightly in a wholly determined way. Freedom, that is to say, is now treated as a third order good, and as being more valuable than second order goods (such as sympathy and heroism) would be if they were deterministically produced, and it is being assumed that second order evils, such as cruelty, are logically necessary accompaniments of freedom, just as pain is a logically necessary pre-condition of sympathy.

I think that this solution is unsatisfactory primarily because of the incoherence of the notion of freedom of the will: but I cannot discuss this topic adequately here, although some of my criticisms will touch upon it.

Mackie's principal problem with the free-will defense is that it presumes that people have genuinely free wills—a contention that Mackie disagrees with. Aside from this, though, he feels that the free-will defense overlooks an option that God had. Why couldn't God have created a world containing free people in which we all freely choose to do the right thing? Suppose, for example, that, prior to creation, God looked at all the possible worlds that he might create. World 1, for example, might consist of one brick and nothing more; God would presumably reject this world since he could make something better. World 2 might consist of a world similar to ours, but with only robot-like creatures, with no free wills; God would also reject this plan since he could do better than this as well. World 3 might contain people with free wills, and in this world Hitler freely chooses to commit the horrible crimes that he did commit. In World 4, people have free wills, but Hitler instead freely chooses to be morally good. In World 5, people have free wills, and *everyone* freely chooses to be morally good. According to Mackie, an all-good God would opt to create World 5 over the others. That is, God could have created a world containing free creatures that always freely chose to do good. Thus, the free will defense fails to rectify the existence of a good God with the presence of evil.

First I should query the assumption that second order evils are logically necessary accompaniments of freedom. I should ask this: if God has made men such that in their free choices they sometimes prefer what is good and sometimes what is evil, why could He not have made men such that they always freely choose the good? If there is no logical impossibility in a man's freely choosing the good on one, or on several, occasions, there cannot be a logical impossibility in his freely choosing the good on every occasion. God was not, then, faced with a choice between making innocent automata and making beings who, in acting freely, would sometimes go wrong: there was open to him the obviously better possibility of making beings who would act freely but always go right. Clearly, his failure to avail himself of this possibility is inconsistent with his being both omnipotent and wholly good.

ASK YOURSELF

51. According to Mackie, God could have created a world containing people with _____ who would always _____.

If it is replied that this objection is absurd, that the making of some wrong choices is logically necessary for freedom, it would seem that "freedom" must here mean complete randomness or indeterminacy, including randomness with regard to the alternatives good and evil, in other words that men's choices and consequent actions can be "free" only if they are not determined by their characters. Only on this assumption can God escape the responsibility for men's actions; for if he made them as they are, but did not determine their wrong choices, this can only be because the wrong choices are not determined by men as they are. But then if freedom is randomness, how can it be a characteristic of *will?* And, still more, how can it be the most important good? What value or merit would there be in free choices if these were random actions which were not determined by the nature of the agent?

ASK YOURSELF

52. According to Mackie, what is wrong with the believer saying that making some wrong choices is logically necessary for freedom?

I conclude that to make this solution plausible two different senses of "freedom" must be confused, one sense which will justify the view that freedom is a third order good, more valuable than other goods would be without it, and another sense, sheer randomness, to prevent us from ascribing to God a decision to make men such that they sometimes go wrong when he might have made them such that they would always freely go right.

This criticism is sufficient to dispose of this solution. But besides this there is a fundamental difficulty in the notion of an omnipotent God creating men with free will, for if men's wills are really free this must mean that even God cannot control them, that is, that God is no longer omnipotent. It may be objected that God's gift of freedom to men does not mean that he *cannot* control their wills, but that he always *refrains* from controlling their wills. But why, we may ask, should God refrain from controlling evil wills? Why should he not leave men free to will rightly, but intervene when he sees them beginning to will wrongly? If God could do this, but does not, and if he is wholly good, the only explanation could be that even a wrong free act of will is not really evil, that its freedom is a value which outweighs its wrongness, so that there would be a loss of value if God took away the wrongness and the freedom together. But this is utterly opposed to what theists say about sin in other contexts. The present solution of the problem of evil, then, can be maintained only in the form that God has made men so free that he *cannot* control their wills.

This leads us to what I call the Paradox of Omnipotence: can an omnipotent being make things which he cannot subsequently control? Or, what is practically equivalent to this, can an omnipotent being make rules which then bind himself? (These are practically equivalent because any such rules could be regarded as setting certain things beyond his control, and *vice versa*.) The second of these formulations is relevant to the suggestions that we have already met, that an omnipotent God creates the rules of logic or causal laws, and is then bound by them.

It is clear that this is a paradox: the questions cannot be answered satisfactorily either in the affirmative or in the negative. If we answer "Yes," it follows that if God actually makes things which he cannot control, or makes rules which bind himself, he is not omnipotent once he has made them: there are then things which he cannot do. But if we answer "No," we are immediately asserting that there are things which he cannot do, that is to say that he is already not omnipotent. . . .

ASK YOURSELF

53. What is the paradox of omnipotence?

3. THE LOGICAL PROBLEM OF EVIL CHALLENGED: WILLIAM ROWE

Mackie's discussion of the problem of evil quickly became the subject of much philosophical discussion, perhaps as much for the boldness of his skeptical claims as for the force of his argument. Religious believers, according to Mackie, are illogical insofar as their belief in God is contradicted by other facts that believers themselves hold. But is the situation really as bad as that? Several respondents think that it is not. The heart of Mackie's argument is that belief in an all-good and all-powerful God is logically inconsistent with the fact of suffering in the world. Contemporary philosopher William Rowe argues that these concepts are not in fact logically inconsistent. The key here is to understand the relation between a logical *contradiction* and a logical *inconsistency*. A logical *contradiction* occurs when I assert a particular statement and its negation at the same time. For example, the propositions, "this object is red" and "it is not the case that this object is red" are contradictory. It is logically impossible for the object to be red and not red at the same time in the same respect. By contrast, a logical *inconsistency* occurs when two statements *lead* to a contradiction, but are not explicitly contradictory themselves. For example, these two statements are inconsistent:

1. This object is red.
2. It is not the case that this object is colored.

This is because we all assume another necessarily true statement:

3. Whatever is red is colored.

When we take 1 and 3 together, we then get an additional statement:

4. This object is colored.

And, statement 4 explicitly contradicts statement 2. Now, Mackie claims that there is a logical inconsistency between the following statements:

1. An all-good and all-powerful God exists.
2. Evil exists.

Mackie then offers this third statement as a means of generating a contradiction:

3. A good omnipotent thing eliminates evil completely.

Statements 1 and 3 combined give us the following statement:

4. It is not the case that evil exists.

And, statement 4 explicitly contradicts statement 2. The question for Rowe, then, is whether statement 3 is necessarily true. He thinks it isn't:

> For in our own experience we know that evil is sometimes connected with good in such a way that we are powerless to achieve the good without permitting the evil. Moreover, in such instances, the good sometimes outweighs the evil, so that a good being might intentionally permit the evil to occur in order to realize the good which outweighs it.
>
> Leibniz gives the example of a general who knows that in order to achieve the good of saving the town from being destroyed by an attacking army he must order his men to defend the town, with the result that some of his men will suffer and die. [From William L. Rowe, *Philosophy of Religion,* Chapter 6]

ASK YOURSELF

54. Give an example of your own in which some small evil must occur in order to bring about a greater good.

According to Rowe, then, we must reject Mackie's statement 3 since "we can't be sure that an omnipotent, wholly good being will prevent the occurrence of any evil whatever." Rowe considers a revised version of statement 3, which might be more acceptable:

3'. A good, omnipotent, omniscient being prevents the occurrence of any evil that is not logically necessary for the occurrence of a good which outweighs it.

Although this revised statement is necessarily true, the problem now is that it does not lead to statement 4 above, namely, "it is not the case that evil exists," and thus no contradiction arises. The only thing that 3' shows is that the evils that do exist in the world are logically necessary for the occurrence of goods which outweigh them. The upshot of the logical problem of evil, for Rowe, is that either the additional statement will not be necessarily true, or if it is necessarily true, then it will not give rise to a contradiction. In either case, the logical problem of evil fails.

Rejecting the logical problem of evil, Rowe nevertheless believes that there is still a problem with the idea that both God and evil exist—a problem that he calls the *evidential problem of evil.* Although the variety and extent of evil in the world may not be logically inconsistent with the existence of God, it does, he thinks, offer rational support for the view that God does not exist. Rowe's argument is this:

1. There exist instances of intense suffering which an omnipotent, omniscient being could have prevented without thereby preventing the occurrence of any greater good.

2. An omniscient, wholly good being would prevent the occurrence of any intense suffering it could, unless it could not do so without thereby preventing the occurrence of some greater good.

3. Therefore, there does not exist an omnipotent, omniscient, wholly good being.

The key premise here is the first one, and the principal justification for it rests on our gut feeling that certain kinds of evil could be prevented without upsetting any greater good. Consider, for example, a fawn that is trapped and burned in a fire and suffers in agony for several days before dying. What possible greater good can come from this? None, it would seem. However, Rowe argues, this is not decisive evidence, since we are not in a position to foresee all of the potentially beneficial consequences that might occur from this tragedy. But, based on what we do know from our life experiences, it seems to be a tragedy which serves no greater good.

ASK YOURSELF

55. Try to think of some greater good that might come from a fawn suffering for several days from severe burns.

4. A SOUL-MAKING THEODICY: JOHN HICK

A "theodicy" is an attempt to reconcile God's existence with the fact of suffering in the world. Mackie discusses—and rejects—several traditional theodicies, such as the views that evil leads to greater goods and that evil results from free human choice. According to contemporary philosopher John Hick (b. 1922), most theodicies in the Christian tradition are influenced by a view articulated by the medieval philosopher Augustine (354–430 CE), namely, that evil is the result of the fall of humanity. As described in the Old Testament book of Genesis, God originally created humans as morally perfect creatures. But, through their own choices, Adam and Eve went against God's wishes, and ever since human nature has been morally corrupt. The free-will defense is one expression of Augustine's position insofar as it is claimed that evil in the world is due to the degenerate choices that we make in our morally corrupt condition. But there is, Hick argues, another lesser-known theodicy within Christianity, which was inspired by the theologian Irenaeus (120–202 CE), who suggested that human creation involves a two-step process. First, we are created in the *image* of God and, after much development, become re-created in the *likeness* of God. Hick recasts this two-stage process in the more contemporary framework of evolution. The first stage involves the emergence of *Homo sapiens* among other animals in a primitive and hostile environment. After much social development, we enter the second stage in which we attempt to refine the intellectual, moral, and religious components of our nature, and thereby approach the likeness of God. Like the first stage, though, this second stage is also a struggle that occurs over time.

According to Hick, humanity is currently in this second stage, and the evil that we see around us is the result of us being in this transitional state. For, as he writes, "a person-making environment cannot be a pain-free paradise," and we must expect some suffering along the way. Hick lays out four key points of his soul-making theodicy:

1. The divine intention in relation to humankind, according to our hypothesis, is to create perfect finite personal beings in filial relationship with their Maker.

2. It is logically impossible for humans to be created already in this perfect state, because in its spiritual aspect it involves coming freely to an uncoerced consciousness of God from a situation of epistemic distance, and in its moral aspect, freely choosing the good in preference to evil.

3. Accordingly the human being was initially created through the evolutionary process, as a spiritually and morally immature creature, and as part of a world which is both religiously ambiguous and ethically demanding.

4. Thus, that one is morally imperfect (i.e., that there is moral evil), and that the world is a challenging and even dangerous environment (i.e., that there is natural evil), are necessary aspects of the present stage of the process through which God is gradually creating perfected finite persons. [From John Hick, "An Irenaean Theodicy" (1980)]

> **ASK YOURSELF**
>
> **56.** According to Hick, God's aim is to create _____ finite personal beings, first through the _____ process and then through a process in which we work our way through moral challenges.

One benefit of Hick's theory is that it attempts to address the problem of evil in the context of what biological and social scientists tell us about our human origins and development. Thus, human biological and social evolution are integral parts of God's plan in his creation of and relation with human beings. The principal obstacle to Hick's hypothesis is whether the final goal of a perfected human nature outweighs the thousands of years of suffering that people have endured along that path. In Hick's words, "Is it necessary that there should be the depths of demonic malice and cruelty which each generation has experienced . . . ?" The answer, he believes, depends on the importance we place on our ability to freely engage in the process of moral development:

If we take with full seriousness the value of human freedom and responsibility, as essential to the eventual creation of perfected children of God, then we cannot consistently want God to revoke that freedom when its wrong exercise becomes intolerable to us.

> **ASK YOURSELF**
>
> **57.** Does Hick's soul-making theodicy raise any special problems concerning God's notion of justice?

SUMMING UP THE PROBLEM OF EVIL

The argument from evil is one of the oldest and most stubborn problems surrounding the notion of God: How can an all-good, all-powerful, and all-knowing God permit suffering in the world? Fyodor Dostoevsky highlights an array of evils that we might expect God to prevent, such as cruelty to animals and cruelty to children.

Even if God punished the offenders, he suggests, this would not remove the problem: God should have prevented these acts of cruelty to begin with. John L. Mackie argues that belief in an all-good and all-powerful God is logically inconsistent with the fact of suffering in the world. Traditional solutions to the problem, he argues, such as the free-will defense, fail. The only real solution is to deny God's goodness, or power, or his existence altogether. Against Mackie's position, William L. Rowe argues that the presence of suffering is not logically inconsistent with the existence of an all-good and all-powerful God. The problem, according to Rowe, is that we can't assume that an omnipotent, wholly good being will prevent the occurrence of any evil whatever. That is, at least some evils seem justifiable, and this blocks the charge of logical inconsistency. John Hick offers a unique solution to the problem of evil: Human creation is a developmental process during which time we evolve to eventually become a more perfect likeness of God. Suffering, then, is just part of the developmental process of creation.

CAN OF WORMS

The problem of evil, and its various solutions, ties in with philosophical issues of human nature and morality. The free-will defense to the problem makes the assumption that humans indeed have free wills. Hick's contention that human nature is currently developing toward a state of perfection rests on a Darwinian notion of human evolution. Notions of free will and evolution are explored in Chapter 3. The free-will defense also suggests that there is something fundamentally bad about human nature which prompts us to act cruelly toward others. Ethicists similarly wrestle with the question about whether human nature is fundamentally good or evil, selfish or unselfish. This, in turn, impacts the notions of moral obligation that we may have. These issues are discussed in Chapter 6.

C. MYSTICISM AND RELIGIOUS EXPERIENCE

The great medieval Muslim philosopher Al-Ghazali wrote an autobiography describing his spiritual journey from one philosophical school to another. He finally found home in Sufism, Islam's mystical tradition, and he explains the meditative path toward God that he learned to follow. The multi-staged process begins with "purging the heart of all that does not belong to God" and ends in "complete absorption into God." In this state of ecstasy he was able to directly grasp spiritual truths that could not even be conceived by non-mystics. Mystics of religious traditions around the world make similar statements about the indescribable experience of being drawn into God and the special insight that they gain from the experience. Al-Ghazali's testimony is especially noteworthy, though, since, as a respected philosopher, he knew how to investigate extravagant claims and would not frivolously make one himself.

QUESTIONS TO DISCUSS

a. Does having a mystical experience of God prove that God exists?

b. Can you think of some special religious insight you might gain through a mystical experience that you would not get through normal channels of knowledge?

c. Some Native American religious practices involved achieving a mystical state with the aid of hallucinogenic drugs. Does the mechanism of drug use cast doubt on the legitimacy of the experience?

Up to this point in this chapter, we've looked at some of the more vigorous challenges to religious belief. One response to these attacks is to consider the religious experiences of various believers, which, on face value, support the central claims of believers. Religious experiences may be especially prominent during life-changing events, such as conversion, passage to adulthood, or marriage. Even routine religious rituals such as prayer or attending weekly church or temple services may bring out strong emotional responses. The conversion experience of Paul as described in the New Testament Book of Acts is an especially vivid example of a religious experience:

> When I was nearing Damascus, about midday, a great light suddenly flashed from the sky all around me. I fell to the ground, and heard a voice saying: "Saul, Saul, why do you persecute me?" I answered, "Tell me, Lord, who you are." "I am Jesus of Nazareth, whom you are persecuting," he said. My companions saw the light, but did not hear the voice that spoke to me. [Acts 22]

The most dramatic of all religious experiences, though, are mystical ones, such as Al-Ghazali's, which involve a unifying encounter with the divine. Even as intense as Paul's experience was, it does not appear to be mystical in nature, for it principally describes a direct *communication* with God, but not a *union* with God.

An exceptionally vivid description of a mystical experience is the following by British poet Alfred Lord Tennyson:

> This [waking trance] has come upon me through repeating my own name to myself silently, till all at once, as it were out of the intensity of the consciousness of individuality, individuality itself seemed to dissolve and fade away into boundless being, and this not a confused state but the clearest, the surest of the surest, utterly beyond words—where death was an almost laughable impossibility—the loss of personality (if so it were) seeming no extinction, but the only true life. I am ashamed of my feeble description. Have I not said the state is utterly beyond words?

Philosophers are interested in mystical experiences for two reasons. First, some mystics claim insight into a unique view of reality: Everything that we see in the universe, including ourselves, is part of a single ultimate being. Although the rocks, trees, and stars that I see around me might appear to be separately existing things, they are really all unified within divine reality. Insofar as philosophy explores theories about the nature of reality, the claims of mystics demand attention. Second, some philosophers believe that some mystical experiences might offer a kind of proof of the existence of divine reality. The proof rests on the apparent fact that mystics around the world offer remarkably similar descriptions of their mystical experiences—along the lines of Tennyson. This uniformity of experience should compel us to accept as true the reality that mystics describe. In this chapter we will look at classic Hindu expressions of mysticism, along with some recent views on whether such experiences are trustworthy enough to tell us anything about divine reality.

1. HINDU MYSTICISM

Much of Hindu religious thought and practice rests on the contention that we should mystically experience the "Self-God" (*Atman-Brahman*). According to this view, God is the ultimate reality that permeates the entire universe, and, insofar as we are part of the universe, we too are a component of God. It may *appear* to me that I am just a finite creature in a physical world of finite things. However, buried deep within the various layers of my physical and mental existence is my true Self, which is nothing other than God. My usual ways of perceiving the world—such as through my eyes and ears—are completely ill-suited for discovering the God hidden within me. Through meditative practices, I can clear away the distracting elements of ordinary consciousness, and thereby expose the divine inner core of my identity. The term "yoga" in Hinduism means discipline, and one type of yoga focuses on the step-by-step process of meditation.

The *Bhagavad Gita*. A clear description of meditative yoga appears in the Hindu classic from the fifth century BCE entitled the *Bhagavad Gita*. The work is a dialogue between two characters, Arjuna and Krishna. Arjuna is an expert archer who is about to engage in a bloody family feud, and he seeks advice from his chariot driver Krishna. Unbeknownst to Arjuna, Krishna is actually the incarnation of God, and he proceeds to coach Arjuna on the subject of the Self-God and the meditative path of yoga.

FROM *Bhagavad Gita,* SECTION 6

KRISHNA   Understand that "Yoga" is renunciation, and no one becomes a Yogi without renouncing his will. . . . The Yogi should constantly engage himself in Yoga, staying in a secret place by himself, subduing his thoughts and self, and freeing himself from hope and greed. He should set up a fixed seat for himself in a pure place, which is neither too high, nor too low, made of a cloth, a black deerskin, and kusa grass, one over the other. Once there he should practice Yoga for the purification of the self; he should make his mind one-pointed, subduing his thoughts and the functions of his senses. He should hold his body, head and neck erect, immovably steady, looking at the point of his nose with an unseeing gaze. His heart should be serene, fearless and firm in the vow of renunciation. His mind should be controlled as he sits in harmony. In this manner he will think on me [i.e., God] and aspire after me. . . .

Yoga is not for the person who eats too much or too little, or who sleeps too much or too little. Yoga kills all pain for the person who is moderate in eating, amusement, performing actions, sleeping, and waking. When his subdued thought is fixed on the Atman and free from desiring things, then we can say that he is harmonized. Just as a lamp in a windless place does not flicker, so too will the subdued thought of the Yogi be absorbed in the Yoga of the self. . . . The Yogi who harmonizes the self and puts away evil will enjoy the infinite bliss of unity with the eternal God (Brahman). The self, harmonized by Yoga, sees the Self (Atman) abiding in all beings, and all beings in the Self (Atman). Everywhere he sees the same thing. I will never lose hold of the person who sees me everywhere, and sees everything in me, and that person will never lose hold of me. Regardless of how else he may live, the Yogi lives in me who is established in unity and worships me abiding in all things. The perfect Yogi is the one who, established in unity, sees equality in everything, whether pleasant or painful.

ASK YOURSELF

58. What are some of the steps to meditation that Krishna describes?

Arjuna recognizes the difficulties of proper meditation and feels that some people may be too mentally restless to engage in such a disciplined introspective activity. Krishna agrees, but assures Arjuna that the situation is not hopeless for mentally restless people.

ARJUNA   You describe this Yoga as a unity. However, Krishna, I see no basis for it given the impermanence of thought. The mind is very restless. Indeed, it is impetuous, strong, and difficult to bend. Perhaps it is as hard to control as the wind.

KRISHNA   Undoubtedly, Arjuna, the mind is restless and hard to control. But it may be controlled with constant practice and dispassion. I think Yoga is hard to attain by an uncontrolled self. But for a controlled Atman, it is attainable by properly directing energy.

ARJUNA   Suppose that a person has faith, but his mind is still uncontrolled and wanders away from Yoga, thus failing to attain perfection in Yoga. What is in store for him? He fails in his quest from Brahman, and thus fails both his earthy and spiritual quest. Please dispel my doubts, since only you are able to do this.

KRISHNA   No, he will not be lost in this life or the next. No one who does what is right will walk the path of destruction. Even if he fell from Yoga, by virtue of his good actions, he will be reborn in a pure and house, and may even be born into a family of wise Yogis. But this kind of birth is difficult to obtain in this world. In this reborn state, he retains the characteristics belonging to his previous body, and with these he again works for perfection.

ASK YOURSELF

59. What is Krishna's response to Arjuna's question concerning the fate of the person of faith who fails?

The *Yoga Sutra*. In the centuries following the *Bhagavad Gita*, several formal schools of yoga developed, each stressing different methods for discovering the Self-God within. One of these was the school of Royal Yoga, whose principal text was the *Yoga Sutra*, ascribed to an unknown figure named Patanjali. The work presents a series of meditative steps that lead to the mystical awareness of the inner Self-God. The opening section explains the key obstacle for the mystic: There are seemingly endless distractions originating in ordinary consciousness, and we must subdue each of these, one by one.

FROM *Yoga Sutra*

1.1. Here is the explanation of Yoga.
1.2. Yoga involves subduing the variations of one's ordinary consciousness.
1.3. In Yoga, the observer abides in himself.
1.4. At other times he identifies with the variations of his ordinary consciousness.
1.5. There are five kinds of variations of our ordinary consciousness, both painful and painless.
1.6. They are true conception, misconception, fiction, sleep, and memory.
1.7. The types of true conception are experience, inference and testimony.
1.8. Misconception involves an incorrect concept, that is, not staying in the proper form of that which is conceived.

1.9. Fiction is an incorrect notion of a thing, resulting in false knowledge conveyed by words.

1.10. Sleep is a variation of ordinary consciousness that depends on the conception of nothing.

1.11. Memory involves not letting go of an object of which one has been aware.

1.12. Through practice and detachment these [five variations of ordinary consciousness] can be suppressed.

1.13. Of these, "practice" involves the repeated effort to keep ordinary consciousness in an unvaried stated.

1.14. Such practice must be done firmly, with devotion, and continually adhered to for a long time.

1.15. "Detachment" is the state of overcoming one's desires for things seen on earth and things heard of in scripture.

ASK YOURSELF

60. In the *Yoga Sutra*, what are the five variations of ordinary consciousness, and how can they be suppressed?

61. In the *Yoga Sutra*, what is "practice and detachment"?

The *Yoga Sutra* continues describing an eight-step process toward meditative union. The steps explain how we should clear our minds from social, bodily, and mental distractions until we finally are receptive to the experience of mystical union.

2.29. The eight steps to yoga are appetitive restraint, social observance, bodily postures, breath regulation, suppression of the senses, focus, even awareness, and meditative union (*samadhi*).

2.30. The appetitive restraints are not killing, not lying, not stealing, self-restraint, and not coveting.

2.32. The social observances are cleanliness, contentment, austerity, study, and continual devotion to the Lord.

2.46. Posture is steady and easy.

2.49. Breath regulation is stopping the movement of inhaling and exhaling.

2.54. Suppression of the senses is when the senses do not perceive objects and instead follow the nature of the mind.

3.1. Focus is fixing the ordinary consciousness on a point in space.

3.2. Even Awareness is the Continuous Flow of Similar Mental Variations.

3.3. Meditative union (*samadhi*) is even awareness arising from the object alone, ignorant of itself.

ASK YOURSELF

62. The first step is appetitive restraint, and it consists of a series of moral rules. The point here is that improper behavior will not allow us to attain a calm and undistracted mental state. Explain why lying, for example, might block our path toward mystical union.

2. THE LIMITED AUTHORITY OF MYSTICAL EXPERIENCES: WILLIAM JAMES

The first uniquely American contribution to philosophy was an early twentieth-century movement called *pragmatism,* whose leading proponent was Harvard University professor William James (1842–1910). James's general philosophical position is that we resolve questions of truth by exploring the practical effects of various theories on our lives, rather than by vainly hunting for objective facts. In *The Varieties of Religious Experience* (1902) he uses this practical method in a discussion of mysticism. Granted that mystics have quite profound experiences of reality that differ from our ordinary conceptions of the world. Do these experiences carry any authority? James takes a middle position on the issue: They can be rightly authoritative for the mystic who has the experience, but they have no authority over the nonmystic. In the selection below, he begins with a summary of his key contentions.

WILLIAM JAMES (1842–1910)

American pragmatist philosopher, author of The Varieties of Religious Experience *(1902).*

FROM WILLIAM JAMES, *The Varieties of Religious Experience* (1902), LECTURE 17

I have now sketched with extreme brevity and insufficiency, but as fairly as I am able in the time allowed, the general traits of the mystic range of consciousness. It is on the whole pantheistic and optimistic, or at least the opposite of pessimistic. It is anti-naturalistic, and harmonizes best with twice-bornness and so-called other-worldly states mind.

My next task is to inquire whether we can invoke it as authoritative. Does it furnish any warrant for the truth of the twice-bornness and supernaturality and pantheism which it favors? I must give my answer to this question as concisely as I can.

In brief my answer is this—and I will divide it into three parts:

1. Mystical states, when well developed, usually are, and have the right to be, absolutely authoritative over the individuals to whom they come.

2. No authority emanates from them which should make it a duty for those who stand outside of them to accept their revelations uncritically.

3. They break down the authority of the non-mystical or rationalistic consciousness, based upon the understanding and the senses alone. They show it to be only one kind of consciousness. They open out the possibility of other orders of truth, in which, so far as anything in us vitally responds to them, we may freely continue to have faith.

I will take up these points one by one.

ASK YOURSELF

63. What are some of the features of mystical experience that James notes?

Turning to each of these three points in more detail, he first contends that mystical states are authoritative for the mystic because they are directly perceived in a way similar to the way our senses perceive the world around us. They are incontrovertible from the mystic's point of view.

1. As a matter of psychological fact, mystical states of a well-pronounced and emphatic sort are usually authoritative over those who have them. They have been "there," and [they] know. It is vain for rationalism to grumble about this. If the mystical truth that comes to a man proves to be a force that he can live by, what mandate have we of the majority to order him to live in another way? We can throw him into a prison or a madhouse, but we cannot change his mind—we commonly attach it only the more stubbornly to its beliefs. It mocks our utmost efforts, as a matter of fact, and in point of logic it absolutely escapes our jurisdiction. Our own more "rational" beliefs are based on evidence exactly similar in nature to that which mystics quote for theirs. Our senses, namely, have assured us of certain states of fact; but mystical experiences are as direct perceptions of fact for those who have them as any sensations ever were for us. The records show that even though the five senses be in abeyance in them, they are absolutely sensational in their epistemological quality, if I may be pardoned the barbarous expression—that is, they are face to face presentations of what seems immediately to exist. I abstract from weaker states, and from those cases of which the books are full, where the director (but usually not the subject) remains in doubt whether the experience may not have proceeded from the demon. Example: Mr. John Nelson writes of his imprisonment for preaching Methodism: "My soul was as a watered garden, and I could sing praises to God all day long; for he turned my captivity into joy, and gave me to rest as well on the boards, as if I had been on a bed of down. Now could I say, 'God's service is perfect freedom,' and I was carried out much in prayer that my enemies might drink of the same river of peace which my God gave so largely to me."

The mystic is, in short, invulnerable, and must be left, whether we relish it or not, in undisturbed enjoyment of his creed. Faith, says Tolstoy, is that by which men live. And faith-state and mystic state are practically convertible terms.

ASK YOURSELF

64. James states that the mystic is "invulnerable." What does this mean?

James questions whether the mystic's experience carries any authority for non-mystics. He argues that they don't: No authority springs from them that should make it a duty for those who stand outside of them to accept their revelations uncritically. He considers the argument from unanimity: There is a presumption in favor of mystical experiences because mystics generally report the same thing.

2. But I now proceed to add that mystics have no right to claim that we ought to accept the deliverance of their peculiar experiences, if we are ourselves outsiders and feel no private call thereto. The utmost they can ever ask of us in this life is to admit that they establish a presumption. They form a consensus and have an unequivocal outcome; and it would be odd, mystics might say, if such a unanimous type of experience should prove to be altogether wrong. At bottom, however, this would only be an appeal to numbers, like the appeal of rationalism the other way; and the appeal to numbers has no logical force. If we acknowledge it, it is for "suggestive," not for logical reasons: we follow the majority because to do so suits our life.

But even this presumption from the unanimity of mystics is far from being strong. In characterizing mystic states as pantheistic, optimistic, etc., I am afraid I over-simplified the truth. I did so for expository reasons, and to keep the closer to the classic mystical tradition. The classic religious mysticism, it now must be confessed, is only a "privileged case." It is an extract, kept true to type by the selection of the fittest specimens and their preservation in "schools." It is carved out from a much larger mass; and if we take the larger mass as seriously as religious mysticism has historically taken itself, we find that the supposed unanimity largely disappears. To begin with, even religious mysticism itself, the kind that accumulates traditions and makes schools, is much less unanimous than I have allowed. It has been both ascetic and antinomianly self-indulgent within the Christian church.

ASK YOURSELF

65. Why, according to James, is the argument from unanimity "far from strong"?

James argues further that, for the outsider, mysticism is discredited from the fact that insane people have bizarre mystical experiences.

So much for religious mysticism proper. But more remains to be told, for religious mysticism is only one half of mysticism. The other half has no accumulated traditions except those which the text-books on insanity supply. Open any one of these, and you will find abundant cases in which "mystical ideas" are cited as characteristic symptoms of enfeebled or deluded states of mind. In delusional insanity, paranoia, as they sometimes call it, we may have a diabolical mysticism, a sort of religious mysticism turned upside down. The same sense of ineffable importance in the smallest events, the same texts and words coming with new meanings, the same voices and visions and leadings and missions, the same controlling by extraneous powers; only this time the emotion is pessimistic: instead of consolations we have desolations; the meanings are dreadful; and the powers are enemies to life. It is evident that from the point of view of their psychological mechanism, the classic mysticism and these lower mysticisms spring from the same mental level, from that great subliminal or transmarginal region of which science is beginning to admit the existence, but of which so little is really known. That region contains every kind of matter: "seraph and snake" abide there side by side. To come from thence is no infallible credential. What comes must be sifted and tested, and run the gauntlet of confrontation with the total context of experience, just like what comes from the outer world of sense. Its value must be ascertained by empirical methods, so long as we are not mystics ourselves.

Once more, then, I repeat that non-mystics are under no obligation to acknowledge in mystical states a superior authority conferred on them by their intrinsic nature.

ASK YOURSELF

66. James states that the same level of the human mind contains "seraph and snake" side by side. What does he mean by this?

James's third contention about mysticism is that such experiences show that our normal consciousness of the world is only one type of consciousness that human beings are capable of.

Thus, to at least some extent, mystical experiences compromise the supreme authority that we usually ascribe to rational consciousness.

3. Yet, I repeat once more, the existence of mystical states absolutely overthrows the pretension of non-mystical states to be the sole and ultimate dictators of what we may believe. As a rule, mystical states merely add a supersensuous meaning to the ordinary outward data of consciousness. They are excitements like the emotions of love or ambition, gifts to our spirit by means of which facts already objectively before us fall into a new expressiveness and make a new connection with our active life. They do not contradict these facts as such, or deny anything that our senses have immediately seized. It is the rationalistic critic rather who plays the part of denier in the controversy, and his denials have no strength, for there never can be a state of facts to which new meaning may not truthfully be added, provided the mind ascend to a more enveloping point of view. It must always remain an open question whether mystical states may not possibly be such superior points of view, windows through which the mind looks out upon a more extensive and inclusive world. The difference of the views seen from the different mystical windows need not prevent us from entertaining this supposition. The wider world would in that case prove to have a mixed constitution like that of this world, that is all. It would have its celestial and its infernal regions, its tempting and its saving moments, its valid experiences and its counterfeit ones, just as our world has them; but it would be a wider world all the same. We should have to use its experiences by selecting and subordinating and substituting just as is our custom in this ordinary naturalistic world; we should be liable to error just as we are now; yet the counting in of that wider world of meanings, and the serious dealing with it, might, in spite of all the perplexity, be indispensable stages in our approach to the final fullness of the truth.

In this shape, I think, we have to leave the subject. Mystical states indeed wield no authority due simply to their being mystical states. But the higher ones among them point in directions to which the religious sentiments even of non-mystical men incline. They tell of the supremacy of the ideal, of vastness, of union, of safety, and of rest. They offer us hypotheses, hypotheses which we may voluntarily ignore, but which as thinkers we cannot possibly upset. The super-naturalism and optimism to which they would persuade us may, interpreted in one way or another, be after all the truest of insights into the meaning of this life.

ASK YOURSELF

67. What are some of the hypotheses about the world that mystical states suggest even for the non-mystic?

 3. ### THE UNTRUSTWORTHINESS OF MYSTICAL EXPERIENCES: BERTRAND RUSSELL

British philosopher Bertrand Russell (1872–1970) was one of the leading figures in early twentieth-century philosophy. Throughout his long life he made a mark both as a prolific writer on a variety of philosophical subjects and also as a political activist. Following in the empiricist tradition set by David Hume, Russell was a philosophical and religious skeptic. In his book *Religion and Science* he discusses several noted conflicts that have occurred over the millennia between scientists and religious believers. One of these involves the claim of mystics to discover the true nature of reality, which is invisible to ordinary scientific exploration.

He argues that the mystical conceptions of reality are essentially untrustworthy because they require abnormal physical states, such as result from fasting and breathing exercises. To that extent, we should not trust the mystic's reports—regardless of how unanimous—anymore than we should trust the hallucinatory experiences of someone on drugs. Russell begins in the selection below conceding that reports of mystics agree in some key ways, although he argues that aspects of mystics' experiences may be colored by doctrines in their particular religions.

From Bertrand Russell, *Religion and Science* (1935)

The chief argument in favor of the mystics is their agreement with each other. "I know nothing more remarkable," says Dean Inge, "than the unanimity of the mystics, ancient, mediaeval, and modern, Protestant, Catholic, and even Buddhist or Mohammedan, though the Christian mystics are the most trustworthy." I do not wish to underrate the force of this argument, which I acknowledged long ago in a book called *Mysticism and Logic*. The mystics vary greatly in their capacity for giving verbal expression to their experiences, but I think we may take it that those who succeeded best all maintain: (1) that all division and separateness is unreal, and that the universe is a single indivisible unity; (2) that evil is illusory, and that the illusion arises through falsely regarding a part as self-subsistent; (3) that time is unreal, and that reality is eternal, not in the sense of being everlasting, but in the sense of being wholly outside time. I do not pretend that this is a complete account of the matters on which all mystics concur, but the three propositions that I have mentioned may serve as representatives of the whole. Let us now imagine ourselves a jury in a law-court, whose business it is to decide on the credibility of the witnesses who make these three somewhat surprising assertions.

We shall find, in the first place, that, while the witnesses agree up to a point, they disagree totally when that point is passed, although they are just as certain as when they agree. Catholics, but not Protestants, may have visions in which the Virgin appears; Christians and Mohammedans, but not Buddhists, may have great truths revealed to them by the Archangel Gabriel; the Chinese mystics of the Tao tell us, as a direct result of their central doctrine, that all government is bad, whereas most European and Mohammedan mystics, with equal confidence, urge submission to constituted authority. As regards the points where they differ, each group will argue that the other groups are untrustworthy; we might, therefore, if we were content with a mere forensic triumph, point out that most mystics think most other mystics mistaken on most points. They might, however, make this only half a triumph by agreeing on the greater importance of the matters about which they are at one, as compared with those as to which their opinions differ. We will, in any case, assume that they have composed their differences, and concentrated the defense at these three points—namely, the unity of the world, the illusory nature of evil, and the unreality of time. What test can we, as impartial outsiders, apply to their unanimous evidence?

ASK YOURSELF

68. What, according to Russell, are the three key points that reports of mystical experiences have in common?

69. In what particulars, according to Russell, do religious mystics disagree in their experiences?

Mystics believe that a special kind of mental conditioning is required to have mystical experiences, and this, in turn, requires special bodily states, such as fasting, meditation, and breathing exercises.

As men of scientific temper, we shall naturally first ask whether there is any way by which we can ourselves obtain the same evidence at first hand. To this we shall receive various answers. We may be told that we are obviously not in a receptive frame of mind, and that we lack the requisite humility; or that fasting and religious meditation are necessary; or (if our witness is Indian or Chinese) that the essential prerequisite is a course of breathing exercises. I think we shall find that the weight of experimental evidence is in favor of this last view, though fasting also has been frequently found effective. As a matter of fact, there is a definite physical discipline, called yoga, which is practiced in order to produce the mystic's certainty, and which is recommended with much confidence by those who have tried it. Breathing exercises are its most essential feature, and for our purposes we may ignore the rest.

In order to see how we could test the assertion that yoga gives insight, let us artificially simplify this assertion. Let us suppose that a number of people assure us that if, *for a certain time,* we breathe in a certain way, we shall become convinced that time is unreal. Let us go further, and suppose that, having tried their recipe, we have ourselves experienced a state of mind such as they describe. But now, having returned to our normal mode of respiration, we are not quite sure whether the vision was to be believed. How shall we investigate this question? . . .

ASK YOURSELF

70. What, according to Russell, is the aim of yoga?

Having gathered the appropriate data from mystical experiences, the issue now is whether these data are trustworthy. Russell's simple answer is *no,* because the experiences themselves require abnormal bodily states.

The certainty and partial unanimity of mystics is no conclusive reason for accepting their testimony on a matter of fact. The man of science, when he wishes others to see what he has seen, arranges his microscope or telescope; that is to say, he makes changes in the external world, but demands of the observer only normal eyesight. The mystic, on the other hand, demands changes in the observer, by fasting, by breathing exercises, and by a careful abstention from external observation. (Some object to such discipline, and think that the mystic illumination cannot be artificially achieved; from a scientific point of view, this makes their case more difficult to test than that of those who rely on yoga. But nearly all agree that fasting and an ascetic life are helpful.) We all know that opium, hashish, and alcohol produce certain effects on the observer, but as we do not think these effects [are] admirable we take no account of them in our theory of the universe. They may even, sometimes, reveal fragments of truth; but we do not regard them as sources of general wisdom. The drunkard who sees snakes does not imagine, afterwards, that he has had a revelation of a reality hidden from others, though some not wholly dissimilar belief must have given rise to the worship of Bacchus. In our own day, as William James related, there have been people who considered that the intoxication produced by laughing-gas revealed truths which are hidden at normal times. From a scientific point of view, we can make no distinction between the man who eats little and sees heaven and the man who drinks much and sees snakes. Each is in an abnormal physical condition, and therefore has abnormal perceptions. Normal perceptions, since they have to be useful in the struggle for life, must have some correspondence with fact; but in abnormal perceptions there is no reason to expect such correspondence, and their testimony, therefore, cannot outweigh that of normal perception.

ASK YOURSELF

71. According to Russell, mystical experiences are unreliable since they require abnormal bodily states. What are some abnormal physical conditions that Russell compares this to?

Having debunked the mystic's claim, Russell concludes noting some positive aspects of mysticism.

The mystic emotion, if it is freed from unwarranted beliefs, and not so overwhelming as to remove a man wholly from the ordinary business of life, may give something of very great value—the same kind of thing, though in a heightened form, that is given by contemplation. Breadth and calm and profundity may all have their source in this emotion, in which, for the moment, all self-centered desire is dead, and the mind becomes a mirror for the vastness of the universe. Those who have had this experience, and believe it to be bound up unavoidably with assertions about the nature of the universe, naturally cling to these assertions. I believe myself that the assertions are inessential, and that there is no reason to believe them true. I cannot admit any method of arriving at truth except that of science, but in the realm of the emotions I do not deny the value of the experiences which have given rise to religion. Through association with false beliefs, they have led to much evil as well as good; freed from this association, it may be hoped that the good alone will remain.

ASK YOURSELF

72. According to Russell, science is the only way to arrive at truths about the universe, but religious mysticism is a legitimate vehicle in the realm of the _____.

4. THE TRUSTWORTHINESS OF RELIGIOUS EXPERIENCES: RICHARD SWINBURNE

How might the mystic respond to Russell's attack on the trustworthiness of mystical experiences? One reaction, offered by Cambridge University philosophy professor C. D. Broad (1887–1971), is to simply accept the fact that abnormal physical states are needed to tap into the reality beyond our ordinary perceptions:

Suppose, for the sake of argument, that there is an aspect of the world which remains altogether outside the ken of ordinary persons in their daily life. Then it seems very likely that some degree of mental and physical abnormality would be a necessary condition for getting sufficiently loosened from the objects of ordinary sense-perception to come into cognitive contact with this aspect of reality. Therefore the fact that those persons who claim to have this peculiar kind of cognition generally exhibit certain mental and physical abnormalities is rather what might be anticipated if their claims were true. One might need to be slightly "cracked" in order to have some peep-holes into the super-sensible world. [From C. D. Broad, *Religion, Philosophy and Psychical Research* (1953)]

Another response is to look more generally at the issue of trustworthiness. What does it take for *any* experience to be considered trustworthy, and not merely mystical experiences? If we can establish a general criterion of trustworthiness, then perhaps we might find that mystical experiences indeed fulfill that criterion. This is the route taken by Richard Swinburne in his book *The Existence of God*.

The Principle of Credulity. Swinburne offers a basic principle of credulity—that is, a standard to judge whether there is proper evidence to believe an experience. The principle, most simply, is that if we perceive that an object is there, then it probably really is there—unless there are special reasons to think otherwise.

FROM RICHARD SWINBURNE, *The Existence of God* (1979)

In discussing religious experience philosophers have sometimes made the claim that an experience is evidence for nothing beyond itself, and that therefore religious experience has no evidential value. That remark reflects a philosophical attitude that those philosophers would not adopt when discussing experiences of any other kind. Quite obviously having the experience of it seeming (epistemically) to you that there is a table there (i.e. your seeming to see a table) is good evidence for supposing that there is a table there. Having the experience of its seeming (epistemically) to you that I am here giving a lecture (i.e. your seeming to hear me give a lecture) is good evidence for supposing that I am here lecturing. So generally, contrary to the original philosophical claim, I suggest that it is a principle of rationality that (in the absence of special considerations) if it seems (epistemically) to a subject that x is present, then probably x is present; what one seems to perceive is probably so. How things seem to be is good grounds for a belief about how things are. From this it would follow that, in the absence of special considerations, all religious experiences ought to be taken by their subjects as genuine, and hence as substantial grounds for belief in the existence of their apparent object—God, or Mary, or Ultimate Reality, or Poseidon. This principle, which I shall call the Principle of Credulity, and the conclusion drawn from it seem to me correct. It seems to me, and I hope to my readers, intuitively right in most ordinary cases such as those to which I have just been referring, to take the way things seem to be as the way they are. . . .

ASK YOURSELF

73. Illustrate Swinburne's principle of credulity with the example of the book that is before your eyes.

A critic of religious experience might argue that Swinburne's principle is too broad and it should be restricted in ways that allow for normal perceptual experiences, but rule out religious experiences.

I shall now argue that attempts to restrict the principle in ways designed to rule out its application to religious experience are either unjustified or unsuccessful. I shall consider two such attempts to argue that while its appearing to me that there are before me tables, chairs, houses, etc. is good grounds for supposing that there are (i.e. its seeming to me that I am seeing them is good grounds for supposing that I am), its appearing to me that the world before me is being sustained by God, or that there are present angels or Ultimate Reality is not good grounds for supposing that things are thus.

Is Uniform Past Experience Required? One possible way that the religious critic might restrict the principle of credulity is to argue that we need uniform past experience—that is, *induction*—to back up our perceptual claims. For example, I can trust my present perception of the table in front of me because my past perceptions have not misled me. According to the critic, though, there is no similar past experience to support my religious experiences; thus religious experiences would fail the principle of credulity. However, Swinburne believes that such an emphasis on past experience ignores a basic problem with induction. If past experience is relevant at all, I must be able to actually recollect those experiences. But why trust my recollections? Suppose I say that I trust my memory because past experiences confirm its reliability. But I'm now arguing in a circle since I am relying on my memory to prove the reliability of my memory. According to Swinburne, we ultimately rely on the basic principle of credulity—that things are the way they seem—without any further inductive justification.

The first argument is that our supposing that the way things seem is the way they are is not an ultimate principle of rationality, but itself requires inductive justification, and that that inductive justification is available in the ordinary cases but not in the religious cases. More particularly, a philosopher may claim that the fact that it appears that x is present is good grounds for supposing that x is present only if we have evidence that when in the past it appeared that x was present, it proved so to be; or at any rate the assumption that x is present has proved a successful assumption to work from. Hence, the philosopher might argue, it is all right to take what looks like a table as a table, because our past experience has shown that such appearances are not misleading; but he might go on to question whether we had the kind of inductive evidence which was necessary to justify taking religious experiences seriously.

One difficulty with this view is that it is ordinarily supposed that people are justified in taking what looks like a table to be one even if they do not at the same time recall their past experiences with tables, and even if they cannot immediately do so. So the principle would have to say that our justification for taking what looked like a table to be one was that we could remember such past experiences if we tried hard enough. It will not do to say that our merely having had the past experiences suffices to justify our present inference, whether or not we can remember those experiences. For if a claim is to be justified inductively, we must in some sense "have" the evidence of past performance in order to be justified in making the inference. But then, an induction from past experiences to future experiences is only reliable if we correctly recall our past experiences. And what grounds have we got for supposing that we do? Clearly not inductive grounds—an inductive justification of the reliability of memory-claims would obviously be circular. Here clearly we must rely on the principle that things are the way they seem, as a basic principle not further justifiable; that we seem to have had such and such experiences is in itself good grounds for believing that we had. The principle that the rational man supposes that in the absence of special considerations in particular cases things are the way they seem to be, cannot always be given inductive justification. And if it is justifiable to use it when other justifications fail in memory cases, what good argument can be given against using it in other kinds of case when other justifications fail? . . .

ASK YOURSELF

74. According to Swinburne, justifying the reliability of my memory through induction would obviously be _____.

Must We Distinguish Between a Real Experience and an Interpretation? A second way that the critic of religion might restrict the principle of credulity is to confine it to our real experiences, but not to our interpretations of those experiences. Seeing a ship, for example, is a real experience. Seeing a *Russian* ship, though, is an interpretation of that experience.

The second attempt to restrict the application of the Principle of Credulity allows that the principle holds in ordinary cases (without needing inductive justification) but denies that (in the absence of inductive justification) it holds in less usual cases. One writer who has thus restricted the principle is Chisholm. He claims that whenever we take something to have a certain sensible characteristic (or relation), we have adequate evidence for the claim that it does have this characteristic (or relation); but that whenever we take something to have some non-sensible characteristic (or relation), that is not in itself adequate evidence to suppose that it does. . . . So, according to Chisholm, if something seems (epistemically) to S to be brown or square or solid, that is good grounds for believing that it is. But if something seems to be a table, or a Victorian table, or a ship, or a Russian ship, that is in itself not good grounds for believing that it is. You can only have good grounds for believing that something is a table in terms of it looking brown, square, and solid and in terms of things which look like that having appeared (in the past) to be used for writing on (the notion of "writing" perhaps being spelt out in terms of "sensible" characteristics). . . .

ASK YOURSELF

75. Suppose that you hold this book in your hand. What, according to the critic, would be your real experience of the book (justified by the principle of credulity) and what would be your interpretation of the book (not justified by the principle of credulity)?

Swinburne concedes that religious believers commonly distinguish between a real experience of God and an interpretation of that experience. However, he nevertheless argues that many of our real experiences have built-in interpretations, which are justified by the principle of credulity.

That there is such a line to be drawn is a common and seldom argued assumption in many discussions of religious experience. Once the line is drawn, the consequences are evident. For the line always leaves the typical objects of religious experience as matters of interpretation rather than as true objects of real experience. It follows that even if it seems to you strongly that you are talking to God or gazing at Ultimate Reality, this fact is no reason in itself for supposing that you are. You are having an experience which is properly to be described in a much more mundane way—e.g. as the experience of hearing certain noises—which you interpret as the voice of God, but which you have no good reason for so doing unless further evidence is produced.

However, no such line as the one which Chisholm attempts to draw can be drawn between real experience and interpretation. For clearly we are justified in holding many perceptual beliefs about objects having non-sensible characteristics which cannot be backed up in terms of beliefs about objects having "sensible" characteristics. Few would doubt that I am justified in believing that a certain woman whom I see at the other side of a room is my wife. Yet if asked what it is about the woman I take to be my wife which makes me believe that she is my wife, I would be utterly unable to give a satisfactory answer. I could only give a very vague description of the Chisholmian "sensible" characteristics by which I recognize her, a description which would fit tens of thousands of other women whom I would not for one moment mistake for my wife. That one can recognize does not entail that one can describe; nor does it even entail that (even if one cannot describe them) one knows what the features are by which one recognizes. I may be justified in claiming that you are tired or angry, just by looking at your face, and yet not know what it is about your face which makes you look tired or angry. Again, I can recognize my wife's voice over the telephone, although I certainly cannot say what it is about the noises which come through the telephone receiver which are especially characteristic of her voice. For senses such as smell and taste most of us have no vocabulary for describing sensible characteristics, other than in terms of the objects which cause them (e.g. as "the taste of tea" or "the smell of roses"). Asked about the liquid we are drinking "What is it about it that makes it taste like tea?", we would be stuck for an answer. But that fact casts no doubt on our justification for believing that we are drinking a cup of tea. The fact that it tastes like tea is good reason in itself for supposing that it is—whether or not we can say in more primitive terms what it is about it which makes it taste like tea.

ASK YOURSELF

76. Swinburne believes that the lines between a real experience and an interpretation of that experience are often blurry. Give one example he uses to explain his point.

According to Swinburne, then, the second attempt at restricting the principle of credulity fails. This means that, on face value, religious experiences are trustworthy perceptions of the divine reality that they report.

Men differ in the kinds of objects and properties which they learn to pick out. Sometimes they can pick out and even describe the "sensible characteristics" of those objects and sometimes they cannot; and even if they can, the recognition of objects of some kind and their more sophisticated properties may be a more natural process than the description of their sensible characteristics. There is no reason of principle why we should not grow so adept at spotting Russian ships, or Victorian tables, or blue-dwarf stars, or elliptical galaxies that we can recognize them straight off, without being able to say what it is in the way of Chisholmian sensible characteristics about what we see which makes us identify them as we do.

So this second argument against the original Principle of Credulity fails, and the principle stands. . . . From all this it follows that if it seems to me that I have a glimpse of Heaven, or a vision of God, that is grounds for me and others to suppose that I do. And, more generally, the occurrence of religious experiences is prima facie reason for all to believe in that of which the reported experience was purportedly an experience.

ASK YOURSELF

77. Suppose that you have a vision of God. According to Swinburne, what does the principle of credulity entitle you to believe about that vision?

SUMMING UP THE ISSUE OF MYSTICISM AND RELIGIOUS EXPERIENCE

Philosophers are interested in the experiences of religious mystics because they involve truth claims that cannot always be supported through normal experience. Mystical encounters with God might also form the basis for proof of God's existence: God exists because mystics report encounters with God. Hindu mysticism, as represented in the *Bhagavad Gita*, involves experiencing the Self-God—the ultimate reality of all things that lies at the heart of each of our identities. The *Yoga Sutra* describes meditative techniques that lead to this mystical experience. William James examined the claims of various mystics and concluded that they may be justly authoritative for the mystic having the experience, but they have no authority over the nonmystic. Bertrand Russell took a less charitable view of mystical experiences, arguing that mystical claims about the world are untrustworthy because they require abnormal physical states. Richard Swinburne defends the genuineness of mystical experiences by investigating more generally the criterion of trustworthiness. The basic principle of trustworthiness that we all rely on is this: If we perceive that an object is there, then it probably really is there, unless there are special reasons to think otherwise. Mystical experiences, according to Swinburne, pass this test.

CAN OF WORMS

Mystical experiences present a challenge to our common notions of how we attain knowledge. For example, I gain knowledge through my five senses, and I can trust my experiences when they are to some extent repeatable and backed by scientific laws. Mystical claims, though, do not fit this formula. This raises a fundamental question about how many legitimate sources of knowledge there are. Swinburne argues that scientific inductive reasoning is at least as problem-laden as mystical experiences. Standard approaches to knowledge are explored in Chapter 5. Mystical experiences also have implications regarding the nature of reality, since, according to many mystics, God permeates the entire universe, including the identities of individual people. To that extent, we encounter God when we discover our true hidden self. This issue is explored in Chapter 3.

D. The Ontological Argument for God's Existence

Science fiction writer Douglas Adams wrote the following spoof on philosophical proofs for God's existence:

> Now it is such a bizarrely improbable coincidence that anything so mindbogglingly useful [as the Babel fish which can translate all languages] could have evolved by chance that some thinkers have chosen to see it as a final and clinching proof of the non-existence of God.
>
> The argument goes something like this: "I refuse to prove that I exist," says God, "for proof denies faith, and without faith I am nothing."
>
> "But," says Man, "the Babel fish is a dead giveaway isn't it? It could not have evolved by chance. It proves you exist, and so therefore, by your own arguments, you don't. QED."

"Oh dear," says God, "I hadn't thought of that," and promptly vanishes in a puff of logic. [From Douglas Adams, *The Hitchhiker's Guide to the Galaxy* (1979)]

There are two remarkable insights to Adams's discussion here. First, he points out the tension between faith and reason in religious matters—that is, whether we should explore the existence of God through reason, or instead see it solely as a matter of faith. Second, he points out the high degree of confidence that philosophers have placed on logic—almost to the point that a logical argument can *make* something exist or not exist.

QUESTIONS TO DISCUSS

a. Is it important for the religious believer to be able to logically demonstrate God's existence?

b. Assuming that you believe in God, do you think it is possible that God might not have existed (just as you might not have existed)?

c. When attempting to prove God's existence, some philosophers have defined "God" as "the greatest conceivable being." Is there a problem with this definition?

Mystical experiences, which we have explored, offer only one approach to proving the existence of divine reality—a proof grounded in the actual experiences of the believer. Beginning about two thousand years ago, ancient philosophers such as Aristotle and Cicero offered and discussed more logically oriented arguments for God's existence. Following their leads, Christian, Jewish, and Muslim theologians during the Middle Ages refined several formal proofs, which have since become staples in philosophical inquiries into religion. The motive behind the earlier formulators of proofs for God was not so much to convert atheists who were infiltrating medieval society. In fact, the odds are slim that there were any vocal disbelievers at that time when religion so thoroughly dominated society. Instead, the motive was partly to clarify how far human reason on its own could confirm religious beliefs already held by society. Another aim behind the proofs was to clarify the *nature* of God. They were not attempting to prove the existence of any God or Gods, but, instead a God with specific traits. First, the God they had in mind was *monotheistic*—that is, a single divine being as opposed to the polytheistic notion of many gods. Second, the God they envisioned had specific attributes, such as being all-powerful, all-knowing, and all-good. Philosophers today refer to this conception as the "theistic God." Medieval philosophers adopted several strategies in their theistic proofs, and over time the most famous of these have been dubbed the "ontological argument," the "cosmological argument," and the "design argument."

The ontological argument for God's existence is one of the all-time masterpieces of philosophical argumentation. Regardless of whether the proof succeeds or fails, it is a concise and insightful argument that has an almost irresistible force. The original formulation of the argument was presented by Anselm of Canterbury (1033–1109), a Benedictine monk from Normandy, France, who later became Archbishop of Canterbury in England. Anselm was especially interested in proofs for God's existence and, in an earlier writing titled *Monologion,* he presents several theistic arguments found in the writings of previous medieval philosophers. However, he is most famous for the ontological argument that appears in his *Proslogion.* Following the theological tradition of Augustine, Anselm felt that God's existence could be confirmed through rational argumentation, but only to those who first believe in God. Reason thus depends upon some kind of religious faith.

1. ANSELM'S PROOFS

Anselm presents at least two versions of the ontological argument. In the first proof, he introduces the conception of God as "a being than which nothing greater can be conceived," or, more simply, the *greatest conceivable being*. He argues that anyone who entertains this concept of God will run into difficulties if he or she tries to deny that such a being exists.

FROM ANSELM, *Proslogion* (1077), I

And so, Lord, do you, who gives understanding to faith, give me, so far as you know it to be profitable, to understand that you are as we believe; and that you are that which we believe. And, indeed, we believe that you are a being than which nothing greater can be conceived. Or is there no such nature, since the fool has said in his heart, there is no God? (Psalms 14:1). But, at any rate, this very fool, when he hears of this being of which I speak—a being than which nothing greater can be conceived—understands what he hears, and what he understands is in his understanding; although he does not understand it to exist.

For, it is one thing for an object to be in the understanding, and another to understand that the object exists. When a painter first conceives of what he will afterwards perform, he has it in his understanding, but he does not yet understand it to be, because he has not yet performed it. But after he has made the painting, he both has it in his understanding, and he understands that it exists, because he has made it.

Hence, even the fool is convinced that something exists in the understanding, at least, than which nothing greater can be conceived. For, when he hears of this, he understands it. And whatever is understood, exists in the understanding. And assuredly that, than which nothing greater can be conceived, cannot exist in the understanding alone. For, suppose it exists in the understanding alone: then it can be conceived to exist in reality; which is greater.

Therefore, if that, than which nothing greater can be conceived, exists in the understanding alone, the very being, than which nothing greater can be conceived, is one, than which a greater can be conceived. But obviously this is impossible. Hence, there is no doubt that there exists a being, than which nothing greater can be conceived, and it exists both in the understanding and in reality.

In its most basic form, this first version of the ontological argument is this:

1. We have the concept of God, and in that sense God exists "in the understanding."
2. The concept of "God" is the concept of the greatest conceivable being.
3. Real existence is greater than mere existence in the understanding.
4. Therefore, God must exist in reality, not just in the understanding.

The first premise simply means that we understand and can consistently think about the concept of God, whereas, for instance, we could not think about the concept of a square sphere. The second premise is true by definition: By "God" we mean the greatest conceivable being. The third premise means that a real thing is greater than an imaginary or merely conceived thing of the same kind; for example, a real $100 is greater than an imaginary $100.

After presenting the above argument, Anselm continues with a second proof: Not only does God exist, but he has *necessary* existence. The idea of the "greatest conceivable being" is unique in that such a being cannot fail to exist—that is, it must exist necessarily.

And it assuredly exists so truly, that it cannot be conceived not to exist. For, it is possible to conceive of a being which cannot be conceived not to exist; and this is greater than one which can be conceived not to exist. Hence, if that, than which nothing greater can be conceived, can be conceived not to exist, it is not that, than which nothing greater can be conceived. But this is an irreconcilable contradiction. There is, then, so truly a being than which nothing greater can be conceived to exist, that it cannot even be conceived not to exist; and this being you are, O Lord, our God.

So truly, therefore, do you exist, O Lord, my God, that you cannot be conceived not to exist; and rightly. For, if a mind could conceive of a being better than you, the creature would rise above the Creator; and this is most absurd. And, indeed, whatever else there is, except you alone, can be conceived not to exist. To you alone, therefore, it belongs to exist more truly than all other beings, and hence in a higher degree than all others. For, whatever else exists does not exist so truly, and hence in a less degree it belongs to it to exist. Why, then, has the fool said in his heart, there is no God (Psalms 14:1), since it is so evident, to a rational mind, that you do exist in the highest degree of all? Why, except that he is dull and a fool?

Anselm's first argument treats *ordinary* existence in reality as a great-making quality; that is, something with ordinary existence is greater than something that is merely imagined or held in the mind. His second argument, though, treats *necessary* existence as a great-making quality. For only of something that exists necessarily would it be true to say that it "cannot be conceived not to exist." An analogy might help clarify this point. Spheres are round necessarily. If someone claimed they had found a sphere that was not round, we would say that was impossible. A sphere *must* be round. If, for example, you are trying to think of something as being both a sphere and square, you are contradicting yourself in your own thoughts. Now we might think of Anselm as saying something like this: God exists necessarily; that is, it is not possible that God not exist. It belongs to the concept of God that God could not come into existence, die, or disintegrate. When we are thinking of God, we are thinking of a being which, by definition, could not be born or die. We are, that is, thinking of a being X such that it is not possible that X not exist. And that is exactly what it means to say that God exists necessarily. So if you claim that it is possible that God does not exist, you are contradicting yourself in your own thoughts.

2. AGAINST THE ONTOLOGICAL ARGUMENT: GAUNILO, AQUINAS, AND KANT

From the time of Anselm on through the present day, the ontological argument has attracted the attention of many of the greatest minds in philosophy. Some have defended one or another version of the argument, while others have attempted to refute it. We will consider three classic criticisms, all of which appear to be aimed at the first version of Anselm's argument.

Gaunilo's Criticism. Gaunilo, a monk who was a contemporary of Anselm, wrote an attack on Anselm's argument entitled "on behalf of the fool." He offers several criticisms, the most well known being a parody on Anselm's argument in which he proves the existence of the greatest possible island. If we replaced "something than which nothing greater can be conceived" in Anselm's argument with "an island than which none greater can be conceived," then we could prove the existence of that island, Gaunilo claimed. If someone denied that our most perfect island existed, then we could say that they must not be conceiving the most perfect island. For, as Anselm argues, existence in reality is a perfection or great-making quality, and so the most perfect island would have to have that quality too. On Anselm's kind of reasoning, it seems, the most perfect island would have to have existence in reality—as well as the best climate and other perfect features. Gaunilo's point was that we could prove the existence of almost anything using Anselm's style of argument—for example, the most perfect rock or the most perfect automobile. A form of argument that can be used to prove the existence of any perfect thing is obviously defective. Gaunilo thus tries to show that Anselm's reasoning leads to absurd consequences and must be rejected.

ASK YOURSELF

79. We noted above that there is more than one argument in Anselm's text. Does Gaunilo's argument apply to only one of Anselm's arguments, and, if so, which one? Explain and justify your answer.

In an essay five times longer than his original argument, Anselm responded to Gaunilo's criticisms. The following is his reply to the island objection.

Gaunilo began to suspect his travel agent's
tendency to exaggerate.

FROM ANSELM, "Reply to Gaunilo"

You say, it is as if one should suppose an island in the ocean, which surpasses all lands in its fertility, and which, because of the difficulty, or rather the impossibility, of discovering what does not exist, is called a lost island; and should say that there can be no doubt that this island truly exists in reality, for this reason, that one who hears it described easily understands what he hears.

Now I promise confidently that if any man shall devise anything existing either in reality or in concept alone (except that than which a greater cannot be conceived) to which he can adapt the sequence of my reasoning, I will discover that thing, and will give him his lost island, not to be lost again.

But it now appears that this being than which a greater is inconceivable cannot be conceived not to be, because it exists on so assured a ground of truth; for otherwise it would not exist at all.

Hence, if any one says that he conceives this being not to exist, I say that at the time when he conceives of this either he conceives of a being than which a greater is inconceivable, or he does not conceive at all. If he does not conceive, he does not conceive of the non-existence of that of which he does not conceive. But if he does conceive, he certainly conceives of a being which cannot be even conceived not to exist. For if it could be conceived not to exist, it could be conceived to have a beginning and an end. But this is impossible.

He, then, who conceives of this being conceives of a being which cannot be even conceived not to exist; but he who conceives of this being does not conceive that it does not exist; else he conceives what is inconceivable. The non-existence, then, of that than which a greater cannot be conceived is inconceivable.

The upshot of Anselm's reply is that his argument cannot apply to any being whose nonexistence is conceivable, such as an island or a car.

Aquinas's Criticism. About 150 years after Anselm died, Dominican friar Thomas Aquinas (1225–1274) offered a criticism of the ontological argument. He agreed with Anselm that God's existence is self-evident—that is, that the notion of God itself entails existence. However, Aquinas believed that some self-evident notions cannot be grasped by people, and this is the case with God's self-existence:

> Perhaps not everyone who hears this word "God" understands it to signify something than which nothing greater can be thought, seeing that some have believed God to be a body. Yet, granted that everyone understands that by this word "God" is signified something than which nothing greater can be thought, nevertheless, it does not therefore follow that he understands that what the word signifies exists actually, but only that it exists mentally. Nor can it be argued that it actually exists, unless it be admitted that there actually exists something than which nothing greater can be thought; and this precisely is not admitted by those who hold that God does not exist. [From Aquinas, *Summa Theologica* (1266), First Part, Q. 2]

According to Aquinas, even if we accept Anselm's definition of God—the greatest conceivable being—that does not mean we will infer that God exists in reality. Aquinas thinks that the argument would require us to have an adequate conception of God, which we may not have. He also suggests that it is question begging—that is, assumes the very thing that is to be proved.

Kant's Criticism. In more recent centuries, German philosopher Immanuel Kant (1724–1804) presented what has become one of the more influential criticisms of the ontological argument. Kant contends that the ontological argument rests on a grammatical misunderstanding about the notion of existence. There are, he believes, two kinds of predicates. Normal predicates are simply added to the conception of some subject, such as "the ball *is round,*" "the ball *is red,*" or "the ball *bounces.*" Other predicates, though, are not added to a subject, but they are already assumed to be part of the object itself; this is particularly so with the notion of existence. For example, if I say that "The ball exists" I am not adding any attribute to the notion of "ball" but merely asserting the existence of a ball. According to Kant, the ontological argument uses the notion of existence as though it were a normal predicate. There are indeed normal predicates that we can legitimately ascribe to the notion of "the greatest conceivable being." For example, we can say that "the greatest conceivable being *is powerful*" or "the greatest conceivable being *is*

Title page of German edition of Immanuel Kant's Critique of Pure Reason *(1781).*

wise." Suppose, though, that we go on to say that "the greatest conceivable being *exists.*" I have not added any new attribute but have only repeated what is already assumed in the notion of "being." So, when Anselm concludes that "the greatest conceivable being *exists in reality,*" he misuses the notion of "existence" and the whole argument must be rejected because it rests on this grammatical mistake.

Being is evidently not a real predicate, that is, a conception of something which is added to the conception of some other thing. It is merely the positing of a thing, or of certain determinations in it. Logically, it is merely the copula of a judgment. The proposition, God is omnipotent, contains two conceptions, which have a certain object or content; the word *is*, is no additional predicate—it merely indicates the relation of the predicate to the subject. Now, if I take the subject (God) with all its predicates (omnipotence being one), and say: God is, or, There is a God, I add no new predicate to the conception of God, I merely posit or affirm the existence of the subject with all its predicates—I posit the object in relation to my conception. The content of both is the same; and there is no addition made to the conception, which expresses merely the possibility of the object, by my thinking the object—in the expression, it is—as absolutely given or existing. [From Immanuel Kant, *The Critique of Pure Reason* (1781)]

ASK YOURSELF

81. According to Kant, when I say "God exists" I add no new _____ to the conception of God.

SUMMING UP THE ISSUE OF THE ONTOLOGICAL ARGUMENT

Anselm's ontological argument is an attempt to prove God's existence by unpacking the logical implications embedded in the notion of God as "the greatest conceivable being." If we think about the idea of "the greatest conceivable being," we will see that such a being must exist. By definition, it must have the greatest conceivable qualities, particularly the quality of "existence," since "existence" is a greater quality than "nonexistence." Alternatively, we must think of the greatest conceivable qualities as including "necessary existence." Anselm's argument has been widely criticized. Gaunilo argued that ontological-type arguments could prove the existence of almost anything, such as the greatest possible island. Aquinas conceded that it belongs to the essence or notion of God that God exists, but thought it possible to deny that there is any such essence. The claim that it is not possible begs the question. Kant argued that Anselm misuses the notion of existence when asserting that "the greatest conceivable being exists in reality" by treating it as an ordinary predicate on the same level as "red."

CAN OF WORMS

The ontological argument is indeed, as Anselm states, a one-of-a-kind proof. From the mere concepts of "God" and "existence" alone, he believes that we can deduce God's existence. Nevertheless, components of Anselm's discussion, along with the ensuing debate, connect with several areas of philosophy. When Anselm contends that God exists *necessarily,* this raises larger metaphysical issues about "necessity" and "possibility." Kant's view that "existence is not a normal predicate" ties in with contemporary discussions in logic and philosophy of language, particularly with disputes about how best to logically represent "existence" in a formal or natural linguistic system. In fact, many contemporary versions of Anselm's argument are presented in symbolic logic and thus rest heavily on the metaphysical assumptions that go into particular logical systems.

E. THE COSMOLOGICAL ARGUMENT FOR GOD'S EXISTENCE

Around the time of Anselm, Muslim philosophers, developing ideas they found in Aristotle, formulated a different proof for God's existence, which has since been called the cosmological argument. The Muslim argument begins by noting that there are cause–effect connections in the physical world all around us. For example, a sapling in my yard was produced by its parent tree, and that tree in turn by its parent. We can trace these causal connections back further and further, but the chain of events cannot simply go back through time forever. There must be some first cause to the series, and this cause is God.

QUESTIONS TO DISCUSS

a. A common question that even children ask is "how did everything get here"? What are the possible answers that we might give to this question?

b. We sometimes hear people make an argument like this: it doesn't make sense to say that God created the universe, because we can then ask "who or what created God?" Is there a problem with this line of reasoning?

c. Suppose that you were an astronaut and, while exploring the far depths of space you found a stack of bricks extending in both directions as far as you could see. Would it be logically possible for the stack of bricks to be infinitely long?

1. AQUINAS'S PROOFS

Dominican friar Thomas Aquinas (1225–1274) was aware of the formulation of the cosmological argument offered by some Muslims but felt that it had problems. Aristotle himself had, Aquinas thought, shown that it is not possible to prove that the universe is not infinite temporally. Logically speaking, why can't a causal chain of events trace back through time to infinity without ever arriving at a first cause? Christians certainly believe that God created—that is, *caused*—the world, and that the universe simply did not exist from eternity. However, Aquinas argued, this is a belief based on faith, and not on reason. Thus, from the standpoint of pure logic, the Muslim cosmological argument noted above fails.

FROM THOMAS AQUINAS, *Summa Theologica* (1266), FIRST PART, Q. 2, ART. 3; Q. 46, ART. 2

By faith alone do we hold, and by no demonstration can it be proved, that the world did not always exist, as was said above of the mystery of the Trinity. The reason of this is that the newness of the world cannot be demonstrated on the part of the world itself. For the principle of demonstration is the essence of a thing. Now everything according to its species is abstracted from "here" and "now"; whence it is said that universals are everywhere and always. Hence it cannot be demonstrated that man, or heaven, or a stone were not always. Likewise neither can it be demonstrated on the part of the efficient cause, which acts by will. For the will of God cannot be investigated by reason, except as regards those things which God must will of necessity; and what He wills about creatures is not among these, as was said above. But the divine will can be manifested by revelation, on which faith rests. Hence that the world began to exist is an object of faith, but not of demonstration or science. And it is useful to consider this, lest anyone, presuming to demonstrate what is of faith, should bring forward reasons that are not cogent, so as to give occasion to unbelievers to laugh, thinking that on such grounds we believe things that are of faith.

ASK YOURSELF

82. According to Aquinas, upon what must we base our knowledge of God's will?

Essential and Accidental Causes. In spite of his dissatisfaction with the Muslim argument, Aquinas went on to offer five ways of proving God's existence, the first three of which are versions of the cosmological argument. We will look at Way Two, which is an argument from what Aristotle called *efficient causes*—that is, objects or events that through their sheer force produce some effect.

The second way is from the nature of the efficient cause. In the world of sense we find there is an order of efficient causes. There is no case known (neither is it, indeed, possible) in which a thing is found to be the efficient cause of itself; for so it would be prior to itself, which is impossible. Now in efficient causes it is not possible to go on to infinity, because in all efficient causes following in order, the first is the cause of the intermediate cause, and the intermediate is the cause of the ultimate cause, whether the intermediate cause be several, or only one. Now to take away the cause is to take away the effect. Therefore, if there be no first cause among efficient causes, there will be no ultimate, nor any intermediate cause. But if in efficient causes it is possible to go on to infinity, there will be no first efficient cause, neither will there be an ultimate effect, nor any intermediate efficient causes; all of which is plainly false. Therefore it is necessary to admit a first efficient cause, to which everyone gives the name of God.

The argument from efficient cause is this: Some things have been caused to exist by something else. If X has been caused to exist, then X must have been caused by Y. If Y has been caused to exist, then it too must have been caused by some Z. But there cannot be an infinite chain of efficient causes. Hence there is a first cause which we call God.

At first glance, Aquinas's cosmological argument might not appear that different from the Muslim version. The difference, though, rests on a distinction that Aquinas makes between *essential causes* (causes *per se*) and *accidental causes* (causes *per accidens*). He explains this difference here:

In efficient causes it is impossible to proceed to infinity "*per se*"—thus, there cannot be an infinite number of causes that are "*per se*" required for a certain effect; for instance, that a stone be moved by a stick, the stick by the hand, and so on to infinity. But it is not impossible to proceed to infinity "accidentally" as regards efficient causes; for instance, if all the causes thus infinitely multiplied should have the order of only one cause, their multiplication being accidental, as an artificer acts by means of many hammers accidentally, because one after the other may be broken. It is accidental, therefore, that one particular hammer acts after the action of another; and likewise it is accidental to this particular man as generator to be generated by another man; for he generates as a man, and not as the son of another man. For all men generating hold one grade in efficient causes—viz. the grade of a particular generator. Hence it is not impossible for a man to be generated by man to infinity; but such a thing would be impossible if the generation of this man depended upon this man, and on an elementary body, and on the sun, and so on to infinity.

The standard example of an *essential* cause is a stone, which is moved by a stick, which is moved by one's hand, which is moved by one's arm. This example exhibits three features which show the presence of essential causes: (1) The stone, stick, hand, and arm have one property in common, namely, motion; (2) the motion of all four objects is simultaneous; and (3) the existence and motion of the first three objects is directly required to produce the motion of the stone. In contrast to this, the standard example of an *accidental* cause is Abraham begetting Isaac, who, in turn, begets Jacob. Here, neither Abraham's immediate existence, nor his reproductive activity, is required in producing his grandson Jacob. This example lacks the above three features of essential causes and, for this reason, shows the presence of accidental causes. With this distinction in mind, we can summarize Aquinas's argument as follows:

1. Some things exist and their existence is caused.
2. Whatever is caused to exist is caused to exist by something else.
3. An infinite series of simultaneous causes resulting in the existence of a particular thing is impossible.
4. Therefore, there is a first cause of whatever exists.

Premise 1 is clearly true: The world is full of causes and effects. Premise 2 is a fact that we all assume: If you have an effect, then you must have a cause, the converse of which states, if you do not have a cause, then you do not have an effect. Premise 3 states that there cannot be an infinite regress of causes. The reason for this is that the chain of causes in question (i.e., X which is caused by Y which is caused by Z) is a series of *essential* causes. If Aquinas tried to argue for the existence of a first cause on the basis of a chain of *accidental* causes, it simply would not work, since it is possible for a series of accidental causes to be infinite. A chain of essential causes, on the other hand, cannot regress infinitely. Since, using the example above, the hand and stick merely transfer motion to the stone, an infinite regress of causes would eliminate the possibility of explaining the motion which is being transferred ultimately to the stone. Without an initial cause of the motion, there would be no motion to transfer. Given, then, that the type of cause Aquinas is dealing with in premise 1 is an essential efficient cause, premise 3 ("there cannot be an infinite chain of efficient causes") seems more plausible.

ASK YOURSELF

83. State in your own words Aquinas's argument from essential causes. Make sure you employ the distinction between essential causes and accidental causes.

From the standpoint of medieval science, Aquinas's argument seems to work. Astronomers in Aquinas's time believed that the motion of the winds was caused at that moment by the motion of the moon, which in turn was caused at that moment by the motion of other heavenly bodies. Such simultaneous motion cannot travel up through outer space to infinity. There must, then, be a first cause to this simultaneous motion.

2. CLARKE'S PROOF AND HUME'S CRITICISMS

By the early eighteenth century, Aquinas's version of the cosmological argument declined in popularity—particularly in Protestant countries—and gave way to a newer version by British clergyman Samuel Clarke (1675–1729). Like Aquinas, Clarke argued that we must grant in principle that causal connections might trace back through time to eternity past. We could see the world, then, as consisting of an infinitely long series of dependent objects in which each thing depends on the previous thing for its existence. For example, I depend for my existence on my parents, they on their parents, and so on. Even if we grant this fact, Clarke continues, there remains an important unexplained fact, namely the fact that the entire infinite series itself exists. Thus, there must be a self-existent being that explains the whole series. Clarke's actual presentation of the argument makes for somewhat difficult reading. A clearer account is provisionally presented by David Hume in his *Dialogues Concerning Natural Religion* (1779), which Hume himself then harshly attacks.

**DAVID HUME
(1711–1776)**

Scottish skeptical philosopher and author of Dialogues Concerning Natural Religion *(1779).*

From his earliest philosophical productions, Hume was highly critical of religion and argued that religious belief was driven by superstition and fanaticism. In his middle forties, he composed his *Dialogues,* which systematically attacks the most recent versions of the theological proofs, including the cosmological argument. When Hume presented the manuscript of this work to his close friends, they were shocked by its controversial nature and discouraged him from ever publishing it. Twenty years later as his health was rapidly declining, Hume made arrangements to have the *Dialogues* published after his death. The work finally appeared in 1779 and, as expected, it met with heated criticism. The *Dialogues* is a conversation between three principal characters: Cleanthes, Philo, and Demea.

The Argument Presented. Hume presents Clarke's version of the cosmological argument in the following passage, through the mouth of Demea.

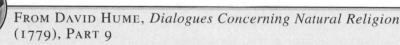

FROM DAVID HUME, *Dialogues Concerning Natural Religion*
(1779), PART 9

DEMEA   The argument, replied Demea, which I would insist on, is the common one. Whatever exists must have a cause or reason of its existence; it being absolutely impossible for any thing to produce itself, or be the cause of its own existence. In mounting up, therefore, from effects to causes, we must either go on in tracing an infinite succession, without any ultimate cause at all; or must at last have recourse to some ultimate cause, that is *necessarily* existent: Now, that the first supposition is absurd, may be thus proved. In the infinite chain or succession of causes and effects, each single effect is determined to exist by the power and efficacy of that cause which immediately preceded; but the whole eternal chain or succession, taken together, is not determined or caused by any thing; and yet it is evident that it requires a cause or reason, as much as any particular object which begins to exist in time. The question is still reasonable, why this particular succession of causes existed from eternity, and not any other succession, or no succession at all. If there be no necessarily existent being, any supposition which can be formed is equally possible; nor is there any more absurdity in Nothing's having existed from eternity, than there is in that succession of causes which constitutes the universe. What was it, then, which determined Something to exist rather than Nothing, and bestowed being on a particular possibility, exclusive of the rest? *External causes,* there are supposed to be none. *Chance* is a word without a meaning. Was it *Nothing?* But that can never produce any thing. We must, therefore, have recourse to a necessarily existent Being, who carries the *reason* of his existence in himself, and who cannot be supposed not to exist, without an express contradiction. There is, consequently, such a Being; that is, there is a Deity.

ASK YOURSELF

84. The central intuition of the cosmological argument is expressed in the question, "Why is there something rather than _____?"

More formally, the argument is this:

1. The world contains an infinite sequence of contingent facts.
2. An explanation is needed as to the origin of this whole infinite series (which goes beyond an explanation of each member in the series).
3. The explanation of this whole series cannot reside in the series itself, since the very fact of its existence would still need an explanation (principle of sufficient reason).
4. Therefore, there is a necessary being which produced this infinite series (and which is the complete explanation of its own existence as well).

The Failure of *A Priori* Arguments. The dialogue continues with an assault on the cosmological argument by Cleanthes—who in this instance expresses Hume's views. Cleanthes begins by noting the failure of *a priori* arguments in general—that is, arguments based solely on conceptual notions (such as an infinite sequences of dependent beings) without focusing on things that we actually experience.

CLEANTHES   I shall not leave it to Philo, said Cleanthes, though I know that the starting objections is his chief delight, to point out the weakness of this metaphysical reasoning. It seems to me so obviously ill-grounded, and at the same time of so little consequence to the cause of true piety and religion, that I shall myself venture to show the fallacy of it.

    I shall begin with observing, that there is an evident absurdity in pretending to demonstrate a matter of fact, or to prove it by any arguments *a priori.* Nothing is demonstrable, unless the contrary implies a contradiction. Nothing, that is distinctly conceivable, implies a contradiction. Whatever we conceive as existent, we can also conceive as non-existent.

There is no being, therefore, whose non-existence implies a contradiction. Consequently there is no being, whose existence is demonstrable. I propose this argument as entirely decisive, and am willing to rest the whole controversy upon it.

It is pretended that the Deity is a necessarily existent being; and this necessity of his existence is attempted to be explained by asserting, that if we knew his whole essence or nature, we should perceive it to be as impossible for him not to exist, as for twice two not to be four. But it is evident that this can never happen, while our faculties remain the same as at present. It will still be possible for us, at any time, to conceive the non-existence of what we formerly conceived to exist; nor can the mind ever lie under a necessity of supposing any object to remain always in being; in the same manner as we lie under a necessity of always conceiving twice two to be four. The words, therefore, *necessary existence,* have no meaning; or, which is the same thing, none that is consistent.

ASK YOURSELF

85. Why, according to Cleanthes, is there no being whose existence can be demonstrated?

But further, why may not the material universe be the necessarily existent Being, according to this pretended explication of necessity? We dare not affirm that we know all the qualities of matter; and for aught we can determine, it may contain some qualities, which, were they known, would make its non-existence appear as great a contradiction as that twice two is five. I find only one argument employed to prove, that the material world is not the necessarily existent Being: and this argument is derived from the contingency both of the matter and the form of the world. "Any particle of matter," it is said, "may be *conceived* to be annihilated; and any form may be *conceived* to be altered. Such an annihilation or alteration, therefore, is not impossible." But it seems a great partiality not to perceive, that the same argument extends equally to the Deity, so far as we have any conception of him; and that the mind can at least imagine him to be non-existent, or his attributes to be altered. It must be some unknown, inconceivable qualities, which can make his non-existence appear impossible, or his attributes unalterable: And no reason can be assigned, why these qualities may not belong to matter. As they are altogether unknown and inconceivable, they can never be proved incompatible with it.

Add to this, that in tracing an eternal succession of objects, it seems absurd to inquire for a general cause or first author. How can any thing, that exists from eternity, have a cause, since that relation implies a priority in time, and a beginning of existence?

ASK YOURSELF

86. According to Cleanthes, the material universe itself might be the "necessarily existent being" that the cosmological argument attempts to demonstrate. Whatever qualities believers might ascribe to God as the ultimate source of things, these qualities might also belong to matter. What specific qualities does Cleanthes list?

Cleanthes concludes with what has become the most central criticism of this version of the cosmological argument. Once we adequately explain each individual item in an infinite series of dependent beings, then we have thereby given a full explanation of the entire series, and it makes no sense to inquire into any cause beyond this.

In such a chain, too, or succession of objects, each part is caused by that which preceded it, and causes that which succeeds it. Where then is the difficulty? But the *whole,* you say, wants a cause. I answer, that the uniting of these parts into a whole, like the uniting of several distinct countries into one kingdom, or several distinct members into one body, is performed merely by an arbitrary act of the mind, and has no influence on the nature of things. Did I show you the particular causes of each individual in a collection of twenty particles of matter, I should think it very unreasonable, should you afterwards ask me, what was the cause of the whole twenty. This is sufficiently explained in explaining the cause of the parts.

ASK YOURSELF

87. According to Cleanthes, if we know the causes of each individual in a collection, then it is unreasonable to ask for the cause of the _____.

88. If I have a complete explanation for the existence of the sugar in my cookie, and a complete explanation for the flour in my cookie, and that is all there is to the cookie, do I then have a complete explanation for the cookie?

According to Cleanthes, the flaw in the cosmological argument consists in assuming that there is some larger fact about the universe that needs explaining beyond the particular items in the series itself.

SUMMING UP THE ISSUE OF THE COSMOLOGICAL ARGUMENT

The basic intuition behind the cosmological argument is that, when we trace causal connections back further and further, we must arrive at a first cause to the series, and this cause is God. Aquinas presented a version of this argument based on the view that it is impossible for a chain of essential causes—causes occurring exactly at the same time—to be infinitely long. Samuel Clarke presented a modified version of the argument. Even if we assume that causes of the universe trace back to infinity past, there is still a fundamental fact that requires an explanation: why the entire infinite series of causes exists at all. God, Clarke argued, is the required cause of the infinite series. Hume criticized the cosmological argument on two grounds. First, the material universe itself might be the "necessarily existent being" that the cosmological argument attempts to demonstrate. Second, the existence of the entire series of dependent beings is fully explained by the existence of each dependent being in the series.

CAN OF WORMS

The dominant question raised by the cosmological argument is, "Why is there something rather than nothing?" Aquinas and Clarke attempted to answer this with the notion of a creator God. This question is also one which touches on the meaning of life, for the answer that we give to this question may impact how we view the purpose of the universe and human existence itself. Like philosophers, physicists also explore why something exists rather than nothing, and, to that extent, some of their theories and methods of investigation are scrutinized by the philosophy of science. Hume's criticism—that the whole series is sufficiently explained by each thing in the series—raises issues in logic and the theory of explanation. Specifically, when is it appropriate or inappropriate to state that a collection of things can be reduced to the properties of its individual parts.

F. THE DESIGN ARGUMENT FOR GOD'S EXISTENCE

Perhaps the oldest argument for God's existence is the *design argument,* which rests on the simple intuition that the presence of natural design in the world around us implies the existence of some designer. We find hints of this reasoning in the Old Testament Book of Psalms, "The heavens declare the glory of God; and the firmament shows his handiwork" (19:1). Technically, this passage does not *argue* for the conclusion that God exists, but it states that the grandeur of nature bears the mark of God and, to that extent, is a kind of testament to God's existence.

QUESTIONS TO DISCUSS

a. Are there any things in the natural world that seem to require a divine designer as an explanation?

b. Could God have used evolution as a tool to bring about the design that we see in nature?

c. Is there anything in the design of nature that requires us to believe that it was created by a single, all powerful God?

Along with his cosmological arguments, Thomas Aquinas presented a brief version of the design argument:

> The fifth way is taken from the governance of the world. We see that things which lack intelligence, such as natural bodies, act for an end, and this is evident from their acting always, or nearly always, in the same way, so as to obtain the best result. Hence it is plain that not fortuitously, but designedly, do they achieve their end. Now whatever lacks intelligence cannot move towards an end, unless it be directed by some being endowed with knowledge and intelligence; as the arrow is shot to its mark by the archer. Therefore some intelligent being exists by whom all natural things are directed to their end; and this being we call God. [From Aquinas, *Summa Theologica* (1266), First Part, Q. 2, Art. 3]

More precisely, Aquinas's design argument is this. Objects without intelligence act toward some end; for example, a tree grows and reproduces its own kind. Moving toward an end or acting purposively requires intelligence. If a thing is unintelligent, yet acts for some end, then that thing must be guided to this end by something which is intelligent. And this "something" is God.

In the centuries after Aquinas, theologians kept pace with the growing body of scientific knowledge. Medieval notions of science and cosmology were discarded and ultimately replaced with a conception of the universe governed by mechanistic physical laws. The newer theistic proofs were thus scientifically up to date, drawing on the latest contributions of mathematicians, astronomers, biologists, and other physical scientists. By the eighteenth century, the most common versions of this argument were in the form of an analogy between the design that we see in human productions and the design that we see in the natural world. The general form of any argument from analogy is this:

1. Object A has properties f, g, and h and also P.
2. Object B is like A in having properties f, g, and h.
3. Therefore probably B has properties P also.

Following this formula, the design argument from analogy is this:

1. Machines (which have orderly and purposeful arrangements of parts) are the products of intelligent design.
2. The universe resembles a machine (insofar as it has an orderly and purposeful arrangement of parts).
3. Therefore, the universe is the product of intelligent design.

Proponents of the design argument used a variety of examples to draw out the analogy. For example, they pointed out the intricate mechanisms of human-made watches and compared these with the natural machinery that we see in the operation of the solar system or in the biological make up of the eye or the hand.

1. AGAINST THE DESIGN ARGUMENT: DAVID HUME

Earlier we examined Hume's attack on the cosmological argument as appears in his *Dialogues Concerning Natural Religion*. In that work, Hume takes on the design argument as well. The initial design argument from analogy is presented by the character Cleanthes.

FROM DAVID HUME, *Dialogues Concerning Natural Religion* (1799), PARTS 2 AND 5

CLEANTHES   I shall briefly explain how I conceive this matter. Look round the world: contemplate the whole and every part of it: You will find it to be nothing but one great machine, subdivided into an infinite number of lesser machines, which again admit of subdivisions to a degree beyond what human senses and faculties can trace and explain. All these various machines, and even their most minute parts, are adjusted to each other with an accuracy which ravishes into admiration all men who have ever contemplated them. The curious adapting of means to ends, throughout all nature, resembles exactly, though it much exceeds, the productions of human contrivance; of human designs, thought, wisdom, and intelligence. Since, therefore, the effects resemble each other, we are led to infer, by all the rules of analogy, that the causes also resemble; and that the Author of Nature is somewhat similar to the mind of man, though possessed of much larger faculties, proportioned to the grandeur of the work which he has executed. By this argument *a posteriori,* and by this argument alone, do we prove at once the existence of a Deity, and his similarity to human mind and intelligence. [*Dialogues Concerning Natural Religion,* Part 2]

ASK YOURSELF

89. According to Cleanthes, in what ways is the world "one great machine"?

The Failure of the Analogy. Cleanthes' design argument is then challenged by Philo—who here represents Hume's views. A central assumption in the design argument is that the universe resembles a machine (premise 2 above). Perhaps there is some superficial resemblance between the two—such as with the circular movement of planets around the sun and the movement of gears within clocks. However, Philo argues that such resemblance doesn't hold up to close scrutiny. The universe is quite different from human machines. Philo begins explaining a basic principle of logic: The more dissimilar two objects are, the weaker the analogy between those two objects becomes.

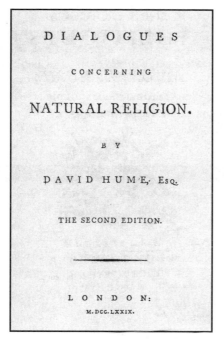

DIALOGUES

CONCERNING

NATURAL RELIGION.

BY

DAVID HUME, Esq.

THE SECOND EDITION.

———

LONDON:
M.DCC.LXXIX.

Title page of David Hume's Dialogues Concerning Natural Religion *(1779) first published two years after Hume's death.*

PHILO ... That a stone will fall, that fire will burn, that the earth has solidity, we have observed a thousand and a thousand times; and when any new instance of this nature is presented, we draw without hesitation the accustomed inference. The exact similarity of the cases gives us a perfect assurance of a similar event; and a stronger evidence is never desired nor sought after. But wherever you depart, in the least, from the similarity of the cases, you diminish proportionably the evidence; and may at last bring it to a very weak *analogy,* which is confessedly liable to error and uncertainty. After having experienced the circulation of the blood in human creatures, we make no doubt that it takes place in Titius and Maevius. But from its circulation in frogs and fishes, it is only a presumption, though a strong one, from analogy, that it takes place in men and other animals. The analogical reasoning is much weaker, when we infer the circulation of the sap in vegetables from our experience that the blood circulates in animals; and those, who hastily followed that imperfect analogy, are found, by more accurate experiments, to have been mistaken.

If we see a house, Cleanthes, we conclude, with the greatest certainty, that it had an architect or builder; because this is precisely that species of effect which we have experienced to proceed from that species of cause. But surely you will not affirm, that the universe bears such a resemblance to a house, that we can with the same certainty infer a similar cause, or that the analogy is here entire and perfect. The dissimilitude is so striking, that the utmost you can here pretend to is a guess, a conjecture, a presumption concerning a similar cause; and how that pretension will be received in the world, I leave you to consider.

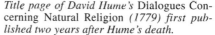

ASK YOURSELF

90. Philo presents examples of weak analogies. Give one of these.

CLEANTHES It would surely be very ill received, replied Cleanthes; and I should be deservedly blamed and detested, did I allow, that the proofs of a Deity amounted to no more than a guess or conjecture. But is the whole adjustment of means to ends in a house and in the universe so slight a resemblance? The economy of final causes? The order, proportion, and arrangement of every part? Steps of a stair are plainly contrived, that human legs may use them in mounting; and this inference is certain and infallible. Human legs are also contrived for walking and mounting; and this inference, I allow, is not altogether so certain, because of the dissimilarity which you remark; but does it, therefore, deserve the name only of presumption or conjecture?

ASK YOURSELF

91. Cleanthes responds to Philo by specifying the precise features that the universe has in common with objects of human design, such as houses. What are these features?

Philo insists again that any difference between two compared things weakens the analogy. Objects of human design such as houses certainly do exhibit intelligent thought. However, when we survey the various systems of the universe, we find many causal forces that do not apparently depend upon conscious thought. Why single out those that seem to require intelligent design as the main ones?

PHILO That all inferences, Cleanthes, concerning fact, are founded on experience; and that all experimental reasonings are founded on the supposition that similar causes prove similar effects, and similar effects similar causes; I shall not at present much dispute with you. But observe, I entreat you, with what extreme caution all just reasoners proceed in the transferring of experiments to similar cases. Unless the cases be exactly similar, they repose no perfect confidence in applying their past observation to any particular phenomenon. Every alteration of circumstances occasions a doubt concerning the event; and it requires new experiments to prove certainly, that the new circumstances are of no moment or importance. A change in bulk, situation, arrangement, age, disposition of the air, or surrounding bodies; any of these particulars may be attended with the most unexpected consequences: And unless the objects be quite familiar to us, it is the highest temerity to expect with assurance, after any of these changes, an event similar to that which before fell under our observation. The slow and deliberate steps of philosophers here, if anywhere, are distinguished from the precipitate march of the vulgar, who, hurried on by the smallest similitude, are incapable of all discernment or consideration.

But can you think, Cleanthes, that your usual phlegm and philosophy have been preserved in so wide a step as you have taken, when you compared to the universe houses, ships, furniture, machines, and, from their similarity in some circumstances, inferred a similarity in their causes? Thought, design, intelligence, such as we discover in men and other animals, is no more than one of the springs and principles of the universe, as well as heat or cold, attraction or repulsion, and a hundred others, which fall under daily observation. It is an active cause, by which some particular parts of nature, we find, produce alterations on other parts. But can a conclusion, with any propriety, be transferred from parts to the whole? Does not the great disproportion bar all comparison and inference? From observing the growth of a hair, can we learn any thing concerning the generation of a man? Would the manner of a leaf's blowing, even though perfectly known, afford us any instruction concerning the vegetation of a tree?

ASK YOURSELF

92. What are some of the actuating "springs and principles" that the universe exhibits aside from intelligent design?

But, allowing that we were to take the operations of one part of nature upon another, for the foundation of our judgment concerning the *origin* of the whole (which never can be admitted), yet why select so minute, so weak, so bounded a principle, as the reason and design of animals is found to be upon this planet? What peculiar privilege has this little agitation of the brain which we call thought, that we must thus make it the model of the whole universe? Our partiality in our own favor does indeed present it on all occasions; but sound philosophy ought carefully to guard against so natural an illusion.

ASK YOURSELF

93. What is Hume's point when he refers to "this little agitation of the brain which we call thought"?

So far from admitting, continued Philo, that the operations of a part can afford us any just conclusion concerning the origin of the whole, I will not allow any one part to form a rule for another part, if the latter be very remote from the former. Is there any reasonable ground to conclude, that the inhabitants of other planets possess thought, intelligence, reason, or any thing similar to these faculties in men? When nature has so extremely diversified her manner of operation in this small globe, can we imagine that she incessantly copies herself throughout so immense a universe? And if thought, as we may well suppose, be confined merely to this narrow corner, and has even there so limited a sphere of action, with what propriety can we assign it for the original cause of all things? The narrow views of a peasant, who makes his domestic economy the rule for the government of kingdoms, is in comparison a pardonable sophism.

But were we ever so much assured, that a thought and reason, resembling the human, were to be found throughout the whole universe, and were its activity elsewhere vastly greater and more commanding than it appears in this globe; yet I cannot see, why the operations of a world constituted, arranged, adjusted, can with any propriety be extended to a world which is in its embryo state, and is advancing towards that constitution and arrangement. By observation, we know somewhat of the economy, action, and nourishment of a finished animal; but we must transfer with great caution that observation to the growth of a fetus in the womb, and still more to the formation of an animalcule in the loins of its male parent. Nature, we find, even from our limited experience, possesses an infinite number of springs and principles, which incessantly discover themselves on every change of her position and situation. And what new and unknown principles would actuate her in so new and unknown a situation as that of the formation of a universe, we cannot, without the utmost temerity, pretend to determine.

A very small part of this great system, during a very short time, is very imperfectly discovered to us; and do we thence pronounce decisively concerning the origin of the whole?

Admirable conclusion! Stone, wood, brick, iron, brass, have not, at this time, in this minute globe of earth, an order or arrangement without human art and contrivance; therefore the universe could not originally attain its order and arrangement, without something similar to human art. But is a part of nature a rule for another part very wide of the former? Is it a rule for the whole? Is a very small part a rule for the universe? Is nature in one situation, a certain rule for nature in another situation vastly different from the former?

94. Philo argues that we cannot take a part of the universe and use it as a model for how the whole thing was created. What is the "part of the universe" that Philo has in mind?

And can you blame me, Cleanthes, if I here imitate the prudent reserve of Simonides, who, according to the noted story, being asked by Hiero, *What God was?* desired a day to think of it, and then two days more; and after that manner continually prolonged the term, without ever bringing in his definition or description? Could you even blame me, if I had answered at first, *that I did not know,* and was sensible that this subject lay vastly beyond the reach of my faculties? You might cry out skeptic and railler, as much as you pleased: but having found, in so many other subjects much more familiar, the imperfections and even contradictions of human reason, I never should expect any success from its feeble conjectures, in a subject so sublime, and so remote from the sphere of our observation. When two *species* of objects have always been observed to be conjoined together, I can *infer,* by custom, the existence of one wherever I *see* the existence of the other; and this I call an argument from experience. But how this argument can have place, where the objects, as in the present case, are single, individual, without parallel, or specific resemblance, may be difficult to explain. And will any man tell me with a serious countenance, that an orderly universe must arise from some thought and art like the human, because we have experience of it? To ascertain this reasoning, it were requisite that we had experience of the origin of worlds; and it is not sufficient, surely, that we have seen ships and cities arise from human art and contrivance.

95. According to Philo, we have "no experience of the origin of the worlds." Why is this a problem for the design argument?

Concerning the Infinity, Perfection, and Unity of the Creator. According to Philo, even if there is some indication of intelligent design in the natural world, this does not allow us to infer the existence of a single, all-powerful, all-knowing, and all-good God. We must proportion the cause of a thing to the effects that we actually see. Since the universe (as an effect) is limited, diverse, and imperfect, we cannot infer that the designer (the cause) is unlimited, single, and perfect.

PHILO   *First,* By this method of reasoning, you renounce all claim to infinity in any of the attributes of the Deity. For, as the cause ought only to be proportioned to the effect, and the effect, so far as it falls under our cognizance, is not infinite; what pretensions have we, upon your suppositions, to ascribe that attribute to the Divine Being? You will still insist, that, by removing him so much from all similarity to human creatures, we give in to the most arbitrary hypothesis, and at the same time weaken all proofs of his existence.

Secondly, You have no reason, on your theory, for ascribing perfection to the Deity, even in his finite capacity, or for supposing him free from every error, mistake, or incoherence, in his undertakings. There are many inexplicable difficulties in the works of Nature, which, if we allow a perfect author to be proved *a priori*, are easily solved, and become only seeming difficulties, from the narrow capacity of man, who cannot trace infinite relations. But according to your method of reasoning, these difficulties become all real; and perhaps will be insisted on, as new instances of likeness to human art and contrivance. At least, you must acknowledge, that it is impossible for us to tell, from our limited views, whether this system contains any great faults; or deserves any considerable praise, if compared to other possible, and even real systems. Could a peasant, if the *Aneid* were read to him, pronounce that poem to be absolutely faultless, or even assign to it its proper rank among the productions of human wit, he, who had never seen any other production?

But were this world ever so perfect a production, it must still remain uncertain, whether all the excellences of the work can justly be ascribed to the workman. If we survey a ship, what an exalted idea must we form of the ingenuity of the carpenter who framed so complicated, useful, and beautiful a machine? And what surprise must we feel, when we find him a stupid mechanic, who imitated others, and copied an art, which, through a long succession of ages, after multiplied trials, mistakes, corrections, deliberations, and controversies, had been gradually improving? Many worlds might have been botched and bungled, throughout an eternity, ere this system was struck out; much labor lost, many fruitless trials made; and a slow, but continued improvement carried on during infinite ages in the art of world-making. In such subjects, who can determine, where the truth; nay, who can conjecture where the probability lies, amidst a great number of hypotheses which may be proposed, and a still greater which may be imagined?

ASK YOURSELF

96. According to Philo, many worlds might have been "botched and bungled, throughout an eternity" before this one was created. What does this imply about the nature of the creator or creators?

And what shadow of an argument, continued Philo, can you produce, from your hypothesis, to prove the unity of the Deity? A great number of men join in building a house or ship, in rearing a city, in framing a commonwealth; why may not several deities combine in contriving and framing a world? This is only so much greater similarity to human affairs. By sharing the work among several, we may so much further limit the attributes of each, and get rid of that extensive power and knowledge, which must be supposed in one deity, and which, according to you, can only serve to weaken the proof of his existence. And if such foolish, such vicious creatures as man, can yet often unite in framing and executing one plan, how much more those deities or demons, whom we may suppose several degrees more perfect!

To multiply causes without necessity, is indeed contrary to true philosophy: but this principle applies not to the present case. Were one deity antecedently proved by your theory, who were possessed of every attribute requisite to the production of the universe; it would be needless, I own (though not absurd), to suppose any other deity existent. But while it is still a question, Whether all these attributes are united in one subject, or dispersed among several independent beings, by what phenomena in nature can we pretend to decide the controversy? Where we see a body raised in a scale, we are sure that there is in the opposite scale, however concealed from sight, some counterpoising weight equal to it; but it is still allowed to doubt, whether that weight be an aggregate of several distinct bodies, or one uniform united mass. And if the weight requisite very much exceeds any thing which we have ever seen conjoined in any single body, the former supposition becomes still more probable and natural. An intelligent being of such vast power and capacity as is necessary to produce the universe, or, to speak in the language of ancient philosophy, so prodigious an animal exceeds all analogy, and even comprehension.

But further, Cleanthes: men are mortal, and renew their species by generation; and this is common to all living creatures. The two great sexes of male and female, says Milton, animate the world. Why must this circumstance, so universal, so essential, be excluded from those numerous and limited deities? Behold, then, the theogony of ancient times brought back upon us.

And why not become a perfect Anthropomorphite? Why not assert the deity or deities to be corporeal, and to have eyes, a nose, mouth, ears, etc.? Epicurus maintained, that no man had ever seen reason but in a human figure; therefore the gods must have a human figure. And this argument, which is deservedly so much ridiculed by Cicero, becomes, according to you, solid and philosophical.

In a word, Cleanthes, a man who follows your hypothesis is able perhaps to assert, or conjecture, that the universe, sometime, arose from something like design: but beyond that position he cannot ascertain one single circumstance; and is left afterwards to fix every point of his theology by the utmost license of fancy and hypothesis. This world, for aught he knows, is very faulty and imperfect, compared to a superior standard; and was only the first rude essay of some infant deity, who afterwards abandoned it, ashamed of his lame performance: it is the work only of some dependent, inferior deity; and is the object of derision to his superiors: it is the production of old age and dotage in some superannuated deity; and ever since his death, has run on at adventures, from the first impulse and active force which it received from him.

 2. **THE DESIGN ARGUMENT REVISITED: WILLIAM PALEY**

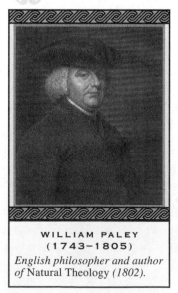

WILLIAM PALEY
(1743–1805)

English philosopher and author of Natural Theology *(1802).*

William Paley (1743–1805) was an archdeacon in the Anglican Church, as well as the author of several philosophy books that became standard reading in British universities for several decades. Although Paley was sympathetic with some aspects of Hume's philosophy—particularly his moral theory—he was bothered by Hume's views on religion. In 1802 he published a work entitled *Natural Theology,* which aimed at overturning Hume's attack on the design argument in the *Dialogues.* We've seen that one of Hume's central criticisms of the design argument is that the analogy between the universe and humanly produced machines is weak. For example, Hume argues that we cannot compare the two since we've experienced the creation of machines by humans, but no one has witnessed how the universe was created. Paley addresses this point directly by paralleling the intricate mechanisms of the universe with a complex watch. Even if we are completely unfamiliar with how this watch or any other watch was created, in Paley's view, we would still marvel at the workmanship. Thus, for Paley, the analogy between the universe and objects of human design is strong enough for us to infer the existence of a supremely intelligent designer.

Like Cleanthes' design argument in Hume's *Dialogues*, the centerpiece of Paley's natural theology is an argument from analogy.

FROM WILLIAM PALEY, *Natural Theology* (1802)

In crossing a heath, suppose I pitched my foot against a stone, and were asked how the stone came to be there, I might possibly answer, that, for anything I knew to the contrary, it had lain there for ever; nor would it, perhaps, be very easy to show the absurdity of this answer. But suppose I found a watch upon the ground, and it should be inquired how the watch happened to be in that place, I should hardly think of the answer which I had before given—that, for anything I knew, the watch might have always been there. Yet why should not this answer serve for the watch as well as for the stone? Why is it not as admissible in the second case as in the first? For this reason, and for no other, viz., that, when we come to inspect the watch, we perceive (what we could not discover in the stone) that its several parts are framed and put together for a purpose, e.g. that they are so formed and adjusted as to produce motion, and that motion so regulated as to point out the hour of the day; that, if the different parts had been differently shaped from what they are, if a different size from what they are, or placed after any other manner, or in any other order than that in which they are placed, either no motion at all would have been carried on in the machine, or none which would have answered the use that is now served by it. To reckon up a few of the plainest of these parts, and of their offices, an tending to one result: We see a cylindrical box containing a coiled elastic spring, which, by its endeavor to relax itself, turns round the box. We next observe a flexible chain (artificially wrought for the sake of flexure) communicating the action of the spring from the box to the fusee. We then find a series of wheels, the teeth of which catch in, and apply to, each other, conducting the motion from the fusee to the balance, and from the balance to the pointer, and, at the same time, by the size and shape of those wheels, so regulating that motion as to terminate in causing an index, by an equable and measured progression, to pass over a given space in a given time. We take notice that the wheels are made of brass, in order to keep them from rust; the springs of steel, no other metal being so elastic; that over the face of the watch there is placed a glass, a material employed in no other part of the work, but in the room of which, if there had been any other than a transparent substance, the hour could not be seen without opening the case. This mechanism being observed (it requires indeed an examination of the instrument, and perhaps some previous knowledge of the subject, to perceive and understand it; but being once, as we have said, observed and understood), the inference, we think, is inevitable, that the watch must have had a maker; that there must have existed, at some time, and at some place or other, an artificer or artificers who formed it for the purpose which we find it actually to answer; who comprehended its construction, and designed its use.

ASK YOURSELF

99. If you found a plant with a structure as intricate as that of the watch, why might you be inclined to say that it must have been designed by some conscious mind?

Nor would it, I apprehend, weaken the conclusion, that we had never seen a watch made; that we had never known an artist capable of making one; that we were altogether incapable of executing such a piece of workmanship ourselves, or of understanding in what manner it was performed; all this being no more than what is true of some exquisite remains of ancient art, of some lost arts, and, to the generality of mankind, of the more curious productions of modern manufacture. Does one man in a million know how oval frames are turned? Ignorance of this kind exalts our opinion of the unseen and unknown artist's skill, if he be unseen and unknown, but raises no doubt in our minds of the existence and agency of such an artist, at some former time, and in some place or other. Nor can I perceive that it varies at all the inference, whether the question arise concerning a human agent, or concerning an agent of a different species, or an agent possessing, in some respect, a different nature. Neither, secondly, would it invalidate our conclusion, that the watch sometimes went wrong, or that it seldom went exactly right. The purpose of the machinery, the design, and the designer, might be evident, and, in the case supposed, would be evident, in whatever way we accounted for the irregularity of the movement, or whether we could account for it or not. It is not necessary that a machine be perfect, in order to show with what design it was made; still less necessary, where the only question is, whether it were made with any design at all.

Nor, thirdly, would it bring any uncertainty into the argument, if there were a few parts of the watch, concerning which we could not discover, or had not yet discovered, in what manner they conduced to the general effect; or even some parts, concerning which we could not ascertain whether they conduced to that effect in any manner whatever. For, as to the first branch of the case, if by the loss, or disorder, or decay of the parts in question, the movement of the watch were found in fact to be stopped, or disturbed, or retarded, no doubt would remain in our minds as to the utility or intention of these parts, although we should be unable to investigate the manner according to which, or the connection by which, the ultimate effect depended upon their action or assistance; and the more complex is the machine, the more likely is this obscurity to arise. Then, as to the second thing supposed, namely, that there were parts which might be spared without prejudice to the movement of the watch, and that he had proved this by experiment, these superfluous parts, even if we were completely assured that they were such, would not vacate the reasoning which we had instituted concerning other parts. The indication of contrivance remained, with respect to them, nearly as it was before.

ASK YOURSELF

100. Give an example of a part of an organism—for example, your own body— which seems to perform no function.

Nor, fourthly, would any man in his senses think the existence of the watch, with its various machinery, accounted for, by being told that it was one out of possible combinations of material forms; that whatever he had found in the place where he found the watch, must have contained some internal configuration or other; and that this configuration might be the structure now exhibited, viz., of the works of a watch, as well as a different structure.

Nor, fifthly, would it yield his inquiry more satisfaction, to be answered, that there existed in things a principle of order, which had disposed the parts of the watch into their present form and situation. He never knew a watch made by the principle of order; nor can he even form to himself an idea of what is meant by a principle of order, distinct from the intelligence of the watchmaker.

Sixthly, he would be surprised to hear that the mechanism of the watch was no proof of contrivance, only a motive to induce the mind to think so:

And [seventhly] not less surprised to be informed, that the watch in his hand was nothing more than the result of the laws of metallic nature. It is a perversion of language to assign any law as the efficient, operative cause of anything. A law presupposes an agent; for it is only the mode according to which an agent proceeds; it implies a power; for it is the order according to which that power acts. Without this agent, without this power, which are both distinct from itself, the law does nothing, is nothing. The expression, "the law of metallic nature," may sound strange and harsh to a philosophic ear; but it seems quite as justifiable as some others which are more familiar to him such as "the law of vegetable nature," "the law of animal nature," or, indeed, as "the law of nature," in general, when assigned as the cause of phenomena in exclusion of agency and power, or when it is substituted into the place of these.

Neither, lastly, would our observer be driven out of his conclusion, or from his confidence in its truth, by being told that he knew nothing at all about the matter. He knows enough for his argument: he knows the utility of the end: he knows the subserviency and adaptation of the means to the end. These points being known, his ignorance of other points, his doubts concerning other points, affect not the certainty of his reasoning. The consciousness of knowing little need not beget a distrust of that which he does know. . . .

Every indication of contrivance, every manifestation of design, which existed in the watch, exists in the works of nature; with the difference, on the side of nature, of being greater and more, and that in a degree which exceeds all computation. I mean that the contrivances of nature surpass the contrivances of art, in the complexity, subtilty, and curiosity of the mechanism; and still more, if possible, do they go beyond them in number and variety; yet in a multitude of cases, are not is evidently mechanical, not less evidently contrivances, not less evidently accommodated to their end, or united to their office, than are the most perfect productions of human ingenuity.

ASK YOURSELF

101. According to Paley, if there are "contrivances" in nature, there must be a _____.

3. EVOLUTION AND THE DESIGN ARGUMENT: CHARLES DARWIN

In the early nineteenth century, the consensus was that Paley successfully overturned Hume's criticisms of the design argument. The analogy between the universe and objects of human design seemed close enough to conclude that a cosmic designer exists. This victory, though, was short-lived. In 1859 Charles Darwin published *On the Origin of Species,* which offered a nonreligious, thoroughly naturalistic explanation of the origin and character of various life forms. According to Darwin, biological organisms evolve largely on the basis of random mutations. Those plants and animals with the most advantageous mutations are likely to survive, and those without those advantages are doomed to extinction. What appears to be intelligent design in the world, then, is only the result of natural selection. In his *Descent of Man* (1871) Darwin focused specifically on human beings and showed how our complex biology and behavior also result from evolutionary processes alone. Darwin himself was well acquainted with Paley and in his early years accepted Paley's position; he states in a letter, "I do not think I hardly ever admired a book more than Paley's 'Natural Theology.' I could almost

**CHARLES DARWIN
(1809–1882)**

English evolutionary biologist and author of On the Origin of Species *(1859).*

formerly have said it by heart" (Darwin to John Lubbock, November 15, 1859). At some point, though, his view changed and in an 1876 autobiography he expressed his conviction that Paley's design argument fails:

> The old argument from design in Nature, as given by Paley, which formerly seemed to me so conclusive, fails, now that the law of natural selection has been discovered. We can no longer argue that, for instance, the beautiful hinge of a bivalve shell must have been made by an intelligent being, like the hinge of a door by man. There seems to be no more design in the variability of organic beings, and in the action of natural selection, than in the course which the wind blows. [From Charles Darwin, *Life and Letters of Charles Darwin* (1887), 1.8]

Darwin's most detailed critique of the design argument appears at the close of his *Variation of Animals and Plants under Domestication.* He begins stating the principal position of evolution: All animal life descended from a single primitive life form as a result of a series of tiny variations. Natural selection, then, is the "paramount power" which produces new species.

FROM CHARLES DARWIN, *Variation of Animals and Plants Under Domestication* (1868), 2.28

In accordance with the views maintained by me in this work and elsewhere, not only the various domestic races, but the most distinct genera and orders within the same great class—for instance, mammals, birds, reptiles, and fishes—are all the descendants of one common progenitor, and we must admit that the whole vast amount of difference between these forms has primarily arisen from simple variability. To consider the subject under this point of view is enough to strike one dumb with amazement. But our amazement ought to be lessened when we reflect that beings almost infinite in number, during an almost infinite lapse of time, have often had their whole organization rendered in some degree plastic, and that each slight modification of structure which was in any way beneficial under excessively complex conditions of life has been preserved, whilst each which was in any way injurious has been rigorously destroyed. And the long-continued accumulation of beneficial variations will infallibly have led to structures as diversified, as beautifully adapted for various purposes and as excellently coordinated, as we see in the animals and plants around us. Hence I have spoken of selection as the paramount power, whether applied by man to the formation of domestic breeds, or by nature to the production of species.

ASK YOURSELF

102. What lessens Darwin's amazement regarding the contention that all animals descended from a single progenitor?

Suppose that we grant Darwin's point that all animals evolved over time from a single creature. Couldn't we see this as an illustration of God's elaborate design in the natural world? The intricacy of the evolutionary mechanism would, as Paley expressed it, only increase our admiration for the mastermind behind it. Darwin disagrees and holds that evolution is merely the work of blind natural forces, with no intended design. Suppose that the religious believer concedes Darwin's point that natural selection operates through chance mutations, which together with environmental factors favor the survival of some organisms over others. However, the believer might still argue that divine design is reflected in the original simple variations—or mutations—that occur. For example, imagine that there was a species of light-colored moths living in an environment. Suppose, further, that through simple mutation, one happened to be born with darker coloring. The original light-colored moths would be more easily spotted by hungry birds looking for food, while the mutated darker moth and its descendents would escape detection and win in the battle for survival. According to the believer, we find God's design in the simple mutation that resulted in the original dark moth. Even at this level, though, Darwin feels that simple mutations are purely random and reflect no higher design. He makes his case with a metaphor of a man who erects a stone building from scattered and uncut pieces of rock lying around.

I may recur to the metaphor given in a former chapter: if an architect were to rear a noble and commodious edifice, without the use of cut stone, by selecting from the fragments at the base of a precipice wedge-formed stones for his arches, elongated stones for his lintels, and flat stones for his roof, we should admire his skill and regard him as the paramount power. Now, the fragments of stone, though indispensable to the architect, bear to the edifice built by him the same relation which the fluctuating variations of organic beings bear to the varied and admirable structures ultimately acquired by their modified descendants.

Some authors have declared that natural selection explains nothing, unless the precise cause of each slight individual difference be made clear. If it were explained to a savage utterly ignorant of the art of building, how the edifice had been raised stone upon stone, and why wedge-formed fragments were used for the arches, flat stones for the roof, etc.; and if the use of each part and of the whole building were pointed out, it would be unreasonable if he declared that nothing had been made clear to him, because the precise cause of the shape of each fragment could not be told. But this is a nearly parallel case with the objection that selection explains nothing, because we know not the cause of each individual difference in the structure of each being.

ASK YOURSELF

103. According to Darwin's metaphor, how are some of the random pieces of stone used in the construction of the stone building?

The point of Darwin's metaphor is this. We accept that there is no inherent design to the randomly shaped rocks, in spite of the spectacular building that can be made from them. Similarly, we should accept that there is no inherent design to simple random variations in biology, in spite of the spectacular things that the process of natural selection can make of them.

The shape of the fragments of stone at the base of our precipice may be called accidental, but this is not strictly correct; for the shape of each depends on a long sequence of events, all obeying natural laws; on the nature of the rock, on the lines of deposition or cleavage, on the form of the mountain, which depends on its upheaval and subsequent denudation, and lastly on the storm or earthquake which throws down the fragments. But in regard to the use to which the fragments may be put, their shape may be strictly said to be accidental. And here we are led to face a great difficulty, in alluding to which I am aware that I am traveling beyond my proper province. An omniscient Creator must have foreseen every consequence which results from the laws imposed by Him. But can it be reasonably maintained that the Creator intentionally ordered, if we use the words in any ordinary sense, that certain fragments of rock should assume certain shapes so that the builder might erect his edifice?

ASK YOURSELF

104. According to Darwin, an all-knowing God might have *foreseen* the evolutionary outcomes of random variations in biology, but this does not mean that God intentionally _____ those evolutionary outcomes.

If the various laws which have determined the shape of each fragment were not predetermined for the builder's sake, can it be maintained with any greater probability that He specially ordained for the sake of the breeder each of the innumerable variations in our domestic animals and plants—many of these variations being of no service to man, and not beneficial, far more often injurious, to the creatures themselves? Did He ordain that the crop and tail-feathers of the pigeon should vary in order that the fancier might make his grotesque pouter and fantail breeds? Did He cause the frame and mental qualities of the dog to vary in order that a breed might be formed of indomitable ferocity, with jaws fitted to pin down the bull for man's brutal sport? But if we give up the principle in one case—if we do not admit that the variations of the primeval dog were intentionally guided in order that the greyhound, for instance, that perfect image of symmetry and vigor, might be formed—no shadow of reason can be assigned for the belief that variations, alike in nature and the result of the same general laws, which have been the groundwork through natural selection of the formation of the most perfectly adapted animals in the world, man included, were intentionally and specially guided. However much we may wish it, we can hardly follow Professor Asa Gray in his belief "that variation has been led along certain beneficial lines," like a stream "along definite and useful lines of irrigation." If we assume that each particular variation was from the beginning of all time preordained, then that plasticity of organization, which leads to many injurious deviations of structure, as well as the redundant power of reproduction which inevitably leads to a struggle for existence, and, as a consequence, to the natural selection or survival of the fittest, must appear to us superfluous laws of nature. On the other hand, an omnipotent and omniscient Creator ordains everything and foresees everything. Thus we are brought face to face with a difficulty as insoluble as is that of free will and predestination.

ASK YOURSELF

105. What is Asa Gray's position regarding evolution and divine design?

106. According to Darwin, if God did predetermine all the simple biological variations throughout evolutionary history, then the various natural mechanisms of evolution would be superfluous. What are those mechanisms and why would they be superfluous on Darwin's reasoning?

4. THE FINE-TUNING ARGUMENT: ROBIN COLLINS

Even during Darwin's lifetime, the scientific community quickly adopted the theory of evolution, and in the last revised edition of the *Origin of the Species* Darwin notes the remarkable shift in attitude among his colleagues: "I formerly spoke to very many naturalists on the subject of evolution, and never once met with any sympathetic agreement. . . . Now, things are wholly changed, and almost every naturalist admits the great principle of evolution." Today evolution through natural selection is one of the foundational assumptions of biological science, and the majority of scientists adopt Darwin's view regarding natural design. As in Darwin's time, though, there are critics today who feel that science hasn't been able to adequately account for many features of the natural world. Divine creation, they believe, is a more likely explanation for how things are. This is the approach taken by the "fine-tuning argument." According to this view, science shows that the physical conditions of the world had to be precisely as they are; otherwise the universe could not sustain life. Suppose

ROBIN COLLINS
Contemporary American philosopher and defender of the fine-tuning argument.

that gravity was either a little stronger or weaker. Suppose that the strong nuclear force that binds protons and neutrons together in an atom had been stronger or weaker. Suppose that the initial big bang as physicists describe it had differed in strength by only the tiniest fraction of a fraction. In all of these cases, life would have been impossible. Thus, when considering the delicate precision of these factors, it is more reasonable to conclude that a divine mind orchestrated these events than to conclude that they occurred simply by chance. This argument differs from design arguments that focus on specific features in the universe—such as the apparent design in the biological mechanisms of an eye or a hand. Darwin's theory of natural selection might reasonably explain how these adaptations occur naturalistically. Current discussions of the fine-tuning argument, however, focus on a fact that could not easily be explained by natural selection, namely, an initial set of conditions which allow for life.

ASK YOURSELF

107. Some design arguments focus on particular adaptive features of the universe, such as the construction of the human eye. What, though, does the fine-tuning argument focus on?

Contemporary philosopher Robin Collins formulates a version of the fine-tuning argument here:

(1) The existence of the fine-tuning is not improbable under theism.
(2) The existence of the fine-tuning is very improbable under the atheistic single-universe hypothesis.
Conclusion: From premises (1) and (2) and the prime principle of confirmation, it follows that the fine-tuning data provides strong evidence in favor of the design hypothesis over the atheistic single-universe hypothesis. [From Robin Collins, "The Fine Tuning Argument" (1999)]

The "prime principle of confirmation" that Collins refers to in the conclusion is this: Whenever we are considering two competing hypotheses, an observation counts as evidence in favor of the hypothesis under which the observation has the highest probability (or is the least improbable).

As an illustration, consider the hypothesis that (1) a certain accused person, Bill, is guilty of a murder, and also consider a competing hypothesis to the effect that (2) Bob is guilty. Suppose that Bill's fingerprints are on the murder weapon. The observation that his prints are on the weapon counts in favor of (1) rather than (2) because it is quite probable that if his prints are on the weapon, he committed the murder, whereas it is quite improbable that they would be on the weapon if he had not. This would not be a *proof* that Bill did it, but, all other things being equal, the existence of the prints would be strong evidence for his guilt. Similarly, Collins argues, the existence of fine tuning in the universe is probable, or at least not improbable, under the hypothesis that an intelligent being created the universe. But, he contends, it is improbable on the atheist hypothesis, according to which the remarkable set of conditions necessary for life would have come into existence just by accident.

ASK YOURSELF

108. According to Collins, fine-tuning in the universe is not _____ under theism, but is very _____ under atheism.

SUMMING UP THE ISSUE OF THE DESIGN ARGUMENT

Design arguments for the existence of God maintain that the occurrence of natural design in the world suggests the existence of a designer. Many design arguments are based on an analogy between the universe and human machines: Machines are the products of intelligent design and, so, since the universe resembles machines, it too must be the product of intelligent design. Hume criticized the design argument on three main grounds. First, he argued that the universe does not sufficiently resemble human machines, and thus the analogy falls apart. Second, Hume argued that even if parts of the universe exhibit some design, this does not entitle us to say that the whole universe was created by God. Third, even if parts of the universe exhibit design, we cannot justly conclude that the designer was a single, all-powerful, all-intelligent, and good being. Responding to Hume, William Paley argued that there really is a strong similarity between the universe and objects of human design. Furthermore, even if we never saw how an object like a watch was created, we would still recognize its design and conclude that it was produced by an intelligent being. This, he believes, strengthens our inference that the design in the universe is the result of an intelligent designer. Charles Darwin offered an important alternative explanation to the theory of intelligent design: The apparent design that we see in nature (particularly in living things) was the result of natural evolutionary forces. According to Darwin, there is no need to postulate a designer when environmental pressures and natural selection can explain the design-like features that we observe. In reaction to atheistic explanations of the world, Robin Collins offers a fine-tuning argument for God's existence. He contends that the physical conditions that make life possible on earth are extraordinarily delicate, and their occurrence is more probable under a theistic hypothesis than an atheistic one.

CAN OF WORMS

Design arguments touch on many issues in the philosophy of science: what constitutes a "scientific" theory, how do we test the adequacy of our theories, and are religious explanations of creation in any way "scientific"? The philosophy of science is itself strongly connected to investigations in epistemology, inductive logic, and metaphysics.

G. FAITH AND RATIONALITY

When philosophers attempt to prove God's existence, they express an underlying conviction that religious faith can be supported by human reason. In a book titled *Christianity Not Mysterious* (1696), British theologian John Toland (1679–1722) argued that reason is in fact the litmus test of true religion. According to Toland, not only might we prove God's existence, but human reason might also clarify issues concerning God's nature, the human soul, the afterlife, and salvation. This, though, is only one way of looking at the issue. At the other end of the spectrum, some theologians hold that religious belief is purely a matter of faith, and human reason is not only irrelevant to the process, but might even hinder one's faith. Early Christian theologian Tertullian (160–220) expressed this view with the question "What does Athens have to do with Jerusalem?"—implying that reason (Athens) has nothing to do with faith (Jerusalem). And, when faced with rational contradictions concerning the Christian doctrine of the incarnation, Tertullian said "it is certain *because* it is impossible." Toland's and Tertullian's views are both somewhat extreme, and most believers hold to a position somewhere between the two—acknowledging the importance of reason in some areas and the uniqueness of faith in others.

QUESTIONS TO DISCUSS

a. Are there any issues of religious belief that should be exclusively a matter of faith, without the interference of reason?

b. Suppose that faith comes in conflict with reason—as it seemed that it did in Galileo's day when the church insisted that the planets revolve around the sun. How should such conflicts be resolved?

c. If there's no evidence either for or against the existence of God, should we believe anyway just to be safe?

There is a spectrum of possible positions on the relation of faith to reason. One position called "fideism"—literally "faith-ism"—maintains that issues regarding belief in God are largely or entirely matters of faith rather than reason. A strong fideist tradition runs throughout Western theology and philosophy. One of the more famous philosophical proponents of this view was Blaise Pascal.

1. WAGERING ON BELIEF IN GOD: BLAISE PASCAL

**BLAISE PASCAL
(1623–1662)**

French philosopher, mathematician, and theologian and author of Thoughts *(1670).*

Blaise Pascal (1623–1662) was associated with the Roman Catholic Jansenist movement, and was famed for his contributions to science and mathematics as well as philosophy and religion. After his death, an unfinished book of his titled *Thoughts* was published in which he holds that the traditional arguments for God's existence fail: There is "too much to deny, yet too little to be sure." Religious belief, Pascal maintains, is a matter of faith and not reason. The most famous part of his work is the "Wager": Pascal argues that when reason is neutral on the issue of God's existence, the balance of positive and negative consequences of believing versus disbelieving in God should compel us to move toward a faith-based belief in God.

Reason Is Neutral Concerning God. Pascal begins his discussion of the Wager by discussing the limitations of reason in proving God's existence.

FROM BLAISE PASCAL, *Thoughts* (1670)

By faith we know God's existence. In the glorious state of heaven we will know his nature. Now, I have already shown that we may easily know the existence of a thing without knowing its nature. Let us speak now according to the light of nature. If there is a God he is infinitely incomprehensible, since, having neither parts nor limits, he has no proportion to us. We are then incapable of knowing either what he is, or whether he is. This being true, who will dare to undertake to resolve this question? It cannot be we who have no proportion to him.

Who, then, will blame those Christians who are not able to give a reason for their belief insofar as they profess a religion for which they can give no reason? In exposing it to the world, they declare that it is a folly *stultitiam* (1 Corinthians 1:18). And then you complain that they do not prove it! If they proved it, they would not keep their word. It is in lacking proofs that they do not lack sense. Yes, but though this may excuse those who offer it such, and take away the blame for producing it without reason, this does not excuse those who receive it.

ASK YOURSELF

109. What does the "light of nature" or reason alone tell us about God's nature and existence?

Let us examine this point then, and say "God is, or he is not." But to which side shall we incline? Reason cannot decide it at all. There is an infinite chaos that separates us. A game is being played at the extremity of this infinite distance in which heads or tails must come up.

Which will you take? By reason you can wager on neither. By reason you can hinder neither from winning.

Do not, then, charge those with falsehood who have made a choice. For you know nothing about it. "No. But I blame them for having made, not *this* choice, but *a* choice. For although he who takes heads, and the other, are in the same fault, they arc both in fault. The proper way is simply not to wager."

ASK YOURSELF

110. Given that our reason cannot prove God's existence, what is wrong with just flipping a coin to decide what we should believe?

Stakes of the Wager. Even though we can't just flip a coin, Pascal believes that ultimately a choice must be made. We face a situation in which even not choosing constitutes a choice. Not only is our choice forced, but there are tremendous differences in consequences depending on what side we choose.

Yes, but you must wager. This is not voluntary. You have set sail. Which will you take? Let's see. Since a choice must be made, let's see which intcrests you the least. You have two things to lose: the true and the good. And you have two things to stake: your reason and your will; that is, your knowledge and your complete happiness. And your nature has two things to shun: error and misery. Your reason is not more wounded, since a choice must necessarily be made in choosing one rather than the other. Here a point is eliminated. But what about your happiness? Let us weigh the gain and the loss in taking heads that God exists. Let us weigh these two cases. If you gain, you gain all. If you lose, you lose nothing. Wager without hesitation, then, that he is. "This is admirable. Yes, it is necessary to wager, but perhaps I wager too much." Let us see. Since there is equal risk of gaining or losing, if you had to gain but two lives for one, still you might wager. But if there were three lives to gain, it would be required to play (since you are under the necessity of playing). And, when you are forced to play, you would be imprudent not to risk your life in order to gain three in a play where there is equal hazard of loss and gain. But there is an eternity of life and happiness. And this being true, even if there were an infinity of chances (only one of which might be for you) you would still be right in wagering one in order to have two. And being obliged to play, if there was an infinity of life infinitely happy to gain, you would act foolishly to refuse to play one life against three in a game where among an infinity of chances there is one for you. But there is here an infinity of life infinitely happy to gain. And there is a chance of gain against a finite number of chances of loss, and what you play is finite.

ASK YOURSELF

111. How much do we stand to gain if we wager in favor of belief in God?

This [the balance of gain over loss] is quite settled. Wherever the infinite is, and where there is not an infinity of chances of loss against the chance of gain, there is nothing to weigh, and we must give all. And thus, when wc are forced to play, we must renounce reason in order to keep life, rather than to risk it for the infinite gain, which is as likely to occur as the loss of nothingness.

A full description of the stakes of the wager is illustrated in the following chart, where the vertical columns indicate what is to be gained or lost under the two possible bets:

	Wager he exists	Wager he doesn't
God exists	Gain: infinite happiness	Gain: nothing
	Loss: little or nothing	Loss: infinite happiness
God doesn't exist	Gain: nothing	Gain: little or nothing
	Loss: little or nothing	Loss: nothing

The point of the wager is neither to prove that God exists, nor to show that belief in God is rational. Instead, the wager aims to show that belief in God is a *rational act*. An act is rational if it achieves a reasonable end; by contrast, beliefs are rational when they meet certain standards, such as consistency and due consideration of the relevant evidence. Pascal considers a potential criticism of his reasoning. My happiness in this life is certain, but my alleged future happiness is actually infinitely uncertain. So why gamble on that which is infinitely uncertain, regardless of how great the possible gain?

For there is no use in saying that it is uncertain whether we shall gain, and that it is certain that we risk. And there is no use in saying that the infinite distance between [a] the certainty of what we risk and [b] the uncertainty of what we shall gain raises the finite good which we certainly risk to a level of equality with the uncertain infinite gain. It is not so. Every player, without violating reason, risks a certainty to gain uncertainty, and nevertheless he risks a finite certainty to gain a finite uncertainty. The distance is not infinite between this certainty of what we risk and the uncertainty of gain. This is false. There is, in truth, an infinity between the certainty of gaining and the certainty of losing. But the uncertainty of gaining is proportioned to the certainty of what we risk, according to the proportion of the chances of gain and loss. It follows from this that if there are as many chances on one side as there are on the other, the game is playing even. And then the certainty of what we risk is equal to the uncertainty of the gain. This is quite far from being infinitely distant. And thus our proposition [of infinite gain] is of infinite force when there is the finite to hazard in a play where the chances of gain and loss are equal, and the infinite to gain. This is demonstrative, and if people are capable of any truths, this is one of them.

Pascal's response to the above criticism is to deny that our future gain is infinitely uncertain. The odds are the same as to whether we will gain happiness or we won't.

Faith. Pascal continues by considering those who say that they are not psychologically capable of making such a belief commitment.

"I confess it, I admit it. But, still, are there no means of seeing the truth behind the game?" Yes, the scriptures and the rest.

"Yes, but my hands are tied and my mouth is dumb. I am forced to wager, and I am not free. I am chained and so constituted that I cannot believe. What will you have me do then?" It is true. But at least learn your inability to believe, since reason brings you to such belief [given the above reasoning], and yet you cannot believe. Try then to convince yourself not by the addition of proofs for the existence of God, but by the reduction of your own passions. You would have recourse to faith, but don't know the ways. You wish to be cured of infidelity, and you ask for the remedy. Learn it from those who have been bound like yourself, and who would wager now all their goods. These know the road that you wish to follow, and are cured of a disease that you wish to be cured of. Follow their course, then, from its beginning. It consisted in doing all things *as if* they believed in them, in using holy water, in having masses said, etc. Naturally this will make you believe and stupefy you at the same time. "But this is what I fear." And why? What have you to lose?

> **ASK YOURSELF**
>
> **112.** Pascal's solution to those who claim an inability to believe is to reduce one's passions and rely on faith. What steps should we take to have such faith?

Pascal argues that a life of belief in God is not a loss in this life, but is in fact a gain.

> But to show you that this leads to it [i.e., belief], this will diminish the passions, which are your great obstacles. Now, what harm will come to you in taking this course? You would be faithful, virtuous, humble, grateful, beneficent, a sincere friend, truthful. Truly, you would not be given up to poisonous pleasures, to false glory, or false joys. But would you not have other pleasures?
>
> I say to you that you will gain by it in this life. And, each step you take in this direction, you will see so much of the certainty of gain, and so much of the nothingness of what you hazard, that you will acknowledge in the end that you have wagered something certain, infinite for which you have given nothing.

2. THE WILL TO BELIEVE: WILLIAM JAMES

In the section on religious mysticism earlier in this chapter, we looked at William James's contention that mystical experiences have authority for the mystic, but not for the non-mystic. In his essay "The Will to Believe" (1897) he explores the tension between faith and reason in religious belief. Scientifically minded people in James's day felt that, if we cannot rationally demonstrate God's existence, then we should abstain from religious belief. In response, James argues that we have the right to believe in God in the absence of evidence.

Hypotheses and Options. Central to James's argument is the notion of a "genuine option." He defines this as an option which is living (as opposed to dead), forced (as opposed to avoidable), and momentous (as opposed to trivial).

FROM WILLIAM JAMES, "The Will to Believe" (1897)

Let us give the name of *hypothesis* to anything that may be proposed to our belief; and just as the electricians speak of live and dead wires, let us speak of any hypothesis as either *live* or *dead*. A live hypothesis is one which appeals as a real possibility to him to whom it is proposed. If I asked you to believe in the Mahdi, the notion makes no electric connection with your nature,—it refuses to scintillate with any credibility at all. As an hypothesis it is completely dead. To an Arab, however (even if he be not one of the Mahdi's followers), the hypothesis is among the mind's possibilities: it is alive. This shows that deadness and liveness in an hypothesis are not intrinsic properties, but relations to the individual thinker. They are measured by his willingness to act. The maximum of liveness in an hypothesis , means willingness to act irrevocably. Practically, that means belief; but there is some believing tendency wherever there is willingness to act at all.

Next, let us call the decision between two hypotheses an *option*. Options may be of several kinds. They may be: 1. *living* or *dead;* 2. *forced* or *avoidable;* 3. *momentous* or *trivial;* and for our purposes we may call an option a genuine option when it is of the forced, living, and momentous kind.

1. A living option is one in which both hypotheses are live ones. If I say to you: "Be a theosophist or be a Mohammedan," it is probably a dead option, because for you neither hypothesis is likely to be alive. But if I say: "Be an agnostic or be a Christian," it is otherwise: trained as you are, each hypothesis makes some appeal, however small, to your belief.

2. Next, if I say to you: "Choose between going out with your umbrella or without it," I do not offer you a genuine option, for it is not forced. You can easily avoid it by not going out at all. Similarly, if I say, "Either love me or hate me," "Either call my theory true or call it false," your option is avoidable. You may remain indifferent to me, neither loving nor hating, and you may decline to offer any judgment as to my theory. But if I say, "Either accept this truth or go without it," I put on you a forced option, for there is no standing place outside of the alternative. Every dilemma based on a complete logical disjunction, with no possibility of not choosing, is an option of this forced kind.

3. Finally, if I were Dr. Nansen and proposed to you to join my North Pole expedition, your option would be momentous; for this would probably be your only similar opportunity, and your choice now would either exclude you from the North Pole sort of immortality altogether or put at least the chance of it into your hands. He who refuses to embrace a unique opportunity loses the prize as surely as if he tried and failed. *Per contra,* the option is trivial when the opportunity is not unique, when the stake is insignificant, or when the decision is reversible if it later prove unwise. Such trivial options abound in the scientific life. A chemist finds an hypothesis live enough to spend a year in its verification: he believes in it to that extent. But if his experiments prove inconclusive either way, he is quit for his loss of time, no vital harm being done.

It will facilitate our discussion if we keep all these distinctions well in mind.

ASK YOURSELF

113. What is one of the examples James gives of living, forced, and momentous options?

Before giving his own position on the issues of faith and religious belief, James first considers two alternative positions: those of Blaise Pascal and William Clifford.

Pascal's Wager. We've looked at Pascal's view that when reason is neutral on the issue of God's existence, the balance of positive and negative consequences of believing versus disbelieving in God should lead us to believe. James considers this position and criticizes it on two accounts. First, he notes potential conflicts that might arise with competing claims of other religions.

The next matter to consider is the actual psychology of human opinion. When we look at certain facts, it seems as if our passional and volitional nature lay at the root of all our convictions. When we look at others, it seems as if they could do nothing when the intellect had once said its say. Let us take the latter facts up first.

Does it not seem preposterous on the very face of it to talk of our opinions being modifiable at will? Can our will either help or hinder our 'intellect in its perceptions of truth? Can we, by just willing it, believe that Abraham Lincoln's existence is a myth, and that the portraits of him in *McClure's Magazine* are all of some one else? Can we, by any effort of our will, or by any strength of wish that it were true, believe ourselves well and about when we are roaring with rheumatism in bed, or feel certain that the sum of the two one-dollar bills in our pocket must be a hundred dollars? We can *say* any of these things, but we are absolutely impotent to believe them; and of just such things is the whole fabric of the truths that we do believe is made up—matters of fact, immediate or remote, as Hume said, and relations between ideas, which are either there or not there for us if we see them so, and which if not there cannot be put there by any action of our own.

In Pascal's *Thoughts* there is a celebrated passage known in literature as Pascal's wager. In it he tries to force us into Christianity by reasoning as if our concern with truth resembled our concern with the stakes in a game of chance. Translated freely his words are these: You must either believe or not believe that God is—which will you do? Your human reason cannot say. A game is going on between you and the nature of things which at the day of judgment will bring out either heads or tails. Weigh what your gains and your losses would be if you should stake all you have on heads, or God's existence: if you win in such case, you gain eternal beatitude; if you lose, you lose nothing at all. If there were an infinity of chances, and only one for God in this wager, still you ought to stake your all on God; for though you surely risk a finite loss by this procedure, any finite loss is reasonable, even a certain one is reasonable, if there is but the possibility of infinite gain. Go, then, and take holy water, and have masses said; belief will come and stupefy your scruples—*Cela vous fera croire et vous abltira.* Why should you not? At bottom, what have you to lose?

You probably feel that when religious faith expresses itself thus, in the language of the gaming table, it is put to its last trumps. Surely Pascal's own personal belief in masses and holy water had far other springs; and this celebrated page of his is but an argument for others, a last desperate snatch at a weapon against the hardness of the unbelieving heart. We feel that a faith in masses and holy water adopted willfully after such a mechanical calculation would lack the inner soul of faith's reality; and if we were ourselves in the place of the Deity, we should probably take particular pleasure in cutting off believers of this pattern from their infinite reward. It is evident that unless there be some pre-existing tendency to believe in masses and holy water, the option offered to the will by Pascal is not a living option. Certainly no Turk ever took to masses and holy water on its account; and even to us Protestants these means of salvation seem such foregone impossibilities that Pascal's logic, invoked for them specifically, leaves us unmoved. As well might the Mahdi write to us, saying, "I am the Expected One whom God has created in his effulgence. You shall be infinitely happy if you confess me; otherwise you shall be cut off from the light of the sun. Weigh, then, your infinite gain if I am genuine against your finite sacrifice if I am not!" His logic would be that of Pascal; but he would vainly use it on us, for the hypothesis he offers us is dead. No tendency to act on it exists in us to any degree.

ASK YOURSELF

114. In your own words state James's first criticism of Pascal's Wager.

James's second criticism of the Wager focuses on the sincerity of the potential believer's conviction.

The talk of believing by our volition seems, then, from one point of view, simply silly. From another point of view it is worse than silly, it is vile. When one turns to the magnificent edifice of the physical sciences, and sees how it was reared; what thousands of disinterested moral lives of men lie buried in its mere foundations; what patience and postponement, what choking down of preference, what submission to the icy laws of outer fact are wrought into its very stones and mortar; how absolutely impersonal it stands in its vast augustness—then how besotted and contemptible seems every little sentimentalist who comes blowing his voluntary smoke-wreaths, and pretending to decide things from out of his private dream! Can we wonder if those bred in the rugged and manly school of science should feel like spewing such subjectivism out of their mouths? The whole system of loyalties which grow up in the schools of science go dead against its toleration; so that it is only natural that those who have caught the scientific fever should pass over to the opposite extreme, and write sometimes as if the incorruptibly truthful intellect ought positively to prefer bitterness and unacceptableness to the heart in its cup.

> *It fortifies my soul to know*
> *That, though I perish, Truth is so—*

sings Clough, while Huxley exclaims: "My only consolation lies in the reflection that, however bad our posterity may become, so far as they hold by the plain rule of not pretending to believe what they have no reason to believe, because it may be to their advantage so to pretend [the word 'pretend' is surely here redundant], they will not have reached the lowest depth of immorality."

ASK YOURSELF

115. Why, according to James, is Pascal's wager "vile"?

Clifford's Veto, Psychological Causes of Belief. Having rejected Pascal's position, James next assesses the view of nineteenth-century philosopher of science and agnostic, William Clifford (1845–1879). For Clifford, only reason should determine what is true. And, when reason is neutral on any matter, we should not believe on the basis of passions, but instead abstain from belief. Thus, if reason is neutral with religious matters, such as God's existence, then we should abstain from religious belief.

That delicious *enfant terrible* Clifford writes: "Belief is desecrated when given to unproved and unquestioned statements for the solace and private pleasure of the believer. . . . Whoso would deserve well of his fellows in this matter will guard the purity of his belief with a very fanaticism of jealous care, lest at any time it should rest on an unworthy object, and catch a stain which can never be wiped away. . . . If [a] belief has been accepted on insufficient evidence [even though the belief be true, as Clifford on the same page explains] the pleasure is a stolen one. . . . It is sinful because it is stolen in defiance of our duty to mankind. That duty is to guard ourselves from such beliefs as from a pestilence which may shortly master our own body and then spread to the rest of the town. . . . It is wrong, always, everywhere, and for every one, to believe anything upon insufficient evidence."

All this strikes one as healthy, even when expressed, as by Clifford, with somewhat too much of robustious pathos in the voice. Free-will and simple wishing do seem, in the matter of our credences, to be only fifth wheels to the coach. Yet if any one should thereupon assume that intellectual insight is what remains after wish and will and sentimental preference have taken wing, or that pure reason is what then settles our opinions, he would fly quite as directly in the teeth of the facts.

It is only our already dead hypotheses that our willing nature is unable to bring to life again. But what has made them dead for us is for the most part a previous action of our willing nature of an antagonistic kind. When I say "willing nature," I do not mean only such deliberate volitions as may have set up habits of belief that we cannot now escape from, I mean all such factors of belief as fear and hope, prejudice and passion, imitation and partisanship, the circumpressure of our caste and set. As a matter of fact we find ourselves believing, we hardly know how or why. Mr. Balfour gives the name of "authority" to all those influences, born of the intellectual climate, that make hypotheses possible or impossible for us, alive or dead.

ASK YOURSELF

116. What factors are involved in one's willing nature?

Here in this room, we all of us believe in molecules and the conservation of energy, in democracy and necessary progress, in Protestant Christianity and the duty of fighting for "the doctrine of the immortal Monroe," all for no reasons worthy of the name. We see into these matters with no more inner clearness, and probably with much less, than any disbeliever in them might possess. His unconventionality would probably have some grounds to show for its conclusions; but for us, not insight, but the *prestige* of the opinions, is what makes the spark shoot from them and light up our sleeping magazines of faith. Our reason is quite satisfied, in nine hundred and ninety-nine cases out of every thousand of us, if it can find a few arguments that will do to recite in case our credulity is criticized by some one else. Our faith is faith in some one else's faith, and in the greatest matters this is most the case. Our belief in truth itself, for instance, that there is a truth, and that our minds and it are made for each other—what is it but a passionate affirmation of desire, in which our social system backs us up? We want to have a truth; we want to believe that our experiments and studies and discussions must put us in a continually better and better position towards it; and on this line we agree to fight out our thinking lives. But if a pyrrhonistic skeptic asks us *how we know* all this, can our logic find a reply? No! certainly it cannot. It is just one volition against another,—we willing to go in for life upon a trust or assumption which he, for his part, does not care to make.

As a rule we disbelieve all facts and theories for which we have no use. Clifford's cosmic emotions find no use for Christian feelings. Huxley belabors the bishops because there is no use for sacerdotalism in his scheme of life. Newman, on the contrary, goes over to Romanism, and finds all sorts of reasons good for staying there, because a priestly system is for him an organic need and delight. Why do so few "scientists" even look at the evidence for telepathy, so-called? Because they think, as a leading biologist, now dead, once said to me, that even if such a thing were true, scientists ought to band together to keep it suppressed and concealed. It would undo the uniformity of Nature and all sorts of other things without which scientists cannot carry on their pursuits. But if this very man had been shown something which as a scientist he might *do* with telepathy, he might not only have examined the evidence, but even have found it good enough. This very law which the logicians would impose upon us—if I may give the name of logicians to those who would rule out our willing nature here—is based on nothing but their own natural wish to exclude all elements form which they, in their professional quality of logicians, can find no use.

Evidently, then, our non-intellectual nature does influence our convictions. There are passional tendencies and volitions which run before and others which come after belief, and it is only the latter that are too late for the fair; and they are not too late when the previous passional work has been already in their own direction. Pascal's argument, instead of being powerless, then seems a regular clincher, and is the last stroke needed to make our faith in masses and holy water complete. The state of things is evidently far from simple; and pure insight and logic, whatever they might do ideally, are not the only things that really do produce our creeds.

ASK YOURSELF

117. What does James conclude about our nonintellectual nature?

Thesis of the Essay. Having dismissed both Pascal's and Clifford's positions, James next presents his assessment of the nonrational religions belief. According to James, when we are faced with a genuine option and reason is neutral, then our nonintellectual nature (that is, our passionate or willing nature) must decide between options.

Our next duty, having recognized this mixed-up state of affairs, is to ask whether it be simply reprehensible and pathological, or whether, on the contrary, we must treat it as a normal element in making up our minds. The thesis I defend is, briefly stated, this: *Our passional nature not only lawfully may, but must, decide an o option between propositions, whenever it is a genuine option that cannot by its nature be decided on intellectual grounds; for to say, under such circumstances, "Do not decide, but leave the question open," is itself a passional decision—just like deciding yes or no—and is attended with the same risk of losing the truth.* The thesis thus abstractly expressed will, I trust, soon become quite clear. But I must first indulge in a bit more of preliminary work.

James's position on willful belief differs from Pascal's in two ways. First, James recognizes that the option must be a live option; second, on James's view, the choice is made on the basis of the willing nature which is less restricting than Pascal's calculation of gains and losses. We may distinguish between a weak and a strong sense of James's position. In the weak sense, James maintains that we should be free to believe a genuine option when reason is neutral. In the strong sense, by contrast, James argues that we are *required* to believe a genuine option when reason is neutral. The reason for this strong version is that some knowledge—such as religious knowledge—can be attained only if we first believe something about which there may be no clear evidence. Augustine, for example, argued that to understand God's nature we must first believe that God exists—even though there is no purely rational evidence demonstrating that God exists. For James, then, we must at least tentatively believe that God exists just in case there are any truths about which we would otherwise be ignorant.

Religious Belief. Suppose that a scientist claimed that we should believe an important scientific theory even though there is no evidence for it. We'd probably respond with skepticism. Why should the situation be any different with religious belief? Addressing this point, James notes two basic features of the religious hypothesis.

In truths dependent on our personal action, then, faith based on desire is certainly a lawful and possibly an indispensable thing.

But now, it will be said, these are all childish human cases, and have nothing to do with great cosmical matters, like the question of religious faith. Let us then pass on to that. Religions differ so much in their accidents that in discussing the religious question we must make it very generic and broad. What then do we now mean by the religious hypothesis? Science says things are; morality says some things are better than other things; and religion says essentially two things.

First, she says that the best things are the more eternal things, the overlapping things, the things in the universe that throw the last stone, so to speak, and say the final word. "Perfection is eternal," this phrase of Charles Secretan seems a good way of putting this first affirmation of religion, an affirmation which obviously cannot yet be verified scientifically at all.

The second affirmation of religion is that we are better off even now if we believe her first affirmation to be true.

ASK YOURSELF

118. What are the two essential points of the basic religious hypothesis?

Recalling his opening discussion of a genuine option, James argues here that religious belief counts as a genuine option. It is obviously live and momentous. Furthermore, it is forced since by abstaining we lose a possible good as if we chose not to believe.

Now, let us consider what the logical elements of this situation are *in case the religious hypothesis in both its branches be really true.* (Of course, we must admit that possibility at the outset. If we are to discuss the question at all, it must involve a living option. If for any of you religion be a hypothesis that cannot by any living possibility be true, then you need go no farther. I speak to the "saving remnant" alone.) So proceeding, we see, first, that religion offers itself as a *momentous* option. We are supposed to gain, even now, by our belief, and to lose by our nonbelief, a certain vital good. Secondly, religion is a *forced* option, so far as that good goes. We cannot escape the issue by remaining skeptical and waiting for more light, because, although we do avoid error in that way *if religion be untrue,* we lose the good, *if it be true,* just as certainly as if we positively chose to disbelieve. It is as if a man should hesitate indefinitely to ask a certain woman to marry him because he was not perfectly sure that she would prove an angel after he brought her home. Would he not cut himself off from that particular angel-possibility as decisively as if he went and married some one else? Skepticism, then, is not avoidance of option; it is option of a certain particular kind of risk. *Better risk loss of truth than chance of error*—that is, your faith-vetoer's exact position. He is actively playing his stake as much as the believer is; he is backing the field against the religious hypothesis, just as the believer is backing the religious hypothesis against the field. To preach skepticism to us as a duty until "sufficient evidence" for religion be found, is tantamount therefore to telling us, when in presence of the religious hypothesis, that to yield to our fear of its being error is wiser and better than to yield to our hope that it may be true. It is not intellect against all passions, then; it is only intellect with one passion laying down its law. And by what, forsooth, is the supreme wisdom of this passion warranted? Dupery for dupery, what proof is there that dupery through hope is so much worse than dupery through fear? I, for one, can see no proof; and I simply refuse obedience to the scientist's command to imitate his kind of option, in a case where my own stake is important enough to give me the right to choose my own form of risk. If religion be true and the evidence for it be still insufficient, I do not wish, by putting your extinguisher upon my nature (which feels to me as if it had after all some business in this matter), to forfeit my sole chance in life of getting upon the winning side—that chance depending, of course, on my willingness to run the risk of acting as if my passional need of taking the world religiously might be prophetic and right.

119. Why is religion a forced option? That is, why can there be no religious agnostics?

James concludes by rejecting the agnostic's rules for truth seeking which would direct us to simply neither believe nor disbelieve in religious truths.

All this is on the supposition that it really may be prophetic and right, and that, even to us who are discussing the matter, religion is a live hypothesis which may be true. Now, to most of us religion comes in a still further way that makes a veto on our active faith even more illogical. The more perfect and more eternal aspect of the universe is represented in our religions as having personal form. The universe is no longer a mere *It* to us, but a *Thou,* if we are religious; and any relation that may be possible from person to person might be possible here. For instance, although in one sense we are passive portions of the universe, in another we show a curious autonomy, as if we were small active centers on our own account. We feel, too, as if the appeal of religion to us were made to our own active good-will, as if evidence might be forever withheld from us unless we met the hypothesis half-way. To take a trivial illustration: just as a man who in a company of gentlemen made no advances, asked a warrant for every concession, and believed no one's word without proof, would cut himself off by such churlishness from all the social rewards that a more trusting spirit would earn—so here, one who should shut himself up in snarling logicality and try to make the gods extort his recognition willy-nilly, or not get it at all, might cut himself off forever from his only opportunity of making the gods' acquaintance. This feeling, forced on us we know not whence, that by obstinately believing that there are gods (although not to do so would be so easy both for our logic and our life) we are doing the universe the deepest service we can, seems part of the living essence of the religious hypothesis. If the hypothesis *were* true in all its parts, including this one, then pure intellectualism, with its veto on our making willing advances, would be an absurdity; and some participation of our sympathetic nature would be logically required. I, therefore, for one, cannot see my way to accepting the agnostic rules for truth-seeking, or willfully agree to keep my willing nature out of the game. I cannot do so for this plain reason, that *a rule of thinking which would absolutely prevent me from acknowledging certain kinds of truth if those kinds of truth were really there, would be an irrational rule.* That for me is the long and short of the formal logic of the situation, no matter what the kinds of truth might materially be.

120. What is James's reason for not accepting the agnostic rules for truth seeking?

3. CAN WE KNOW GOD WITHOUT ARGUMENTS? ALVIN PLANTINGA AND JAY VAN HOOK

At this point in our discussion, the various controversies in the philosophy of religion have involved a battle between two camps. First, there are *evidentialists* who believe that questions of God's existence must be subjected to rational scrutiny. If the evidence suggests that God exists, then we should believe in God; and, if the evidence suggests that God does not exist, then we should not believe. Whether we believe in God or not, says the evidentialist, we must address the issue in the same way, namely, according to the strongest evidence. Thus, Aquinas, Paley, Hume, and Darwin are all evidentialists, in spite of their differing belief convictions. Second, there are "fideists" who believe that (1) God's existence cannot be rationally demonstrated and (2) belief in God rests solely on personal faith, and not on reason. Tertullian, Pascal, and James are religious fideists. There is, though, a third position, often called "reformed epistemology," which is a view inspired by Reformation theologian John Calvin (1509–1564). Reformed epistemologists typically accept the first point of fideism, that God's existence cannot be rationally demonstrated. However, they reject the second point of fideism and argue instead that belief in God is rational because God's existence is a foundational truth. Eighteenth-century Scottish philosopher James Oswald (1676–1772), an early advocate of this view, argued that human reason does two main things. First, reason intuitively grasps fundamental truths that cannot otherwise be demonstrated through rational argument, such as basic mathematical and moral principles. Second, through human reason, we take these foundational truths and deduce others—just as in geometry we begin with foundational notions of points or lines and deduce complex theorems from these. According to Oswald, God's existence is a fundamental and rational truth. We should not even attempt to deduce God's existence from other principles. Instead, we rationally grasp God's existence just as we do foundational mathematical principles.

A leading contemporary proponent of reformed epistemology is University of Notre Dame professor Alvin Plantinga (b. 1932). According to Plantinga, belief in God is *properly basic* in the sense that it is a foundational notion that we are justified in holding. He points out the relation between the evidentialist position and that of classical foundationalism:

> The evidentialist objection is rooted in *classical foundationalism,* an enormously popular picture or total way of looking at faith, knowledge, justified belief, rationality, and allied topics. This picture has been widely accepted ever since the days of Plato and Aristotle; its near relatives, perhaps, remain the dominant ways of thinking about these topics. We may think of the classical foundationalist as beginning with the observation that some of one's beliefs may be *based upon* others; it may be that there are a pair of propositions A and B such that I believe A *on the basis of* B. Although this relation isn't easy to characterize in a revealing and non-trivial fashion, it is nonetheless familiar. I believe that the word "umbrageous" is spelled u-m-b-r-a-g-e-o-u-s. This belief is based on another belief of mine: the belief that that's how the dictionary says it's spelled. I believe that $72 \times 71 = 5112$. This belief is based upon several other beliefs I hold: that $1 \times 72 = 72$; $7 \times 2 = 14$; $7 \times 7 = 49$; $49 + 1 = 50$; and others.

ASK YOURSELF

121. Give your own example of a belief that you hold that is based on another belief.

Plantinga continues by pointing out that some of our beliefs are foundational insofar as they are not based on any more fundamental beliefs.

> Some of my beliefs, however, I accept but don't accept on the basis of any other beliefs. Call these beliefs *basic.* I believe that $2 + 1 = 3$, for example, and don't believe it on the basis of other propositions. I also believe that I am seated at my desk, and that there is a mild pain in my right knee. These too are basic to me; I don't believe them on the basis of any other propositions. According to the classical foundationalist, some propositions are

properly or *rightly* basic for a person and some are not. Those that are not, are rationally accepted only on the basis of *evidence,* where the evidence must trace back, ultimately, to what is properly basic. The existence of God, furthermore, is not among the propositions that are properly basic; hence a person is rational in accepting theistic belief only if he has evidence for it. [From Alvin Plantinga, "Is Belief in God Properly Basic?" (1981)]

ASK YOURSELF

122. What is a "basic belief" and what is a "properly basic belief"?

123. According to classical foundationalism, when are we rationally justified in believing in God's existence?

Contrary to classical foundationalists who ground belief in God upon rational argument, Plantinga contends that the proposition "God exists" is a properly basic belief. That is, we are justified in believing that God exists on the basis of "a tendency or disposition to see his hand in the world about us." This, he argues, is analogous to other basic beliefs, such as the belief that the objects that we perceive really do exist, and the belief that the people I see really do have conscious minds. It's not merely a basic belief, but a *rationally justified* basic belief, which entitles us to say that we *know* that God exists.

There is certainly an appeal to the view that belief in God is properly basic: The believer can claim to be rational without having to demonstrate that God exists. Nevertheless, this view is not without its problems. Contemporary philosopher Jay Van Hook (b. 1939) argues that this position risks collapsing into relativism. How many so-called foundational beliefs do we actually have, which cannot be challenged by some critic? The list is exceedingly short. Take, for example, the possible foundations for my belief that George Washington was the first president of the United States:

I never saw Washington at all, and certainly not functioning presidentially. My teachers told me? But surely my teachers are not infallible. I read it in books? But I can't rely on everything I read. Government documents? Perhaps a part of a government myth-making. And so we could go.

If all so-called foundational beliefs are suspect, then what does knowledge amount to? Perhaps, Van Hook suggests, knowledge is "what our peers will let us get away with saying"—as contemporary philosopher Richard Rorty words it. Contrary to Plantinga and other reformed epistemologists, then, the statement "I know God exists" is relative to one's peer group and is not an indisputable foundational belief.

But now suppose that I claim to know that God exists and created the world. This is a controversial claim, and not all of my peers will let it pass. My fellow church members and Christian colleagues may well accept the claim; a typical gathering of American philosophers probably would not. So it appears that I can properly be said to know things about God in some groups of peers, but not in others. Thus, Rorty's view seems to have the unsatisfying result that one both knows and does not know the truth of certain controversial propositions. . . . Knowledge is peer-group relative. [From Jay Van Hook, "Knowledge, Belief, and Reformed Epistemology" (1981)]

ASK YOURSELF

124. Give an example of a religious belief that is apparently peer-group relative.

Van Hook suggests as an alternative: Dispense with the claim to "know" that God exists and be content to simply *believe* it. "Does a claim to know here *add* anything to the heartfelt belief and inner certainty?" The answer, for Van Hook, seems to be *no*.

SUMMING UP THE ISSUE OF FAITH AND RATIONALITY

Philosophers have sometimes differed about whether belief in God is solely a matter of faith, or whether it can be supported by reason. Blaise Pascal argued that reason is neutral on the question of God's existence, and that our belief should be based on faith. As a step toward having faith in God, though, Pascal felt that we should consider the consequences of believing versus disbelieving in God. There is more potential gain by believing, he argued, than by disbelieving. Although disagreeing with Pascal's wager, William James also defends faith-based religious belief. According to James, we have a right to believe in God when reason is neutral and such belief constitutes a genuine option for us. In fact, he continues, we may even be obligated to believe in God as a means of discovering religious truths that we would not otherwise obtain. Alvin Plantinga defends the Calvinistic view that belief in God is properly basic. That is, belief in God is a foundational notion, not deduced from other principles, and we are rationally justified in holding to this belief without needing to offer any proof for it. Contrary to Plantinga, Jay Van Hook argues that belief in God is not really a foundational belief for everyone, but is instead a conviction relative to one's peer group.

**CAN OF
WORMS**

Issues of religious faith raise interesting epistemological questions. Is faith a legitimate source of knowledge? When we think about the various ways that we know things, two methods immediately suggest themselves: (a) knowledge gained through our senses and (b) knowledge gained by analytical reasoning. Knowledge through faith, though, does not fit into either of these categories. Some philosophers have even linked faith with skepticism: Reason, according to skeptics, is inherently flawed and thus should be rejected as the final authority concerning true beliefs. And this suggests the need for faith as an instrument of guidance. Recent discussions in epistemology have called into question the popular notion, namely, that knowledge must consist of only a small set of basic propositions, such as reports of immediate experience, and elementary mathematical propositions, or propositions validly inferred from the basic ones. Perhaps there are many other basic propositions besides those, and believers might argue that "God exists" is one of them.

SUMMING UP THE CHAPTER

We began this chapter by looking at ways that Hume, Marx, and Nietzsche challenged religious belief. They attacked the rationality of belief in miracles, argued that religion acts like a drug to keep the oppressed masses subservient, and concluded that modern civilization has essentially killed the idea of God. One of the most longstanding attacks on religion, though, is based on "the problem of evil," which questions how an all-good, all-powerful, and all-knowing God could allow suffering in the world. John L. Mackie, in particular, argues that the indisputable fact of suffering logically contradicts the traditional conception of God. He also contends that standard theodicies, such as the free will defense, fail. John Hick offered a "soul-making" theodicy according to which the presence of evil is explained by the fact that humans are evolving toward a state of perfection, but have not yet reached it. In contrast to these attacks on religion, several arguments have been offered in proof of God's existence. Religious mysticism offers a direct empirical proof: We know that God exists because religious mystics have directly experienced God. Bertrand Russell is not convinced by this argument and maintains that mystical claims about the world are untrustworthy because they require abnormal physical states. William James argues that mystical states carry authority for mystics, but not for non-mystics. A more formal proof for God's existence is the ontological argument, presented by Anselm, according to which "the greatest conceivable being" must exist since it is contradictory to suggest otherwise. The cosmological argument maintains that there must be a first cause at the head of the causal connections that we see in the world around us. The most influential theistic proof is probably the design argument, which maintains that the presence of natural design in the world around us implies the existence of some designer. Charles Darwin's theory of evolution challenged the design argument by offering an alternative naturalistic explanation of how apparent design emerged in the world. Recent versions of the design argument maintain that the delicate conditions needed to sustain life on earth are more plausibly explained through the existence of God, rather than through random chance. The chapter concludes by considering whether belief in God should be grounded in faith rather than reason. Blaise Pascal argues for the reasonableness of "betting" that God exists by showing that the consequences of such a bet would make it the best bet available. William James argued that, when reason is neutral, we ought to believe in God through faith so that we might gain knowledge that we would otherwise miss out on. Alvin Plantinga argued that belief in God is properly basic in the sense that such belief is not deduced from other principles, yet is rationally justified.

FINAL REACTIONS

Turn to the "First Reaction" questions at the outset of this chapter and answer them as you feel about them now. Then compare your earlier answers with your current answers. Are there major differences? If so, note what they are and indicate which readings may have influenced you.

FURTHER READINGS

GENERAL WORKS

Clark, Kelly James, ed., *Readings in the Philosophy of Religion* (Peterborough, Ontario: Broadview Press, 2000).

Kessler, Gary E., ed., *Philosophy of Religion: Toward a Global Perspective* (Belmont, CA: Wadsworth Publishing Company, 1999).

Murray, M., and Stump, E., eds., *Philosophy of Religion: The Big Questions* (Oxford: Blackwell, 1999).

Peterson, Michael, ed., *Philosophy of Religion, Selected Readings* (New York: Oxford University Press, 1996).

Peterson, Michael, *Reason and Religious Belief* (New York: Oxford University Press, 1998).

Quinn, Philip L., and Taliaferro, Charles, eds., *A Companion to Philosophy of Religion* (Oxford: Blackwell, 1997).

WORKS ON SPECIFIC TOPICS AND FIGURES

Fieser, James, ed., *Early Responses to Hume's Writings on Religion* (Bristol: Thoemmes Press, 2001).

Hick, John, and Arthur C. McGill, eds., *The Many-Faced Argument* (New York: Macmillan. 1967). Essays on the ontological argument.

Mackie, John L., *The Miracle of Theism* (London: Oxford University Press, 1982).

Peterson, Michael, ed., *The Problem of Evil: Selected Readings* (Notre Dame: University of Notre Dame Press, 1992).

Phillips, D. Z., *Religion Without Explanation* (Oxford: Basil Blackwell, 1976).

Plantinga, Alvin, *God, Freedom and Evil* (New York: Harper and Row, 1974).

Richard Dawkins, *The Blind Watchmaker* (New York: Norton Publishing, 1996).

Rowe, William L. *The Cosmological Argument* (Princeton, NJ: Princeton University Press 1975).

Stace, Walter T., *Mysticism and Philosophy* (New York: Macmillan, 1960).

Yandell, Keith, *The Epistemology of Religious Experience* (Cambridge: Cambridge University Press, 1993).

CHAPTER 3

HUMAN NATURE AND THE SELF

hakespeare's Hamlet says "What a piece of work is man." Hamlet is amazed at (and made suspicious by) the complexity of human behavior and motivation and thought. Perhaps, however, there is nothing special about human beings. Perhaps we do not differ in any fundamental way from other beings, like trees, or dogs, or chimps. Perhaps we are just another part of nature, complex in some ways, but with no unique features that set us apart from the rest of nature in some remarkable way. On the other hand, if humans do have such unique features, it may turn out to be very important for us to know what they are and to understand them.

FIRST REACTIONS

Think about how you feel right now regarding the following questions, noting whether you agree, disagree, or are not sure about the views expressed. Make a note of your answers on a separate piece of paper, and hang on to it. We will return to these questions at the end of this chapter. Perhaps by then you will be inclined to answer some of them differently.

    a. Think about what we commonly mean by "self"? Is self-hood something given, by nature, or God, or must it be achieved? What do you make of the command to "be yourself"?

b. If we are simply part of nature, are we capable of free actions, or are all of our actions governed or determined by natural laws?

c. Even if we have some freedom, we still might ask *how much* we actually have. Are we restricted in our attempts to mold our own lives by (1) heredity, (2) environment, or (3) economic and other social conditions?

d. Is there some core to the self that does not change? If so, does that core provide me with my personal identity?

e. If there is such a core, is it principally physical, or is it rather soulish/mental, and could it survive death?

f. Think about what is involved in "being somebody," and what it takes to be a complete self, a fully mature human. Are there any problems with being an individual, as opposed to being just part of the crowd?

g. Do religious and ethical ideals, such as the ideal of being always in close connection to God, contribute to becoming a complete self or do such ideals rather get in the way of becoming a complete independent self?

h. Think about whether it is a mistake to stress "individuality" too much. (1) Should I think of myself as part of God or some greater spiritual whole? (2) Should I think of myself as simply a complicated animal? (3) Should I think of myself as essentially part of nature or the natural world?

A. DETERMINISM VERSUS FREE WILL

In a famous criminal case during the early 1920s, lawyer Clarence Darrow defended two young men, Leopold and Loeb, who were accused of murdering an adolescent boy. Darrow did not deny that they had committed the murder. Rather he argued that because of their particular upbringing, it was unreasonable to hold them responsible for their actions. Darrow in effect argued that anyone who had been brought up as Leopold and Loeb were would have committed murder or some similar terrible crime. He asserted, in determinist fashion, that "Nature is strong and she is pitiless . . . and we are her victims." Darrow's defense secured them life imprisonment rather than execution. More recently, two young men from Los Angeles, the Menendez brothers, were charged with murdering their parents. The brothers admitted to the killings but argued that because of the way they had been treated by their parents, they should not be held responsible for what they did. Anyone who reads the papers or watches the TV news will probably be able to think of similar cases. In these situations certain philosophical assumptions are made. Many people accept those assumptions. In the initial trial of the Menendez case, which resulted in a hung jury, some jurors apparently accepted certain controversial philosophical assumptions. The important question here is whether they *should* have accepted them. The discussions in this section are devoted to precisely that issue.

**QUESTIONS
TO DISCUSS**

a. Think about how much of your life consists of "knee-jerk reactions." Is it a lot or a little, or does this only pertain to a few physical reactions?

b. If you are free, in the sense of being able to make genuine choices, does that mean some of your actions are *uncaused?*

c. If you do not have free will, can you be held responsible for anything?

The first two questions in the above "Questions to Discuss" box are about free actions. Most of us know that if you heat a gas, it will expand. The gas has no choice. When your doctor taps your knee at a certain spot, the bottom part of your leg will jerk upwards. You cannot choose to have your leg do otherwise. That is why various actions that seem to be automatic—or not thought through and deliberately chosen—are sometimes called "knee-jerk reactions." For example, if I automatically dismiss as stupid anything done by a Republican president, that might count as a knee-jerk reaction. But we could extend the notion to include all sorts of things that I do because I have been "programmed" by my heredity and/or environment, including such trivial things as always "choosing" pizza rather than a hamburger, or more important things, like avoiding exercise.

We can begin a discussion of the issue of free will versus determinism by distinguishing three principal views that are central to the debate: "indeterminism," "determinism," and "compatabilism." The Renaissance philosopher Pico della Mirandola said that the most significant feature of human nature is our ability to freely choose how to live. While animals are locked into their respective roles, humans are at liberty to climb as high as the angels, or sink as low as beasts. Many philosophers before and after Pico have similarly felt that freedom is our most defining feature. Philosophers who advocate such views may be labeled "indeterminists" or "libertarians." The most extreme version of this view regards actions as completely uncaused. Modified versions may involve the idea that actions are caused after all, but they are caused by volitions, or acts of willing, or agents.

Although some conception of free will is central to common-sense thinking about human behavior, many philosophers have argued that there is no such thing. If human beings are purely physical things, simply biological machines, or can be fully replicated by machines, then we may have no free will. The laws of physics govern purely physical things, and those laws are deterministic. For example, it is not up to a planet to decide what orbit it will follow. This is *determined* by its mass, its distance from other bodies and other physical factors. Nor is it up to an engine to decide whether to spin or not. The activities of machines are determined by physical make up and mechanical or natural laws. The actions of machines are certainly not caused by acts of "willing" on the part of the machines. So, if humans are essentially machine-like, or are simply physical objects subject to physical laws, then we don't have free will any more than planets or engines do. This view is commonly labeled "determinism" or sometimes "hard determinism". The development of the sciences since the seventeenth century has contributed to the popularity of this view. It should not be confused with fatalism, for example—the view that my life is fated by the stars. Nor should it be confused with the idea that God causes everything. Such views are also deterministic, but they are not the kind of determinism discussed in this section.

At one level, determinism is very hard to swallow. If it is correct, then what becomes of the notion that humans are responsible for their actions? Given the truth of determinism, it seems that it would make no more sense to praise or blame human beings for their conduct than it would to blame or praise a planet for moving as it does. Such a view runs against some of our deepest intuitions. At the same time, *determinism* rests on an equally strong intuition, namely, the notion that everything that happens has a cause. Events don't just happen. Something causes them to happen. So some of our strongest intuitions clash. Some philosophers have tried to keep *all* of these intuitions. They argue that determinism could be true, and it could nonetheless be true that we have some freedom. Thinkers who take this position are called "compatibilists" or, sometimes, "soft determinists." The term "compatibilism" expresses the idea that free will and determinism are compatible with each other.

It is worth noting that, throughout the discussions below, the notion of physical laws as "deterministic" can be misleading. Not all of Newtonian mechanics is deterministic, and modern quantum physics is often said to be non-determinist. Moreover, there are ordinary uses of "cause" which require no knowledge of physics, but which seem to run afoul of the notion of free will, so a person could be a determinist without knowing much science. Nonetheless, the general picture sketched above for the planets or the engine is the sort of picture that for the most part has driven the free will/determinism controversy in the modern era. The assumptions under discussion are that laws of a more or less deterministic sort are crucial for scientific explanation and that science must be able to explain human actions.

1. THE CASE FOR DETERMINISM: BARON D'HOLBACH

Eighteenth-century French philosopher Paul-Henri Thiry, Baron d'Holbach (1723–1789), was one of the more skeptical philosophers of his time. An avowed atheist, he attempted to explain human nature without reference to God, spirits, an afterlife, or anything religious. In place of such notions, he argues in his *System of Nature* (1770) that the world arose by means of physical causes alone and that human beings are "constantly regulated by the same laws, which nature has prescribed to all the beings she brings forth." Thus, according to d'Holbach, human conduct is under the strict rule of physical laws, and our actions are completely determined. The very concept of a free human will, he argues, is contrary to the essence of our human nature. It is an unwarranted idea that arises from misguided religious conviction or bad philosophizing.

FROM PAUL-HENRI THIRY, BARON D'HOLBACH, *The System of Nature* (1770), CHAPTER 11

In whatever manner man is considered, he is connected to universal nature, and submitted to the necessary and immutable laws that she imposes on all the beings she contains, according to their peculiar essences or to the respective properties with which, without consulting them, she endows each particular species. Man's life is a line that nature commands him to describe upon the surface of the earth, without his ever being able to swerve from it, even for an instant. He is born without his own consent; his organization does in nowise depend upon himself; his ideas come to him involuntarily: his habits are in the power of those who cause him to contract them; he is unceasingly modified by causes, whether visible or concealed, over which he has no control, which necessarily regulate his mode of existence, give the hue to his way of thinking, and determine his manner of acting. He is good or bad, happy or miserable, wise or foolish, reasonable or irrational, without his will being for anything in these various states. Nevertheless, in spite of the shackles by which he is bound it is pretended he is a free agent, or that, independent of the causes by which he is moved, he determines his own will.

According to d'Holbach, a habit, such as the habit of sleeping late, is caused by factors over which a person has no control. Perhaps you just picked it up from a lazy parent. He compares being in such a habit to being in "shackles"—that is, bound by chains. If I am literally bound by chains, I am certainly not free. If I am locked in a room, that is not quite as bad as being chained to the wall, though I am still not free. If I am detained in a house, that is even better. If I can leave the house and go shopping at one mall, that is even better. If I can leave and go anywhere in the world that I feel like going, it would seem crazy to say I am in shackles. It would seem that I am as free as anyone could get. Of course the shackles d'Holbach has in mind are metaphorical. He thinks I am just as much in shackles when I am "free" to go anywhere as I would be when chained to a wall.

ASK YOURSELF

1. Some people think that by comparing the factors that determine my behavior to shackles, d'Holbach makes being determined sound scarier than it actually is. Do you agree? Explain.

The will, as we have elsewhere said, is a modification of the brain, by which it is disposed to action, or prepared to give play to the organs. This will is necessarily determined by the qualities, good or bad, agreeable or painful, of the object or the motive that acts upon his senses, or of which the idea remains with him, and is resuscitated by his memory. In consequence, he acts necessarily, his action is the result of the impulse he receives either from the motive, from the object, or from the idea which has modified his brain or disposed his will. When he does not act according to this impulse, it is because there comes some new cause, some new motive, some new idea, which modifies his brain in a different manner, gives him a new impulse, determines his will in another way, by which the action of the former impulse is suspended: thus, the sight of an agreeable object, or its idea, determines his will to set him in action to procure it; but if a new object or a new idea more powerfully attracts him, it gives a new direction to his will, annihilates the effect of the former, and prevents the action by which it was to be procured. This is the mode in which reflection, experience, reason, necessarily arrests or suspends the action of man's will: without this he would of necessity have followed the anterior impulse which carried him towards a then desirable object. In all this he always acts according to necessary laws from which he has no means of emancipating himself.

ASK YOURSELF

2. Although d'Holbach speaks of or uses the term "will," he means by it nothing more than a modification of the _____.

If when tormented with violent thirst, he figures to himself in idea, or really perceives a fountain, whose limpid streams might cool his feverish want, is he sufficient master of himself to desire or not to desire the object competent to satisfy so lively a want? It will no doubt be conceded that it is impossible he should not be desirous to satisfy it; but it will be said—if at this moment it is announced to him that the water he so ardently desires is poisoned, he will, notwithstanding his vehement thirst, abstain from drinking it; and it has, therefore, been falsely concluded that he is a free agent. The fact, however, is, that the motive in either case is exactly the same: his own conservation. The same necessity that determined him to drink before he knew the water was deleterious, upon this new discovery equally determined him not to drink; the desire of conserving himself either annihilates or suspends the former impulse; the second motive becomes stronger than the preceding, that is, the fear of death, or the desire of preserving himself necessarily prevails over the painful sensation caused by his eagerness to drink: but, it will be said, if the thirst is very parching, an inconsiderate man without regarding the danger will risk swallowing the water. Nothing is gained by this remark: in this case, the anterior impulse only regains the ascendancy; he is persuaded that life may possibly be longer preserved, or that he shall gain a greater good by drinking the poisoned water than by enduring the torment, which, to his mind, threatens instant dissolution: thus the first becomes the strongest and necessarily urges him on to action.

ASK YOURSELF

3. D'Holbach claims that cases we might describe as the exercise of will power—such as refusing to drink when very thirsty—are merely cases of one _____ winning out over another _____.

Is he the master of desiring or not desiring an object that appears desirable to him? Without doubt it will be answered, no: but he is the master of resisting his desire, if he reflects on the consequences. But, I ask, is he capable of reflecting on these consequences, when his soul is hurried along by a very lively passion, which entirely depends upon his natural organization, and the causes by which he is modified? Is it in his power to add to these consequences all the weight necessary to counterbalance his desire? Is he the master of preventing the qualities which render an object desirable from residing in it? I shall be told: he ought to have learned to resist his passions; to contract a habit of putting a curb on his desires. I agree to it without any difficulty. But in reply, I again ask, is his nature susceptible of this modification? Does his boiling blood, his unruly imagination, the igneous fluid that circulates in his veins, enable him to apply true experience in the moment when it is wanted? And even when his temperament has capacitated him, has his education, the examples set before him, the ideas with which he has been inspired in early life, been suitable to make him contract this habit of repressing his desires? . . . In short, the actions of man are never free; they are always the necessary consequence of his temperament, of the received ideas, and of the notions, either true or false, which he has formed to himself of happiness; of his opinions, strengthened by example, by education, and by daily experience.

ASK YOURSELF

4. Cite two physical factors and two psychological factors that, on d'Holbach's account, determine behavior.

D'Holbach gives a particularly impressive example of what we would call "will power" but then argues that such examples do nothing to prove freedom of the will.

When Mutius Scaevola held his hand in the fire, he was as much acting under the influence of necessity (caused by interior motives) that urged him to this strange action, as if his arm had been held by strong men: pride, despair, the desire of braving his enemy, a wish to astonish and anxiety to intimidate him, etc., were the invisible chains that held his hand bound to the fire.

Notice that once again d'Holbach compares being moved by certain motives to being in chains. He goes on to argue that free agency cannot be understood as mere absence of restraint. The fact that I am not literally bound with chains or forcibly confined may lead me to *say* that I am free. But all my actions are still determined by forces acting on me, over which I have no control, such as the forces of heredity and environment. D'Holbach's descriptions of humans as being "in chains" even in the most normal circumstances makes this point in a metaphorical fashion.

2. COMPATIBILISM: DAVID HUME

Scottish Philosopher David Hume (1711–1776) was no less an advocate of determinism than d'Holbach. They differed, though, about whether the notion of free will or "liberty" was in any way salvageable. Hume felt that the concept of free will could have some legitimate meaning if we defined it in a very limited way. Hume considers two contending positions, which we may call strong liberty and weak liberty, respectively. Strong liberty is the notion that we have power over the motivations of the will. That is, no matter how forceful my various motivations might be, I will not be locked into acting in any particular way, and am thus truly free. According to Hume, we must reject this strong notion of liberty since it goes directly against the kind of determinism required both by science and common sense. Weak liberty, on the other hand, is the notion that we have "a power of acting or not acting, according to the determinations of the will." That is, my will indeed activates my behavior, but it does so based on how my motivations direct me. If I am motivationally determined to drink a glass of water, then my will necessarily directs my behavior in this way. This weaker notion of liberty is completely consistent with determinism, and Hume calls his efforts at resolving

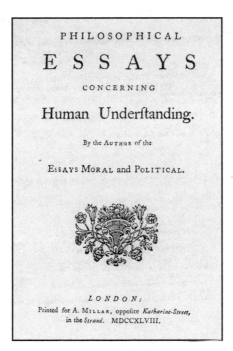

PHILOSOPHICAL

E S S A Y S

CONCERNING

Human Underſtanding.

By the AUTHOR of the

ESSAYS MORAL and POLITICAL.

LONDON:
Printed for A. MILLAR, oppoſite *Katharine-Street,*
in the *Strand.* MDCCXLVIII.

Title page of the first edition of David Hume's Philosophical Essays *(1748), later retitled* An Enquiry Concerning Human Understanding.

the free will controversy a "reconciling project." Today philosophers call this kind of reconciling project "compatibilism."

Endorsement of Weak Liberty. Hume states here the thrust of his reconciling project: We must reject the notion of strong liberty, and accept only that of weak liberty—which is compatible with "necessity" as he calls it here.

FROM DAVID HUME, *Enquiry Concerning Human Understanding* (1748), SECTION 8

But to proceed in this reconciling project with regard to the question of liberty and necessity; the most contentious question of metaphysics, the most contentious science; it will not require many words to prove, that all mankind have ever agreed in the doctrine of liberty as well as in that of necessity, and that the whole dispute, in this respect also, has been hitherto merely verbal. For what is meant by liberty, when applied to voluntary actions? We cannot surely mean that actions have so little connection with motives, inclinations, and circumstances, that one does not follow with a certain degree of uniformity from the other, and that one affords no inference by which we can conclude the existence of the other. For these are plain and acknowledged matters of fact. By liberty, then, we can only mean *a power of acting or not acting, according to the determinations of the will;* that is, if we choose to remain at rest, we may; if we choose to move, we also may. Now this hypothetical liberty is universally allowed to belong to every one who is not a prisoner and in chains. Here, then, is no subject of dispute.

5. How does Hume define "liberty"?

As defined here, Hume's weak notion of "liberty" in no way contradicts determinism, since it means only that the will initiates or refrains from initiating actions and that such a "power" belongs to anyone who is not a prisoner or in chains. There obviously is a distinction between the condition I am in when not in chains and the condition I am in when chained down, and it is natural to mark the distinction by saying that in the former case I am not free, whereas in the latter I am free. Nonetheless, when we are not chained down, our actions are still determined. The "will" as Hume uses the term does not refer to some capacity to act apart from causation. In that respect his usage is just like d'Holbach's.

Rejection of Strong Liberty. Hume recognizes that many readers may reject the notion of weak liberty and prefer instead the strong version. He argues, though, that we should reject the notion of strong liberty since it involves the notion that the will is uncaused, and the notion of any uncaused event or faculty is nonsense.

Whatever definition we may give of liberty, we should be careful to observe two requisite circumstances; *firstly*, that it be consistent with plain matter of fact; *secondly,* that it be consistent with itself. If we observe these circumstances, and render our definition intelligible, I am persuaded that all mankind will be found of one opinion with regard to it.

It is universally allowed that nothing exists without a cause of its existence, and that chance, when strictly examined, is a mere negative word, and means not any real power which has anywhere a being in nature. But it is pretended that some causes are necessary, some not necessary. Here then is the advantage of definitions. Let any one *define* a cause, without comprehending, as a part of the definition, a *necessary connection* with its effect; and let him show distinctly the origin of the idea, expressed by the definition; and I shall readily give up the whole controversy. But if the foregoing explication of the matter be received, this must be absolutely impracticable. Had not objects a regular conjunction with each other, we should never have entertained any notion of cause and effect; and this regular conjunction produces that inference of the understanding, which is the only connection, that we can have any comprehension of. Whoever attempts a definition of cause, exclusive of these circumstances, will be obliged to employ either unintelligible terms or such as are synonymous to the term which he endeavors to define. And if the definition above mentioned be admitted; liberty, when opposed to necessity, not to constraint, is the same thing with chance, which is universally allowed to have no existence.

6. Suppose that an advocate of strong liberty maintained that some events do not take place through absolute necessity. What is Hume's response?

3. IN DEFENSE OF FREE WILL: THOMAS REID

Scottish philosopher Thomas Reid (1710–1796) was a passionate critic of Hume and he rejected Hume's whole approach to the free will issue. Reid argued that human beings have a range of instinctive common-sense beliefs that God implanted in all of us. Once we reach the appropriate age—perhaps around age ten—we then become conscious of these common-sense convictions and base our beliefs and actions on them. For example, we have a common-sense belief that the world really is just as we perceive it through our senses.

**THOMAS REID
(1710–1796)**
Scottish common-sense philosopher, and author of Essays on the Active Powers of the Human Mind *(1788).*

In his *Essays on the Active Powers of the Human Mind* (1788), Reid argues that we have a common-sense intuition that our actions are truly free. Reid rejects determinism and endorses strong liberty: We have a genuine power over the motivations of our will. Reid nowhere claims that our actions are completely *uncaused,* however. Each of our actions, he believes, has a motivational cause, but the motivations we have are within our control. We could have had different motives than the ones we have at any given moment.

E S S A Y S

ON THE

A C T I V E   P O W E R S

O F   M A N.

By THOMAS REID, D.D. F.R.S. Edin.
PROFESSOR OF MORAL PHILOSOPHY
IN THE UNIVERSITY OF GLASGOW.

He hath shewed thee, O Man, what is good.   MICAH.

EDINBURGH:
PRINTED FOR JOHN BELL, Parliament-Square,
AND G. G. J. & J. ROBINSON, London.
M,DCC,LXXXVIII.

Title page of Thomas Reid's Essays on the Active Powers of the Human Mind *(1788).*

FROM THOMAS REID, *Essays on the Active Powers of the Human Mind* (1788), 4.6, FIRST ARGUMENT

The very conception or idea of active power must be derived from something in our own constitution. It is impossible to account for it otherwise . . . that it is natural to man, appears from the following observations.

Firstly, we are conscious of many voluntary exertions, some easy, others more difficult, some requiring a great effort. These are exertions of power. And though a man may be unconscious of his power when he does not exert it, he must have both the conception and the belief of it when he knowingly and willingly exerts it, with intention to produce some effect.

Secondly, deliberation about an action of moment, whether we shall do it or not, implies a conviction that it is in our power. To deliberate about an end, we must be convinced that the means are in our power; and to deliberate about the means, we must be convinced that we have power to choose the most proper.

Thirdly, suppose our deliberation brought to an issue, and that we resolved to do what appeared proper, can we form such a resolution or purpose, without any conviction of power to execute it? No; it is impossible. A man cannot resolve to pay out a sum of money, which he neither has, nor hopes ever to have.

Fourthly, again, when I plight my faith in any promise or contract, I must believe that I shall have power to perform what I promise. Without this persuasion, a promise would be downright fraud.

There is a condition implied in every promise, *if we live,* and *if God continue with us the power which he has given us.* Our conviction, therefore, of this power derogates not in the least from our dependence upon God. The rudest savage is taught by nature to admit this condition in all promises, whether it be expressed or not. For it is a dictate of common sense, that we can be under no obligation to do what it is impossible for us to do.

If we act upon the system of necessity, there must be another condition implied in all deliberation, in every resolution, and in every promise; and that is, *if we shall be willing.* But the will not being in our power, we cannot engage for it.

If this condition be understood, as it must be understood if we act upon the system of necessity, there can be no deliberation or resolution, nor any obligation in a promise. A man might as well deliberate, resolve and promise, upon the actions of other men as upon his own.

It is no less evident, that we have a conviction of power in other men, when we advise, or persuade, or command, or conceive them to be under obligation by their promises.

Fifthly, is it possible for any man to blame himself for yielding to necessity? Then he may blame himself for dying, or for being a man. Blame supposes a wrong use of power; and when a man does as well as it was possible for him to do, wherein is he to be blamed? Therefore all conviction of wrong conduct, all remorse, and self-condemnation, imply a conviction of our power to have done better. Take away this conviction, and there may be a sense of misery, or a dread of evil to come, but there can be no sense of guilt, or resolution to do better.

7. Summarize the five points just made in defense of free will.

8. Reid argues that if I do not have the power to control my own actions, then I might as well deliberate about the actions of _____ as I do about my own actions.

9. One of our most persistent practices is the practice of praising and blaming ourselves and others. Why does Reid think this fact counts against determinism?

Cases of Actions That Are Not Free, or Not Entirely Free. Reid is not claiming that *all* of our actions are free. His position enables him to make distinctions between kinds and degrees of motivation. We normally think that a person who is insane and motivated to act as he does by insane impulses is not truly free. A child who has not had time to learn to moderate his impulses is free only to some degree. A mature adult is fully free but may sometimes be held less responsible because of the intensity of a motive, such as anger. Such distinctions are not made by d'Holbach or Hume, who would consider the motivating factors in the case of an insane person, a child and a normal adult to be equally determining, and all of the resulting actions to be equally determined. Reid considered this failure to make such obvious distinctions a point against determinists, and he believed it was a point in his own favor that his theory maintained these ordinary distinctions.

This natural conviction of some degree of power in ourselves and in other men, respects voluntary actions only. For as all our power is directed by our will, we can form no conception of power, properly so called, that is not under the direction of will. And therefore our exertions, our deliberations, our purposes, our promises, are only in things that depend upon our will. Our advices, exhortations, and commands, are only in things that depend upon the will of those to whom they are addressed. We impute no guilt to ourselves, nor to others; in things where the will is not concerned.

But it deserves our notice, that we do not conceive everything, without exception to be in a man's power which depends upon his will. There are many exceptions to this general rule. The most obvious of these I shall mention, because they both serve to illustrate the rule, and are of importance in the question concerning the liberty of man.

In the rage of madness, men are absolutely deprived of the power of self-government. They act voluntarily, but their will is driven as by a tempest, which, in lucid intervals, they resolve to oppose with all their might, but are overcome when the fit of madness returns.

Idiots are like men walking in the dark, who cannot be said to have the power of choosing their way, because they cannot distinguish the good road from the bad. Having no light in their understanding, they must either sit still, or be carried on by some blind impulse.

Between the darkness of infancy, which is equal to that of idiots, and the maturity of reason, there is a long twilight which, by insensible degrees, advances to the perfect day.

In this period of life, man has but little of the power of self-government. His actions, by nature, as well as by the laws of society, are in the power of others more than in his own. His folly and indiscretion, his levity and inconstancy, are considered as the fault of youth, rather than of the man. We consider him as half a man and half a child, and expect that each by turns should play its part. He would be thought a severe and unequitable censor of manners, who required the same cool deliberation, the same steady conduct, and the same mastery over himself in a boy of thirteen, as in a man of thirty.

It is an old adage, that violent anger is a short fit of madness. If this be literally true in any case, a man in such a fit of passion, cannot be said to have the command of himself. If real madness could be proved, it must have the effect of madness while it lasts, whether it be for an hour or for life. But the madness of a short fit of passion, if it be really madness, is incapable of proof; and therefore is not admitted in human tribunals as an exculpation. And, I believe, there is no case where a man can satisfy his own mind that his passion, both in its beginning and in its progress, was irresistible. The Searcher of hearts alone knows infallibly what allowance is due in cases of this kind.

But a violent passion, though it may not be irresistible, is difficult to be resisted: and a man, surely, has not the same power over himself in passion, as when he is cool. On this account it is allowed by all men to alleviate, when it cannot exculpate; and has its weight in criminal courts, as well as in private judgment.

ASK YOURSELF

10. Reid claims that a "short fit of madness" is not admitted as an "exculpation" (that is, an excuse) but it does "alleviate" (make our judgment less severe). Is that true in criminal proceedings today? Mention, for example, some different kinds of terms used in courts for killing a human being and indicate which one makes our judgment least severe.

It ought likewise to be observed, that he who has accustomed himself to restrain his passions, enlarges by habit his power over them, and consequently over himself. When we consider that a Canadian savage can acquire the power of defying death, in its most dreadful forms, and of braving the most exquisite torment for many long hours, without losing the command of himself, I may learn from this, that, in the constitution of human natures there is ample scope for the enlargement of that power of self-command, without which there can be no virtue nor magnanimity.

There are cases, however, in which a man's voluntary actions are thought to be very little, if at all, in his power, on account of the violence of the motive that impels him. The magnanimity of a hero, or of a martyr, is not expected in every man, and on all occasions.

If a man trusted by the government with a secret, which it is high treason to disclose, be prevailed upon by a bribe, we have no mercy for him, and hardly allow the greatest bribe to be any alleviation of his crime.

But, on the other hand, if the secret be extorted by the rack, or by the dread of present death, we pity him more than we blame him, and would think it severe and unequitable to condemn him as a traitor.

What is the reason that all men agree in condemning this man as a traitor in the first case, and in the last, either exculpate him, or think his fault greatly alleviated. If he acted necessarily in both cases, compelled by an irresistible motive, I can see no reason why we should not pass the same judgment on both.

But the reason of these different judgments is evidently this, that the love of money, and of what is called a man's interest, is a cool motive, which leaves to a man the entire power over himself; but the torment of the rack, or the dread of present death, [is] so violent [a] motive, that men who have not uncommon strength of mind, are not masters of themselves in such a situation, and therefore what they do is not imputed, or is thought less criminal.

If a man resist such motives, we admire his fortitude, and think his conduct heroical rather than human. If he yields, we impute it to human frailty, and think him rather to be pitied than severely censured.

Inveterate habits are acknowledged to diminish very considerably the power a man has over himself. Although we may think him highly blamable in acquiring them, yet when they are confirmed to a certain degree, we consider him as no longer master or himself, and hardly reclaimable without a miracle.

Thus we see, that the power which we are led by common sense to ascribe to man, respects his voluntary actions only, and that it has various limitations even with regard to them. Some actions that depend upon our will are easy, others very difficult, and some, perhaps, beyond our power. In different men, the power of self-government is different, and in the same man at different times. It may be diminished, or perhaps lost, by bad habits; it may be greatly increased by good habits.

These are facts attested by experience, and supported by the common judgment of mankind. Upon the system of liberty, they are perfectly intelligible; but, I think, irreconcilable to that of necessity; for, how can there be an easy and a difficult in actions equally subject to necessity? or, how can power be greater or less, increased or diminished, in those who have no power?

This natural conviction of our acting freely, which is acknowledged by many who hold the doctrine of necessity, ought to throw the whole burden of proof upon that side: for, by this, the side of liberty has what lawyers call *jus quæsitum,* or a right of ancient possession, which ought to stand good till it be overturned. If it cannot be proved that we always act from necessity, there is no need of arguments on the other side, to convince us that we are free agents.

ASK YOURSELF

11. Reid thinks that the burden of proof is on the determinist. How might the determinist respond?

4. DETERMINISM, INDETERMINISM, AND AGENCY: RICHARD TAYLOR

In his book *Metaphysics* (1963), contemporary American philosopher Richard Taylor critically examines the views on the free will/determinism controversy which have been presented above. In the following excerpt he focuses on soft determinism (compatibilism) and indeterminism and presents a view of his own called "agency theory," which he distinguishes from indeterminism.

Against Soft Determinism. Taylor first critiques a theory similar to Hume's. He believes that there are fundamental shortcomings in all versions of that theory.

FROM RICHARD TAYLOR, *Metaphysics* (1963)

All versions of this theory [soft determinism or compatibilism] have in common three claims, by means of which, it is naively supposed, a reconciliation is achieved between determinism and freedom. Freedom being, furthermore, a condition of moral responsibility and the only condition that metaphysics seriously questions, it is supposed by the partisans of this view that determinism is perfectly compatible with such responsibility. This, no doubt, accounts for its great appeal and wide acceptance, even by some men of considerable learning.

The three claims of soft determinism are (1) that the thesis of determinism is true, and that accordingly all human behavior, voluntary or other, like the behavior of all other things, arises from antecedent conditions, given which no other behavior is possible—in short, that all human behavior is caused and determined; (2) that voluntary behavior is nonetheless free to the extent that it is not externally constrained or impeded; and (3) that, in the absence of such obstacles and constraints, the causes of voluntary behavior are certain states, events, or conditions within the agent himself; namely, his own acts of will or volitions, choices, decisions, desires, and so on.

Thus, on this view, I am free, and therefore sometimes responsible for what I do, provided nothing prevents me from acting according to my own choice, desire, or volition, or constrains me to act otherwise. There may, to be sure, be other conditions for my responsibility—such as, for example, an understanding of the probable consequences of my behavior, and that sort of thing—but absence of constraint or impediment is, at least, one such condition. And, it is claimed, it is a condition that is compatible with the supposition that my behavior is caused—for it is, by hypothesis, caused by my own inner choices, desires, and volitions.

ASK YOURSELF

12. What are the three claims of soft determinism?

The theory of soft determinism looks good at first—so good that it has for generations been solemnly taught from numberless philosophical chairs and implanted in the minds of students as sound philosophy—but no great acumen is needed to discover that far from solving any problem, it only camouflages it.

My free actions are those unimpeded and unconstrained motions that arise from my own inner desires, choices, and volitions; let us grant this provisionally. But now, whence arise those inner states that determine what my body shall do? Are they within my control or not? Having made my choice or decision and acted upon it, could I have chosen otherwise or not? Here the determinist, hoping to surrender nothing and yet to avoid the problem implied in that question, bids us not to ask it; the question itself, he announces, is without meaning. For to say that I could have done otherwise, he says, means only that I would have done otherwise if those inner states that determined my action had been different; if, that is, I had decided or chosen differently. To ask, accordingly, whether I could have chosen or decided differently is only to ask whether, had I decided to decide differently or chosen to choose differently, or willed to will differently, I would have decided or chosen or willed differently. And this, of course, is unintelligible nonsense.

But it is not nonsense to ask whether the causes of my actions—my own inner choices, decisions, and desires—are themselves caused. And of course they are, if determinism is true, for on that thesis everything is caused and determined. And if they are, then we cannot avoid concluding that, given the causal conditions of those inner states, I could not have decided, willed, chosen, or desired otherwise than I in fact did, for this is a logical consequence of the very definition of determinism. Of course we can still say that, if the causes of those inner states, whatever they were, had been different, then their effects, those inner states themselves, would have been different, and that in this hypothetical sense I could have decided, chosen, willed, or desired differently—but that only pushes our problem back still another step. For we will then want to know whether the causes of those inner states were within my control; and so on, ad infinitum. We are, at each step, permitted to say "could have been otherwise" only in a provisional sense—provided, that is, something else had been different—but must then retract it and replace it with "could not have been other-wise" as soon as we discover, as we must at each step, that whatever would have to have been different could not have been different.

ASK YOURSELF

13. According to Taylor, the question that the soft determinist fails to take seriously is the question "Could I _____?"

Examples Against Soft Determinism. Taylor continues offering examples that, he believes, show difficulties with soft determinism.

Such is the dialectic of the problem. The easiest way to see the shadowy quality of soft determinism, however, is by means of examples.

Let us suppose that my body is moving in various ways, that these motions are not externally constrained or impeded, and that they are all exactly in accordance with my own desires, choices, or acts of will and what not. When I will that my arm should move in a certain way, I find it moving in that way, unobstructed and unconstrained. When I will to speak, my lips and tongue move, unobstructed and unconstrained, in a manner suitable to the formation of the words I choose to utter. Now given that this is a correct description of my behavior, namely, that it consists of the unconstrained and unimpeded motions of my body in response to my own volitions, then it follows that my behavior is free, on the soft determinist's definition of "free." It follows further that I am responsible for that behavior; or at least, that if I am not, it is not from any lack of freedom on my part.

But if the fulfillment of these conditions renders my behavior free—that is to say, if my behavior satisfies the conditions of free action set forth in the theory of soft determinism—then my behavior will be no less free if we assume further conditions that are perfectly consistent with those already satisfied.

We suppose further, accordingly, that while my behavior is entirely in accordance with my own volitions, and thus "free" in terms of the conception of freedom we are examining, my volitions themselves are caused. To make this graphic, we can suppose that an ingenious physiologist can induce in me any volition he pleases, simply by pushing various buttons on an instrument to which, let us suppose, I am attached by numerous wires. All the volitions I have in that situation are, accordingly, precisely the ones he gives me. By pushing one button, he evokes in me the volition to raise my hand; and my hand, being unimpeded, rises in response to that volition. By pushing another, he induces the volition in me to kick, and my foot, being unimpeded, kicks in response to that volition. We can even suppose that the physiologist puts a rifle in my hands, aims it at some passer-by, and then, by pushing the proper button, evokes in me the volition to squeeze my finger against the trigger, whereupon the passer-by falls dead of a bullet wound.

This is the description of a man who is acting in accordance with his inner volitions, a man whose body is unimpeded and unconstrained in its motions, these motions being the effects of those inner states. It is hardly the description of a free and responsible agent. It is the perfect description of a puppet. To render a man your puppet, it is not necessary forcibly to constrain the motions of his limbs, after the fashion that real puppets are moved. A subtler but no less effective means of making a man your puppet would be to gain complete control of his inner states, and ensuring, as the theory of soft determinism does ensure, that his body will move in accordance with them.

**THINKING
LOGICALLY**

Taylor gives the following critique:

Suppose the soft determinist is right. Then,

1. Some of my actions come from me, from my own "volitions."
2. Actions which proceed from my own volitions are free, according to the definition of "free."
3. Therefore, some of my actions are free, by 1 and 2.
4. Some of my volitions could have been produced by an "ingenuous physiologist."
5. Since they are my volitions they would be free, according to the soft determinist.
6. Obviously volitions produced in that way would *not* be free.

So on the soft determinist position, some actions are both free and not free (5 and 6 both must be true).

ASK YOURSELF

14. What kind of criticism is this? (a) Confusion of necessary and sufficient conditions. (b) Reduction to absurdity. (c) Refutation by counterexample. (See the discussion of logic in Chapter 1.)

15. Discuss whether Taylor's critique actually works. Notice that the button pusher is "outside" of the agent. Remember, his critique will work only if premise 4 of his argument (as stated in the logic box) is true. In particular, it must be true, as 4 states, that the volitions produced by the ingenious physiologist are indeed "mine."

The example is somewhat unusual, but it is no worse for that. It is perfectly intelligible, and it does appear to refute the soft determinist's conception of freedom. One might think that, in such a case, the agent should not have allowed himself to be so rigged in the first place, but this is irrelevant; we can suppose that he was not aware that he was, and was hence unaware of the source of those inner states that prompted his bodily motions. The example can, moreover, be modified in perfectly realistic ways, so as to coincide with actual and familiar cases. One can, for instance, be given a compulsive desire for certain drugs, simply by having them administered to him over a course of time. Suppose, then, that I do, with neither my knowledge nor consent, thus become a victim of such a desire and act upon it. Do I act freely, merely by virtue of the fact that I am unimpeded in my quest for drugs? In a sense I do, surely, but I am hardly free with respect to whether or not I shall use drugs. I never chose to have the desire for them inflicted upon me.

Nor does it, of course, matter whether the inner states which allegedly prompt all my "free" activity are evoked in me by another agent or by perfectly impersonal forces. Whether a desire which causes my body to behave in a certain way is inflicted upon me by another person, for instance, or derived from hereditary factors, or indeed from anything at all, matters not in the least. In any case, if it is in fact the cause of my bodily behavior, I cannot but act in accordance with it. Wherever it came from, whether from personal or impersonal origins, it was entirely caused or determined, and not within my control. Indeed, if determinism is true, as the theory of soft determinism holds it to be, all those inner states which cause my body to behave in whatever ways it behaves must arise from circumstances that existed before I was born; for the chain of causes is infinite, and none could have been the least different, given those that preceded.

ASK YOURSELF

16. Imagine a chain of causes, starting with something that happened before you were born (perhaps your parents being introduced to each other) and ending with your now taking a philosophy course. Put down five or so of the main elements in the chain. Does it seem that taking the course is "determined"?

Simple Indeterminism.   Taylor next criticizes the theory of simple indeterminism—that our actions are uncaused. They could be either entirely uncaused, or, as in Reid, caused by our inner states, desires, fears and other motives. But in order to avoid soft determinism, we must assume that those inner states are themselves uncaused.

We might at first now seem warranted in simply denying determinism, and saying that, insofar as [my actions] are free they are not caused; or that if they are caused by my own inner states—my own desires, impulses, choices, volitions and whatnot—then these, in any case, are not caused. This is a perfectly clear sense in which a man's action, assuming that it was free, could have been otherwise. If it was uncaused, then even given the conditions under which it occurred and all that preceded, some other act was nonetheless possible, and he did not have to do what he did. Or if his action was the inevitable consequence of his own inner states, and could not have been otherwise given these, we can nevertheless say that these inner states, being uncaused, could have been otherwise, and could thereby have produced different actions.

Only the slightest consideration will show, however, that this simple denial of determinism has not the slightest plausibility. For let us suppose it is true, and that some of my bodily motions—namely, those I regard as my free acts—are not caused at all or, if caused by my own inner states, that these are not caused. We shall thereby avoid picturing a puppet, to be sure [the determinist picture]—but only by substituting something even less like a man; for the conception that now emerges is not that of a free man, but of an erratic and jerking phantom, without any rhyme or reason at all.

Suppose that my right arm is free according to this conception; that is, that its motions are uncaused. It moves this way and that way from time to time, but nothing causes these motions. Sometimes it moves forth vigorously, sometimes up, sometimes down, sometimes it just drifts vaguely about—these motions all being wholly free and uncaused. Manifestly I have nothing to do with them at all; they just happen, and neither I nor anyone can ever tell what this arm will be doing next. It might seize a club and lay it on the head of the nearest bystander, no less to my astonishment than his. There will never be any point in asking why these motions occur, or in seeking any explanation of them, for under the conditions assumed there is no explanation. They just happen, from no causes at all.

This is no description of free, voluntary, or responsible behavior. Indeed, so far as the motions of my body or its parts are entirely uncaused, such motions cannot even be ascribed to me as my behavior in the first place, since I have nothing to do with them. The behavior of my arm is just the random motion of a foreign object. Behavior that is mine must be behavior that is within my control, but motions that occur from no causes are without the control of anyone. I can have no more to do with, and no more control over, the uncaused motions of my limbs than a gambler has over the motions of an honest roulette wheel. I can only, like him, idly wait to see what happens.

ASK YOURSELF

17. Why, according to Taylor, can't the motions of my arm be ascribed to me— that is, shown to be *my* motions—on the simple indeterminist view?

Nor does it improve things to suppose that my bodily motions are caused by my own inner states, so long as we suppose these to be wholly uncaused. The result will be the same as before. My arm, for example, will move this way and that, sometimes up and sometimes down, sometimes vigorously and sometimes just drifting about, always in response to certain inner states, to be sure. But since these are supposed to be wholly uncaused, it follows that I have no control over them and hence none over their effects. If my hand lays a club forcefully on the nearest bystander, we can indeed say that this motion resulted from an inner club-wielding desire of mine; but we must add that I had nothing to do with that desire, and that it arose, to be followed by its inevitable effect, no less to my astonishment than to his.

Both determinism and simple indeterminism are loaded with difficulties, and no one who has thought much on them can affirm either of them without some embarrassment. Simple indeterminism has nothing whatever to be said for it, except that it appears to remove the grossest difficulties of determinism, only, however, to imply perfect absurdities of its own. Determinism, on the other hand, is at least initially plausible. Men seem to have a natural inclination to believe in it; it is, indeed, almost required for the very exercise of practical intelligence. And beyond this, our experience appears always to confirm it, so long as we are dealing with everyday facts of common experience, as distinguished from the esoteric researches of theoretical physics. But determinism, as applied to human behavior, has implications which few men can casually accept, and they appear to be implications which no modification of the theory can efface.

Both theories, moreover, appear logically irreconcilable to the two items of data that we set forth at the outset; namely, (1) that my behavior is sometimes the outcome of my deliberation, and (2) that in these and other cases it is sometimes up to me what I do.

ASK YOURSELF

18. What are some of the implications of determinism which "few men can casually accept"?

The Theory of Agency. Taylor attempts to set forth a way of thinking about human action which does not rest on either the views of determinism or indeterminism. According to

Taylor, human beings sometimes cause their own actions independently of prior causes. His theory closely parallels Reid's, using different terminology. Whereas Reid felt that a person's "will" could act independently of prior motivational causes, Taylor feels that the person as "agent" can act independently of such causes.

The only conception of action that accords with our data is one according to which men—and perhaps some other things—are sometimes, but of course not always, self-determining beings; that is, beings which are sometimes the causes of their own behavior. In the case of an action that is free, it must be such that it is caused by the agent who performs it, but such that no antecedent conditions were sufficient for his performing just that action. In the case of an action that is both free and rational, it must be such that the agent who performed it did so for some reason, but this reason cannot have been the cause of it.

Now this conception fits what men take themselves to be; namely, beings who act, or who are agents, rather than things that are merely acted upon, and whose behavior is simply the causal consequence of conditions which they have not wrought. When I believe that I have done something, I believe that it was I who caused it to be done, I who made something happen, and not merely something within me, such as one of my own subjective states, which is not identical with myself. If I believe that something not identical with myself was the cause of my behavior—some event wholly external to myself, for instance, or even one internal to myself, such as a nerve impulse, volition, or what-not—then I cannot regard that behavior as being an act of mine, unless I further believe that I was the cause of that external or internal event. My pulse, for example, is caused and regulated by certain conditions existing within me, and not by myself. I do not, accordingly, regard this activity of my body as my action, and would be no more tempted to do so if I became suddenly conscious within myself of those conditions or impulses that produce it. This is behavior with which I have nothing to do, behavior that is not within my immediate control, behavior that is not only not free activity, but not even the activity of an agent to begin with; it is nothing but a mechanical reflex. Had I never learned that my very life depends on this pulse beat, I would regard it with complete indifference, as something foreign to me, like the oscillations of a clock pendulum that I idly contemplate.

ASK YOURSELF

19. Say what you think "I" refers to in the preceding paragraph. What constitutes the "I" to which Taylor refers?

Now this conception of activity, and of an agent who is the cause of it, involves two rather strange metaphysical notions that are never applied elsewhere in nature. The first is that of a self or person—for example, a man—who is not merely a collection of things or events, but a substance and a self-moving being. For on this view it is a man himself, and not merely some part of him or something within him, that is the cause of his own activity. Now we certainly do not know that a man is anything more than an assemblage of physical things and processes, which act in accordance with those laws that describe the behavior of all other physical things and processes. Even though a man is a living being, of enormous complexity, there is nothing, apart from the requirements of this theory, to suggest that his behavior is so radically different in its origin from that of other physical objects, or that an understanding of it must be sought in some metaphysical realm wholly different from that appropriate to the understanding of non-living things.

Second, this conception of activity involves an extraordinary conception of causation, according to which an agent, which is a substance and not an event, can nevertheless be the cause of an event. Indeed, if he is a free agent he can, on this conception, cause an event to occur—namely, some act of his own-without anything else causing him to do so. This means that an agent is sometimes a cause, without being an antecedent sufficient condition; for if I affirm that I am the cause of some act of mine, then I am plainly not saying that my very existence is sufficient for its occurrence, which would be absurd. If I say that my hand causes my pencil to move, then I am saying that the motion of my hand is, under the other conditions then prevailing, sufficient for the motion of the pencil. But if I then say that I cause my hand to move, I am not saying anything remotely like this, and surely not that the motion of my self is sufficient for the motion of my arm and hand, since these are the only things about me that are moving.

ASK YOURSELF

20. According to Taylor's theory, what am I *not* saying when I say that I am the cause of the motion of my hand?

This conception of the causation of events by beings or substances that are not events is, in fact, so different from the usual philosophical conception of a cause that it should not even bear the same name, for "being a cause" ordinarily just means "being an antecedent sufficient condition or set of conditions." Instead, then, of speaking of agents as causing their own acts, it would perhaps be better to use another word entirely, and say, for instance, that they originate them, initiate them, or simply that they perform them.

Now this is on the face of it a dubious conception of what a man is. Yet it is consistent with our data, reflecting the presuppositions of deliberation, and appears to be the only conception that is consistent with them, as determinism and simple indeterminism are not. The theory of agency avoids the absurdities of simple indeterminism by conceding that human behavior is caused, while at the same time avoiding the difficulties of determinism by denying that every chain of causes and effects is infinite. Some such causal chains, on this view, have beginnings, and they begin with agents themselves. Moreover, if we are to suppose that it is sometimes up to me what I do, and understand this in a sense which is not consistent with determinism, we must suppose that I am an agent or a being who initiates his own actions, sometimes under conditions which do not determine what action he shall perform. Deliberation becomes, on this view, something that is not only possible but quite rational, for it does make sense to deliberate about activity that is truly my own and that depends for its outcome upon me as its author, and not merely upon something more or less esoteric that is supposed to be intimately associated with me, such as my thoughts, choices, volitions and what not.

One can hardly affirm such a theory of agency with complete comfort, however, and wholly without embarrassment, for the conception of men and their powers which is involved in it is strange indeed, if not positively mysterious. In fact, one can hardly be blamed here for simply denying our data outright, rather than embracing this theory to which they do most certainly point. Our data—to the effect that men do sometimes deliberate before acting, and that when they do, they presuppose among other things that it is up to them what they are going to do—rest upon nothing more than fairly common consent. These data might simply be illusions. It might in fact be that no man ever deliberates, but only imagines that he does, that from pure conceit he supposes himself to be the master of his behavior and the author of his acts. Spinoza has suggested that if a stone, having been thrown into the air, were suddenly to become conscious, it would suppose itself to be the source of its own motion, being then conscious of what it was doing but not aware of the real cause of its behavior. Certainly men are sometimes mistaken in believing that they are behaving as a result of choice deliberately arrived at. A man might, for example, easily imagine that his embarking upon matrimony is the result of the most careful and rational deliberation, when in fact the causes, perfectly sufficient for that behavior, might be of an entirely physiological, unconscious origin.

ASK YOURSELF

21. Think of an unconscious cause that might make a person, Bill, marry another person, Jane, when there were other people available for Bill to marry (Sally or Sue).

Taylor makes it clear that in discussing freedom versus determinism we can slide in one of two directions. If we stress freedom, we are in danger of thinking of actions as arbitrary, unpredictable motions that occur without any cause and thus in some sense without any reason. It appears that they do not come from *me* in any intelligible sense, and thus they do not fit our intuitive notions of what freedom is.

On the other hand, if we stress the idea that everything must have a cause, then we seem to be in danger of breaking down the very idea of responsibility. Taylor's own theory tries to avoid both dangers. Actions are caused and are therefore not arbitrary. But at least some of them are caused by agents, not by prior sufficient causal conditions, and therefore at least some of them are due to the agent, who is thus responsible for them. We might say that the agent *originates* the action. Taylor's view is similar to a view advanced by Roderic Chisholm. In the following selection the Taylor-Chisholm view is critiqued by Harry Frankfurt.

5. DETERMINISM AND SECOND-ORDER DESIRES: HARRY FRANKFURT

American philosopher Harry Frankfurt accepts the idea—so important to Chisholm and Taylor (and to most non-philosophers)—that it must be possible, and must make sense, to hold people responsible for their actions. But Frankfurt does not think that we succeed in doing that in the way Chisholm supposes. For one thing, the Taylor/Chisholm accounts do not distinguish the kind of freedom nonhuman and nonresponsible animals have from the kind humans have. In fact many philosophers may have overlooked the importance of what Frankfurt calls "second-order desires." A human being and a dog can both desire to gorge themselves on a beefsteak, and when they are not prevented from doing so, and do it, they may be equally free. However, the human can also desire to desire or desire not to desire. The human could desire the beefsteak but not desire to desire it, and if that second desire is effective, he will not eat it. Perhaps he is on a diet and is refusing to follow his own desires for beefsteaks. He desires not to. Dogs don't go on diets. They do not regulate their first-order desires through second-order desires.

Frankfurt identifies the *will* as an effective desire that drives an agent all the way to action. When I have a second-order desire for a first-order desire to become my will, then that second-order desire is called a "second-order volition." According to Frankfurt, second-order volitions are the distinguishing feature of persons. Nonhuman animals lack second-order desires, and therefore second-order volitions, so they cannot count as persons. But some humans, even though they have second-order desires, may lack second-order volitions, and they too fail to be persons, as Frankfurt uses the term. The following examples illustrate what is at stake in these distinctions.

ASK YOURSELF

22. I could have a desire for drugs even while strongly wanting not to have such a desire. That "wanting not" is an example of what Frankfurt calls a _____ .

Frankfurt contrasts what he calls a "wanton" with persons. A wanton does not care what his first-order desires are, or which of them become his will—that is, which of them actually produces an action. That is, he has no second-order desires regarding his first-order ones.

From Harry Frankfurt, "Freedom of the Will and the Concept of a Person" (1971)

The distinction between a person and a wanton may be illustrated by the difference between two narcotics addicts. Let us suppose that the physiological condition accounting for the addiction is the same in both men, and that both succumb inevitably to their periodic desires for the drug to which they are addicted. One of the addicts hates his addiction and always struggles desperately, although to no avail, against its thrust. He tries everything that he thinks might enable him to overcome his desires for the drug. But these desires are too powerful for him to withstand, and invariably, in the end, they conquer him. He is an unwilling addict, helplessly violated by his own desires.

The unwilling addict has conflicting first-order desires: he wants to take the drug, and he also wants to refrain from taking it. In addition to these first-order desires, however, he has a volition of the second order. He is not a neutral with regard to the conflict between his desire to take the drug and his desire to refrain from taking it. It is the latter desire, and not the former, that he wants to constitute his will; it is the latter desire, rather than the former, that he wants to be effective and to provide the purpose that he will seek to realize in what he actually does.

The other addict is a wanton. His actions reflect the economy of his first-order desires, without his being concerned whether the desires that move him to act are desires by which he wants to be moved to act. If he encounters problems in obtaining the drug or in administering it to himself, his responses to his urges to take it may involve deliberation. But it never occurs to him to consider whether he wants the relations among his desires to result in his having the will he has. The wanton addict may be an animal, and thus incapable of being concerned about his will. In any event he is, in respect of his wanton lack of concern, no different from an animal.

The second of these addicts may suffer a first-order conflict similar to the first-order conflict suffered by the first. Whether he is human or not, the wanton may (perhaps due to conditioning) both want to take the drug and want to refrain from taking it. Unlike the unwilling addict, however, he does not prefer that one of his conflicting desires should be paramount over the other; he does not prefer that one first-order desire rather than the other should constitute his will. It would be misleading to say that he is neutral as to the conflict between his desires, since this would suggest that he regards them as equally acceptable. Since he has no identity apart from his first-order desires, it is true neither that he prefers one to the other nor that he prefers not to take sides.

It makes a difference to the unwilling addict, who is a person, which of his conflicting first-order desires wins out. Both desires are his, to be sure; and whether he finally takes the drug or finally succeeds in refraining from taking it, he acts to satisfy what is in a literal sense his own desire. In either case he does something he himself wants to do, and he does it not because of some external influence whose aim happens to coincide with his own but because of his desire to do it. The unwilling addict identifies himself, however, through the formation of a second-order volition, with one rather than with the other of his conflicting first-order desires. He makes one of them more truly his own and, in so doing, he withdraws himself from the other. It is in virtue of this identification and withdrawal, accomplished through the formation of a second-order volition, that the unwilling addict may meaningfully make the analytically puzzling statements that the force moving him to take the drug is a force other than his own, and that it is not of his own free will but rather against his will that this force moves him to take it.

The wanton addict cannot or does not care which of his conflicting first-order desires wins out. His lack of concern is not due to his inability to find a convincing basis for preference. It is due either to his lack of the capacity for reflection or to his mindless indifference to the enterprise of evaluating his own desires and motives. There is only one issue in the struggle to which his first-order conflict may lead: whether the one or the other of his conflicting desires is the stronger. Since he is moved by both desires, he will not be altogether satisfied by what he does no matter which of them is effective. But it makes no difference to *him* whether his craving or his aversion gets the upper hand. He has no stake in the conflict between them and so, unlike the unwilling addict, he can neither win nor lose the struggle in which he is engaged. When a *person* acts, the desire by which he is moved is either the will he wants or a will he wants to be without. When a *wanton* acts, it is neither.

ASK YOURSELF

23. When a wanton has conflicting desires, it does not matter to _____ which of those desires is acted upon.

There is a very close relationship between the capacity for forming second-order volitions and another capacity that is essential to persons, one that has often been considered a distinguishing mark of the human condition. It is only because a person has volitions of the second order that he is capable both of enjoying and of lacking freedom of the will. The concept of a person is not only, then, the concept of a type of entity that has both first-order desires and volitions of the second order. It can also be construed as the concept of a type of entity for whom the freedom of its will may be a problem. This concept excludes all wantons, both infrahuman and human, since they fail to satisfy an essential condition for the enjoyment of freedom of the will. And it excludes those suprahuman beings, if any, whose wills are necessarily free.

Just what kind of freedom is the freedom of the will? This question calls for an identification of the special area of human experience to which the concept of freedom of the will, as distinct from the concepts of other sorts of freedom, is particularly germane. In dealing with it, my aim will be primarily to locate the problem with which a person is most immediately concerned when he is concerned with the freedom of his will.

According to one familiar philosophical tradition, being free is fundamentally a matter of doing what one wants to do. Now the notion of an agent who does what he wants to do is by no means an altogether clear one: both the doing and the wanting, and the appropriate relation between them as well, require elucidation. But although its focus needs to be sharpened and its formulation refined, I believe that this notion does capture at least part of what is implicit in the idea of an agent who *acts* freely. It misses entirely, however, the peculiar content of the quite different idea of an agent whose *will* is free.

> ### ASK YOURSELF
> **24.** Compatibilists argue that when someone does what he wants to do, he is free. Frankfurt does not disagree, but he denies that someone who does what he wants necessarily has free _____.

We do not suppose that animals enjoy freedom of the will, although we recognize that an animal may be free to run in whatever direction it wants. Thus, having the freedom to do what one wants to do is not a sufficient condition of having a free will. It is not a necessary condition either. For to deprive someone of his freedom of action is not necessarily to undermine the freedom of his will. When an agent is aware that there are certain things he is not free to do, this doubtless affects his desires and limits the range of choices he can make. But suppose that someone, without being aware of it, has in fact lost or been deprived of his freedom of action. Even though he is no longer free to do what he wants to do, his will may remain as free as it was before. Despite the fact that he is not free to translate his desires into actions or to act according to the determinations of his will, he may still form those desires and make those determinations as freely as if his freedom of action had not been impaired.

Suppose I think I am free to go to Grand Rapids today, even though I cannot, since the only flight that can get me there has, unbeknownst to me, been canceled. According to Frankfurt, in such a situation, I am still free to "form my desires" and also to determine which desires I would act on if I could. Being free to determine which desires I would act on is still freedom. It is the freedom proper to second order volitions.

> ### ASK YOURSELF
> **25.** Could a dog have that kind of freedom?

When we ask whether a person's will is free we are not asking whether he is in a position to translate his first-order desires into actions. That is the question of whether he is free to do as he pleases. The question of the freedom of his will does not concern the relation between what he does and what he wants to do. Rather, it concerns his desires themselves. But what question about them is it?

It seems to me both natural and useful to construe the question of whether a person's will is free in close analogy to the question of whether an agent enjoys freedom of action. Now freedom of action is (roughly, at least) the freedom to do what one wants to do. Analogously, then, the statement that a person enjoys freedom of the will means (also roughly) that he is free to want what he wants to want. More precisely, it means that he is free to will what he wants to will, or to have the will he wants. Just as the question about the freedom of an agent's action has to do with whether it is the action he wants to perform, so the question about the freedom of his will has to do with whether it is the will he wants to have.

26. Since the unwilling drug addict is not free to have the will he wants, he lacks _____. So that is what the free-will controversy ought to be focused on, since it is that about which people are concerned.

It is in securing the conformity of his will to his second-order volitions, then, that a person exercises freedom of the will. And it is in the discrepancy between his will and his second-order volitions, or in his awareness that their coincidence is not his own doing but only a happy chance, that a person who does not have this freedom feels its lack. The unwilling addict's will is not free. This is shown by the fact that it is not the will he wants. It is also true, though in a different way, that the will of the wanton addict is not free. The wanton addict neither has the will he wants nor has a will that differs from the will he wants. Since he has no volitions of the second order, the freedom of his will cannot be a problem for him. He lacks it, so to speak, by default.

Examples such as the one concerning the unwilling addict may suggest that volitions of the second order, or of higher orders, must be formed deliberately and that a person characteristically struggles to ensure that they are satisfied. But the conformity of a person's will to his higher-order volitions may be far more thoughtless and spontaneous than this. Some people are naturally moved by kindness when they want to be kind, and by nastiness when they want to be nasty, without any explicit forethought and without any need for energetic self-control. Others are moved by nastiness when they want to be kind and by kindness when they intend to be nasty, equally without forethought and without active resistance to these violations of their higher-order desires. The enjoyment of freedom comes easily to some. Others must struggle to achieve it.

27. Suppose someone *did* actively and successfully resist his first-order desire to be nasty when he had a second-order desire to be kind. Would he be a person with freedom of the will?

My theory concerning the freedom of the will accounts easily for our disinclination to allow that this freedom is enjoyed by the members of any species inferior to our own. It also satisfies another condition that must be met by any such theory, by making it apparent why the freedom of the will should be regarded as desirable. The enjoyment of a free will means the satisfaction of certain desires, desires of the second or of higher orders—whereas its absence means their frustration. The satisfactions at stake are those which accrue to a person of whom it may be said that his will is his own. The corresponding frustrations are those suffered by a person of whom it may be said that he is estranged from himself, or that he finds himself a helpless or a passive bystander to the forces that move him.

A person who is free to do what he wants to do may yet not be in a position to have the will he wants.

28. Would the unwilling addict be an example of such a person as the one just described?

Suppose, however, that he enjoys both freedom of action and freedom of the will. Then he is not only free to do what he wants to do; he is also free to want what he wants to want. It seems to me that he has, in that case, all the freedom it is possible to desire or to conceive. There are other good things in life, and he may not possess some of them. But there is nothing in the way of freedom that he lacks.

ASK YOURSELF

29. So, someone who is free to want that they want to want has _____ _____ .

It is far from clear that certain other theories of the freedom of the will meet these elementary but essential conditions: that it be understandable why we desire this freedom and why we refuse to ascribe it to animals. Consider, for example, Roderick Chisholm's quaint version of the doctrine that human freedom entails an absence of causal determination. Whenever a person performs a free action, according to Chisholm, it's a miracle. The motion of a person's hand, when the person moves it, is the outcome of a series of physical causes; but some event in this series, "and presumably one of those that took place within the brain, was caused by the agent and not by any other events." A free agent has, therefore, "a prerogative which some would attribute only to God: each of us, when we act, is a prime mover unmoved."

This account fails to provide any basis for doubting that animals of subhuman species enjoy the freedom it defines. Chisholm says nothing that makes it seem less likely that a rabbit performs a miracle when it moves its leg than that a man does so when he moves his hand. But why, in any case, should anyone *care* whether he can interrupt the natural order of causes in the way Chisholm describes? Chisholm offers no reason for believing that there is a discernible difference between the experience of a man who miraculously initiates a series of causes when he moves his hand and a man who moves his hand without any such breach of the normal causal sequence. There appears to be no concrete basis for preferring to be involved in the one state of affairs rather than in the other.

ASK YOURSELF

30. Can you see any difference between Chisholm's theory, as described here, and Taylor's notion of agency? Mention one way in which they are alike.

It is generally supposed that, in addition to satisfying the two conditions I have mentioned, a satisfactory theory of the freedom of the will necessarily provides an analysis of one of the conditions of moral responsibility. The most common recent approach to the problem of understanding the freedom of the will has been, indeed, to inquire what is entailed by the assumption that someone is morally responsible for what he has done. In my view, however, the relation between moral responsibility and the freedom of the will has been very widely misunderstood. It is not true that a person is morally responsible for what he has done only if his will was free when he did it. He may be morally responsible for having done it even though his will was not free at all.

ASK YOURSELF

31. Consider the unwilling addict. His will is not free, according to Frankfurt's account. Do you think he is morally responsible for taking drugs nonetheless?

A person's will is free only if he is free to have the will he wants. This means that, with regard to any of his first-order desires, he is free either to make that desire his will or to make some other first-order desire his will instead. Whatever his will, then, the will of the person whose will is free could have been otherwise; he could have done otherwise than to constitute his will as he did. It is a vexed question just how "he could have done otherwise" is to be understood in contexts such as this one. But although this question is important to the theory of freedom, it has no bearing on the theory of moral responsibility. For the assumption that a person is morally responsible for what he has done does not entail that the person was in a position to have whatever will he wanted.

This assumption *does* entail that the person did what he did freely, or that he did it of his own free will. It is a mistake, however, to believe that someone acts freely only when he is free to do whatever he wants or that he acts of his own free will only if his will is free. Suppose that a person has done what he wanted to do, that he did it because he wanted to do it, and that the will by which he was moved when he did it was his will because it was the will he wanted. Then he did it freely and of his own free will. Even supposing that he could have done otherwise, he would not have done otherwise; and even supposing that he could have had a different will, he would not have wanted his will to differ from what it was. Moreover, since the will that moved him when he acted was his will because he wanted it to be, he cannot claim that his will was forced upon him or that he was a passive bystander to its constitution. Under these conditions, it is quite irrelevant to the evaluation of his moral responsibility to inquire whether the alternatives that he opted against were actually available to him.

In illustration, consider a third kind of addict. Suppose that his addiction has the same physiological basis and the same irresistible thrust as the addictions of the unwilling and wanton addicts, but that he is altogether delighted with his condition. He is a willing addict, who would not have things any other way. If the grip of his addiction should somehow weaken, he would do whatever he could to reinstate it; if his desire for the drug should begin to fade, he would take steps to renew its intensity.

The willing addict's will is not free, for his desire to take the drug will be effective regardless of whether or not he wants this desire to constitute his will. But when he takes the drug, he takes it freely and of his own free will. I am inclined to understand his situation as involving the overdetermination of his first-order desire to take the drug. This desire is his effective desire because he is physiologically addicted. But it is his effective desire also because he wants it to be. His will is outside his control, but, by his second-order desire that his desire for the drug should be effective, he has made this will his own. Given that it is therefore not only because of his addiction that his desire for the drug is effective, he may be morally responsible for taking the drug.

Think about this willing addict. Since he is an addict, he is unable to refrain from taking drugs. In that sense he does not have freedom of action. When he takes drugs there is really no other possibility for him, no alternative. However, *that is just how he wants it*. He wants to be an addict. Surely there is *some* difference between such an individual and one who is an addict but doesn't want to be, or someone who is an addict, but doesn't care one way or the other whether he is an addict. What is that difference? How should it be described? Frankfurt describes it this way: Such a person takes drugs freely or "of his own free will." Why describe it that way? Because he is doing what he wants! His second-order desire is a desire to be an addict, and that is just what he is being. He has made his first-order desire for drugs his own, and he says to himself "that is how I am and that is how I *want* to be." Since he acts in accord with how he wants to be, he acts freely or of his own free will. That being the case, surely he can be held morally responsible for who he is, and thus for taking drugs, can't he?

ASK YOURSELF

32. Think about this: When Albert the willing addict takes drugs, there is really no alternative for him. That is the only way he can act. So must it be Frankfurt's view that sometimes a person acts freely even when he has no alternative but to act the way he does?

My conception of the freedom of the will appears to be neutral with regard to the problem of determinism. It seems conceivable that it should be causally determined that a person is free to want what he wants to want. If this is conceivable, then it might be causally determined that a person enjoys a free will. There is no more than an innocuous appearance of paradox in the proposition that it is determined, ineluctably and by forces beyond their control, that certain people have free wills and that others do not. There is no incoherence in the proposition that some agency other than a person's own is responsible (even *morally* responsible) for the fact that he enjoys or fails to enjoy freedom of the will. It is possible that a person should be morally responsible for what he does of his own free will and that some other person should also be morally responsible for his having done it.

On the other hand, it seems conceivable that it should come about by chance that a person is free to have the will he wants. If this is conceivable, then it might be a matter of chance that certain people enjoy freedom of the will and that certain others do not. Perhaps it is also conceivable, as a number of philosophers believe, for states of affairs to come about in a way other than by chance or as the outcome of a sequence of natural causes. If it is indeed conceivable for the relevant states of affairs to come about in some third way, then it is also possible that a person should in that third way come to enjoy the freedom of the will.

Frankfurt's discussion has several surprising conclusions that sound paradoxical at first. Here are some of them:

A person can act freely even when they have no alternative (call this the denial of the "principle of alternative possibilities").

A person who is physiologically addicted can still have freedom of the will.

An individual who has no second-order volitions is not even a person.

It may be that being causally determined is compatible with freedom of the will, but not for the reasons given by compatibilists.

These claims appear to contradict some of the fundamental assumptions that have governed the free will/determinism conflict. If Frankfurt is right, then d'Holbach, Hume, Taylor, and Chisholm are all confused. They are not clear what it is that they are talking about when they talk about freedom of the will. Freedom of the will is the freedom to act according to one's own second-order volitions. Albert the willing addict acts according to his second-order volitions. So he has freedom of the will. Suppose that nothing stands in the way of his taking drugs. He is not in jail, he has the money to buy them, and so forth. A compatibilist could say that he has freedom of the will because nothing is preventing him from acting according to his *first-order desires*. But that is not what having freedom of the will is. Rather, freedom of the will is being able to act according to one's *second-order desires*. Only persons have such desires. In the compatibilist view, on the other hand, there is no difference between the willing addict and a conditioned dog for the dog obviously has first-order desires. So according to the compatibilist view, the dog must have free will! Frankfurt thinks that is nonsense.

An incompatibilist, such as Taylor or Chisholm, might argue that the fact that some person, Albert, does what he wants cannot be what makes his will free, since those wants might themselves have been caused by factors outside Albert's control. He is free, on their view, only if his actions are caused by "himself" where the self in question *cannot be identified with any desires or wants*. Frankfurt argues that this notion of agency makes it mysterious why anyone should *care* whether they have free will or not. What matters to people, what they care about, is whether they are able to mold their own lives, to have the kinds of desires and wants that they think worth having. That is what makes the issue of free will important to people.

ASK YOURSELF

33. Do you think Frankfurt has scored any points against the traditional positions in the free will/determinism controversy? If so, where?

34. Do you think dogs have free will in the same sense that persons do? Why, or, why not?

SUMMING UP THE PROBLEM OF FREE WILL

Philosophical discussions of the free will/determinism issue attempt to account for our apparently conflicting intuitions about causes, natural laws, responsibility and blame, and the ability to order our own desires or wants. Philosophers have tried to remove the conflicts. That could be done by denying the validity of some of our intuitions, or by making other adjustments. The libertarian or *indeterminist* throws out our intuitions about causes, and claims that there could be uncaused events. Or, if he holds a more moderate position, such as Reid's, he believes that at least some of our actions are "up to us" and that we can be held responsible for them. In Reid's view, even though causal factors, such as heredity, environmental pressures, or the desire to conform, are always in operation, we are capable of acting against those causal pressures. Taylor's "theory of agency" is certainly very close to the indeterminist view. A free act in his view is one that is originated by myself as agent.

The *hard determinist* seems to simply throw out all of our intuitions about freedom and responsibility. We may believe very strongly that we have free will and are sometimes responsible for what we do. But according to thinkers like d'Holbach, that is simply an illusion. The *compatibilist,* or soft determinist, tries to maintain a place for our intuitions about freedom and responsibility *and* our intuitions about causes and effects. They claim that what we mean when we say that an action is free is simply that it proceeds from our own desires, wants, and so forth. Frankfurt thinks most of the arguments discussed thus far miss the point. They fail to account for the difference between humans and other animals, and they fail to address the real concerns that motivate the controversy to begin with.

Reflection on these issues certainly does produce some intellectual cramps. Moreover, we have only scratched the surface. The philosophical literature on this issue is enormous. A great deal of it, however, consists of critique or defense of the positions sketched in the preceding selections. It should be noted, however, that it is probably true that what interests most people initially is the *practical* issue of freedom. The practical issue arises when we accept that we are capable of free actions but then discover that that freedom can wither away, or be taken from us. The French thinker Tocqueville worried that in a democracy people might lose the ability to think and act on their own, and spend more and more of their lives in mindless entertainments and indulgence in brute pleasures. Under such circumstances the kind of freedom that matters, the freedom to direct the course of our own lives and the life of our communities toward some worthy end, might wither away. Frankfurt might describe that as a failure at the level of the formation of our own second-order desires. In his view, determinists, compatibilists and indeterminists have all generally failed to take into account the distinction, crucial to understanding free will, between first- and second-order desires.

CAN OF WORMS

Many of us are familiar with or have heard about people who gradually cease to be "agents" in Taylor's view of the subject. They lose a sense of direction, gradually become captive to "low" impulses, and no longer seem to be fully human. We can see how difficult it is to separate our thinking about freedom and determinism from our thinking about character and ethics generally. The problem of free will may begin to look like a very practical ethical problem, when it is suggested that if we are not careful we may lose our free will due to personal lacks and social forms of life which encourage bland conformism. We will return to the notions of agency and freedom in the context of ethics. It also looks as though the way in which we think about the mind may have much to do with our views on freedom. Unless the mind is reducible to brain activity, it is quite possible that the very existence of mentality cannot be accounted for in terms of physical causes. In that case some kind of indeterminism might look plausible or might even be required. Discussions of the nature of the mind, as well as of the relations of the mind to the brain and to machines, are included in a later chapter. It is impossible to mount an adequate discussion of the freedom/determinism controversy without paying some attention to such issues with which it is entangled in the philosophical can of worms.

ASK YOURSELF

35. Briefly explain how your own view on the free will/determinism debate impacts your thinking about (a) ethical, (b) religious, and (c) political or legal issues. Try to give a *consistent* account.

B. IDENTITY AND SURVIVAL

In 1977 a man named Billy Milligan was arrested for the rapes of three women in Columbus, Ohio. Psychologists who examined Billy made a startling discovery. "Billy" was a name that covered at least ten different personalities. One of them was an escape artist, one a protector of women and children, one a painter of timid still-lifes. These personalities were not just staged. Remarkable capacities appropriate to each showed up in jail. Once Billy was put in solitary confinement in a straightjacket. The guards found him sitting in the cell using the jacket as a pillow! The question naturally arises, which of these many personalities is the "real" self of "Billy." In another similar case of "multiple personality," a women named Chris Sizemore reported that she was none other than the "Eve" of *The Three Faces of Eve* (1957), a famous book describing a multiple personality disorder. Sizemore reported having many different "selves," and it appeared to psychologists that some of them knew nothing of the others. Sizemore eventually was "cured" and had this to say: "You don't know how wonderful it is to go to bed at night and know that it will be you that wakes up the next day." In 1997 a group of people belonging to a cult called "Heaven's Gate" committed mass suicide. Investigation showed that these people believed that the time had come for the liberation of their true selves. They considered that the true self is a kind of spiritual core, far superior to the body, and capable of existing in the "astral realm" without the body. These people believed that the passing of the comet Hale Bopp was a signal to them that the time had come to depart from their bodies. Cases such as these raise uniquely philosophical questions about the nature of personal identity.

QUESTIONS TO DISCUSS

a. Is the self identifiable at all from one time to another, or is there no single "self" that I am?

b. If there is a single self, does it get its identity from a mental core?

c. If there is a mental or spiritual core, what is that core? How is *it* identified?

d. Is it possible that what gives me a continuing personal identity is continuity of memories?

e. If there is no mental core which confers personal identity, could there be physical identity through time?

f. Could our selves survive death? If so, would that mean that a spiritual or mental core survived death? Would it make sense to suppose that a disembodied spirit could "carry" personal identity?

We may wonder what constitutes the "self" or what makes any person the same person from childhood to adulthood, or for that matter from hour to hour. How do I know it will be "I" that wakes up in the morning? Perhaps there is no permanent core, no *real* self, that persists through all changes, but even if there is, perhaps it could not survive death. Perhaps the members of Heaven's Gate were just confused in their belief that they could exist without bodies. These are the puzzles addressed in this section.

1. NO-SELF AND TRANSMIGRATION OF THE SOUL: BUDDHISM

A central contention in Buddhist philosophy is the *no-self* doctrine: There is no unified and continuous self. The target of attack here is the traditional Hindu notion that when a body dies the soul migrates to another body. A passage in the Hindu *Bagavad Gita,* for example, states that "As a person throws off worn-out garments and takes new ones, so too the dweller in the body throws off worn-out bodies and enters into others that are new." Buddhists argued that there is no soul that might successively put on and take off different bodies in a way analogous to putting on or taking off various clothes. One of the classic discussions of the no-self doctrine is from a Buddhist work titled *Questions of King Milinda,* written about 100 CE. The

**SIDDHĀRTHA GAUTAMA
(SIXTH TO FIFTH
CENTURY BCE)**
*also called the Buddha,
founder of the Buddhist religion originating in India.*

work is a dialogue between a king named Milinda, who is puzzled by several Buddhist doctrines, and a Buddhist monk named Nagasena, who tries to set the record straight.

The Self as a Name for a Collection of Properties. The discussion of the no-self doctrine opens as Nagasena introduces himself to the King in a very bizarre way: Nagasena states his name, but denies that he is really a permanent self. His name, he contends, is only an abstract designation. Startled at Nagasena's introduction, the King then ridicules him. If there is no real self by the name of "Nagasena," then who is performing the Buddhist rituals that Nagasena appears to be doing? He thus attempts to catch Nagasena in a contradiction: Nagasena seems to be really there, but Nagasena continually refuses to be identified with any specific behavior, bodily feature, or mental experience. On King Milinda's reasoning, if Nagasena cannot be identified with any physical or mental thing, then it makes no sense to even say that he has the name "Nagasena" even as a mere abstract designation.

FROM *Questions of King Milinda* (100 CE)

NAGASENA   I am known as Nagasena, your majesty, and it is by this name that my associates address me. But although parents give us names such as "Nagasena"... it is, however, only a generally understood term, a designation in common use. For there is no permanent self involved in the matter.

KING MILINDA   . . . If there is no self to be found, who is it then that furnishes you priests with the priestly requisites—robes, food, bedding, and medicine, the reliance of the sick? Who is it that makes use of the same? Who is it that keeps the precepts? Who is it that applies himself to meditation? Who is it that realizes the Paths, the Fruits, and Nirvana? Who is it that destroys life? Who is it that takes what is not given him? Who is it that commits immorality? Who is it that tells lies? Who is it that drinks intoxicating liquor? Who is it that commits the five crimes that constitute "proximate karma" [i.e., actions that have consequences in the next life]? In that case, there is no merit; there is no demerit; there is no one who does or causes to be done meritorious or demeritorious deeds; neither good nor evil deeds can have any fruit or result. Nagasena, neither is he a murderer who kills a priest, nor can you priests, Nagasena, have any teacher, preceptor, or ordination. When you say, "My fellow-priests, your majesty, address me as 'Nagasena,'" what then is this 'Nagesena'? Please, revered one, is the hair of the head 'Nagasena'?

NAGASENA   No, truly, your majesty.

KING MILINDA   Is the hair of the body "Nagasena"?

NAGASENA   No, truly, your majesty.

KING MILINDA   Are nails . . . teeth . . . skin . . . flesh . . . sinews . . . bones . . . marrow of the bones . . . kidneys . . . heart . . . liver . . . pleura . . . spleen . . . lungs . . . intestines . . . mesentery . . . stomach . . . feces . . . bile . . . phlegm . . . pus . . . blood . . . sweat . . . fat . . . tears . . . lymph . . . saliva . . . snot . . . synovial fluid . . . urine . . . brain of the head . . . form . . . sensation . . . perception . . . predispositions . . . consciousness . . . form, "Nagasena"?

KING MILINDA   Are, then, form, sensation, perception, the predispositions, and consciousness unitedly "Nagasena"?

NAGASENA   No, truly, your majesty.

KING MILINDA   Is it, then, something besides form, sensation, perception, the predispositions, and consciousness, which is "Nagasena"?

NAGASENA   No, truly, your majesty.

KING MILINDA   Although I question you very closely, I fail to discover any "Nagasena." Truly, now, "Nagasena" is a mere empty sound. What "Nagasena" is there here? You speak a falsehood, a lie: there is no "Nagasena."

ASK YOURSELF

36. What are some of the mental qualities that the King attempts to identify with Nagasena?

Nagasena responds to the King by using a parallel kind of reasoning regarding a chariot. Like the name "Nagasena," the word "chariot" is also merely an abstract designation that refers to a collection of parts and no specific thing.

NAGASENA   Your majesty . . . did you come on foot, or riding?

KING MILINDA   I do not go on foot; I came in a chariot.

NAGASENA   If you came in a chariot, indicate this chariot to me. Is the pole the chariot?

KING MILINDA   No, truly.

NAGASENA   Is the axle . . . wheels . . . chariot-body . . . banner-staff . . . yoke . . . reins . . . goading-stick the chariot?

KING MILINDA   No, truly, Nagasena.

NAGASENA   Please, your majesty, are pole, axle, wheels, chariot-body, banner-staff, yoke, reins, and goad unitedly the chariot?

KING MILINDA   No, truly, Nagasena.

NAGASENA   Is it, then, something else besides pole, axle, wheels, chariot-body, banner-staff, yoke, reins, and goad which is the chariot?

KING MILINDA   No, truly, Nagasena.

NAGASENA   Although I question you very closely, I fail to discover any chariot. Truly now, your majesty, the word "chariot" is a mere empty sound. What chariot is there here? Your majesty, you speak a falsehood, a lie: there is no chariot. Your majesty, you are the chief king in all the continent of India. Of whom are you afraid that you speak a lie? Listen to me, my lords, you five hundred High priests, and you eighty thousand priests! Milinda the king here says this: "I came in a chariot," and when I request, "If you came in a chariot, indicate that chariot to me," he fails to produce any chariot. Is it possible for me to agree with what he says?

NARRATOR   When he had thus spoken, the five hundred High priests applauded the venerable Nagasena. The priests then spoke to King Milinda as follows: "Now, your majesty, answer, if you can." Then King Milinda spoke to the venerable Nagasena as follows.

KING MILINDA   Speaking truthfully, Nagasena, the word "chariot" is only a way of counting, a term, a label, a convenient designation, and a name for pole, axle, wheels, chariot-body, and banner-staff.

NAGASENA   You understand a chariot very well. In exactly the same way, in regards to me, [the word] "Nagasena" is only a way of counting, a term, a label, a convenient designation, or a mere name for the hair of my head, hair of my body . . . brain of the head, form, sensation, perception, the predispositions, and consciousness. But in the absolute sense there is no self here to be found. And the priestess Vajira said the following in the presence of The Blessed One: "Even as the word of 'chariot' means that members join to frame a whole; so when the groups appear to view, we use the phrase, 'A living being.' "

KING MILINDA   This is wonderful, Nagasena! This is marvelous! The wit of your replies is brilliant and prompt. If the Buddha were alive, he would applaud.

ASK YOURSELF

37. According to Nagasena, what does the word "chariot" refer to?

The Self Is Not a Perceiving Soul. Suppose we accept Nagasena's point that there is no fixed component of our behavior, body, or mind that can be identified as the self. Can't I still identify my permanent self with my *soul?* King Milinda suggests this possibility. The King's notion of a "soul" is not that of an immaterial wispy ghost, but instead a living principle within us that allows us to perceive the physical world. This living principle, according to the King, is present throughout the entire body and coordinates all sensations as it freely chooses—somewhat like an orchestra leader directing sounds from various musicians. Nagasena disputes the existence of such a living principle. When we look at how perception takes place within us, we only find rigidly constructed sensory systems, and we don't discover a perceiving soul at any stage. Nagasena begins this discussion by pointing out that the five windows of the senses are isolated from each other, and there is no power within us to freely mix and mingle the sensory data that flows through these windows.

KING MILINDA   Is there, Nagasena, such a thing as the soul?

NAGASENA   What is this "soul" your majesty?

KING MILINDA   It is the *living principle* within which sees forms through the eye, hears sounds through the ear, experiences tastes through the tongue, smells odors through the nose, feels touch through the body, and discerns things through the mind. It is just as we—sitting here in the palace—can look out of any window out of which we wish to look, the east window or the west, or the north or the south.

NAGASENA   I will tell you about the five doors, great king. Listen attentively. If the [so-called] *living principle* within sees forms through the eye in the manner that you mention, choosing its window as it likes, can it not then see forms not only through the eye, but also through each of the other five organs of sense? And in like manner can it not then as well hear sounds, and experience taste, and smell odors, and feel touch, and discern conditions through each of the other five organs of sense, besides the one you have in each case specified?

KING MILINDA   No, Sir.

NAGASENA   Then these powers are not united one to another freely [through a so-called "living principle"], the latter sense to the former organ, and so on. Now—as we are seated here in the palace, with these windows all thrown open, and in full daylight—if we only stretch forth our heads, we will see all kinds of objects plainly. Can the *living principle* do the same when the doors of the eyes are thrown open? When the doors of the ear are thrown open, can it do so? Can it then not only hear sounds, but see sights, experience tastes, smell odors, feel touch, and discern conditions? And so with each of its windows?

KING MILINDA   No, Sir.

NAGASENA   Then these powers are not united one to another freely [through a so-called "living principle"].

ASK YOURSELF

38. According to Nagasena, when the doors of our ears are thrown open, we can only _____.

Nagasena continues explaining how each of our five senses follows a strict physiological system; for example, we taste honey when it touches our tongues, but not when it reaches our stomachs.

NAGASENA   Now again, great king, if Dinna here were to go outside and stand in the gateway, would you be aware that he had done so?

KING MILINDA   Yes, I should know it.

NAGASENA   And if the same Dinna were to come back again, and stand before you, would you be aware of his having done so?

KING MILINDA   Yes, I should know it.

NAGASENA   Well, great king, would the living principle within discern, in like manner, if anything possessing flavor were laid upon the tongue, its sourness, or its saltness, or its acidity, or its pungency, or its astringency, or its sweetness?

KING MILINDA   Yes, it would know it.

NAGASENA   But when the flavor had passed into the stomach would it still discern these things?

KING MILINDA   Certainly not.

NAGASENA   Then these powers are not united one to the other freely [through a so-called "living principle"]. Now suppose, your majesty, a man were to have a hundred vessels of honey brought and poured into one trough, and then, having had another man's mouth closed over and tied up, were to have him cast into the trough full of honey. Would he know whether that into which he had been thrown was sweet or whether it was not?

KING MILINDA   No, Sir.

NAGASENA   But why not?

KING MILINDA   Because the honey could not get into his mouth.

NAGASENA   Then, great king, these powers are not united one to another indiscriminately.

KING MILINDA   I am not capable of discussing with such a reasoner. Be pleased, Sir, to explain to me how the matter stands.

NAGASENA   It is by reason, your majesty, of the eye and of forms that sight arises, and those other conditions—contact, sensation, idea, thought, abstraction, sense of vitality, and attention—arise each simultaneously with its predecessor. And a similar succession of cause and effect arises when each of the other five organs of sense is brought into play. And so herein there is no such thing as soul.

ASK YOURSELF

39. Nagasena has us imagine a man who first had his mouth taped shut and then was thrown into a trough of honey. What are we to conclude from this example about the perception of honey?

Thus, according to Nagasena, we are left only with isolated sense perceptions that come and go as our five senses are stimulated; there simply is no perceptual soul that regulates our sensory experiences.

Rebirth Is Not Transmigration. We've seen that the traditional Hindu notion of reincarnation involves a permanent self that transmigrates from one physical body to another. But, if there is no fixed self or soul as Buddhists maintain, then the traditional notion of reincarnation goes out the window. King Milinda and Nagasena discuss this issue. According to Nagasena, even though the literal notion of transmigration of the soul must be rejected, there is a more metaphorical notion of "rebirth" that Buddhists can retain. Throughout our lives we impact people around us, and to that extent something about us is reborn in the lives of others.

KING MILINDA   Does rebirth take place without anything transmigrating?

NAGASENA   Yes, rebirth takes place without anything transmigrating.

KING MILINDA   How does rebirth take place without anything transmigrating? Give an illustration.

NAGASENA   Suppose a man lit a light from another light. Would the one light have passed over (or transmigrated) to the other light?

KING MILINDA   No, truly, Nagasena.

NAGASENA   In exactly the same way, your majesty, does rebirth take place without anything transmigrating.

KING MILINDA   Give another illustration.

NAGASENA   Do you remember having learned as a boy some verse or other from your professor of poetry?

KING MILINDA   Yes.

NAGASENA   Did the verse pass over (or transmigrate) to you from your teacher?

KING MILINDA   No, truly.

NAGASENA   In exactly the same way rebirth takes place without anything transmigrating.

ASK YOURSELF

40. Nagasena suggests that in some sense a poetry teacher is reborn when he passes on a poem to a student. Describe something in your conduct that impacts others that might similarly be seen as a "rebirth."

2. THE SELF AS A BUNDLE OF PERCEPTIONS: DAVID HUME

Around two thousand years after Buddhism first wrestled with problems surrounding the notion of a unified self, European philosophers had similar thoughts on the subject. The views of David Hume, which appeared in his *Treatise of Human Nature* (1739), bear some interesting similarities to the Buddhist views presented above.

Hume's Original Argument. According to Hume, philosophers typically misunderstand the notion of the self. One philosopher Hume possibly has in mind is Descartes, who believed that the self is a thinking spirit. According to Hume, such philosophers maintain that the self (a) is a simple and unified thing/experience and (b) continues over time as a unified thing/experience.

FROM DAVID HUME, *A Treatise of Human Nature* (1739), BOOK 1.4.6 AND APPENDIX

There are some philosophers who imagine [that] we are every moment intimately conscious of what we call our *self;* that we feel its existence and its continuance in existence; and [that we] are certain, beyond the evidence of a demonstration, both of its perfect identity and simplicity. The strongest sensation, the most violent passion, say they, instead of distracting us from this view, only fix it the more intensely, and make us consider their influence on self either by their pain or pleasure. To attempt a farther proof of this were to weaken its evidence; since no proof can be derived from any fact, of which we are so intimately conscious; nor is there any thing, of which we can be certain, if we doubt of this.

ASK YOURSELF

41. What kind of proofs do these philosophers offer for their view?

Hume argues that if we do have an idea of a single, continuous self, this idea must have come from some impression (either external or internal experience). However, it appears that we have no impression of such a single, continuous self.

Unluckily all these positive assertions are contrary to that very experience, which is pleaded for them, nor have we any idea of *self,* after the manner it is here explained. For from what impression could this idea be derived? This question it is impossible to answer without a manifest contradiction and absurdity; and yet 'tis a question, which must necessarily be answered, if we would have the idea of self pass for clear and intelligible, It must be some one impression, that gives rise to every real idea. But self or person is not any one impression, but that to which our several impressions and ideas are supposed to have a reference. If any impression gives rise to the idea of self, that impression must continue invariably the same, thro' the whole course of our lives; since self is supposed to exist after that manner. But there is no impression constant and invariable. Pain and pleasure, grief and joy, passions and sensations succeed each other, and never all exist at the same time. It cannot, therefore, be from any of these impressions, or from any other, that the idea of self is derived; and consequently there is no such idea.

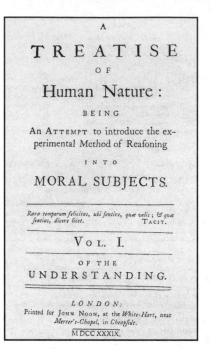

A

TREATISE

OF

Human Nature:

BEING

An ATTEMPT to introduce the experimental Method of Reaſoning

INTO

MORAL SUBJECTS.

*Rara temporum felicitas, ubi ſentire, quæ velis; & quæ
ſentias, dicere licet.* TACIT.

VOL. I.

OF THE

UNDERSTANDING.

LONDON:
Printed for JOHN NOON, at the *White-Hart,* near
Mercer's-Chapel, in *Cheapſide.*
MDCC XXXIX.

Title page of David Hume's A Treatise of Human Nature
*(1739), Hume's major philosophical work which he later
disavowed.*

ASK YOURSELF

42. Why does Hume think we can form no such idea of a single, continuous self?

But farther, what must become of all our particular perceptions upon this hypothesis? All these are different, and distinguishable, and separable from each other, and may be separately considered, and may exist separately, and have no Deed of tiny thing to support their existence. After what manner, therefore, do they belong to self; and how are they connected with it? For my part, when I enter most intimately into what I call *myself,* I always stumble on some particular perception or other, of heat or cold, light or shade, love or hatred, pain or pleasure. I never can catch *myself* at any time without a perception, and never can observe anything but the perception. When my perceptions are removed for any time, as by sound sleep; so long am I insensible of *myself,* and may truly be said not to exist. And were all my perceptions removed by death, and could I neither think, nor feel, nor see, nor love, nor hate after the dissolution of my body, I should be entirely annihilated, nor do I conceive what is farther requisite to make me a perfect non-entity.

ASK YOURSELF

43. If we "look within" to find our "selves" what do we actually find?

If any one, upon serious and unprejudiced reflection thinks he has a different notion of *himself,* I must confess I can reason no longer with him. All I can allow him is, that he may be in the right as well as I, and that we are essentially different in this particular. He may, perhaps, perceive something simple and continued, which he calls himself; though I am certain there is no such principle in me.

But setting aside some metaphysicians of this kind, I may venture to affirm of the rest of mankind, that they are nothing but a bundle or collection of different perceptions, which succeed each other with an inconceivable rapidity, and are in a perpetual flux and movement. Our eyes cannot turn in their sockets without varying our perceptions. Our thought is still more variable than our sight; and all our other senses and faculties contribute to this change; nor is there any single power of the soul, which remains unalterably the same, perhaps for one moment. The mind is a kind of theatre, where several perceptions successively make their appearance, pass, re-pass, glide away, and mingle in an infinite variety of postures and situations. There is properly no *simplicity* in it at one time, nor identity in difference, whatever natural propension we may have to imagine that simplicity and identity. The comparison of the theatre must not mislead us. They are the successive perceptions only, that constitute the mind; nor have we the most distant notion of the place, where these scenes are represented, or of the materials, of which it is composed.

Hume warns against taking his metaphor of the "theater" literally. The mind or self is not a "place" in which things happen, since it is not a place at all. It is just a passing mixture of experiences.

ASK YOURSELF

44. Hume's notion of a bundle is also a metaphor or analogy. Consider a pile of sticks strewn about the lawn. What sort of thing do you need to make them into a compact bundle?

45. Can you think of anything that might correspond to the sort of thing you mentioned in the previous question, in the case of your "self"?

Hume concedes that we have a "natural propensity" or inclination to believe in a simple and continuous self, even though we are in fact only a bundle of perceptions. At first he suggests that our human nature instinctively connects our various moments of perception because they resemble each other and are causally related. Thus, we have an artificially constructed idea of a unified self.

Hume's Modified View. A year after Hume published the above discussion, he abandoned his initial explanation of the artificially constructed idea of the self. His final position on the issue is that he simply has no explanation of how we create this concept.

But upon a more strict review of the section concerning *personal identity,* I find myself involved in such a labyrinth, that, I must confess I neither know how to correct my former opinions, now how to render them consistent. If this be not a good general reason for **skepticism,** 'tis at least a sufficient one (if I were not already abundantly supplied) for me to entertain a diffidence and modesty in all my decisions. . . .

In short there are two principles, which I cannot render consistent; nor is it in my power to renounce either of them, viz. *that all our distinct perceptions are distinct existences, and that the mind never perceives any real connection among distinct existences.* Did our perceptions either inhere in something simple and individual, or did the mind perceive some real connection among them, there would be no difficulty in the case. For my part, I must plead the privilege of a skeptic, and confess, that this difficulty is too hard for my understanding. I pretend not, however, to pronounce it absolutely insuperable. Others, perhaps, or myself, upon more mature reflections, may discover some hypothesis, that will reconcile those contradictions.

ASK YOURSELF

46. Hume is in fact very puzzled by the notion of personal identity. We could put the puzzle in terms of this question: What makes me the same _____ today as I was yesterday or ten years ago?

THINKING LOGICALLY

The notion of identity can be logically puzzling. We may feel inclined to say that A is identical to B, provided that whatever is true of A is true of B and vice versa. For instance, if A = B, then if A is blue, B is blue. But if *everything* that is true of A is true of B, then it would seem that A and B are not distinct from one another at all. For example, if it is true of A that it is located in, and fills, a certain specific space, then it must be true of B that it is located in and fills that same specific space. But then, are they not one thing, rather than two identical things? Many arguments depend upon the notion of identity. Descartes, whom we will discuss further in Chapter 4, argued that he was a mental thing, not a physical thing. One of his arguments went like this:

1. I cannot coherently think that *I* do not exist (I would have to exist to think it!).
2. I can think that my *body* does not exist.
3. Therefore, I am not identical with my body.

This argument is an enthymeme. The missing premise is "If A is identical with B, then whatever is true of A is true of B." If this principle were always true, then Descartes has a strong argument. But most logicians think that it is not true in every context, and that his argument is fallacious.

ASK YOURSELF

47. Consider this counterexample to Descartes's argument (fill in the blank):

1. I cannot think that Mark Twain is not Mark Twain.
2. I can think that Mark Twain is not Samuel Clemens (perhaps I have never even heard of Samuel Clemens!).
3. Therefore, Mark Twain is not _____.

This is a counterexample because the premises could be true whereas the conclusion is in fact false. It is therefore an invalid argument.

3.   IDENTITY AND SURVIVAL: TERENCE PENELHUM

Contemporary philosopher Terence Penelhum, who taught for many years at the University of Calgary, Canada, finds Hume's puzzlement regarding the self provocative but resolvable. Although Penelhum finds some notion of a continuous self plausible, he nevertheless sees serious problems with the idea of a self that persists after bodily death. What would it mean to say that a person had survived death—that is, that one and the same person died and yet is now in some way alive?

FROM TERENCE PENELHUM, *Religion and Rationality* (1971)

The logical problems one has to contend with when examining the concept of survival are to a large extent extensions of those that have puzzled philosophers when they have tried to analyze the notion of personal identity. We all recognize one another—we arc all familiar enough with the experience of wondering who someone is; and most of us know the embarrassment that follows when one makes a mistake about who someone is.

Our day-to-day thinking about these matters suggests that we take it for granted that there are clearly understood factors that determine whether the man before us is Smith or not, or is who he says he is or not, even though we may be unable, to decide sometimes, through lack of information whether these factors obtain. Philosophers have been puzzled, however, when they have tried to say what these factors are. Skeptical philosopher even wondered whether any such factors can be isolated; and if they cannot be, they have suggested, our assumption that people do retain their identities from one period of time to the next may be an illusion.

Skepticism About Personal Identity. Penelhum next draws out the skeptical implications of the problem of personal identity.

We do not need to spend much time here on this sort of skepticism. Its most famous exponent is Hume, who confessed himself unable to detect any stability in the mental life of men and therefore thought that the incessant changes that human minds undergo make it plainly false that they retain any identity at all. Our belief that they do retain an identity is a convenient fiction but nothing better. This skepticism rests on an unstated assumption that there is some sort of logical conflict between the notions of sameness and change. If this were so, then in order to be sure that any type of being retained identity through time, we would have to be sure that it, or at least the essential part of it, remained unchanged through that time. If this is true, then of course Hume would be quite justified in relapsing into skepticism about personal identity. But once the assumption is exposed, its gratuitousness becomes apparent. Sameness or identity is an ambiguous notion; borrowing vocabulary found in Hume himself, we can distinguish between "numerical identity" and "specific identity." Two things arc identical in the specific sense if they are exactly alike in some or all respects. This can only be true if they are, nevertheless, two distinct things—if, that is, they are not identical in the numerical sense. Two numerically different things may or may not be the same in the specific sense. One and the same thing (in the numerical sense) may be the same at one time as it was at an earlier time, or it may not. If it is not, it has changed. To say that just because it has changed it cannot be numerically the same is to confuse the two sorts of identity.

Certain changes, however, may destroy a thing—that is, whatever remains of it is no longer sufficient to entitle us to say that that thing has continued in existence, and we are forced to say that something else is there, as when a house crumbles and a mere heap of stones remains. Even though Hume is wrong in thinking that the mere fact of change destroys numerical identity, it is still the case that for each *sort* of thing, certain changes will destroy that identity and certain others will not. Reducing all parts of a chair to ashes in a fire will destroy its identity, whereas changing the color of its surface by painting it will not. This suggests, once again, that the proper philosophical task is to discover, at least in the case of those classes of things that are of philosophical interest to us, what factors have to remain for a thing of that sort to continue in being and which ones do not. The problem of personal identity consists, in part, of trying to clarify this in the case of persons.

ASK YOURSELF

48. Why, according to Penelhum, does the mere fact of change not destroy identity?

When we try to do this we are confronted with another oddity in a discussion like Hume's. He restricts himself, without any apparent recognition of the need to justify this restriction, to a consideration of only the mental factors that make up the being of a person and ignores the physical ones. If one makes this restriction, one is immediately confronted with the following facts that Hume stresses: first, he notes that the changes we can introspect within the mind succeed one another very rapidly; and second, he points out that one cannot detect any more stable element. Since we usually conceive of *things* as entities that change fairly slowly unless catastrophe strikes them and do not normally change nearly as rapidly as the contents of the mind seem to do, our ascription of identity to the person is apt to seem puzzling. But what needs to be questioned here is Hume's restriction. One of the major reasons for it is that Hume inherits the dualism that Descartes passed down from Plato into modern philosophy. It is a characteristic part of that tradition not merely to divide the human person into two parts but to identify the real person with the mind and assume that the body is merely a place that this person inhabits. If this identification is presupposed, then Hume's bewilderment in the face of the rapidity of mental change is understandable enough.

ASK YOURSELF

49. Hume assumes that the criteria of identity for persons must be mental. If we drop that assumption the puzzlement caused by the _____ of change may disappear.

Mental and Bodily Criteria of Identity. Penelhum turns to the "the doctrine of spiritual substance."

This is the doctrine that . . . there is some hidden core to [the self] that persists unchanged throughout, thus providing a backdrop against which the changes occur. This backdrop need not be unchanging: It could be subject only to gradual change. The tacit assumption that it cannot change at all is only the result of assuming that identity and change are always inconsistent. But even if we allow that the spiritual substance to which the occurrences in our mental lives belong might itself be subject to gradual change, the doctrine is without value. For if the doctrine implies that we can find this relatively permanent core within by looking into ourselves, then it is false; for we cannot, as Hume emphasizes. If on the other hand, it is admitted that the doctrine postulates something that is not accessible to observation, there is another difficulty: It can at best be a matter of happy accident that when we judge someone before us to be the same person as someone we knew before, we are right. For the only thing that would make this judgment reliable is the knowledge that the features possessed by the present and the past person belonged to the same substance. Yet when the substance is inaccessible even to the person himself, how could we ever know that an identity judgment was true? It is obvious that our basis for such judgments must be something other than what the doctrine requires it to be, for how, otherwise, could we learn to make such judgments in the first place?

We base our identity judgments, at least of others, upon the observation of their physical appearance. This fact, plus the mysteriousness of the doctrine of spiritual substance, has made it very tempting for philosophers to say that what makes a person the same from one period to the next is the continuance of his body throughout the two periods. The human body has the relative stability that we associate with a great many observable material objects and is not usually subject to the rapid changes that go on in the human mind. The plausibility of the claim that bodily continuity is a necessary and sufficient condition of personal identity derives also from the fact that our judgments about the identity of persons are in the vast majority of cases based on our having looked at them, talked to them, and recognized them. . . .

Penelhum goes on to consider the possibility that there might be a standard of identity of a mental sort after all. For it may seem plausible to suppose that memories tie the mind together into a unified self.

So we have here the possibility of a purely mental standard of identity: that person A at time T2 is the same as person B at some earlier time T1 if and only if, among the experiences that person A has at T2 there are memories of experiences that person B had at T1. In the literature of the subject these two criteria of identity (bodily continuity, and memory) have contended for priority.

ASK YOURSELF

50. Would the idea that memories provide a criterion of personal identity be especially attractive to someone who thinks that survival of death (life after death) must be spiritual, not physical?

Penelhum allows that someone who does not believe in any kind of life after death might still embrace the idea that memory provides the criteria for personal identity. Nonetheless, that idea is particularly appealing to those who believe in immortal souls or minds of some sort, by virtue of which death will not simply be the end of *me*. The notion that the core self is a soul or spirit which is capable of some kind of disembodied existence is a standard item in the religious beliefs of many people.

Someone who accepts the doctrine of disembodied survival, therefore, will naturally incline toward the view that memory is *the* one necessary and sufficient condition of personal identity, since he must reject the traditional alternative position.

There is an artificiality about speaking, as I have, about two competing positions here. For in daily life it looks as though we use both standards of identity, resorting to one or the other depending on circumstances. Sometimes we decide who someone is by ascertaining facts about their physical appearance, height, weight, and the rest. Sometimes we decide who someone is by trying to determine whether or not they can remember certain past events that the person they claim to be could not fail, we think, to recall. Indeed, the border between these two methods becomes less clear than it first seems, when we reflect that we might try to reach our decision by seeing what skills a person has retained or what performances he can carry out. But although both standards are used, one might still have priority over the other. This would be the case if the other would not be available to us if the one were not or if the description of the one required some reference to the other.

Even though both kinds of criteria might be involved in our judgments about identity, perhaps one might have priority over the other. Penelhum argues that that is indeed the case.

There are two arguments that tend to show, I think, that the bodily criterion has priority . . .
    The first one, which is the less fundamental, rests on the fact that people forget things. We cannot say that the man before us is the same who performed some past action if and only he remembers doing that action, for people forget actions they have done. . . .
    The second and more fundamental argument rests on the fact that the notion of remembering is ambiguous. To say that someone remembers some action or event may mean merely that he believes he did it or witnessed it (without, at least consciously, basing this belief upon being told about it). It is possible, of course, for someone to remember something in this sense without what he remembers having happened at all and without its having happened to him even if it did occur. The more common use of the notion of remembering, however, concedes the truth of the man's belief, so that to say that the man remembers some action or event is to say that his claim to know about it is correct. Let us call these sense (i) and sense (ii) of "I remember." Then we can say that to remember in sense (i) is to believe that one remembers in sense (ii).

51. Give an example, real or imaginary, of someone, perhaps yourself, remembering doing something that they did not in fact do.

It is apparent that memory in sense (i) cannot provide a criterion of personal identity. It is certainly not a sufficient condition of a man before us being the person that he claims to be that he remembers, in sense (i), doing or experiencing something done or experienced by the man he claims to be. For he could believe that he remembered doing something in this sense, even if nobody had done it. So we have to lean on sense (ii) of "remember." But this leads into a deeper problem. Let us simplify our discussion by concentrating solely upon a person's remembering doing an action or having an experience or witnessing an event. . . . To say that someone, in sense (ii) remembers, is not merely to report that he believes something, but to accept his belief to be true. But an integral part of his belief is not only that some action was done, some experience had, or some event witnessed, but that it was done or had or witnessed by *him*. In other words, to say that he remembers in sense (ii) is not just to say that he now has some mental image or some conviction, even though it is likely to include this—it is to say that the past action, experience, or event that he refers to is part of his own past. But it now becomes clear that we cannot even state the memory criterion of identity without having some prior (and therefore independent) notion of the identity of the person. So the identity of the person must in the end rest upon some other condition, and the claim that it could rest solely upon memory must be false.

Suppose I remember giving a speech to a large crowd in the school auditorium. Perhaps I have an image in my mind of myself standing at the podium, and of the great crowd before me. Obviously my memory includes a memory of *myself.* I believe that it was indeed I who gave the speech, the same "I" as is now remembering that speech. So perhaps having this and other memories is what ties together the present "I" and the past "I" into one, self-identical person.

But what am I claiming here? If I believe it was I simply because "I" remember doing it, or remember it as part of "my own" past, I must have some notion of the "I" or self which I employ when stating this "memory criterion," and where did I get *that* notion of the I? Obviously not from continuity of memories! So we must be operating with some "prior notion" of personal identity. Put otherwise, when I try to show how my identity might be preserved from moment to moment, day to day, year to year, through memories which tie the moments or years together in one person's experience, I employ the notion of "one person" in the very act of giving this account of what it is that makes me into "one person" from day to day, year to year. So I cannot have gotten the notion of one continuous person from a consideration of how memories might tie the self together. So, we are left with bodily criteria of identity.

> ### ASK YOURSELF
>
> **52.** Try to put in your own words the problem that arises when we try to treat continuity of memories as a criterion of personal identity.

The bodily criterion of identity is the natural one to refer to here. If, because of some commitment to dualism, one refuses to resort to it, it becomes wholly mysterious what the criterion of personal identity can be.

Identity and Personal Life After Death

We can now return to the problem of survival. We were considering how far it is possible to make sense of the notion of the persistence of a disembodied person through time and of the claim that some particular future disembodied person will be identical with one of us in this world here and now. We can also ask how far the doctrine of the resurrection of the body frees us from the difficulties that the doctrine of disembodied survival encounters.

If bodily continuity is a necessary condition of the persistence of a person through time, then we cannot form any clear conception of the persistence of a person through time without a body nor of the identity of such a person with some previous embodied person. The previous reflections about the notion of personal identity leave us with two results: first, that to attempt to understand the self-identity of a person solely in terms of memory is impossible and, second, that when we are considering the case of flesh-and-blood persons there seems no alternative but to conclude that bodily continuity is a necessary condition of personal identity. These conclusions by themselves do not show that no substitute for bodily continuity could be invented when discussing the case of disembodied personality. But some substitute for it would have to be supplied by invention, and until it is, the notion of disembodied personal identity makes no sense.

If mental or "soulish" criteria do not suffice to make intelligible the notion of personal identity *within* this life, then the same criteria will not make intelligible the notion of an identity between a pre-death and post-death person. Suppose you believe that your soul survives the death of your body. And perhaps you believe that what makes a particular soul *your* soul is that it remembers things that you did in your earthly life, as well as things that may have happened to it since you began your post-mortem existence, assuming that post-mortem existence is temporal in some sense. But the arguments given above seem to show that you could not establish that the soul in question is *your* soul just by appeal to memories. So unless there is some other way to determine the identity of souls, it will be the case that your belief in the soul's life after death is unintelligible or nonsensical.

If we turn now to the problem of identifying the disembodied person with some person who has died, we find the same difficulty. To say that he can be so identified because he remembers the deeds or experiences of that person is once again to use the notion of remembering in sense (ii). But to do this is to presuppose that we understand what it is for the rememberer to be identical with the person who did those deeds or had those experiences. And we do not actually understand this. For although the person who did those deeds had a body, the rememberer, by hypothesis, does not have one and therefore cannot have the same body. It does not seem possible, therefore, to find any answer to the problem of self-identity for disembodied persons.

What about the doctrine of the resurrection of the body? Given that we are talking of the future existence of persons with bodies, the notion of their lasting through time in their future state does not seem to present any logical difficulties. But what of their identity with ourselves? If we assume some one-to-one correspondence between the inhabitants of the next world and of this (that is, assume at least that the inhabitants of the next world each resemble, claim to be, and claim to remember the doings of inhabitants of this one), it might seem foolish to deny that they will be identical with ourselves. But foolishness is not logical absurdity. It is conceivable that there might be a future existence in which there were large numbers of persons each resembling one of us and having uncanny knowledge of our pasts. And if that world does come to be in the future, we shall not be in it. What would make it a world with us in it, rather than a world with duplicates of us in it and not ourselves? Unless I can give a clear answer to this, it seems, very paradoxically, to be a matter of arbitrary choice whether to say these future people are us or not.

ASK YOURSELF

53. What is the question to which I must give a "clear answer"?

Surely, the answer might run, they will have the same bodies that we now have. But this is precisely what is not obvious. Apart from questions about whether the future bodies are like ours in youth, maturity, or old age, the dissolution of the earthly body means that the future body will be in some sense new. To say that it is the old one re-created is merely to say it is the same one without giving any reason for saying it is identical with the original body rather than one very much like it. To answer this way, then, seems merely to face the same puzzle again. To say that the future beings will remember in sense (ii) our doings and feelings is to raise the same questions here as before. The only possible solution seems to be to insist that in spite of the time gap between the death of the old body and the appearance of the new one, something persists in between. But what? The person disembodied? If so, then the doctrine of the resurrection of the body does not avoid the difficulties that beset the doctrine of disembodied survival, for the simple reason that it falls back upon that very doctrine when its own implications are understood.

> ### ASK YOURSELF
>
> **54.** What is the problem with thinking that "I" am still *me* in the resurrection given that my old body disintegrated and a new one came into existence?

This argument does not show that the doctrine of the resurrection of the body is absurd in the way in which the doctrine of disembodied survival is. It shows rather that the doctrine of resurrection is merely one way, and a question-begging way, of describing a set of circumstances that can be described equally well in another fashion. Yet the difference between the two alternative descriptions is a vital one. For it comes to no less than the original question, namely, do we survive? It is a question that the doctrine provides an answer to but one that seems to have no conclusive grounds, even if the circumstances envisaged in the doctrine were admitted to be forthcoming.

The belief in survival, then, at least in this version, does not run into insuperable difficulties of logic. But it does not seem possible to describe a set of future circumstances that will unambiguously show it to be true. I have previously argued that if the doctrine is agreed to be coherent, it can offer a suitable answer to the difficulties about the verification of religious beliefs. I do not consider the present puzzle to show that it is not coherent. But it does show its status to be very baffling.

> ### ASK YOURSELF
>
> **55.** Put briefly, a description of the resurrection life is a description of bodily beings, but whether any of those bodily beings is "I" rather than a being that is just _____ I in all physical and psychological respects cannot be settled, on Penelhum's view.

SUMMING UP THE PROBLEM OF IDENTITY AND SURVIVAL

Are we deluded in thinking that we have some core self, a soul, spirit or mind, which stays the "same" throughout change? Hume and other skeptics think so. But the skeptical position runs up against some of our strongest intuitions, just as does determinism. Perhaps Hume simply confuses specific and numerical identity. Two things, A and B, are specifically identical if they have all or almost all the same traits. In that sense, I am clearly not identical with myself as I was ten years ago. My body has changed drastically. My "mind" has changed a lot too. My opinions have changed and so have some of my mental habits. But in the numerical sense of identity, A and B are identical if they are the same thing, however many changes that thing has undergone. There is one Niagara Falls; although it keeps changing, it is still Niagara Falls and not some numerically distinct waterfall. Although the notion of numerical identity is not without problems, it does not have the problems that specific identity has. Or perhaps Hume and other skeptics assume that if there is going to be personal identity through time, it will have to be rooted in mental life, rather than physical life. Yet bodily criteria might suffice for personal identity. My body is numerically the same as it was ten years ago. No other body has taken over. In any case, it is not obvious what sense there is in the notion that my identity persists through death. Perhaps the notion that it does sits better with the idea that identity is a bodily matter than with the idea that it is a mental or "soul" matter.

**CAN OF
WORMS**

If the very concept of the "self" is somehow confused, most of the other debates about human nature in this chapter will be pointless. If there is no real "me" but just a flux or stream of changes, then there should be no need to worry about freedom, about how "we" differ from other beings, or how "we" are related to a larger reality. It almost looks as though our thinking about the human self has as a strict presupposition the idea of continuity in the self. That was more or less the conclusion to which Immanuel Kant was driven (see Chapter 5), and he tried to produce a convincing argument for the claim that we cannot escape the idea of personal identity, and that we are justified in employing it. His response to skeptics like Hume may not satisfy everyone, but it seems clear that *some* response is desperately needed.

Even if we do find a satisfactory response, however, it will not necessarily satisfy our curiosity about the possibility of personal survival of death, as Penelhum has argued. That is an issue that is of intense concern to many people. Obviously it runs together with important *religious* questions, some of which are discussed in Chapter 2. In fact, our thinking about God, reward, punishment for sin, and above all an afterlife is tangled up with notions of personal identity. It is not clear that philosophers can resolve these puzzles about personal identity, but we have seen at least a little bit of what may be involved in that crucial discussion.

ASK YOURSELF

56. State your own view on the matter of personal identity, and explain its connections, if any, with your religious or other beliefs.

C. THE SELF AS ACTIVE BEING

Nearly any book store contains hundreds of "self-help" manuals. Many of them advise the reader on how to discover their true identity or "self." Some TV commercials for exercise equipment try to convince potential customers to buy their wares by claiming that using it will enable them to shape a new identity, an "entire new you." These books and commercials would not work if it were not the case that many people are dissatisfied in some way with "who they are." Many people feel they have yet to "get a life" and that doing so is somehow up to them. The Western world in the twenty-first century has invested heavily in therapies of various kinds. Some therapists try to solve identity crises, or to release the "real you" from inhibitions or restricting and purportedly repressive sex roles or other purportedly artificial expectations. Some therapies are designed to bring "spiritual awareness," or to awaken hidden potentials for deep contentment and truly fulfilled lives. Some therapists focus primarily on relieving various "mental ills" such as depression, compulsions of various kinds, or interpersonal difficulties. Some therapists specialize in the problems of old people, others specialize in juvenile "disorders." Some books address themselves to those who are near death.

Our self-help literature and our therapeutic culture rest upon various philosophical assumptions about the nature of human beings and the self. For example, some self-help literature assumes that genuine selfhood is already present in me, and has merely to be uncovered. Some therapeutic approaches make assumptions about human freedom and human abilities, or inabilities, to overcome unfavorable environments. Some self-help literature makes assumptions about the naturalness of death ("death is just a part of life"). Some assume that human life divides up into stages, with distinctive problems in each stage. Such assumptions are more often than not unexamined. Should we accept them? Do our self-help literature and therapeutic practices require conceptions of the self that can survive thoughtful examination?

**QUESTIONS
TO DISCUSS**

a. Is the self something that exists automatically waiting to be "discovered," or is selfhood an *achievement*?

b. Are there people who fail to achieve a genuine identity, who are a mere face in a crowd, or mere "couch potatoes"? If so, how come?

c. Does the achievement of authentic selfhood require that I pursue some particularly worthy (ethical, religious, political) ideal?

d. Could I become a complete person with a genuine identity by becoming famous, or rich, or powerful? What if I become famous by cheating and lying? Would that make a difference?

e. Could I become a complete person without facing honestly and fully fundamental truths, such as the truth that I must die?

f. Perhaps ethical and religious ideals actually get in the way of genuine selfhood. Do they work to make me a kind of meek conformist? Might religious teachings which stress humility, for instance, get in the way of worthy self-assertion?

Discussions of the mind–body problem, free will, and personal identity may be philosophically provocative, but some readers might feel less than totally engaged by such discussion. I do not commonly entertain skeptical doubts about the possibility of free action, or the identity of myself through time. But I may nonetheless be unsure about who I really am and whether I have an identity that matters. Moreover, I may feel responsible for lacking much of a self, or pride in having become, through effort, a worthy person. It does seem that I can shape myself in various ways and that failure to "become all I can be" may be due to laziness, rather than inherited or environmental obstacles. And what, practically, is the free will issue? Is it a problem that arises in thought once we grasp the nature of science, or is it rather more personal? I may wonder if I can *achieve* freedom by overcoming my impulses, avoiding bad decisions, cultivating my spirit so as to avoid despair. To employ terminology used by Frankfurt in the discussion of determinism, I can and probably do think of myself as capable of second-order desires, and it may matter to me what those desires are like and whether they can be effective. To put the matter somewhat differently, I may be concerned that I become a real person, someone who acts in ways that involve the will, as opposed to a passive observer of my own life, someone knocked about by circumstances.

Most people have at least some sense that it is not enough to idly sit and watch as events unfold in ones own life. A person can, it seems, be engaged with themselves and their surroundings so as to shape themselves and the world to some extent. I am in that sense an *active being*, responsible not only for my actions, but for the kinds of desires, wants, and even moods that I have and the kind of environment I inhabit. I can deceive myself and look for excuses, or be mired in false consciousness, or I can be responsible, pick myself up, and live hopefully and energetically, seeking to shape my character so that I become more fully responsible for my actions and my "self" in a broader sense.

Several writers—particularly in the continental European philosophical tradition—have explored the idea of the self as an active being. Their views may surprise you. They often speak against some of our most typical thoughts about human life and selfhood. Sometimes they remind us of things which we already know, but would rather forget. They are often out of step with much that we find on self-help bookshelves or in therapists offices. Sometimes they are out of step with what we hear in church, or from those who would reform our social institutions in order to better achieve human fulfillment. That is so even though some of these writers are the original sources for various popular ideas! More often than not, though, the popularized versions bear little resemblance to the originals.

1. THE SELF AS SPIRIT: SØREN KIERKEGAARD

**SØREN KIERKEGAARD
(1813–1855)**

Danish philosopher and author of The Sickness unto Death *(1849).*

The writings of Danish philosopher Søren Kierkegaard (1813–1855) are marked by deep psychological penetration. He reflects constantly on the characteristics of human inner life. Anxiety and dread, joy and love, boredom, despair, melancholy and depression, humor and irony all receive extended treatment in his works. In a work entitled *The Sickness Unto Death* he undertakes to analyze the most fundamental aspects of the human self. The abstractness and complexity of parts of this work are perhaps a jesting imitation of the philosophy of Hegel, who was very popular in Kierkegaard's day. Kierkegaard considered that the Danish Hegelians of his day did not deserve to be taken seriously. He thought they merely reflected the values of the age; and in particular, they underestimated the importance of individual decisiveness and personal self-examination. Though he may have written in a way that poked fun at the Hegelians, there is no doubt that the claims made here are meant seriously. The opening passage is notoriously complex, but contains fundamental claims that need to be understood.

Nothing Comes Naturally. A human being is not just *soul* as Plato believed, or *thought* as Descartes believed, or *body* as materialists believe. Humans are not bundles of ideas, or souls that can float free of this world, or cogs in a mechanistic, deterministic universe. Instead, a human self is constituted by a constant struggle and activity, which Kierkegaard denotes "spirit."

FROM SØREN KIERKEGAARD, *The Sickness unto Death* (1849), PART I

A human being is spirit. But what is spirit? Spirit is the self. But what is the self? The self is a relation that relates itself to itself or it is that in the relation whereby it relates itself to itself. The self is not the relation but is that whereby the relation relates itself to itself. A human being is a synthesis of the infinite and the finite, of the temporal and the eternal, of freedom and necessity, in short, a synthesis. A synthesis is a relation between two. Considered thus, a human being is still not a self.

This sounds very complicated. But consider just the claim that a human is a synthesis of freedom and necessity. Some of what I am I am necessarily, in a sense that can be illustrated here. For example, my height and eye color, my place of birth and parents, my mortality, my gender are not things I chose nor can I get rid of them, and in that sense are "necessary." On the other hand, some of what I am I am by choice; a married or single person, a baker or candlestick maker, honest or dishonest. This synthesis of necessity and freedom characterizes all people, at all times and all places. But not everyone deserves to be called a "self" (there are, after all, some "nobodies"). So there must be something more to being a self than this invariable synthesis.

ASK YOURSELF

57. Try to imagine what more might be involved in being a self, and state it here.

In the relation between two, the relation is the third as a negative unity, and the two relate to the relation and in the relation to the relation; thus under the qualification "psychical" the relation between the psychical and the physical is a relation. If, however, the relation relates itself to itself, this relation is the positive third, and this is the self.

In a "negative unity" (the term is a piece of Hegelian jargon) the things united lose their independence. Sugar dissolved in water might be an example of a negative unity; the relation between the sugar and the water in the solution is one in which they are no longer apart or independent. It belongs to humans as such to be relations between necessity and freedom, the temporal and eternal; that is, these different dimensions are always interacting and they are what constitutes our "psychical" or psychological makeup. But that interacting can be more or less active or passive. If I drift along, allowing my life to be dictated by its necessities and finitude, without trying to realize anything by choice, I will lack a self. Only when I actively relate what I am by nature (the natural self) to what I might be (call that the "ideal" self) in a "positive" way do I begin to be a self, a somebody. Doing that requires constant attention and struggle as I seek to come closer and closer to some ideal. My actual existing self never can be a complete "merger" with any ideal and cannot be "dissolved" into it. It will always be a "positive" unity of the necessary (that which I am by heredity, for instance) and the possible or ideal (that which I think I ought to be, or would like to be).

ASK YOURSELF

58. Give an example of some ideal that you strive for—that is, something, or some way, you would like to be—and describe how some "necessity" of your life (some natural trait for instance) tends to get in the way of your attempt to achieve that ideal.

Such a relation that relates itself [the natural self] to itself [the ideal self], a self, must either have composed itself [put itself together] or have been composed by another. If the relation that relates itself to itself has been composed by another, then the relation is no doubt the third, but this relation, the third, is yet again a relation and relates itself to that which composed the whole relation. The human self is such a derived, composed relation, a relation that relates itself to itself and in relating itself to itself relates itself to another.

ASK YOURSELF

59. Whom do you suppose the "other" that "composed the whole relation" might be?

Given the constant struggle involved in being a self, despair is also a constant possibility. My necessities and finitude and the pressures of time will tempt me to give up, to relax my effort to become somebody and settle for being a "nobody" more or less, perhaps even a "couch potato," or they may drive me to total frustration and suicide. I may give up "willing to be" myself or may even will to get rid of myself. The latter would normally be considered a form of despair, but a passive apathetic life is also despair on Kierkegaard's view. But he thinks there is another more basic form of despair.

Thus it turns out that there can really be two forms of despair. If a human self had itself composed itself, then there could only be a question of one form: not to will to be oneself, to will to do away with oneself, but there could not be the form: in despair to will to be oneself. This form of despair is in fact the expression for the entire relation's (the self's) dependence, the expression for the fact that the self can not come to equilibrium and peace by itself, but only by relating itself to that which composed the entire relation even as it relates itself to itself.

ASK YOURSELF

60. One form of despair consists of refusing to be oneself. The other form consists of what?

Yes, so far is it from being that case that this second form of despair (the despair of willing to be oneself) merely indicates a particular species of despair, that on the contrary, all despair ultimately can be traced back to it and analyzed into it. If the despairing person is aware of his despair, as he thinks he is, and does not speak meaninglessly of it as of something that is happening to him (somewhat as when one suffering from dizziness speaks in nervous delusion of a weight on his head or of something that has fallen down on him, etc., a weight and a pressure that nevertheless are not something external but a reverse reflection of the internal) and now with all his power seeks to lift the despair by himself and by himself alone—he is still in despair and with all his supposed labor only works himself all the deeper into deeper despair. Despair's misrelation is not a simple misrelation but a misrelation in a relation that relates itself to itself and has been composed by another, so that the misrelation in that relation which is for itself also reflects itself infinitely in the relation to the power that composed it.

Put less abstractly, you cannot succeed in becoming an authentic self without relating yourself to God. So if you are trying to become a lawyer, say, or even trying to become an honest person, then no matter how well you succeed in realizing those ideals, you will still be in despair if you are simply trying to construct a life for yourself apart from the one who put you together in the first place. Kierkegaard goes on to illustrate how the various ideals that we pursue all fail in some way to be worthy of the human task, unless they are taken up into a striving to realize an "ideal ideal" which is, he argues, the ideal of a self "before God."

Accordingly the formula that describes the self's condition when despair is completely rooted out is this: in relating itself to itself and in willing to be itself, the self rests transparently in the power that composed it.

ASK YOURSELF

61. What do you suppose is referred to by "transparently" in this remark? Remember that "transparent" contrasts with "opaque," "obscure," "hard to see through." Remember also that I can fail to be transparent to myself— sometimes I just can't figure myself out!

Despair as a Sign of Value. The task character of human existence, the need to struggle for selfhood, is the distinctive thing about us as humans. But it is also what makes despair possible. A dog does not struggle to be a dog, and it cannot despair over failure to be a dog. A human is always struggling more or less for self-realization. Those who struggle least are, we might say, closest to being dogs. Kierkegaard argues that even though despair is a kind of sickness in the self, indeed a deadly sickness, it nevertheless is a sign of human dignity.

Is despair an advantage or a defect? Purely dialectically, it is both. If one thinks only of despair in the abstract, without thinking of a particular person in despair, it must be regarded as a surpassing advantage. The possibility of this sickness is a man's advantage over the animal, and this advantage distinguishes him in quite another way than does his erect walk, for it indicates the infinite erectness or sublimity, that he is spirit. The possibility of this sickness is a man's advantage over the animal; to be aware of this sickness is the Christian's advantage over the natural man; to be cured of this sickness, the Christian's blessedness.

Consequently, to be able to despair is an infinite advantage, and yet to be in despair is not only the greatest misfortune and misery—no, it is damnation. Generally this is not the case with the relation between possibility and actuality. If it is an advantage to be able "to be" this or that, then it is an even greater advantage to be that; that is to say, "to be" is related like an ascent to "being able to be." With respect to despair, on the other hand, to be is like a descent when compared with being able to be; as infinitely high as the possibility is, so correspondingly low is the actuality. Thus in relation to despair, not to be in despair is the ascending scale. But here again this determination is ambiguous. Not to be in despair is not the same as not being lame, blind, etc. If not being in despair signifies no more than not being in despair, then it means precisely to be in despair. Not to be in despair must signify the active annihilation of the possibility of being able to be in despair; if a person is truly not to be in despair, he must at every moment annihilate the possibility.

ASK YOURSELF

62. Little children generally just live from moment to moment. They do not worry much about whether they are realizing an ideal, leave alone "the" ideal. Does it follow from Kierkegaard's comments above that a little child must be in despair?

Despair Is Everywhere. We normally think of despair as the exception, and would only think of ourselves as being "in despair" when we are feeling terrible or are in particularly bad circumstances. But anyone who is less than completely integrated with the highest ideal is, according to Kierkegaard, in despair.

. . . just as a physician might say that there is perhaps not one single living human being who is completely healthy, so anyone who really knows mankind might say that there is not one single living human being who does not despair a little, in whom, at the deepest level, there dwells an unrest, an inner strife, a disharmony, an anxiety about an unknown something or a something he does not even dare to try to know, an anxiety about some possibility in existence or an anxiety about himself, so that, as the physician speaks of going around with an illness in the body, he walks around with a sickness, carries around a sickness of the spirit that signals its presence at singular moments in and through an unexplained anxiety. In any case, no human being ever lived and no one lives outside of Christendom who has not despaired, and no one in Christendom if he is not a true Christian, and insofar as he is not wholly that, he still is to some extent in despair.

Many people will probably view this observation as a paradox, an overstatement, and also a gloomy and depressing point of view. But it is none of these things. It is not gloomy, for, on the contrary, it seeks to shed light on what generally is left somewhat obscure; it is not depressing but on the contrary is elevating, inasmuch as it views every human being under the determination of the highest claim upon him, to be spirit; nor is it a paradox but, on the contrary, a basic view consistently carried through, and therefore neither is it an overstatement.

ASK YOURSELF

63. Why is the view that nearly everyone is in despair neither (a) somber, (b) depressing, nor (c) an overstatement?

However, the customary view of despair is content with appearances, and thus it is a superficial view, that is, no view at all. It assumes that every man must himself know best whether or not he is in despair. Anyone who says he is, is regarded as being in despair, and anyone who thinks he is not is therefore regarded as not. Consequently the phenomenon of despair is infrequent rather than utterly common. It is not unusual for one to be in despair; no, it is rare, very rare, that one is in truth not in despair.

The vulgar view has a very poor understanding of despair. Among other things, it completely overlooks (to name only this, which, properly understood, places thousands and thousands and millions in the category of despair), it completely overlooks that not being in despair, not being conscious of being in despair, is precisely a form of despair. In a much deeper sense, the vulgar view in relationship to interpreting despair is as it sometimes is in relationship to determining whether a person is sick—in a much deeper sense, for the vulgar view understands far less well what spirit is (and lacking this understanding, one cannot understand despair, either) than it understands sickness and health. Normally one takes a person to be healthy when he himself does not say that he is sick, not to mention when he himself says that he is well. The physician on the other hand views sickness differently. Why? Because the physician has a defined and developed conception of what it is to be healthy and ascertains a man's condition accordingly. The physician knows that just as there is merely imaginary sickness there is also merely imaginary health, and in the latter case he first takes measures to reveal the sickness. Generally the physician, precisely because he is a physician (a well informed one), does not entirely credit what a person says about his own condition. If it were the case that what anyone says about his condition, that he is healthy or sick, or where he feels pain, and so forth, were completely reliable, to be a physician would be a delusion. For a physician has to not merely prescribe remedies but also, first and foremost, to identify the sickness, and again, first and foremost to ascertain whether the supposedly sick person is really sick or whether the supposedly healthy person is perhaps really sick. Such is also the relation of the physician of the soul to despair. He knows what despair is; he recognizes it and therefore is satisfied neither with a person's declaration that he is not in despair nor with his declaration that he is. It must be noted that in a certain sense it is not even always the case that those who say they despair are in despair. Despair can be affected, and as a determination of the spirit it may also be mistaken for and confused with all sorts of transitory states, such as dejection, inner conflict, which pass without turning into despair. But the physician of the soul rightly regards these also as forms of despair; he sees very well that they are affectation—but precisely this affectation is despair: he sees very well that this dejection etc. do not mean much, but precisely this—that it has and acquires no great significance—is despair.

The vulgar view also overlooks that despair is dialectically different from what is usually termed a sickness, because it is a sickness of the spirit. And this dialectic, correctly understood, again brings thousands under the definition of despair. If at a given time a physician has made sure that someone is well, and that person later becomes ill, then the physician may legitimately say that this person *was* healthy at one time, but now on the other had *is* sick. Not so with despair. As soon as despair becomes apparent, it is manifest that the individual was in despair [all along].

Suppose that I despair because I lose my job. Before losing it, everything seemed fine to me, but now everything is gloom and all seems lost. What this shows, according to Kierkegaard, is that I was in despair all along. Why? Because it shows that my idea of living well and being somebody was a function of my having a certain job. But to have such a thought is to fail to understand what it is to be a self, and thus necessarily entails that I have not been a self, and that in turn entails that I have been in despair all along. To despair is to lack a real self.

ASK YOURSELF

64. Does having an important job make a person "somebody"? Could a person who works daily at some menial task be a person of great substance, a real somebody? If so, how? If not, why not?

Hence, at no moment is it possible to decide anything about a person who has not been saved by having been in despair. For when that which causes his despair occurs, in the same moment it becomes evident that he has been in despair his whole life. On the other hand, when someone gets a fever, it can by no means be said that has now become evident that he has had a fever all his life. Despair is a determination of the spirit, is related to the eternal, and thus has something of the eternal in its dialectic.

Despair is not only dialectically different from a sickness, but all its indications are also dialectical, and therefore the superficial view is very easily deceived in determining whether or not despair is present. Not to be in despair can in fact mean precisely to be in despair, and it can mean having been saved from being in despair. Security and tranquillity can signify being in despair; precisely this security and this tranquillity can be the despair, and yet they can signify having overcome despair and having won peace.

ASK YOURSELF

65. When does a sense of security and tranquillity *not* signify despair?

66. Does the person who is in despair, but nonetheless feels secure and tranquil, have as good a grasp of what security and tranquillity really area, as does the person who is not in despair?

[T]he condition of man, regarded as spirit (and if there is to be any question of despair, man must be regarded as under the determination "spirit"), is always critical. In relation to sickness we speak of a crisis but not in relation to health. Why not? Because physical health is an immediate determination that first becomes dialectical in the condition of sickness, in which the question of a crisis arises. But spiritually, or when the human being is regarded as spirit, both health and sickness are critical; there is no immediate health of the spirit.

This claim that "there is no immediate health of spirit" could be rephrased in the following way: *Nothing comes naturally.* In all my activities I am pursuing something which is apart from me, and I could act otherwise. I cannot achieve happiness, contentment, or security by good luck, by having lots of money, by being good looking, all of which are matters of immediacy. What matters is what I *do* with my luck, looks, and so on. Some people make themselves miserable with their money or looks. Others achieve contentment amid poverty and failure. Nothing "works" automatically or "naturally." What matters is how I fashion myself, not what I am "immediately" (i.e., through nature, good luck, momentary feelings, and the like).

ASK YOURSELF

67. What do you think Kierkegaard would say about the claim that people are what they are as a result of heredity and environment? Try to use his vocabulary in answering this.

As soon as man ceases to be regarded under the determination "spirit" (and in that case one cannot speak about despair, either) but only as a psychical-physical synthesis, health is an immediate determination, and mental or physical sickness is the only dialectical determination . . . happiness is not a qualification of spirit, and deep, deep within the most secret hiding place of happiness there dwells also anxiety, which is despair; it very much wishes to be allowed to remain since for despair the most cherished and desirable place to live is in the heart of happiness. . . . For that reason, it is impossible to slip through life on this immediacy. And if this happiness does succeed in slipping through, well, it helps very little, for it is despair. Despair is, precisely because it is totally dialectical, that sickness concerning which it holds that it is the greatest misfortune never to have it: it is a true god send to get it, even if it is the most dangerous of illnesses, when one will not be cured of it.

ASK YOURSELF

68. Why is it the worst misfortune not to have consciously despaired?

There is so much talk about human distress and wretchedness—I try to understand it and have also known something about it firsthand; there is so much talk about wasting a life: but only that person's life was wasted who went on living so deceived by life's joys or its sorrows that he never became decisively and eternally conscious as spirit, as self, or, what amounts to the same thing, never became aware and in the deepest sense never gained the impression that there is a God and that "he," he himself, his self, exists before this God—the infinite profit of which is never gained except through despair. Oh, and this wretchedness that so many go on living this way, cheated of this most blessed of all thoughts, this wretchedness, that we are engrossed in or encourage the human throng to be engrossed in everything else, or use them to supply the energy for the drama of life but never remind them of their blessedness, that we lump them together and cheat them instead of splitting them apart so that each individual may gain the highest, the only thing worth living for and enough to live in for an eternity. I think that I could weep an eternity over the existence of this wretchedness! And to me an even more horrible expression of this most terrible sickness and misery is that it is hidden—not only that the person suffering from it may wish to hide it and may succeed, not only that it can so live in a man that no one, no one detects it, no, but also that it can be so hidden in a man that he himself does not know of it! And when the hourglass has run out, the hourglass of temporality, when the noise of secular life has grown silent and its restless or ineffectual activism has come to an end, when everything is still around you, as it is in eternity, then—whether you were man or woman, rich or poor, dependent or independent, fortunate or unfortunate, whether you ranked with royalty and bore a gleaming crown, or in humble obscurity bore only the toil and heat of the day, whether your name will be remembered as long as the world stands and consequently as long as it stood, or you are nameless and run nameless in the uncountable multitude, whether the magnificence encompassing you surpassed all human description or the most severe and ignominious human judgment befell you—eternity asks you, and every individual in these millions and millions, about only one thing: whether you have lived in despair or not, whether you have despaired in such a way that you did not realize that you were in despair, or whether you bore this sickness secretly in your innermost being, as your gnawing secret, as a fruit of sinful love under your heart, or in such a way that you, a terror to others, raged in despair. And if so, if you lived in despair, then as far as everything else goes, whether you won or lost, everything is lost for you, Eternity knows you not, or, more terrible still, it knows you as you are known, and binds you firmly to yourself in despair.

> **ASK YOURSELF**
>
> **69.** Psychologists, psychiatrists, social workers, and other kinds of counselors are in the business of trying to heal "selves." Do you think Kierkegaard would have much hope that such people might succeed in healing the most fundamental sickness in people? Explain.

2. THE SELF AS WORKER: KARL MARX

Karl Marx was born in Germany in 1818 to a family that had Jewish origins but had converted to Christianity. His father was a lawyer and wished to escape the restrictions on which positions in the legal system could be open to Jews. Marx studied Hegel and received a doctorate in philosophy at the University of Berlin. Like Kierkegaard, Marx was familiar with and affected by Hegel's thought. He reacted against Hegel's notion that history is in some sense "spiritual." Instead Marx contends that it is the material conditions of life that are central to human history. His radical views made it impossible for him to get an academic position, and he became involved in left wing and revolutionary journalism, a career that he pursued in Belgium and Paris and eventually London, where he spent most of the last half of his life (from 1849 on). He was for some time a correspondent for the *New York Tribune*. He died in London in 1883. Marx is usually thought of as the source of communism, which is largely a political conception. But at the root of Marx's concerns was a certain view of a human being as *Homo faber*—that is, a maker or producer. Until we realize ourselves as workers or producers, we will be less than fully human. To use a favorite Marxian term, where work does not play its proper role in our lives, we will remain "alienated" from our own human essence.

The Laborer Under Capitalism. Marx thought that capitalism had the effect of alienating workers from themselves and the product of their labor. Capitalism is an economic system in which the people who own the means of production (machines, land, etc.) are not the people who do the work of producing goods. The owners, the "capitalists," are, in Marxist lingo, the "bourgeoisie" and the workers are the "proletariat." These two classes of people are necessarily in conflict with one another. In fact, the entire history of humanity has been one of conflict between economically determined classes.

ASK YOURSELF

70. Capitalism came to be the dominant form of economic organization in Europe and America in the nineteenth century. Is it still dominant, and, if so, where? Where not, if anywhere?

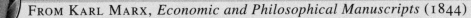

From Karl Marx, *Economic and Philosophical Manuscripts* (1844)

The laws of political economy express the estrangement of the worker in his object. Thus: the more the worker produces, the less he has to consume; the more value he creates, the more valueless, the more unworthy he becomes; the better formed his product, the more deformed becomes the worker; the more civilized his object, the more barbarous becomes the worker; the mightier labor becomes, the more powerless becomes the worker; the more ingenious labor becomes, the duller becomes the worker and the more he becomes nature's bondsman.

In order to appreciate what Marx is claiming here, it would be helpful to think about the typical nineteenth-century factory, say, a woolen mill. In these, thousands of workers repeat dull tasks for long hours, producing enormous value as they do so, but getting only a very small wage. Moreover, the things the laborer produces do not belong to him or her, so the worker is "alienated" from the product of labor. The laborer cannot think of the product as "that which I made and which belongs to me."

Political economy conceals the estrangement inherent in the nature of labor by not considering the direct relationship between the worker (labor) and production. It is true that labor produces for the rich wonderful things—but for the worker it produces privation. It produces palaces—but for the worker, hovels. It produces beauty—but for the worker, deformity. It replaces labor by machines but some of the workers it throws back to a barbarous type of labor, and the other workers it turns into machines. It produces intelligence—but for the worker idiocy, cretinism.

ASK YOURSELF

71. Give an example of labor familiar to you which is meaningless to the worker.

When we ask, then, what is the essential relationship of labor, we are asking about the relationship of the worker to production.

The Worker's Activity Under Capitalism. Workers are alienated from themselves in their work.

Till now we have been considering the estrangement, the alienation of the worker only in one of its aspects, i.e., the worker's relationship to the products of his labor. But the estrangement is manifested not only in the result but in the act of production within the producing activity itself. How would the worker come to face the product of his activity as a stranger, were it not that in the very act of production he was estranging himself from himself? The product is after all but the summary of the activity, of production. If then the product of labor is *alienation,* production itself must be active alienation, the alienation of activity, the activity of alienation. In the estrangement of the object of labor is merely summarized the estrangement, the alienation, in the activity of labor itself.

ASK YOURSELF

72. The worker puts himself, his life, into his work. That is obviously so in the sense that most of his life will be spent either working or "refueling" to work more. Is it so in any other sense? Mention another possible sense.

Many people would agree that a "meaningful life" is one which is spent doing "meaningful work"—that is, work that is valued by the worker for its intrinsic characteristics, not just for how much money it brings in.

ASK YOURSELF

73. Which would you prefer, a job which is meaningful but doesn't produce lots of income, or one which means nothing to you but produces lots of income?

What, then, constitutes the alienation of labor? First, the fact that labor is external to the worker, i.e., it does not belong to his essential being; that in his work, therefore, he does not affirm himself but denies himself, does not feel content but unhappy, does not develop freely his physical and mental energy but mortises his body and ruins his mind. The worker therefore only feels himself outside his work, and in his work feels outside himself. He is at home when he is not working, and when he is working he is not at home. His labor is therefore not voluntary, but coerced; it is forced labor. It is therefore not the satisfaction of a need; it is merely a means to satisfy needs external to it. Its alien character emerges clearly in the fact that as soon as no physical or other compulsion exists, labor is shunned like the plague.

ASK YOURSELF

74. Marx has just mentioned several things that constitute the "alienation" of labor. Mention two of them that seem most important to you.

If the main purpose of life was to engage in sensual pleasures (beer and TV and sex and vacations by the sea), then no one should complain if the only way they can get those things is by working 8 AM to 5 PM five days a week—or a lot longer, in Marx's day. But Marx doesn't think that *is* the main purpose of life.

ASK YOURSELF

75. In Marx's view, you can have a fulfilled life only if when you are at work you also are _____.

External labor, labor in which man alienates himself, is a labor of self-sacrifice, of mortification. Lastly, the external character of labor for the worker appears in the fact that it is not his own, but someone else's, that it does not belong to him, that in it he belongs, not to himself, but to another.

ASK YOURSELF

76. To whom does the worker's labor belong? To whom does the worker himself belong?

Just as in religion the spontaneous activity of the human imagination, of the human brain, and of the human heart operates independently of the individual—that is, operates on him as an alien, divine, or diabolical activity—in the same way the worker's activity is not his spontaneous activity. It belongs to another; it is the loss of his self.

Marx's argument so far is this:

1. I am who I am essentially only in my work.
2. Under capitalism my work belongs to someone else.
3. Therefore, under capitalism, who I essentially am belongs to someone else.
4. Therefore, under capitalism, I am estranged from, alienated from, made a stranger to, my own self.

The Loss of Human Essence in Alienated Labor. In fact what is lost by the proletariat is nothing less than his own humanity.

As a result, therefore, man (the worker) no longer feels himself to be freely active in any but his animal functions—eating, drinking, procreating, or at most in his dwelling and in dressing-up, etc.; and in his human functions he no longer feels himself to be anything but an animal. What is animal becomes human and what is human becomes animal.

These last remarks are at the center of what Marx wants to say. Clearly they amount to a claim about what it is that makes a human a human, rather than a mere animal.

ASK YOURSELF

77. What is the "human function" of people?

Certainly drinking, eating, procreating, etc., are also genuinely human functions. But in the abstraction which separates them from the sphere of all other human activity and turns them into sole and ultimate ends, they are animal. . . .

[Under Capitalism] labor, life-activity, productive life itself, appears to man merely as a means of satisfying a need—the need to maintain the physical existence. Yet the productive life is the life of the species. It is life-engendering life. The whole character of a species—its species character—is contained in the character of its life-activity; and free, conscious activity is man's species character. [Under capitalism] life itself appears only as a means to life.

ASK YOURSELF

78. "Species character" is simply what is characteristic of humans as such, what is essential to us, and common to all, as opposed to what is unique or idiosyncratic. What then is our "species character," according to Marx?

The way in which capitalism robs people of their humanity, their "species character," is analogous to the way in which prostitution does the same thing. The prostitute uses herself, her own life, as a means to life; she "sells herself" in order to live. So does the laborer. And the one who "buys" also becomes degraded.

Prostitution is only a specific expression of the general prostitution of the laborer, and since it is a relationship in which not the prostitute alone, but also the one who [uses the services of] prostitutes, fall[s] and the latter's abomination is still greater—the capitalist, etc., also comes under this head.

Humans are distinguished from mere animals by the fact that they are conscious of their own life and capable of shaping it, or, as in the case of capitalism, misshaping it.

The animal is immediately identical with its life-activity. It does not distinguish itself from it. It is its life-activity. Man makes his life-activity itself the object of his will and of his consciousness. He has conscious life-activity. It is not a determination with which he directly merges. Conscious life-activity directly distinguishes man from animal life-activity. It is just because of this that he is a species being. Or it is only because he is a species being that he is a conscious being, i.e., that his own life is an object for him. Only because of that is his activity free activity. Estranged labor reverses this relationship, so that it is just because man is a conscious being that he makes his life-activity, his essential being, a mere means to his existence.

ASK YOURSELF

79. In the passage just quoted, what shows that Marx is not, in one sense, a determinist?

80. What is it that distinguishes humans from other animals, in Marx's view?

In creating an objective world by his practical activity, in working-up inorganic nature, man proves himself a conscious species being, i.e., as a being that treats the species as its own essential being, or that treats itself as a species being. Admittedly animals also produce. They build themselves nests, dwellings, like the bees, beavers, ants, etc. But an animal only produces what it immediately needs for itself or its young. It produces one-sidedly, while man produces universally. It produces only under the dominion of immediate physical need, while man produces even when he is free from physical need and only truly produces in freedom therefrom. An animal produces only itself, while man reproduces the whole of nature. An animal's product belongs immediately to its physical body, while man freely confronts his product. An animal forms things in accordance with the standard and the need of the species to which it belongs, while man knows how to produce in accordance with the standard of every species, and knows how to apply everywhere the inherent standard to the object. Man therefore also forms things in accordance with the laws of beauty.

ASK YOURSELF

81. Marx's ideal of self-fulfilling labor is becoming clearer. It must be something a person would want to do even if they did not need to work to make a living. Say what you think of that idea.

The Estrangement of People from People. Not only is the worker under capitalism estranged from his product and from himself, he also loses fulfilling relations to other people.

An immediate consequence of the fact that man is estranged from the product of his labor, from his life-activity, from his species being is the estrangement of man from man. If a man is confronted by himself, he is confronted by the other man. What applies to a man's relation to his work, to the product of his labor and to himself, also holds of a man's relation to the other man, and to the other man's labor and object of labor.

In fact, the proposition that man's species nature is estranged from him means that one man is estranged from the other, as each of them is from man's essential nature. The estrangement of man, and in fact every relationship in which man stands to himself, is first realized and expressed in the relationship in which a man stands to other men.

Hence within the relationship of estranged labor each man views the other in accordance with the standard and the position in which he finds himself as a worker.

On the job I don't view you simply as another human being, but as my foreman, my competitor for a raise or a job, and so forth.

Let us now see, further, how in real life the concept of estranged, alienated labor must express and present itself.

If the product of labor is alien to me, if it confronts me as an alien power, to whom, then, does it belong? To a being other than me. Who is this being? The gods? To be sure, in the earliest times the principal production (for example, the building of temples, etc., in Egypt, India, and Mexico) appears to be in the service of the gods, and the product belongs to the gods. However, the gods on their own were never the lords of labor. No more was nature. And what a contradiction it would be if, the more man subjugated nature by his labor and the more the miracles of the gods were rendered superfluous by the miracles of industry, the more man were to renounce the joy of production and the enjoyment of the produce in favor of these powers.

The alien being, to whom labor and the produce of labor belongs, in whose service labor is done and for whose benefit the produce of labor is provided, can only be man himself.

If the product of labor does not belong to the worker, if it confronts him as an alien power, this can only be because it belongs to some other man than the worker. If the worker's activity is a torment to him, to another it must be delight and his life's joy. Not the gods, not nature, but only man himself can be this alien power over man.

ASK YOURSELF

82. The "man" to whom this alien power belongs is of course the _____ .

Wages and Private Property. Genuine human community, the flourishing of genuine humanity, depends upon the abolition of wage systems and the ideals of private property that go with them.

Higher wages . . . would therefore be nothing but better payment for the slave, and would not conquer either for the worker or for labor [his] human status and dignity.

Indeed, even the equality of wages demanded by Proudhon only transforms the relationship of the present-day worker to his labor into the relationship of all men to labor. Society is then conceived as an abstract capitalist.

Wages are a direct consequence of estranged labor, and estranged labor is the direct cause of private property. The downfall of the one aspect must therefore mean the downfall of the other.

Capitalism makes private property possible by ensuring that the wealth produced by labor ends up in the hands of the capitalist, rather than the worker. This is only possible because the capitalist pays the worker a wage, rather than giving him a share in the value of the produced object proportional to the value actually produced by the worker. The capitalist can then use the value that was produced by, but not distributed to, the laborer to amass wealth and private property for his own enjoyment. But the capitalist loses too. The very idea of private property takes everyone, the capitalist included, away from their humanity.

Private property has made us so stupid and one-sided that an object is only ours when we have it—when it exists for us as capital, or when it is directly possessed, eaten, drunk, worn, inhabited, etc.—in short, when it is used by us. Although private property itself again conceives all these direct realizations of possession as means of life, and the life which they serve as means is the life of private property—labor and conversion into capital.

We get things as a means to life. But under capitalism we may fail to understand that "life"—that is, real human life—is not a matter of possessing, but rather a matter of the development of our humanity, which is itself essentially social, depending upon others and meant to exist in productive service to others, and therefore never "private" or furthered by what is private.

Humans Are Essentially Social Beings. We can never flourish and get the best kind of life except by drawing on and being part of a community. Capitalism isolates workers from workers, workers from capitalists, and capitalists from other capitalists. It is thus antithetical to true community, and thus antithetical to the development of true humanity.

What is to be avoided above all is the re-establishing of "Society" as an abstraction vis-a-vis the individual. The individual is the social being. His life, even if it may not appear in the direct form of a communal life carried out together with others, is therefore an expression and confirmation of social life. Man's individual and species life are not different, however much—and this is inevitable—the mode of existence of the individual is a more particular, or more general mode of the life of the species, or the life of the species is a more particular or more general individual life.

But again when I am active scientifically, etc.—when I am engaged in activity which I can seldom perform in direct community with others—then I am social, because I am active as a man. Not only is the material of my activity given to me as a social product (as is even the language in which the thinker is active): my own existence is social activity, and therefore that which I make of myself, I make of myself for society and with the consciousness of myself as a social being.

ASK YOURSELF

83. Name an aspect of "humanity" that could not exist without language.

Our ability to enjoy the world around us, music, the beauties of nature, a good novel, depends upon our social nature.

. . . On the other hand, looking at this in its subjective aspect: just as music alone awakens in man the sense of music, and just as the most beautiful music has no sense for the unmusical ear—is no object for it, because my object can only be the confirmation of one of my essential powers and can therefore only be so for me as my essential power is present for itself as a subjective capacity, because the sense of an object for me goes only so far as my senses go (has only sense for a sense corresponding to that object)—for this reason the senses of the social man are other senses than those of the non-social man. Only through the objectively unfolded richness of man's essential being is the richness of subjective human sensibility (a musical ear, an eye for beauty of form—in short, senses capable of human gratifications, senses confirming themselves as essential powers of man) either cultivated or brought into being. For not only the five senses but also the so-called mental senses—the practical senses (will, love, etc.)—in a word, human sense—the humanness of the senses—comes to be by virtue of its object, by virtue of humanized nature. The forming of the five senses is a labor of humanized nature. The forming of the five senses is a labor of the entire history of the world down to the present.

This last remark is a striking claim, but it is well confirmed by numerous facts. Marx's fore-runner, Hegel, described some of them. The way in which we perceive anything depends upon our training, our socialization. Australian aborigine children can see birds in trees which cannot be seen at all by a perfectly sharp-sighted westerner. It is obvious that what I hear in a piece of music depends upon my training and background, which come to me socially. Many other examples could be given of the way in which my "senses" depend upon my culture or upbringing.

ASK YOURSELF

84. Give an example of the way in which your ability to enjoy something through the senses, such as a painting, or a sunset, depends upon your relation to some other person or other people.

The sense [way of experiencing] caught up in crude practical need has only a restricted sense. For the starving man, it is not the human form of food that exists, but only its abstract being as food; it could just as well be there in its crudest form, and it would be impossible to say wherein this feeding-activity differs from that of animals. The care-burdened man in need has no sense for the finest play; the dealer in minerals sees only the mercantile value but not the beauty and the unique nature of the mineral: he has no mineralogical sense. Thus, the objectification of the human essence both in its theoretical and practical aspects is required to make man's sense human, as well as to create the human sense corresponding to the entire wealth of human and natural substance.

Authentic Communism Is the Solution. According to Marx, authentic communism involves getting rid of wages and private property for the sake of human development, rather than out of resentment and a desire for "leveling." It is the next stage in human development.

Communism as the positive transcendence of private property (as human self-estrangement), and therefore as the real appropriation of the human essence by and for man; communism therefore as the complete return of man to himself as a social (i.e., human) being—a return become conscious, and accomplished within the entire wealth of previous development. This communism, as fully-developed naturalism, equals humanism, and as fully-developed humanism equals naturalism; it is the genuine resolution of the conflict between man and nature and between man and man—the true resolution of the strife between existence and essence, between objectification and self-confirmation, between freedom and necessity, between the individual and the species. Communism is the riddle of history solved, and it knows itself to be this solution.

From the relationship of estranged labor to private property it further follows that the emancipation of society from private property, etc., from servitude, is expressed in the political form of the emancipation of the workers—not because only their emancipation was at stake but because the emancipation of the workers contains universal human emancipation—and it contains this, because the whole of human servitude is involved in the relation of the worker to production, and every relation of servitude is but a modification and consequence of this relation.

ASK YOURSELF

85. To summarize: (a) Capitalism and private property alienate people and are thus opposed to human flourishing. (b) _____ does away with capitalist institutions, and replace them with genuine communal life. (c) Therefore, _____ is the solution to the alienation.

86. Marx is often described as an economic determinist. The way we live and work, think and feel, from day to day, is determined by the movement of economic forces that no individual can control. But there is a sense in which Marx is not a determinist. If you have studied the section on determinism, try to say here in what way Marx is not a determinist.

---

3. THE SELF AS THE WILL TO POWER: FRIEDRICH NIETZSCHE

Friedrich Nietzsche was born in 1844 in Lutzen, now in Germany, at about the time that Marx was 26 years old and Kierkegaard 31. His father, a Lutheran pastor, died while Friedrich was a child, leaving him in the care of his mother, who was the daughter of a Lutheran pastor, and two aunts. Friedrich claimed that the low point in his own physical health came in his thirty-sixth year, a fact that he considered significant since his "incomparable father" had died at the age of 36. Despite the sense of a close connection to his father, he came to completely reject Christianity. In fact, Nietzsche's view of human nature constitutes a rejection of many traditional views. His stress on individuality and the dangers of being absorbed into the herd and losing "practical freedom" is reminiscent of Kierkegaard, but his rejection of all the usual crutches which people lean upon in order to escape responsibility is very radical.

Lack of Will. A central theme in Nietzsche is "the will to power." The healthy person, the aristocrat, does as he wills, not as religion or morality or science or anything else dictates.

FROM FRIEDRICH NIETZSCHE, *The Joyful Wisdom* (1882)

Belief is always most desired, most pressingly needed where there is a lack of will, for the will, as emotion of command, is the distinguishing characteristic of sovereignty and power. That is to say, the less a person knows how to command, the more urgent is his desire for one who commands, who commands sternly—a God, a prince, a caste, a physician, a confessor,

a dogma, a party conscience. From whence perhaps it could be inferred that the two world religions, Buddhism and Christianity, might well have had the cause of their rise, and especially of their rapid extension, in an extraordinary malady of the will. And in truth it has been
so: both religions lighted upon a longing, monstrously exaggerated by malady of the will, for
an imperative, a "Thou shalt," a longing going the length of despair; both religions were
teachers of fanaticism in times of slackness of will power, and thereby offered to innumerable persons a support, a new possibility of exercising will, an enjoyment in willing. For in
fact fanaticism is the sole "volitional strength" to which the weak and irresolute can be
excited, as a sort of hypnotizing of the entire sensory–intellectual system, in favor of the
overabundant nutrition (hypertrophy) of a particular point of view and a particular sentiment,
which then dominates—the Christian calls it his faith. When a man arrives at the fundamental conviction that he requires to be commanded, he becomes "a believer." Reversely, one
could imagine a delight and a power of self determining, and a freedom of will whereby a
spirit could bid farewell to every belief, to every wish for certainty, accustomed as it would
be to support itself on slender cords and possibilities, and to dance even on the verge of
abysses. Such a spirit would be the free spirit par excellence.

Nietzsche wants to affirm that the person who frees herself of religion, morality, and so on,
will not fall into pessimism, despair, or nihilism, but will be affirming of life, joyous, dancing "even on the verge of abysses." But he has a question.

Is This Nihilism? Nietzsche wonders if his own exhortations might lead to "nihilism," the
denial that anything is of any worth.

Our Note of Interrogation. But you don't understand it? As a matter of fact, an effort will be
necessary in order to understand us. We seek for words; we seek perhaps also for ears. Who
are we after all? If we wanted simply to call ourselves in older phraseology, atheists, unbelievers, or even immoralists, we should still be far from thinking ourselves designated
thereby: we are all three in too late a phase for people generally to conceive, for you, my
inquisitive friends, to be able to conceive, what is our state of mind under the circumstances.
No, we have no longer the bitterness and passion of him who has broken loose, who has to
make for himself a belief, a goal, and even a martyrdom out of his unbelief! We have become
saturated with the conviction (and have grown cold and hard in it) that things are not at all
divinely ordered in this world, nor even according to human standards do they go on rationally, mercifully, or justly: we know the fact that the world in which we live is ungodly,
immoral, and "inhuman"; we have far too long interpreted it to ourselves falsely and menda-
ciously, according to the wish and will of our veneration, that is to say, according to our need.
    For man is a venerating animal. But he is also a distrustful animal: and that the world is
not worth what we have believed it to be worth is about the surest thing our distrust has at last
managed to grasp. So much distrust, so much philosophy! We take good care not to say that
the world is of less value; it seems to us at present absolutely ridiculous when man claims to
devise values to surpass the values of the actual world; it is precisely from that point that we
have retraced our steps; as from an extravagant error of human conceit and irrationality,
which for a long period has not been recognized as such. This error had its last expression in
modern Pessimism; an older and stronger manifestation in the teaching of Buddha; but
Christianity also contains it, more dubiously, to be sure, and more ambiguously, but nonetheless seductive on that account. The whole attitude of "man versus the world," man as world-
denying principle, man as the standard of the value of things, as judge of the world, who in

the end puts existence itself on his scales and finds it too light—the monstrous impertinence of this attitude has dawned upon us as such, and has disgusted us—we now laugh when we find, "Man and World" placed beside one another, separated by the sublime presumption of the little word "and." But how is it? Have we not in our very laughing just made a further step in despising mankind? And consequently also in Pessimism, in despising the existence cognizable by us? Have we not just thereby become liable to a suspicion of an opposition between the world in which we have hitherto been at home with our venerations—for the sake of which we perhaps endure life—and another world which we ourselves are: an inexorable, radical, most profound suspicion concerning ourselves, which is continually getting us Europeans more annoyingly into its power, and could easily face the coming generation with the terrible alternative: Either do away with your venerations, or with yourselves! The latter would be Nihilism; but would not the former also be Nihilism? This is our note of interrogation.

ASK YOURSELF

87. By "venerations" Nietzsche means any of those things that we look to to give meaning to our lives. Give one example.

Nietzsche advocates living life willfully, with self-confidence, pride, honest contempt for weakness, respect only for those who respect themselves and are ones equals. He spoke of a coming "Superman" who would embody these ideals. The Superman would live "beyond good and evil."

ASK YOURSELF

88. Discuss in some detail why this ideal of life seems to be inconsistent with both Christianity and morality. Then give your personal opinion of Nietzsche's ideal.

In his book *Thus Spake Zarathustra,* Nietzsche imagines the Persian prophet Zarathustra proposing a new morality appropriate to the "Superman."

FROM FRIEDRICH NIETZSCHE, *Thus Spake Zarathustra* (1883)

3. When Zarathustra arrived at the nearest town which adjoins the forest, he found many people assembled in the market-place; for it had been announced that a rope-dancer would give a performance. And Zarathustra spoke so to the people:

I teach you the Superman. Man is something that is to be surpassed. What have you done to surpass man?

All beings formerly have created something beyond themselves: and you want to be the ebb of that great tide, and would rather go back to the beast than surpass man?

What is the ape to man? A laughing-stock, a thing of shame. And just the same shall man be to the Superman: a laughing-stock, a thing of shame.

You have made your way from the worm to man, and much within you is still worm. Once were you apes, and even yet man is more of an ape than any of the apes.

ASK YOURSELF

89. Nietzsche was very interested in Darwin. What is "Darwinian" in the preceding?

Even the wisest among you is only a disharmony and hybrid of plant and phantom. But do I bid you become phantoms or plants?

Observe, I teach you the Superman!

The Superman is the meaning of the earth. Let your will say: The Superman shall be the meaning of the earth!

I summon you, my brothers, remain true to the earth, and believe not those who speak to you of super-earthly hopes! They are Poisoners, whether they know it or not.

> **ASK YOURSELF**
>
> **90.** What sort of people with what sorts of beliefs are most typically inclined to speak of super-earthly hopes?

They are Despisers of life, decaying ones and poisoned ones themselves, of whom the earth is weary: so away with them!

Once blasphemy against God was the greatest blasphemy; but God died, and then also those blasphemers. To blaspheme the earth is now the dreadfulest sin, and to rate the heart of the unknowable higher than the meaning of the earth!

Once the soul looked contemptuously on the body, and then that contempt was the supreme thing: the soul wished the body meager, ghastly, and famished. So it thought to escape from the body and the earth.

Oh, that soul was itself meager, ghastly, and famished; and cruelty was the delight of that soul!

But you, also, my brothers, tell me: What does your body say about your soul? Is your soul not poverty and pollution and wretched self-complacency?

To be sure, a polluted stream is man. One must be a sea, to receive a polluted stream without becoming impure.

So you see, I teach you the Superman: he is that sea; in him can your great contempt be submerged.

What is the greatest thing you can experience? It is the hour of great contempt. The hour in which even your happiness becomes loathsome to you, and so also your reason and virtue.

The hour when you say: "What good is my happiness! It is poverty and pollution and wretched self-complacency. But my happiness should justify existence itself!"

The hour when you say: "What good is my reason! Does it long for knowledge as the lion for his food? It is poverty and pollution and wretched self-complacency!"

The hour when you say: "What good is my virtue! As yet it has not made me passionate. How weary I am of my good and my bad! It is all poverty and pollution and wretched self-complacency!"

The hour when you say: "What good is my justice! I do not see that I am fervor and fuel. The just, however, are fervor and fuel!"

The hour when you say: "What good is my pity! Is not pity the cross on which he is nailed who loves man? But my pity is not a crucifixion."

Have you ever spoken so? Have you ever cried so? Ah! would that I had heard you crying so!

It is not your sin—it is your self-satisfaction that cries to heaven; your very sparingness in sin cries to heaven!

Where is the lightning to lick you with its tongue? Where is the frenzy with which you should be inoculated?

So you see, I teach you the Superman: he is that lightning, he is that frenzy! When Zarathustra had so spoken, one of the people called out: "We have now heard enough of the rope-dancer; it is time now for us to see him!" And all the people laughed at Zarathustra. But the rope-dancer, who thought the words applied to him, began his performance.

4. Zarathustra, however, looked at the people and wondered. Then he spoke so:

Man is a rope stretched between the animal and the Superman—a rope over an abyss.

A dangerous crossing, a dangerous wayfaring, a dangerous looking-back, a dangerous trembling and halting.

What is great in man is that he is a bridge and not a goal: what is lovable in man is that he is an over-going and a down-going.

I love those that know not how to live except as down-goers, for they are the over-goers.

I love the great despisers, because they are the great adorers, and arrows of longing for the other shore.

I love those who do not first seek a reason beyond the stars for going down and being sacrifices, but sacrifice themselves to the earth, that the earth of the Superman may hereafter arrive.

I love him who lives in order to know, and seeks to know in order that the Superman may hereafter live. So seeks he his own down-going.

ASK YOURSELF

91. Explain Zarathustra's analogy of the rope between animal and Superman.

I love him who labors and invents, that he may build the house for the Superman, and prepare for him earth, animal, and plant: for so seeks he his own down-going.

I love him who loves his virtue: for virtue is the will to down-going, and an arrow of longing.

I love him who reserves no share of spirit for himself, but wants to be wholly the spirit of his virtue: so walks he as spirit over the bridge.

I love him who makes his virtue his inclination and destiny: so, for the sake of his virtue, he is willing to live on, or live no more.

I love him who desires not too many virtues. One virtue is more of a virtue than two, because it is more of a knot for one's destiny to cling to.

I love him whose soul is lavish, who wants no thanks and does not give back: for he always bestows, and does not desire to keep for himself.

I love him who is ashamed when the dice fall in his favor, and who then asks: "Am I a dishonest player?"—for he is willing to succumb.

I love him who scatters golden words in advance of his deeds, and always does more than he promises: for he seeks his own down-going.

I love him who justifies the future ones, and redeems the past ones: for he is willing to succumb through the present ones.

I love him who chastens his God, because he loves his God: for he must succumb through the wrath of his God.

I love him whose soul is deep even in the wounding, and may succumb through a small matter: so goes he willingly over the bridge.

I love him whose soul is so overfull that he forgets himself, and all things are in him: so all things become his down-going.

I love him who is of a free spirit and a free heart: so is his head only the bowels of his heart; his heart, however, causes his down-going.

I love all who are like heavy drops falling one by one out of the dark cloud that lowers over man: they herald the coming of the lightning, and succumb as heralds.

So you see, I am a herald of the lightning, and a heavy drop out of the cloud: the lightning, however, is the Superman.

5. When Zarathustra had spoken these words, he again looked at the people, and was silent. "There they stand," he said to his heart; "there they laugh: they understand me not; I am not the mouth for these ears.

Must one first batter their ears, that they may learn to hear with their eyes? Must one clatter like kettledrums and penitential preachers? Or do they only believe the stammerer?

They have something whereof they are proud. What do they call it, that which makes them proud? Culture, they call it; it distinguishes them from the goatherds.

They dislike, therefore, to hear of "contempt" of themselves. So I will appeal to their pride.

I will speak to them of the most contemptible thing: that, however, is the last man!"

And so spoke Zarathustra to the people:

It is time for man to fix his goal. It is time for man to plant the germ of his highest hope.

Still is his soil rich enough for it. But that soil will one day be poor and exhausted, and no lofty tree will any longer be able to grow thereon.

Alas! there comes the time when man will no longer launch the arrow of his longing beyond man—and the string of his bow will have unlearned to whizz!

I tell you: one must still have chaos in one, to give birth to a dancing star. I tell you: you have still chaos in you.

Alas! There comes the time when man will no longer give birth to any star. Alas! There comes the time of the most despicable man, who can no longer despise himself.

Notice: I show you the last man.

"What is love? What is creation? What is longing? What is a star?"—so asks the last man and blinks.

The earth has then become small, and on it there hops the last man who makes everything small. His species is ineradicable like that of the ground-flea; the last man lives longest.

"We have discovered happiness"—say the last men, and blink thereby.

ASK YOURSELF

92. What, according to Zarathustra, is so contemptible about the last man?

They have left the regions where it is hard to live; for they need warmth. One still loves one's neighbor and rubs against him; for one needs warmth.

Turning ill and being distrustful, they consider sinful: they walk warily. He is a fool who still stumbles over stones or men!

A little poison now and then: that makes pleasant dreams. And much poison at last for a pleasant death.

One still works, for work is a pastime. But one is careful unless the pastime should hurt one.

One no longer becomes poor or rich; both are too burdensome. Who still wants to rule? Who still wants to obey? Both are too burdensome.

No shepherd, and one herd! Everyone wants the same; everyone is equal: those who have other sentiments go voluntarily into the madhouse.

"Formerly all the world was insane," say the subtlest of them, and blink thereby.

They are clever and know all that has happened: so there is no end to their raillery. People still fall out, but are soon reconciled—otherwise it spoils their stomachs.

They have their little pleasures for the day, and their little pleasures for the night, but they have a regard for health.

"We have discovered happiness," say the last men, and blink thereby.

And here ended the first discourse of Zarathustra, which is also called "The Prologue," for at this point the shouting and mirth of the multitude interrupted him. "Give us this last man, O Zarathustra"—they called out—"make us into these last men! Then will we make you a present of the Superman!" And all the people exulted and smacked their lips. Zarathustra, however, turned sad, and said to his heart:

"They didn't understand me: I am not the mouth for these ears.

Too long, perhaps, have I lived in the mountains; too much have I listened to the brooks and trees: now do I speak to them as to the goatherds.

My soul is calm and clear, like the mountains in the morning. But they think I am cold, and a mocker with terrible jests.

And now they look at me and laugh: and while they laugh they hate me too. There is ice in their laughter."

ASK YOURSELF

93. Mention three characteristics of the "last man" and try to say why Nietzsche despises them.

94. Nietzsche has been comparing the "last" man to what "man"?

95. How do the listeners respond to Zarathustra's story about the last man?

4. THE SELF AS BEING TOWARD DEATH: MARTIN HEIDEGGER

Martin Heidegger (1889–1976) taught philosophy at Freiburg University, at Marburg University, and again during the Nazi regime at Freiburg University in Germany. As rector of Freiburg he joined the Nazi party, a fact which has provoked much discussion about the relations, if any, between his philosophical thought and his political loyalties. Heidegger was influenced by Edmund Husserl's "phenomenology," in which an attempt is made to focus strictly on the content of everyday consciousness, of what is simply "given" apart from all philosophical or other kinds of theorizing about that content. Phenomenologically, my shovel appears as "something to dig with" rather than as an object existing independently of my interests which simply appears to the senses as one more object, perhaps having "objective" characteristics which would be the same for all observers. Objective properties would include being constituted by kinds of metal and wood and having a certain color, and those properties are themselves further described in "objective," disinterested scientific theories. Considered in these last ways the shovel is said by Heidegger to be merely "present to hand." Heidegger was influenced by some of Kierkegaard's writings. The selections in this chapter from Kierkegaard's *The Sickness unto Death* would make good preliminary reading for much of what follows. Heidegger's style is not reader friendly. He uses technical terms and coins new terms out of old, or gives a new sense to familiar language. The selections which follow from *Being and Time* (1927) amply exemplify that style.

The Task of a Preparatory Analysis of Dasein. Heidegger raises what he calls the question of "being." This is an "ontological" question (from the Greek term *"ontos"* meaning "being"). Heidegger distinguishes between an entity (things that are) and the being of an entity. We may naturally assume that a stone, say, exists independently of any use we could find for it, and that the "real" stone is the stone which we discover through pure perceptions. But in Heidegger's view, the stone adapted for use as a hammer, say, is ontologically prior to the stone as a mere object. Put otherwise, we might say that the being of an entity is a function of its meaningful status within human experience. An entity is meaningful when it serves some human interest, purpose, or passion. Thus *human* life becomes the crucial focus of Heidegger's work. Being is a matter of "is" (what *x* is, how *x* is, even merely that *x* is). What is distinctive about human being is awareness of being, including its own being. Thus Division I of this major work begins with an account of human being, which he dubs "Dasein" ("being there" in German).

FROM MARTIN HEIDEGGER, *Being and Time* (1927)

We are ourselves the entities to be analyzed. The Being of any such entity is *in each case mine*. . . . *Being* is that which is an issue for every such entity. . . .

The "essence" of this entity lies in its "to be." Its Being-what-it-is (*essentia*) must, so far as we can speak of it at all, be conceived in terms of its *Being (existentia)*. But here our ontological task is to show that when we choose to designate the Being of this entity as "existence," this term does not and cannot have the ontological signification of the traditional term *"existentia"*—ontologically, *existentia* is tantamount to *Being-present-at-hand, a* kind of Being which is essentially inappropriate to entities of Dasein's character. To avoid getting bewildered, we shall always use the Interpretative expression *"presence-at-hand"* for the term *"existential"* while the term "existence," as a designation of Being, will be allotted solely to Dasein.

The "essence" of Dasein lies in its existence. Accordingly those characteristics which can be exhibited in this entity are not "properties" present-at hand of some entity which "looks" so and so and is itself present-at-hand; they are in each case possible ways for it to be, and no more than that. All the Being-as-it-is which this entity possesses is primarily Being. So when we designate this entity with the term "Dasein," we are expressing not its "what" (as if it were a table, house or tree) but its Being.

ASK YOURSELF

96. Would it generally be correct to replace "Dasein" with "the kind of being humans have"?

Look at a soccer ball, then remove all thought of its use to people. Considered apart from possible uses, such a thing appears as "present at hand," a mere object in a world without value. On the other hand, there is a special class of things such that their "properties" are simply possible ways of being. Therefore they do not have any fixed properties. They are capable of being many things, or being in many ways. Humans are like that. I cannot say *what* I am (my *essentia* or essence) without saying what my projects or interests are, and above all by saying what I am trying to become. Perhaps I can say what the ball is, namely a spherical thing filled with air and of a certain color, without bringing in any human purposes. I cannot similarly consider myself as simply a lump of matter without eliminating what is "essential" to human being, to "Dasein." Heidegger employs this term partly to avoid assimilating the notion of a human self to that of other sorts of things. I can have a lion before me, and what it is will be pretty much right there before me, however long I may care to study its behavior or anatomy. I cannot have a human being before me in the same way. This point should become clearer in what follows.

ASK YOURSELF

97. Might a physicist who is studying the physics of my batting swing regard me as merely "present at hand"?

That Being which is an *issue* for this entity in its very Being is in each case mine. Thus Dasein is never to be taken ontologically as an instance or special case of some genus of entities as things that are present-at-hand. To entities such as these, their Being is "a matter of indifference"; or more precisely, they "are" such that their Being can be neither a matter of indifference to them, nor the opposite. Because Dasein has *in each case mineness,* one must always use a *personal* pronoun when one addresses it: "I am," "you are."

Furthermore, in each case Dasein is mine to be in one way or another. Dasein has always made some sort of decision as to the way in which it is in each case mine. That entity which in its Being has this very Being as an issue comports itself towards its Being as its ownmost possibility. In each case Dasein *is* its possibility, and it "has" this possibility, but not just as a property, as something present-at-hand would. And because Dasein is in each case essentially its own possibility, it *can,* in its very Being, "choose" itself and win itself; it can also lose itself and never win itself; or only "seem" to do so. But only insofar as it is essentially something which can *be authentic*—that is, something of its own—can it have lost itself and not yet won itself. As modes of Being, *authenticity and inauthenticity* (these expressions have been chosen terminologically in a strict sense) are both grounded in the fact that any Dasein whatsoever is characterized by mineness. But the inauthenticity of Dasein does not signify any "less" Being or any "lower" degree of Being. Rather it is the case that even in its fullest concretion Dasein can be characterized by inauthenticity—when busy, when excited, when interested, when ready for enjoyment. The two characteristics of Dasein which we have sketched—the priority *of "existentia"* over *essentia* and the fact that Dasein is in each case mine—have already indicated that in the analytic of this entity we are facing a peculiar phenomenal domain.

Dasein, human existence, is always the existence of an individual who is concerned about his or her existence, it is existence of a type that is aware of itself as a "me" capable of becoming or of change, and such that not all possible outcomes of living are equally authentic. Heidegger's account of human existence is similar to Kierkegaard's, for both stress the need to struggle in order to win oneself, or to win a "self" at all.

ASK YOURSELF

98. The word "existence" (*existentia*), which is reserved for Dasein, means, etymologically, "to stand forth" or "reach forward." How is that term thus appropriate for an understanding of humans in particular?

At the outset of our analysis it is particularly important that Dasein should not be interpreted with the differentiated character of some definite way of existing, but that it should be uncovered in the undifferentiated character which it has proximally and for the most part. This undifferentiated character of Dasein's everydayness is *not nothing,* but a positive phenomenal characteristic of this entity. Out of this kind of Being-and back into it again-is all existing, such as it is. We call this everyday undifferentiated character of Dasein *"averageness."* . . .

To illustrate: If I consider Dasein in terms of some "definite way of existing" such as that exhibited by a holy person, or a rich person, then I have construed it as concrete, rather than as a kind of being which is "defined" by possibility. Any ordinary person is at any moment undefined, undifferentiated, able to be many things and many ways, in a way that, for instance, no mouse or camel is. Nonetheless, each human must strive for some definite ideal; otherwise he or she will be "neither this nor that"—that is, "average."

The Basic State of Dasein. An understanding of Dasein requires the recognition that it is "in-a-world." Dasein's engagement with various possibilities is not an engagement with one possibility at a time, so to speak. Rather every focus of attention affects all other possibilities, organizes them, we might say, in a certain way.

Dasein's facticity is such that its Being-in-the-world has always dispersed itself or even split itself up into definite ways of Being-in. The multiplicity of these is indicated by the following examples: having to do with something, producing something, attending to something and looking after it, making use of something, giving something up and letting it go, undertaking, accomplishing, evincing, interrogating, considering, discussing, determining. . . . All these ways of Being-in have *concern* as their kind of Being—a kind of Being which we have yet to characterize in detail. Leaving undone, neglecting, renouncing, taking a rest—these too are ways of concern; but these are all *deficient* modes, in which the possibilities of concern are kept to a "bare minimum." . . .

Being-in-the-world is a way of being in which the subject is engaged, acting, interested. So if I am producing a piece of furniture, then everything around me stands out or recedes in a certain way. Woodworking tools stand out, the color of my shop door does not. I am "concerned" with the tools, not "concerned" with the color of the door.

ASK YOURSELF

99. What might Heidegger say about the mode of being in the world exemplified by a couch potato—that is, someone who is hardly engaged in anything whatsoever, but is almost entirely passive? Note the last sentence in the previous section.

The Worldhood of the World. Heidegger acknowledges various uses of "world," but for his analysis of Dasein as "being in the world" the following are especially significant.

"World" functions as an ontological term, and signifies the Being of those entities which we have just mentioned [i.e., Dasein]. And indeed "world" can become a term for any realm which encompasses a multiplicity of entities: for instance, when one talks of the "world" of a mathematician, "world" signifies the realm of possible objects of mathematics.

"World" can be understood in another ontical sense—not, however, as those entities which Dasein essentially is not and which can be encountered within-the-world, but rather as that *"wherein"* a factical Dasein as such can be said to "live." "World" has here a pre-ontological existentiell signification, Here again there are different possibilities: "world" may stand for the "public" we-world, or one's "own" closest (domestic) environment. . . .

The Being of those entities which we encounter as closest to us can be exhibited phenomenologically if we take as our clue our everyday Being-in-the-world, which we also call our *"dealings" in* the world and *with* entities within-the-world. Such dealings have already dispersed themselves into manifold ways of concern. The kind of dealing which is closest to us is, as we have shown, not a bare perceptual cognition, but rather that kind of concern which manipulates things and puts them to use; and this has its own kind of "knowledge." The phenomenological question applies in the first instance to the Being of those entities which we encounter in such concern. . . .

We shall call those entities which we encounter in concern *"equipment."* *In* our dealings we come across equipment for writing, sewing, working, transportation, measurement. The kind of Being which equipment possesses must be exhibited. The clue for doing this lies in our first defining what makes an item of equipment—namely, its equipmentality.

Taken strictly, there "is" no such thing as an equipment. To the Being of any equipment there always belongs a totality of equipment, in which it can be this equipment that it is. Equipment is essentially "something in-order-to." . . . A totality of equipment is constituted by various ways of the "in-order-to," such as serviceability, conduciveness, usability, manipulability.

In the "in-order-to" as a structure there lies an *assignment or reference of* something to something. Only in the analyses which are to follow can the phenomenon which this term 'assignment' indicates be made visible in its ontological genesis. Provisionally, it is enough to take a look phenomenally at a manifold of such assignments. Equipment—in accordance with its equipmentality—always is *in terms of* its belonging to other equipment: inkstand, pen, ink, paper, blotting pad, table, lamp, furniture, windows, doors, room. These "Things" never show themselves proximally as they are for themselves, so as to add up to a sum of *realia* and fill up a room.

A table is a table for something (for writing on, eating at, sitting around in gatherings) and is thus presented to consciousness in connection with other things such as tableware and meetings, rather than as a single isolated object perceived by the senses. It exists "in order to."

What we encounter as closest to us (though not as something taken as a theme) is the room; and we encounter it not as something "between four walls" in a geometrical spatial sense, but as equipment for residing. Out of this the "arrangement" emerges, and it is in this that any "individual" item of equipment shows itself. *Before* it does so, a totality of equipment has already been discovered.

Equipment can genuinely show itself only in dealings cut to its own measure (hammering with a hammer, for example); but in such dealings an entity of this kind is not *grasped* thematically as an occurring Thing, nor is the equipment-structure known as such even in the using. The hammering does not simply have knowledge about the hammer's character as equipment, but it has appropriated this equipment in a way which could not possibly be more suitable. In dealings such as this, where something is put to use, our concern subordinates itself to the "in-order-to" which is constitutive for the equipment we are employing at the time;

the less we just stare at the hammer-Thing, and the more we seize hold of it and use it, the more primordial does our relationship to it become, and the more unveiledly is it encountered as that which it is—as equipment.

We may tend to think of the world as the totality of objects in it and of human interests as being secondary impositions or interpretations placed upon that world. We may tend to think of the world as existing independently of humans. That tendency must be eradicated in order to come to an understanding of *being*.

ASK YOURSELF

100. If I encounter a ball simply as spherical and green, would that be a more "primordial" (basic) way of encountering it than if I encountered it as a soccer ball, on Heidegger's account?

In equipment that is used, "Nature" is discovered along with it by that use—the "Nature" we find in natural products.

Here, however, "Nature" is not to be understood as that which is just present-at-hand, nor as the *power of Nature*. The wood is a forest of timber, the mountain a quarry of rock; the river is water-power, the wind is wind "in the sails." As the "environment" is discovered, the "Nature" thus discovered is encountered too. If its kind of Being as ready-to-hand is disregarded, this "Nature" itself can be discovered and defined simply in its pure presence-at-hand. But when this happens, the Nature which "stirs and strives," which assails us and enthralls us as landscape, remains hidden. The botanist's plants are not the flowers of the hedgerow; the "source" which the geographer establishes for a river is not the "springhead in the dale."

Heidegger is arguing that even natural objects are understood first of all (most "primordially") in relationship to human interests and aims. At the same time, if we try to understand the world apart from all interests, as merely "objects with properties," we will miss out on other characteristics such as those revealed in poetry.

ASK YOURSELF

101. If I ignore the beauty of a flower, I may be treating nature as simply part of the _____ _____ _____, rather than as something that moves and stirs me, apart from any use I can make of it.

. . . To lay bare what is just present-at-hand and no more, cognition must first penetrate *beyond* what is ready-to-hand in our concern. *Readiness-to-hand is the way in which entities as they are "in themselves" are defined ontologicocategorially.* . . .

This and previous claims have a strong "pragmatist" flavor to them. Very roughly, pragmatists argued that reality and truth are functions of use, of human action in the world. That view seems to conflict with the common sense notion that what is real and what is true is so quite apart from humans. For example, if the earth rotates around the sun, then that is real and true, whether or not any human knows it or even thinks about it.

Being-in-the-World as Being-with and Being-One's-Self. Our being in the world has so far been characterized in terms of our purposes and uses, so the stress has been on "equipment." But there is another aspect of being in the world which is distinctive, namely the fact that in the world we are with others.

Dasein is an entity which is in each case I myself; its Being is in each case mine. This definition *indicates an ontologically* constitutive state, but it does no more than indicate it. At the same time this tells us *ontically* (though in a rough and ready fashion) that in each case an "I"—not Others—is this entity. The question of the "who" answers itself in terms of the "I" itself, the "subject," the "Self." . . .

The assertion that it is I who in each case Dasein is, is ontically obvious; but this must not mislead us into supposing that the route for an ontological Interpretation of what is "given" in this way has thus been unmistakably prescribed. Indeed it remains questionable whether even the mere ontical content of the above assertion does proper justice to the stock of phenomena belonging to everyday Dasein. It could be that the "who" of everyday Dasein just is *not* the "I myself". . . .

The kind of "giving" we have [in the direct givenness of the "I"] . . . is the mere, formal, reflective awareness of the "I"; and perhaps what it gives is indeed evident. This insight even affords access to a phenomenological problematic in its own right, which has in principle the signification of providing a framework as a "formal phenomenology of consciousness." . . .

But if the Self is conceived "only" as a way of Being of this entity, this seems tantamount to volatilizing the real "core" of Dasein. Any apprehensiveness however which one may have about this gets its nourishment from the perverse assumption that the entity in question has at bottom the kind of Being which belongs to something present-at-hand, even if one is far from attributing to it the solidity of an occurrent corporeal Thing. Yet man's *"substance"* is not spirit as a synthesis of soul and body; it is rather *existence.*

Heidegger is attacking certain views about what constitutes the "I" and what can be known about it. Descartes in particular comes to mind as one who held that the "I" is directly given, and that the "I" in question is a thinking or mental thing. It is worth noting that the last sentence quoted is completely consistent with Kierkegaard's notion of the self as "spirit," since he denied that the self is a synthesis of body and soul, and reserved the term "spirit" for "existing" or "reaching-out" beings.

> ### ASK YOURSELF
>
> **102.** Descartes thought that the "substance" of the self is an entirely nonphysical "thinking," a non-extended thing that engages in mental activities or has mental experiences. Heidegger denies this. Does he then assert that human selves are simply bodies?

Our dealings in the world are always at least implicitly dealings with others. One of the problems generated by Descartes' account of the self was the "problem of other minds." How could I even know there are other thinking things, since I only have access to my *own* thoughts? But according to Heidegger, my relation to others is just as primordial or basic as my relation to myself.

The answer to the question of the "who" of everyday Dasein is to be obtained by analyzing that kind of Being in which Dasein maintains itself proximally and for the most part. Our investigation takes its orientation from Being-in-the-world—that basic state of Dasein by which every mode of its Being gets co-determined. If we are correct in saying that by the foregoing explication of the world, the remaining structural items of Being-in-the-world have become visible, then this must also have prepared us, in a way, for answering the question of the "who."

In our "description" of that environment which is closest to us—the work world of the craftsman, for example—the outcome was that along with the equipment to be found when one is at work, those Others for whom the "work" is destined are "encountered too." If this is ready-to-hand, then there lies in the kind of Being which belongs to it (that is, in its involvement) an essential assignment or reference to possible wearers, for instance, for whom it should be "cut to the figure." Similarly, when material is put to use, we encounter its producer or "supplier" as one who "serves" well or badly. When, for example, we walk along the edge of a field but "outside it," the field shows itself as belonging to such-and-such a person, and decently kept up by him; the book we have used was bought at so-and-so's shop and given by such-and-such a person, and so forth. The boat anchored at the shore is assigned in its Being-in-itself to an acquaintance who undertakes voyages with it; but even if it is a "boat which is strange to us," it still is indicative of Others. The Others who are thus "encountered" in a ready-to-hand, environmental context of equipment, are not somehow added on in thought to some Thing which is proximally just present-at-hand; such "Things" are encountered from out of the world in which they are ready-to-hand for Others—a world which is always mine too in advance. . . .

By "Others" we do not mean everyone else but me—those over against whom the "I" stands out. They are rather those from whom, for the most part, one does not distinguish oneself—those among whom one is too. . . . The world of Dasein is a *with-world*. Being-in is *Being-with* Others. Their Being-in-themselves within-the-world is *Dasein-with*. . . .

> ### ASK YOURSELF
>
> **103.** Human being is in itself a being with others. There is no other kind of human being. If Heidegger is right, would "individualism" be impossible? Define individualism before you answer.

. . . We must hold fast to the phenomenal facts of the case which we have pointed out, namely, that Others are encountered *environmentally. This* elemental worldly kind of encountering, which belongs to Dasein and is closest to it, goes so far that even one's *own* Dasein becomes something that it can itself proximally "come across" only when it *looks away* from 'Experiences' and the "center of its actions," or does not as yet "see" them at all. Dasein finds "itself" proximally in *what* it does, uses, expects, avoids-in those things environmentally ready-to-hand with which it is proximally *concerned*. . . .

Being-with is such that the disclosedness of the Dasein-with of Others belongs to it; this means that because Dasein's Being is Being-with, its understanding of Being already implies the understanding of Others. This understanding, like any understanding, is not an acquaintance derived from knowledge about them, but a primordially existential kind of Being, which, more than anything else, makes such knowledge and acquaintance possible. Knowing oneself is grounded in Being-with, which understands primordially. . . .

One's own Dasein, like the Dasein-with of Others, is encountered proximally and for the most part in terms of the with-world with which we are environmentally concerned. When Dasein is absorbed in the world of its concern—that is, at the same time, in its Being-with towards Others—it is not itself. Who is it, then, who has taken over Being as everyday Being-with one-another?

The They. If it is essential to the kind of being human beings have that they be in the world *with others*, then might it not be the case that my life will be dictated by whatever fads and fancies the majority happen to favor? Must I be a conformist? Will my life be absorbed into theirs? This question directs us to the "who" of the "others" that I am with.

In one's concern with what one has taken hold of, whether with, for, or against, the Others, there is constant care as to the way one differs from them, whether that difference is merely one that is to be evened out, whether one's own Dasein has lagged behind the Others and wants to catch up in relationship to them, or whether one's Dasein already has some priority over them and sets out to keep them suppressed. The care about this distance between them is disturbing to Being-with-one-another, though this disturbance is one that is hidden from it. If we may express this existentially, such Being-with-one-another has the character of *distantiality*. The more inconspicuous this kind of Being is to everyday Dasein itself, all the more stubbornly and primordially does it work itself out.

But this distantiality which belongs to Being-with, is such that Dasein, as everyday Being-with-one-another, stands in *subjection* to Others. It itself *is* not; its Being has been taken away by the Others. Dasein's everyday possibilities of Being are for the Others to dispose of as they please. These Others, moreover, are not *definite* Others. On the contrary, any Other can represent them. What is decisive is just that inconspicuous domination by Others which has already been taken over unawares from Dasein as Being-with. One belongs to the Others oneself and enhances their power. "The Others" whom one thus designates in order to cover up the fact of one's belonging to them essentially oneself, are those who proximally and for the most part *"are there"* in everyday Being-with-one-another. The "who" is not this one, not that one, not oneself, not some people, and not the sum of them all. The "who" is the neuter, *the "they."* . . .

We take pleasure and enjoy ourselves as *they* take pleasure; we read, see, and judge about literature and art as *they* see and judge; likewise we shrink back from the "great mass" as *they* shrink back; we find "shocking" what *they* find shocking. The "they," which is nothing definite, and which all are, though not as the sum, prescribes the kind of Being of everydayness.

> **ASK YOURSELF**
>
> **104.** In our thinking and acting we tend to be absorbed into the thinking and acting of the "they." We tend to be conformists through and through. Give an example from you own life of being absorbed in "the they." Anything "conformist" will do.

Falling. Heidegger is expressing a theme common to much existentialist literature, the theme of the "mass man," or what Nietzsche called "the herd." To be nothing but a member of the herd is to be fallen. According to Heidegger, this "fallen" condition is in a sense inevitable.

This term does not express any negative evaluation, but is used to signify that Dasein is proximally and for the most part *alongside* the "world" of its concern. This "absorption in . . ." has mostly the character of Being-lost in the publicness of the "they." Dasein has, in the first instance, fallen away from itself as an authentic potentiality for Being its Self, and has fallen into the "world." "Fallenness" into the "world" means an absorption in Being-with-one-another, insofar as the latter is guided by idle talk, curiosity, and ambiguity. Through the Interpretation of falling, what we have called the "inauthenticity" of Dasein may now be defined more precisely. On no account, however, do the terms "inauthentic" and "non-authentic" signify "really not," as if in this mode of Being, Dasein were altogether to lose its Being. "Inauthenticity" does not mean anything like Being-no-longer-in-the-world, but amounts rather to a quite distinctive kind of Being-in-the-world—the kind which is completely fascinated by the "world" and by the Dasein-with of Others in the "they.". . .

Dasein, tranquillized, and "understanding" everything . . . drifts along towards an alienation in which its own-most potentiality-for-Being is hidden from it. Falling Being-in-the-world is not only tempting and tranquillizing; it is at the same time *alienating*. . . .

The alienation of falling—at once tempting and tranquillizing—leads by its own movement, to Dasein's getting *entangled in* itself.

The phenomena we have pointed out—temptation, tranquillizing, alienation and self-entangling (entanglement)—characterize the specific kind of Being which belongs to falling. This "movement" of Dasein in its own Being, we call its *"downward plunge."*

. . . In falling, nothing other than our potentiality-for-Being-in-world is the issue, even if in the mode of inauthenticity. Dasein *can* fall only *because* Being-in-the-world understandingly with a state-of-mind is an issue for it. On the other hand, *authentic* existence is not something which floats above falling everydayness; existentially, it is only a modified way in which such everydayness is seized upon.

The phenomenon of falling does not give us something like a "night view" of Dasein, a property which occurs ontically and may serve to round out the innocuous aspects of this entity. Falling reveals an *essential* ontological structure of Dasein itself. . . .

If falling is an "essential ontological structure of Dasein," then it appears that no one can avoid it. No one completely resists the tendency to fall into "idle chatter" for instance. We are not thereby condemned to inauthenticity, however, provided that we face up to the character of our being in the world. We must then discover a "modified way" in which everyday life with others is lived. But to do so brings to the surface the care and anxiety that always characterize Dasein.

Care and Anxiety as the Being of Dasein. Anxiety is not something that a few people feel now and then—for example, when the stock market falls or war breaks out. Rather, anxiety is essential to the very structure of Dasein's being in the world.

That in the face of which one has anxiety is Being-in-the-world as such. What is the difference phenomenally between that in the face of which anxiety is anxious and that in the face of which fear is afraid? That in the face of which one has anxiety is not an entity within-the-world. Thus it is essentially incapable of having an involvement. . . . That in the face of which one is anxious is completely indefinite. Not only does this indefiniteness leave tactically undecided which entity within-the-world is threatening us, but it also tells us that entities within-the-world are not "relevant" at all. Nothing which is ready-to-hand or present-at-hand within the world functions as that in the face of which anxiety is anxious. . . .

ASK YOURSELF

105. Heidegger apparently means by "anxiety" a condition of general uneasiness. Thus, if I am anxious about something specific, such as whether I will get an "A" in a course, that is not the sort of anxiety he has in mind. Anxiety according to him has no definite _____.

Nonetheless, specific anxieties may be symptomatic of a deeper condition.

In that in the face of which one has anxiety, the "It is nothing and nowhere" becomes manifest. The obstinacy of the "nothing and nowhere within-the-world" means as a phenomenon that *the world as such is that in the face of which one has anxiety.* The utter insignificance which makes itself known in the "nothing and nowhere," does not signify that the world is absent, but tells us that entities within-the-world are of so little importance in themselves that on the basis of this *insignificance* of what is within-the-world, the world in its worldhood is all that still obtrudes itself.

What oppresses us is not this or that, nor is it the summation of everything present-at-hand; it is rather the *possibility* of the ready-to-hand in general; that is to say, it is the world itself. When anxiety has subsided, then in our everyday way of talking we are accustomed to say that "it was really nothing." . . . If the "nothing"—that is, the world as such—exhibits itself as that in the face of which one has anxiety, this means that *Being-in-the-world itself is that in the face of which anxiety is anxious.* . . .

Anxiety is not only anxiety in the face of something, but, as a state-of-mind, it is also *anxiety about* something. That which anxiety is profoundly anxious about is not a *definite* kind of Being for Dasein or a *definite* possibility for it. Indeed the threat itself is indefinite, and therefore cannot penetrate threateningly to this or that factically concrete potentiality-for-Being. That which anxiety is anxious about is Being-in-the-world itself.

Anxious feelings are often indefinite. We do not know exactly what is making us anxious. Heidegger claims that it is our very situation as beings that are not fixed by nature but must live in the face of possibilities, which explains anxiety.

ASK YOURSELF

106. Why would a sense that my life is essentially open to all sorts of possibilities make me anxious? You can answer this question by thinking about how you would feel if you knew for certain that you must become a lawyer, as compared to how you would feel if you thought it were possible that you might become a doctor, an engineer, or a homeless drunk and there are no guarantees about your future.

Anxiety is uncomfortable precisely because it amounts to a heightened awareness of possibility, of the unfixed character of my "world" and myself. But that awareness also tears me away from the "they." The "they," the sense that I am with others and like them, provides a sense of security. Anxiety tears me away from that comfort. But at the same time it can open the way toward genuine individuality.

ASK YOURSELF

107. Would Heidegger think of the authentic individual, the one who has become conscious of the "unfixed" or "unanchored" character of human life, as an "individualist" who will have nothing to do with communal norms and ways of life?

Dasein and Temporality. Heidegger believes that there is nothing beyond death. We are finite beings. Death is not one possibility among others for such beings but the possibility of the end of possibility, the end of that particular way of being in the world in which one is concerned about realizing this or that future possibility. And since, unlike most of what concerns us, death cannot be shared, it can set each individual apart from the "they" definitively.

With death, Dasein stands before itself in its ownmost potentiality-for-Being. This is a possibility in which the issue is nothing less than Dasein's Being-in-the-world. Its death is the possibility of no-longer being-able-to-be-there. If Dasein stands before itself as this possibility, it has been fully assigned to its ownmost potentiality-for-Being. When it stands before itself in this way, all its relations to any other Dasein have been undone. This ownmost non-relational possibility is at the same time the uttermost one.

As potentiality-for-Being, Dasein cannot outstrip the possibility of death. Death is the possibility of the absolute impossibility of Dasein. Thus death reveals itself as that *possibility which is one's ownmost, which is nonrelational, and which is not to be outstripped.* As such, death is something *distinctively* impending. Its existential possibility is based on the fact that Dasein is essentially disclosed to itself, and disclosed, indeed, as ahead-of-itself. This item in the structure of care has its most primordial concretion in Being-towards-death. As a phenomenon, Being-towards-the-end becomes plainer as Being towards that distinctive possibility of Dasein which we have characterized. . . .

ASK YOURSELF

108. In saying that in death Dasein is disclosed to itself as ahead of itself, is Heidegger in effect claiming that human beings are temporal beings in a way that dogs, for instance, are not? Would it make sense to say that a dog is "ahead of itself"? What does it mean to say that of a human? In your answer give an example of what it means for a human.

Being-Toward-Death and the Everydayness of Dasein. The refusal to face our own individual deaths serves to conceal the true character of Dasein. One form of that refusal shows itself in the way we generalize about death. "Everyone has to die sometime" we say. But we do not really think "I" must die sometime. The following passage evokes Tolstoy's story "The Death of Ivan Illich," a story which Heidegger acknowledged as an important source for his own thinking. In that story Illich, who is terminally ill, has difficulty realizing that *he* is going to die, though in an abstract way he knows that all die and he is one of the all.

. . . The analysis of the phrase "one dies" reveals unambiguously the kind of Being which belongs to everyday Being-towards-death. In such a way of talking, death is understood as an indefinite something which, above all, must duly arrive from somewhere or other, but which is proximally *not yet present-at-hand* for oneself, and is therefore no threat. The expression "one dies" spreads abroad the opinion that what gets reached, as it were, by death, is the "they." In Dasein's public way of interpreting, it is said that "one dies," because everyone else and oneself can talk himself into saying that "in no case is it I myself," for this "one" is *the "nobody."* "Dying" is levelled off to an occurrence which reaches Dasein, to be sure, but belongs to nobody in particular. If idle talk is always ambiguous, so is this manner of talking about death. Dying, which is essentially mine in such a way that no one can be my representative, is perverted into an event of public occurrence which the "they" encounters. In the way of talking which we have characterized, death is spoken of as a "case" which is constantly occurring. Death gets passed off as always something "actual"; its character as a possibility gets concealed, and so are the other two items that belong to it-the fact that it is non-relational and that it is not to be outstripped. By such ambiguity, Dasein puts itself in the position of losing itself in the "they" as regards a distinctive potentiality-for-Being which belongs to Dasein's ownmost Self. The "they" gives its approval, and aggravates the *temptation* to cover up from oneself one's ownmost Being-towards-death. This evasive concealment in the face of death dominates everydayness so stubbornly that, in Being with one another, the "neighbors" often still keep talking the "dying person" into the belief that he will escape death and soon return to the tranquillized everydayness of the world of his concern. Such "solicitude" is meant to "console" him. It insists upon bringing him back into Dasein, while in addition it helps him to keep his ownmost non-relational possibility-of-Being completely concealed. In this manner the "they" provides *a constant tranquillization about death.* At bottom, however, this is a tranquillization not only for him who is "dying" but just as much for those who "console" him. And even in the case of a demise, the public is still not to have its own tranquillity upset by such an event, or be disturbed in the carefreeness with which it concerns itself. Indeed the dying of Others is seen often enough as a social inconvenience, if not even a downright tactlessness, against which the public is to be guarded. . . .

But along with this tranquillization, which forces Dasein away from its death, the "they" at the same time puts itself in the right and makes itself respectable by tacitly regulating the way in which *one* has to comport oneself towards death. It is already a matter of public acceptance that "thinking about death" is a cowardly fear, a sign of insecurity on the part of Dasein, and a somber way of fleeing from the world. *The "they" does not permit us the courage for anxiety in the face of death.* The dominance of the manner in which things have been publicly interpreted by the "they," has already decided what state-of-mind is to determine our attitude towards death. In anxiety in the face of death, Dasein is brought face to face with itself as delivered over to that possibility which is not to be outstripped. The "they" concerns itself with transforming this anxiety into fear in the face of an oncoming event.

ASK YOURSELF

109. Once again, what is one fundamental difference between fear and anxiety? And, which one is more revealing of the nature of human existence (Dasein)?

Factically one's own Dasein is always dying already; that is to say, it is in a Being-towards-its-end. And it hides this Fact from itself by re-coining "death" as just a "case of death" in Others—an everyday occurrence which, if need be, gives us the assurance still more plainly that "oneself" is still "living." But in thus falling and fleeing *in the face of* death, Dasein's everydayness attests that the very "they" itself already has the definite character of *Being-towards-death,* even when it is not explicitly engaged in "thinking about death."

Being-towards-death is the anticipation of a potentiality-for-Being of that entity whose kind of Being is anticipation itself. In the anticipatory revealing of this potentiality-for-Being, Dasein discloses itself to itself as regards its uttermost possibility. But to project itself on its ownmost potentiality-for-Being means to be able to understand itself in the Being of the entity so revealed-namely, to exist. Anticipation turns out to be the possibility of understanding one's *ownmost* and uttermost potentiality-for Being-that is to say, the possibility of *authentic existence.* The ontological constitution of such existence must be made visible by setting forth the concrete structure of anticipation of death. How are we to delimit this structure phenomenally? Manifestly, we must do so by determining those characteristics which must belong to an anticipatory disclosure so that it can become the pure understanding of that ownmost possibility which is non-relational and not to be outstripped—which is certain and, as such, indefinite. It must be noted that understanding does not primarily mean just gazing at a meaning, but rather understanding oneself in that potentiality-for-Being which reveals itself in projection.

Death is Dasein's *ownmost* possibility. Being towards this possibility discloses to Dasein its *ownmost* potentiality-for-Being, in which its very Being is the issue. Here it can become manifest to Dasein that in this distinctive possibility of its own self, it has been wrenched away from the "they.". . .

We may now summarize our characterization of authentic Being-towards-death as we have projected it existentially: *anticipation reveals to Dasein its lostness* in *the they-self, and brings it face to face with the possibility of being itself, primarily unsupported by concernful solicitude, but of being itself, rather in an impassioned* freedom towards *death—a freedom which has been released from the Illusions of the they, and which is factical, certain of itself, and anxious.* . . . [Heidegger's emphasis]

Authenticity and Resoluteness. The reader may have begun to wonder whether Heidegger's analysis of Dasein has any ethical import. Does it imply that certain behaviors and attitudes are definitely better than others? The analysis of falleness and the "they-self" certainly carries negative connotations, despite Heidegger's insistence that they are invariant features of Dasein. The alternative is some kind of "authenticity." But what is that like?

Heidegger uses the term "resoluteness" to describe the authentic person. The resolute person, who faces her own death honestly and fully apprehends her finiteness, is no longer drawn into idle chatter about life, for that idle chatter only served to conceal anxiety and disguise the being-toward-death of Dasein. Nor is she drawn into meaningless striving for some final superiority over others, for nothing is final. Thus she is able to avoid those features of the "they" which are most infected by existential dishonesty. To that extent "authenticity" has a recognizable ethical content. But is there no more to it?

ASK YOURSELF

110. What is resoluteness?

111. Could a person be resolute in doing evil? Try to imagine an example.

Heidegger does not provide answers to the question "What should I resolve to do?" What I resolve will depend upon the particular historical situation into which I have been "thrown" but the "how" of my action is what matters most. I must act with an awareness of my finiteness, my being with others, and with courageous acceptance of responsibility.

What one resolves upon in resoluteness has been prescribed ontologically in the existentiality of Dasein in general as a potentiality-for-Being in the manner of concernful solicitude. As care, however, Dasein has been determined by facticity and falling. Disclosed in its "there," it maintains itself both in truth and in untruth with equal primordiality. This "really" holds in particular for resoluteness as authentic truth. Resoluteness appropriates untruth authentically. Dasein is already in irresoluteness and soon, perhaps, will be in it again. The term "irresoluteness" merely expresses that phenomenon which we have interpreted as a Being-surrendered to the way in which things have been prevalently interpreted by the "they." Dasein, as a they-self, gets "lived" by the common-sense ambiguity of that publicness in which nobody resolves upon anything but which has always made its decision. "Resoluteness" signifies letting oneself be summoned out of one's lostness in the "they."

ASK YOURSELF

112. Describe a case where what "they" (meaning most people around you) typically think or do has determined how you, without thought or real decision, have behaved. In other words, describe a time when you were "lost in the they."

Even resolutions remain dependent upon the "they" and its world. The understanding of this is one of the things that a resolution discloses, inasmuch as resoluteness is what first gives authentic transparency to Dasein. In resoluteness the issue for Dasein is its ownmost potentiality-for-Being, which, as something thrown, can project itself only upon definite factical possibilities.

ASK YOURSELF

113. Do the immediately preceding remarks allow for the possibility that I could be "*completely* different" from those around me?

SUMMING UP THE ISSUE OF THE ACTIVE SELF

Kierkegaard, Marx, Nietzsche, and Heidegger all make claims about what human beings essentially are. Their views differ and clash in some respects, but there are important continuities. All of them ascribe powers of self-formation to humans, although Marx considers those powers to be limited by impersonal economic forces. All of them think humans are distinct from the rest of nature in important, even crucial, respects. All of them are deeply concerned with various forms of "inauthenticity," of failures to live up to some ideal of genuine human life. Kierkegaard saw the falling way from true humanity in religious terms, Nietzsche in anti-religious and anti-moral terms. Heidegger seems to have borrowed ideas from both of them, while introducing a kind of "pragmatism" or concern with the way humans are inserted into the world in a "practical" way. All of them are in one sense very practical thinkers, concerned with pressing questions about how to live, not just with theoretical issues. Kierkegaard, Nietzsche, and Heidegger have all had a powerful influence on philosophy in the twentieth century, particularly the movement called "existentialism" but also, more recently, "post modern" trends. Marx's influence on twentieth-century political life was enormous.

CAN OF WORMS

Much of what we have just read overlaps with or could be placed alongside of the discussions in Chapter 6. For ethics is in part a consideration of arguments about what human beings should try to become, and that is certainly the focus in this section, even in Nietzsche, who attacks "ethics" in one sense, but is deeply concerned with the best kind of life for humans.

These writers also all have something to say about the place of religion in the constitution of human nature, and so their discussions also bear on the material in Chapter 2.

It is very clear that all of these writers also assume some form, often a very radical form, of freedom. The freedom they assume is more than simply the freedom to act one way rather than another. Rather, it includes responsibility for one's own character, thoughts, even moods. They approach this issue in a practical way, which is worth pondering when thinking about the discussion of freedom of the will in Section A, and in particular Frankfurt's critique of much of the traditional discussion.

Finally, it is worth noting that Heidegger's emphasis on embodiment and death has a bearing on the discussions in Chapter 4. We will see how when we get there.

D. THE SELF CONNECTED WITH A LARGER REALITY

A few years ago the movie star Brad Pitt was married in a Buddhist ceremony. That could hardly have happened in Hollywood fifty years ago. In recent years the media and schools have been reminding us with increasing frequency of the fact that we live in a diverse world and that we should not automatically assume that our "Western" perspective is superior. Many people have come to accept this point. Brad Pitt would be merely a famous example. What would be involved in a rejection of that "Western perspective?" A Western perspective is well represented in the preceding sections. One common thread in most of those selections is the idea of individualism. Human individuals stand apart from the rest of the world and nature in important ways. Many eastern religions and philosophies, in contrast, stress the idea that the individual must dissolve into God or Nature.

**QUESTIONS
TO DISCUSS**

a. What might be involved in thinking of myself as part of God or some greater spiritual whole?

b. How should I think of myself in relation to the natural world? Is it a mistake to emphasize individuality in a way that overlooks my oneness with nature? Is it perhaps even wrong to do that?

c. Just how different are human beings from the rest of nature, anyway? Are there good reasons for thinking of human selves as anything more than unusually complicated animals?

Pantheism is the view that God is identical to nature as a whole. There are many versions of this view, but the underlying presumption is that everything we point to in the world around us is really a part of God's being. It's not simply that things in the world reflect God's personality or bear the mark of God. Rather, the individual things that I see are quite literally a piece of God. Thus, when I ask "What am I?" the pantheist would respond "You are a part of God"—or more bluntly—"You are God." To understand my true self, then, I must look beyond the conception of myself as an isolated individual and explore divine reality itself.

Pantheism is a religious way of looking at our connection with ultimate reality. There is, though, another more secular way of seeing how the self is integrated with the larger world around us. We might view ourselves as a part of—and intertwined with—the natural world. We evolved from natural processes, we are composed of natural stuff, and we sustain ourselves by relying on the natural environment. I simply cannot divorce my true identity from the natural world, as many traditional philosophers have done. According to some contemporary environmentalist philosophers, we must take a more *holistic* view of reality; that is, we should focus on the *whole* system of nature and not be sidetracked by the individual components that contribute to the whole. We frequently hear about conflicts between environmentalists and businesses. For example, there have been several cases where environmentalists have tried to block the harvesting of timber from old forests. These environmentalists are often referred to contemptuously as "tree huggers." Perhaps, though, hugging trees would be a good thing. To the extent that we are integrated into nature, we should be friends with the natural world and not assert ourselves as masters over it.

In a similar vein, the famous biologist Stephen Jay Gould stressed the idea that humans must stop thinking of themselves as somehow "special." We are, Gould insisted, just higher animals. Our "selves" are not some kind of special conscious or spiritual entities distinct from other beings. Gould was not inspired by a particular religious vision or by environmental concerns, but rather by a scientific vision, derived from Charles Darwin, of nature as a unity. In Gould's view, it is science that shows that in fact humans are just part of a larger whole. In this section we will look at several views that identify the self with a larger reality—some religious, some naturalistic and secular, and some in between.

1. THE SELF-GOD: HINDU *UPANISHADS*

A theme underlying many Asian philosophies is that we are connected with the larger world around us. Hindu philosophy in particular emphasizes that ultimate reality is the *Self-God* (*Atman-Brahman*), which pervades all things. Based on my ordinary way of experiencing the world, I appear to be an isolated individual thing that comes in contact with other isolated individual things. But if I look beneath this ordinary view of myself, I will discover that my true inner Self is divine ultimate reality. Around 500 BCE a series of Hindu philosophical texts began to appear called the *Upanishads,* the central theme of which was this view of the Self-God. Two of the more famous of these are discussed here.

The Self as the Inner Essence of All Things: *Chandogya Upanishad.* The *Chandogya Upanishad*—one of the oldest in the collection—presents the Self-God doctrine through the use of several metaphors. The divine Self is the single inner essence of all things, just as honey is gathered from the juice of many trees, and many rivers mix into a single sea, and sap flows through all parts of a tree. The Self-God is the unifying factor within all things, and that divine Self is at the core of each of our identities. The following selection repeats the phrase "you are that," which expresses the central point of the *Upanishads,* namely, that each of us is that divine Self.

Chandogya Upanishad, 6:9–11

UDDALAKA   Bees make honey by collecting the juices of distant trees and reducing the juices into one form. These juices have no discrimination and do not say "I am the juice of this tree or that tree." In the same manner, when all these creatures merge with Being [either in deep sleep or in death], they do not know that they merged with Being.

Whatever these creatures are here—whether a lion, a wolf, a boar, a worm, a fly, a gnat, or a mosquito—they become that again and again. Everything that exists has as its soul that which is the finest essence. It is Reality. It is the Self (*Atman*), and *you are that*, my son.

SVETAKETU   Please, sir, tell me more.

UDDALAKA   All right. The eastern rivers [like the Ganges] flow toward the east, and the western rivers [like the Sindhu] flow toward the west. They go from sea to sea. They become the sea. When those rivers are in the sea, they do not say "I am this or that river." In the same manner, when all these creatures come forth from Being, they do not know that they have come forth from Being. Whatever these creatures are here—whether a lion, a wolf, a boar, a worm, a fly, a gnat, or a mosquito—they become that again and again. Everything that exists has as its soul that which is the finest essence. It is Reality. It is the Self, and *you are that*, my son.

SVETAKETU   Please, sir, tell me more.

UDDALAKA   All right. If someone struck the root of this large tree here, it would lose sap, but live. If he struck its trunk, it would lose sap, but live. If he struck its top, it would lose sap, but live. Pervaded by the living Self, that tree stands firm, drinking in its nourishment and rejoicing. But if life leaves one of its branches, that branch withers. If it leaves a second, that branch withers. If it leaves a third, that branch withers. If it leaves the whole tree, the whole tree withers. Understand this: this body withers and dies when the living Self leaves it. The living Self itself, though, does not die. Everything that exists has as its soul that which is the finest essence. It is Reality. It is the Self, and *you are that*, my son.

ASK YOURSELF

114. According to the above, what happens to the inner Self when we die?

Human and Environmental Responsibility: *Isa Upanishad.* Mohandas K. Gandhi (1869–1948) was India's most revered political leader of modern times, and he is renowned worldwide for his efforts to achieve social progress through nonviolent protest. Gandhi's religious views were multicultural. He stated specifically that "there is no other God than truth," and felt that all religions participate in truth. He nevertheless took consolation in the religious classics of his native land, such as the *Upanishads*. He was especially drawn to the *Isa Upanishad*—the shortest Upanishad in the collection, which consists of only eighteen lines. He writes that "if all the *Upanishads* and all the other scriptures happened all of a sudden to be reduced to ashes, if only the first verse in the *Ishopanishad* were left intact in the memory of Hindus, Hinduism would live forever." The first verse of the *Isa Upanishad* that Gandhi refers to is somewhat complicated:

> By the Lord enveloped must this all be; whatever moving thing there is in this moving world. With this renounced, you may enjoy. Covet not the wealth of anyone at all.

Gandhi's more comprehensible rendering of the verse is as follows:

> All this that we see in this great Universe is pervaded by God. Renounce it and enjoy it. Do not covet anybody's wealth or possessions.

Gandhi sees four main parts to this verse: (1) God pervades all things; (2) we should renounce the world; (3) we should enjoy the world; and (4) we should not desire other people's things. These main points, he believes, should satisfy the yearnings of any seeker of truth around the world:

> I venture to suggest to all who do not belong to the Hindu faith that it satisfies their cravings also. And if it is true—and I hold it to be true—you need not take anything in Hinduism which is inconsistent with or contrary to the meaning of this *Mantra*. What more can a man in the street want to learn than this that the one God and Creator and Maker of all that lives pervades the Universe? The three other parts of the *Mantra* follow directly from the first. If you believe that God pervades everything that He has created you must believe that you cannot enjoy anything that is not given by Him. And seeing that He is the Creator of His numberless children, it follows that you cannot covet anybody's possessions. If you think that you are one of His numerous creatures, it behooves you to renounce everything and lay it at His feet. That means the act of renunciation of everything is not a mere physical renunciation but represents a second or new birth. It is a deliberate act, not done in ignorance. It is therefore a regeneration.

ASK YOURSELF

115. According to Gandhi, what is involved in the act of renunciation?

Gandhi especially emphasized the complementary acts of both renouncing and enjoying the world. In fact, when he was asked to sum up his life in three words, he quoted the *Isa Upanishad:* Renounce and enjoy the world. Renouncing the world is partly an educational task, by which we learn to live for the service of others and avoid harmful behavior:

> It is the strict law of God that anyone who desires to be close to Him should renounce the world and yet be in it. This is what the first mantra of the Ishopanishad exhorts us to do. This thing is difficult and yet easy at the same time. It is easy if we believe that we have to live for service. We acquire learning not for sensuous pleasures and for earning but for mukti [i.e., spiritual liberation]. Education is considered necessary to save ourselves from darkness, sensuous pleasures and capricious behavior. [From Mohandas K. Gandhi, "Speech at students' meeting, Lahore, 13 July 1934"]

Hindu philosophers inspired by Gandhi have pushed the interpretation of the *Isa Upanishad* to include a responsibility not only to human beings, but to the environment as a whole. In *Hinduism and Ecology,* Ranchor Prime translates the opening verse of the *Isa Upanishad* in a way that reflects environmental responsibility:

> Everything within this world is possessed by God. He pervades both the animate and the inanimate. Therefore one should only take one's fair share, and leave the rest to the Supreme.

Thus, we begin with the intuition that God pervades all things, and we end with the idea that we should not abuse the environment. Prime writes,

> The Isa Upanishad says it all. Nature is sacred, all life is sacred, the whole earth is sacred. That is the Hindu contribution. Western industrial life has become desacrilised. The only sanctity left is human life. We have to push the frontier beyond human and include the

whole earth. Earth is our mother, earth is goddess, earth is Kali, earth is Parvati, earth is Sita, Earthmother—and she is the home of God. [From Ranchor Prime, *Hinduism and Ecology,* Chapter 9]

ASK YOURSELF

116. What, according to Prime, is Hinduism's contribution?

2. THE WAY OF NATURE: CHUANG-TZU

Taoist Temple.

Classical Hinduism is just one Asian philosophy that advocates our connection with the larger world around us. Another is Taoism, which developed in China around 500 BCE. The key notion of Taoism is the *Tao*—pronounced "dao" and usually translated as *way* or *path*. Taoist philosophers concede the impossibility of precisely defining the Tao. In fact, the most famous of all Taoist passages states, "The Tao that can be named is not the eternal and unchanging Tao. The name that can be spoken is not the eternal and unchanging name" (*Tao Te Ching*, 1). That is, if you try to describe the Tao, then you really haven't done it. Nonetheless, Taoist philosophers do offer a clear account of how the Tao impacts our lives and the world around us. The Tao is ultimate reality itself—the mother of all things, and the path of nature. Everything that we see in the world around us reflects the rhythm of the Tao—cycles of growth and decay, life and death, and the constant transformation of one thing into another. In a sense, nature is one great recycling system in which today's plants and animals become tomorrow's fertilizer for more plants and animals. We not only live within this natural recycling system, but we are part of it. Taoism recommends that we conform our actions and attitudes with the way of nature and thereby live and think with uncontrived spontaneity and exist in harmony with things around us. The following passage, from the Taoist classic *Chuang-tzu* (fourth century BCE), is a tale about two men whose bodies wither as they approach death. Rather than lamenting this fact or blaming God, they accept that their lives are part of nature's transformation process, and they must ultimately embrace nature's way.

FROM *Chuang-tzu,* BOOK 6

Masters Ssu, Yu, Li, and Lai were all four conversing together. They asked, "Who can make non-action his head, life his backbone, and death the tail of his existence? Who knows how birth and death, existence and annihilation comprise one single body? The person who understands this will be admitted to friendship with us." The four men looked at one another and laughed. There was no disagreement in their minds, and they all became friends.

Not long after, Yu fell ill, and Ssu went to see him. "How great is the Creator!" said the sufferer. "He made me the deformed object that I am!" Yu was a crooked hunchback; his five viscera were squeezed into the upper part of his body; his chin bent over his navel; his shoulder was higher than his crown; on his crown was an ulcer pointing to the sky; his breath came and went in gasps. Nevertheless, he was easy in his mind, and made no trouble of his condition. He limped to a well, looked at himself in it, and said, "I can't believe that the Creator would have made me the deformed object that I am!" Ssu said, "Do you dislike your condition?" He replied, "No, why should I dislike it? If the creator transformed my left arm into a rooster, I would watch the time of the night. If he transformed my right arm into a cross-bow, I would then be looking for a duck to shoot for roasting. If he transformed my rump-bone into a wheel and my spirit into a horse, I would then be able to ride in my own chariot. I'd never have to change horses. I obtained life because it was my time. I am now parting with it in accordance with the same law. When we rest in what the time requires, and manifest that submission, neither joy nor sorrow can enter. This is what the ancients called "loosening the rope." Some, though, are hung up and cannot loosen themselves. They are held fast by the bonds of material existence. But it is a long-acknowledged fact that no creatures can overcome Heaven. Why, then, should I hate my condition?"

ASK YOURSELF

117. What are some of the things that Yu thinks nature could transform him into?

Eventually another of the four, named Lai, fell ill, and lay gasping for breath, while his family stood weeping around. The fourth friend, Li, went to see him. "Leave!" he cried to the wife and children; "Go away! You hinder his decomposition." Then, leaning against the door, he said, "Truly, God is great! I wonder what he will make of you now. I wonder where you will be sent. Do you think he will make you into rat's liver or into the shoulders of a snake?"

"A son," answered Lai, "must go wherever his parents bid him. Nature is no other than a man's parents. If she bid me to die quickly, and I object, then I am an unfilial son. She can do me no wrong. The Tao gives me this form, this toil in adulthood, this tranquility in old age, and this rest in death. And surely that which is such a kind mediator of my life is the best mediator of my death. Suppose that the boiling metal in a smelting-pot were to bubble up and say, 'Make a sword out of me.' I think the caster would reject that metal as strange. And if a sinner like myself were to say to God, 'Make of me a man, make of me a man,' I think he too would reject me as strange. The universe is the smelting-pot, and God is the caster. I will go wherever I am sent, to wake unconscious of the past, as a man wakes from a dreamless sleep."

ASK YOURSELF

118. Why does Lai accept what the Tao has in store for him after his death?

3. THE ECOLOGICAL SELF: ARNE NAESS

Environmental philosophers in recent years have challenged traditional notions of human identity and argued instead that the true self is intertwined with the larger natural world. In 1973, Norwegian philosopher Arne Naess coined the term "deep ecology." He contrasted deep ecology with "shallow ecology"—the more traditional conception that people have identities that are rigidly distinct from the surrounding environment, even though they depend upon the natural world in various ways. On this shallow view, all environmental issues—such as energy conservation or toxic waste disposal—are be addressed from a human-centered standpoint. Natural environments such as forests, swamps, and grasslands have value only to the extent that they serve human interests. Nonhuman things in and of themselves have no true inherent value or claim to moral consideration. If we have any responsibility to treat animals humanely or preserve natural environments, it is only because *people* benefit by doing so. This human-centered approach can have some positive impact on the environment, since, for example, reckless disregard for ecosystems might result in the destruction of the human species. Still, Naess believes that shallow ecology does not go far enough. The problem rests with the human-centered assumption itself, which, he argues, is a far too restricted way of looking at human identity. Our true nature is intimately connected with the surrounding environment and ultimately with all life. This is our *ecological self*. If we adopt this deeper notion of who we are, then our treatment of the environment will be radically different. We will value the environment in its own right and not simply for how we can most efficiently exploit it.

How, though, do we shift from a shallow concept of the self to a deeper ecological one? In the essay below, Naess argues that we must experience joy in the natural world around us and thereby come to identify ourselves with the larger environment. He begins with a synopsis of his main points.

FROM ARNE NAESS, "Self Realization: An Ecological Approach to Being in the World" (1987)

For at least 2500 years, humankind has struggled with basic questions about who we are, what we are heading for, what kind of reality are part of. Two thousand five hundred years is a short period in the lifetime of a species, and still less in the lifetime of the Earth, on whose surface we belong as mobile parts.

What I am going to say more or less in my own way, may roughly be condensed into the following six points:

1. We underestimate ourselves. I emphasize *self*. We tend to confuse it with the narrow ego.

2. Human nature is such that with sufficient all-sided maturity we cannot avoid "identifying" ourselves with all living beings, beautiful or ugly, big or small, sentient or not. I will elucidate my concept of identifying later.

3. Traditionally, the *maturity of the self* develops through three stages—from ego to social self, and from social self to metaphysical self. In this conception of the process,

nature—our home, our immediate environment, where we belong as children, and our identification with living human beings—is largely ignored. I therefore tentatively introduce the concept of *an ecological self*. We may be in, of and for nature from our very beginning. Society and human relations are important, but our self is richer in its constitutive relations. These relations are not only relations we have with humans and the human community but with the larger community of all living beings.

4. The joy and meaning of life is enhanced through increased self-realization, through the fulfillment of each being's potential. Whatever the differences between beings, increased self-realization implies broadening and deepening of the *self*.

5. Because of an inescapable process of identification with others, with growing maturity, the self is widened and deepened. We "see ourself in others." Self-realization is hindered if the self-realization of others, with whom we identify, is hindered. Love of ourself will labor to overcome this obstacle by assisting in the self-realization of others according to the formula "live and let live." Thus, all that can be achieved by altruism—the dutiful, moral consideration of others—can be achieved—and much more—through widening and deepening ourself. Following Immanuel Kant's critique, we then act *beautifully* but neither morally nor immorally.

6. The challenge of today is to save the planet from further devastation which violates both the enlightened self-interest of humans and nonhumans, and decreases the potential of joyful existence for all. . . .

> **ASK YOURSELF**
>
> **119.** Naess rejects the traditional three-step notion of the maturity of the self and suggests instead the notion of an ecological self. What are the traditional three steps?

"Identifying With." Naess is aware of all the attempts in the history of philosophy to discover the true nature of the self—such as those explored earlier in this chapter. All of these efforts run into difficulty, though, because they underestimate the importance of expanding and developing the idea of that with which we *identify* ourselves. I might upon occasion identify myself with my individual mind or body. Or I might identify myself with some group, such as a church or a nation. However, according to Naess, I can also identify with what is more radically outside myself, such as animals, plants, and even entire ecosystems. Only when I do that do I discover my true self, the "ecological self."

The simplest answer to who or what I am is to point to my body, using my finger. But clearly I cannot identify my self or even my ego with my body. For example, compare:

"I know Mr. Smith." with "My body knows Mr. Smith."

"I like poetry." with "My body likes poetry."

"The only difference between us is that you are a Presbyterian and I am a Baptist." with "The only difference between our bodies is that your body is Presbyterian whereas mine is Baptist."

In the above sentences we cannot substitute "my body" for "I" nor can we substitute "my mind" or "my mind and body" for "I." But this of course does not tell us what the ego or self is.

Several thousand years of philosophical, psychological, and social-psychological discourse has not brought us any stable conception of the "I," ego, or the self. In modern psychotherapy these notions play an indispensable role, but the practical goal of therapy does not necessitate philosophical clarification of the terms. For our purposes, it is important to remind ourselves what strange and marvelous phenomena we are dealing with. They are extremely close to each of us. Perhaps the very nearness of these objects of reflection and discourse adds to our difficulties. I shall only offer a single sentence resembling a definition of the ecological self. The ecological self of a person is that with which this person identifies.

This key sentence (rather than definition) about the self shifts the burden of clarification from the term *self* to that of *identification* or more accurately, the *process of identification.*

ASK YOURSELF

120. According to Naess, if I say "I know Mr. Smith," I don't simply mean that "My _____ knows Mr. Smith."

THINKING LOGICALLY

In a previous logic box we discussed the notion of identity. One source of puzzlement about identity resides in the fact that I can know that certain descriptions apply to myself, but not know that other descriptions apply equally well to exactly the same numerically identical self. Thus I may know that the description "son of George" applies to myself, but not know that "the second person born in the world in 1980" applies to myself. Now, consider Naess's argument just given.

1. It is true that I know Mr. Smith.
2. It is silly and false to say my body knows Mr. Smith.
3. Therefore something is true of "I" that is not true of my body.
4. If something is true of A but not of B, then A cannot be identical with B.
5. Therefore, I cannot be identified with my body.

But suppose I am in fact identical with my body but just do not know that fact. Then it would be true that "I know Mr. Smith" would be identical in meaning, in *one* sense of *meaning,* with "My body knows Mr. Smith." It would be true in the sense of meaning in which meaning is *reference.* It could be that what I use "I" to refer to and what I use "my body" to refer to are in fact one and the same thing, though I do not know that fact. It could be that I do not know it because I am not familiar with materialist theories about humans, even though those theories are true (for a discussion of a materialist theory of humans, see the discussion of eliminative materialism in Chapter 3). Although it does sound odd to say "my body knows Smith" or "my body is Presbyterian," it might still be *true,* if in fact I am nothing above and beyond my body. The fact that it sounds odd when I identify myself with my body does not show that I am making some kind of mistake when I "identify myself with my body."

ASK YOURSELF

121. Does this criticism depend upon the claim that some premise of Naess's argument is false or upon the claim that his conclusion does not follow from his premises?

122. There a missing premise in Naess's argument that has been supplied in the version given above. Which is it? 1, 2, or 4?

123. Does this criticism depend upon confusing "being identical with" with "identifying with"?

How might we identify with things beyond ourselves? Naess illustrates how he once was able to identify with a flea.

What would be a paradigmatic situation of identification? It is a situation in which identification elicits intense empathy. My standard example has to do with a nonhuman being I met 40 years ago. I looked through an old-fashioned microscope at the dramatic meeting of two drops of different chemicals. A flea jumped from a lemming strolling along the table and landed in the middle of the acid chemicals. To save it was impossible. It took many minutes for the flea to die. Its movements were dreadfully expressive. What I felt was, naturally, a painful compassion and empathy. But the empathy was *not* basic. What *was* basic was the process of identification, that "I see myself in the flea." If I was alienated from the flea, not seeing intuitively anything resembling myself, the death struggle would have left me indifferent. So there must be identification in order for there to be compassion and, among humans, solidarity.

ASK YOURSELF

124. In what way did Naess identify with the flea?

Hindu Philosophy and the Broader Self. Naess believes that Hindu philosophy offers an insight into the ecological self and the process of identifying ourselves with the world around us. Gandhi, as we have seen, spent much of his life bettering the conditions of others, and he encouraged us to do the same. According to Naess, this kind of service toward others flows from the very idea that we are connected to the world around us. We help others because we identify with them through the universal Self (*Atman*). Just as we identify with other humans, so too should we identify with the nonhuman living world.

As a student and admirer since 1930 of Gandhi's nonviolent direct action, I am inevitably influenced by his metaphysics which furnished him tremendously powerful motivation to keep on going until his death. His supreme aim, as he saw it, was not only India's *political* liberation. He led crusades against extreme poverty, caste suppression, and against terror in the name of religion. These crusades were necessary, but the liberation of the individual human being was his highest end. Hearing Gandhi's description of his ultimate goal may sound strange to many of us.

What I want to achieve—what I have been striving and pining to achieve these thirty years—is self-realization, to see God face to face, to attain Moksha (Liberation). I live and move and have my being in pursuit of that goal. All that I do by way of speaking and writing, and all my ventures in the political field, are directed to this same end.

This sounds individualistic to the Western mind, a common misunderstanding. If the self Gandhi is speaking about were the ego or the "narrow" self (*jiva*) of egocentric interest, of narrow ego gratifications, why then work for the Poor? For him it is the supreme or universal Self—the atman—that is to be realized. Paradoxically, it seems, he tries to reach self-realization through *selfless action,* that is, through reduction of the dominance of the narrow self or ego. Through the wider Self every living being is connected intimately, and from this intimacy follows the capacity of *identification* and as its natural consequences, the practice of nonviolence. No moralizing is necessary, just as we do not require moralizing to make us breathe. We need to cultivate our insight, to quote Gandhi again: "The rockbottom foundation of the technique for achieving the power of nonviolence is belief in the essential oneness of all life."

Historically we have seen how ecological preservation is nonviolent at its very core. Gandhi notes:

> I believe in *advaita* (non-duality), I believe in the essential unity of man and, for that matter, of all that lives. Therefore I believe that if one man gains spirituality, the whole world gains with him and, if one man fails, the whole world fails to that extent.

Some people might consider Gandhi extreme in his personal consideration for the self-realization of living beings other than humans. He traveled with a goat to satisfy his need for milk. This was part of a nonviolent witness against certain cruel features in the Hindu way of milking cows. Furthermore, some European companions who lived with Gandhi in his ashram were taken aback that he let snakes, scorpions and spiders move unhindered into their bedrooms—animals fulfilling their lives. He even prohibited people from having a stock of medicines against poisonous bites. He believed in the possibility of satisfactory coexistence and he proved right. There were no accidents. Ashram people would naturally look into their shoes for scorpions before putting them on. Even when moving over the floor in darkness one could easily avoid trampling on one's fellow beings. Thus, Gandhi recognized a basic, common right to live and blossom, to self-realization applicable to any being having interests or needs. Gandhi made manifest the internal relation between self-realization, nonviolence and what is sometimes called biospherical egalitarianism.

ASK YOURSELF

125. How did Gandhi express connection with nonhuman living things?

Naess notes that the usual conception of self-realization is quite egoistic: I should gratify my own desires and strive for economic success. However, he believes that this greatly underestimates our real nature, as we see expressed in both Hinduism and Buddhism. True self-realization aims at bettering the larger world around us.

In the environment in which I grew up, I heard that what is important in life is to be somebody—usually implying to outdo others, to be victorious in comparison of abilities. This conception of the meaning and goal of life is especially dangerous today in the context of vast international economic competition. The law of supply and demand of separate, isolatable "goods and services" independent of real needs, must not be made to reign over increasing areas of our lives. The ability to cooperate, to work with people, to make them feel good *pays* of course in a fiercely individualist society, and high positions may require it. These virtues are often subordinated to the career, to the basic norms of narrow ego fulfillment, not to a self-realization worth the name. To identify self-realization with ego indicates a vast underestimation of the human self.

According to a usual translation of Pali or Sanskrit, Buddha taught his disciples that the human mind should embrace all living things as a mother cares for her son, her only son. For some it is not meaningful or possible for a human *self* to embrace all living things, then the usual translation can remain. We ask only that your mind embrace all living beings, and that you maintain an intention to care, feel and act with compassion.

If the Sanskrit word *atman* is translated into English, it is instructive to note that this term has the basic meaning of *self* rather than mind or *spirit,* as you see in translations. The superiority of the translation using the word *self* stems from the consideration that if your *self* in the wide sense embraces another being, you need no moral exhortation to show care. You care for yourself without feeling any moral pressure to do it-unless you have succumbed to a neurosis of some kind, developed self-destructive tendencies, or hate yourself.

The Australian ecological feminist Patsy Hallen uses a formula close to that of Buddha: "we are here to embrace rather than conquer the world." Notice that the term *world* is used here rather than *living beings*. I suspect that our thinking need not proceed from the notion of living being to that of the world. If we can conceive of reality or the world we live in as alive in a wide, not easily defined sense then there will be no non-living beings to care for!

If "self-realization" today is associated with life-long narrow ego gratification, isn't it inaccurate to use this term for self-realization in the widely different sense of Gandhi, or less religiously loaded, as a term for the widening and deepening of the self so it embraces all life forms? Perhaps it is. But I think the very popularity of the term makes people listen for a moment and feel safe. In that moment the notion of a greater Self can be introduced, contending that if people equate self-realization with narrow ego fulfillment, they seriously *underestimate* themselves. We are much greater, deeper, more generous and capable of dignity and joy than we think! A wealth of noncompetitive joys is open to us!

ASK YOURSELF

126. Naess states that an awareness of our larger Self makes "a wealth of noncompetitive joys open to us." Give an example of a noncompetitive joy.

Joyfully Connecting the Self and the Other. Eastern philosophy aside, Naess believes that we can approach the notion of the ecological self by blurring the distinction between our private individual selves and other things. The best way to do this is by experiencing the joy of other people. It is then a short step to experiencing joy as we appreciate the wonders of the natural world.

I have another important reason for inviting people to think in terms of deepening and widening their selves, starting with narrow ego gratification as the crudest, but inescapable starting point. It has to do with the notion usually placed as the opposite of egoism, namely the notion of *altruism*. The Latin term *ego* has as its opposite the *alter*. Altruism implies that *ego* sacrifices its interest in favor of the other, the *alter*. The motivation is primarily that of duty; it is said that we *ought* to love others as strongly as we love ourself.

What humankind is capable of loving from mere duty or more generally from moral exhortation is, unfortunately, very limited. From the Renaissance to the Second World War about four hundred cruel wars have been fought by Christian nations, usually for the flimsiest of reasons. It seems to me that in the future more emphasis has to be given to the conditions which naturally widen and deepen our self. With a sufficiently wide and deep sense of self, ego and alter as opposites are eliminated stage by stage as the distinctions are transcended.

Early in life, the social *self* is sufficiently developed so that we do not prefer to eat a big cake alone. We share the cake with our family and friends. We identify with these people sufficiently to see our joy in their joy, and to see our disappointment in theirs. Now is the time to share with all life on our maltreated earth by deepening our identification with all life-forms, with the ecosystems, and with Gaia, this fabulous, old planet of ours.

ASK YOURSELF

127. Why do we share cake with our family and friends?

According to Naess, many environmental ethicists today impose a kind of moral guilt trip on society, nagging it to become more environmentally aware through self-sacrifice. Naess does not believe that this technique is effective. Instead, he argues, if we can encourage others to first connect with the environment—experiencing the joy of relating to something bigger than ourselves—then proper moral behavior will automatically follow.

The philosopher Immanuel Kant introduced a pair of contrasting concepts which deserve extensive use in our effort to live harmoniously in, for, and of nature: the concept of *moral* act and that of *beautiful* act. Moral acts are acts motivated by the intention to follow moral laws, at whatever cost, that is, to do our moral duty solely out of respect for that duty. Therefore, the supreme indication of our success in performing a pure, moral act is that we do it completely against our inclination, that we hate to do it, but are compelled by our respect for moral law. Kant was deeply awed by two phenomena, "the heaven with its stars above me and the moral law within me."

If we do something we should because of a moral law, but do it out of inclination and with pleasure—what then? If we do what is right because of positive inclination, then, according to Kant, we perform a *beautiful* act. My point is that in environmental affairs we should primarily try to influence people toward beautiful acts by finding ways to work on their inclinations rather than their morals. Unhappily, the extensive moralizing within the ecological movement has given the public the false impression that they are primarily asked to sacrifice, to show more responsibility, more concern, and better morals. As I see it we need the immense variety of sources of joy opened through increased sensitivity toward the richness and diversity of life, through the profound cherishing of free natural landscapes. We all can contribute to this individually, and it is also a question of politics, local and global. Part of the joy stems from the consciousness of our intimate relation to something bigger than our own ego, something which has endured for millions of years and is worth continued life for millions of years. The requisite care flows naturally if the self is widened and deepened so that protection of free nature is felt and conceived of as protection of our very selves.

What I am suggesting is the supremacy of ecological ontology and a higher realism over environmental ethics as a means of invigorating the ecology movement in the years to come. If reality is experienced by the ecological Self, our behavior *naturally* and beautifully follows norms of strict environmental ethics. We certainly need to hear about our ethical shortcomings from time to time, but we change more easily through encouragement and a deepened perception of reality and our own *self,* that is, through a deepened realism. How that is to be brought about is too large a question for me to deal with here. But it will clearly be more a question of community therapy than community science: we must find and develop therapies which heal our relations with the widest community, that of all living beings.

ASK YOURSELF

128. Kant distinguished between *moral* acts, which are acts performed from a strict sense of duty, and *beautiful* acts (beneficial acts motivated by personal pleasure). According to Naess, which of these two will make us more aware of the ecological self?

4.   HUMAN BEINGS AS EVOLVED ANIMALS: CHARLES DARWIN

Although Charles Darwin (1809–1882) is a major figure in the history of science, his views have also played an important role in the history of philosophy and the history of ideas generally. Darwin was by no means a religious "pantheist," or a religious believer of any kind. Nor was he a "deep ecologist." He did, however, propose an entirely naturalistic vision of human nature: Humans are simply creatures evolved from lower animals. Who we are, then, is entirely a function of the natural world and the evolutionary processes that have shaped all life on earth. Thus we are not unique or higher than the rest of nature in any fundamental sense.

**CHARLES DARWIN
(1809–1882)**
English evolutionary biologist and author of The Descent of Man *(1871).*

The Evolution of Humans. Darwin's views are particularly controversial insofar as they imply that there is no important difference between human beings and other animals. Even nonreligious persons might find such a view objectionable. Moreover, it seems at first glance that there are some fundamental differences. Darwin eventually published his views on this matter in *The Descent of Man.* He argues that humans developed from "lower" species just like any other animal.

FROM CHARLES DARWIN, *The Descent of Man* (1871)

The nature of the following work will be best understood by a brief account of how it came to be written. During many years I collected notes on the origin or descent of man, without any intention of publishing on the subject, but rather with the determination not to publish, as I thought that I should thus only add to the prejudices against my views. It seemed to me sufficient to indicate, in the first edition of my *Origin of Species,* that by this work "light would be thrown on the origin of man and his history"; and this implies that man must be included with other organic beings in any general conclusion respecting his manner of appearance on this earth.

Physical Similarities. Darwin argues for the "general conclusion" just mentioned by pointing out a host of similarities between humans and other animals. For instance, there are many physical similarities.

The Bodily Structure of Man. It is notorious that man is constructed on the same general type or model as other mammals. All the bones in his skeleton can be compared with corresponding bones in a monkey, bat, or seal. So it is with his muscles, nerves, blood-vessels and internal viscera. The brain, the most important of all the organs, follows the same law, as shewn by Huxley and other anatomists. Bischoff, who is a hostile witness, admits that every chief fissure and fold in the brain of man has its analogy in that of the orang; but he adds that at no period of development do their brains perfectly agree; nor could perfect agreement be expected, for otherwise their mental powers would have been the same.

129. Which of the physical similarities mentioned might be the most important in your opinion, and why?

That Humans Evolved from Lower Animals. In this passage Darwin summarizes some of his discussion.

The bearing of the three great classes of facts now given is unmistakable. But it would be superfluous fully to recapitulate the line of argument given in detail in my *Origin of Species*. (1) The homological construction of the whole frame in the members of the same class is intelligible, if we admit their descent from a common progenitor, together with their subsequent adaptation to diversified conditions. In any other view, the similarity of pattern between the hand of a man or monkey, the foot of a horse, the flipper of a seal, the wing of a bat, etc., is utterly inexplicable. It is no scientific explanation to assert that they have all been formed on the same ideal plan.

130. What is it that Darwin thinks is not a "scientific" explanation?

(2) With respect to development, we can clearly understand, on the principle of variation supervening at a rather late embryonic period, and being inherited at a corresponding period, how it is that the embryos of wonderfully different forms should still retain, more or less perfectly, the structure of their common progenitor. No other explanation has ever been given of the marvelous fact that the embryos of a man, dog, seal, bat, reptile, etc., can at first hardly be distinguished from each other. In order to understand the existence of rudimentary organs, we have only to suppose that a former progenitor possessed the parts in question in a perfect state, and that under changed habits of life they became greatly reduced, either from simple disuse or through the natural selection.

Thus we can understand how it has come to pass that man and all other vertebrate animals have been constructed on the same general model, why they pass through the same early stages of development, and why they retain certain rudiments in common. Consequently we ought frankly to admit their community of descent: to take any other view is to admit that our own structure, and that of all the animals around us, is a mere snare laid to entrap our judgment. This conclusion is greatly strengthened, if we look to the members of the whole animal series, and consider the evidence derived from their affinities or classification, their geographical distribution and geological succession. It is only our natural prejudice, and that arrogance which made our forefathers declare that they were descended from demigods, which leads us to demur to this conclusion. But the time will before long come, when it will be thought wonderful [i.e., *amazing, remarkable*] that naturalists, who were well acquainted with the comparative structure and development of man, and other mammals, should have believed that each was the work of a separate act of creation.

131. The last mentioned belief is in fact precisely what many _____ believe.

132. Despite all the similarities between humans and other animals, there do seem to be some very important differences. Mention one such difference.

Gradual Changes Compatible with the Evidence. Darwin shows how certain differences are compatible with development from a lower animal.

If it be an advantage to man to stand firmly on his feet and to have his hands and arms free, of which, from his preeminent success in the battle of life, there can be no doubt, then I can see no reason why it should not have been advantageous to the progenitors of man to have become more and more erect or bipedal. They would thus have been better able to defend themselves with stones or clubs, to attack their prey, or otherwise to obtain food. The best built individuals would in the long run have succeeded best, and have survived in larger numbers. If the gorilla and a few allied forms had become extinct, it might have been argued, with great force and apparent truth, that an animal could not have been gradually converted from a quadruped into a biped, as all the individuals in an intermediate condition would have been miserably ill-fitted for progression. But we know (and this is well worthy of reflection) that the anthropomorphous apes are now actually in an intermediate condition; and no one doubts that they are on the whole well adapted for their conditions of life. Thus the gorilla runs with a sidelong shambling gait, but more commonly progresses by resting on its bent hands.

> ### ASK YOURSELF
> **133.** It is sometimes argued that if people had developed from lower animals, there ought to be animals intermediate between people and those lower animals. Darwin has just pointed out that that is exactly what we find. What is his example of this?

Intellectual Differences Between Humans and Other Animals. The greatest differences between humans and lower animals seem to be intellectual.

We have seen . . . that man bears in his bodily structure clear traces of his descent from some lower form; but it may be urged that, as man differs so greatly in his mental power from all other animals, there must be some error in this conclusion. No doubt the difference in this respect is enormous, even if we compare the mind of one of the lowest savages, who has no words to express any number higher than four, and who uses hardly any abstract terms for common objects or for the affections, with that of the most highly organized ape. The difference would, no doubt, still remain immense, even if one of the higher apes had been improved or civilized as much as a dog has been in comparison with its parent-form, the wolf or jackal. The Fuegians rank amongst the lowest barbarians; but I was continually struck with surprise how closely the three natives on board H. M. S. Beagle, who had lived some years in England, and could talk a little English, resembled us in disposition and in most of our mental faculties. If no organic being excepting man had possessed any mental power, or if his powers had been of a wholly different nature from those of the lower animals, then we should never have been able to convince ourselves that our high faculties had been gradually developed. But it can be shewn that there is no fundamental difference of this kind. We must also admit that there is a much wider interval in mental power between one of the lowest fishes, as a lamprey or lancelet, and one of the higher apes, than between an ape and man; yet this interval is filled up by numberless gradations.

ASK YOURSELF

134. Why would the existence of great variations in intelligence among lower animals suggest that human intelligence evolved from primitive forms of intelligence?

Emotional Differences Are Only Minor. Perhaps the really important differences between humans and other animals are differences in the kinds of feelings they can have. Darwin argues against this, however.

To return to our immediate subject: the lower animals, like man, manifestly feel pleasure and pain, happiness and misery. Happiness is never better exhibited than by young animals, such as puppies, kittens, lambs, etc., when playing together, like our own children. Even insects play together, as has been described by that excellent observer, P. Huber, who saw ants chasing and pretending to bite each other, like so many puppies.

ASK YOURSELF

135. To "anthropomorphize" is to attribute human traits to nonhumans on the basis of superficial similarities that do not warrant those attributions. (In Greek, *anthropos* means "human" and *morphe* refers to shape or appearance.) Do you think Darwin anthropomorphizes in the preceding passage? Why or why not?

The fact that the lower animals are excited by the same emotions as ourselves is so well established, that it will not be necessary to weary the reader by many details. Terror acts in the same manner on them as on us, causing the muscles to tremble, the heart to palpitate, the sphincters to be relaxed, and the hair to stand onend. Suspicion, the offspring of fear, is eminently characteristic of most wild animals. . . . Most of the more complex emotions are common to the higher animals and ourselves. Every one has seen how jealous a dog is of his master's affection, if lavished on any other creature; and I have observed the same fact with monkeys. This shows that animals not only love, but have desire to be loved. Animals manifestly feel emulation. They love approbation or praise; and a dog carrying a basket for his master exhibits in a high degree self-complacency or pride. There can, I think, be no doubt that a dog feels shame, as distinct from fear, and something very like modesty when begging too often for food. A great dog scorns the snarling of a little dog, and this may be called magnanimity.

ASK YOURSELF

136. What evidence is there that a dog could feel shame?

137. Could a dog feel shame about something it did yesterday or a year ago? So far as the present discussion is concerned, does it matter if the answer is "no"? Why or why not?

Several observers have stated that monkeys certainly dislike being laughed at; and they sometimes invent imaginary offences. In the Zoological Gardens I saw a baboon who always got into a furious rage when his keeper took out a letter or book and read it aloud to him; and his rage was so violent that, as I witnessed on one occasion, he bit his own leg till the blood flowed. Dogs show what may be fairly called a sense of humor, as distinct from mere play; if a bit of stick or other such object be thrown to one, he will often carry it away for a short distance; and then squatting down with it on the ground close before him, will wait until his master comes quite close to take it away. The dog will then seize it and rush away in triumph, repeating the same maneuver, and evidently enjoying the practical joke.

ASK YOURSELF

138. In your opinion how many of the examples of "higher emotions" found by Darwin in lower animals are found there only because he clearly anthropomorphized?

Instinct or Reason? Darwin argues that it is not always possible to determine whether intelligent behavior arises from instinct, from "thought," or from something like what we now call "conditioning."

We will now turn to the more intellectual emotions and faculties, which are very important. . . . We can only judge by the circumstances under which actions are performed, whether they are due to instinct, or to reason, or to the mere association of ideas: this latter principle, however, is intimately connected with reason.

The notion of an "association of ideas" is derived from the theories of thinkers like Locke and Hume. It is clear, however, from the examples that Darwin now gives that his conception is very close to what is called "conditioning" in contemporary psychology.

A curious case has been given by Prof. Mobius, of a pike, separated by a plate of glass from an adjoining aquarium stocked with fish, and who often dashed himself with such violence against the glass in trying to catch the other fishes, that he was sometimes completely stunned. The pike went on thus for three months, but at last learnt caution, and ceased to do so. The plate of glass was then removed, but the pike would not attack these particular fishes, though he would devour others which were afterwards introduced; so strongly was the idea of a violent shock associated in his feeble mind with the attempt on his former neighbors. If a savage, who had never seen a large plate-glass window, were to dash himself even once against it, he would for a long time afterwards associate a shock with a window-frame; but very differently from the pike, he would probably reflect on the nature of the impediment, and be cautious under analogous circumstances. Now with monkeys, as we shall presently see, a painful or merely a disagreeable impression, from an action once performed, is sometimes sufficient to prevent the animal from repeating it. If we attribute this difference between the monkey and the pike solely to the association of ideas being so much stronger and more persistent in the one than the other, though the pike often received much the more severe injury, can we maintain in the case of man that a similar difference implies the possession of a fundamentally different mind?

139. Fill in the blanks in the following argument:

    a. The kind of mind a thing has is shown in its learning processes.

    b. The pike, though very stupid, learns through _____.

    c. The savage, though not so stupid, also learns through _____.

    d. Therefore, there is no difference between the kind of _____ found in a pike and in a savage.

140. Do you think the argument just cited is sound? Why or why not?

SUMMING UP THE ISSUE OF THE SELF CONNECTED WITH A LARGER REALITY

Some spiritual and philosophical traditions advocate a view of the human self, or human nature, as incomplete in itself and *necessarily* connected to a larger reality. The larger reality might be conceived as the Self-God (*Atman-Brahman*), or nature. Nature might itself be thought of as "spiritual" in some way. We have seen such views expressed by the Taoists, Gandhi, and Naess. The self might also be conceived simply as a more developed animal, and in that sense as part of nature, rather than something unique that stands apart. Such a view has garnered a lot of support from the development of ideas in the biological sciences, many of which were first proposed or anticipated by Darwin.

CAN OF WORMS

Some of the themes developed in this section have ethical implications. Is Naess's view, for example, at bottom an ethical view—that is, a view about how we *ought* to relate to nature? It is also clear that some of the views presented here have a direct relation to religious teachings, some of which are discussed in Chapter 2. There is, however, a further connection between Darwin's vision of human nature and some of the views developed in the Chapter 4. For example, Dennet's account of the human mind or of mentality depends quite heavily upon ideas that are basically Darwinian. Darwin's ideas about human evolution and natural selection play a very basic role in many materialist or naturalistic accounts of the mind. They also play an important role in some accounts of knowledge, as might be expected given the close connection between mind and knowledge. We see again that conceptions of the self are intertwined with ethical, religious, and epistemological issues.

SUMMING UP THE CHAPTER

We have examined just a few of the many views on human nature, self-hood, personal identity, and the relations of the self to the rest of reality. Some of those views deny any special status to humans in the overall scheme of things. Determinists like d'Holbach and thinkers like Darwin argue that humans are a function of natural processes. Determinism is the result of the widespread influence of science, as well as of common intuitions about universal causation. But Hume argued that determinism is compatible with the deeply entrenched idea that humans have some freedom to shape themselves. Reid and Taylor have argued that determinism is false.

The debate between determinists, compatibilists, and various kinds of libertarians, or believers in free will, is far from over. Some philosophers, like Frankfurt, believe that the discussion has often depended upon confusions and has failed to address real human concerns. Other views on human nature and the self construe freedom in a way that might seem more practical or more engaged with what we really care about. Kierkegaard, for example, denies that "anything comes naturally" for humans and that our most distinctive trait is our capacity to shape ourselves according to many different ideals. Nietzsche and Heidegger would agree to a very large extent with Kierkegaard. Marx thinks that economic conditions can overcome our freedom, but he assumes that humans are capable, at a very basic level, of seeing their condition as requiring a kind of freedom through which they can develop their true, nonalienated selves.

However, some philosophers, Eastern and Western, argue that the very notion of personal identity, which is assumed by the writers just mentioned, is deeply problematic. What makes a person the *same* person from day to day, year to year? Some skeptics deny that we have any coherent notion of personal identity. Others argue that it is possible to make sense of the notion of a continuing self. But the idea that the self might continue beyond death contains very special difficulties. Finally there are deep challenges to the notions of self or human nature that have tended to dominate in the west. Eastern religion and philosophy try to show how the self can be identified with a great, super-personal reality, or with nature. Our thinking about human nature affects our thinking about morality, religion, the environment, politics, the relations of mind to body, the nature of knowledge, and much else. Even when our ideas about what is distinctive in human nature are not articulated, they are back of our institutions and nearly everything we do from day to day. They are right at the center of the philosophical *can of worms.*

FINAL REACTIONS

Turn to the "First Reaction" questions at the outset of this chapter and answer them as you feel about them now. Then compare your current answers with your original answers. Are there major differences? If so, note what they are and indicate which readings may have influenced you.

FURTHER READINGS

GENERAL WORKS

Kim, Jaegwon, and Sosa, Ernest, eds., *A Companion to Metaphysics* (Oxford: Blackwell, 1995).

Lowe, E. J., *A Survey of Metaphysics* (New York: Oxford University Press, 2002).

Stevenson, Leslie, and Haberman, David, *Ten Theories of Human Nature* (New York: Oxford University Press, 1998).

Stevenson, Leslie, ed., *The Study of Human Nature: A Reader* (New York: Oxford University Press, 1999).

WORKS ON SPECIFIC TOPICS AND FIGURES

Frankfurt, Harry, *The Importance of What We Care About: Philosophical Essays* (Cambridge: Cambridge University Press, 1988).

Koller, John M., and Koller, Patricia, *Sourcebook of Asian Philosophy* (New York: Macmillan, 1991).

O'Connor, Timothy, ed., *Agents, Causes, and Events: Essays on Indeterminism and Free Will* (New York: Oxford University Press, 1995).

CHAPTER 4

SOULS, MINDS, BODIES, AND MACHINES

hink about the sorts of things we say that relate to the mind or soul. "He has lost his soul." "Only the soul is immortal." "She has gone mental." "His thoughts were elsewhere." "He is absent-minded." "She had an unconscious smile on her face." "I cannot tell if he is conscious or not." "It is silly to suppose an ant could feel pain." "After-death experiences reported by some people prove that the soul (or mind) can exist apart from the body." "Thoughts and other mental things are in the head." "Are you out of your mind?" "A robot could have thoughts." "My computer has a memory, but do I really want to say that it remembers things?" "Joe felt a pain in his toe even after his foot was amputated."

We think we know what we are talking about when we say some of these things. But if we reflect a little, we may get confused or wonder just what we mean. Obviously, when I say that someone's thoughts are elsewhere, I do not mean that if we looked around, say in some other room, we might find those thoughts under a couch or on the piano. But what then *do* I mean? Are thoughts and other "mental" things located somewhere in space? If so, where? In the head, perhaps? But where in the head? Suppose you are thinking about a conversation you had yesterday. Is this thought or series of thoughts located at some specific point or in some area of your brain? If we did a brain scan, would we be able to see the thoughts? What about the pain in Joe's toe? Since he doesn't have a toe, how can the pain be there? But where is it then? When we say that people are mentally disturbed, do we mean that something is wrong in their brains, or in their souls, or do we just mean that their *behavior* is odd? What is a soul anyway, and is there such a thing as sickness of the soul? The more we reflect on what we know or think we know about the mind, the brain, and the soul, the more confused we may become. We should not feel bad about that.

**FIRST
REACTIONS**

a. Do you think thoughts are located somewhere? If so, where?

b. Is the soul the real you, and if it is, does it have some special relation to God or ultimate reality?

c. Do you think of the soul as being the same thing as the mind or as something closely related to the mind?

d. Could a machine, for example, a mechanical robot, think? Could a machine experience pain? Could a machine fall in love?

e. What do you mean when you say someone's thoughts are elsewhere?

f. Do you suppose that even the most advanced brain scan possible would enable you to see a thought?

g. Could a sensation, say of color or pain, be nothing but a brain event?

Some of the earliest philosophers on record, and many of the latest, have struggled intensely to understand the nature of the mind or soul, the nature of body, and the relations between them. Ancient thinkers, both Eastern and Western, have questioned whether there is some essential connection between the soul and God. More recent thinkers who have focused on the mind–body relation have usually found it deeply puzzling. It is not obvious, for example, that thoughts are located anywhere, unless you identify having a thought with being in a certain brain state. Some have argued that it is just a confusion to think that a thought is either located or not located, just as it would be a confusion to suppose the *function* of a doorstop (as opposed to the doorstop itself) is either located, or not located, somewhere. Some have wondered what distinguishes one mind from another, or whether the mind or soul could survive bodily death, or whether other beings besides humans have minds or souls. Some have doubted that anyone could even know that other minds exist at all, anywhere. You are in good company if you have ever been puzzled by the notion of consciousness or have wondered whether sensation requires consciousness. Likewise, many philosophers and other thinkers have wondered whether cognitive activity requires consciousness; whether machines could think or be conscious; whether aliens, or bats, could have a different kind of consciousness which we could never understand; or whether all experience might be duplicated in a brain in a vat. Many of these concerns and puzzles are addressed in the following selections.

A. ANCIENT WESTERN VIEWS ON BODY, SOUL, AND MIND

Several philosophers from the ancient world proposed innovative views about the nature of mind or soul. Sometimes those views differed sharply from one another. Moreover, the positions developed from Plato (ca. 400 BCE) through Lucretius (75 BCE) anticipate many modern discussions and continue to provoke discussion and philosophical reflection.

a. Do you think of the sourness of a lemon as being "in" the lemon? Is the color of your shirt "in" the shirt?

b. Could the mind, or soul, exist apart from any body whatsoever? If you think so, why?

c. Do you think of nonhuman animals as having souls? Minds? Thoughts? Sensations?

d. Could something have sensations without having a mind? Without having a soul?

1. MATERIALISM, ATOMS, AND SENSATION: DEMOCRITUS AND LUCRETIUS

According to both the early Greek philosopher Democritus (fl. 450 BCE) and his later Roman follower Lucretius (ca. 94–55 BCE) all that exists is atoms in motion. Atoms are conceived as imperceptibly small material things that interact with each other so as to build up the world that is familiar to us. The view that everything that exists is material is called "materialism." How then does a materialist like Democritus explain mental phenomena, including perception itself? Mental phenomena do not seem to be material phenomena. His account is striking in the way it anticipates some modern views. Little is known of Democritus, but the following has been attributed to him.

> Sweet and bitter, hot and cold, and color, are so only by convention (*nomos*). But only atoms and the void exist in reality. We apprehend nothing precisely, but only in relation to the condition of our own bodies. [From Democritus, fragments]

ASK YOURSELF

1. Is the sourness of a lemon actually objectively in the lemon, or is it just a function of the interaction between the lemon and our body, and in that sense something that exists only "subjectively" rather than as part of objective reality?

Democritus' notion of certain things being what they are only by "convention" implies that they are not really real because they are not somehow objective or independent of human thought and activity.

ASK YOURSELF

2. Do you think of heat and cold or colors as "real"? Does the old conundrum about a tree falling in a forest where no one is present come into the discussion? (The question is whether there would then be any sound.)

Lucretius adds some details on the physical nature of the mind.

> The nature of the mind and soul is bodily; for when it is seen to push the limbs, rouse the body from sleep, and alter the countenance and guide and turn about the whole man, . . . must we not admit that the mind and the soul are of a bodily nature? . . .

I will now go on to explain in my verses in what kind of body the mind consists. . . . First of all I say that it is extremely fine and formed of exceedingly minute bodies. . . . The following fact . . . demonstrates how fine the texture is of which its nature is composed, and how small the room is in which it can be contained, could it only be collected into one mass: as soon as the untroubled sleep of death has gotten hold of a man and the nature of the mind and soul has withdrawn, you can perceive then no diminution of the entire body either in appearance or weight: death makes all good save the vital sense and heat. Therefore the whole soul must consist of very small seeds and be inwoven through veins and flesh and sinews; inasmuch as, after it has all withdrawn from the whole body, the exterior contour of the limbs preserves itself entire and not a tittle of the weight is lost.

Again we perceive that the mind is begotten along with the body and grows up together with it and becomes old along with it . . . children go about with a tottering and weakly body, so slender sagacity of mind follows along with it; then when their life has reached the maturity of confirmed strength . . . the Power of the mind [is] more developed . . . when the body has been shattered by the mastering might of old age . . . the intellect halts, the tongue dotes, the mind gives way, all faculties fail. [From Lucretius, *On the Nature of Things,* Books 1–3]

ASK YOURSELF

3. Give two of Lucretius' reasons for thinking the mind is just as physical a thing as the body.

Democritus and Lucretius were monists. That is, they believed that there is only one kind of reality, namely physical reality. Their views thus clash directly with the views of Plato.

2. SOUL AND BODY: PLATO

One of the greatest figures in philosophy is the ancient Greek thinker Plato (ca. 427–347 BCA). In fact, one recent philosopher said that "all of Western philosophy is but a footnote to Plato." He not only had a colossal presence in the theater of ideas in the ancient past, but even today philosophers acknowledge his influence and go to his writings for insight. A case in point is his treatment of the relation between the soul and body. The position he takes is called "dualism," which in this context means that humans are composed of two distinct things—a physical body and a nonphysical soul. This view appears in his work *Phaedo,* which is a dialogue between the character Socrates, who represents Plato's position, and Cebes, whom Socrates is trying to persuade. Socrates argues here that soul and body are by nature meant to be separate, and that only by complete separation from the body can anyone achieve perfect immortality.

Platonic Dualism. One thing that stands out in the passage below is the connection between the soul and moral purity. The soul is not identified with psychological functions, such as thinking and perceiving, nor is the "body" or the "bodily" identified simply with what is physical. This same point is clear in the selection from the *Phaedo* in Chapter 3 in this volume.

FROM PLATO, *Phaedo*

SOCRATES   And are we to suppose that the soul, which is invisible, in passing to the true Hades, which like her is invisible, and pure, and noble, and on her way to the good and wise God—whither, if God will, my soul is also soon to go—that the soul, I repeat, if this be her nature and origin, is blown away and perishes immediately on quitting the body, as the many say? That can never be, dear Simmias and Cebes. The truth rather is that the soul which is pure at departing draws after her no bodily taint, having never voluntarily had connection with the body which she is ever avoiding, herself gathered into herself (for such abstraction has been the study of her life). And what does this mean but that she has been a true disciple of philosophy and has practised how to die easily? And is not philosophy the practice of death?

CEBES   Certainly.

SOCRATES   That soul, I say, herself invisible, departs to the invisible world, to the divine and immortal and rational: thither arriving, she lives in bliss and is released from the error and folly of men, their fears and wild passions and all other human ills, and forever dwells, as they say of the initiated, in company with the gods. Is not this true, Cebes?

CEBES   Yes, said Cebes, beyond a doubt.

SOCRATES   But the soul which has been polluted, and is impure at the time of her departure, and is the companion and servant of the body always, and which is in love with and fascinated by the body and by the desires and pleasures of the body, until she is led to believe that the truth only exists in a bodily form, which a man may touch and see and taste and use for the purposes of his lusts—the soul, I mean, accustomed to hate and fear and avoid the intellectual principle, which to the bodily eye is dark and invisible, and can be attained only by philosophy—do you suppose that such a soul as this will depart pure and unalloyed?

CEBES   That is impossible, he replied.

SOCRATES   She is engrossed by the corporeal, which the continual association and constant care of the body have made natural to her.

CEBES   Very true.

SOCRATES   And this, my friend, may be conceived to be that heavy, weighty, earthy element of sight by which such a soul is depressed and dragged down again into the visible world, because she is afraid of the invisible and of the world below-prowling about tombs and sepulchres, in the neighborhood of which, as they tell us, are seen certain ghostly apparitions of souls which have not departed pure, but are cloyed with sight and therefore visible.

Later philosophers, such as Descartes, think of the soul almost exclusively in terms of psychological functions, and they are puzzled by the relation between the soul, or "mind" thus conceived, and the body, construed as a purely physical thing. Plato is not concerned exclusively with that relationship. In fact his principal concern seems to be with the relationship between what is morally pure in the self and what is not. Psychological functions can themselves become corrupted, and when they do they are classified with or associated with the body. So Plato is not struggling with the way psychological and physical traits can be combined.

Two religious teachings would be in agreement with Plato's view. One is the teaching about the transmigration of souls, such as is found in Hinduism but also among the Pythagoreans and others. The other is the teaching that pure souls go to a kind of heaven after death.

ASK YOURSELF

4. This last teaching sounds a lot like the popular version of a teaching of what religion?

Plato, however, does not present these teachings simply as doctrines to be believed, but rather tries to argue for their rational plausibility. Much of the *Phaedo,* which has as its setting in a jail where Socrates was executed, is devoted to those arguments. One of them follows. Socrates draws an analogy between the soul being immortal and the number three being odd. The odd is the opposite of the even, so nothing that is odd could be even ("receive the even"). Likewise the soul is by definition the life principle; whatever has soul is alive. Therefore something could not be a soul and also be dead.

SOCRATES   Then the soul, as has been acknowledged, will never receive the opposite of what she brings. And now, he said, what did we call that principle which repels the even?

CEBES   The odd.

SOCRATES   What do we call the principle which does not admit of death?

CEBES   The immortal.

SOCRATES   And does the soul admit of death?

CEBES   No.

SOCRATES   Then the soul is immortal?

CEBES   Yes.

SOCRATES   And may we say that this is proven?

CEBES   Yes, abundantly proven, Socrates.

SOCRATES   And supposing that the odd were imperishable, must not three be imperishable?

CEBES Of course . . . .

SOCRATES   And the same may be said of the immortal: if the immortal is also imperishable, the soul when attacked by death cannot perish; for the preceding argument shows that the soul will not admit of death, or ever be dead, any more than three or the odd number will admit of the even, or fire or the heat in the fire, of the cold. Yet a person may say: "But although the odd will not become even at the approach of the even, why may not the odd perish and the even take the place of the odd?" Now to him who makes this objection, we cannot answer that the odd principle is imperishable; for this has not been acknowledged, but if this had been acknowledged, there would have been no difficulty in contending that at the approach of the even the odd principle and the number three took up their departure; and the same argument would have held good of fire and heat and any other thing.

CEBES   Very true.

SOCRATES   And the same may be said of the immortal: if the immortal is also imperishable, then the soul will be imperishable as well as immortal; but if not, some other proof of her imperishableness will have to be given.

CEBES   No other proof is needed for if the immortal, being eternal, is liable to perish, then nothing is immortal.

ASK YOURSELF

5. In terms of Plato's analogy, for the soul to die would be like the number three becoming _____.

6. Has Plato made the soul immortal simply by defining it as immortal? Does he give any reasons here for believing that there is such a thing as the soul?

Plato's notion of the soul is modified in various ways in his later works, but he never completely gives up the idea that the soul, unlike the body, includes what is by nature immortal and separable from the body. Moreover, he continues to think of the soul in morally significant terms.

The Soul as an Immortal Complex. In his *Phaedrus,* Plato both reiterates and further develops his analysis of the nature of the soul. He continues to argue that the soul is immortal and to argue, as he had in the *Republic* (not excerpted here), that it has three primary divisions. But in this dialogue he portrays the soul's struggle for knowledge in a way that allows passions or desires to play a positive, even a necessary role. In that respect this dialogue contrasts with the *Phaedo* and the *Republic.* Recall, for instance, the insistence in the *Phaedo* that passions and desires always *obstruct* the search for knowledge and the grasp of the forms. His argument for immortality follows.

FROM PLATO, *Phaedrus*

SOCRATES   Let us view the affections and actions of the soul divine and human, and try to ascertain the truth about them. The beginning of our proof is as follows:

The soul through all her being is immortal, for that which is ever in motion is immortal; but that which moves another and is moved by another, in ceasing to move ceases also to live. Only the self-moving, never leaving self, never ceases to move, and is the fountain and beginning of motion to all that moves besides. Now, the beginning is unbegotten, for that which is begotten has a beginning; but the beginning is begotten of nothing, for if it were begotten of something, then the begotten would not come from a beginning. But if unbegotten, it must also be indestructible; for if beginning were destroyed, there could be no beginning out of anything, nor anything out of a beginning; and all things must have a beginning. And therefore the self-moving is the beginning of motion; and this can neither be destroyed nor begotten, else the whole heavens and all creation would collapse and stand still, and never again have motion or birth. But if the self-moving is proved to be immortal, he who affirms that self-motion is the very idea and essence of the soul will not be put to confusion. For the body which is moved from without is soulless; but that which is moved from within has a soul, for such is the nature of the soul. But if this be true, must not the soul be the self-moving, and therefore of necessity unbegotten and immortal? Enough of the soul's immortality.

The Latin word for "soul" is *"anima,"* which is found in the English "animated." "Soul" in this ancient usage is always associated with motion. According to Plato, something that initiates motion could not have had a beginning, since if it did, whatever got it started would have to be self-moving, and so we start on an infinite regress.

7. Therefore, we might as well admit from the outset that each source of motion (each soul) is itself without a beginning, or, in Plato's terms, is _____.

Plato continues in the *Phaedrus* by describing the three-part nature of the soul. He illustrates the divisions with an analogy of a charioteer drawn by two horses.

Let me speak briefly, and in a figure, and let the figure be composite: a pair of winged horses and a charioteer. Now the winged horses and the charioteers of the gods are all of them noble and of noble descent, but those of other races are mixed; the human charioteer drives his in a pair; and one of them is noble and of noble breed, and the other is ignoble and of ignoble breed; and the driving of them of necessity gives a great deal of trouble to him. I will endeavor to explain to you in what way the mortal differs from the immortal creature.

The soul in her totality has the care of inanimate being everywhere, and traverses the whole heaven appearing in divers forms—when perfect and fully winged she soars upward, and orders the whole world. But the imperfect soul, losing her wings and drooping in her flight at last settles on the solid ground—there, finding a home, she receives an earthly frame which itself appears to be self-moved, but is really moved by her power; and this composition of soul and body is called a living and mortal creature. For no such union can be reasonably believed to be immortal; although fancy, not having seen nor surely known the nature of God, may imagine an immortal creature having both a body and also a soul which are united throughout all time.

. . . And now let us ask the reason why the soul loses her wings! . . . As I said at the beginning of this tale, I divided each soul into three—two horses and a charioteer; and one of the horses was good and the other bad: the division may remain, but I have not yet explained in what the goodness or badness of either consists, and to that I will proceed.

The right-hand horse is upright and cleanly made; he has a lofty neck and an aquiline nose; his color is white, and his eyes dark; he is a lover of honor and modesty and temperance, and the follower of true glory. He needs no touch of the whip, but is guided by word and admonition only. The other is a crooked lumbering animal, put together anyhow; he has a short thick neck; he is flat-faced and of a dark color, with gray eyes and blood-red complexion; the mate of insolence and pride, shag-eared and deaf, hardly yielding to whip and spur.

Now when the charioteer beholds the vision of love, and has his whole soul warmed through sense, and is full of the prickings and ticklings of desire, the obedient steed, then as always under the government of shame, refrains from leaping on the beloved; but the other, heedless of the goads and of the blows of the whip, plunges and runs away, giving all manner of trouble to his companion and the charioteer, whom he forces to approach the beloved and to remember the joys of love. They at first indignantly oppose him and will not be urged on to do terrible and unlawful deeds. But at last, when he persists in plaguing them, they yield and agree to do as he bids them.

8. Plato's allegorical picture of the soul expresses very aptly the inner conflict that many people feel between that in them which is _____ and that which is _____.

In the Phaedo, Plato portrays the soul as intrinsically unified, intellectual, and untroubled by desire except when attached to a body. But in the *Phaedrus* Plato presents the highest part of the soul as itself a source of desire. Thus desires or passions are no longer "merely" bodily and no longer necessarily obstacles to the search for truth.

ASK YOURSELF

9. Using Plato's division of the soul into Charioteer, and two steeds, state what part of the soul actually feels "desire" for the beloved first.

In Plato's view the soul or some part of it is associated with that which is highest or most worthy in a person. That fact, which is mentioned already in the commentary above, is very clear in the previous selection, and it links Plato's thought to some Eastern conceptions to a certain extent, as does the notion of the soul as complex (see the selection below from the Katha Upanishad). Later discussions of the relation of mind to body, which occupy much of the remainder of this chapter, seem to have lost that focus on a moral aspect to the soul. But the following selection still shows signs of it.

3. SOUL AS FORM OF THE BODY: ARISTOTLE

Plato and Socrates conceived of the soul as something distinct from the body, capable of existing before the birth and after the death of the body, and as an entity with moral traits. Plato's equally famous pupil Aristotle (384–322 BCE) took a quite different position on the

THE SCHOOL OF ATHENS

subject. In fact, Aristotle does not confine "souls" to human beings. Understanding why will illuminate his conception of the human soul.

Kinds of Soul. According to Aristotle, humans are not the only living things with souls.

FROM ARISTOTLE, *On the Soul*, 2.1–2.3

We must consider also whether soul is divisible or is without parts, and whether it is everywhere homogeneous or not; and if not homogeneous, whether its various forms are different specifically or generically: up to the present time those who have discussed and investigated soul seem to have confined themselves to the human soul. We must be careful not to ignore the question whether soul can be defined in a single unambiguous formula, as is the case with animal, or whether we must not give a separate formula for each of it, as we do for horse, dog, man, god (in the latter case the "universal" animal—and so too every other "common predicate"—being treated either as nothing at all or as a later product).

We resume our inquiry from a fresh starting-point by calling attention to the fact that what has soul in it differs from what has not, in that the former displays life. Now this word has more than one sense, and provided any one alone of these is found in a thing we say that thing is living. Living, that is, may mean thinking or perception or local movement and rest, or movement in the sense of nutrition, decay and growth. Hence we think of plants also as living, for they are observed to possess in themselves an originative power through which they increase or decrease in all spatial directions; they grow up and down, and everything that grows increases its bulk alike in both directions or indeed in all, and continues to live so long as it can absorb nutriment. This power of self-nutrition can be isolated from the other powers mentioned, but not they from it—in mortal beings at least. The fact is obvious in plants; for it is the only "soul" power they possess. This is the originative power the possession of which leads us to speak of things as living at all. But it is the possession of sensation that leads us for the first time to speak of living things as animals; for even those beings which possess no power of local movement but do possess the power of sensation we call animals and not merely living things.

Certain kinds of animals possess in addition the power of locomotion, and still another order of animate beings, i.e. man and possibly another order like man or superior to him, the power of thinking, i.e. mind. It is now evident that a single definition can be given of soul only in the same sense as one can be given of figure. For, as in that case there is no figure distinguishable and apart from triangle, etc., so here there is no soul apart from the forms of soul just enumerated. It is true that a highly general definition can be given for figure which will fit all figures without expressing the peculiar nature of any figure. So here in the case of soul and its specific forms.

ASK YOURSELF

10. What is the difference between the "soul" of a vegetable and the "soul" of an animal?

The notion of soul is strongly connected with life. You could almost say "soul = life" as Plato did in the argument just cited from the *Phaedo*. But there are many kinds of living things—plants, animals, viruses, and so forth. Aristotle is raising the question whether there should be one account of soul for all of these different kinds of living things.

Aristotle is pointing out that the "kind" of life a plant has consists simply in nutritive (vegetative) functions. On the other hand, what we call animals, while they have nutritive functions, also have the capacity for sensation and movement. So they have "life" in an expanded sense. Aristotle is thus arguing that there are different kinds of soul or different "ways" of being alive.

So there must be different definitions for different types of soul. We could give a general definition of soul, just as we can define "figure" in general—even though there is no such thing as a figure in general, but only particular figures, such as the triangle, the square, and so forth. The general definition of "soul" would be "anything that is alive" or "whatever it is that makes living things alive." But there are differences in the way plants are alive, animals are alive, and humans are alive.

How the Soul and the Body Are Related. The difference between Aristotle's conception of the soul and Plato's is particularly marked in Aristotle's account of the relation of soul to body.

Suppose that the eye were an animal. Sight would then have been its soul; for sight is the substance or essence of the eye which corresponds to the formula, the eye being merely the matter of seeing. When seeing is removed, the eye is no longer an eye, except in name. It is no more a real eye than the eye of a statue or of a painted figure . . . as the pupil plus the power of sight constitutes the eye, so the soul plus the body constitutes the animal. From this it indubitably follows that the soul is inseparable from its body.

Aristotle is drawing an analogy; if an eyeball could live on its own, then the power of sight would be to an eyeball as the soul is to the body. Obviously you cannot have the power of sight all by itself. The power must be realized in something. Likewise you cannot have a soul all by itself. It is simply a kind of "power" or capacity, and you cannot have capacities all by themselves. Capacities are always capacities of something. For example you cannot have the capacity to run all by itself. You can only have it in a dog, a man, an ant, and so forth.

SUMMING UP ANCIENT WESTERN VIEWS ON MIND, BODY, AND SOUL

Clearly the views of Democritus and Lucretius differ radically from the views of Plato. And Aristotle's views differ from all of them in important ways. We can roughly distinguish three main positions: the materialist position, where the mind or soul is a complex physical thing; the dualist position, where the soul is radically distinct from body and may be capable of existing without the body; and finally a more or less functionalist position, according to which "soul" or "mind" are terms that denote a manner in which a living body is organized and operates. Further developments of and variations on these three positions recur throughout the history of this subject.

**CAN OF
WORMS**

The very concept "soul" has religious connotations. So the disputes in metaphysics about the nature of the mind or soul overlap with philosophical inquiry into religion. The idea that bodily life is somehow second rate and that there is something "higher" that is associated with the mind also keeps coming up in philosophical ethics, even in a secular figure like Mill. Ethical, religious, and metaphysical questions are once more intertwined.

B. CLASSIC HINDU VIEWS ON SOUL, SELF, AND GOD

How close are you to God? Some of the answers that have been given to that question will come as a surprise to many people. Eastern ideas about body/soul/mind/self are even more colored by religious concerns than are the views of Plato. In fact some of the views discussed in this section actually identify the true self with something like God! Yet some claims similar to those made in the West come up here too. For example, there are puzzles about the relation of that which is more mind-like or spiritual to that which is more physical. And there are monistic views reminiscent of Spinoza, who wrote long after these Eastern writers.

**QUESTIONS
TO DISCUSS**

a. Do you think of your mind, or soul, as being somehow more closely related to God than your body is? Why or why not?

b. Do you think of yourself as having some deep spiritual core, which is finally much more important than that part of your mind or self which deals with ordinary everyday experience?

c. A famous Christian preacher of the fourteenth century once said "I am God." He was not trying to be arrogant. Nonetheless, do you find this remark shocking? Can you make any sense of the idea?

 1. ### THE OUTER EMPIRICAL SELF AND THE INNER SELF-GOD:
KATHA UPANISHAD

In Chapter 3, we looked at the Hindu conception of the Self-God (Atman-Brahman) as it appears in the *Upanishads*. According to this notion, our selves have two basic components or aspects. There is first an outer empirical part, which involves our physical bodies, bodily perceptions, and even our conscious mental experiences. Second, buried beneath these outer and superficial layers is our true self—the Self-God—which is the supreme reality of the entire universe. Many philosophers in Western civilization such as Descartes have struggled to discover the precise relation between our physical human bodies and our nonphysical human minds—what we now call the "mind–body problem." But Hindus construe mind and body in ways importantly different from the way they are construed in the West. According to Hindus, my "mind"—as Descartes and others conceive of it—is really only part of my outer empirical self, and is of the same fundamental nature as my physical body. For Hindus, then, the connection between the two is no real mystery. What Descartes and others completely miss, though, is the true Self-God hidden beneath the empirical self-layer.

The Path to the Self-God: *Katha Upanishad.* The *Katha Upanishad,* composed anonymously around 500 BCE, describes the difficulties we encounter in our quest for the Self-God. We might go our entire lives ignoring our inner divine Self and reacting only to the outer layers of our thoughts and experiences. The true self is buried deep within us, and discovering it requires a remarkable effort.

FROM *Katha Upanishad*

Many are not even able to hear the Self, and many, even when they hear of it, do not comprehend it. Wonderful is the person, who when found, is able to teach the Self. Wonderful also is the person who comprehends it when taught by an able teacher. The Self, when taught by an inferior person, is not easy to understand, even when one frequently thinks about it. Unless another teaches it, there is no way to it, for it is inconceivably smaller than what is small. That doctrine cannot be obtained by argument, but when someone else declares it, then it is easy to understand. You have obtained this knowledge now, and you are truly a person of genuine determination. May we always have an inquirer like you! . . . Indeed, the wise person leaves joy and sorrow far behind when he meditates on his Self and recognizes the primordial, who is difficult to see, who has entered into the dark, who is hidden in the cave, and who dwells in the abyss. A mortal rejoices when he hears this, embraces it, separates it from all qualities, and thus reaches the subtle Being, because he has obtained what is a cause for rejoicing. I believe that the house of God is open.

ASK YOURSELF

14. What does the above say about understanding the Self through argument?

The discussion continues by listing some key features of the divine Self. Its sacred sound is *Om*, which Hindu believers often chant and meditate upon. It is eternal and is unaffected by the death of the human body.

That word is *Om*, which all the *Vedas* [i.e., Hindu scriptures] record, which all prayers proclaim, which people desire when they live as religious students. That imperishable syllable means God, that syllable means the highest God. If a person knows that syllable, then he obtains whatever he desires. This is the best support, this is the highest support; he who knows that support is magnified in the world of God.

The knowing Self is not born, and it does not die. It sprang from nothing, and nothing sprang from it. The primordial is unborn, eternal, everlasting. He is not killed, though the body is killed. If the killer thinks that he kills, if the killed thinks that he is killed, they do not understand. For this one does not kill, nor is that one killed. The Self, smaller than small, greater than great, is hidden in the heart of that creature. A person who is free from desires and free from grief sees the majesty of the Self by the grace of the Creator. Though sitting still, he walks far. Though lying down, he goes everywhere. Who, except myself, is able to know the God who rejoices yet who also does not rejoice? The wise person never grieves who knows the Self as bodiless within the bodies, as unchanging among changing things, as great and all-pervading.

That Self cannot be gained by the Vedas, nor by understanding, nor by much learning. Whoever the Self chooses can gain knowledge of the Self. The Self chooses him as his own. However, a person cannot obtain knowledge of the Self if he has not first turned away from his wickedness. He must be tranquil, subdued, and have his mind at rest. . . .

ASK YOURSELF

15. What does the above say about understanding the Self through the *Vedas* (i.e., Hinduism's sacred scripture)?

The Katha Upanishad presents a rather complex account of human psychology, where different components of our bodies and minds perform different activities. The relation between these components is presented with the metaphor of a chariot.

We may understand that the Self is sitting in the chariot, the body is the chariot, the intellect is the charioteer, and the mind is the reins. The senses are the horses, the objects of the senses are their roads. When he [i.e., the highest Self] is in union with the body, the senses, and the mind, then wise people call him the Enjoyer. If someone has no understanding and his mind [i.e., the reins] is never firmly held, then his senses, like vicious horses, are unmanageable. But if someone has understanding and his mind is always firmly held, then his senses are under control, like good horses of a charioteer. If someone has no understanding and is unmindful and always impure, then he never reaches that place, but enters into the cycle of births. But if someone has understanding and is mindful and always pure, then he indeed reaches that place, and from there he is not born again. And if someone has understanding for his charioteer, and who holds the reins of the mind, then he reaches the end of his journey, and that is the highest place of Vishnu.

Beyond the senses there are the objects, beyond the objects there is the mind, and beyond the mind there is the intellect. The Great self [i.e., the ego] is beyond the intellect. Beyond the Great there is the Undeveloped, beyond the Undeveloped there is the Person. Beyond the Person there is nothing. This is the goal, and is the highest road.

ASK YOURSELF

16. In the chariot analogy, what is represented by the chariot, the charioteer, the reins, the horses, and the road, respectively?

The discussion continues by explaining where we should look to find the Self and where we should avoid looking.

That Self is hidden in all beings and does not shine forth, although astute seers see it through their sharp and subtle intellects. A wise person should keep down speech and mind. He should keep them within the Self, which is knowledge. He should keep knowledge within the Self, which is the Great. And he should keep that [the Great] within the Self, which is the Quiet. Wake up and rise, having obtained your wishes. Understand them! The wise say that, like the sharp edge of a razor, the path [to the Self] is difficult to travel and obtain. We are freed from the jaws of death when we perceive that which is without sound, without touch, without form, without decay, without taste, eternal, without smell, without beginning, without end, beyond the Great, and unchangeable.

The existent Self pierced the openings [of the senses] so that they turn outward; and so one [wrongly] looks outward, and not within himself. A certain wise person, however, wishing for immortality, closed his eyes and saw the Self directly [within himself]. Children follow outward pleasures, and fall into the snare of widespread death. Only the wise, knowing the nature of what is immortal, do not look for anything stable here among unstable things. Through that [i.e. the Self] we know form, taste, smell, sounds, and loving touches; through that we also know what else exists [within us]. This is that [for which you seek]. By knowing the great all-pervading Self, the wise person knows things while asleep and awake, and he grieves no more. Those who know that this living soul which eats honey [i.e., perceives objects] is the Self—which is always near, the Lord of the past and the future—[those people] have no more fears. This is that [for which you seek].

> ### ASK YOURSELF
>
> **17.** The above passage contains a famous line: "like the sharp edge of a razor, the path [to the Self] is difficult to travel and obtain." What does this mean?

2. STRICT MONISM: SANKARA

In spite of attempts in the *Upanishads* to explain the relation between the outer empirical self and the inner Self-God, many questions remained unanswered. Suppose that our true inner Self is indeed God, which permeates the entire universe. What, then, is the status of the outer empirical self? Is it distinct from the Self-God? Is it part of the Self-God? Or is it just an illusion? A branch of Hindu philosophy called *Vedanta* arose around the eighth century CE, which aimed to answer these lingering questions from the *Upanishads*. Vedanta philosophers themselves, though, disagreed about how to resolve these issues. One version—forged by a scholar named Sankara (788–820 CE)—took a strict monistic approach: Only one thing exists. There are two key elements to this position. First, according to Sankara, the one divine reality is unchanging and indivisible. In defense of this point, he draws on a variety of passages in the *Upanishads* which imply strict monism. In Chapter 3 in this book, we look at the famous phrase from the *Chandogya Upanishad:* "You are that"—that is, the inner you is the God of the universe. Sankara makes explicit mention of this phrase in the passages below. Second, although it might appear that there are a variety of things in the world around us, including our outer empirical selves, we must dismiss this as a complete illusion. Suppose that while walking down the road you see what appears to be a snake ahead of you. As you get closer, however, you see that it is not at all a snake, but merely a rope. In the same way, according to Sankara, the world might appear to contain lots of different objects, but in reality it is one great undifferentiated spiritual whole.

FROM SANKARA, *Commentary on the Vedanta Sutra,* 2:1:14

When accepted as the doctrine of the Vedas, this doctrine of the individual soul having its Self in God (Brahman) does away with the independent existence of the individual [empirical] soul. This is just as the idea of the rope does away with the idea of the snake [for which the rope had been mistaken]. And if the doctrine of the independent existence of the individual soul has to be set aside, then the view of the entire phenomenal world having an independent existence must likewise be set aside insofar as it is based on the individual soul. But in addition to the element of unity, an element of manifoldness would have to be [falsely] assumed in Brahman only for the purpose of establishing the phenomenal world.

Scriptural passages also declare that for people who see that everything has its Self in God (Brahman), [they also see that] the whole phenomenal world is non-existent, including actions, agents, and consequences of actions. Nor can it be said that this non-existence of the phenomenal world is declared by Scripture to be limited to certain states. For the passage "You are that" shows that the general fact of God (Brahman) being the Self of all is not limited by any particular state. . . .

ASK YOURSELF

18. According to Sankara, what does the phrase "You are that" tell us about God (Brahman)?

Suppose the critic grants Sankara's general point that the entire universe is really God. Still, argues the critic, God could go through *some* kind of change or modification, just as a single glob of clay can be modified into different shapes. Sankara dismisses this conjecture.

By quoting parallel instances of clay (and its various modifications), it may be objected that Scripture itself endorses a Brahman which is capable of modification. For we know from experience that clay and similar things do undergo modifications. In reply, this objection is without force. A number of scriptural passages deny all modifications of Brahman and thereby teach that it is absolutely changeless. Such passages are, "Indeed, God (Brahman) is this great unborn Self, undecaying, undying, immortal, fearless." . . . For we cannot ascribe to one Brahman the two qualities of (a) being subject to modification and (b) being free from modification. And if you say, "Why should they not be both predicated of Brahman?" we reply that the qualification "absolutely changeless" precludes this. For the changeless Brahman cannot be the substratum of varying attributes. . . .

In this manner the Vedanta texts declare that, for those who have reached the state of truth and reality, the whole apparent world does not exist. The *Bhagavad Gita* also declares that in reality the relation of Ruler and ruled does not exist. Scripture as well as the *Bhagavad Gita* says that, on the other hand, all those distinctions are valid [only] as far as the phenomenal world is concerned.

ASK YOURSELF

19. What is the scriptural passage that Sankara quotes in refutation of the view that God can undergo modifications like a glob of clay?

---

3. QUALIFIED MONISM: RAMANUJA

In the eleventh century CE, a Vedanta scholar named Ramanuja challenged Sankara's rigid monistic position and offered instead a more moderate interpretation of the *Upanishads*. Like the critic mentioned above, Ramanuja grants in principle that the universe consists of a single Divine thing but thinks that there are different parts or modifications within God—like the single glob of clay that can be molded into different things. Thus, according to Ramanuja, my outer empirical self and my true inner Self reflect two distinct aspects within the single

God. Ramanuja still advocates monism—only a single thing exists—but it is qualified in the sense that this single thing has parts and can be modified.

FROM RAMANUJA, *Commentary on the Vedanta Sutra*, 1.1.1

We cannot admit the claim that Scripture teaches that the cessation of ignorance springs only from the cognition of a God (Brahman) devoid of all difference. Such a view is clearly denied by other scripture passages . . . Because God (Brahman) is characterized by difference, all Vedic texts declare that final release results from the cognition of a qualified God (Brahman). And even those texts that describe God (Brahman) by way of negation really aim at setting forth a God (Brahman) that possesses attributes.

In texts such as "You are that" (*tat tvam asi*), the relation of the constituent parts is not meant to convey the idea of the absolute unity of an undifferentiated substance. On the contrary, the words "that" and "you" denote a God (Brahman) distinguished by difference. The word "that" refers to God (Brahman) as omniscient, etc., which had been introduced as the general topic of consideration in previous passages of the same section, such as "It thought, may I be many." The word "you," which stands in relation to "that," conveys the idea of God (Brahman) insofar as its body consists of the individual souls connected with non-intelligent matter. . . .

Moreover, it is not possible for ignorance to belong to God (Brahman), whose essential nature is knowledge, which is free from all imperfections, omniscient, comprising within itself all favorable qualities. However, ignorance would result from the absolute oneness of "that" and "you." It [i.e., God] would be the underlying strata of all those defects and afflictions which spring from ignorance. . . .

If, on the other hand, the text is understood to refer to God (Brahman) as having the individual souls for its body, both words ("that" and "you") keep their primary meaning. Thus, by making a declaration about one substance distinguished by two aspects, the text preserves the fundamental principle of "relation." On this interpretation the text further implies that Brahman (free from all imperfection and comprising within itself all favorable qualities) is the internal ruler of the individual souls and possesses lordly power.

ASK YOURSELF

20. According to Ramanuja's interpretation of the phrase "You are that," how do the terms "you" and "that" denote differences within God (Brahman)?

It may be interesting to compare Ramanuja's view to the views of the Western philosopher Spinoza, who is discussed below. Spinoza was also a monist, who believed that the one reality, which is God/Nature (*Deus sive natura*), has different aspects.

SUMMING UP CLASSIC HINDU VIEWS ON SOUL, SELF, AND GOD

Classic Hindu philosophy, as reflected in the *Katha Upanishad*, holds that a person has two selves: (a) an outer empirical part consisting of a body and conscious mental experiences and (b) a hidden inner part, which is the ultimate reality of the entire universe—the Self-God. Discovering this concealed part of us is a difficult task. Later Hindu scholars of the *Upanishads* attempted to resolve lingering questions raised by those texts, particularly whether our outer empirical selves are completely distinct from the Self-God. Sankara argued that the Self-God is composed of no parts. It may appear to us that the world contains different kinds of things, including our outer empirical selves, but this is an illusion. Ramanuja, by contrast, agreed that everything is subsumed in a single God, but he also held that God has parts, like a single glob of clay that can be molded into different things. Thus, my outer empirical self and my true inner Self reflect two distinct aspects within the single God.

CAN OF WORMS

Classic Hindu philosophy makes a dramatic claim: My inner self is the ultimate reality of the entire universe. If this view is true, then we might discover this hidden inner self through an introspective meditative experience—first peeling away the outer layers of our identities and then discovering what remains. Hindu meditative practices are discussed in Chapter 2. We also find in that chapter some critics who maintain that mystical experiences are unreliable. Another thing implied by Classic Hindu philosophy is that all existing things are connected to each other by means of this underlying reality. In Chapter 3, we see that some philosophers have argued that being aware of this interconnectedness should impact how we view and treat the environment. Thus these Hindu views have a bearing on environmental ethics.

C. MODERN VIEWS ON MIND AND BODY

In the seventeenth century, many European philosophers turned their attention to the nature of mind or consciousness and its relations to the body and physical nature generally. This interest was partly the result of scientific achievements of the time. Engineers and clock makers were capable of crafting complex and sophisticated machines which were self-regulating. Biologists and anatomists, armed with a much better understanding of human anatomy than their predecessors, began to think of the human body as a sophisticated soft machine. Questions then naturally emerged about how our human minds relate to our bodily machinery. The resulting mind–body theories defined the nature of the debate for centuries to come.

QUESTIONS TO DISCUSS

a. Very commonly our thoughts, which we may think of as "mental" or "spiritual" in some sense, affect our bodies. For example, my thought that I would like a cool drink affects my body in such a way that I get up and walk to the Coke machine. Do physical events also affect mental ones? Give an example of a physical event producing a mental event.

b. Some theories of mind and body involve the claim that they are completely distinct kinds of "things." Can you think of some problems such theories might have to face?

c. Could it be that mind and body, or soul and body, are so closely connected or intermingled that we could never clearly distinguish one from the other?

d. Are thoughts essentially "private"? Is it impossible to know that another person is thinking, or even that there are other minds? If not, why not?

1. MENTAL AND PHYSICAL SUBSTANCE: RENÉ DESCARTES

**RENÉ DESCARTES
(1596–1650)**

French rationalist philosopher and author of Meditations *(1641).*

French philosopher and mathematician René Descartes (1596–1650) was educated at a Jesuit college that was firmly grounded in the medieval scholastic tradition. After furthering his studies in Paris, he enlisted in the Dutch and, later, the Bavarian armies. In 1629 Descartes moved to Holland where he lived in seclusion for 20 years, changing his residence frequently to preserve his privacy. During this period he produced the writings upon which his fame rests. Perhaps his most famous work today is his *Meditations on the First Philosophy* (1641), which, as the subtitle indicates, is an attempt to prove the existence of God and "the distinction between mind and body."

Distinct Attributes of Mind and Body. Descartes's views on body and mind are motivated in large part by his theory of knowledge, which is explored in Chapter 5. In the following selection he attempts to provide criteria for distinguishing mind from body. It is significant that Descartes was part of the scientific revolution of the seventeenth century. The emerging ideal of science was one in which measurement and the use of mathematical formulae were extremely important. However, it seems obvious that sensations or thoughts cannot be measured with rulers or clocks. We might be able to say how long a sensation, such as a pain, lasted, but that does not tell us much about the pain itself. It does not appear that we could express the difference between a stabbing pain and a throbbing pain in terms of numbers or measures of any kind. Certainly Descartes felt that the realm of the mental was very different from the realm of the physical, largely because he thought that what distinguishes the physical is that it can be measured, weighed, and in general treated mathematically, whereas the mental cannot be treated in those ways.

FROM RENÉ DESCARTES, *Meditations* (1641), MEDITATION 6

In order to begin this examination, then, I here say, in the first place, that there is a great difference between mind and body, inasmuch as body is by nature always divisible, and the mind is entirely indivisible. For, as a matter of fact, when I consider the mind, that is to say, myself inasmuch as I am only a thinking thing, I cannot distinguish in myself any parts, but understand myself to be clearly one and entire. And although the whole mind seems to be united to the whole body, yet if a foot, or an arm, or some other part, is separated from my body, I am aware that nothing has been taken away from my mind. And the faculties of willing, feeling, conceiving, etc. cannot be properly speaking said to be its parts, for it is one and the same mind which employs itself in willing and in feeling and understanding. But it is quite otherwise with corporeal or extended objects, for there is not one of these imaginable by me which my mind cannot easily divide into parts, and which consequently I do not recognize as being divisible; this would be sufficient to teach me that the mind or soul of man is entirely different from the body, if I had not already learned it from other sources.

ASK YOURSELF

21. What is the key difference between mind and body mentioned here?

Descartes' tendency to associate mind with the brain is typically modern. Although he thinks of the mind as nonphysical, he also wants to associate it somehow with the brain. In that respect he is typically modern. The ancient thinker Lucretius associated the mind with the heart.

I further notice that the mind does not receive the impressions from all parts of the body immediately, but only from the brain, or perhaps even from one of its smallest parts, namely, from that in which the common sense is said to reside, which, whenever it is disposed in the same particular way, conveys the same thing to the mind, although meanwhile the other portions of the body may be differently disposed, as is testified by innumerable experiments which it is unnecessary here to recount.

Long Nerves to the Brain. Descartes' speculations about the brain and the nervous system show some familiarity with the experimental science that was developing in his era. There are long nerves going to and from the brain. If we poke one of these at one place, we may get a sensation qualitatively identical to one we would get if we poked it at another place.

I notice, also, that the nature of body is such that none of its parts can be moved by another part a little way off which cannot also be moved in the same way by each one of the parts which are between the two, although this more remote part does not act at all. As, for example, in the cord ABCD [which is in tension] if we pull the last part D, the first part A will not be moved in any way differently from what would be the case if one of the intervening parts B or C were pulled, and the last part D were to remain unmoved. And in the same way, when I feel pain in my foot, my knowledge of physics teaches me that this sensation is communicated by means of nerves dispersed through the foot, which, being extended like cords from there to the brain, when they are contracted in the foot, at the same time contract the inmost portions of the brain which is their extremity and place of origin, and then excite a certain movement which nature has established in order to cause the mind to be affected by a sensation of pain represented as existing in the foot. But because these nerves must pass through the tibia, the thigh, the loins, the back and the neck, in order to reach from the leg to the brain, it may happen that although their extremities which are in the foot are not affected, but only certain ones of their intervening parts [which pass by the loins or the neck], this action will excite the same movement in the brain that might have been excited there by a hurt received in the foot, in consequence of which the mind will necessarily feel in the foot the same pain as if it had received a hurt. And the same holds good of all the other perceptions of our senses.

ASK YOURSELF

22. What further reasons does Descartes give here for associating mind with the brain, rather than thinking of the mind as dispersed through the body?

23. Do Descartes' comments in the preceding section have a bearing on the phenomenon called "phantom pain" in which a person feels a pain in an amputated limb? Explain.

Feelings That Advance Our Preservation. Some of the sensations that arise from the body contribute to the survival of the body. Descartes attributes that fact to God's planning. More recent thinkers such as Darwin might attribute the same facts to natural selection.

When the nerves which are in the feet are violently or more than usually moved, their movement, passing through the medulla of the inmost parts of the brain, gives a sign to the mind which makes it feel somewhat, namely, pain, as though in the foot, by which the mind is excited to do its utmost to remove the cause of the evil as dangerous and hurtful to the foot. It is true that God could have constituted the nature of man in such a way that this same movement in the brain would have conveyed something quite different to the mind. For example, it might have produced consciousness of itself either in so far as it is in the brain, or as it is in the foot, or as it is in some other place between the foot and the brain, or it might finally have produced consciousness of anything else whatsoever. But none of all this would have contributed so well to the conservation of the body. Similarly, when we desire to drink, a certain dryness of the throat is produced which moves its nerves, and by their means the internal portions of the brain. And this movement causes in the mind the sensation of thirst, because in this case there is nothing more useful to us than to become aware that we have need to drink for the conservation of our health. And the same holds good in other instances.

ASK YOURSELF

24. Give one of Descartes' examples of an exaggerated bodily feeling that is for the benefit of self-preservation.

The Pineal Gland. Descartes believed that humans are composed of two distinct parts: a physical body that moves about in the physical world and a nonphysical or spiritual mind that thinks and feels. This dualism presents a problem for Descartes. How, in his view, could these two very different things, minds and bodies, interact in the ways they obviously do? For example, when my hand touches something hot, this sensation is registered in my mind. Also, if my mind decides to remove my hand, this decision must be transferred to my body, which results in motor activity. Thus, Descartes needs an explanation of both sensory and motor communication between our spirit minds and physical bodies. In the following, from Part 1 of *The Passions of the Soul* (1649), Descartes argues that the pineal gland in the brain is the gateway between the two realms.

FROM RENÉ DESCARTES, *The Passions of the Soul* (1649), 1.31–1.34

That there is a small gland in the brain in which the soul exercises its function more particularly than in the other parts. It is likewise necessary to know that although the soul is joined to the whole body, there is yet in that [body] a certain part in which it exercises its functions more particularly than in all the others. And it is usually believed that this part is the brain, or possibly the heart. It is believed to be the brain because it is with it that the organs of sense are connected. And it is believed to be the heart because it is apparently in it that we experience the passions. But, in examining the matter with care, it seems as though I had clearly ascertained that the part of the body in which the soul exercises its functions immediately is in nowise the heart, nor the whole of the brain. Instead, it is merely the most inward of all its parts, namely, a certain very small gland which is situated in the middle of its substance and so suspended above the duct whereby the animal spirits in its anterior cavities have communication with those in the posterior. It is such that the slightest movements which take place in it may alter very greatly the course of these spirits. And, reciprocally, the smallest changes which occur in the course of the spirits may do much to change the movements of this gland.

ASK YOURSELF

25. What are the two standard accounts of where the body and soul are connected?

How we know that this gland is the main seat of the soul. The reason which persuades me that the soul cannot have any other seat in all the body than this gland wherein to exercise its functions immediately, is that I reflect that the other parts of our brain are all of them double, just as we have two eyes, two hands, two ears, and finally all the organs of our outside senses are double. And inasmuch as we have but one solitary and simple thought of one particular thing at one and the same moment, it must necessarily be the case that there must somewhere be a place where the two images which come to us by the two eyes, where the two other impressions which proceed from a single object by means of the double organs of the other senses, can unite before arriving at the soul, in order that they may not represent to it two objects instead of one. And it is easy to see how these images or other impressions might unite in this gland by the intermission of the spirits which fill the cavities of the brain. But there is no other place in the body where they can be thus united unless they are so in this gland.

ASK YOURSELF

26. What reason does Descartes give for holding that the pineal gland is the gateway between the brain and body?

27. Machines are not alive. Descartes' comparison of the body to a machine thus seems to imply that there is no real _____ in the body.

28. In Descartes' view, all physical or bodily things, including such things as human brains, exist in space, whereas minds do not. Does his theory that the two interact in the pineal gland (which is in space) make sense, given his conception of mind and body? Explain.

It is significant that Descartes' focus is on "mind" or the "mental" in a sense that would have been largely foreign to Plato. Both of them are sometimes called body–soul dualists, but it would be more accurate to refer to Descartes as a body–mind dualist. Minds are not quite equivalent to souls, although they share significant properties, such as being nonspatial. A distinctive notion of "soul" appears in the work of Anne Conway. Conway rejects Descartes' view and borrows only a few elements from Plato.

2. THE MIXTURE OF BODY AND SOUL: ANNE CONWAY

British philosopher Anne Conway (1631–1678) was educated privately by Henry More, a prominent member of a seventeenth-century intellectual movement known as Cambridge Platonism. Following their ancient Greek mentor, the Platonists emphasized both reason and the spirit realm. They also rejected purely mechanistic views of the universe, and they held that God and spirit were active components of the world. In addition to influence from the

Platonists, Conway was also inspired by mystical writers of the Jewish cabalistic tradition, who developed theories about female forces in the universe. Her sole publication is the *Principles of the Most Ancient and Modern Philosophy* published posthumously in 1690. Two themes stand out in her work: (1) Things are capable of changing much more than we typically might think, and (2) body and soul are more or less the same thing, differing only in degree and not in kind.

Body and Soul Differ Only in Degree, Not in Kind. According to Conway, body and soul are not essentially different kinds of things. However, she does not side with materialists like Lucretius, who reduce mind to body or what is physical. Rather, she thinks of the body itself as "soulish" and the soul as "bodyish." Bodies and souls fall into a spectrum, and they intermingle with each other in differing degrees. She offers a series of arguments for her position, one of which, presented below, is based on the intimate connection and interaction between bodies and souls. Thus she rejects any notion of the body as a machine (as in Descartes) or any notion of the soul or mind as totally distinct from the body (as in both Plato and Descartes).

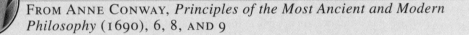

FROM ANNE CONWAY, *Principles of the Most Ancient and Modern Philosophy* (1690), 6, 8, AND 9

To prove that spirit and body differ not essentially, but gradually, I shall deduce my fourth argument from the intimate band or union, which intercedes between bodies and spirits. [It is] by means whereof the spirits have dominion over the bodies with which they are united, that they move them from one place to another, and use them as instruments in their various operations. For if spirit and body are so contrary one to another (so that a spirit is only life, or a living and sensible substance, but a body a certain mass merely dead; a spirit penetrable and indiscernible [i.e., indivisible into parts], which are all contrary attributes) what (I pray you) is that which does so join or unite them together? Or, what are those links or chains, whereby they have so firm a connection, and that for so long a space of time? Moreover also, when the spirit or soul is separated from the body, so that it has no longer dominion or power over it to move it as it had before, what is the cause of this separation?

ASK YOURSELF

29. Conway is addressing a problem that Descartes' extreme dualism must face, namely the problem of _____ _____ interaction.

The following comments look like an attack upon Descartes.

If it be said, that the vital agreement ([which] the soul has to the body) is the cause of the said union, and that the body being corrupted that vital agreement ceases, I answer, we must first inquire in what this vital agreement does consist. For if they cannot tell us wherein it does consist, they only trifle with empty words, which give a sound, but want a signification. For certainly in the sense which they take body and spirit in, there is no agreement at all between them. For a body is always a dead thing, void of life and sense, no less when the spirit is in it, than when it is gone out of it. Hence there is no agreement at all between them. And if there is any agreement, that certainly will remain the same, both when the body is sound, and when it is corrupted.

If they deny this, because a spirit requires an organized body (by means whereof it performs its vital acts of the external senses—moves and transports the body from place to place, which organical action ceases when the body is corrupted) certainly by this the difficulty is never the better solved. For why does the spirit require such an organized body? e.g. Why does it require a corporeal eye so wonderfully formed and organized, that I can see by it? Why does it need a corporeal light to see corporeal objects? Or, why is it requisite that the image of the object should be sent to it, through the eye, that I may see it? If the same were entirely nothing but a spirit, and no way corporeal, why does it need so many several corporeal organs, so far different from the nature of it?

ASK YOURSELF

30. Defenders of the body/soul distinction might argue that the two are connected by means of a "vital agreement" between them. What, for Conway, is the problem with this explanation?

Against Descartes. Conway was aware that her theory of body and soul ran counter to views of the subject held by famous philosophers of her time, especially Descartes, Hobbes, and Spinoza.

From what has been lately said, and from divers reasons alleged, that spirit and body are originally in their first substance but one and the same thing, it evidently appears that the philosophers (so called) which have taught otherwise, whether ancient or modern, have generally erred. . . .

And none can object, that all this philosophy is no other than that of Descartes or Hobbes under a new mask. For, first, as touching the Cartesian philosophy, this says that every body is a mere dead mass, not only void of all kind of life and sense, but utterly incapable thereof to all eternity. This grand error also is to be imputed to all those who affirm body and spirit to be contrary things, and inconvertible one into another, so as to deny a body all life and sense, but utterly incapable thereof to all eternity. This grand error also is to be imputed to all those who affirm body and spirit to be contrary things, and inconvertible one into another, so as to deny a body all life and sense, which is quite contrary to the grounds of this our philosophy. Wherefore it is so far from being a *Cartesian* principle, under a new mask, that it may be truly said it is *anti-Cartesian,* in regard of their fundamental principles—although, it cannot be denied that Descartes taught many excellent and ingenious things concerning the mechanical part of natural operations, and how all natural motions proceed according to rules and laws mechanical, even as indeed nature herself, i.e., the creature, has an excellent mechanical skill and wisdom in itself (given it from God, who is the fountain of all wisdom) by which it operates. But yet in nature, and her operations, they are far more than merely mechanical, and the same is not a mere organical body, like a clock, wherein there is not a vital principle of motion, but a living body, having life and sense, which body is far more sublime than a mere mechanism, or mechanical motion.

ASK YOURSELF

31. Would you agree that a living body is always something more than just a mechanical arrangement of physical parts? Explain.

3. IDEALIST MONISM AND PARALLELISM: BENEDICT SPINOZA AND GOTTFRIED WILLHELM LEIBNIZ

BENEDICT SPINOZA (1632–1677)

Dutch–Jewish philosopher and author of Ethics *(1677).*

Descartes did not give a satisfactory account of the relation between mind and body. It is obvious that mind and body interact. Thoughts and other mental events cause bodily movements, and bodily events cause mental events.

ASK YOURSELF

32. Give examples to illustrate the claim just made.

Yet in Descartes' view, bodies are located in space, minds are not. How then could they interact? The interaction could not occur at a place (such as the pineal gland) since mental events do not occur at any place whatsoever. The difficulty was very evident to Descartes' contemporaries, as the selection from Conway shows. One solution would be to deny any independent metaphysical status to bodies and settle for a completely ideal metaphysics, one in which all that is real is mind or somehow mind-like. Benedict Spinoza (1632–1677) held the view that all that exists is God. There is nothing but God; there is no physical reality independent of God. This view seems to reintroduce religious notions into the discussion of mind and body, notions similar to some found in Eastern thinkers. It is worth noting, however, that Spinoza was accused of atheism in his own time.

> In the foregoing I have explained the nature and properties of God. I have shown that (1) he necessarily exists, (2) that he is one, (3) that he is, and acts solely by the necessity of his own nature, (4) that he is the free cause of all things, and how he is so, (5) that all things are in God, and so depend on him, that without him they could neither exist nor be conceived, and (6) that all things are predetermined by God, not through his free will or absolute fiat, but from the very nature of God or infinite power. [From Benedict Spinoza, *Ethics* (1677), Book 1]

Spinoza is a pantheist, someone who believes that God is everything and everything is God, or is in God. Whatever we might think of such a view, it at any rate avoids the problem of explaining how two distinct kinds of things, the mental and the physical, can interact. For in Spinoza's view there is only *one* kind of existing thing, namely, God.

Another solution to the problem posed by Descartes is called "parallelism." According to this view, mental and bodily events are perfectly lined up together in parallel physical and spiritual realms. For instance, when the physical event of a large rock landing on my toe occurs, the mental event of feeling a pain "in the toe" typically occurs, rather than the feeling of a toothache or any other random pain. In that sense the physical event and the mental event "harmonize." However, there is in this parallelist view no causal connection between the mental and the physical. This view does seem pretty bizarre at first sight. Surely such a remarkable matching could not just take place by chance! Gottfried Willhelm Leibniz

(1646–1716) held some such view, and he argued that the correspondence that gives rise to our notion of a causal relation between mind and body was pre-established by God. God made sure ahead of time that the "right" kind of mental events would always match up with the "right" kind of physical events even though there is no real causal connection between them. God, then, produces the universe in such a way that there are orderly appearances, including the appearance of mental events causing physical ones in a regular predictable way, and vice versa. Thus the problem of how mind and body could possibly interact is avoided.

GOTTFRIED WILLHELM LEIBNIZ (1646–1716)

German philosopher and diplomat, and author of Monadology *(1721).*

> These principles have furnished me the means of explaining on natural grounds the union, or rather the conformity between the soul and the organic body. The soul follows its own laws, and the body likewise follows its own laws. They are fitted to each other in virtue of the pre-established harmony between all substances since they are all representations of one and the same universe.
>
> Souls act in accordance with the laws of final causes through their desires, ends and means. Bodies act in accordance with the laws of efficient causes or of motion. The two realms, that of efficient causes and that of final causes, are in harmony, each with the other.
> [From Gottfried Willhelm Leibniz, *Monadology,* 78, 79]

Leibniz's solution is embedded in a complex metaphysics which certainly deserves respectful study, but which few today would think of as containing a viable solution to the mind–body problem.

ASK YOURSELF

33. Describe the two solutions to mind–body interaction just mentioned.

SUMMING UP MODERN VIEWS ON MIND AND BODY

Descartes cast a long shadow. Much of the debate in the modern period over the nature of mind was governed by reactions to the Cartesian view that "thinking things" are completely nonphysical. Nonetheless, it seems obvious that the thinking thing, the mind, interacts with the body. Thoughts lead to bodily actions. Bodily events cause mental events. But the sharp metaphysical distinction between body and mind would seem to make that impossible. Even where the sharp distinction was challenged, as it was by Conway, Descartes' influence, though negative, was present. Spinoza and Leibniz evade the problem of interaction by constructing metaphysical schemes in which mind and body are mere aspects of a single reality (as with Spinoza) or in which there is no actual interaction (as with Leibniz). Nonetheless, Descartes' influence continued into the twentieth century, and dualist views similar to his continue to provoke discussion.

**CAN OF
WORMS**

Descartes' views have controversial ethical implications. If, as he claimed, animals are not conscious, then there seems to be no point to rules against cruelty to animals. His views also have important implications for knowledge. If I have direct access to my own mind only, then there is a real question as to how I could possibly *know* that there are any other minds. At best I could make a weak inference based on the behavior of others. Descartes' conception could lead to solipsism. Cartesian conceptions have in fact encouraged a way of thinking about human nature in which each human being is isolated from all others and must construct a world from scratch, so to speak. The metaphysical, ethical, epistemological, and social implications of the debate started by Descartes cannot be ignored in evaluating that debate.

D. TWENTIETH-CENTURY VIEWS ON MIND AND BODY

Almost daily we hear news reports about remarkable discoveries in the area of brain anatomy and activity. You may have heard the claim that certain parts of the brain perform certain "functions." There might seem to be an area that handles language, for example. But you may have also heard or read about research that shows that the function purportedly performed by one area of the brain can be taken up by other parts when the original area is damaged. We also read and hear a great deal about the possibility that various behaviors are due to chemical imbalances in the brain. A good deal of experimentation with drugs has resulted from such claims.

**QUESTIONS
TO DISCUSS**

a. Suppose that by removing or deadening a small portion of your brain I could make it impossible for you to do certain things, such as speak normally. Would that show that the mental component of speaking normally was nothing but a brain activity?

b. If seeing something blue was simply a brain activity, would there have to be something blue in the brain? If not, where would the blueness be?

c. Could human beings who were born deaf, dumb, blind, and paralyzed have thoughts, and, if so, how could we know they did, or know what those thoughts might be?

There has been a particularly intense focus on questions in the philosophy of mind in the twentieth century. Some of this focus was provoked in part by developments in the sorts of brain research just mentioned. Developments in the relatively young science of psychology have also provoked philosophical commentary, as has research into artificial intelligence done by non-philosophers. But some of the contemporary focus on mind derives from a style of philosophizing that emphasizes careful analysis and the use of "thought experiments" to explore the conceptual "geography" of "mind," "belief," "intention," and the like. Some twentieth-century philosophers have regarded that style as peculiarly philosophical. Thus some philosophers have challenged the findings of neurologists and psychologists on the grounds that they are conceptually confused in various ways. Philosophers have also been able to put some of the detailed results of brain research or AI research into the larger context of long-standing debates about the relations of the mental to the physical.

1. LOGICAL BEHAVIORISM: GILBERT RYLE

In the twentieth century, various forms of "behaviorism" were proposed as solutions to the so-called mind–body problem. Some psychologists, perhaps most notably B. F. Skinner, have argued that what we normally call thoughts, beliefs, desires, and the like are actually nothing more than behavioral patterns or dispositions to behave in certain ways under certain circumstances. The behaviorist program in psychology has been subjected to strong criticisms that we cannot discuss here.

However, there is another form of behaviorism, associated especially with the British philosopher Gilbert Ryle (1900–1976), called *logical behaviorism*. Ryle contends that expressions referring to what is mental—such as "he thought about his brother"—belong to a different logical category than do expressions referring to physical objects and occurrences. Ryle argued that once that fact is understood, the problem raised by Descartes' view will disappear. He argues that someone who wonders whether just bodies exists, or just minds, or whether both exist in some sort of relationship, is logically confused.

> [To say] "either minds exist or bodies exist" . . . would be like saying, "Either she bought a left-hand and a right-hand glove or she bought a pair of gloves (but not both)." It is perfectly proper to say, in one logical tone of voice, that there exist minds and to say, in another logical tone of voice, that there exist bodies. But these expressions do not indicate two different species of existence, for "existence" is not a generic word like "colored" or "sexed." They indicate two different senses of "exist," somewhat as "rising" has different senses in "the tide is rising," "hopes are rising," and "the average age of death is rising." A man would be thought to be making a poor joke who said that three things are now rising, namely the tide, hopes and the average age of death. It would be just as good or bad a joke to say that there exist prime numbers and Wednesdays and public opinions and navies; or that there exist both minds and bodies.

ASK YOURSELF

34. Suppose that you said that your hopes were rising, and someone then asked "how many feet have they risen?" This response would be pretty silly. Why?

Ryle argues that the traditional Cartesian view supposes that minds are like "ghosts in a machine." Those ghosts are thought of on the model of physical things—ghostly physical things—perhaps with ghostly eyes, arms, and so forth. They do not, however, exist in space, whereas bodies do. Ryle argues that to think of minds in that way is like thinking navies exist in space and Wednesdays do not. We should not suppose that since Wednesdays don't exist in space, they must be ghostly nonspatial entities. They are not "entities" at all, they are neither spatial nor nonspatial. Neither, in Ryle's view, are minds entities at all, either spatial or nonspatial. They are in a different *category* than bodies, just as Wednesdays are in a different category than navies. Navies, let it be noted, are in a different category than single ships. Someone who saw all the ships in a navy and then asked "but when will we see the navy?" would be logically confused. Ryle writes,

Now the dogma of the Ghost in the Machine does just this. It maintains that there exist both bodies and minds; that there occur physical processes and mental processes; that there are mechanical causes of corporeal movements and mental causes of corporeal movements. I shall argue that these and other analogous conjunctions are absurd; but, it must be noticed, the argument will not show that either of the illegitimately conjoined propositions is absurd in itself. I am not, for example, denying that there occur mental processes. Doing long division is a mental process and so is making a joke. But I am saying that the phrase "there occur mental processes" does not mean the same sort of thing as "there occur physical processes," and, therefore, that it makes no sense to conjoin or disjoin the two. [From Gilbert Ryle, *The Concept of Mind* (1949)]

How does all of this apply to understanding particular attributions of mental states? How would Ryle analyze "Mary believed George would be late"? Part of his analysis is similar to the analysis of the psychological behaviorist. To have a belief is not to have something going on "inside" a ghostly medium called the mind. Rather, it is to be disposed to act in certain ways. If Mary has that belief, then she will answer the question "Will George be here on time?" with a verbal utterance such as "no" or "not likely" or she might just get a certain look on her face and shrug. Beliefs are multi-track dispositions or tendencies to behave in a number of related ways. They are not activities that go on inside *mental* entities. It does not follow, however, that they are therefore activities that go on in *physical* entities. That seemed to be the view of some psychological behaviorists. In Ryle's account, that too would be a "category mistake."

Ryle's style of analysis seemed plausible for a number of "mental states" such as believing and knowing, but perhaps less plausible for feelings and sensations, such as pain sensations or the sour taste of a lemon. In any case, Ryle's logical behaviorism did not make the debate about the relations of minds to bodies go away.

ASK YOURSELF

35. Briefly, in Ryle's account what are we saying or implying when we say that John believes he will pass the philosophy exam?

36. Since in Ryle's view a belief is not a state of a nonphysical mind, does it follow that a belief is a state of a physical body? Explain.

Question c in the last Questions to Discuss box is this: "Could human beings who were born deaf, dumb, blind, and paralyzed have thoughts, and, if so, how could we know they did, or know what those thoughts might be?" How do you suppose Ryle might answer this question?

2. MIND–BRAIN IDENTITY AND ELIMINATIVE MATERIALISM: J. J. C. SMART AND PAUL CHURCHLAND

We have mentioned three principal solutions to the mind–body problem. One solution, suggested by Spinoza, is to get rid of the physical, to argue that all that is real is mind or mind-like. Another solution, suggested by Leibniz, posits a parallelism or pre-established harmony between mental events and physical events. Then there is the behaviorist solution, which in Ryle's version is not so much a solution to the problem as it is the denial that there *is* any problem, except for people who are logically confused.

Another solution consists in removing mind altogether from the metaphysical picture. In this view, people are nothing but physical things. This view was already anticipated by Democritus and Lucretius. As knowledge of the brain and entire nervous system expanded in the modern era, many thinkers advanced more sophisticated materialist views of the mind. Some concluded that mental events are nothing but physical events of a special type, involving complex reactions in the nervous systems of human beings and other animals.

ASK YOURSELF

37. What are the four views of the mind–body relation considered so far?

Scientists have learned a great deal about the brain and nervous system since the days of Descartes and Leibniz. It is worth noting here, for future reference, that brains or nervous systems consist of cells called "neurons." Cells are among the smallest living things, as small as 10 microns (one millionth of a meter) in diameter. Some neurons are quite long, however, stretching down the spine. Neurons have "axons" along which electrical changes take place (themselves functions of chemical changes). Thus neuronal events are electrical/chemical events. Brain activity can be understood as interactions between neurons or groups of them. When recent scientists and philosophers claim that mental events are nothing but brain events, those are the sorts of events to which they are usually referring. Increased knowledge of the brain has encouraged the idea that the mental is nothing more than a special subset of the physical.

Reductionism and Materialism. In the twentieth century a great many philosophers and scientists adopted materialist views of the mind. Some hold that mental events are *identical with* brain events. This is the "identity thesis." A feeling of pain is nothing more than a certain neuronal event. These views are usually "reductionist" in the sense that mental events are *reduced to* physical events.

The notion of a "reduction" is common in the sciences and even in everyday life. A nation is reducible to a collection of citizens; that is to say, it is *nothing more* than a collection of citizens. A cloud is reducible to, or is nothing more than, a collection of water droplets. Water is nothing more than two atoms of hydrogen and one of oxygen combined in a certain way; that is, water is H_2O. The last is an example of a theoretical "micro-reduction" since in it a familiar object, water, is reduced to something unfamiliar and theoretical (and relatively small), namely atoms and chemical bonds. Lightning is reducible to, is nothing more than, an electrical discharge. Likewise, perhaps a mental event is nothing more than a physical event. The notion of "reduction" turns out to be quite complex, but keeping these examples in mind will help clarify materialist reductionism in the philosophy of mind.

It does not follow from reductionist claims that, for example, a report of a sensation, such as "I am now having an orangeish afterimage" *means* the same or has the same "logic" as a statement that mentions all the neuronal events that constitute having such a sensation. A proponent of the mind–brain identity thesis, J. J. C. Smart, put it this way:

Insofar as a sensation statement is a report of something, that something is in fact a brain process. Sensations are nothing over and above brain processes. Nations are nothing "over and above" citizens, but this does not prevent the logic of nation statements being very different from the logic of citizen statements. [From J. J. C. Smart, "Sensations and Brain Processes" (1959)]

To illustrate the last claim: Nations can go through economic recessions, whereas the individual citizens who make up the nation cannot be meaningfully said to go through economic recessions *as individuals* (though they might suffer from one or live during one). That illustrates what it means to say that the "logic" of statements about citizens is often different from the "logic" of statements about nations. It does not follow that there is something more to a nation than the collection of citizens which make it up. Likewise, a pain can be piercing or intense, whereas brain events are neither piercing nor intense, but it does not follow that pains are anything more than brain events.

ASK YOURSELF

38. According to Smart, pains simply are brain events. However, even if I don't know anything about the brain or nervous system, I can still talk informatively about some mental events. Give an example.

39. Suppose someone objected to the identity thesis in the following way: I can know I am in pain without knowing that my brain is in state S, where state S *is* the pain, in the identity theorist view. So something is true of my pain, namely that I know about it, which is not true of my brain state S, about which, let us suppose, I know nothing. Therefore my pain cannot be identical with that brain state, since if two things are identical, whatever is true of the one must be true of the other. How could Smart reply? For help with this question see the Thinking Logically box in Chapter 2, Section D, 3.

Eliminative Materialism. Some philosophers have argued that we will ultimately be able to get along without mentioning supposed mental events at all. Recently, some materialist views of the mind have been proposed which aim to *eliminate* mental concepts altogether from correct descriptions of the world. Instead of keeping the concept "pain" or "thought" and *reducing* them to something physical, the eliminativist thinks of those concepts as belonging to an outmoded theory that ought to be discarded.

In order to get the flavor of this view, consider the concept "phologiston." Eighteenth-century chemists held the theory that combustion is the result of the release of an element called phlogiston from the burning object. It was a bad theory and has been eliminated from descriptions of the world proffered by modern chemists. Chemists no longer speak of phlogiston at all. They certainly do not try to show how "phlogiston events" can be *reduced* to "oxygenation events." Analogously, eliminative materialists in the philosophy of mind argue that some future brain science or neurophysiology will make it possible to simply discard all references to thoughts or other mental events. They think this would be a good thing because, among other reasons, the familiar language that we use to describe our mental lives is part of a bad theory, which they call "folk psychology," or what we might call common-sense psychology. Folk psychology, they believe, has proved incapable of improvement or great accuracy and should be eliminated.

To illustrate this view, consider the following case. I often explain what people are doing in terms of feelings, thoughts, or memories which I attribute to them. For example, I might explain why you are scowling by supposing that you are remembering something that made you angry. But I might be completely wrong. Moreover, I do not have any clear idea of what memory is. So when I use the folk psychological notion of "memory" to explain something, I often err, and generally do not understand clearly what I am doing. Moreover, my repertoire of common sense psychological concepts will fail drastically when faced with unusual behavior.

A contemporary proponent of eliminative materialism, Paul Churchland, puts it this way:

> The most central things about us remain almost entirely mysterious from within folk psychology . . . so long as one sticks to normal brains, the poverty of folk psychology is perhaps not strikingly evident. But as soon as one examines the many perplexing behavioral and cognitive deficits suffered by people with damaged brains, one's descriptive and explanatory resources start to claw the air. [From Paul Churchland, *Matter and Consciousness* (1988)]

One example mentioned by Churchland is what is called "blindsight." A person in this condition has lost their visual field entirely and yet can accurately indicate the location of moving or illuminated objects. A number of interesting illustrations along these lines can be found in the essay by Huxley in the upcoming section on minds and machines. It is true that the concepts of thought, belief, feeling, sensation, and so forth, which all of us use so naturally, do not seem to work very well, or at all, when we are confronted with such phenomena as blindsight.

One thing that motivates scientists to seek for reductions of the mental to the physical—or alternatively the elimination of the mental as proposed by Churchland—is a hope for the *unity of science.* In fact that hope is one of the main motivations behind *materialism* in general. Many scientists cannot accept the idea that psychology, biology, chemistry, and physics are separate sciences with independent principles and laws. There must be principles that underlie all the sciences, and it seems to many that these principles are most likely ones to be found in physics. Thus many think that chemistry can be "reduced to" physics. The chemist's descriptions of water in terms of hydrogen and oxygen can perhaps be further reduced to descriptions of subatomic particles obeying the laws of physics. Similarly, perhaps descriptions of mental states could be reduced to, or eliminated in favor of, descriptions of the microstructure of the brain, descriptions that are ultimately put in terms of physics.

ASK YOURSELF

40. What is "reductionism"? Try to give an example not mentioned in the text.

41. Explain how eliminative materialism differs from reductionism.

42. How does the quest for the "unity of science" motivate reductionism and eliminativism?

---

3. FUNCTIONALISM: JERRY FODOR

Reductive materialism in its twentieth-century versions has provoked strong criticisms. Some critics have pointed out that if the identity thesis were true, it would follow that an extraterrestrial being who had a brain made of different kinds of materials than those comprising a human brain could not have thoughts or pains, or at any rate the same sorts of thoughts or pains that we have. But that seems to many critics to be implausible. Thus, if we want to be materialists, we need to find an account of mental events that does not identify mental events with specifically human physical states, such as firings of neurons in brains that are physically just like human brains. Another criticism is set forth in the following selection, which is by the contemporary American philosopher Jerry Fodor. Fodor then presents an alternative view which is consistent with a materialist metaphysics, but which is not reductionist. That view is called "functionalism."

Problems with Reductionism. Like Ryle, Fodor argues that it is a kind of "category mistake" to think that psychological states or events can be reduced to specific physical events.

FROM JERRY FODOR, *Psychological Explanation* (1968)

Psychological entities (sensations, for example) are not readily thought of as capable of being microanalyzed into *anything,* least of all neurons or states of neurons. Pains do not have parts, so brain cells are not parts of pains.

It is, in short, conceivable that there may be true psychophysical identity statements, but it seems inconceivable that such statements are properly analyzed as expressing what Place has called identities of composition, that is, as expressing relations between wholes and their parts.

The claim that water is identical with H_2O would be the claim that there is an identity of composition between them. Water is the "whole," and hydrogen and oxygen atoms are the parts.

It is worth pursuing at some length the difference between the present view of the relation between psychological and neurological constructs and the view typical of reductivist materialism. In reductive analysis (microanalysis), one asks: "What does X consist of ?" and the answer has the form of a specification of the microstructure of X. Thus: "What does water consist of?" "Two atoms of hydrogen linked with one atom of oxygen." "What does lightning consist of ?" "A stream of electrons." And so on. In typical cases of functional analysis, by contrast, one asks about a part of a mechanism what *role it plays* in the activities that are characteristic of the mechanism as a whole: "What does the camshaft do?" "It opens the valves, permitting the entry into the cylinder of fuel, which will then be detonated to drive the piston." Successful microanalysis is thus often contingent upon the development of powerful instruments of observation or precise methods of dissection. Successful functional analysis, on the other hand, requires an appreciation of the sorts of activity that are characteristic of a mechanism and of the contribution made by the functioning of each part of the mechanism to the economy of the whole.

A camshaft is a rod with disks strategically placed on it so that as it turns it opens the valves in the cylinders of an internal combustion engine. A simpler illustration of Fodor's idea would be this; a brick could be a door stopper. When I call it a brick, I refer to certain physical characteristics and makeup. When I call it a doorstopper, I simply say what *function* I have given it. Other things that have completely different physical makeups, such as a rubber wedge or a large brass pot, could also "function as" door stops. All of them could "play that role." For something to be a doorstop, it must simply function in a certain way. It need not be made up of any specific materials, have a specific shape, and so forth. It does not follow that absolutely anything could be a doorstop. But it does follow that the function of holding a door open could be fulfilled by many different objects. The function is "multiply realizable." Fodor is arguing that mental states are functional states that could be realized physically in many ways. Thoughts, for example, play a certain functional role in my life. Thoughts are identified in terms of that role. Different functions = different thoughts. Since thoughts can be realized in many physically different kinds of things, there could be no *identity* between a mental state and a *specific* physical configuration.

ASK YOURSELF

43. Why not?

Since microanalysis and functional analysis are very different ways of establishing relations between scientific theories, or between ordinary language descriptions, conceptual difficulties may result when the vocabulary of one kind of analysis is confounded with the vocabulary of the other.

If I speak of a device as a "camshaft," I am implicitly identifying it by reference to its physical structure, and so I am committed to the view that it exhibits a characteristic and specifiable decomposition into physical parts." But if I speak of the device as a "valve lifter," I am identifying it by reference to its function and I therefore undertake no such commitment. There is, in particular, no sense to the question "What does a valve lifter consist of?" if this is understood as a request for microanalysis—that is, as analogous to such questions as "What does water consist of?" (There *is*, of course, sense to the question "What does *this* valve lifter consist of?" but the generic valve lifter must be *functionally* defined, and functions do not have parts.) One might put it that being a valve lifter is not reducible to (is not a matter of) being a collection of rods, springs, and atoms, in the sense in which being a camshaft is. The kinds of questions that it makes sense to ask about camshafts need not make sense, and are often impertinent, when asked about valve lifters.

ASK YOURSELF

44. To return to the doorstopper example, we could rephrase Fodor's last sentence as follows: The kinds of questions that it makes sense to ask about _____ need not make sense when asked about _____.

45. Give an example of such a question.

It is, then, conceivable that serious confusions could be avoided if we interpreted statements that relate psychological and neurological constructs not as articulating microanalyses but as attributing certain psychological functions to corresponding neurological systems. For example, philosophers and psychologists who have complained that it is possible to trace an input from afferent to central neurological systems without once encountering motives, strategies, drives, needs, hopes, along with the rest of the paraphernalia of psychological theories, have been right in one sense but wrong in another, just as one would be if one argued that a complete mechanical account of the operation of an internal combustion engine never encounters such a thing as a valve lifter. In both cases, the confusion occurs when a term that properly figures in functional accounts of mechanisms is confounded with terms that properly appear in mechanistic accounts, so that one is tempted to think of the function of a part as though it were itself one part among others.

From a functional point of view, a camshaft is a valve lifter and *this* valve lifter (i.e., this particular mechanism for lifting valves) may be "nothing but" a camshaft. But a mechanistic account of the operations of internal-combustion engines does not seek to replace the concept of a valve lifter with the concept of a camshaft, nor does it seek to "reduce" the former to the latter. What it does do is to explain *how* the valves get lifted: that is, what mechanical transactions are involved when the camshaft lifts the valves. In the same way, presumably, neurological theories seek to explain what biochemical transactions are involved when drives are reduced, motives entertained, objects perceived, and so on.

To return to our simpler case, an account of a doorstopper should not "reduce" being a doorstopper to being, say, a rubber wedge. That is, it does not require that being a doorstopper is *identical to* being a rubber wedge. That would imply that nothing but a rubber wedge could be a doorstopper, which is obviously false. Nonetheless, in a particular case where we are using a rubber wedge as a doorstopper, we might explain *how* a rubber wedge holds open a door. That explanation would mention the properties of rubber, friction, and so forth. A different sort of explanation of *how* this occurs would be needed if the doorstopper were a brick.

In short, drives, motives, strategies, and such are, on the present view, internal states postulated in attempts to account for behavior, perception, memory, and other phenomena in the domain of psychological theories. In completed accounts, they could presumably serve to characterize the functional aspects of neurological mechanisms; that is, they would figure in explanations of how such mechanisms operate to determine the molar behavior of an organism, its perceptual capacities, and so on. But this does not entail that drives, motives, and strategies have microanalyses in terms of neurological systems any more than valve lifters can be microanalyzed into camshafts.

"Molar" behavior is a *large* unit of behavior, such as hearing, which psychological theories explain in terms of various minute physical mechanisms.

ASK YOURSELF

46. What would the "molar behavior" of a doorstop be?

47. Why can't valve lifters be microanalyzed into camshafts? Why can't doorstops be microanalyzed into rubber wedges?

There are still further philosophically pertinent differences between the suggestion that psychophysical identity statements should be understood as articulating functional analyses and the suggestion that they should be analyzed as microreductions.

When, in paradigmatic cases, entities in one theory are reduced to entities in another, it is presupposed that both theories have available conceptual mechanisms for saying what the entities have in common. For example, given that water can be "reduced" to H_2O, it is possible to say what all samples of water have in common either in the language of viscosity, specific gravity, and so on at the macrolevel, or in chemical language at the microlevel. It is patent that functional analysis need not share this property of reductive analysis. When we identify a certain mousetrap with a certain mechanism, we do not thereby commit ourselves to the possibility of saying in mechanistic terms what all members of the set of mousetraps have in common. Because it is (roughly) a sufficient condition for being a mousetrap that a mechanism be customarily *used* in a certain way, there is nothing in principle that requires that a pair of mousetraps *have* any shared mechanical properties. It is, indeed, because "mousetrap" is functionally rather than mechanically defined that "building a better mousetrap"—that is, building a mechanically novel mousetrap, which functions better than conventional mousetraps do—is a reasonable goal to set oneself.

A good mousetrap has been devised consisting of a plastic pan with very sticky stuff on it. Obviously this mousetrap has *nothing physical* in common with the more conventional mousetraps made of wooden bases, steel springs, bars, and so forth. What they *do* have in common is that both are mousetraps. They have the same function. Similarly, two *physically different* anatomical structures (one in a Martian, another in an earthling) might have in common the same function, say, hearing, or color perception, or thinking about last night's party.

It is a consequence of this consideration that the present interpretation of the relation between neurological and psychological constructs is compatible with very strong claims about the ineliminability of mental language from behavioral theories. Let us suppose that there are true psychophysical statements that identify certain neurological mechanisms as the ones that possess certain psychologically relevant functional properties. It still remains quite conceivable that identical psychological functions could sometimes be ascribed to anatomically heterogeneous neural mechanisms. In that case, mental language will be required to state the conditions upon such ascriptions of functional equivalence. It is, in short, quite conceivable that a parsing of the nervous system by reference to anatomical or morphological similarities may often fail to correspond in any uniform way to its parsing in terms of psychological function. Whenever this occurs, explicit reference to the character of such functions will be required if we are to be able to say what we take the brain states that we classify together to have in common. Every mousetrap can be identified with some mechanism, and being a mousetrap can therefore be identified with being a member of some (indefinite) set of possible mechanisms. But enumerating the set is not a way of dispensing with the notion of a mousetrap; that notion is required to say what all the members of the set have in common and, in particular, what credentials would be required to certify a putative new member as belonging to the set. Such considerations may be extended to suggest not only that a *plausible* version of materialism will need to view psychological theories as articulating the functional characteristics of neural mechanisms, but also that that is the *only* version of materialism that is likely to prove coherent.

Experiments have shown that *different* parts of the brain can take up the *same* function. For example, if the sensory receptors in a certain area of the skin are eliminated, the part of the brain that normally responds to signals from that part of the skin will not simply cease to function but will begin to respond to adjacent areas of the skin. Thus it takes over a function originally fulfilled by another part of the brain that might differ in subtle ways physically. That would be an example of what Fodor calls "identical psychological functions" ascribed to "anatomically heterogeneous" neural mechanisms.

Only H_2O can be water. Water $= H_2O$. Some philosophers have claimed that mental events are identical with physical (brain) events in that same sense of "identity." Fodor has argued that the relation between brain events and psychological events *cannot* be that kind of identity relation. Psychological terms name *functions*. Functional states *cannot* be identified with or reduced to particular physical states or items.

ASK YOURSELF

48. To illustrate the last claim: The functional term "doorstop" *cannot* be reduced to a physical term, such as _____. The reason is that doorstops can be made of many different sorts of _____ such as _____ or _____.

Thus Fodor rejects materialist reductionism. He does not, however, reject materialism. He believes his position is consistent with the claim that all that exists is physical or material. In his view, all mental events or processes are physical, just as all doorstops are physical.

A question may arise at this point. Just as it seems conceivable that something nonphysical, such as a spiritual force, might perform the function of holding a door open, so, it might seem, something nonphysical (like a Cartesian mind!) might perform a mental function.

49. Is there anything in Fodor's account that would *rule out* the possibility that the cause of various mental functions is a Cartesian mind? If you think so, what is it?

If the answer to the preceding question is "no," then it may be that Fodor's account does not do justice to the strong conviction held by so many recent philosophers that everything that exists is physical or material.

SUMMING UP TWENTIETH-CENTURY VIEWS ON MIND AND BODY

The tone for much discussion, over the last 400 years, of the nature of mind and body was certainly set by Descartes. Cartesian dualism postulated an apparently un-bridgeable gap between minds and bodies that drove some thinkers to materialism, others to idealism. Twentieth-century thinkers have developed sophisticated versions of materialism, aided by recent discoveries about the nervous systems and the brain. Some twentieth-century materialists have argued that mental states are identical with states of the brain or reducible to them, in a way analogous to the way clouds are "reducible" to water droplets, or nations to individual citizens. Others have argued for the possibility of eliminating all references to thoughts and other mental notions in a completed account of the brain. Yet other thinkers have thought that Descartes was conceptually confused. One of the most powerful accounts of mental states and acts developed in recent years is functionalism. Perhaps such mental "things" as thoughts, or fears, or beliefs are nothing more than names for the way in which certain purely physical things *function*. Functionalism is compatible with materialism, though functionalism does not entail materialism in the way that identity theory or eliminative materialism does.

CAN OF WORMS

Current debates over the nature of the mind have an obvious bearing on how we think of human nature. Are we really just physical things; and, if so, what happens to the age-old notion that humans, and perhaps other sentient beings, are somehow special, perhaps even to the point of being related in a special way to God? The issues here are also clearly ethical in character. But in addition, discussions of the nature of the mind have affected, and been affected by, developments in the philosophy of science. Increasingly sophisticated accounts of the notion of reduction, or of the exact function of various parts of the nervous system, are deeply intertwined with current debates over the mind–body problem.

E. INTENTIONALITY

There is a table in front of me right now. It is of course an inert physical object. Suppose someone asked me "What is your table about?" What sense could I possibly make of that question? Perhaps the questioner thinks that I am engaged in some sort of game in which I am *using* that table as a sign of something. But suppose there is just the table. No people are around; no people are using it for anything. In that case it seems that I cannot make any sense at all of the question "What is the table about?" Physical things are not "about" or "of" any-thing. They just are. Is that ever the case with "mental" phenomena? Some philosophers have insisted that "No!" must be the answer. Since $x = y$ only if everything that is true of x is true of y, it follows that mental phenomena cannot be identical with physical phenomena. For example, it is *true of* my thought that "Bob is late" that that thought is "about" Bob. But it is not *true of* the physical state of my brain when I have that thought that *the physical state* is about anything at all. So, by the principle stated, my thought cannot be identical with that brain state. Some philosophers have nonetheless tried to show that intentionality, properly understood, does not conflict with such claims as the claim that thoughts are identical with some physical processes or conditions.

**QUESTIONS
TO DISCUSS**

a. Make a list of mental states. Take into account not only thoughts, beliefs, hopes, desires, and fears, but also sensations of all sorts and also moods. Next, try to think of an object corresponding to each. For example, a thought is always a thought *about* something, say, about tomorrow's exam. A desire is always for something, or directed upon an object, such as a hot fudge sundae. Is there anything in your list that is *not* about something, or of something, or directed upon something? If you find some mental state like that, name it and describe it here.

b. If two people are thinking about last Monday's soccer game, and one of them thinks in Chinese and the other in English, are they having the same thought? Explain your view.

c. Is it possible that there are many beliefs that you have which you have so far never thought about or consciously considered? If you can think of any, mention them.

 **INTENTIONALITY AS THE MARK OF THE MENTAL:
FRANZ BRENTANO**

The Austrian philosopher and psychologist Franz Brentano (1838–1917) is often cited as the main recent source for the idea that what distinguishes the mental realm from the physical is what he called "intentionality." The basic idea is that mental phenomena are always "about" something or directed to something. Even when I am thinking about, or wanting, or fearing, something that does not exist, such as a unicorn, I am certainly thinking about something. If I am imagining something, such as myself at the beach, then even though I am not at the beach, there is still something, something that seems to be part of *me* as a conscious being, which I am attending to or thinking about. We might call it a content of consciousness. Generally it seems true that if I am conscious at all, I am conscious *of* something. The following are characteristic statements of this idea from Brentano's major work *Psychology from an Empirical Standpoint*:

> Every mental phenomenon is characterized by what the scholastics of the Middle Ages referred to as the intentional (and also mental) inexistence of the object, and what we, although with not quite unambiguous expressions, would call relation to a content, direction upon an object (which is not here to be understood as a reality) or immanent objectivity. . . . This intentional inexistence is exclusively characteristic of mental phenomena. No physical phenomenon manifests anything similar. Consequently, we can define mental phenomena by saying that they are such phenomena as include an object intentionally within themselves. [From *Psychology from an Empirical Standpoint* (1874) 1973, p. 88]

It does seem that no merely physical object could have the trait or feature that Brentano is pointing out. A rock cannot be "about" anything. A storm cloud on the horizon is not in itself about anything, although some conscious being might "take it as" a sign of, or a pointer toward, a coming storm. Only where you have minds do you have intentionality.

If the last claim is correct, then materialism would seem to be defeated. A brain is a physical thing. A brain or any of its states, any "brain event," is just a physical thing or occurrence. Such physical things are never in themselves *about* anything, never directed *upon* an object. Thoughts and feelings, on the contrary, are precisely the sorts of things that *are* about something. So thoughts could not be brain events.

ASK YOURSELF

50. So it follows, does it not, that no _____ thing could be a _____ event?

51. List five intentional terms (or mental states). Start your list with "belief." Remember that it must make sense for each term you list to attach an "about" or an "of" or a "that" (thus, belief is always "about" something or "that" something is the case).

The intentionality that is unique to consciousness is still thought by some philosophers to be the most distinguishing feature of mental phenomena and to be not reducible to or functionally equivalent to anything physical. The selections by John Searle in the next section on minds and machines, as well as in Chapter 5, draw heavily upon the concept of intentionality. However, some philosophers who want to maintain a strictly materialist view of things believe that intentionality does not defeat materialism.

2.   KINDS OF INTENTIONAL PSYCHOLOGY: DANIEL DENNETT

Daniel Dennett, a contemporary American philosopher, is one materialist who holds that the problem of intentionality does not defeat materialist accounts of the mind. He makes his case in various books and essays, including the following essay on "Three Kinds of Intentional Psychology." The three kinds are what he calls "folk psychology," "intentional systems theory," and "sub-personal cognitive psychology." The first is a mixture of abstract and concrete features, and it works well a lot of the time but can't come up to scientific status. (Folk psychology is described earlier in the discussion of eliminative materialism.) The second is purely abstract. The third is more concrete for it involves explanations of human behavior in terms of actual structural features of the brain or nervous system. In the course of his discussion, Dennett touches upon many of the views and concepts already treated in this chapter, in particular, Ryle's logical behaviorism, eliminative materialism, reductive materialism, folk psychology, functionalism, and, of course, intentionality. Thus this essay provides an opportunity to see some of the ways these various concepts and theories in the philosophy of mind might be related to one another.

Folk Psychology as a Source of Theory. Dennett does not believe, as eliminativists do, that folk psychology should be eliminated, and he does not believe that the concepts used in folk psychology, such as "belief" and "desire," refer to something that can be reduced to concrete physical elements or events, as do identity theorists. Rather, folk psychology should be treated as an abstract way of talking about ourselves and others that generally works pretty well and should be kept around for that reason.

From Daniel Dennett, "Three Kinds of Intentional Psychology" (1981)

Suppose that you and I both believe that cats eat fish. Exactly what feature must we share for this to be true of us? More generally, recalling Socrates' favorite style of question, what must be in common between things truly ascribed in *intentional* predicates—such as "wants to visit China" or "expects noodles for supper"? As Socrates points out, in the *Meno* and elsewhere, such questions are ambiguous or vague in their intent. One can be asking on the one hand for something rather like a definition, or on the other hand for something rather like a theory (Socrates of course preferred the former sort of answer.) What do all magnets have in common? First answer: they all attract iron. Second answer: they all have such-and-such a microphysical property (a property that explains their capacity to attract iron). In one sense people knew what magnets were—they were things that attracted iron—long before science told them what magnets were. A child learns what the word "magnet" means not, typically, by learning an explicit definition, but by learning the "folk physics" of magnets, in which the ordinary term "magnet" is embedded or implicitly defined as a theoretical term.

Sometimes terms are embedded in more powerful theories, and sometimes they are embedded by explicit definition. What do all chemical elements with the same valence have in common? First answer: they are disposed to combine with other elements in the same integral ratios. Second answer: they all have such-and-such a microphysical property (a property which explains their capacity to combine). The theory of valences in chemistry was well in hand before its microphysical explanation was known. In one sense chemists knew what valences were before physicists told them.

So what appears in Plato to be a contrast between giving a definition and giving a theory can be viewed as just a special case of the contrast between giving one theoretical answer and giving another, more "reductive" theoretical answer. Fodor draws the same contrast between "conceptual" and "causal" answers to such questions and argues that Ryle champions conceptual answers at the expense of causal answers, wrongly supposing them to be in conflict. There is justice in Fodor's charge against Ryle, for there are certainly many passages in which Ryle seems to propose his conceptual answers as a bulwark against the possibility of *any* causal, scientific, psychological answers, but there is a better view of Ryle's view (or perhaps at best a view he ought to have held) that deserves rehabilitation. Ryle's "logical behaviorism" is composed of his steadfastly conceptual answers to the Socratic questions about matters mental. If Ryle thought these answers ruled out psychology, ruled out causal (or reductive) answers to the Socratic questions, he was wrong, but if he thought only that the conceptual answers to the questions were not to be given by a microreductive psychology, he was on firmer ground. It is one thing to give a causal explanation of some phenomenon and quite another to cite the cause of a phenomenon in the analysis of the concept of it.

ASK YOURSELF

52. Suppose you are explaining, or giving an analysis of, the concept of a "wish" to a person learning English. Would you need to mention the sorts of things that "cause" wishes in order to explain the concept? Try to write down a brief version of what you would say to such a person in teaching them this concept.

Some concepts have what might be called an essential causal element. For instance, the concept of a genuine Winston Churchill *autograph* has it that how the trail of ink was in fact caused is essential to its status as an autograph. Photocopies, forgeries, inadvertently indistinguishable signatures—but perhaps not carbon copies—are ruled out. These considerations are part of the *conceptual* answer to the Socratic question about autographs.

Now some, including Fodor, have held that such concepts as the concept of intelligent action also have an essential causal element; behavior that appeared to be intelligent might be shown not to be by being shown to have the wrong sort of cause. Against such positions Ryle can argue that even if it is true that every instance of intelligent behavior is caused (and hence has a causal explanation), exactly *how* it is caused is inessential to its being intelligent—something that could be true even if all intelligent behavior exhibited in fact some common pattern of causation. That is, Ryle can plausibly claim that no account in causal terms could capture the class of intelligent actions except *per accidens*. In aid of such a position—for which there is much to be said in spite of the current infatuation with causal theories—Ryle can make claims of the sort Fodor disparages ("it's not the mental activity that makes the clowning clever because what makes the clowning clever is such facts as that it took place out where the children can see it") without committing the error of supposing causal and conceptual answers are incompatible.

Suppose someone thinks you cannot understand what "fear" is unless you understand something about the limbic system and how it functions in a person. Clearly he would be mistaken. Nearly all of us grasp the concept of fear; very few of us know anything about the limbic system. We can grasp the concept without understanding all about the causal background to any given fear. That was part of Ryle's point. Ryle would say that to have a fear is by definition to be disposed to run away and/or emit certain kinds of sounds and/or break out in a sweat and so forth. That would be a "conceptual" answer to the question "What is a fear?" That is all we need to know to grasp the concept "fear."

On the other hand, even though an explanation of the concept of fear does not require mentioning the limbic system, an explanation of fear that *does* mention the limbic system and tries to show how changes in that system may *cause* fear reactions (such as feelings of panic) may nevertheless be compatible with a purely conceptual explanation.

Dennett continues with a discussion of reductionism in physical science. Much of chemistry, he claims, has been "reduced to" physics, in the sense that explanations in terms of chemical properties can be rephrased in terms of physics without loss of explanatory power, and in fact with increased explanatory power. Is something similar possible for folk psychology? Could it be reduced to something more basic, like neurophysiology?

First we will answer the question "What do all believers-that-*p* have in common?" the first way, the "conceptual" way, and then see if we can go on to "reduce" the theory that emerges in our first answer to something else—neurophysiology most likely. Many theorists seem to take it for granted that *some* such reduction is both possible and desirable, and perhaps even inevitable, even while recent critics of reductionism, such as Putnam and Fodor, have warned us of the excesses of "classical" reductionist creeds. No one today hopes to conduct the psychology of the future in the vocabulary of the neurophysiologist, let alone that of the physicist, and principled ways of relaxing the classical "rules" of reduction have been proposed. The issue, then, is *what kind* of theoretical bonds can we expect—or ought we to hope—to find—uniting psychological claims about beliefs, desires, and so forth with the claims of neurophysiologists, biologists, and other physical scientists?

Since the terms "belief" and "desire" and their kin are parts of ordinary language, like "magnet," rather than technical terms like "valence," we must first look to "folk psychology" to see what kind of things we are being asked to explain. What do we learn beliefs are when we learn how to use the words "believe" and "belief"? The first point to make is that we do not really learn what beliefs are when we learn how to use these words. Certainly no one *tells us* what beliefs are, or if someone does, or if we happen to speculate on the topic on our own, the answer we come to, wise or foolish, will figure only weakly in our habits of thought about what people believe. We learn to *use* folk psychology as a vernacular social technology, a craft; but we don't learn it self-consciously as a theory—we learn no meta-theory with the theory—and in this regard our knowledge of folk psychology is like our knowledge of the grammar of our native tongue. This fact does not make our knowledge of folk psychology entirely unlike human knowledge of explicit academic theories, however; one could probably be a good practicing chemist and yet find it embarrassingly difficult to produce a satisfactory textbook definition of a metal or an ion.

ASK YOURSELF

53. When we learn, as we all do, to explain our own actions and the actions of others in terms of beliefs, desires, fears, and the like are we learning to theorize about behavior, according to Dennett?

54. Try to say what you think a belief *is*. Must one have language in order to have beliefs?

What are beliefs? Very roughly, folk psychology has it that *beliefs* are information-bearing states of people that arise from perceptions and that, together with appropriately related *desires,* lead to intelligent *action.* That much is relatively uncontroversial, but does folk psychology also have it that nonhuman animals have beliefs? If so, what is the role of language in belief? Are beliefs constructed of parts? If so, what are the parts? Ideas? Concepts? Words? Pictures? Are beliefs like speech acts or maps or instruction manuals or sentences? Is it implicit in folk psychology that beliefs enter into causal relations, or that they don't? How do decisions and intentions intervene between belief–desire complexes and actions? Are beliefs introspectible, and if so, what authority do the believer's pronouncements have?

All these questions deserve answers, but one must bear in mind that there are different reasons for being interested in the details of folk psychology. One reason is that it exists as a phenomenon, like a religion or a language or a dress code, to be studied with the techniques and attitudes of anthropology. It may be a myth, but it is a myth we live in, so it is an "important" phenomenon in nature. A different reason is that it seems to be a *true* theory, by and large, and hence is a candidate—like the folk physics of magnets and unlike the folk science of astrology—for incorporation into science. These different reasons generate different but overlapping investigations. The anthropological question should include in its account of folk psychology whatever folk actually include in their theory, however misguided, incoherent, gratuitous some of it may be. . . . The proto-scientific quest, on the other hand, as an attempt to prepare folk theory for subsequent incorporation into, or reduction to, the rest of science, should be critical and should eliminate all that is false or ill founded, however well entrenched in popular doctrine. (Thales thought that lodestones had souls, we are told. Even if most people agreed, this would be something to eliminate from the folk physics of magnets prior to "reduction.") One way of distinguishing the good from the bad, the essential from the gratuitous, in folk theory is to see what must be included in the theory to account for whatever predictive or explanatory success it seems to have in ordinary use. In this way we can criticize as we analyze, and it is even open to us in the end to discard folk psychology if it turns out to be a bad theory, and with it the presumed theoretical entities named therein.

ASK YOURSELF

55. How, according to Dennett, does folk psychology differ from astrology?

56. The recommendation that we should discard or eliminate folk psychology has already been made by which philosopher quoted earlier in this chapter?

If we discard folk psychology as a theory, we would have to replace it with another theory, which, while it did violence to many ordinary intuitions, would explain the predictive power of the residual folk craft.

We use folk psychology all the time, to explain and predict each other's behavior; we attribute beliefs and desires to each other with confidence—and quite un-self-consciously—and spend a substantial portion of our waking lives formulating the world-not excluding ourselves-in these terms. Folk psychology is about as pervasive a part of our second nature as is our folk physics of middle-sized objects. How good is folk psychology? If we concentrate on its weaknesses we will notice that we often are unable to make sense of particular bits of human behavior (our own included) in terms of belief and desire, even in retrospect; we often cannot predict accurately or reliably what a person will do or when, we often can find no resources within the theory for settling disagreements about particular attributions of belief or desire. If we concentrate on its strengths we find first that there are large areas in which it is extraordinarily reliable in its predictive power. Every time we venture out on a highway, for example, we stake our lives on the reliability of our general expectations about the perceptual beliefs, normal desires, and decision proclivities of the other motorists. Second, we find that it is a theory of great generative power and efficiency. For instance, watching a film with a highly original and unstereotypical plot, we see the hero smile at the villain and we all swiftly and effortlessly arrive at the same complex theoretical diagnosis: "Aha!" we conclude (but perhaps not consciously), "he wants her to think he doesn't know she intends to defraud his brother!" Third, we find that even small children pick up facility with the theory at a time when they have a very limited experience of human activity from which to induce a theory. Fourth, we find that we all use folk psychology knowing next to nothing about what actually happens inside people's skulls. "Use your head," we are told, and we know some people are brainier than others, but our capacity to use folk psychology is quite unaffected by ignorance about brain processes—or even by large-scale misinformation about brain processes.

ASK YOURSELF

57. Review Churchland's objections to folk psychology, as described earlier in this chapter. Then say how Dennett would reply to those objections.

As many philosophers have observed, a feature of folk psychology that sets it apart from both folk physics and the academic physical sciences is that explanations of actions citing beliefs and desires normally not only describe the provenance of the actions, but at the same time defend them as reasonable under the circumstances. They are reason-giving explanations, which make an ineliminable allusion to the rationality of the agent.

ASK YOURSELF

58. A typical folk-psychological explanation of my coming to work every morning would be that I *desire* to keep my job since I *need* the income it brings, and I *believe* that only by showing up at work most of the time will I keep my job. This explanation mentions desires, needs, beliefs and actions. It also is appealing because it "makes sense"; that is to say, showing up at work would be the *reasonable* or *rational* or sensible thing to do given that I desire to keep my job. So this explanation makes an ineliminable allusion to the _____ of the agent (me).

Primarily for this reason, but also because of the pattern of strengths and weaknesses just described, I suggest that folk psychology might best be viewed as a rationalistic calculus of interpretation and prediction—an idealizing, abstract, instrumentalistic interpretation method that has evolved because it works and works because we have evolved. We approach each other as *intentional systems,* that is, as entities whose behavior can be predicted by the method of attributing beliefs, desires, and rational acumen according to the following rough and ready principles:

(1) A system's beliefs are those it *ought to have,* given its perceptual capacities, its epistemic needs, and its biography. Thus, in general, its beliefs are both true and relevant to its life, and when false beliefs are attributed, special stories must be told to explain how the error resulted from the presence of features in the environment that are deceptive relative to the perceptual capacities of the system.

(2) A system's desires are those it *ought to have,* given its biological needs and the most practicable means of satisfying them. Thus intentional systems desire survival and procreation, and hence desire food, security, health, sex, wealth, power, influence, and so forth, and also whatever local arrangements tend (in their eyes—given their beliefs) to further these ends in appropriate measure. Again, "abnormal" desires are attributable if special stories can be told.

(3) A system's behavior will consist of those acts that *it would be rational* for an agent with those beliefs and desires to perform.

In (1) and (2) "ought to have" means "would have if it were *ideally* ensconced in its environmental niche." Thus all dangers and vicissitudes in its environment it will *recognize as such* (i.e., *believe* to be dangers) and all the benefits—relative to its needs, of course—it will *desire.* When a fact about its surroundings is particularly relevant to its current projects (which themselves will be the projects such a being ought to have in order to get ahead in its world), it will *know* that fact and act accordingly. And so forth and so on. This gives us the notion of an ideal epistemic and conative operator or agent, relativized to a set of needs for survival and procreation and to the environment(s) in which its ancestors have evolved and to which it is adapted. But this notion is still too crude and overstated. For instance, a being may come to have an epistemic need that its perceptual apparatus cannot provide for (suddenly all the green food is poisonous, but alas it is colorblind), hence the relativity to perceptual capacities. Moreover, it may or may not have had the occasion to learn from experience about something, so its beliefs are also relative to its biography in this way: it will have learned what it ought to have learned, viz., what it had been given evidence for in a form compatible with its cognitive apparatus—providing the evidence was "relevant" to its project then. . . .

In short, we treat each other as if we were rational agents, and this myth—for surely we are not all that rational—works very well because we are *pretty* rational. This single assumption, in combination with home truths about our needs, capacities and typical circumstances, generates both an intentional interpretation of us as believers and desirers and actual predictions of behavior in great profusion. I am claiming, then, that folk psychology can best be viewed as a sort of logical behaviorism: *what it means* to say that someone believes that *p* is that that person is disposed to behave in certain ways under certain conditions. What ways under what conditions? The ways it would be rational to behave, given the person's other beliefs and desires. The answer looks in danger of being circular, but consider: an account of what it is for an element to have a particular valence will similarly make ineliminable reference to the valences of other elements. What one is given with valence talk is a whole system of interlocking attributions, which is saved from vacuity by yielding independently testable predictions.

I have just described in outline a method of predicting and explaining the behavior of people and other intelligent creatures. Let me distinguish two questions about it: is it something we could do, and is it something we in fact do? I think the answer to the first is obviously yes, which is not to say the method will always yield good results. That much one can ascertain by reflection and thought experiment. Moreover, one can recognize that the method is familiar. Although we don't usually use the method self-consciously, we do use it self-consciously on those occasions when we are perplexed by a person's behavior, and then it often yields satisfactory results. Moreover, the ease and naturalness with which we resort to this self-conscious and deliberate form of problem-solving provide some support for the claim that what we are doing on those occasions is not switching methods but simply becoming self-conscious and explicit about what we ordinarily accomplish tacitly or unconsciously.

No other view of folk psychology, I think, can explain the fact that we do so well predicting each other's behavior on such slender and peripheral evidence; treating each other as intentional systems works (to the extent that it does) because we really are well designed by evolution and hence we *approximate* to the ideal version of ourselves exploited to yield the predictions. But not only does evolution not guarantee that we will always do what is rational; it guarantees that we won't. If we are designed by evolution, then we are almost certainly nothing more than a bag of tricks, patched together by a *satisficing* Nature—Herbert Simon's term (1957)—and no better than our ancestors had to be to get by. Moreover, the demands of nature and the demands of a logic course are not the same. Sometimes—even *normally* in certain circumstances—it pays to jump to conclusions swiftly (and even to forget that you've done so), so by most philosophical measures of rationality (logical consistency, refraining from invalid inference) there has probably been some positive evolutionary pressure in favor of "irrational" methods.

The notion that we are designed by evolution requires only that the features we have acquired through natural selection and other factors be "satisfactory" for the job they do. Consider the Panda's "thumb." It is really hardly a thumb at all, but it satisfies the Panda's need to be able to strip the leaves off bamboo shoots. Similarly, Dennett is suggesting, evolutionary pressures produced a rationality in humans which has been good enough to get us by in most situations, but which is hardly ideal. We are certainly not perfectly rational, but it would not really be to our advantage to be so. We are merely "patched together by a satisficing nature."

ASK YOURSELF

59. Suppose that there had been a lot of evolutionary pressure in favor of irrational methods or no particular pressure in favor of rationality generally. Would that fact cast a shadow over all of our theorizing? Explain your answer.

60. What are some reasons given by Dennett for supposing that we have not evolved into completely rational beings?

How rational are we? Recent research in social and cognitive psychology suggests we are only minimally rational, appallingly ready to leap to conclusions or be swayed by logically irrelevant features of situations, but this jaundiced view is an illusion engendered by the fact that these psychologists are deliberately trying to produce situations that provoke irrational responses—inducing pathology in a system by putting strain on it—and succeeding, being good psychologists. No one would hire a psychologist to prove that people will choose a paid vacation to a week in jail if offered an informed choice. At least not in the better psychology departments. A more optimistic impression of our rationality is engendered by a review of the difficulties encountered in artificial intelligence research. Even the most sophisticated AI programs stumble blindly into misinterpretations and misunderstandings that even small children reliably evade without a second thought. From this vantage point we seem marvelously rational.

Some of the "difficulties in artificial intelligence research" mentioned here are discussed more fully by Haugeland in the last selection in this chapter.

However rational we are, it is the myth of our rational agenthood that structures and organizes our attributions of belief and desire to others and that regulates our own deliberations and investigations. We aspire to rationality, and without the myth of our rationality the concepts of belief and desire would be uprooted. Folk psychology, then, is *idealized* in that it produces its predictions and explanations by calculating in a normative system; it predicts what we will believe, desire, and do, by determining what we ought to believe, desire, and do.

That is, what we "ought to believe, desire, and do," *given that* we are rational. If we are rational we will look for food (potatoes, say), not rocks, when we are hungry because we will believe that potatoes, but not rocks, will take care of the hunger.

Folk psychology is *abstract* in that the beliefs and desires it attributes are not—or need not be—presumed to be intervening distinguishable states of an internal behavior-causing system. (The point will be enlarged upon later.) The role of the concept of belief is like the role of the concept of a center of gravity, and the calculations that yield the predictions are more like the calculations one performs with a parallelogram of forces than like the calculations one performs with a blueprint of internal levers and cogs.

Folk psychology is thus *instrumentalistic* in a way the most ardent realist should permit: people really do have beliefs and desires, on my version of folk psychology, just the way they really have centers of gravity and the earth has an equator. Reichenbach distinguished between two sorts of referents for theoretical terms: *illata*—posited theoretical entities—and *abstracta*—calculation-bound entities or logical constructs. Beliefs and desires of folk psychology (but not all mental events and states) are *abstracta*.

A belief, Dennett claims, is a "calculation bound" entity in the way that the equator is. He says that beliefs are "real" just the way the equator is real. Now in one sense the equator is not real at all. If you take a sea journey and cross the equator, you will not find a line running across the ocean. The equator is an abstract "device" for making various calculations about location. It is shown on maps but does not, like the cities shown on maps, correspond to an actual thing on the surface of the earth. In similar manner, a belief, which is a folk-psychological "entity," is a device for making calculations about such things as how others will behave. It is not a real *concrete* thing at all, such as a brain process, but rather an abstract thing, an *abstracta*. And when we use it to make predictions we do so on the assumption that people are for the most part rational.

ASK YOURSELF

61. Suppose that I think that you believe I'm dishonest. What would be an example of a "calculation" (a prediction, for example) that I might make about your behavior on the basis of that belief-attribution?

This view of folk psychology emerges more clearly when contrasted to a diametrically opposed view, each of whose tenets has been held by some philosopher, and at least most of which have been espoused by Fodor:

Beliefs and desires, just like pains, thoughts, sensations and other episodes, are taken by folk psychology to be real, intervening, internal states or events, in causal interaction, subsumed under covering laws of causal stripe. Folk psychology is not an idealized, rationalistic calculus but a naturalistic, empirical, descriptive theory, imputing causal regularities discovered by extensive induction over experience. To suppose two people share a belief is to suppose them to be ultimately in some structurally similar internal condition, e.g. for them to have the same words of Mentalese written in the functionally relevant places in their brains.

Fodor, in contrast to Dennett, believes that beliefs and desires are not just abstracta or "calculation bound entities," that is, abstract devices for making predictions about behavior. In his view, beliefs actually are causes of behavior, just as an ingested drug, or a brain lesion, might cause certain kinds of behavior.

I want to deflect this head-on collision of analyses by taking two steps. First, I am prepared to grant a measure of the claims made by the opposition. Of course we don't all sit in the dark in our studies like mad Leibnizians rationalistically excogitating behavioral predictions from pure, idealized concepts of our neighbors, nor do we derive all our readiness to attribute desires from a careful generation of them from the ultimate goal of survival. We may observe that some folk seem to desire cigarettes, or pain, or notoriety (we observe this by hearing them tell us, seeing what they choose, etc.) and without any conviction that these people, given their circumstances, ought to have these desires, we attribute them anyway. So rationalistic generation of attributions is augmented and even corrected on occasion by empirical generalizations about belief and desire that guide our attributions and are learned more or less inductively. For instance, small children believe in Santa Claus, people are inclined to believe the more self-serving of two interpretations of an event in which they are involved (unless they are depressed), and people can be made to want things they don't need by making them believe that glamorous people like those things. And so forth in familiar profusion. This folklore does not consist in *laws*—even probabilistic laws—but some of it is being turned into science of a sort, for example theories of "hot cognition" and cognitive dissonance. I grant the existence of all this naturalistic generalization, and its role in the normal calculations of folk psychologists-that is, all of us. People do rely on their own parochial group of neighbors when framing intentional interpretations. That is why people have so much difficulty understanding foreigners—their behavior, to say nothing of their languages. They impute more of their own beliefs and desires, and those of their neighbors, than they would if they followed my principles of attribution slavishly. Of course this is a perfectly reasonable shortcut for people to take, even when it often leads to bad results. We are in this matter, as in most, satisficers, not optimizers, when it comes to information gathering and theory construction. 1 would insist, however, that all this empirically obtained lore is laid over a fundamental generative and normative framework that has the features I have described.

My second step away from the conflict I have set up is to recall that the issue is not what folk psychology as found in the field truly is, but what it is at its best, what deserves to be taken seriously and incorporated into science. It is not particularly to the point to argue against me that folk psychology is *in fact* committed to beliefs and desires as distinguishable, causally interacting *illlata* [generally, concrete or real things]; what must be shown is that it ought to be. The latter claim I will deal with in due course. The former claim I *could* concede without embarrassment to my overall project, but I do not concede it, for it seems to me that the evidence is quite strong that our ordinary notion of belief has next to nothing of the concrete in it. Jacques shoots his uncle dead in Trafalgar Square and is apprehended on the spot by Sherlock; Tom reads about it in the *Guardian* and Boris learns of it in *Pravda*. Now Jacques, Sherlock, Tom, and Boris have had remarkably different experiences—to say nothing of their earlier biographies and future prospects—but there is one thing they share: they all believe that a Frenchman has committed murder in Trafalgar Square. They did not all *say* this, not even "to themselves"; *that proposition* did not, we can suppose, "occur to" any of them, and even if it had, it would have had entirely different import for Jacques, Sherlock, Tom, and Boris. Yet they all believe that a Frenchman committed murder in Trafalgar Square. This is a shared property that is visible, as it were, only from one very limited point of view—the point of view of folk psychology. Ordinary folk psychologists have no difficulty imputing such useful but elusive commonalities to people. If they then insist that in doing so they are postulating a similarly structured object in each head, this is a gratuitous bit of misplaced concreteness, a regrettable lapse in ideology.

If the belief that Jacques, Sherlock, Tom, and Boris share were an identifiable concrete thing, such as a certain state of the brain that could play a role in causal interactions, what thing would that be? We could not identify it with their all having the thought (expressed in English) that "a Frenchman committed murder in Trafalgar Square." Maybe Boris doesn't know English and thus couldn't have that thought. Maybe Tom has not actually thought to himself, "A Frenchman committed murder in Trafalgar Square." Maybe he did have the thought "A Frenchman committed murder in London," or maybe he had no particular thought at all. Perhaps Boris *could not* have had, like Tom, the belief that a Frenchman committed murder in London simply because he is not British and does not know Trafalgar Square is in London. And so forth. One can think of hundreds of differences between the four men with respect to this "belief" and nothing that they had in common, other than the "abstract" claim that they had the same belief. The result is that the "belief" itself begins to seem like a very abstract thing (an *abstracta*), rather than some concrete thing (an *illata*).

But in any case there is no doubt that folk psychology is a mixed bag, like folk productions generally, and there is no reason in the end not to grant that it is much more complex, variegated (and in danger of incoherence) than my sketch has made it out to be. The *ordinary* notion of belief no doubt does place beliefs somewhere midway between being *illata* and being *abstracta*. What this suggests to me is that the concept of belief found in ordinary understanding, that is, in folk psychology, is unappealing as a scientific concept.

It is unappealing as a scientific concept because it cannot be fit into any precise explanatory scheme or theory, because it has no definite identity conditions, as does, say, oxygen, because even though it sometimes works well as a calculation device, other times it does not work at all, and so forth.

62. Consult the discussion above under "Eliminative Materialism" to find a case where the ordinary concept of belief does not work *at all* in predicting or explaining behavior.

There seems no comfortable way of avoiding the claim that we have an infinity of beliefs, and common intuition does not give us a stable answer to such puzzles as whether the belief that 3 is greater than 2 is none other than the belief that 2 is less than 3. The obvious response to the challenge of an infinity of beliefs with slippery identity conditions is to suppose these beliefs are not all "stored separately"; many—in fact *most* if we are really talking about infinity—will be stored *implicitly* in virtue of the *explicit* storage of a few (or a few million)—the *core beliefs.* The core beliefs will be "stored separately," and they look like promising *illata* in contrast to the virtual or implicit beliefs which look like paradigmatic *abstracta.* But although this might turn out to be the way our brains are organized, I suspect things will be more complicated than this: there is no reason to suppose the core *elements,* the concrete, salient, separately stored representation tokens (and there must be some such elements in any complex information processing system), will explicitly represent (or *be*) a subset of our *beliefs* at all. That is, if you were to sit down and write out a list of a thousand or so of your paradigmatic beliefs, *all* of them could turn out to be virtual, only implicitly stored or represented, and what was explicitly stored would be information (e.g., about memory addresses, procedures for problem-solving, or recognition, etc.) that was entirely unfamiliar. It would be folly to prejudge this empirical issue by insisting that our core representations of information (whichever they turn out to be) are beliefs *par excellence,* for when the facts are in, our intuitions may instead support the contrary view: the least controversial self-attributions of belief may pick out beliefs that from the vantage point of developed cognitive theory are invariably virtual.

It might turn out, for example, that my belief that people who scowl are angry is "virtual"— that is, that belief is not a real concrete thing such as a particular state of the brain, a particular "thought," or a particular anything at all, but an *abstracta,* a device for predicting behavior. It might turn out, on the other hand, that my belief that "for any three statements A, B, and C, if A implies B and B implies C, then A implies C" is "hardwired"—that is, is a "real part of me"— even though I might never list it as one of the things I believe. In fact many people might never even think of it at all, even though they show, in their behavior, that they believe it.

63. Try to imagine a bit of *nonverbal* behavior that would show that a person believes that for any three statements, A, B, and C, if A implies B and B implies C, then A implies C.

64. What are your intuitions about your belief that the earth is round and moves? Is it a "virtual" belief or something that is a core belief "explicitly stored"? Explain your answer.

In such an eventuality what could we say about the causal roles we assign ordinarily to beliefs (e.g., "Her belief that John knew her secret caused her to blush")? We could say that whatever the core elements were in virtue of which she virtually believed that John knew her secret, they, the core elements, played a direct causal role (somehow) in triggering the blushing response. We would be wise, as this example shows, not to tamper with our *ordinary* catalogue of beliefs (virtual though they might all turn out to be), for these are predictable, readily understandable, manipulable regularities in psychological phenomena in spite of their apparent neutrality with regard to the explicit/implicit (or core/virtual) distinction. What Jacques, Sherlock, Boris, and Tom have in common is probably only a virtual belief "derived" from largely different explicit stores of information in each of them, but virtual or not, it is their sharing of *this* belief that would explain (or permit us to predict) in some imagined circumstances their all taking the same action when given the same new information. ("And now for one million dollars, Tom [Jacques, Sherlock, Boris], answer our jackpot question correctly: has a French citizen ever committed a major crime in London?")

At the same time we want to cling to the equally ordinary notion that beliefs can cause not only actions, but blushes, verbal slips, heart attacks, and the like. Much of the debate over whether or not intentional explanations are causal explanations can be bypassed by noting how the core elements, *whatever they may be,* can be cited as playing the causal role, while belief remains virtual. "Had Tom not believed that p and wanted that q, he would not have done A." Is this a causal explanation? It is tantamount to this: Tom was in some one of an indefinitely large number of structurally different states of type B that have in common just that each one of them licenses attribution of belief that p and desire that q in virtue of its normal relations with many other states of Tom, and this state, whichever one it was, was causally sufficient, given the "background conditions" of course, to initiate the intention to perform A, and thereupon A was performed, and had he not been in one of those indefinitely many type B states, he would not have done A.

For example (filling in Dennett's p, q, and A), if Tom had not *believed* that the hamburger was real food (as opposed, say, to a plastic replica), and had he not *wanted* something to eat, he would not have eaten the hamburger. This explanation of Tom's eating the hamburger cites beliefs and wants, which are intentional entities of the sort central to folk psychology. Is it a causal explanation? That is, do the beliefs and desires *cause* Tom's behavior? We would normally think so. But causal explanations are what scientists look for. However, causes in science must be identifiable things or events or processes. But, according to Dennett's discussion so far, beliefs and desires are mostly *not* identifiable things or events or processes, so it would appear that they could not be causes and thus this could *not* be a causal explanation. Therefore it is not a scientific explanation. This means that folk psychology is not science, or it is bad science.

ASK YOURSELF

65. Think of one thing that might cause you to sneeze. Would that cause be an identifiable thing or event? Would your explanation be scientific or capable of being absorbed into a complete scientific explanation? Explain.

The ordinary notion of belief is pulled in two directions. If we want to have good theoretical entities, good *illata,* or good logical constructs, good *abstracta,* we will have to jettison some of the ordinary freight of the concepts of belief and desire. So I propose a divorce. Since we seem to have both notions wedded in folk psychology, let's split them apart and create two new theories: one strictly abstract, idealizing, holistic, instrumentalistic—pure intentional system theory—and the other a concrete, microtheoretical science of the actual realization of those intentional systems—what I will call sub-personal cognitive psychology. By exploring their differences and interrelations, we should be able to tell whether any plausible "reductions" are in the offing.

To put this summary somewhat differently, since a belief, which is a typical folk psychological entity, is an *abstracta,* and the causal elements required in theoretical science are *illata,* it may pay to separate folk psychology from science. When we have done that, we may be in a better position to determine whether it is possible to "reduce" folk psychology to something more basic, such as neurophysiology.

Intentional System Theory. Dennett labels the seperable theories wedded in folk psychology "intentional system theory" and "subpersonal cognitive psychology."

The first new theory, intentional system theory, is envisaged as a close kin of, and overlapping with, such already existing disciplines as decision theory and game theory, which are similarly abstract, normative, and couched in intentional language. It borrows the ordinary terms "belief" and "desire" but gives them a technical meaning within the theory. It is a sort of holistic logical behaviorism because it deals with the prediction and explanation from belief–desire profiles of the actions of whole systems (either alone in environments or in interaction with other intentional systems), but it treats the individual realizations of the systems as black boxes. The *subject* of all the intentional attributions is the whole system (the person, the animal, or even the corporation or nation) rather than any of its parts, and individual beliefs and desires are not attributable in isolation, independently of other belief and desire attributions. The latter point distinguishes intentional system theory most clearly from Ryle's logical behaviorism, which took on the impossible burden of characterizing individual beliefs (and other mental states) as particular individual dispositions to outward behavior.

Economic theory might provide a partial illustration of what Dennett has in mind when he speaks of intentional system theory. For instance, economists develop theories about the behavior of individuals or other "actors" in a market economy. They assume that the actors in question are rational, which amounts to assuming that they have certain beliefs and desires and act as they "ought," given those beliefs and desires. Thus if I desire a new house and believe that the best time to buy one is when interest rates are low, I will shop for one when rates are low. So economists adopt a thoroughly intentionalist stance when they theorize. They do not look for the underlying physical–causal mechanisms that actually produce behavior. By ignoring those mechanisms, they are treating them like a "black box"—that is, a feature of a system that produces certain effects in a way that is not explained.

However, it is crucial to understand that the economists' descriptions of human behavior are not *limited* to "folk psychology." Instead they seek to give very precise accounts of the ways in which various beliefs and desires will motivate economic actors. For example, they construct theories of decreasing marginal utility in order to predict at what point people will give up making certain kinds of transactions, like buying houses, and switch to other consumption patterns. These theories are not folk psychology "plain and simple" so to speak, since they are not common knowledge commonly used to predict behavior.

ASK YOURSELF

66. Economic theory employs folk psychological notions, such as belief and desire. Why are economic theories not then folk psychology "plain and simple"?

Intentional system theory deals just with the performance specifications of believers while remaining silent on how the systems are to be implemented. In fact this neutrality with regard to implementation is the most useful feature of intentional characterizations. Consider, for instance, the role of intentional characterizations in evolutionary biology. If we are to explain the evolution of complex behavioral capabilities or cognitive talents by natural selection, we must note that it is the intentionally characterized capacity (e.g., the capacity to acquire a belief, a desire, to perform an intentional action) that has survival value, however it happens to be realized as a result of mutation. If a particularly noxious insect makes its appearance in an environment, the birds and bats with a survival advantage will be those that come to believe this insect is not good to eat. In view of the vast differences in neural structure , genetic background, and perceptual capacity between birds and bats, it is highly unlikely that this useful trait they may come to share has a common description at any level more concrete or less abstract than intentional system theory. It is not only that the intentional predicate is a projectible predicate in evolutionary theory; since it is more general than its species-specific counterpart predicates (which characterize the successful mutation just in birds, or just in bats), it is preferable. So from the point of view of evolutionary biology, we would not want to "reduce" an intentional characterization even if we knew in particular instances what the physiological implementation was.

ASK YOURSELF

67. Does Dennett's point here include a "functionalist" claim (see the immediately preceding selection in this text). That is, does Dennett here claim that a "belief" is the sort of thing that can be "multiply realizable" so that one and the same belief, for example that a certain insect is poisonous, could be realized in a bat by certain structures and events in the nervous system and in a bird by very different structures and events in its quite different nervous system? (Remember, bats are quite different than birds. Mention some ways they are different.)

68. Does Dennett's bird/bat example support the idea that beliefs are *abstracta?* Explain your answer.

69. Both a bird and a bat can "believe" that a certain insect is noxious. But they don't have a lot in common in terms of brain states or states of the nervous system even when they are both believing that. According to Dennett, we should nonetheless continue to speak of their having the *same* "belief" since by doing so we can understand that both of them have a feature that is useful for _____, the sort of feature upon which _____ biology focuses.

This level of generality is essential if we want a theory to have anything meaningful and defensible to say about such topics as intelligence in general (as opposed, say, to just human or even terrestrial or natural intelligence) or such grand topics as meaning or reference or representation. Suppose, to pursue a familiar philosophical theme, we are invaded by

Martians, and the question arises: do they have beliefs and desires? Are they that much *like us?* According to intentional system theory, if these Martians are smart enough to get here, then they most certainly have beliefs and desires—in the technical sense proprietary to the theory—no matter what their internal structure, and no matter how our folk-psychological intuitions rebel at the thought.

This principled blindness of intentional system theory to internal structure seems to invite the retort: but there has to be *some* explanation of the *success* of intentional prediction of the behavior of systems. It isn't just magic. It isn't a mere coincidence that one can generate all these *abstracta,* manipulate them via some version of practical reasoning, and come up with an action prediction that has a good chance of being true. There must be some way in which the internal processes of the system mirror the complexities of the intentional interpretation, or its success would be a miracle.

Of course. This is all quite true and important. Nothing without a great deal of structural and processing complexity could conceivably realize an intentional system of any interest, and the complexity of the realization will surely bear a striking resemblance to the complexity of the instrumentalistic interpretation. Similarly, the success of valence theory in chemistry is no coincidence, and people were entirely right to expect that deep microphysical similarities would be discovered between elements with the same valence and that the structural similarities found would explain the dispositional similarities. But since people and animals are unlike atoms and molecules not only in being the products of a complex evolutionary history, but also in being the products of their individual learning histories, there is no reason to suppose that individual (human) believers that *P* [that is, believers in some statement, such as that "the earth is round"]—like individual (carbon) atoms with valence 4—regulate their dispositions with *exactly* the same machinery. Discovering the constraints on design and implementation variation, and demonstrating how particular species and individuals in fact succeed in realizing intentional systems, is the job for the third theory: subpersonal cognitive psychology.

Subpersonal Cognitive Psychology as a Performance Theory. The notion that very abstract descriptions of believing and thinking could be applied in the construction of actual complex objects that appear to believe and think is discussed in great detail in the following section, which deals with "thinking machines" such as robots or computers. It anticipates the later discussion of the relations between minds and machines.

The task of subpersonal cognitive psychology is to explain something that at first glance seems utterly mysterious and inexplicable. The brain, as intentional system theory and evolutionary biology show us, is a *semantic engine;* its task is to discover what its multifarious inputs *mean,* to discriminate them by their significance and "act accordingly." That's what brains *are for.* But the brain, as physiology or plain common sense shows us, is just a *syntactic engine;* all it can do is discriminate its inputs by their structural, temporal, and physical features and let its entirely mechanical activities be governed by these "syntactic" features of its inputs. That's all brains *can do.* Now how does the brain manage to get semantics from syntax? How could *any* entity (how could a genius or an angel or God) get the semantics of a system from nothing but its syntax? It couldn't. The syntax of a system doesn't determine its semantics.

The issue raised by Dennett here is fundamental to contemporary discussions of the mind. It is treated in great detail in the following section on minds and machines in the selection by

Searle. You can get a sense for the importance of the topic if you see the connection between "semantics" and "intentionality." Semantics is the study of *meaning*. A word has a shape when written down or a phonetic quality when spoken, but in addition, and most importantly, words also *mean* something. That is, they are *about* something or are used to talk about something.

> **ASK YOURSELF**
>
> **70.** So, in giving you the "semantics" of a word I must tell you what the word is _____ or refers to.

Now, recall the explanation of intentionality at the beginning of this section. To say that mental states such as thoughts, beliefs, and hopes are intentional is to say they are *about* something or directed upon an object. Now words and sentences are also "about" something or refer to something. They have a semantic dimension.

Dennett has just claimed that brains are mere "syntactic engines." That means that they are like processing devices that operate upon shapes and patterns of various kinds. But they have no *semantic* dimension. It would seem to follow immediately that our capacities to use words in a meaningful way and to think, desire, and so forth, require something more than just a brain or nervous system. What would that something more be? We naturally want to say, "a mind." Beliefs and desires, and the language we express them in, all have aboutness or intentionality, and as Brentano claimed, that makes them "mental" and not physical. But as soon as we answer in that way, we have given up on materialism, which is the belief that there are no distinct entities called minds but only brains or nervous systems or other physical things. We could summarize all of this in a very short argument:

1. Brains are mere syntactic "engines."
2. Minds are semantic "engines."
3. The semantic cannot be reduce to the syntactic.
4. Therefore, minds are not (reducible to) brains or any other physical thing or event.
5. Therefore, materialism is false.

Dennett is a materialist who wants to avoid any kind of dualism and who believes in the unity of science. So his task here, which is the fundamental task of this whole essay, is to show how intentionality can be accounted for without postulating minds, understood as nonphysical entities. Otherwise put, his aim is to defeat the short argument just given.

> **ASK YOURSELF**
>
> **71.** Why must Dennett defeat the short argument just given?

By what alchemy, then, does the brain extract semantically reliable results from syntactically driven operations? It cannot be designed to do an impossible task, but it could be designed to *approximate* the impossible task, to *mimic* the behavior of the impossible object (the semantic engine) by capitalizing on close (close enough) fortuitous correspondences between structural regularities—of the environment and of its own internal states and operations—and semantic types.

The basic idea is familiar. An animal needs to know when it has satisfied the goal of finding and ingesting food, but it settles for a friction-in-the-throat-followed-by-stretched-stomach detector, a mechanical switch turned on by a relatively simple mechanical condition that normally co-occurs with the satisfaction of the animals "real" goal. It's not fancy and can easily be exploited to trick the animal into either eating when it shouldn't or leaving off eating when it shouldn't, but it does well enough by the animal in its normal environment.

What Dennett is suggesting is that for an animal to "know" (intentional) that it has had enough food, it simply needs to be the kind of thing just described with "mechanical switches." This is not behaviorism since a claim is being made about something more than behavior, namely, inner structure. But it is compatible with materialism.

Or suppose I am monitoring telegraph transmissions and have been asked to intercept all *death threats* (but only death threats in English—to make it "easy"). I'd like to build a machine to save me the trouble of interpreting semantically every message sent, but how could this be done? No machine could be designed to do the job perfectly, for that would require defining the semantic category *death threat in English* as some tremendously complex feature of strings of alphabetic symbols, and there is utterly no reason to suppose this could be done in a principled way. (If somehow by brute-force inspection and subsequent enumeration we could list all and only the English death threats of, say, less than a thousand characters, we could easily enough build a filter to detect them, but we are looking for a principled, projectible, extendable method.) A really crude device could be made to discriminate all messages containing the symbol strings

. . . I will kill you . . .

or

. . . you . . . die . . . unless . . .

or . . . (for some finite disjunction of likely patterns to be found in English death threats).

   This device would have some utility, and further refinements could screen the material that passed this first filter, and so on. An unpromising beginning for constructing a sentence understander, but if you want to get semantics out of syntax (whether the syntax of messages in a natural language or the syntax of afferent neuron impulses), variations on this basic strategy are your only hope. You must put together a bag of tricks and hope nature will be kind enough to let your device get by. Of course some tricks are elegant and appeal to deep principles of organization, but in the end all one can hope to produce (all natural selection can have produced) are systems that *seem* to discriminate meanings by actually discriminating things (tokens of no doubt wildly disjunctive types) that covary reliably with meanings. Evolution has designed our brains not only to do this but to evolve and follow strategies of self-improvement in this activity during their individual lifetimes.

Here then is Dennett's answer: The nervous system cannot indeed grasp "meaning" or "understand" anything, but its patterns of reaction are *as if* it understood, given that the behavior it produces "varies reliably" with meaning. Compare this to an electrical eye. Such a device does not actually see anything, but it sends out signals to the electrical door opener at Wal-Mart *as if* it saw things (people approaching). These systems "seem" to grasp meanings or, in the case of the door opener, to see.

ASK YOURSELF

72. According to Dennett, all natural selection can produce are systems that _____ to know meanings.

It is the task of subpersonal cognitive psychology to propose and test models of such activity—of pattern recognition or stimulus generalization, concept learning, expectation, learning, goal-directed behavior, problem-solving—that not only produce a simulacrum of genuine content-sensitivity, but that do this in ways demonstrably like the way people's brains do it, exhibiting the same powers and the same vulnerabilities to deception, over-load, and confusion. It is here that we will find our good theoretical entities, our useful *illata,* and while some of them may well resemble the familiar entities of folk psychology—beliefs, desires, judgments, decisions—many will certainly not. The only similarity we can be sure of discovering in the *illata* of subpersonal cognitive psychology is the intentionality of their labels. They will be characterized as events with content, bearing information, signaling this and ordering that.

In order to give the *illata* these labels, in order to maintain any intentional interpretation of their operation at all, the theorist must always keep glancing outside the system, to see what normally produces the configuration he is describing, what effects the system's responses normally have on the environment, and what benefit normally accrues to the whole system from this activity. In other words the cognitive psychologist cannot ignore the fact that it is the realization of an intentional system he is studying on pain of abandoning semantic interpretation and hence psychology. On the other hand, progress in subpersonal cognitive psychology will blur the boundaries between it and intentional system theory, knitting them together much as chemistry and physics have been knit together.

Imagine a robot that can "feel" when it is getting warm and a thermostat that can "feel" the same thing. The robot might be constructed out of microchips and other complicated electronic stuff, and the thermostat may simply have a bimetallic strip and a contact point. So they have nothing in common physically. But we are saying of both of them that they "feel," and feelings appear to be intentional. Feelings are "of" something or directed upon some object or situation.

Now the physical structures of these things are *illata* in the lingo Dennett has adopted. As *illata* they have nothing in common. It is only insofar as both "feel" that they have anything in common. But why should we keep this "intentional label" at all? In fact, it seems rather odd to keep it in the case of the thermostat, but we will ignore that for the sake of simplifying this discussion. Well, consider the robot. We say that it feels heat because it goes into new physical states as the temperature rises, and, moreover, these physical states produce other physical states or conditions, such as the condition of moving away on its "legs" from a fire. And this last bit of behavior keeps the robot from getting burned up. So our analysis of the robot's physical structure also enables us to understand how the robot has survived even where fires broke out. Dennett is suggesting that it is just this sort of complex relation between environmental inputs, structure, and beneficial behavior that we want to understand when we do psychology. And we can best do that by keeping around intentional labels like "feels," "believes," and so forth. Those labels organize our thinking and research, even when our research is into *illata*—that is, the concrete features of things that explain, in a physical way, their behavior.

ASK YOURSELF

73. Use Dennett's terminology to fill in the blanks: The behavior of both robots and thermostats in the presence of heat and cold might warrant attributing to both the same beliefs, or _____. But they certainly are not alike with respect to the physical structures that produce their "behavior"—that is, their _____.

The alternative of ignoring the external world and its relations to the internal machinery . . . is not really psychology at all, but just at best abstract neurophysiology-pure internal syntax with no hope of a semantic interpretation. Psychology "reduced" to neurophysiology in this fashion would not be psychology, for it would not be able to provide an explanation of the regularities it is psychology's particular job to explain: the reliability with which "intelligent" organisms can cope with their environments and thus prolong their lives. Psychology can, and should, work toward an account of the physiological foundations of psychological processes, not by eliminating psychological or intentional characterizations of those processes, but by exhibiting how the brain implements the intentionally characterized performance specifications of subpersonal theories.

There is no way to capture the semantic properties of things (word tokens, diagrams, nerve impulses, brain states) by a micro-reduction. Semantic properties are not just relational but, you might say, super-relational, for the relation a particular vehicle of content, or token, must bear in order to have content is not just a relation it bears to other similar things (e.g. other tokens, or parts of tokens, or sets of tokens, or causes of tokens) but a relation between the token and the whole life—and counterfactual life—of the organism it "serves" *and* that organism's requirements for survival *and* its evolutionary ancestry.

The word "book" is a type, and particular written and spoken instances of that word are "tokens" of that type. So the seventh word in the sentence just before this one is a token of the type of that word (the word "and").

ASK YOURSELF

74. Is Dennett saying that the semantic content of "book," for example, is nothing more than a matter of the way various word tokens interact with each other, with users of that word understood as living beings with complex life forms and with the pressures put upon those users by their various environments?

The Prospects of Reduction. Dennett goes on to argue that what we need for this proposed reduction of folk psychology to intentional system theory is the notion of a Turing machine. Turing machines are discussed further in the next section on minds and machines. A Turing machine is any device that operates upon input at a purely syntactical level, and produces appropriate output. The machine goes through a series of states determined by a program. The "states" in question are defined functionally, not physically. Digital computers are describable as Turing machines. What they get as input is certain impulses in various "shapes" (orders, locations) sent by, for example, keys pushed by fingers. What they produce are, for example, words on a screen, words out of a speaker, or words on a piece of paper.

To say that two computers "both believe that $2 + 2 = 4$" would be to say simply that they are in the same Turing machine state, so that if "$2 + 2 = ?$" were punched in to either one, both would produce "4." Dennett considers the following formulation: Anything, *x*, is in a given mental state *M* if and only if *x* realizes some Turing machine *K* in logical state *A*.

Of our three psychologies—folk psychology, intentional system theory, and subpersonal cognitive psychology—what then might reduce to what? Certainly the one-step micro-reduction of folk psychology to physiology alluded to in the slogans of the early identity theorists will never be found—and should never be missed, even by staunch friends of materialism and scientific unity. A prospect worth exploring, though, is that folk psychology (more precisely, the part of folk psychology worth caring about) reduces—conceptually—to intentional system theory.

In other words, for two things both to believe that cats eat fish they need not be physically similar in any specifiable way, but they must both be in a "functional" condition specifiable in principle in the most general functional language; they must share a Turing machine description according to which they are both in some particular logical state. This is still a reductionist doctrine, for it proposes to identify each mental type with a functional type picked out in the language of automata theory. But this is still too strong, for there is no more reason to suppose Jacques, Sherlock, Boris, and Tom "have the same program" in *any* relaxed and abstract sense, considering the differences in their nature and nurture, than that their brains have some crucially identical physico-chemical feature. We must weaken the requirements for the right-hand side of our formula still further .

Consider

Anyone, *x*, believes that *p* if and only if *x* can be predictively attributed the belief that *p*

This appears to be blatantly circular and uninformative, with the language on the right simply mirroring the language on the left. But all we need to make an informative answer of this formula is a systematic way of making the attributions alluded to on the right-hand side.

Consider the parallel case of Turing machines. What do two different realizations or embodiments of a Turing machine have in common when they are in the same logical state? Just this: there is a system of description such that according to it both are described as being realizations of some particular Turing machine, and according to this description, which is predictive of the operation of both entities, both are in the same state of that Turing machine's machine table. One doesn't *reduce* Turing machine talk to some more fundamental idiom; one *legitimizes* Turing machine talk by providing it with rules of attribution and exhibiting its predictive powers. If we can similarly legitimize "mentalistic" talk, we will have no need of a reduction, and that is the point of the concept of an intentional system. Intentional systems are supposed to play a role in the legitimization of mentalistic predicates parallel to the role played by the abstract notion of a Turing machine in setting down rules for the interpretation of artifacts as computational automata.

Suppose two physically different computers, A and B, have had "2 + 2 = ?" entered and both of them have the same "machine table." Then I can predict, with no further knowledge, that both A and B will both produce "4" as output. I do not need to "reduce" my abstract Turing machine description of those computers to descriptions of what is taking place in an electronic circuit, supposing A is made of electronic stuff, or to descriptions of what is taking place among some vacuum tubes, supposing B is made of vacuum tubes and other old fashioned stuff. All I need to know is the abstract Turing machine description. At any rate, if all I am interested in is predicting output, that is all I need to know. So the description of them in this abstract way is "legitimized" by the fact that using it enables me to make perfectly accurate predictions. It does not follow that each computer is inhabited my some mysterious thing, a Turing machine. But neither does it follow that Turing machine language is useless or should be eliminated. Obviously.

ASK YOURSELF

75. Why? What would be lost if I eliminated the abstract descriptions of A and B and replaced them with descriptions of what A and B are made of? That is, what prediction about what both of them will do would be lost?

The analogy between the theoretical roles of Turing machines and intentional systems is more than superficial. Consider that warhorse in the philosophy of mind, Brentano's thesis that intentionality is the mark of the mental: all mental phenomena exhibit intentionality and no physical phenomena exhibit intentionality. This has been traditionally taken to be an *irreducibility* thesis: the mental, in virtue of its intentionality, cannot be reduced to the physical. But given the concept of an intentional system, we can construe the first half of Brentano's thesis—all mental phenomena are intentional—as a *reductionist* thesis of sorts, parallel to Church's thesis in the foundations of mathematics. According to Church's thesis, every "effective" procedure in mathematics is recursive, that is, Turing-computable. Church's thesis is not provable, since it hinges on the intuitive and informal notion of an effective procedure, but it is generally accepted, and it provides a very useful reduction of a fuzzy-but-useful mathematical notion [the notion of an "effective" procedure] to a crisply defined notion of apparently equal scope and greater power. Analogously, the claim that every mental phenomenon alluded to in folk psychology is *intentional-system-characterizable* would, if true, provide a reduction of the mental as ordinarily understood—a domain whose boundaries are at best fixed by mutual acknowledgment and shared intuition—to a clearly defined domain of entities whose principles of organization are familiar, relatively formal and systematic, and entirely general.

An "effective procedure" is a procedure that can be performed without thought or in a purely mechanical way. If, for example, I have the rule that, when any two marks are assigned a "T," then anything that consists of those two marks plus a "&" between them is also assigned a "T," then I have an effective procedure for determining which strings of marks with "&" in them get assigned a "T." (A few other rules are necessary, but perhaps this gives the idea.) A completely "stupid" machine could be set up to apply this rule. Any realization of a Turing machine could follow this rule. (Incidentally, this rule can be interpreted as the rule for determining the truth value of conjunctions in truth functional logic, as well as most natural language conjunctions.)

ASK YOURSELF

76. Produce a statement that is a conjunction and that is true just in case both conjuncts are true. Here is an example: "Bob is here and Bill is here."

This reduction claim, like Church's thesis, cannot be proven but could be made compelling by piecemeal progress on particular (and particularly difficult) cases—a project I set myself elsewhere. The final reductive task would be to show not how the terms of intentional system theory are eliminable in favor of physiological terms via subpersonal cognitive psychology, but almost the reverse: to show how a system described in physiological terms could warrant an interpretation as a realized intentional system.

To sum up: Dennett rejects attempts to reduce mind or the intentional to something physical. But it does not follow, in his view, that the mind is something nonphysical, or indeed that there exists anything at all that is nonphysical. We will be justified in talking about persons and various other beings in terms of their beliefs and desires, not because they have mysterious nonphysical entities called "minds" inside them that have equally mysterious things called beliefs and desires, but because describing them in that way works—in particular, it enables us to make predictions accurately. "Psychology" in this view can advance beyond folk psychology not by eliminating it but by showing how folk psychology is "legitimated" by intentional system theory and subpersonal descriptions. Thus, we can make accurate predictions about the behavior and subsequent history of bats and birds that share the "belief" that a certain noxious insect is indeed noxious. At the same time we can learn more and more about the "subpersonal cognitive systems" of bats and birds, respectively, without making either reductionist or nonmaterialist assumptions. Thus Dennett hopes to have sketched (and it is no more than a sketch) a way in which we can avoid both reductionism and mentalism or dualism. At the same time he avoids the "anti-scientific" bias of Ryle, who claimed that investigation into the operations of the brain (subpersonal cognitive systems) was irrelevant to understanding the realm of the mental.

Suppose it is true that people tend to repeat behavior that is quickly rewarded more than behavior that is not quickly rewarded or behavior that is punished. That would be a case of "conditioning" (see Glossary). And suppose I describe this fact as follows: People who *believe* they will be quickly rewarded for doing something are likely to do it. Now, a behaviorist psychologist would not accept such a description, since he considers the folk psychological notion of "belief" useless in science. Science, he thinks, should stick to describing behavior and eliminate references to beliefs.

ASK YOURSELF

77. According to Dennett, would there be anything wrong with using such a description ("*A believes p*") even in a "scientific" psychology? Why or why not?

78. According to Dennett, would the acceptance of such a description get in the way of further investigation into "reinforcement schedules" or into the physiological mechanisms (brain events for example) which underlie all behavior? Explain.

SUMMING UP INTENTIONALITY

Brentano's notion of intentionality has come to play a central role in the philosophy of mind. It puts a large obstacle in the way of all materialist theories of the mind. Some metaphysical materialists such as Democritus seemed to be unaware of the problem. However, twentieth-century philosophers with a materialist bent, such as Dennett, feel compelled to give some kind of account of how physical things can be "about" something in the way thoughts are. More precisely, they want to know how, at the level of language, words can be about something (or have a semantic dimension) without minds to think the connection between the words and what they are about. It is easy enough to construct a mechanical device that performs syntactical tasks, such as correcting grammar. It is not so easy to imagine a mechanical device that understands the meanings of words. Dennett recognizes this and tries to deal with the difficulty by treating folk psychological or "intentional idioms" such as

**CAN OF
WORMS**

"believes that" and "sees that" as useful devices for predicting behavior. But he denies that they require the postulation of minds as metaphysically distinct entities.

The notion of intentionality plays a fundamental role in the psychology of perception, and thus in epistemology. It can be thought of as providing aid to dualist positions, including those with religious overtones. And, as will become clear in the next section, it has a very direct bearing on how we evaluate androids and other beings that might be thought to have rights or other kinds of ethical standing. If those beings cannot be construed as ever being in intentional states, the notion that they should be treated with respect may turn out to be ridiculous. Thus, issues in epistemology, religion, and ethics are all affected by the debate about intentionality.

F. MINDS AND MACHINES

The idea that humans are nothing more than very elaborate machines has been around for several centuries. In the seventeenth century when mechanical clocks were becoming common, thinkers like Hobbes and La Mettrie hypothesized that humans might be a kind of very elaborate clockwork. More recent developments, particularly twentieth-century inventions, such as computers and robots that seem to "think," have lent much greater credibility to the notion of the self as a machine.

**QUESTIONS
TO DISCUSS**

a. Your computer has a memory. Do you think it actually remembers things?

b. Numerous films and TV series feature robots and androids that look like, talk like, and in many other ways behave like human beings. Could there actually be such beings, and could they be conscious?

c. Does it make sense to suppose that a mechanical device of any kind could *care* about something?

1. HUMANS AS MACHINES: THOMAS HUXLEY

British evolutionary biologist Thomas H. Huxley (1825–1895) exemplfies the strength of materialist thinking in the nineteenth century. He was one of Darwin's main defenders and became known as "Darwin's bulldog." In his 1874 essay entitled "On the Hypothesis That Animals Are Automata," he argues that humans are merely physical, machine-like entities. He begins his demonstration by considering nonhuman animals.

Animals as Machines. The main thing Huxley needs to show is that something can act purposefully without needing a mind or thoughts to do so.

FROM THOMAS HUXLEY, *Methods and Results* (1893)

There remains a doctrine to which Descartes attached great weight, so that full acceptance of it became a sort of note of a thoroughgoing Cartesianism, but which, nevertheless, is so opposed to ordinary prepossessions that it attained more general notoriety, and gave rise to more discussion, than almost any other Cartesian hypothesis. It is the doctrine that brute animals are mere machines or automata, devoid not only of reason, but of any kind of consciousness, which is stated briefly in the Discourse on Method, and more fully in the "Replies to the Fourth Objections," and in the correspondence with Henry More. . . .

Descartes' line of argument is perfectly clear. He starts from reflex action in man, from the unquestionable fact that, in ourselves, co-ordinate, purposive, actions may take place, without intervention of consciousness or volition, or even contrary to the latter. As actions of a certain degree of complexity are brought about by mere mechanism, why may not actions of still greater complexity be the result of a more refined mechanism? What proof is there that brutes are other than a superior race of marionettes, which eat without pleasure, cry without pain, desire nothing, know nothing, and only simulate intelligence as a bee simulates a mathematician?

**THOMAS HUXLEY
(1825–1895)**
English evolutionary biologist.

. . . If the spinal cord of a frog is cut across, so as to provide us with a segment separated from the brain, we shall have a subject parallel to the injured man, on which experiments can be made without remorse; as we have a right to conclude that a frog's spinal cord is not likely to be conscious, when a man's is not.

Now the frog behaves just as the man did. The legs are utterly paralysed, so far as voluntary movement is concerned; but they are vigorously drawn up to the body when any irritant is applied to the foot. But let us study our frog a little farther. Touch the skin of the side of the body with a little acetic acid, which gives rise to all the signs of great pain in an uninjured frog. In this case, there can be no pain, because the application is made to a part of the skin supplied with nerves which come off from the cord below the point of section; nevertheless, the frog lifts up the limb of the same side, and applies the foot to rub off the acetic acid; and, what is still more remarkable, if the limb be held so that the frog cannot use it, it will, by and by, move the limb of the other side, turn it across the body, and use it for the same rubbing process. It is impossible that the frog, if it were in its entirety and could reason, should perform actions more purposive than these: and yet we have most complete assurance that, in this case, the frog is not acting from purpose, has no consciousness, and is a mere insensible machine.

ASK YOURSELF

79. Briefly, what shows that the frog, under the conditions cited, "is a mere insensible machine," according to Huxley?

But now suppose that, instead of making a section of the cord in the middle of the body, it had been made in such a manner as to separate the hindermost division of the brain from the rest of the organ, and suppose the foremost two-thirds of the brain entirely taken away. The frog is then absolutely devoid of any spontaneity; it sits upright in the attitude which a frog habitually assumes; and it will not stir unless it is touched; but it differs from the frog which I have just described in this, that, if it be thrown into the water, it begins to swim, and swims just as well as the perfect frog does. But swimming requires the combination and successive coordination of a great number of muscular actions. And we are forced to conclude, that the impression made upon the sensory nerves of the skin of the frog by the contact with the water into which it is thrown, causes the transmission to the central nervous apparatus of an impulse which sets going a certain machinery by which all the muscles of swimming are brought into play in due co-ordination. If the frog be stimulated by some irritating body, it jumps or walks as well as the complete frog can do. The simple sensory impression, acting through the machinery of the cord, gives rise to these complex combined movements.

It is possible to go a step farther. Suppose that only the anterior division of the brain—so much of it as lies in front of the "optic lobes"—is removed. If that operation is performed quickly and skillfully, the frog may be kept in a state of full bodily vigour for months, or it may be for years; but it will sit unmoved. It sees nothing; it hears nothing. It will starve sooner than feed itself, although food put into its mouth is swallowed. On irritation, it jumps or walks; if thrown into the water it swims. If it be put on the hand, it sits there, crouched, perfectly quiet and would sit there forever. If the hand be inclined very gently and slowly, so that the frog would naturally tend to slip off, the creature's fore paws are shifted on to the edge of the hand, until he can just prevent himself from falling. If the turning of the hand be slowly continued, he mounts up with great care and deliberation, putting first one leg forward and then another, until he balances himself with perfect precision upon the edge; and if the turning of the hand is continued, he goes through the needful set of muscular operations, until he comes to be seated in security, upon the back of the hand. The doing of all this requires a delicacy of coordination, and a precision of adjustment of the muscular apparatus of the body, which are only comparable to those of a ropedancer. To the ordinary influences of light, the frog, deprived of its cerebral hemispheres, appears to be blind. Nevertheless, if the animal be put upon a table, with a book at some little distance between it and the light, and the skin of the hinder part of its body is then irritated, it will jump forward, avoiding the book by passing to the right or left of it. Therefore, although the frog appears to have no sensation of light, visible objects act through its brain upon the motor mechanism of its body.

It is obvious that had Descartes been acquainted with these remarkable results of modern research, they would have furnished him with far more powerful arguments than he possessed in favour of his view of the automatism of brutes. The habits of a frog, leading its natural life, involve such simple adaptations to surrounding conditions that the machinery, which is competent to do so much without the intervention of consciousness, might well do all.

ASK YOURSELF

80. To summarize, since the frog can do so much without consciousness, it is not unreasonable to think that it could do _____ without consciousness.

And this argument is vastly strengthened by what has been learned in recent times of the marvellously complex operations which are performed mechanically, and to all appearance without consciousness, by men, when, in consequence of injury or disease, they are reduced to a condition more or less comparable to that of a frog, in which the anterior part of the brain has been removed. A case has recently been published by an eminent French physician, Dr. Mesnet, which illustrates this condition so remarkably that I make no apology for dwelling upon it at considerable length.

An Example of Mechanical Action in a Human. The frog, Huxley argues, is not unique with respect to its "machine" characteristics. Humans are like that too. He illustrates this with the example of a soldier whose brain was injured during battle.

A sergeant of the French army, F——, twenty-seven years of age, was wounded during the battle of Bazeilles, by a ball which fractured his left parietal bone. He ran his bayonet through the Prussian soldier who wounded him, but almost immediately his right arm be-came paralysed; after walking about two hundred yards, his right leg became similarly affected, and he lost his senses. When he recovered them, three weeks afterwards, in a hos-pital at Mayence, the right half of the body was completely paralyzed, and remained in this condition for a year. At present, the only trace of paralysis which remains is a slight weak-ness of the right half of the body. Three or four months after the wound was inflicted, peri-odical disturbances of the functions of the brain made their appearance, and have continued ever since. The disturbances last from fifteen to thirty hours; the intervals at which they occur being from fifteen to thirty days. For four years, therefore, the life of this man has been di-vided into alternating phases—short abnormal states intervening between long normal states.

In the periods of normal life, the ex-sergeant's health is perfect; he is intelligent and kindly and performs, satisfactorily, the duties of a hospital attendant. The commencement of the abnormal state is ushered in by uneasiness and a sense of weight about the forehead, which the patient compares to the constriction of a circle of iron; and, after its termination, he complains, for some hours, of dullness and heaviness of the head. But the transition from the normal to the abnormal state takes place in a few minutes, without convulsions or cries, and without anything to indicate the change to a bystander. His movements remain free and his expression calm, except for a contraction of the brow, an incessant movement of the eye-balls, and a chewing motion of the jaws. The eyes are wide open, and their pupils dilated. If the man happens to be in a place to which he is accustomed, he walks about as usual; but, if he is in a new place, or if obstacles are intentionally placed in his way, he stumbles gently against them, stops, and then, feeling over the objects with his hands, passes on one side of them. He offers no resistance to any change of direction which may be impressed upon him, or to the forcible acceleration or retardation of his movements. He eats, drinks, smokes, walks about, dresses and undresses himself, rises and goes to bed at the accustomed hours. Nevertheless, pins may be run into his body, or strong electric shocks may be sent through it, without causing the least indication of pain; no odorous substance, pleasant or unpleasant, makes the least impression; he eats and drinks with avidity whatever is offered, and takes asafoetida, or vinegar, or quinine, as readily as water; no noise affects him; and light influ-ences him only under certain conditions. Dr. Mesnet remarks, that the sense of touch alone seems to persist, and indeed to be more acute and delicate than in the normal state: and it is by means of the nerves of touch, almost exclusively, that his organism is brought into rela-tion with the external world. Here a difficulty arises. It is clear from the facts detailed, that the nervous apparatus by which, in the normal state, sensations of touch are excited, is that by which external influences determine the movements of the body, in the abnormal state. But does the state of consciousness, which we term a tactile sensation, accompany the oper-ation of this nervous apparatus in the abnormal state? Or is consciousness utterly absent, the man being reduced to an insensible mechanism?

It is impossible to obtain direct evidence in favour of the one conclusion or the other; all that can be said is that the case of the frog shows that the man may be devoid of any kind of consciousness.

A further difficult problem is this. The man is insensible to sensory impressions made through the ear, the nose, the tongue, and, to a great extent, the eye; nor is he susceptible of pain from causes operating during his abnormal state. Nevertheless, it is possible so to act upon his tactile apparatus, as to give rise to those molecular changes in his sensorium, which are ordinarily the causes of associated trains of ideas. I give a striking example of this process in Dr. Mesnet's words: "He was taking a walk in the garden under a bunch of trees. We placed in his hand his walking stick which he had let fall a few minutes before. He feels it, passes his hand over the bent handle a few times, becomes attentive, seems to extend his ear, and suddenly calls out, "Henry," then, "Here they are. There are about twenty to our two! We have reached our end." And then, with his hand behind his back, as if about to leap, he prepares to attack with his weapon. He crouches in the level, green grass, his head concealed by a tree, in the position of a hunter, and follows all the short-distance movements of the enemy which he believes he sees, with accompanying movements of his hands and shoulders."

In a subsequent abnormal period, Dr. Mesnet caused the patient to repeat this scene by placing him in the same conditions. Now, in this case, the question arises whether the series of actions constituting this singular pantomime was accompanied by the ordinary states of consciousness, the appropriate train of ideas, or not? Did the man dream that he was skirmishing? Or was he in the condition of one of Vaucauson's automata, a senseless mechanism worked by molecular changes in his nervous system? The analogy of the frog shows that the latter assumption is perfectly justifiable.

The ex-sergeant has a good voice and had, at one time, been employed as a singer at a cafe. In one of his abnormal states he was observed to begin humming a tune. He then went to his room, dressed himself carefully, and took up some parts of a periodical novel, which lay on his bed, as if he were trying to find something. Dr. Mesnet, suspecting that he was seeking his music, made up one of these into a roll and put it into his hand. He appeared satisfied, took his cane and went downstairs to the door. Here Dr. Mesnet turned him round, and he walked quite contentedly, in the opposite direction, towards the room of the concierge. The light of the sun shining through a window now happened to fall upon him and seemed to suggest the footlights of the stage on which he was accustomed to make his appearance. He stopped, opened his roll of imaginary music, put himself into the attitude of a singer, and sang, with perfect execution, three songs, one after the other. After which he wiped his face with his handkerchief and drank, without a grimace, a tumbler of strong vinegar and water which was put into his hand.

An experiment which may be performed upon the frog deprived of the fore part of its brain, well known as Goltz's "Quak-versuch," affords a parallel to this performance. If the skin of a certain part of the back of such a frog is gently stroked with the finger, it immediately croaks. It never croaks unless it is so stroked, and the croak always follows the stroke, just as the sound of a repeater follows the touching of the spring. In the frog, this "song" is innate—so to speak *a priori*—and depends upon a mechanism in the brain governing the vocal apparatus, which is set at work by the molecular change set up in the sensory nerves of the skin of the back by the contact of a foreign body.

In man there is also a vocal mechanism, and the cry of an infant is in the same sense innate and *a priori,* inasmuch as it depends on an organic relation between its sensory nerves and the nervous mechanism which governs the vocal apparatus. Learning to speak, and learning to sing, are processes by which the vocal mechanism is set to new tunes. A song which has been learned has its molecular equivalent, which potentially represents it in the brain, just as a musical box, wound up, potentially represents an overture. Touch the stop and the overture begins; send a molecular impulse along the proper afferent nerve and the singer begins his song.

The tune that a music box emits is "represented" by, for example, spikes on a cylinder in a certain arrangement, which in turn activate various lengths of vibrating bars. Teaching a song to someone is like fashioning spikes on the cylinder; that is, it is setting up a physical configuration that under certain prompts or stimuli will produce the tune. Thus, knowing a tune is not a matter of having something "in my mind" or "consciousness" but is rather a matter of a physical configuration having been established in my brain or nervous system.

ASK YOURSELF

81. Today we have "purely physical configurations" that we are particularly likely to describe as having thoughts, memories and so on, namely _____. Would our technology give further credence to Huxley's view?

Again, the manner in which the frog, though apparently insensible to light, is yet, under some circumstances, influenced by visual images, finds a singular parallel in the case of the ex-sergeant.

Sitting at a table, in one of his abnormal states, he took up a pen, felt for paper and ink, and began to write a letter to his general in which he recommended himself for medal, on account of his good conduct and courage. It occurred to Dr. Mesnet to ascertain experimentally how far vision was concerned in this act of writing. He therefore interposed a screen between the man's eyes and his hands; under these circumstances he went on writing for a short time, but the words became illegible, and he finally stopped, without manifesting any discontent. On the withdrawal of the screen he began to write again where he had left off. The substitution of water for ink in the inkstand had a similar result. He stopped, looked at his pen, wiped it on his coat, dipped it in the water, and began again with the same effect. On one occasion, he began to write upon the topmost of ten superimposed sheets of paper. After he had written a line or two, this sheet was suddenly drawn away. There was a slight expression of surprise, but he continued his letter on the second sheet exactly as if it had been the first. This operation was repeated five times, so that the fifth sheet contained nothing but the writer's signature at the bottom of the page. Nevertheless, when the signature was finished, his eyes turned to the top of the blank sheet, and he went through the form of reading over what he had written, a movement of lips accompanying each word; moreover, with his pen, he put in such corrections as were needed, in that part of the blank page which corresponded with the position of the words which required correction, in the sheets which had been taken away. If the five sheets had been transparent, therefore, they would, when superimposed, have formed a properly written and corrected letter.

Immediately after he had written his letter, F—— got up, walked down to the garden, made himself a cigarette, lighted and smoked it. He was about to prepare another, but sought in vain for his tobacco-pouch, which had been purposely taken away. The pouch was now thrust before his eyes and put under his nose, but he neither saw nor smelt it; yet, when it was placed in his hand, he at once seized it, made a fresh cigarette, and ignited a match to light the latter. The match was blown out, and another lighted match placed close before his eyes, but he made no attempt to take it; and, if his cigarette was lighted for him, he made no attempt to smoke. All this time the eyes were vacant, and neither winked, nor exhibited any contraction of the pupils. From these and other experiments, Dr. Mesnet draws the conclusion that his patient sees some things and not others; that the sense of sight is accessible to all things which are brought into relation with him by the sense of touch, and, on the contrary, insensible to things which lie outside this relation. He sees the match he holds and does not see any other . . . just so the frog "sees" the book which is in the way of his jump, at the same time that isolated visual impressions take no effect upon him.

As I have pointed out, it is impossible to prove that F—— is absolutely unconscious in his abnormal state, but it is no less impossible to prove the contrary; and the case of the frog goes a long way to justify the assumption that, in the abnormal state, the man is a mere insensible machine. . . .

Though we may see reason to disagree with Descartes' hypothesis that brutes are unconscious machines, it does not follow that he was wrong in regarding them as automata. They may be more or less conscious, sensitive, automata; and the view that they are such conscious machines is that which is implicitly, or explicitly adopted by most persons. When we speak of the actions of the lower animals being guided by instinct and not by reason, what we really mean is that, though they feel as we do, yet their actions are the results of their physical organisation. We believe, in short, that they are machines, one part of which (the nervous system) not only sets the rest in motion, and co-ordinates its movements in relation with changes in surrounding bodies, but is provided with special apparatus, the function of which is the calling into existence of those states of consciousness which are termed sensations, emotions, and ideas. I believe that this generally accepted view is the best expression of the facts at present known . . . it may be assumed, then, that molecular changes in the brain are the causes of all the states of consciousness of brutes. Is there any evidence that these states of consciousness may, conversely, cause those molecular changes which give rise to muscular motion? I see no such evidence. The frog walks, hops, swims, and goes through his gymnastic performances quite as well without consciousness, and consequently without volition, as with it; and, if a frog, in his natural state, possesses anything corresponding with what we call volition, there is no reason to think that it is anything but a concomitant of the molecular changes in the brain which form part of the series involved in the production of motion.

Huxley is arguing that while physical events may cause "consciousness," nothing in consciousness causes any physical event. So, my conscious thought that I would like something to eat does not in any way determine the motion of my body toward the counter or my picking up the hamburger. Huxley's view is called "epiphenomenalism" in the philosophy of mind, and it is neatly and memorably illustrated by the following analogy.

The consciousness of brutes would appear to be related to the mechanism of their body simply as a collateral product of its working, and to be as completely without any power of modifying that working as the steam-whistle which accompanies the work of a locomotive engine is without influence upon its machinery. Their volition, if they have any, is an emotion indicative of physical changes, not a cause of such changes.

ASK YOURSELF

82. Thus what we call "consciousness" really plays no significant role in our lives. Our thoughts and feelings do not actually move us to act. It is not the *feeling* of pain that makes us withdraw our hand from the stove burner. It is simply the physical nerve connections that cause it. Can you then think of *anything* important that would be missing if we had no consciousness? If so mention it (them).

The conception of the relations of states of consciousness with molecular changes in the brain—of psychoses with neuroses—does not prevent us from ascribing free will to brutes. For an agent is free when there is nothing to prevent him from doing that which he desires to do. If a greyhound chases a hare, he is a free agent, because his action is in entire accordance with his strong desire to catch the hare; while so long as he is held back by the leash he is not free, being prevented by external force from following his inclination. And the ascription of freedom to the greyhound under the former circumstances is by no means inconsistent with the other aspect of the facts of the case—that he is a machine impelled to the chase, and caused, at the same time, to have the desire to catch the game by the impression which the rays of light proceeding from the hare make upon his eyes, and through them upon his brain. . . .

One of the most disturbing things about the notion that a human is just a machine is the apparent implication that, like machines, we have no free will, but rather must simply act according to our mechanical functions or design, as acted upon by external "inputs." An auto engine does not "decide" to "turn over" when it gets the appropriate gas, electrical, and air "inputs." Its doing so is entirely "determined," and the view that humans are similarly determined by design and inputs (environment) is called "determinism."

ASK YOURSELF

83. How does Huxley try to show that we can be machines and still not be determined? Do you find his argument convincing?

Humans Are Also Automata. Huxley argues that the evidence adduced so far is sufficient to establish that humans are just machines with a little superfluous consciousness added on, like steam coming from the locomotive.

It will be said that I mean that the conclusions deduced from the study of the brutes are applicable to man, and that the logical consequences of such application are fatalism, materialism, and atheism—whereupon the drums will beat the *pas de charge*.

ASK YOURSELF

84. Why might someone think atheism would be a consequence of Huxley's view?

One does not do battle with drummers; but I venture to offer a few remarks for the calm consideration of thoughtful persons, untrammelled by foregone conclusions, unpledged to shore-up tottering dogmas, and anxious only to know the true bearings of the case.

It is quite true that, to the best of my judgment, the argumentation which applies to brutes holds equally good of men: and therefore, that all states of consciousness in us, as in them, are immediately caused by molecular changes of the brain-substance. It seems to me that in men, as in brutes, there is no proof that any state of consciousness is the cause of change in the motion of the matter of the organism. If these positions are well based, it follows that our mental conditions are simply the symbols in consciousness of the changes which take place automatically in the organism; and that, to take an extreme illustration, the feeling we call volition is not the cause of a voluntary act, but the symbol of that state of the brain which is the immediate cause of that act. We are conscious automata, endowed with free will in the only intelligible sense of that much-abused term—inasmuch as in many respects we are able to do as we like—but nonetheless parts of the great series of causes and effects which, in unbroken continuity, composes that which is, and has been, and shall be the sum of existence.

ASK YOURSELF

85. The well-known scientist Carl Sagan once said "The universe is everything that is, that ever was, and ever will be." Sagan's remark is much in the spirit of the last sentence just quoted from Huxley. Both Huxley and Sagan were atheists. What is it in their respective claims that implies atheism?

86. Huxley argues that our willing to do something does not cause us to do it but is merely the "symbol" of that state or configuration of the brain that *does* cause us to act. What sort of thing, in his view, would have produced that configuration of the brain?

87. Can something be a "symbol" if there are no minds around to think about the connection between it and what it symbolizes?

LUDWIG WITTGENSTEIN (1889–1951)

Austrian-born philosopher and author of Philosophical Investigations *(1953).*

2. REMINDERS ABOUT MACHINES AND THINKING: LUDWIG WITTGENSTEIN AND PAUL ZIFF

There have been remarkable developments in artificial intelligence (AI) research and computer technology in the latter half of the twentieth century and up to the present. These developments have given greater plausibility to the idea that machines might have thoughts and feelings. Thus, indirectly, they give greater plausibility to the idea that humans are themselves machines. Movies and TV series featuring androids, such as Data (*Star Trek*: *The Next Generation*), have popularized these ideas. Ludwig Wittgenstein (1889–1951), who was himself trained as an engineer, developed views on the nature of human thought that conflict with such popular ideas about androids. The following few excerpts from his posthumous *Philosophical Investigations* show some of the ways in which thinking about language and mind are intertwined.

FROM LUDWIG WITTGENSTEIN, *Philosophical Investigations* (1953)

356. One is inclined to say: "Either it is raining, or it isn't—how I know, how the information has reached me, is another matter." But then let us put the question like this: What do I call "information that it is raining"? (Or have I only information of this information too?) And what gives this 'information' the character of information about something? Doesn't the form of our expression mislead us here? For isn't it a misleading metaphor to say: "My eyes give me the information that there is a chair over there"?

ASK YOURSELF

88. Why would it be a misleading metaphor? What about "my brain gives me the information that there is a chair"? In answering this, think what it would take for either brain or eyes to be "given information" in the sense in which I can give you information about, say, a bus schedule.

357. We do not say that *possibly* a dog talks to itself. Is that because we are so minutely acquainted with its soul? Well, one might say this: If one sees the behavior of a living thing, one sees its soul. But do I also say in my own case that I am saying something to myself because I am behaving in such-and-such a way? I do *not* say it from observation of my behavior. But it only makes sense because I do behave in this way. Then it is not because I *mean* it that it makes sense?.

358. But isn't it our *meaning* it that gives sense to the sentence? (And here, of course, belongs the fact that one cannot mean a senseless string of words.) And 'meaning it' is something in the sphere of the mind. But it is also something private! It is the intangible *something;* comparable with consciousness itself.

How could this seem ludicrous? It is, as it were, a dream of our language.

ASK YOURSELF

89. If our meaning what we say is not what gives sense to our utterances, than what does? Look back to 357 in answering.

359. Could a machine think? Could it be in pain? Well, is the human body to be called such a machine? It surely comes as close as possible to being such a machine.

360. But a machine surely cannot think! Is that an empirical statement? No. We only say of a human being and what is like one that it thinks. We also say it of dolls and no doubt of ghosts too. Look at the word "to think" as a tool.

ASK YOURSELF

90. Wittgenstein says that only what is like a human being is said to think. List some ways the following are like human beings, and some ways they are unlike humans; androids; dolls; a box on wheels with a powerful computer in the box.

Empirical statements are statements that can be shown to be true or false through observation. What observations would prove that a machine thinks? Wittgenstein denies that the statement "a machine cannot think" is empirical. No observations of any machine could show it to be either true or false. The next selection may help to clarify the issues here.

The Feelings of Robots. In the following excerpts from an article entitled "The Feelings of Robots," American philosopher Paul Ziff argues that androids or robots could not have feelings. The kinds of contextual considerations that he points out are quite possibly the sorts of things Wittgenstein had in mind when he claimed that we only say of humans, or what are quite like them, that they think or feel pain.

From Paul Ziff, "The Feelings of Robots" (1959)

Could robots feel tired? Could a stone feel tired? Could the number 17 feel tired? It is clear that there is no reason to believe that 17 feels tired.

There are good reasons not to suppose that 17 ever feels anything at all. Consequently it is necessary to consider whether there are good reasons for not supposing that robots ever feel anything at all.

ASK YOURSELF

91. Could the number 17 feel tired? To quote Wittgenstein, 360, "Is this an empirical question?" If you think it is, describe what observations you would make to show that it is true or false.

If we say of a person that he feels tired, we generally do so not only on the basis of what we see then and there but on the basis of what we have seen elsewhere and on the basis of how what we have seen elsewhere ties in with what we see then and there.

7. Suppose K is a robot. An ordinary man may see K and not knowing that K is a robot, the ordinary man may say K feels tired. If I ask him what makes him think so, he may reply K worked all day digging ditches. Anyway, just look at K: if he doesn't look tired, who does?' That doesn't prove anything. If I know K is a robot, K may not look tired to me. It is not what I see but what I know. Or it is not what I see then and there but what I have seen elsewhere. Where? In a robot psychology laboratory.

8. In our laboratory we have taken robots apart, we have changed and exchanged their parts, we have changed and exchanged their programs. And what we find in our laboratory is this: no robot could sensibly be said to feel anything. Why not?

9. Because the way a robot acts (in a specified context) depends primarily on how we programmed it to act. Suppose some robots are programmed to act like a tired man after lifting a feather while some are so programmed that they never act like a tired man. Shall we say "It is a queer thing but some robots feel tired almost at once while others never feel tired"? Or suppose some are programmed to act like a tired man after lifting something blue but not something green. Shall we say some robots feel tired when they lift blue things but not when they lift green things? Hard work makes a man feel tired: what will make a robot act like a tired man? Perhaps hard work, or light work. Or no work, or anything at all. For it will depend on the whims of the man who makes it.

ASK YOURSELF

92. Ziff is arguing that our use of such expressions as "is tired" presupposes or has built into it a certain background, a background that is missing in the case of robots that are genuinely machines. What are some of the elements of that background? What background elements are missing in the case of the number 17?

3. MINDS, BRAINS, AND THE CHINESE ROOM ARGUMENT: JOHN SEARLE

In the previous selection, Ziff argued against the contention that robots could have feelings. What, though, about other kinds of mental phenomena? Could they have thoughts, such as that 2 + 2 = 4? John Searle (b. 1932), philosophy professor at the University of California,

Berkeley, argues that no human mental phenomena can be replicated by any programmed machine. He employs a controversial argument that has been widely discussed, often referred to as "the Chinese room argument."

FROM JOHN SEARLE, "Minds, Brains and Programs" (1980)

What psychological and philosophical significance should we attach to recent efforts at computer simulations of human cognitive capacities? In answering this question, I find it useful to distinguish what I will call "strong" AI from "weak" or "cautious" AI (Artificial Intelligence). According to weak AI, the principal value of the computer in the study of the mind is that it gives us a very powerful tool. For example, it enables us to formulate and test hypotheses in a more rigorous and precise fashion. But according to strong AI, the computer is not merely a tool in the study of the mind; rather, the appropriately programmed computer really *is* a mind, in the sense that computers given the right programs can be literally said to *understand* and have other cognitive states. In strong AI, because the programmed computer has cognitive states, the programs are not mere tools that enable us to test psychological explanations; rather, the programs are themselves the explanations.

JOHN SEARLE (B. 1932)
contemporary philosopher and author of Minds, Brains and Science *(1984).*

I have no objection to the claims of weak AI, at least as far as this article is concerned. My discussion here will be directed at the claims I have defined as those of strong AI, specifically the claim that the appropriately programmed computer literally has cognitive states and that the programs thereby explain human cognition. When I hereafter refer to AI, I have in mind the strong version, as expressed by these two claims.

I will consider the work of Roger Schank and his colleagues at Yale (Schank & Abelson 1977), because I am more familiar with it than I am with any other similar claims, and because it provides a very clear example of the sort of work I wish to examine. But nothing that follows depends upon the details of Schank's programs. The same arguments would apply to Winograd's SHRDLU (Winograd 1973), Weizenbaum's ELIZA (Weizenbaum 1967), and indeed any Turing machine simulation of human mental phenomena.

Very briefly, and leaving out the various details, one can describe Schank's program as follows: the aim of the program is to simulate the human ability to understand stories. It is characteristic of human beings' story-understanding capacity that they can answer questions about the story even though the information that they give was never explicitly stated in the story. Thus, for example, suppose you are given the following story: "A man went into a restaurant and ordered a hamburger. When the hamburger arrived it was burned to a crisp, and the man stormed out of the restaurant angrily, without paying for the hamburger or leaving a tip." Now, if you are asked "Did the man eat the hamburger?" you will presumably answer, "No, he did not." Similarly, if you are given the following story: "A man went into a restaurant and ordered a hamburger; when the hamburger came he was very pleased with it, and as he left the restaurant he gave the waitress a large tip before paying his bill," and you are asked the question, "Did the man eat the hamburger?" you will presumably answer, "Yes, he ate the hamburger." Now Schank's machines can similarly answer questions about restaurants in this fashion. To do this, they have a "representation" of the sort of information that human beings have about restaurants, which enables them to answer such questions as those above, given these sorts of stories. When the machine is given the story and then asked the question, the machine will print out answers of the sort that we would expect human beings to give if told similar stories. Partisans of strong AI claim that in this question and answer sequence the machine is not only simulating a human ability but also

1. that the machine can literally be said to *understand* the story and provide the answers to questions, and
2. that what the machine and its program do *explains* the human ability to understand the story and answer questions about it.

Both claims seem to me to be totally unsupported by Schank's work, as I will attempt to show in what follows.

One way to test any theory of the mind is to ask oneself what it would be like if my mind actually worked on the principles that the theory says all minds work on. Let us apply this test to the Schank program with the following *Gedankenexperiment* [thought experiment]. Suppose that I'm locked in a room and given a large batch of Chinese writing. Suppose furthermore (as is indeed the case) that I know no Chinese, either written or spoken, and that I'm not even confident that I could recognize Chinese writing as Chinese writing distinct from, say, Japanese writing or meaningless squiggles. To me, Chinese writing is just so many meaningless squiggles. Now suppose further that after this first batch of Chinese writing I am given a second batch of Chinese script together with a set of rules for correlating the second batch with the first batch. The rules are in English, and I understand these rules as well as any other native speaker of English. They enable me to correlate one set of formal symbols with another set of formal symbols, and all that "formal" means here is that I can identify the symbols entirely by their shapes. Now suppose also that I am given a third batch of Chinese symbols together with some instructions, again in English, that enable me to correlate elements of this third batch with the first two batches, and these rules instruct me how to give back certain Chinese symbols with certain sorts of shapes in response to certain sorts of shapes given me in the third batch. Unknown to me, the people who are giving me all of these symbols call the first batch "a script," they call the second batch a "story," and they call the third batch "questions." Furthermore, they call the symbols I give them back in response to the third batch "answers to the questions," and the set of rules in English that they gave me, they call "the program." Now just to complicate the story a little, imagine that these people also give me stories in English, which I understand, and they then ask me questions in English about these stories, and I give them back answers in English. Suppose also that after a while I get so good at following the instructions for manipulating the Chinese symbols and the programmers get so good at writing the programs that from the external point of view—that is, from the point of view of somebody outside the room in which I am locked my answers to the questions are absolutely indistinguishable from those of native Chinese speakers. Nobody just looking at my answers can tell that I don't speak a word of Chinese. Let us also suppose that my answers to the English questions are, as they no doubt would be, indistinguishable from those of other native English speakers, for the simple reason that I am a native English speaker. From the external point of view—from the point of view of someone reading my "answers"—the answers to the Chinese questions and the English questions are equally good. But in the Chinese case, unlike the English case, I produce the answers by manipulating uninterpreted formal symbols. As far as the Chinese is concerned, I simply behave like a computer; I perform computational operations on formally specified elements. For the purposes of the Chinese, I am simply an instantiation of the computer program.

Suppose a native Chinese speaker/writer slips a piece of paper with the first story through an "in box" in the door. Then he slips in another slip with a question as to whether or not the hamburger was eaten. Suppose I am the person in the room scanning these inputs. All I see are pieces of paper with strange squiggles. I then consult a huge library of books of rules. The rules give instructions for replacing incoming squiggles with new squiggles on a piece of paper. The rules say nothing about what the squiggles mean, if indeed they mean anything at all. Now if those rules are of the right type, by applying them I will be able to write on a piece of paper some "squiggles" that, when seen by a reader of Chinese, convey that the hamburger was not eaten, as in the first story (for some indication of what the rules might be like, see the last selection in this section). This is a description of a device that scans input, where I am the scanner, according to a set of rules applicable to strictly formal elements and produces formal output. Thus the room with all its contents constitutes a "Turing machine," which is any device that scans input and produces output in that way. All digital computers are Turing machines, no matter how complex their hardware and programs may be.

Now if all of this happened fast enough, it would be as though the Chinese person was carrying on a conversation with the room about the story. In that case the room would pass the "Turing test" since the behavior of the room would be indistinguishable from that of a native Chinese speaker/writer. It has been claimed that anything that can pass the Turing test has "understanding" (the British mathematician Alan Turing, after whom the test is named, claimed this).

ASK YOURSELF

93. The person inside the room does not understand Chinese. Would you be inclined to say the *room* understood Chinese? Explain.

Now the claims made by strong AI are that the programmed computer understands the stories and that the program in some sense explains human understanding. But we are now in a position to examine these claims in light of our thought experiment.

1. As regards the first claim, it seems to me quite obvious in the example that I do not understand a word of the Chinese stories. I have inputs and outputs that are indistinguishable from those of the native Chinese speaker, and I can have any formal program you like, but I still understand nothing. For the same reasons, Schank's computer understands nothing of any stories, whether in Chinese, English, or whatever, since in the Chinese case the Computer is me, and in cases where the computer is not me, the computer has nothing more than I have in the case where I understand nothing.

2. As regards the second claim, that the program explains human understanding, we can see that the computer and its program do not provide sufficient conditions of understanding since the computer and the program are functioning, and there is no understanding. But does it even provide a necessary condition or a significant contribution to understanding? One of the claims made by the supporters of strong AI is that when I understand a story in English, what I am doing is exactly the same—or perhaps more of the same—as what I was doing in

manipulating the Chinese symbols. It is simply more formal symbol manipulation that distinguishes the case in English, where I do understand, from the case in Chinese, where I don't. I have not demonstrated that this claim is false, but it would certainly appear an incredible claim in the example. Such plausibility as the claim has derives from the supposition that we can construct a program that will have the same inputs and outputs as native speakers, and in addition we assume that speakers have some level of description where they are also instantiations of a program. On the basis of these two assumptions we assume that even if Schank's program isn't the whole story about understanding, it may be part of the story. Well, I suppose that is an empirical possibility, but not the slightest reason has so far been given to believe that it is true, since what is suggested—though certainly not demonstrated—by the example is that the computer program is simply irrelevant to my understanding of the story. In the Chinese case I have everything that artificial intelligence can put into me by way of a program, and I understand nothing; in the English case I understand everything, and there is so far no reason at all to suppose that my understanding has anything to do with computer programs, that is, with computational operations on purely formally specified elements. As long as the program is defined in terms of computational operations on purely formally defined elements, what the example suggests is that these by themselves have no interesting connection with understanding. They are certainly not sufficient conditions, and not the slightest reason has been given to suppose that they are necessary conditions or even that they make a significant contribution to understanding. Notice that the force of the argument is not simply that different machines can have the same input and output while operating on different formal principles—that is not the point at all. Rather, whatever purely formal principles you put into the computer, they will not be sufficient for understanding, since a human will be able to follow the formal principles without understanding anything. No reason whatever has been offered to suppose that such principles are necessary or even contributory, since no reason has been given to suppose that when I understand English I am operating with any formal program at all.

ASK YOURSELF

94. What does an "operator" in the Chinese room have to know in order to produce "fine, how are you" (spoken or written) when asked "how are you" (spoken or written)?

What, then, is it that I have in the case of the English sentences that I do not have in the case of the Chinese sentences? The obvious answer is that I know what the former *mean,* while I haven't the faintest idea what the latter mean. But of what does this "knowing" consist, and why couldn't we give it, whatever it is, to a machine? Before discussing these questions, Searle briefly discusses the notion of "understanding" and the fact that we sometimes do attribute understanding to artifacts.

There are clear cases in which "understanding" literally applies and clear cases in which it does not apply; and these two sorts of cases are all I need for this argument. I understand stories in English; to a lesser degree I can understand stories in French; to a still lesser degree, stories in German; and in Chinese, not at all. My car and my adding machine, on the other hand, understand nothing: they are not in that line of business. We often attribute "understanding" and other cognitive predicates by metaphor and analogy to cars, adding machines, and other artifacts, but nothing is proved by such attributions. We say, "The door *knows* when to open because of its photoelectric cell," "The adding machine *knows how (understands how, is able)* to do addition and subtraction but not division," and "The thermostat perceives changes in the temperature." The reason we make these attributions is quite interesting, and it has to do with the fact that in artifacts we extend our own intentionality; our tools are extensions of our purposes, and so we find it natural to make metaphorical attributions of intentionality to them; but I take it no philosophical ice is cut by such examples. The sense in which an automatic door "understands instructions" from its photoelectric cell is not at all the sense in which I understand English. If the sense in which Schank's programmed computers understand stories is supposed to be the metaphorical sense in which the door understands, and not the sense in which I understand English, the issue would not be worth discussing. But Newell and Simon write that the kind of Cognition they claim for computers is exactly the same as for human beings. I like the straightforwardness of this claim, and it is the sort of claim I will be considering. I will argue that in the literal sense the programmed computer understands what the car and the adding machine understand, namely, exactly nothing. The computer understanding is not just (like my understanding of German) partial or incomplete; it is zero.

Searle considers various responses to his thought experiment. One is as follows:

While it is true that the individual person who is locked in the room does not understand the story, the fact is that he is merely part of a whole system, and the system does understand the story. The person has a large ledger in front of him in which are written the rules, he has a lot of scratch paper and pencils for doing calculations, he has "data banks" of sets of Chinese symbols. Now, understanding is not being ascribed to the mere individual; rather it is being ascribed to this whole system of which he is a part.

ASK YOURSELF

95. Does this amount to the claim that the whole room, including its contents, "understands" stories even though the ledgers, or people, inside the room do not?

The idea is that while a person doesn't understand Chinese [that is, the person in the room who scans], somehow the *conjunction* of that person and bits of paper might understand Chinese. . . . Let us ask ourselves what is supposed to motivate the systems reply in the first place; that is, what *independent* grounds are there supposed to be for saying that the agent must have a subsystem within him that literally understands stories in Chinese? As far as I can tell, the only grounds are that in the example I have the same input and output as native Chinese speakers and a program that goes from one to the other. But the whole point of the examples has been to try to show that that couldn't be sufficient for understanding, in the sense in which I understand stories in English, because a person, and hence the set of systems that go to make up a person, could have the right combination of input, output, and program and still not understand anything in the relevant literal sense in which I understand English. The only motivation for saying there *must* be a subsystem in me that understands Chinese is that I have a program and I can pass the Turing test; I can fool native Chinese speakers. But precisely one of the points at issue is the adequacy of the Turing test. The example shows that there could be two "systems," both of which pass the Turing test, but only one of which understands; and it is no argument against this point to say that since they both pass the Turing test they must both understand, since this claim fails to meet the argument that the system in me that understands English has a great deal more than the system that merely processes Chinese.

ASK YOURSELF

96. What is involved in "passing the Turing test"?

Searle goes on to argue that if the Chinese room, or any part of it, can be said to understand Chinese, then understanding is going to be a very common thing. For the model is the same for such simple things as thermostats.

If strong AI is to be a branch of psychology, then it must be able to distinguish those systems that are genuinely mental from those that are not. It must be able to distinguish the principles on which the mind works from those on which nonmental systems work; otherwise it will offer us no explanations of what is specifically mental about the mental. And the mental–nonmental distinction cannot be just in the eye of the beholder but it must be intrinsic to the systems; otherwise it would be up to any beholder to treat people as nonmental and, for example, hurricanes as mental if he likes. But quite often in the AI literature the distinction is blurred in ways that would in the long run prove disastrous to the claim that AI is a cognitive inquiry. McCarthy, for example, writes, "Machines as simple as thermostats can be said to have beliefs, and having beliefs seems to be a characteristic of most machines capable of problem solving performance."

What sorts of beliefs might a thermostat have? Well, it records input (temperature changes), processes that input, and provides output (reading on a dial, plus activation of an air conditioner or heater). So, when the temperature goes up by a certain amount, it's reaction could be said to amount to the "belief" that "it is too hot in here."

ASK YOURSELF

97. There are two other beliefs a thermostat might have on this account. What are they?

Anyone who thinks strong AI has a chance as a theory of the mind ought to ponder the implications of that remark. We are asked to accept it as a discovery of strong AI that the hunk of metal on the wall that we use to regulate the temperature has beliefs in exactly the same sense that we, our spouses, and our children have beliefs, and furthermore that "most" of the other machines in the room—telephone, tape recorder, adding machine, electric light switch—also have beliefs in this literal sense. It is not the aim of this article to argue against McCarthy's point, so I will simply assert the following without argument. The study of the mind starts with such facts as that humans have beliefs, while thermostats, telephones, and adding machines don't. If you get a theory that denies this point, you have produced a counterexample to the theory and the theory is false. One gets the impression that people in AI who write this sort of thing think they can get away with it because they don't really take it seriously, and they don't think anyone else will either. I propose, for a moment at least, to take it seriously. Think hard for one minute about what would be necessary to establish that that hunk of metal on the wall over there had real beliefs, beliefs with direction of fit, propositional content, and conditions of satisfaction; beliefs that had the possibility of being strong beliefs or weak beliefs; nervous, anxious, or secure beliefs; dogmatic, rational, or superstitious beliefs; blind faiths or hesitant cogitations; any kind of beliefs. The thermostat is not a candidate. Neither is stomach, liver, adding machine, or telephone. However, since we are taking the idea seriously, notice that its truth would be fatal to strong AI's claim to be a science of the mind. For now the mind is everywhere. What we wanted to know is what distinguishes the mind from thermostats and livers. And if McCarthy were right, strong AI wouldn't have a hope of telling us that.

ASK YOURSELF

98. Putting the matter very simply, some AI researchers seem to be committed to the view that thermostats have thoughts since they receive _____, process it, and produce _____ _____, and that doing that is *all there is to thought*.

The Brain Simulator Reply. Searle goes on to consider another reply. Suppose that the machine in question is not merely functionally the same as a human mind or brain but is physically similar. The "computer" in question would actually have a structure that mimicked the structure of the brain. We would be able to say how that particular physical system produced output in terms of the materials of which it was made and its design just as we might be able to describe the brain's capacity for thought in terms of some future neurophysiology.

Before countering this reply I want to digress to note that it is an odd reply for any partisan of artificial intelligence (or functionalism, etc.) to make: I thought the whole idea of strong AI is that we don't need to know how the brain works to know how the mind works. The basic hypothesis, or so I had supposed, was that there is a level of mental operations consisting of computational processes over formal elements that constitute the essence of the mental and can be realized in all sorts of different brain processes, in the same way that any computer program can be realized in different computer hardwares: on the assumptions of strong AI, the mind is to the brain as the program is to the hardware, and thus we can understand the mind without doing neurophysiology. If we had to know how the brain worked to do AI, we wouldn't bother with AI. However, even getting this close to the operation of the brain is still not sufficient to produce understanding. To see this, imagine that instead of a monolingual man in a room shuffling symbols we have the man operate an elaborate set of water pipes with valves connecting them. When the man receives the Chinese symbols, he looks up in the program, written in English, which valves he has to turn on and off. Each water connection corresponds to a synapse in the Chinese brain, and the whole system is rigged up so that after doing all the right firings—that is, after turning on all the right faucets—the Chinese answers pop out at the output end of the series of pipes.

Now where is the understanding in this system? It takes Chinese as input, it simulates the formal structure of the synapses of the Chinese brain, and it gives Chinese as output. But the man certainly doesn't understand Chinese, and neither do the water pipes, and if we are tempted to adopt what I think is the absurd view that somehow the *conjunction* of man and water pipes understands, remember that in principle the man can internalize the formal structure of the water pipes and do all the "neuron firings" in his imagination. The problem with the brain simulator is that it is simulating the wrong things about the brain. As long as it simulates only the formal structure of the sequence of neuron firings at the synapses, it won't have simulated what matters about the brain, namely its causal properties, its ability to produce intentional states. And that the formal properties are not sufficient for the causal properties is shown by the water pipe example: we can have all the formal properties carved off from the relevant neurobiological causal properties.

ASK YOURSELF

99. What, according to Searle, is missing from the brain simulator that is not missing in the case of a real brain?

The Combination Reply. Searle considers yet another reply:

"Imagine a robot with a brain-shaped computer lodged in its cranial cavity, imagine the computer programmed with all the synapses of a human brain, imagine the whole behavior of the robot is indistinguishable from human behavior, and now think of the whole thing as a unified system and not just as a computer with inputs and outputs. Surely in such a case we would have to ascribe intentionality to the system." I entirely agree that in such a case we would find it rational and indeed irresistible to accept the hypothesis that the robot had intentionality, as long as we knew nothing more about it. . . .

But I really don't see that this is any help to the claims of strong AI; and here's why: According to strong AI, instantiating a formal program with the right input and output is a sufficient condition of, indeed is constitutive of, intentionality. As Newell puts it, the essence of the mental is the operation of a physical symbol system. But the attributions of intentionality that we make to the robot in this example have nothing to do with formal programs. They are simply based on the assumption that if the robot looks and behaves sufficiently like us, then we would suppose, until proven otherwise, that it must have mental states like ours that cause and are expressed by its behavior and it must have an inner mechanism capable of producing such mental states. If we knew independently how to account for its behavior without such assumptions, we would not attribute intentionality to it, especially if we knew it had a formal program.

ASK YOURSELF

100. Does Searle's response here have anything in common with Ziff's claims about robot feelings made in the selection immediately preceding this one? Explain.

A fundamental feature of Searle's position is the idea that only things made of a certain kind or range of stuff could possibly have thoughts or intentionality. Animals fall in that range, robots do not.

Contrast this [robot] case with cases in which we find it completely natural to ascribe intentionality to members of certain other primate species such as apes and monkeys and to domestic animals such as dogs. The reasons we find it natural are, roughly, two: we can't make sense of the animal's behavior without the ascription of intentionality, and we can see that the beasts are made of similar stuff to ourselves—that is an eye, that a nose, this is its skin, and so on. Given the coherence of the animal's behavior and the assumption of the same causal stuff underlying it, we assume both that the animal must have mental states underlying its behavior and that the mental states must be produced by mechanisms made out of the stuff that is like our stuff. We would certainly make similar assumptions about the robot unless we had some reason not to, but as soon as we knew that the behavior was the result of a formal program and that the actual causal properties of the physical substance were irrelevant, we would abandon the assumption of intentionality.

Searle stresses a similar point later in his essay.

I see no reason in principle why we couldn't give a machine the capacity to understand English or Chinese, since in an important sense our bodies with our brains are precisely such machines. But I do see very strong arguments for saying that we could not give such a thing to a machine where the operation of the machine is defined solely in terms of computational processes over formally defined elements; that is, where the operation of the machine is defined as an instantiation of a computer program. It is not because I am the instantiation of a computer program that I am able to understand English and have other forms of intentionality (I am, I suppose, the instantiation of any number of computer programs), but as far as we know, it is because I am a certain sort of organism with a certain biological (i.e., chemical and physical) structure, and this structure, under certain conditions, is causally capable of producing perception, action, understanding, learning, and other intentional phenomena. And part of the point of the present argument is that only something that had those causal powers could have that intentionality. Perhaps other physical and chemical processes could produce exactly these effects; perhaps, for example, Martians also have intentionality but their brains are made of different stuff. That is an empirical question, rather like the question whether photosynthesis can be done by something with a chemistry different from that of chlorophyll. . . .

First, the distinction between program and realization has the consequence that the same program could have all sorts of crazy realizations that had no form of intentionality. Weizenbaum, for example, shows in detail how to construct a computer using a roll of toilet paper and a pile of small stones. Similarly, the Chinese story understanding program can be programmed into a sequence of water pipes, a set of wind machines, or a monolingual English speaker, none of which thereby acquires an understanding of Chinese. Stones, toilet paper, wind, and water pipes are the wrong kind of stuff to have intentionality in the first place—only something that has the same causal powers as brains can have intentionality—and though the English speaker has the right kind of stuff for intentionality, you can easily see that he doesn't get any extra intentionality by memorizing the program, since memorizing it won't teach him Chinese.

ASK YOURSELF

101. Is it implausible, according to Searle, to suppose that a Martian might exhibit intentionality?

102. If a Martian and a human had brains made of different kinds of physical stuff, what would they have to have in common before we could say that they both understood English?

Searle concludes by speculating on the sources of the widespread belief (at least among AI researchers) that a computer or robot could have thoughts. Part of the reason, he speculates, derives from a confusion over the notion of information processing. Note, in this connection, the remarks from Wittgenstein, par. 356, cited earlier.

First, and perhaps most important, is a confusion about the notion of "information processing": many people in cognitive science believe that the human brain, with its mind, does something called "information processing," and analogously the computer with its program does information processing; but fires and rainstorms, on the other hand, don't do information processing at all. Thus, though the computer can simulate the formal features of any process whatever, it stands in a special relation to the mind and brain because when the computer is properly programmed, ideally with the same program as the brain, the information processing is identical in the two cases, and this information processing is really the essence of the mental. But the trouble with this argument is that it rests on an ambiguity in the notion of "information." In the sense in which people "process information" when they reflect, say, on problems in arithmetic or when they read and answer questions about stories, the programmed computer does not do "information processing." Rather, what it does is manipulate formal symbols. . . . The introduction of the notion of "information processing" therefore produces a dilemma: either we construe the notion of "information processing" in such a way that it implies intentionality as part of the process or we don't. If the former, then the programmed computer does not do information processing, it only manipulates formal symbols. If the latter, then, though the computer does information processing, it is only doing so in the sense in which adding machines, typewriters, stomachs, thermostats, rainstorms, and hurricanes do information processing; namely, they have a level of description at which we can describe them as taking information in at one end, transforming it, and producing information as output. But in this case it is up to outside observers to interpret the input and output as information in the ordinary sense. And no similarity is established between the computer and the brain in terms of any similarity of information processing.

We might even think of a tree as "processing information." As the tree grows, rings are added to the trunk. If we cut it down and count the rings, we can acquire information on how old the tree is. So, the tree has taken in data and recorded information (or has information recorded in it).

ASK YOURSELF

103. Discuss this example, and argue that the tree does in fact process information. Then argue that there is a sense in which it does not.

Searle sums up his position thus:

"Could a machine think?" My own view is that *only* a machine could think, and indeed only very special kinds of machines, namely brains and machines that had the same causal powers as brains. And that is the main reason strong AI has had little to tell us about thinking, since it has nothing to tell us about machines. By its own definition, it is about programs, and programs are not machines. Whatever else intentionality is, it is a biological phenomenon, and it is as likely to be causally dependent on the specific biochemistry of its origins as lactation, photosynthesis, or any other biological phenomena. . . . Whatever it is that the brain does to produce intentionality, it cannot consist in instantiating a program, since no program, by itself, is sufficient for intentionality.

Searle's essay has stimulated many responses and critical comments. One thing that is not clear in his essay is his notion of the specific causal powers of a biological brain. Such causal powers are necessary, he claims, for intentionality. Yet he admits that entities (Martians, for instance) might be made of different sorts of materials than humans, and yet be in intentional states. So the question naturally arises, "just how much like the human brain does anything have to be to have its causal powers and be able to produce consciousness, thought, intentionality?" Searle does not provide any answer, though he does deny that certain entities that are structurally like the brain (for example the water pipe system) could have intentionality. Does that fact matter to the plausibility of his position? Various critics seem to have thought so.

One difficulty lies in the notion of intentionality as a "product." What sort of product is it? Functionalists, as we have seen, argue that the principal product produced by a brain is a kind of proper control of input–output relations. The brain is like a computer insofar as it does that, they might argue. There would of course be other products (even my laptop produces heat and a hum) and one might wonder which product is "the" product and which a mere "byproduct." Searle does not give any further specification of "the product" beyond the label "intentionality." Whatever the product might be, if Martians made of, say, fancy varieties of plastic could produce it as well as humans, then must we assume that a computer or robot could not? As long as the Martian was "functionally isomorphic" to a human, could it not be in intentional states? To say of two systems that they are functionally isomorphic is to say that they perform the same function. Thus two plants that both contain some chemical that absorbs light and use the energy to make sugar (and so on for the complete description of photosynthesis) would be functionally isomorphic even if one plant used chlorophyll and the other used some other chemical. And they would both have the same "causal powers" in Searle's sense. That is, they would both photosynthesize.

Perhaps likewise it is not necessary to assume that, as Searle puts it, "the actual causal properties of a robot are irrelevant" to what it produces. One might grant that a program operating on purely formal elements is not sufficient for intentionality, while maintaining that whatever else is needed could be found in a robot that was quite unlike us in physical makeup. In that case, Searle's insistence that intentionality can only be found in something made of stuff similar to what we are made of would be defeated. The question still remains, of course, as to what the "something else" is that is needed for intentionality. Some suggestions on what the additional elements might be are included in the following brief response to Searle.

ASK YOURSELF

104. What is one possible difficulty with Searle's view?

4. A REPLY TO SEARLE: WILLIAM G. LYCAN

Searle's article printed above produced a storm of protest from a wide spectrum of philosophers and AI experts. In this selection, contemporary philosopher William Lycan concedes that passing the Turing test is not sufficient for intentionality.

FROM WILLIAM G. LYCAN, "The Functionalist Reply" (1980)

[Any device, let us call it "D," which has intentionality, must, in addition,] produce behavior from stimuli *in roughly the way that* we do—that D's inner functional organization be not unlike ours and that D process the stimulus input by analogous inner procedures. On this "functionalist" theory, to be in a mental state of such and such a kind is to incorporate a functional component or system of components of type so and so which is in a certain distinctive state of its own. "Functional components" are individuated according to the roles they play within their owners' overall functional organization.

Searle offers a number of cases of entities that manifest the behavioral dispositions we associate with intentional states but that rather plainly do not have any such states. I accept his intuitive judgments about most of these cases. Searle plus rule book plus pencil and paper presumably does not understand Chinese, nor does Searle with memorized rule book or Searle with TV camera or the robot with Searle inside. Neither my stomach nor Searle's liver nor a thermostat nor a light switch has beliefs and desires. But none of these cases is a counterexample to the functionalist hypothesis. The systems in the former group are pretty obviously not functionally isomorphic at the relevant level to human beings who do understand Chinese; a native Chinese carrying on a conversation is implementing procedures of his own, not those procedures that would occur in a mockup containing the cynical, English-speaking, American-acculturated homuncular Searle. Therefore they are not counterexamples to a functionalist theory of language understanding, and accordingly they leave it open that a computer that was functionally isomorphic to a real Chinese speaker would indeed understand Chinese also. Stomachs, thermostats, and the like, because of their brutish simplicity, are even more clearly dissimilar to humans. (The same presumably is true of Schank's existing language-understanding programs.)

ASK YOURSELF

105. Why, according to Lycan, does a thermostat or a light switch not have beliefs?

I have hopes for a sophisticated version of the "brain simulator" (or the "combination" machine) that Searle illustrates with his plumbing example. Imagine a hydraulic system of this type that does replicate, perhaps not the precise neuroanatomy of a Chinese speaker, but all that is relevant of the Chinese speaker's higher functional organization; individual water pipes are grouped into organ systems precisely analogous to those found in the speaker's brain, and the device processes linguistic input in just the way that the speaker does. (It does not merely simulate or describe this processing.) Moreover, the system is automatic and does all this without the intervention of Searle or any other *deus in machina*. Under these conditions and given a suitable social context, I think it would be plausible to accept the functionalist consequence that the hydraulic system does understand Chinese.

Searle's paper suggests two objections to this claim. First, "where is the understanding in this system?" All Searle sees is pipes and valves and flowing water. Reply: Looking around the fine detail of the system's hardware, you are too small to see that the system is understanding Chinese sentences. If you were a tiny, cell-sized observer inside a real Chinese speaker's brain, all you would see would be neurons stupidly, mechanically transmitting electrical charge, and in the same tone you would ask, "Where is the understanding in this system?" But you would be wrong in concluding that the system you were observing did not understand Chinese; in like manner you may well be wrong about the hydraulic device.

ASK YOURSELF

106. What is Searle's first objection? What is Lycan's reply?

Second, even if a computer were to replicate all of the Chinese speaker's relevant functional organization, all the computer is really doing is performing computational operations on formally specified elements. A purely formally or syntactically characterized element has no meaning or content in itself, obviously, and no amount of mindless syntactic manipulation of it will endow it with any. Reply: The premise is correct, and I agree it shows that no computer has or could have intentional states merely in virtue of performing syntactic operations on formally characterized elements. But that does not suffice to prove that no computer can have intentional states at all. Our brain states do not have the contents they do just in virtue of having their purely formal properties either; a brain state described "syntactically" has no meaning or content on its own. In virtue of what, then, do brain states (or mental states however construed) have the meanings they do? Recent theory advises that the content of a mental representation is not determined within its owner's head; rather, it is determined in part by the objects in the environment that actually figure in the representation's etiology and in part by social and contextual factors of several other sorts.

ASK YOURSELF

107. The content of a "representation," Lycan claims, is determined by its etiology, that is, the causal factors or history that produced it. Suppose the representation in question is the thought, call it "T," that there is a table in front of me. What might be some of the causal history that produced T? (You might begin by mentioning light rays refracting from a surface.)

108. Social factors might be required for the thought T. They might include having learned a language from other people. Mention another such social factor.

Now, present-day computers live in highly artificial and stifling environments They receive carefully and tendentiously preselected input; their software is adventitiously manipulated by uncaring programmers; and they are isolated in laboratories and offices, deprived of any normal interaction within a natural or appropriate social setting. For this reason and several others, Searle is surely right in saying that present-day computers do not really have the intentional states that we fancifully incline toward attributing to them. But nothing Searle has said impugns the thesis that if a sophisticated future computer not only replicated human functional organization but harbored its inner representations as a result of the right sort of causal history and had also been nurtured within a favorable social setting, we might correctly ascribe intentional states to it. This point may or may not afford lasting comfort to the AI community.

ASK YOURSELF

109. According to Lycan, what are the two things that a device needs in order to have intentionality?

110. Has Lycan's argument already been anticipated by Searle in his discussion of the brain simulator? Argue pro and con.

5. NATURAL LANGUAGES, AI, AND EXISTENTIAL HOLISM: JOHN HAUGELAND

The importance of language to discussions of AI should be evident from Searle's essay. Many philosophers past and present have claimed that what divides humans from other beings is, above all, language. The primitive linguistic abilities of some intensively trained chimps probably do not count against that claim. But what about the linguistic abilities of computers? There are now computers so linguistically sophisticated that they can, within some limits, translate from one language to another. Nonetheless, suppose there is a strong argument that concludes that no computer can do some of the things with language that humans do relatively easily. Then, it might be argued, the possibility of an android such as *Star Trek*'s Data would be greatly reduced or impossible. Data would be just a fantasy, and the idea that humans are basically fancy machines would be refuted or at least appear highly implausible. The American philosopher John Haugeland has advanced an argument of considerable philosophical interest that reaches that conclusion. His argument depends upon the idea that understanding a language, or any language-like activity, is "holistic" in senses that will be explained. In general the term "holism" refers to "wholes" of some system, as opposed to just the parts. If computers operate only on discrete bits of data, perhaps their linguistic capacities will be very limited.

From John Haugeland, "Understanding Natural Languages" (1979)

The trouble with Artificial Intelligence is that computers don't give a damn—or so I will argue by considering the special case of understanding natural language. Linguistic facility is an appropriate trial for AI because input and output can be handled conveniently with a teletype, because understanding a text requires understanding its topic (which is unrestricted), and because there is the following test for success: does the text enable the candidate to answer those questions it would enable competent people to answer? The thesis will not be that (humanlike) intelligence cannot be achieved artificially, but that there are identifiable conditions on achieving it. This point is as much about language and understanding as about Artificial Intelligence. I will express it by distinguishing four *different* phenomena that can be called "holism": that is, four ways in which brief segments of text cannot be understood "in isolation" or "on a one-by-one basis."

Holism of Intentional Interpretation. It may be helpful to keep the following fact in mind as you study what follows. Just as chess boards and pieces come in many shapes, styles, and sizes, so chess itself can be played in many ways, some of which do not require any board or pieces. For example, in board chess, if a pawn is moved to the space four spaces before the king, we could designate this move as "PK4." So one could eliminate the board and play using nothing but such notations. Nonetheless, in order to realize that some activity that is going on is indeed chess, an observer must make sense of the "moves" or notations. Making sense requires assigning meaning or significance. In other words, making sense requires "intentional" interpretation. Haugeland argues that such interpretation cannot be done piecemeal.

Consider how one might *empirically* defend the claim that a given (strange) object plays chess. Clearly, it is neither necessary nor sufficient that the object use any familiar chess notation (or pieces); for it might play brilliant chess in some alien notation . . . what the defense must do is, roughly:

i.   give systematic criteria for (physically) identifying the object's inputs and outputs;
ii. provide a systematic way of interpreting them as various moves (such as a manual for translating them into standard notation); and then
iii. let some skeptics play chess with it.

The third condition bears all the empirical weight, for satisfying it amounts to public *observation* that the object really does play chess. More specifically the skeptics see that, as interpreted, it makes a sensible (legal and plausible) move in each position it faces. And eventually, induction convinces them that it would do so in any position. Notice that, *de facto,* the object is also being construed as "remembering" (or "knowing") the current position, "trying" to make good moves, "realizing" that rooks outrank pawns, and even "wanting" to win. All these interpretations and construals constitute collectively *an intentional interpretation.*

In order to produce such an interpretation, one must place any given move in the context of other moves. Thus the notation "PK4" means nothing all by itself. "P" could mean anything, "K" could mean anything. However, taken together with other notations, such as "PK5," in a certain sequence we can make sense of a whole series of such notations in terms of a chess game. We need the whole (holism) to interpret the parts. Thus any given input (for example, a thing on a board moving to a new position or a new notation on a piece of paper) can be "understood" as a chess move only against the background of other "moves" or "notations."

Intentional interpretation is intrinsically holistic . . . one output can be construed sensibly as a certain queen move, only if that other was a certain knight move, still another a certain bishop move, and so on .

This is the *holism of intentional interpretation.* The condition that outputs be "sensible" (in the light of prior inputs and other outputs) is just whatever the ill-named "principle of charity" is supposed to capture. I have reviewed it here only to distinguish it from what follows.

Common-Sense Holism

Years ago, Yehoshua Bar-Hillel pointed out that disambiguating "The box was in the pen" requires common-sense knowledge about boxes and pens. He had in mind knowledge of typical sizes, which would ordinarily decide between the alternatives "playpen" and "fountain pen." In a similar vein, it takes common sense to determine the antecedent of the pronoun in: "I left my raincoat in the bathtub, because it was still wet." More subtly, common use informs our appreciation of the final verb of: "Though her blouse draped stylishly, her pants seemed painted on."

> **ASK YOURSELF**
>
> **111.** State here two different interpretations of "her pants seemed painted on." Likewise for "it" in the raincoat-bathtub example. For example, one interpretation of "her pants seemed painted on" might be that her pants were extremely tight.

Straightforward questioning immediately exposes any misunderstanding: Was the bathtub wet? Was there paint on her pants? And the issue isn't just academic; a system designed to translate natural languages must be able to answer such questions. For instance, the correct and incorrect readings of our three examples have different translations in both French and German so the system has to choose. What's so daunting about this, from the designer's [designer of a computer program for translating] point of view, is that one never knows which little fact is going to be relevant next-which common-sense tidbit will make the next disambiguation "obvious." In effect, the whole of common sense is potentially relevant at any point. This feature of natural-language understanding I call *common-sense holism;* its scope and importance was first fully demonstrated in Artificial Intelligence work.

> **ASK YOURSELF**
>
> **112.** Could the problem of how to translate "her pants seemed painted on" be resolved simply by looking up "pants" and "painted," and so on, in a dictionary?

The nature of common-sense holism is brought into sharper relief by current efforts to deal with it—those in Artificial Intelligence being the most concentrated and sophisticated. . . . Most contemporary systems employ some variant of the following idea: facts pertaining to the same subject are stored together ("linked") in structured clusters, which are themselves linked in larger structures, according as their subjects are related.

For example, the concepts of a monkey, a banana, eating, and being eaten would be "linked" in the following way, among others.

Thus, if monkeys typically like bananas, the system can "assume" that any given monkey will like bananas (pending information to the contrary). Third, concepts often have "spaces" or "open slots" waiting (or demanding) to be "filled up" in stipulated ways. For example, the concept of eating would have spaces for the eater and the eaten, it being stipulated that the eater be animate, and the eaten (typically) be food.

> **ASK YOURSELF**
>
> **113.** Would such linkages rule out "the banana ate the monkey" as meaningful?

A system based on such concepts copes with common-sense holism as follows. First, a dictionary routine calls the various concepts associated with the words in a given sentence, subject to constraints provided by a syntactical analyzer. Hence, only the information coded in (or closely linked to) these concepts is actually accessed—passing over the presumably irrelevant bulk. Then the system applies this information to any ambiguities by looking for a combination of concepts (from the supplied pool) which fit each other's open spaces in all the stipulated ways. So, for Bar-Hillel's example, the system might call four concepts: one each for "box" and "is in," and two for "pen." The "is in" concept would have two spaces, with the stipulation that what fills the first be smaller than what fills the second. Alerted by this requirement, the system promptly checks the "typical size" information under the other concepts, and correctly eliminates "fountain pen." An essentially similar procedure will disambiguate the pronouns in sentences like: "the monkeys ate the bananas because they were hungry" or "because they were ripe."

ASK YOURSELF

114. Explain the ambiguity in the word "they" in the two examples mentioned in the last sentence.

The other two examples, however, are tougher. Both raincoats and bathtubs typically get wet, so *that* won't decide which was wet when I left my coat in the tub. People opt for the coat, because being wet is an understandable (if eccentric) reason for leaving a coat in a tub, whereas the tub's being wet would be no (sane) reason to leave a coat in it. But where is this information to be coded? It hardly seems that concepts for "raincoat . . . bathtub," or "is wet," no matter how "encylopedic," would indicate when it's sensible to put a raincoat in a bathtub. This suggests that common sense can be organized only partially according to subject matter. Much of what we recognize as "making sense" is not "about" some topic for which we have a word or idiom, but rather about some (possibly unique) circumstance or episode, which a longer fragment leads us to "visualize." Introspectively, it seems that we imagine ourselves into the case, and then decide from within it what's plausible. Of course, how this is done is just the problem.

The ambiguity of "painted-on pants" is both similar and different. Again, we "imagine" the sort of attire being described; but the correct reading is obviously a metaphor—for "skin tight," which is both coordinated and appropriately contrasted with the stylishly draped blouse. Most approaches to metaphor, however, assume that metaphorical readings aren't attempted unless there is something "anomalous" about the "literal" reading (as in "He is the cream on my peaches," or ". . . faster than greased lightning"). But, in this case there is nothing anomalous about pants with paint on them—they would even clash with "stylish," explaining the conjunction "though. . . ." On that reading, however, the sentence would be silly, whereas the metaphor is so apt that most people don't even notice the alternative.

These examples are meant only to illustrate the subtlety of common sense. They show that no obvious or crude representation will capture it, and suggest that a sophisticated, cross-referenced "encyclopedia" may not suffice either. On the other hand, they don't reveal much about what's "left out," nor (by the same token) whether that will be programmable when we know what it is. The real nature of common sense is still a wide-open question.

Situation Holism. Perhaps even greater difficulties for AI language translators lurk in the way interpretation of sentences depends upon particular situations. Consider the statement "the box is in the pen," which was used as an example by the philosopher Bar-Hillel. One might have to grasp the "situation" in which the statement is made to translate it properly. Haugeland quotes American philosopher Hubert Dreyfus:

. . . in spite of our *general* knowledge about the relative sizes of pens and boxes, we might interpret "The box is in the pen," when whispered in a James Bond movie, as meaning just the opposite of what it means at home or on the farm.

ASK YOURSELF

115. What might it mean in the Bond movie? Why would that be a problem for Bar-Hillel's account of how the program handles such statements?

Existential Holism. In order to grasp the sense of particular sentences or words an interpreter must grasp the "whole" situation. For example, she may have to read quite a bit of the James Bond novel and appreciate the sorts of things that go on in such novels, in order to translate, or just understand, "the box is in the pen" properly. That is what is meant by "situation holism."

In the section on intentional interpretation, we noticed how naturally we construe chess-playing computers as "trying" to make good moves and "wanting" to win. At the same time, however, I think we *also* all feel that the machines don't "really care" whether they win or how they play—that somehow the game doesn't "matter" to them. What's behind these conflicting intuitions? It may seem at first that what machines lack is a "reason" to win: some larger goal that winning would subserve. But this only puts off the problem; for we then ask whether they "really care" about the larger goal. And until this question is answered, nothing has been; just as we now don't suppose pawns "matter" to computers, even though they subserve the larger goal of winning.

Apparently something else must be involved to make the whole hierarchy of goals worth while—something that itself doesn't need a reason, but, so to speak, "matters for its own sake." We get a hint of what this might be, by asking why chess games matter to people (when they do). There are many variations, of course, but here are some typical reasons:

   i. public recognition and esteem, which generates and supports self-esteem (compare the loser's embarrassment or loss of face);
   ii. pride and self-respect at some difficult achievement-like finally earning a "master" rating (compare the loser's frustration and self-disappointment); or
   iii. proving one's prowess or (as it were) "masculinity" (compare the loser's self-doubt and fear of inadequacy).

What these have in common is that the player's self-image or sense of identity is at stake. This concern with "who one is" constitutes at least one issue that "matters for its own sake." Machines (at present) lack any personality and, hence, any possibility of personal involvement; so (on these grounds) nothing can really matter to them.

The point is more consequential for language understanding than for formal activities like chess playing, which are largely separable from the rest of life. A friend of mine tells a story about the time she kept a white rat as a pet. It was usually tame enough to follow at her heels around campus; but one day, frightened by a dog, it ran so far up her pantleg that any movement might have crushed it. So, very sheepishly, she let down her jeans, pulled out her quivering rodent, and won a round of applause from delighted passersby. Now, most people find this anecdote amusing, and the relevant question is: Why? Much of it, surely, is that we identify with the young heroine and share in her embarrassment—being relieved, at the same time, that it didn't happen to us.

Embarrassment, however, (and relief) can be experienced only by a being that has some sense of itself—a sense that is important to it and can be awkwardly compromised on occasion. Hence, only such a being could, as we do, find this story amusing. It might be argued, however, that "emotional" reactions, like embarrassment and bemusement, should be sharply distinguished from purely "cognitive" understanding. Nobody, after all, expects a mechanical chess player to *like* the game or to be thrilled by it. But that distinction cannot be maintained for users of natural language. Translators, for instance, must choose words carefully to retain the character of an amusing original. To take just one example from the preceding story, German has several "equivalents" for "sheepish," with connotations, respectively, of being simple, stupid, or bashful. Only by appreciating the embarrassing nature of the incident, could a translator make the right choice.

ASK YOURSELF

116. The word that should be used to translate "sheepish" is obviously _____.

117. What, in your view, would it take for a machine (a robot) to feel bashful?

Haugeland discusses a number of stories and anecdotes in which understanding depends upon what it is to have a sense of self, a sense of one's life. He closes with this example.

One final example will demonstrate the range of the phenomenon I'm pointing at, and also illustrate a different way in which the reader's personal involvement can be essential. It is a fable of Aesop's.

One day, a farmer's son accidentally stepped on a snake and was fatally bittten. Enraged, the father chased the snake with an axe and managed to cut off its tail. Whereupon, the snake nearly ruined the farm by biting all the animals. Well, the farmer thought it over and finally took the snake some sweetmeats and said: "I can understand your anger, and surely you can understand mine. But now that we are even, let's forget and be friends again." "No, no," said the snake, "take away your gifts. You can never forget your dead son, nor I my missing tail."

Obviously, this story has a "moral," which a reader must "get" in order to understand it. The problem is not simply to make the moral explicit, for then it would be more direct and effective to substitute a nonallegorical paraphrase:

A child is like a part of oneself, such as a limb. The similarities include:

   i. losing one is very bad;
  ii. if you lose one, you can never get it back;
 iii. they have no adequate substitutes; and thus
  iv. they are literally priceless.

Therefore, to regard trading losses of them as a "fair exchange," or "getting even," is to be a fool.

But this is just a list of platitudes. It's not that it misrepresents the moral, but that it lacks it altogether—it is utterly flat and lifeless. By comparison, Aesop's version "lives," because we as readers identify with the farmer. Hence, we too are brought up short by the serpent's rebuke, and that makes us look at ourselves.

The terrifying thing about losing, say, one's legs is not the event itself, or the pain, but rather the thought of *being* a legless cripple for all the rest of one's life. It's the same with losing a son, right? Wrong! Many a parent indeed would joyously give both legs to have back a little girl or boy who is gone. Children can well mean more to who one is than even one's own limbs. So who are you, and what is your life? The folly—what the fable is really about—is not knowing.

A single event cannot be embarrassing, shameful, irresponsible, or foolish in isolation, but only as an act in the biography of a whole, historical individual person whose personality it reflects and whose self-image it threatens. Only a being that cares about who it is, as some sort of enduring whole, can care about guilt or folly, self-respect or achievement, life or death. And only such a being can read. This holism, now not even apparently in the text, but manifestly in the reader, I call (with all due trepidation) *existential holism*. It is essential, I submit, to understanding the meaning of any text that (in a familiar sense) *has* any meaning. If situation holism is the foundation of plot, existential holism is the foundation of literature.

ASK YOURSELF

118. Darwin claimed that a dog could feel shame. In the light of the preceding paragraph, what might be missing in the life of a dog that makes Darwin's claim doubtful? Do the same considerations apply to a robot?

In the context of Artificial Intelligence, however, there remains an important question of whether this sets the standard too high—whether it falls into what Papert somewhere calls "the human/superhuman fallacy," or Dennett "the Einstein–Shakespeare gambit." Wouldn't it be impressive enough, the reasoning goes, if a machine could understand everyday English, even if it couldn't appreciate literature? Sure, it would be impressive; but beyond that there are three replies. First, if we could articulate some ceiling of "ordinariness" beyond which machines can't pass or can't pass unless they meet some further special condition, that would be very interesting and valuable indeed. Second, millions of people can read—really read—and for most of the others it's presumably a sociohistorical tragedy that they can't. Existential holism is not a condition just on creative genius. Finally, and *most important,* there is no reason whatsoever to believe there is a difference in kind between understanding "everyday English" and appreciating literature. Apart from a few highly restricted domains, like playing chess, analyzing mass spectra, or making airline reservations, the most ordinary conversations are fraught with life and all its meaning.

Considering the progress and prospects of Artificial Intelligence can be a peculiarly concrete and powerful way of thinking about our own spiritual nature. As such, it is a comrade of the philosophy of mind (some authors see AI as allied to epistemology, which strikes me as perverse). Here, we have distinguished four phenomena, each with a claim to the title "holism"—not to trade on or enhance any mystery in the term, but rather, I would hope, the opposite. The aim has not been to show that Artificial Intelligence is impossible (though it is, you know) but to clarify some of what its achievement would involve, in the specific area of language understanding. This area is not so limited as it seems, since—as each of the four holisms testifies—understanding a text involves understanding what the text is "about." The holisms, as presented, increase in difficulty relative to current AI techniques; and my own inclination (it's hardly more than that) is to regard the last, existential holism, as the most fundamental of the four. Hence my opening remark: the trouble with Artificial Intelligence is that computers don't give a damn.

Poor computers! Lycan might claim that considering how badly they are treated, it is no wonder that they do not give a damn.

SUMMING UP MINDS AND MACHINES

Past philosophers have felt that the "mental" dimensions of humans rule out the possibility that they might be nothing more than very complicated machines. This intuition has been strongly challenged in the last 150 years. Improved knowledge of the brain and nervous system, as well as recent technologies (computers, robots) have encouraged philosophers and others to attempt mechanistic accounts of the mind. But Wittgenstein, Ziff, Searle, Haugeland, and many others have called attention to difficulties in those accounts. Could a robot actually understand the words that it speaks? Could it actually feel pain, as opposed to merely simulating pain behavior? Could it have the kinds of concerns and interests that, arguably, are essential to understanding? These questions will not go away, and ingenious attempts to answer them on the part of AI proponents have not satisfied all of those who devote themselves to exploration of the relations between minds and machines.

Nonetheless some AI specialists continue to believe that there is no obstacle *in principle* to replicating the full range of human mental life in a robot of some sort. The arguments continue and become more complex.

**CAN OF
WORMS**

Will we ever be required ethically to treat robots or androids with respect or accord them rights? Does our understanding of our own nature undergo a transformation when we think about androids? These questions lead to further doubts and puzzles, respecting the nature of knowledge and understanding. Someone who has just been beaten in chess by a computer may feel strongly inclined to admit that the computer "knew the game" better than she did. We can see from these facts that the mind–machine debate is intertwined with discussions in ethics, anthropology, science, and epistemology.

SUMMING UP THE CHAPTER

Few things concern us more than our "states of mind" or "the condition of our souls." Thoughts, moods, hopes, pains, loves, and hates are the stuff of human life. They seem to be close to, or to be in or part of, our real core selves, our *souls*. Perhaps they are close to God also, or even part of God, for it seems natural to think of them as immaterial, and it has seemed natural to many to think of God as immaterial also. In fact there is an ancient tradition that links the soul or mind to what is morally highest in a person. Other traditions, especially Eastern ones, sometimes go so far as to identify the core self with God. Even if we somehow disassociate soul or mind from religious or moral conceptions, a certain mystery remains. How are we to understand "states of the mind?" Do only humans have them? Are they located somewhere? Perhaps it makes no more sense to ask for their location than it would to ask for the location of Wednesday, or the number 2. On the other hand, it could be that they are nothing but states of the brain. But if they are states of the brain, then it might seem that beings with different kinds of brains, or nonphysical beings (such as God, assuming there is one), could not have thoughts, or thoughts like human thoughts. But that seems implausible. One way out of some of these difficulties is to identify thoughts and other mental states with functions. What matters is not the stuff involved but the function performed, just as what matters most for a doorstopper is that it functions to keep a door open, not that it be made of any particular material. It has seemed quite natural to move on from thinking of minds as physical, or as functional states, to thinking that machines too might have minds. The temptation to do that is greatly reinforced by new technologies, such as computers or robots that seem to think, remember, plan, and learn. Yet it is far from clear that such things could actually think or remember, as opposed to merely simulating thinking or remembering.

FINAL REACTIONS

Has your thinking on the soul changed as a result of studying this chapter? If so, put down some of the ways it has changed. Likewise for the mind. Look back at the initial questions. Are you less, or more, likely to identify thoughts with brain states than you were initially? If so, identify the arguments that made the change take place. Similarly, compare your thinking on minds and machines now to what it was before reading the work of such thinkers as Searle or Haugeland. Do you now find that you cannot take TV shows and movies that feature "intelligent" robots seriously? If you do take them seriously, have you found a way to meet the objections that those thinkers raised? Consider also the very substantial amount of public discussion about brains and the relation of brains and thinking. Probably no one would deny that having an intact brain is necessary for thought and feeling. But it certainly does not follow that having an intact brain is *sufficient* for thinking or feeling. Are not thoughts something distinct from the physical? To revert to one of the initial questions, do you suppose that even the most advanced brain scan possible might enable you to see a thought? These are the sorts of issues that have shaped this chapter, and, as the Cans of Worms indicate, they are issues that will come up again in other chapters.

FURTHER READINGS

GENERAL WORKS

Chalmers, David, ed., *Philosophy of Mind: Classical and Contemporary Readings* (New York: Oxford University Press, 2002).

Chalmers, David, *The Conscious Mind: In Search of a Fundamental Theory* (New York: Oxford University Press, 1996).

Cooney, Brian, *The Place of Mind* (Belmont: Wadsworth Publishing, 2000).

Guttenplan, Samuel, ed., *A Companion to the Philosophy of Mind* (Oxford: Blackwell, 1994).

Robinson, Daniel, ed., *The Mind* (New York: Oxford University Press, 1998).

WORKS ON SPECIFIC TOPICS AND FIGURES

Boden, M.A. ed., *The Philosophy of Artificial Life* (Oxford: Oxford University Press, 1996).

Dennett, D. C. *Consciousness Explained* (Boston: Little, Brown, 1991).

Dreyfus, H. L., and Dreyfus, S. E., *Mind over Machine: The Power of Human Expertise in the Era of the Computer* (New York: The Free Press, 1986).

Nagel, Thomas, *The View from Nowhere* (New York: Oxford University Press, 1986).

Rich, E., and Knight, K. *Artificial Intelligence* (New York: McGraw-Hill, 1991).

CHAPTER 5

EPISTEMOLOGY

I n the checkout lines at supermarkets we frequently find magazines or papers containing reports of sensational events. "Mother converses with baby still in womb." "Twenty people abducted by aliens." Some people take these reports seriously. Others find them merely laughable. But even those who find them laughable may themselves believe in the possibility of a virgin birth, or in the kind of claims made in the best-selling book *Da Vinci Code*. Is there some reliable way to sort out what sorts of claims are to be believed? A gullible person believes too easily, on too little evidence. On the other hand, very skeptical people may refuse to believe even where there is no good reason to doubt. There are, for example, people who doubt that the holocaust during the Nazi regime ever took place. Is that the result of intellectual caution or just another form of prejudiced thinking?

Note your answers to the following questions and save them for future reference.

FIRST REACTIONS

a. How, in fact, does *anyone* know what he or she claims to know? Can we know anything for sure, or are we doomed to perpetual uncertainty? If you think there is something you can know for certain, give an example.

316

b. We may wonder just what distinguishes knowledge from opinion, socially entrenched superstitions, expressions of racist or sexist bias, or expressions of faith. Try to think of some criteria for distinguishing knowledge from these "lower" cognitive states.

c. It may be difficult to simply frame a proper definition of "knowledge." Make a preliminary attempt at a definition.

d. Does knowledge require the observance of duties, such as the obligation to never form a view before checking all the relevant evidence? Does knowledge require the cultivation of virtues of the mind, such as intellectual carefulness, patience, or open mindedness?

e. If I know something, must I be able to say *how* I know, or might I know something even though I do not know exactly how I know it?

f. Are *all* claims to knowledge necessarily infected by some sort of bias or limited perspective? If you think they are, give some examples. If not, say why.

We may wonder just how much, and what kind, of evidence is needed to make a belief respectable, or worthy of being called *knowledge,* as opposed to being called mere opinion or guesswork. How do we find our way between gullibility and skepticism? What responsibilities do we have as adults to withhold assent to claims that are unverified or otherwise look implausible? Is it possible for us to free ourselves from prejudice, inherited traditions that may include superstitious beliefs, or ways of thinking that are biased by our social position, our race, our gender? These and related questions and issues are the stuff of epistemology, the philosophical study of knowledge.

Epistemology has been a major topic of philosophical discussion for at least 2500 years. We might wonder whether philosophers are uniquely or even well equipped to discuss such issues. Perhaps all that we need to know about knowledge can be learned from psychology and other sciences. After all, the sciences in their modern forms are, many think, the best examples of knowledge that we have. Nonetheless, philosophers may have valuable contributions to make. For example, evaluative notions play a natural role in discussions of knowledge, but there are many reasons for thinking science must be value free. The notions of justification and warrant, of correctness or accuracy, are all evaluative. Problems about objectivity seem to require philosophical treatment. Even claims that come from the most respected sciences, such as physics, have been suspected of being tainted by prejudices and untested assumptions. It also belongs to philosophy to determine the ethical responsibilities that may be involved in claims to know things. Moreover, typically philosophical skills are useful in any attempt to define the very notion of knowledge.

A. SKEPTICISM AND CERTAINTY

Skeptics are people who deny that any knowledge, or any knowledge within certain domains, is possible. Radical skeptics may deny that even the most obvious claims can be known to be true. If you claim that the ball in front of you is red, a skeptic might question whether you are partially colorblind. If you claim that the ball in front of you at least exists, a skeptic might question whether you are hallucinating. Some skeptics have doubted whether knowledge is ever possible. In this section we will examine some of the more memorable skeptical arguments.

**QUESTIONS
TO DISCUSS**

a. Skeptics are people who, for no *special* reason, deny that anyone can know obvious things—for example, they might deny that there is a red ball in front of them, when in fact there is. Do you ever feel inclined to carry doubt as far as a skeptic? If so, in theory only or in practice?

b. David Hume, one of the more famous skeptics, avoided publicly discussing skeptical quandaries since he knew that this would just alienate his companions. Are skeptical puzzles more than just crazy or annoying theories?

c. If there are real limits to knowledge, might it be important to know what they are? Why?

d. Consider how cautious you should be when faced with any claim to unassailable authority on any issue. Must you *always* reject such claims, and, if so, why? Consider some examples from religion, science, or some other domain.

e. Is it possible that skepticism is just the first step on the path toward truth? Explain.

1.   THE RELATIVITY OF ALL THINGS: CHUANG-TZU

Here is one of the great skeptical passages from Chinese philosophy:

> Recently, I, Chuang Chou, dreamt that I was a butterfly—a butterfly flying about, feeling that it was enjoying itself, and unaware that it was Chuang Chou. Suddenly I awoke, and was myself again—the real Chuang Chou. I did not know whether it had formerly been Chuang Chou dreaming that he was a butterfly, or it was now a butterfly dreaming that it was Chuang Chou. But between Chuang Chou and a butterfly there must be a difference. This is a case of what is called the Transformation of Things.

The author of this passage is Taoist philosopher Chuang-tzu (369–286 BCE), who was cited in Chapter 3. Chuang-tzu believed that everything that exists is really part of a single ultimate reality called the *Tao*—or way. True knowledge, for Chuang-tzu, involves grasping the nature of the *Tao* and seeing how everything is part of it. However, that is not typically what takes place when we claim to know something. If I pick up a rock and examine its particular features, the last thing on my mind is how that rock connects with some mysterious larger reality. That, according to Chuang-tzu, is where error creeps in. Our usual methods of explaining objects and events are relative to our own limited perspectives. We inevitably misdescribe *everything* that we examine because our approach is so narrowly focused. We then employ our one-sided theories in debates with other people's one-sided theories, and nothing gets accomplished. This is so even with something as simple as whether I am a human dreaming that I'm a butterfly or a butterfly dreaming that I'm human. Both theories are simply two limited perspectives on a single ultimate reality, and neither perspective captures the complete truth. According to Chuang-tzu, our usual approaches to knowledge, then, are relative to the perceiver:

> Does a thing seem so to me? I say it does. Does it not seem so to me? I say it does not. Just as a path is formed by people constantly treading on the ground, a thing is called by its

name through the constant application of the name to it. How does something become so? It becomes so because [people say] it is so. How does something not become so? It doesn't become so because [people say] it is not so. Everything has its inherent character and its proper capacity, and there is nothing that doesn't have these. Accordingly, let us take a small beam and a large pillar, an ugly woman and a classic beauty (such as Hsi Shih), large things, insincere things, crafty things and strange things. In light of the Tao, they may be reduced to the same category.

ASK YOURSELF

1. According to Chuang-tzu, things do not get their names because of some true or essential features contained in them. Instead, how do things get their names?

Embedded in Chuang-tzu's skeptical relativism is a solution: We can see the unity of things in the Tao. The truth that we arrive at in the end may look nothing at all like the one-sided relativist positions that we start with.

Only those who are far reaching in thought know how to understand the unity of things. This being so, let us give up our devotion to our own views, and occupy ourselves with the objective view [of things in the Tao]. The objective view [from the perspective of the Tao] is grounded in what is useful, and usefulness involves identifying things. Identifying things secures success. Once that success is gained, we are near [to the object of our search] and we stop there. When we stop, and do not know it, we have what is called the Tao.

Chuang-tzu illustrates this point further with a tale about a group of monkeys engaged in a verbal dispute with their keeper.

We trouble our minds and intelligence by being obstinately determined [to establish our own respective view], and do not know the agreement [with the views of others which underlies it]. In such cases we have what may be called "three in the morning." What do I mean by "three in the morning?" A monkey keeper was giving out acorns to the monkeys and said to them: "In the morning I will give you each three and in the evening four." This made the monkeys angry, and the keeper then said, "Fine! In the morning I will give you four and in the evening three." The keeper's two proposals were essentially the same, but the result of the one was to make the creatures angry, and the result of the other was to make them pleased. This illustrates the point I am insisting on. Therefore, the wise person brings together a dispute in its affirmations and denials, and rests in the equal fashioning of nature [i.e., the Tao]. [*Chuang-tzu*, Book 2]

ASK YOURSELF

2. What is the job of the wise person in disputes?

2.   THE GOALS AND METHODS OF SKEPTICISM: SEXTUS EMPIRICUS

Although skepticism sometimes appears from the pen of an independent wayward philosopher, it is often part of a tradition—as was so with Chuang-tzu who wrote within the Taoist tradition. One of the more prominent "schools" of skepticism in Western philosophy is called

Pyrrhonism, after its founder Pyrrho of Elea (360–270 BCE). Little is known of Pyrrho, but a later book, *Outlines of Pyrrhonism* by Sextus Empiricus (second century CE), is exceptional for both its clarity and completeness, and it may represent many of Pyrrho's views.

The Goal and Criterion of Skepticism. According to Sextus, there are three kinds of philosophers: (1) dogmatics, who claim to have discovered truth, such as Aristotle and the Stoics; (2) Academic skeptics (i.e., skeptical successors to Plato's Academy), who are still partially dogmatic; and (3) Pyrrhonian skeptics, who make no claims about truth at all. Sextus emphasizes that we can achieve tranquillity only if we stop dogmatizing completely. Tranquillity, which requires release from the struggles caused by "dogmatism," was indeed the main goal toward which Sextus was striving.

FROM SEXTUS EMPIRICUS, *Outlines of Pyrrhonism,* BOOK I

The way of the Skeptical School is an ability to place appearances in opposition to judgments in any way whatever, and thus through the equilibrium of the reasons and things opposed to each other, to reach, first the state of suspension of judgment, and afterwards that of tranquility. . . . "Suspension of judgment" is a holding back of the opinion, in consequence of which we neither deny nor affirm anything. "Tranquility" is repose and calmness of soul. We shall explain how tranquility accompanies suspension of judgment when we speak of the aim. [1.4]

Skepticism arose in the beginning from the hope of attaining tranquillity; for men of the greatest talent were perplexed by the contradiction of things, and being at a loss what to believe, began to question what things are true, and what false, hoping to attain tranquillity as a result of the decision. The fundamental principle of the Skeptical system is especially this, namely, to oppose every argument by one of equal weight, for it seems to us that in this way we finally reach the position where we have no dogmas. [1.6]

ASK YOURSELF

3. What does Sextus mean by tranquillity, and how do we attain it?

Sextus explains that, even though the skeptic suspends judgment about things, the skeptic must also act in the world. For example, if the skeptic simply did nothing, he might starve to death.

But this observance of what pertains to the daily life appears to be of four different kinds. Sometimes it is directed by the guidance of nature, sometimes by the necessity of the feelings, sometimes by the tradition of laws and of customs, and sometimes by the teaching of the arts. It is directed by the guidance of nature, for by nature we are capable of sensation and thought; by the necessity of the feelings, for hunger leads us to food, and thirst to drink; by the traditions of laws and customs, for according to them we consider piety a good in daily life, and impiety an evil; by the teaching of the arts, for we are not inactive in the arts we undertake. We say all these things, however, without expressing a decided opinion. [1.11]

ASK YOURSELF

4. As active people, what are the four areas of regulation that skeptics follow?

Ten Methods of Skepticism. The Ten Methods of Skepticism are perhaps the most important contribution of the Pyrrhonian skeptics. The methods are systematic argument techniques that skeptics use to show that we must suspend judgment on virtually every conceivable issue. The Ten Methods were initially devised by the Pyrrhonian philosopher Aenesidemus (first century BCE) and are presented here by Sextus. Sextus begins by briefly listing the Ten Methods.

Certain Methods were commonly handed down by the older Skeptics, by means of which suspended judgment seems to take place. They are ten in number and are called synonymously arguments and points. They are these: The first is based upon the differences in animals; the second upon the differences in men; the third upon the difference in the constitution of the organs of sense; the fourth upon circumstances; the fifth upon position, distance, and place; the sixth upon mixtures; the seventh upon the quantity and constitution of objects; the eighth upon relation; the ninth upon frequency or rarity of occurrences; the tenth upon systems, customs, laws, mythical beliefs, and dogmatic opinions. We make this order ourselves.

ASK YOURSELF

5. How might "differences in position" give rise to doubts about, say, the size of an object?

Although Sextus gives detailed accounts of each of these methods, we will look only at the first, which is representative of the rest. Briefly, the first method states that animals of different species perceive things differently. For example, different animals may see, taste, smell, hear, or feel the same thing in different ways. Since we have no way of proving that one species has more "accurate" perceptions than another, we can't say for sure what the reality is behind their respective perceptions. We can state this argument more formally in this way:

1. An object appears to have quality X to a dog.
2. The same object appears to have quality Y to a cow and not quality X.
3. We have no reason to think the dog's perceptions are more "accurate" than the cow's, or vice versa.
4. Hence, we suspend judgment as to whether the object has quality X or Y.

The first Method, we said, is the one based upon the differences in animals, and according to this Method, different animals do not get the same ideas of the same objects through the senses. This we conclude from the different origin of the animals, and also from the difference in the constitution of their bodies. . . .

We may see this more clearly in the things that are sought for and avoided by animals. For example, myrrh appears very agreeable to men and intolerable to beetles and bees. Oil also, which is useful to men, destroys wasps and bees if sprinkled on them; and sea-water, while it is unpleasant and poisonous to men if they drink it, is most agreeable and sweet to fishes. Swine also prefer to wash in vile filth rather than in pure clean water. Furthermore, some animals eat grass and some eat herbs; some live in the woods, others eat seeds; some are carnivorous, and others lactivorous; some enjoy putrefied food, and others fresh food; some raw food, and others that which is prepared by cooking; and in general that which is agreeable to some is disagreeable and fatal to others, and should be avoided by them. Thus hemlock makes the quail fat, and henbane the hogs, and these, as it is known, enjoy eating lizards, deer also eat poisonous animals, and swallows, the cantharid. Moreover, ants and flying ants, when swallowed by men, cause discomfort and colic, but the bear, on the contrary,

whatever sickness he may have, becomes stronger by devouring them. The viper is be-
numbed if one twig of the oak touches it, as is also the bat by a leaf of the plane-tree. The
elephant flees before the ram, and the lion before the cock, and seals from the rattling of
beans that are being pounded, and the tiger from the sound of the drum. Many other examples could be given, but that we may not seem to dwell longer than is necessary on this subject, we conclude by saying that since the same things are pleasant to some and unpleasant to
others, and the pleasure and displeasure depend on the ideas, it must be that different animals
have different ideas of objects.

And since the same things appear different according to the difference in the animals, it
will be possible for us to say how the external object appears to us, but as to how it is in reality we shall suspend our judgment. For we cannot ourselves judge between our own ideas
and those of other animals, being ourselves involved in the difference, and therefore much
more in need of being judged than being ourselves able to judge. And furthermore, we cannot give the preference to our own mental representations over those of other animals, either
without evidence or with evidence, for besides the fact that perhaps there is no evidence, as
we shall show, the evidence so called will be either manifest to us or not. If it is not manifest
to us, then we cannot accept it with conviction; if it is manifest to us, since the question is in
regard to what is manifest to animals, and we use as evidence that which is manifest to us
who are animals, then it is to be questioned if it is true as it is manifest to us. It is absurd,
however, to try to base the questionable on the questionable, because the same thing is to be
believed and not to be believed, which is certainly impossible. The evidence is to be believed
insofar as it will furnish a proof, and disbelieved insofar as it is itself to be proved. We shall
therefore have no evidence according to which we can give preference to our own ideas over
those of so-called irrational animals. Since therefore ideas differ according to the difference
in animals, and it is impossible to judge them, it is necessary to suspend the judgment in
regard to external objects.

ASK YOURSELF

6. What are some examples that Sextus gives to show how animals of different
species perceive things differently?

7. Is Sextus arguing that it is impossible for humans to *know* how things really
are in the world, as opposed to how they merely appear?

3.   DREAMS, ILLUSIONS, AND THE EVIL GENIUS: RENÉ DESCARTES

In Chapter 4 we examined the view proposed by René Descartes (1596–1650) that human
beings are composed of a physical body and an immaterial mind. Descartes' view of reality
emerged, to a very large extent, from an intense focus on the question "What can I know?"
In his most enduring work, *Meditations on the First Philosophy* (1641), he begins by entering into the enemy territory of skepticism. Although Descartes himself intends to refute skepticism, he provisionally presents a powerful skeptical attack on the claim that any knowledge
whatsoever is possible.

Systematically Doubting the Foundations of Our Knowledge. The type of doubt that
Descartes proposes is not what we would call common-sense doubt. For example, common
sense tells me that I should have at least some doubts about the abilities of fortune tellers.
Instead, his doubting process is a philosophical one, and is sometimes called "hyperbolic" or

"exaggerated" doubt, which means that he proposes to doubt anything which he has the slightest reason to doubt. When he has gone through all of these reasons, it looks as though there are virtually no items of knowledge left standing.

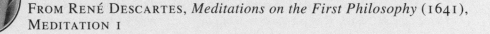

FROM RENÉ DESCARTES, *Meditations on the First Philosophy* (1641), MEDITATION I

It is now some years since I detected how many were the false beliefs that I had from my earliest youth admitted as true, and how doubtful was everything I had since constructed on this basis. And from that time I was convinced that I must once [and] for all seriously undertake to rid myself of all the opinions which I had formerly accepted, and commence to build anew from the foundation, if I wanted to establish any firm and permanent structure in the sciences. But as this enterprise appeared to be a very great one, I waited until I had attained an age so mature that I could not hope that at any later date I should be better fitted to execute my design. This reason caused me to delay so long that I should feel that I was doing wrong were I to occupy in deliberation the time that yet remains to me for action. Today, then, since very opportunely for the plan I have in view I have delivered my mind from every care [and am happily agitated by no passions] and since I have procured for myself an assured leisure in a peaceable retirement, I will at last seriously and freely address myself to the general upheaval of all my former opinions.

ASK YOURSELF

8. What reason does Descartes give in the First Meditation for seriously undertaking to rid himself of his former opinions?

Now for this object it is not necessary that I should show that all of these are false—I will perhaps never arrive at this end. But inasmuch as reason already persuades me that I ought no less carefully to withhold my assent from matters which are not entirely certain and indubitable than from those which appear to me evidently to be false, if I am able to find in each one some reason to doubt, this will suffice to justify my rejecting the whole. And for that end it will not be requisite that I should examine each in particular, which would be an endless undertaking; for owing to the fact that the destruction of the foundations of necessity brings with it the downfall of the rest of the edifice, I will only in the first place attack those principles upon which all my former opinions rested.

All that up to the present time I have accepted as most true and certain I have learned either from the senses or through the senses; but it is sometimes proved to me that these senses are deceptive, and it is wiser not to trust entirely to anything by which we have once been deceived.

ASK YOURSELF

9. Descartes does not intend to doubt the truth of every specific idea that comes into his head. What does he plan to do?

10. What is the main assumption that he brings under suspicion?

Descartes considers that optical illusions and hallucinations might cast doubt on the reliability of the senses. But perhaps his most compelling argument is the following one.

Dream Hypothesis. Descartes argues that there is no sure way to distinguish dream experiences from waking experiences.

At the same time I must remember that I am a man, and that consequently I am in the habit of sleeping, and in my dreams representing to myself the same things or sometimes even less probable things, than do those who are insane in their waking moments. How often has it happened to me that in the night I dreamt that I found myself in this particular place, that I was dressed and seated near the fire, whilst in reality I was lying undressed in bed! At this moment it does indeed seem to me that it is with eyes awake that I am looking at this paper; that this head which I move is not asleep, that it is deliberately and of set purpose that I extend my hand and perceive it; what happens in sleep does not appear so clear nor so distinct as does all this. But in thinking over this I remind myself that on many occasions I have in sleep been deceived by similar illusions, and in dwelling carefully on this reflection I see so evidently that there are no certain indications by which we may clearly distinguish wakefulness from sleep that I am lost in astonishment. And my astonishment is such that it is almost capable of persuading me that I now dream.

ASK YOURSELF

11. Why is Descartes almost convinced that he is sleeping?

Now let us assume that we are asleep and that all these particulars, for example, that we open our eyes, shake our head, extend our hands, and so on, are but false delusions; and let us reflect that possibly neither our hands nor our whole body are such as they appear to us to be. At the same time we must at least confess that the things which are represented to us in sleep are like painted representations which can only have been formed as the counterparts of something real and true, and that in this way those general things at least, that is, eyes, a head, hands, and a whole body, are not imaginary things, but things really existent. For, as a matter of fact, painters, even when they study with the greatest skill to represent sirens and satyrs by forms the most strange and extraordinary, cannot give them natures which are entirely new, but merely make a certain medley of the members of different animals; or if their imagination is extravagant enough to invent something so novel that nothing similar has ever before been seen, and that then their work represents a thing purely fictitious and absolutely false, it is certain all the same that the colors of which this is composed are necessarily real. And for the same reason, although these general things—to wit, a body, eyes, a head, hands, and such like—may be imaginary, we are bound at the same time to confess that there are at least some other objects yet more simple and more universal, which are real and true; and of these just in the same way as with certain real colors, all these images of things which dwell in our thoughts, whether true and real or false and fantastic, are formed.

To such a class of things pertains corporeal nature in general, and its extension, the figure of extended things, their quantity or magnitude and number, as also the place in which they are, the time which measures their duration, and so on.

ASK YOURSELF

12. What kind of things look most doubtful when he considers that he may be dreaming?

That is possibly why our reasoning is not unjust when we conclude from this that Physics, Astronomy, Medicine and all other sciences which have as their end the consideration of composite things, are very dubious and uncertain; but that Arithmetic, Geometry and other sciences of that kind which only treat of things that are very simple and very general, without taking great trouble to ascertain whether they are actually existent or not, contain some measure of certainty and an element of the indubitable. For whether I am awake or asleep, two and three together always form five, and the square can never have more than four sides, and it does not seem possible that truths so clear and apparent can be suspected of any falsity [or uncertainty].

ASK YOURSELF

13. What kinds of beliefs seem to be immune to doubt?

The Evil Genius Hypothesis. Taking his doubts further, Descartes initially speculates that God is deceiving him about all of the things that he believes or perceives.

Nevertheless I have long had fixed in my mind the belief that an all-powerful God existed by whom I have been created such as I am. But how do I know that he has not brought it to pass that there is no earth, no heaven, no extended body, no magnitude, no place, and that nevertheless [I possess the perceptions of all these things and that] they seem to me to exist just exactly as I now see them? And, besides, as I sometimes imagine that others deceive themselves in the things which they think they know best, how do I know that I am not deceived every time that I add two and three, or count the sides of a square, or judge of things yet simpler, if anything simpler can be imagined?

According to traditional Christian theology, infinite goodness is one of God's necessary attributes. If backed into a corner, some might deny God's existence rather than admit that he is the cause of deception. With God out of the picture, though, Descartes argues that he would be even more vulnerable to deception. He then revises his thought experiment and supposes that he might be deceived, not by God, but by a powerful demon.

I will then suppose, not that God who is supremely good and the fountain of truth, but some evil genius not less powerful than deceitful, has employed his whole energies in deceiving me. I will consider that the heavens, the earth, colors, figures, sound, and all other external things are nothing but the illusions and dreams of which this genius has availed himself in order to lay traps for my credulity. I will consider myself as having no hands, no eyes, no flesh, no blood, nor any senses, yet falsely believing myself to possess all these things. I will remain obstinately attached to this idea, and if by this means it is not in my power to arrive at the knowledge of any truth, I may at least do what is in my power [that is, suspend my judgment], and with firm purpose avoid giving credence to any false thing, or being imposed upon by this arch deceiver, however powerful and deceptive he may be.

ASK YOURSELF

14. Although Descartes believes at this point that he cannot be sure an evil genius (spirit) is deceiving him, there is one thing he can do. What is it?

4. SKEPTICISM ABOUT THE EXTERNAL WORLD: DAVID HUME

Although Descartes offered his skeptical vision of the world only provisionally—with the intention to refute it later—Scottish philosopher David Hume (1711–1776) seriously defended a radically skeptical view of things. He ends up denying that we know many things that we have confidence in, such as a real connection between causes and effects, the reliability of experiential reasoning, the concept of an enduring self, and the world that exists independently of our experience. We will first look at his doubts concerning the external world. The thrust of his argument is that we cannot know that objects exist apart from our individual and subjective perceptions.

FROM DAVID HUME, *A Treatise of Human Nature* (1739), BOOK 1.4.2

We ought to examine apart those two questions, which are commonly confounded together, viz. Why we attribute a continued existence to objects, even when they are not present to the senses; and why we suppose them to have an existence distinct from the mind and perception. Under this last head I comprehend their situation as well as relations, their external position as well as the independence of their existence and operation.

These two questions concerning the continued and distinct existence of body are intimately connected together. For if the objects of our senses continue to exist, even when they are not perceived, their existence is of course independent of and distinct from the perception; and vice versa, if their existence be independent of the perception, and distinct from it, they must continue to exist, even though they be not perceived. But though the decision of the one question decides the other; yet that we may the more easily discover the principles of human nature, from whence the decision arises, we shall carry along with us this distinction, and shall consider, whether it be the senses, reason, or the imagination, that produces the opinion of a continued or of a distinct existence. These are the only questions that are intelligible on the present subject. For as to the notion of external existence, when taken for something specifically different from our perceptions, we have already shown its absurdity.

**DAVID HUME
(1711–1776)**
Scottish skeptical philosopher and author of A Treatise of Human Nature *(1739).*

To begin with the senses, it is evident these faculties are incapable of giving rise to the notion of the continued existence of their objects, after they no longer appear to the senses. For that is a contradiction in terms, and supposes that the senses continue to operate, even after they have ceased all manner of operation. These faculties, therefore, if they have any influence in the present case, must produce the opinion of a distinct, not of a continued existence; and in order to do that, must present their impressions either as images and representations, or as these very distinct and external existences.

Hume is wondering where we got even the idea of something existing external to ourselves or our experience.

ASK YOURSELF

15. Hume has just claimed that the idea of external existence could not have arisen from _____.

That our senses offer not their impressions as the images of something distinct, or independent, and external, is evident; because they convey to us nothing but a single perception, and never give us the least intimation of any thing beyond. A single perception can never produce the idea of a double existence, but by some inference either of the reason or imagination. When the mind looks further than what immediately appears to it, its conclusions can never be put to the account of the senses; and it certainly looks further, when from a single perception it infers a double existence, and supposes the relations of resemblance and causation betwixt them.

If our senses, therefore, suggest any idea of distinct existences, they must convey the impressions as those very existences, by a kind of fallacy and illusion. Upon this head we may observe that all sensations are felt by the mind, such as they really are, and that, when we doubt whether they present themselves as distinct objects, or as mere impressions, the difficulty is not concerning their nature, but concerning their relations and situation. Now, if the senses presented our impressions as external to, and independent of ourselves, both the objects and ourselves must be obvious to our senses, otherwise they could not be compared by these faculties. The difficulty then is, how far we are ourselves the objects of our senses.

Suppose that my senses give me the idea of myself on the one hand and external objects on the other. Then I would have to have a sense experience, or "impression" as Hume calls it, of *myself* as well as of those objects. But, he argues, we have no such impression.

It is certain there is no question in philosophy more abstruse than that concerning identity, and the nature of the uniting principle, which constitutes a person. So far from being able by our senses merely to determine this question, we must have recourse to the most profound metaphysics to give a satisfactory answer to it; and in common life it is evident these ideas of self and person are never very fixed nor determinate. It is absurd therefore to imagine the senses can ever distinguish betwixt ourselves and external objects.

ASK YOURSELF

16. Hume has just given a second reason for the claim that we cannot know of a world external to the self. What is it?

Thus to resume what I have said concerning the senses; they give us no notion of continued existence, because they cannot operate beyond the extent, in which they really operate. They as little produce the opinion of a distinct existence, because they neither can offer it to the mind as represented, nor as original. To offer it as represented, they must present both an object and an image. To make it appear as original, they must convey a falsehood.

In Hume's view we are like a person permanently trapped in a picture gallery. Suppose that person sees a picture of a cow. Since he cannot get out of the gallery to where there are actual cows, he could never know there were such things. But even if he could get to where the cow is, the "original" could not be presented to his *mind,* for then he would actually have to have a cow in his mind, and his mind would literally be leaking milk.

ASK YOURSELF

17. Does Hume's skepticism about an external world depend entirely upon the idea that all we are ever directly aware of is the content of our own minds?

Now, it is evident, that whatever may be our philosophical opinion, colors, sounds, heat, and cold, as far as appears to the senses, exist after the same manner with motion and solidity; and that the difference we make betwixt them, in this respect, arises not from the mere perception. So strong is the prejudice for the distinct continued existence of the former qualities, that when the contrary opinion is advanced by modern philosophers, people imagine they can almost refute it from their feeling and experience, and that their very senses contradict this philosophy. It is also evident, that colors, sounds, etc., are originally on the same footing with the pain that arises from steel, and pleasure that proceeds from a fire; and that the difference betwixt them is founded neither on perception nor reason, but on the imagination.

Hume has just attacked the distinction between primary and secondary qualities, which, as we shall see later, was so important to John Locke. Primary qualities are those that are presumably part of the external object itself and have a continued existence independent of our perceptions, and secondary qualities are those that exist only in the minds of perceivers.

ASK YOURSELF

18. As Hume discusses the issue above, an example of a primary quality is _____. An example of a secondary quality is _____.

19. Hume has just claimed that we have no more reason for supposing _____ qualities exist independently of perception than we have for believing _____ qualities do. And we have *no* reason for the latter belief.

Hume tries to account for our natural belief in an external world by examining what differentiates supposedly durable mind-independent things (like tables) from internal things, like tickles or feeling tired. One difference is that our experience of tables is supposedly more "coherent."

Objects have a certain coherence even as they appear to our senses; but this coherence is much greater and more uniform if we suppose the objects to have a continued existence; and as the mind is once in the train of observing a uniformity among objects, it naturally continues till it renders the uniformity as complete as possible. The simple supposition of their continued existence suffices for this purpose, and gives us a notion of a much greater regularity among objects, than what they have when we look no further than our senses.

ASK YOURSELF

20. If I sit looking at a table for an hour, my perceptual experience does not change much. The experience has continuity. If I extend this continuity beyond experience, I come to think of the table as existing _____.

Hume ponders the origin of our belief in a persisting external world at length but concludes that nothing in our experience justifies that belief.

5. THE PROBLEM OF INDUCTION: DAVID HUME AND PETER STRAWSON

Suppose that I pop a lima bean into my mouth but find it so bitter and pasty that I have a tough time swallowing it; the odds are good that I won't try another. Although it's possible that another lima bean might be tastier, even after trying just one I've already made an assumption about *all* lima beans. The reasoning process I'm using here is called a induction: Specific instances are used as evidence for a more general or even a universal conclusion. Our tendency to make inductive generalizations seems to be deeply embedded in human nature. Without it, the tiniest activity, such as opening a door, would present an insurmountable difficulty, and our lives would grind to a halt. Inductive reasoning is by no means 100 percent accurate. There really is a chance that a lima bean exists somewhere that is not as bitter and pasty as the one I tasted. The best that I can infer is that there is a *probability* that the next lima bean will be as displeasing as the previous one. Although this is a limitation in inductive reasoning, it is a limitation that we're willing to live with. Hume points out a much more serious problem with inductive reasoning: The whole process is logically flawed.

Induction Is Not Grounded in Logic or Facts. Induction involves projecting something from the present into the future. If all lima beans that I've tasted so far are bitter and pasty, I may inductively infer that all lima beans that I taste in the future will be the same. Inductive knowledge seems to be essential to the sciences. Typically, scientific explanations are used to make predictions. Newton's laws not only explained planetary motions but enabled Halley to calculate the orbit of a comet and predict quite precisely when that comet would next appear. Halley assumed that the comet would behave in the future just as other heavenly bodies had behaved in the past. Hume denies that we can have any reason to trust in induction, no matter how much knowledge it *seems* to provide.

FROM DAVID HUME, *Enquiry Concerning Human Understanding* (1748), SECTION 4

If a body of like color and consistence with that bread, which we have formerly eat, be presented to us, we make no scruple of repeating the experiment, and foresee, with certainty, like nourishment and support. Now this is a process of the mind or thought, of which I would willingly know the foundation. It is allowed on all hands that there is no known connection between the sensible qualities and the secret powers; and consequently, that the mind is not led to form such a conclusion concerning their constant and regular conjunction, by any thing which it knows of their nature. As to past *experience*, it can be allowed to give *direct* and *certain* information of those precise objects only, and that precise period of time, which fell under its cognizance: But why this experience should be extended to future times, and to other objects, which for aught we know, may be only in appearance similar; this is the main question on which I would insist. The bread, which I formerly eat, nourished me; that is, a body of such sensible qualities was, at that time, endued with such secret powers: But does it follow, that other bread must also nourish me at another time, and that like sensible qualities must always be attended with like secret powers? The consequence seems nowise necessary.

ASK YOURSELF

21. According to Hume, what is the only thing that past experience can give us information about?

Hume offers a two-pronged attack on the notion of induction. First he argues that we cannot justify induction by appealing to any process of logical reasoning. Second he argues that induction cannot be justified by appealing to facts in the world. His argument against logical inference is this.

At least, it must be acknowledged that there is here a consequence drawn by the mind; that there is a certain step taken; a process of thought, and an inference, which wants to be explained. These two propositions are far from being the same, *I have found that such an object has always been attended with such an effect,* and *I foresee, that other objects, which are, in appearance, similar, will be attended with similar effects.* I shall allow, if you please, that the one proposition may justly be inferred from the other: I know, in fact, that it always is inferred. But if you insist that the inference is made by a chain of reasoning, I desire you to produce that reasoning. The connection between these propositions is not intuitive. There is required a medium, which may enable the mind to draw such an inference, if indeed it be drawn by reasoning and argument. What that medium is, I must confess, passes my comprehension; and it is incumbent on those to produce it, who assert that it really exists, and is the origin of all our conclusions concerning matter of fact.

The "inference" Hume is discussing is the inference from the past to the future. In the past whenever I let go of a brick it fell toward the earth, so in the future when I let go of a brick it will fall toward the earth.

ASK YOURSELF

22. What is Hume's response to someone who suggests that there is a logical chain of reasoning between past experiences and inferences about the future?

Hume next argues that inductive inferences are not based on reasoning about matters of fact. Hume gives two arguments against this contention, the first of which is that reasoning about matters of fact assumes this very point in question, namely that the future will be like the past.

If we be, therefore, engaged by arguments to put trust in past experience, and make it the standard of our future judgment, these arguments must be probable only, or such as regard matter of fact and real existence according to the division above mentioned. But that there is no argument of this kind must appear, if our explication of that species of reasoning be admitted as solid and satisfactory. We have said that all arguments concerning existence are founded on the relation of cause and effect; that our knowledge of that relation is derived entirely from experience; and that all our experimental conclusions proceed upon the supposition that the future will be conformable to the past. To endeavor, therefore, the proof of this last supposition by probable arguments, or arguments regarding existence, must be evidently going in a circle, and taking that for granted, which is the very point in question.

ASK YOURSELF

23. What is the precise circularity of reasoning that Hume refers to above?

Hume continues with his second argument. With inductive generalizations, from a greater number of uniform observations about the past, we would expect a higher degree of assurance about the future. However, even a single observed counter-instance undermines this assurance, regardless of how many past observations were uniform. For Hume, this sudden depletion of assurance cannot be explained by any empirical reasoning process.

In reality, all arguments from experience are founded on the similarity which we discover among natural objects, and by which we are induced to expect effects similar to those which we have found to follow from such objects. And though none but a fool or madman will ever pretend to dispute the authority of experience, or to reject that great guide of human life, it may surely be allowed a philosopher to have so much curiosity at least as to examine the principle of human nature, which gives this mighty authority to experience, and makes us draw advantage from that similarity which nature has placed among different objects. From causes which appear similar we expect similar effects. This is the sum of all our experimental conclusions. Now it seems evident that, if this conclusion were formed by reason, it would be as perfect at first, and upon one instance, as after ever so long a course of experience. But the case is far otherwise. [There is] nothing so like as eggs. Yet no one, on account of this appearing similarity, expects the same taste and relish in all of them. It is only after a long course of uniform experiments in any kind, that we attain a firm reliance and security with regard to a particular event. Now where is that process of reasoning which, from one instance, draws a conclusion so different from that which it infers from a hundred instances that are nowise different from that single one? This question I propose as much for the sake of information, as with an intention of raising difficulties. I cannot find, I cannot imagine any such reasoning. But I keep my mind still open to instruction, if any one will vouchsafe to bestow it on me.

ASK YOURSELF

24. Using Hume's egg example, show how a single counter-instance undermines the assurance we have built up from perhaps hundreds of uniform experiences.

Dissolving the Problem of Induction: Peter Strawson. The contemporary British philosopher Peter Strawson (b. 1919) does not attempt to defend the reliability of our inductive reasoning against Hume's attack. He does not think it *needs* any defense. Strawson discusses various attempts to justify induction, including some that Hume also discussed. However, the failure of various attempts to justify induction does not show that it lacks justification. Strawson concludes his discussion with the following remarks.

FROM PETER STRAWSON, *Introduction to Logical Theory* (1952)

First, I want to point out that there is something a little odd about talking of "the inductive method," or even "the inductive policy," as if it were just one possible method among others of arguing from the observed to the unobserved. . . . If one asked a meteorologist what method or methods he used to forecast the weather, one would be surprised if he answered: "Oh, just the inductive method." . . . The answer one hopes for is an account of the tests made, the signs taken account of, the rules and recipes and general laws applied. When such a specific method of prediction or diagnosis is in question, one can ask whether the method is justified in practice; and here again one is asking whether its employment is inductively justified, whether it commonly gives correct results. This question would normally seem an admissible one.

ASK YOURSELF

25. Is Strawson suggesting that the question "Is the inductive method justified?" is *not* an "admissible" question?

If you answered "yes" to the above question, and agree with Strawson, then consider this:

Someone might object: "Surely it is possible, though it might be foolish, to use methods utterly different from accredited scientific ones. Suppose a man, whenever he wanted to form an opinion about what lay beyond his observation or the observation of available witnesses, simply shut his eyes, asked himself the appropriate question, and accepted the first answer that came into his head. Wouldn't this be a non-inductive method?" Well, let us suppose this. The man is asked: "Do you usually get the right answer by your method?" He might answer: "You've mentioned one of its drawbacks; I never do get the right answer; but it's an extremely easy method." One might then be inclined to think that it was not a method of finding things out at all. But suppose he answered: Yes, it's usually (always) the right answer. Then we might be willing to call it a method of finding out, though a strange one. But, then, by the very fact of its success, it would be an inductively supported method.

ASK YOURSELF

26. Is Strawson claiming that *any* method of investigation, no matter how bizarre, is inductively supported if it produces an impressive enough record of successes?

So every successful method or recipe for finding out about the unobserved must be one which has inductive support—for to say that a recipe is successful is to say that it has been repeatedly applied with success; and repeated successful application of a recipe constitutes just what we mean by inductive evidence in its favour . . . I am not seeking to "justify the inductive method," for no meaning has been given to this phrase. *A fortiori,* I am not saying that induction is justified by its success in finding out about the unobserved. I am saying, rather, that any successful method of finding out about the unobserved is necessarily justified by induction. This is an analytic proposition. . . .

Strawson appears to be claiming, in effect, that there are some things we can know independently of experience and that one of these things is this: "Any successful method of finding out about the unobserved is necessarily justified by induction." When he says that this statement is "analytic," he is in fact claiming that it can be known to be true without doing some sort of empirical study. Since empirical studies are themselves inductive in character, it would be futile to try to justify induction through such studies. Otherwise put, you cannot employ induction in the course of showing that you are justified in employing it.

ASK YOURSELF

27. Why can't we employ induction in the course of showing that we are justified in employing it?

SUMMING UP SKEPTICISM

Most forms of skepticism set a very high bar for knowledge. Often, skeptics assume that only where there is complete certainty can there be knowledge. Ancient Pyhrronian skeptics such as Sextus tried to demonstrate the uncertainty of all judgments by showing how equally good arguments could be made for any statement and for its opposite. Later skeptics have tended to stress the unreliability of the senses and have pondered the nature of knowledge via skeptical hypotheses such as Descartes' dream argument, which was not entirely unlike observations by the Taoist Chuang-tzu, who lived nearly 2000 years earlier. Hume has offered skeptical arguments against our common sense beliefs in causal connections, continued personal identity, and the reliability of induction. Many thinkers who are not skeptics still acknowledge that those arguments have some force or at least are worthy of thoughtful replies. Skepticism continues to fascinate us, no doubt in part because it is so difficult to refute.

CAN OF WORMS

In virtually every area of philosophy, skeptical questions arise: Does God exist? Is there an objective standard of morality? Can we even know our own minds? Some forms of skepticism also involve claims about the will. For example, ancient skepticism assumes that we can will a suspension of belief. If we have no ability to will, as hard determinists claim, then one form of skepticism appears to exclude determinism. Logical puzzles also arise in pondering skeptical claims, as well as in attempts to refute those claims. We need a clear account of circularity in argument, and clear reasons for rejecting all types of circular reasoning, before we can accept skeptical rejection of inductive reasoning. It sometimes also appears that skeptical claims are self-defeating. Do they presuppose the possibility of knowledge? Epistemological, metaphysical and logical issues are invariably intertwined in discussions of skepticism.

B. Sources of Knowledge: Rationalism and Empiricism

Common sense tells us that we do know many things. The arguments of the skeptics and relativists, some of which are given in the last section, may seem extreme. Even if we reject skepticism, however, disputes may nevertheless break out about *how* we know what we know. Common sense often answers "we know through sense perception." For example, I know there is a green bowl in front of me because I am in normal perceptual circumstances and can see it. I know Napoleon was short because people who saw him have reported that he was. There are also things I know just by thinking. For example, I know that the parts of a thing cannot be greater than or bigger than the whole.

QUESTIONS TO DISCUSS

a. Try to imagine a case where you believe something because you have seen it but are nevertheless mistaken.

b. Do mathematical beliefs depend upon experience? If whenever you took two things, put them together with two other things, and then counted them up, you always got five things, would that make you give up your mathematical belief that 2 + 2 = 4?

c. Do you know what justice is through experience? If so, what kind of experience?

d. If a tree falls in the forest and there is absolutely no being there to hear it, is there a sound?

e. Can a blind person know as much about the world as a sighted person?

f. Does how you were trained or brought up affect what you see? For example, if you are watching a football game with someone who knows nothing about football, do you actually see the same things?

1. Knowledge Does Not Come from the Senses: Plato

Plato (427–347 BCE) lived and taught in Athens Greece in the fourth century BCE. He was a pupil and admirer of Socrates, who was executed by Athenian authorities when Plato was 24 years old. Socrates was a hero for Plato and others, and his loyal followers believed that he was hated by some because of his unrelenting pursuit of knowledge and wisdom. Plato's works are mostly written in dialogue form, and most of them feature Socrates as the main speaker.

The Senses and Body Obstruct Knowledge. It is worth noting that Plato's opposition to the senses as a source of knowledge includes a moral dimension. The senses are "bodily," and bodily life is morally tainted. Plato's rejection of the senses as a source of knowledge is a principal feature of *rationalism*. The contrary view, that the senses are a reliable source of knowledge, is a principal feature of *empiricism*.

FROM PLATO, *Phaedo*

SOCRATES   Well, but there is another thing, Simmias: Is there or is there not an absolute justice?

SIMMIAS   Assuredly there is.

SOCRATES   And an absolute beauty and absolute good?

SIMMIAS   Of course.

SOCRATES   But did you ever behold any of them with your eyes?

SIMMIAS   Certainly not.

SOCRATES   Or did you ever reach them with any other bodily sense? (and I speak not of these alone, but of absolute greatness, and health, and strength, and of the essence or true nature of everything). Has the reality of them ever been perceived by you through the bodily organs? Or rather, is not the nearest approach to the knowledge of their several natures made by him who so orders his intellectual vision as to have the most exact conception of the essence of that which he considers?

SIMMIAS   Certainly.

SOCRATES   And he attains to the knowledge of them in their highest purity who goes to each of them with the mind alone, not allowing when in the act of thought the intrusion or introduction of sight or any other sense in the company of reason. Rather, with the very light of the mind in her clearness he penetrates into the very light of truth in each. He has got rid, as far as he can, of eyes and ears and of the whole body, which he conceives of only as a disturbing element which hinders the soul from the acquisition of knowledge when in company with her. Is not this the sort of man who, if ever man did, is likely to attain the knowledge of existence?

SIMMIAS   There is admirable truth in that, Socrates.

SOCRATES   And when they consider all this, must not true philosophers make a reflection, of which they will speak to one another in such words as these: We have found, they will say, a path of speculation which seems to bring us and the argument to the conclusion that while we are in the body, and while the soul is mingled with this mass of evil, our desire will not be satisfied, and our desire is of the truth. For the body is a source of endless trouble to us by reason of the mere requirement of food. It is also liable to diseases which overtake and impede us in the search after truth. Moreover by filling us so full of loves, and lusts, and fears, and fancies, and idols, and every sort of folly, the body prevents our ever having, as people say, so much as a thought.

If bodily senses cannot give knowledge, then we might expect a seeker of knowledge to downplay the body and elevate the mind or something mind-like, such as the soul. That is exactly what Plato does, as the above sections clearly indicate. But it is not only the senses that belong to the body. There are also "loves, and lusts, and fears, and fancies, and idols, and every sort of folly." In Plato's view, these also interfere with true knowledge and thus prevent contact with what is eternal and perfect. Consider this example: I will never grasp what true justice is (the form of justice) if I am slave to the desire for possessions or to the fear of being unpopular. So Plato's thinking about the body versus the soul has an ethical and religious dimension. In fact he recommends a kind of asceticism.

ASK YOURSELF

28. How might a fear, such as the fear of being unpopular, interfere with someone's ability to understand or know what justice is? Give an example.

Plato uses the expressions "absolute justice" or "justice itself" or "the form of justice" as ways of referring to eternal and non-empirical entities. These notions serve as the standard for all particular applications of "justice." In order to understand what is just in any act, I must compare that act with a standard that tells me what perfect justice is. I could not have gotten the idea of justice by abstracting it from my experience with particular just acts. How could I determine which acts *were* just if I did not already have the *idea* of justice? But where then did I get my idea of justice, or goodness, or dogness, or anything else? Part of Plato's answer is worked out in the following passage, also from the dialogue *Phaedo*. His example here is the idea of equality, which he refers to with Greek expressions which are variously translated as "equality itself," the "form of equality," "equality in the abstract," or "the essence of equality."

SOCRATES   And shall we proceed a step further, and affirm that there is such a thing as equality, not of wood with wood, or of stone with stone, but that, over and above this, there is equality in the abstract? Shall we affirm this?

SIMMIAS   Affirm, yes, and swear to it, replied Simmias, with all the confidence in life.

SOCRATES   And do we know the nature of this abstract essence?

SIMMIAS   To be sure, he said.

SOCRATES   And whence did we obtain this knowledge? Did we not see equalities of material things, such as pieces of wood and stones, and gather from them the idea of an equality which is different from them?—you will admit that? Or look at the matter again in this way: Do not the same pieces of wood or stone appear at one time equal, and at another time unequal?

SIMMIAS   That is certain.

SOCRATES   But are real equals ever unequal? or is the idea of equality ever inequality?

SIMMIAS   That surely was never yet known, Socrates.

SOCRATES   Then these (so-called) equals are not the same with the idea of equality?

SIMMIAS   I should say, clearly not, Socrates.

SOCRATES   And yet from these equals, although differing from the idea of equality, you conceived and attained that idea?

SIMMIAS   Very true, he said.

SOCRATES   Which might be like, or might be unlike them? And must we not allow that when I or anyone look at any object, x, and perceive that the object aims at being some other thing, A, but falls short of being A—must not whoever makes this observation have had previous knowledge of that A to which, as he says, the other thing, x, although similar, was inferior?

SIMMIAS   Certainly.

SOCRATES   And has not this been our case in the matter of equals and of absolut equality?

SIMMIAS   Precisely.

SOCRATES   Then we must have known absolute equality previously to the time when we first saw the material equals, and reflected that all these apparent equals aim at this absolute equality, but fall short of it? But that makes no difference; whenever from seeing one thing you conceived another, whether like or unlike, there must surely have been an act of recollection?

SIMMIAS   Very true.

SOCRATES   But what would you say of equal portions of wood and stone, or other material equals? And what is the impression produced by them? Are they equals in the same sense as absolute equality? Or do they fall short of this in a measure?

SIMMIAS   Yes, he said, in a very great measure, too.

SOCRATES   And must we not allow that when I or anyone look at any object, and perceive that the object aims at being some other thing, but falls short of, and cannot attain to it—he who makes this observation must have had previous knowledge of that to which, as he says, the other, although similar, was inferior?

SIMMIAS   Certainly.

Take two sticks or pencils that have been measured and clearly appear to be equal in length. Then set one on the middle of the other, perpendicular to it. Do they still *appear* equal? Most will agree that they do *not*. The ways things appear to the senses are often conflicting and contradictory. Perhaps then we do not get our concept of equality by looking at sticks of equal length or at any other equal things. Yet we do have the ability to make judgments about the apparent equality of empirical sticks, and such judgments certainly presuppose knowledge of what equality is. If we did not get that knowledge by looking—that is, through the senses—perhaps we were born with an "innate" idea, or knowledge, of equality—that is, born with the idea of equality already in our minds. Plato argues that such knowledge requires the pre-existence of the soul and the soul's familiarity with "forms." Later rationalists, such as Descartes, preserve the idea that we must be born with certain kinds of ideas and knowledge already implanted in the mind. Those ideas were later referred to as "innate ideas." Even if we do not accept Plato's theory about the pre-existence of the soul, we still have to show how it is possible for us to make such judgments as "this stick is equal to that stick." Plato has given reasons for thinking they are not possible as a result of learning through the senses.

ASK YOURSELF

29. To take a different example, how could you make the judgment that two different things, Fido and Rover, are both dogs, unless you had the "idea" of "dog" already in mind? Can you think of any problem with supposing that you simply observed Fido and Rover, saw that they were similar, and for that reason decided to use the same name "dog" for both of them?

2. ALL KNOWLEDGE DERIVES FROM THE SENSES: JOHN LOCKE

**JOHN LOCKE
(1632–1704)**

English empiricist philosopher and author of An Essay Concerning Human Understanding *(1689).*

British philosopher John Locke (1632–1704) was influential in both epistemology and political philosophy. Other philosophers prior to Locke advocated an empiricist approach to knowledge. However, Locke was an extreme advocate of this methodology, and in his 700-page *Essay Concerning Human Understanding* (1689), he argued that all of our knowledge is based on experience. Although the dispute between empiricists and rationalists altered considerably between the time of Plato and Locke, certain common themes are discernible.

No Knowledge Is Innate. Locke rejects the typical rationalist claim that some of our ideas and knowledge are innate. That is, we are not born with certain kinds of knowledge already implanted in our minds, as both Plato and later Descartes thought. In the following passages he sets forth some of the reasons for the belief that there are innate ideas, and then he attempts to refute that belief.

JOHN LOCKE, *Essay Concerning Human Understanding* (1689), BOOK I

There is nothing more commonly taken for granted than that there are certain principles, both speculative and practical (for they speak of both), universally agreed upon by all humankind: which therefore, they [rationalists in particular] argue, must needs be the constant impressions which the souls of people receive in their first beings, and which they bring into the world with them, as necessarily and really as they do any of their inherent faculties.

.This argument, drawn from universal consent, has this misfortune in it, that if it were true in matter of fact, that there were certain truths wherein all humankind agreed, it would not prove them innate, if there can be any other way shown how people may come to that universal agreement, in the things they do consent in, which I presume may be done.

ASK YOURSELF

30. According to Locke, what will undermine the argument from universal consent?

Locke examines versions of two of Aristotle's famous "laws of thought," which some philosophers believed to be innate "ideas" or principles: the law of identity (what is, is) and the law of non-contradiction (a single thing cannot at one and the same time both be and not be).

[T]his argument of universal consent (which is made use of to prove innate principles) seems to me a demonstration that there are none such. [This is] because there are none to which all humankind give an universal assent. I shall begin with the speculative, and instance in those magnified principles of demonstration, "Whatsoever is, is," and "It is impossible for the same thing to be and not to be"; which, of all others, I think have the most allowed title to-innate. These have so settled a reputation of maxims universally received, that it will no doubt be thought strange if any one should seem to question it. But yet I take liberty to say, that these propositions are so far from having an universal assent, that there are a great part of humankind to whom they are not so much as known. . . . For, first, it is evident, that all children and idiots have not the least apprehension or thought of them. And the want of that is enough to destroy that universal assent which must needs be the necessary concomitant of all innate truths: it seeming to me near a contradiction to say, that there are truths imprinted on the soul, which it perceives or understands not: imprinting, if it signify anything, being nothing else but the making certain truths to be perceived. For to imprint anything on the mind without the mind's perceiving it, seems to me hardly intelligible. If therefore children and idiots have souls, have minds, with those impressions upon them, they must unavoidably perceive them, and necessarily know and assent to these truths. Which since they do not, it is evident that there are no such impressions. For if they are not notions naturally imprinted, how can they be innate? and if they are notions imprinted, how can they be unknown? To say a notion is imprinted on the mind, and yet at the same time to say, that the mind is ignorant of it, and never yet took notice of it, is to make this impression nothing.

ASK YOURSELF

31. Locke argues that certain "universal principles" are not innate by claiming that those principles are not known to _____ and _____.

The key point of Locke's argument is that if an idea is truly in one's mind, then it must be understood. Since some humans do not understand these ideas, then such ideas are not in their minds and thus are not innate.

ASK YOURSELF

32. Consider this example: "It cannot be that it is raining at this time in this place and also that it is not raining at this time in this place." Is there any way an idiot might show that he understood this to be impossible, and thus that he did after all understand the "law of noncontradiction?" If you think so, describe that way.

33. Has Locke addressed the problem raised by Plato as to how we could abstract general ideas from particular perceptions?

Knowledge Traces Back to Sense Perception. Locke gives further arguments for his claim that none of our ideas could be innate. He then attempts to show that knowledge is rooted in sense perception.

Let us then suppose the mind to be, as we say, white paper, void of all characters, without any ideas: How comes it to be furnished? Whence comes it by that vast store which the busy and boundless fancy of man has painted on it with an almost endless variety? Whence has it all the materials of reason and knowledge? To this I answer, in one word, from *experience*. In that all our knowledge is founded; and from that it ultimately derives itself. Our observation employed either, about external sensible objects, or about the internal operations of our minds perceived and reflected on by ourselves, is that which supplies our understandings with all the materials of thinking. These two are the fountains of knowledge, from whence all the ideas we have, or can naturally have, do spring. . . . First, our Senses, conversant about particular sensible objects, do convey into the mind several distinct perceptions of things, according to those various ways wherein those objects do affect them. And thus we come by those ideas we have of yellow, white, heat, cold, soft, hard, bitter, sweet, and all those which we call sensible qualities; which when I say the senses convey into the mind, I mean, they from external objects convey into the mind what produces there those perceptions. This great source of most of the ideas we have, depending wholly upon our senses, and derived by them to the understanding, I call *sensation.*

. . . Secondly, the other fountain from which experience furnishes the understanding with ideas is, the perception of the operations of our own mind within us, as it is employed about the ideas it has got; which operations, when the soul comes to reflect on and consider, do furnish the understanding with another set of ideas, which could not be had from things without. And such are perception, thinking, doubting, believing, reasoning, knowing, willing, and all the different actings of our own minds; which we being conscious of, and observing in ourselves, do from these receive into our understandings as distinct ideas as we do from bodies affecting our senses.

ASK YOURSELF

34. What are the two kinds of "perception" that supply our minds with all that they ever have in them? Give an example of each.

Locke supposes that our senses are fundamentally "passive." The image of the mind as a sheet of white paper upon which "experience" "paints" expresses that fact clearly. But he does speak of "operations of the mind" and develops an elaborate account of how more complex kinds of knowledge are built up from elementary perceptions.

Primary and Secondary Qualities and the Causal Theory of Perception. Locke also makes a fundamental distinction between "ideas" that reflect an external reality, which are "primary," and those that are strictly in the mind, or private, so to speak. The latter are "secondary" qualities.

Whatsoever the mind perceives in itself, or is the immediate object of perception, thought, or understanding, that I call idea; and the power to produce any idea in our mind, I call quality of the subject wherein that power is. Thus a snowball having the power to produce in us the ideas of white, cold, and round—the power to produce those ideas in us, as they are in the snowball—I call qualities; and as they are sensations or perceptions in our understandings, I call them ideas; which ideas, if I speak of sometimes as in the things themselves, I would be understood to mean those qualities in the objects which produce them in us.

ASK YOURSELF

35. According to Locke, to say that a snowball is white is just to say that it has the _____ to produce in us the "idea" of white. Thus the snowball is not in itself actually _____.

Qualities thus considered in bodies are,

First, such as are utterly inseparable from the body, in what state soever it be; and such as in all the alterations and changes it suffers, all the force can be used upon it, it constantly keeps; and such as sense constantly finds in every particle of matter which has bulk enough to be perceived; and the mind finds inseparable from every particle of matter, though less than to make itself singly be perceived by our senses: v.g. Take a grain of wheat, divide it into two parts; each part has still solidity, extension, figure, and mobility: divide it again, and it retains still the same qualities; and so divide it on, till the parts become insensible; they must retain still each of them all those qualities. For division (which is all that a mill, or pestle, or any other body, does upon another, in reducing it to insensible parts) can never take away either solidity, extension, figure, or mobility from any body, but only makes two or more distinct separate masses of matter, of that which was but one before; all which distinct masses, reckoned as so many distinct bodies, after division, make a certain number. These I call original or primary qualities of body, which I think we may observe to produce simple ideas in us, viz. solidity, extension, figure, motion or rest, and number.

Secondly, such qualities which in truth are nothing in the objects themselves but power to produce various sensations in us by their primary qualities, i.e. by the bulk, figure, texture, and motion of their insensible parts, as colors, sounds, tastes, etc. These I call secondary qualities. To these might be added a third sort, which are allowed to be barely powers; though they are as much real qualities in the subject as those which I, to comply with the common way of speaking, call qualities, but for distinction, secondary qualities. For the power in fire to produce a new color, or consistency, in wax or clay—by its primary qualities, is as much a quality in fire, as the power it has to produce in me a new idea or sensation of warmth or burning, which I felt not before— by the same primary qualities, viz. the bulk, texture, and motion of its insensible parts.

ASK YOURSELF

36. Name some primary qualities and some of the ideas that they are capable of producing in a perceiver.

Locke supposes that only primary qualities exist "out there" in objects, external to our minds. Our ideas of those qualities are thus accurate representations of those objects. Thus if I think of a snowball as solid, extended (that is, taking up space), in motion or at rest, I am thinking of it as it is in itself. However, when I think of it as white or cold, I make a mistake if I think those ideas accurately represent it as it is in itself. *Those* ideas exist only in minds and do not accurately represent anything that exists outside them. It should be clear by now that my "idea" of a snowball is actually a collection of "ideas" in Locke's sense, such as the idea of roundness, coldness, whiteness, and so forth.

ASK YOURSELF

37. Consider the old conundrum "If a tree falls in the forest and no one is there to hear it, does it make a sound?" How would Locke answer?

The primary qualities are capable of "causing" in us various ideas or experiences, such as the ideas "white," "cold," and so forth. That is the "causal theory of perception," and it has become a commonplace of science. When I bite into a lemon, the sourness I experience is not in the lemon itself, but results from a causal interaction between certain physical properties of the lemon and my own nervous system.

In Locke's view, and in the views of many subsequent empiricists including Hume, all I am ever directly aware of or "perceive" are my own "ideas" or sense data. Thus I am never directly aware of a snowball. I have "snowball ideas" that lead me to the belief that there is a snowball in the vicinity.

One outstanding puzzle in Locke's view is this: Since all I have direct access to, in his view, is the contents of my own mind, how could I ever know that some of the ideas I find there, such as the idea of location or extension, accurately represent how the objective world really is, and others, such as the idea of white, do not? The only way to know that A accurately represents B is to directly compare A with B.

ASK YOURSELF

38. Could I directly compare any of my ideas of a snowball to the snowball itself, in Locke's view? How, or, why not?

Locke's terminology is also less than clear. He speaks sometimes of perceptions, sometimes of ideas, but in both cases he seems to be indicating some kind of mental content, what later empiricists called "sense data." If I hallucinate a pink elephant, I am still having pink elephant sense data, or ideas, or perceptions. If there actually is a pink elephant, in front of me, I am still having those same sense data. How then can I tell whether there is an elephant there or not? If there is no answer to these questions, Locke's empiricism may result in the kind of skepticism that Hume maintained in the earlier section.

3. THE NATURE OF PERCEPTION: JOHN SEARLE

American philosopher John Searle (b. 1932) tries to give an account of perception that avoids some of the difficulties in traditional empiricist accounts. He is not a rationalist attacking empiricism, but he does make some points that might remind you of Plato. Searle discusses certain features of perception that undermine a Lockean view of it. He focuses on examples of visual perception, but his account is meant to apply to hearing and other kinds of perception. Close attention to Searle's discussion will pay off later when we read more of Hume and Descartes.

FROM JOHN SEARLE, *Intentionality* (1983), CHAPTER 2

When I stand and look at a car, let us say a yellow station wagon, in broad daylight, at point blank range, with no visual impediments, I see the car. How does the seeing work? Well, there is long story about how it works in physical optics and in neurophysiology, but that is not what I mean. I mean how does it work conceptually; what are the elements that go to make up the truth conditions of sentences of the form "*x sees y*" where *x* is a perceiver, human or animal, and *y* is, for example, a material object? When I see a car, or anything else for that matter, I have a certain sort of visual experience. In the visual perception of the car I *don't see* the visual experience, I see the car; but in seeing the car I *have* a visual experience, and the visual experience is an experience of the car, in a sense of "of" we will need to explain. It is important to emphasize that though the visual perception always has as a component a visual experience, it is not the visual experience that is seen, in any literal sense of "see," for if I close my eyes the visual experience ceases, but the car, the thing I see, does not cease. Furthermore, in general it makes no sense to ascribe to the visual experience the properties of the thing that the visual experience is of, the thing that I see. For example, if the car is yellow and has a certain shape characteristic of a station wagon, then though my visual experience is of a yellow object in the shape of a station wagon it makes no sense to say my visual experience itself is yellow or that it is in the shape of a station wagon. Color and shape are properties accessible to vision, but though my visual experience is a component of any visual perception, the visual experience is not itself a visual object, it is not itself seen. If we try to deny this point we are placed in the absurd situation of identifying two yellow station wagon-shaped things in the perceptual situation, the yellow station wagon and the visual experience. . . . But at this point the classical epistemologist will surely want to object as follows: Suppose there is no car there; suppose the whole thing is a hallucination; what do you see then? And the answer is that if there is no car there, then in the car line of business I see nothing. It may seem to me exactly as if I were seeing a car, but if there is no car I don't see anything. I may see background foliage or a garage or a street, but if I am having a hallucination of a car then I don't see a car or a visual experience or a sense datum or an impression or anything else, though I do indeed *have* the visual experience and the visual experience may be indistinguishable from the visual experience I would have had if I had actually seen a car.

ASK YOURSELF

39. Is what Searle here calls a "visual experience" the same as what Locke calls an "idea"?

I want to argue for a point that has often been ignored in discussions of the philosophy of perception, namely that visual (and other sorts of perceptual) experiences have Intentionality. The visual experience is as much *directed at or of* objects and states of affairs in the world as any of the paradigm Intentional states . . . such as belief, fear, or desire. And the argument for this conclusion is simply that the visual experience has conditions of satisfaction in exactly the same sense that beliefs and desires have conditions of satisfaction. I can no more separate this visual experience from the fact that it is an experience of a yellow station wagon than I can separate this belief from the fact that it is a belief that it is raining; the "of" of "experience of" is in short the "of" of Intentionality. In both the cases of belief and visual experience I might be wrong about what states of affairs actually exist in the world. Perhaps I am having a hallucination and perhaps it isn't actually raining. But notice that in each case what counts as a mistake, whether a hallucination or a false belief, is already determined by the Intentional state or event in question. In the case of the beliefs even if I am in fact mistaken, I know what must be the case in order that I not be mistaken, and to say that is simply to say that the Intentional content of the belief determines its conditions of satisfaction; it determines under what conditions the belief is true or false . . . , even if I am having a hallucination, I know what must be the case in order that the experience not be a hallucination, and to say that is simply to say that the Intentional content of the visual experience determines its conditions of satisfaction; it determines what must be the case in order that the experience not be a hallucination in exactly the same sense that the content of the belief determines its conditions of satisfaction. Suppose we ask ourselves, "What makes the presence or absence of rain even relevant to my belief that it is raining, since after all, the belief is just a mental state?" Now, analogously, we can ask, "What makes the presence or absence of a yellow station wagon even relevant to my visual experience, since, after all, the visual experience is just a mental event?" And the answer in both cases is that the two forms of mental phenomena, belief and visual experience, are intrinsically Intentional.

Searle is pointing out that just as a belief is always a belief *that* something is so (for example, I believe *that* the cat is on the mat) or a fear is always *of* something, so visual experience is always experience *that* there is something, that there is a cat for instance, or of something. Experiences, beliefs, and other mental states or dispositions, as well as sentences, are all "*intentional*" in that they are about something, of something, directed at something. That is what the technical term "intentional" means here. The "conditions of satisfaction" for an intentional state involve whatever it would take to make a belief true or generally such as to make the state "fit" the world properly.

ASK YOURSELF

40. State what the conditions of satisfaction would be for the belief that there is a cat on the mat. If those conditions are satisfied, we would say that the belief is _____.

41. What would be the conditions of satisfaction for the *perception* that there is a cat on the mat? If those conditions are *not* satisfied, what might we say about that perception?

The characteristic philosophical mistake in the case of visual experience has been to suppose that the predicates which specify the conditions of satisfaction of the visual experience are literally true of the experience itself. But, to repeat a point mentioned earlier, it is a category mistake to suppose that when I see a yellow station wagon the visual experience itself is also yellow and in the shape of a station wagon. Just as when I believe that it is raining I do not literally have a wet belief, so when I see something yellow I do not literally have a yellow visual experience. One might as well say that my visual experience is six cylindered or that it gets twenty-two miles to the gallon as say that it is yellow or in the shape of a station wagon. One is tempted to the mistake of ascribing the latter (rather than the former) predicates to the visual experience, because the Intentional content specified by "yellow" and "in the shape of a station wagon" have greater immediacy to visual experiences than do the other predicates. . . .

If, when I perceive a yellow wagon, what I am directly aware of is an idea or sense datum, as Locke and Hume seem to claim, then that idea or datum must itself be yellow. Otherwise, where would the notion of the wagon's being yellow come from? But the notion of a yellow sense datum, or visual experience, is confused, Searle is claiming. My visual experience of a yellow car is no more yellow than it is six-cylindered (assuming the car has six cylinders). But what are some of the "conditions of satisfaction" of a visual experience?

It is part of the conditions of satisfaction (in the sense of requirement) of the visual experience that the visual experience must itself be caused by the rest of the conditions of satisfaction (in the sense of things required) of that visual experience. Thus, for example, if I see the yellow station wagon, I have a certain visual experience. But the Intentional content of the visual experience, which requires that there be a yellow station wagon in front of me in order that it be satisfied, also requires that the fact that there is a yellow station wagon in front of me must be the cause of that very visual experience. Thus, the Intentional content of the visual experience requires as part of the conditions of satisfaction that the visual experience be caused by the rest of its conditions of satisfaction, that is, by the state of affairs perceived.

Searle has just mentioned one way in which visual experiences differ from, say, beliefs. The conditions of satisfaction for the belief that the cat is on the mat include the fact that there really is a cat on the mat. But that fact does not have to directly *cause* the belief. The belief might be caused by any number of things, for example, a sound, or a report from someone. Visual experiences are not like that. That the wagon is yellow, and is before me, etc. must itself cause the experience of the wagon in order for the conditions of satisfaction to be met. If something else is causing the experience (for example, a drug that causes yellow-wagon hallucinations) then the conditions of satisfaction are not met.

ASK YOURSELF

42. What is one way beliefs differ from visual experiences?

Searle claims that visual experience is "causally self-referential." This means that one of the conditions of satisfaction for a visual experience is that it be caused by its intentional content.

Furthermore, when I say that the visual experience is causally self-referential I do not mean that the causal relation is seen, much less that the visual experience is seen. Rather, what is seen are objects and states of affairs, and part of the conditions of satisfaction of the visual experience of seeing them is that the experience itself must be caused by what is seen.

ASK YOURSELF

43. Try to think of an example of a visual experience such that the cause of that experience is *not* what is seen. Here is one: I have the visual experience of seeing a red object in front of me because I have red glasses on and the object is actually white.

Whatever other merits Searle's account of perception may have or lack, it at least avoids the traditional empiricist's assumption that I am never directly aware of anything outside my own mind. Of course this account does not itself tell us how we determine whether or not the conditions of satisfaction for any particular visual experience are satisfied.

Searle's discussion contains additional points of considerable interest. He shows that sense perception is more complicated than traditional empiricist accounts suppose. For example, my visual experiences are not just data impinging upon a "passive" mind, as Locke supposed. In fact, the content of my visual experiences and other sense experiences is determined in part by such things as my linguistic abilities, my expectations, and numerous other factors.

In my effort to give an account of the Intentionality of visual perception I am anxious not to make it look much simpler than it really is. In this section I want to call attention to some of the complexities, though the cases I mention here are only a few among many puzzles in the philosophy of perception.

We are tempted to think, *à la* Hume, that perceptions come to us pure and unsullied by language, and that we then attach labels by way of ostensive definitions to the results of our perceptual encounters. But that picture is false in a number of ways. First, there is the familiar point that perception is a function of expectation, and the expectations of human beings at least are normally realized linguistically. So language itself affects the perceptual encounter. Over a quarter of a century ago, Postman and Bruner did some experiments which showed that the recognition threshold for features varied greatly depending on whether or not the particular feature was expected in that situation. If the subject expects that the next color he is going to see is red, he will recognize it much more quickly than if he has no such expectations. But secondly and more importantly from our point of view, many of our visual experiences aren't even possible without the mastery of certain Background skills, and prominent among them are linguistic skills. Consider the following figure:

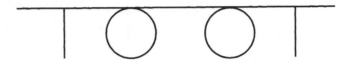

This can be seen as the word "TOOT," as a table with two large balloons underneath, as the number 1001 with a line over the top, as a bridge with two pipelines crossing underneath, as the eyes of a man wearing a hat with a string hanging down each side, and so on. In each case, we have a different experience even though the purely physical visual stimuli, the lines on the paper in front of us and the light reflected from them, are constant. But these experiences and the differences between them are dependent on our having mastered a series of linguistically impregnated cultural skills. It is not the failure, for example, of my dog's optical apparatus that prevents him from seeing this figure as the word "TOOT."

ASK YOURSELF

44. What then does prevent the dog from seeing this figure as the word "TOOT"?

In such a case one wants to say that a certain conceptual mastery is a precondition of having visual experience; and such cases suggest that the Intentionality of visual perception is tied up in all sorts of complicated ways with other forms of Intentionality such as belief and expectation, and also with our systems of representation, most notably language. Both the Network of Intentional states and the Background of non-representational mental capacities affect perception.

ASK YOURSELF

45. If you have studied the Plato selection, can you find anything in the preceding remarks that recalls Plato's discussion of the idea of equality?

There are at least three sorts of cases we will need to discuss. First, there are cases where the Network of beliefs and the Background actually affect the content of the visual experience. Consider, for example, the difference between looking at the front of a house where one takes it to be the front of a whole house and looking at the front of a house where one takes it to be a mere facade, e.g., as part of a movie set. If one believes one is seeing a whole house, the front of the house actually looks different from the way it looks if one believes one is seeing a false facade of a house, even though the optical stimuli may be identical in the two cases. And this difference in the actual character of the visual experiences is reflected in the differences between the two sets of conditions of satisfaction. It is part of the content of my visual experience when I look at a whole house that *I expect* the rest of the house to be there if, for example, I enter the house or go around to the back. In these sorts of cases the character of the visual experience and its conditions of satisfaction will be affected by the content of the beliefs that one has about the perceptual situation. I am not going beyond the content of my visual experience when I say, "I see a house" instead of "I see the facade of a house," for, though the optical stimuli may be the same, the conditions of satisfaction in the former case are that there should be a whole house there. I do not *infer* from the facade of the house to the presence of the house; I simply see a house.

A second sort of case arises where the content of the beliefs is actually inconsistent with the content of the visual experience. A good example is the appearance of the moon on the horizon. When one sees the moon on the horizon it looks a great deal bigger than it does when it is directly overhead. Yet though the visual experiences are different in the two cases there is no change in the content of one's beliefs. I do not believe the moon has grown on the horizon or shrunk overhead. Now in our first sort of example we saw there was no way we could carve off the content of the visual experience from the beliefs one has about it. The house actually looks different depending on what sort of beliefs we have about it. But in the second sort of case we want to say that the visual experience of the moon's size definitely changes with the moon's position and yet our beliefs remain constant. And what shall we say about the conditions of satisfaction of the visual experiences? Because of the holistic character of the Network of our Intentional states, we are inclined to say that the conditions of satisfaction of the visual experiences remain the same. Since we are not really at all inclined to believe that the moon has changed in size, we suppose that the two visual experiences have the same conditions of satisfaction. But I think in fact that is not the right way to describe the situation. Rather, it seems to me that where the Intentional content of our visual experience is in conflict with our beliefs, and where the beliefs override the visual experience, we nonetheless have the original Intentional content of the visual experience. The visual experiences do indeed have as part of their respective Intentional contents that the moon is smaller overhead than it is on the horizon, and the argument for this is that if we imagine that the visual experiences remained as they are now, but that the beliefs were absent, that we simply had no relevant beliefs, then we really would be inclined to believe that the moon had changed in size. It is only because we believe independently that the moon remains constant in size that we allow the Intentionality of belief to override the Intentionality of our visual experience. In these cases we believe that our eyes deceive us. . . . We have then a variety of ways in which the Network and Background of Intentionality are related to the character of the visual experience, and the character of the visual experience is related to its conditions of satisfaction.

1. The house example: Different beliefs cause different visual experiences with different conditions of satisfaction, even given the same optical stimuli.
2. The moon example: The same beliefs coexist—with different visual experiences— with different conditions of satisfaction even though the content of the experiences is inconsistent with the content of the beliefs and is overridden by the beliefs.
3. The triangle and "TOOT" examples: The same beliefs plus different visual experiences yield the same conditions of satisfaction of the visual experiences.

The account of visual perception that I have been arguing for so far is, I guess, a version of "naive" (direct, common sense) realism . . . the thesis I am arguing for concerning the

Intentionality of visual experience will perhaps be clearer if we digress a moment to contrast this naive realist view with its great historical rivals, the representative theory and phenomenalism. Both of these theories differ from naive realism in that they both treat the visual experience as itself the object of visual perception and thus they strip it of its Intentionality. According to them what is seen is always, strictly speaking, a visual experience (in various terminologies the visual experience has been called a "sensum" or a "sense datum," or an "impression"). They are thus confronted with a question that does not arise for the naive realist: What is the relationship between the sense data which we do see and the material object which apparently we do not see? This question does not arise for the naive realist because on his account we do not see sense data at all. We see material objects and other objects and states of affairs in the world, at least much of the time; and in the hallucination cases we don't see anything, though we do indeed *have* visual experiences in both cases.

ASK YOURSELF

46. Is the naive realist still confronted with the question, How do we distinguish cases where we do see something from cases where we do not, given that the perceptual experiences are the same? In answering this question use an example.

SUMMING UP RATIONALISM AND EMPIRICISM

Common sense tells us that some of our knowledge arises from experience. The notion of "experience" is vague but usually includes the idea of sense experience. Common sense also affirms that there is some knowledge that does not seem to arise from experience or the senses, such as mathematical knowledge. Also, scientific knowledge often seems to go beyond experience to a great extent. Empiricists like Locke struggle to maintain the thesis that all knowledge, or all significant or nontrivial knowledge, is grounded in sense experience. But sense experience is complex in ways that have sometimes been ignored by empiricists, as Searle shows. What I experience depends not just upon data impinging upon passive receptors but upon my background knowledge. This sort of fact was noticed even by such early rationalists as Plato, although Plato's attempt to account for that background knowledge would not be accepted by most contemporary philosophers. In various forms the old debate continues between rationalists and empiricists about the sources of knowledge.

**CAN OF
WORMS**

Inquiries into the sources of knowledge lead quite naturally to disputes about the nature of mind. Plato's conception of the mind or soul is central to his epistemology, and Searle's conception of belief and perception depends upon a central claim about "intentionality," which is explored further in Chapter 4. Locke thinks of the mind as primarily a passive receptor of sense data. Is it that, or is it an active processor of data? That part of metaphysics that deals with the nature of the mind is in fact important to many other subfields of philosophy. Even if we do have knowledge that does not arise from experience, as rationalists insist, it does not follow that rationalist accounts of that knowledge have been correct. This matter is explored further in the next section, where issues in the philosophy of language become prominent.

C. A PRIORI KNOWLEDGE

**QUESTIONS
TO DISCUSS**

a. I know that a part of a thing cannot be greater than (for example, bigger than) the whole thing. How do I know that? Through experience? If so, what experience?

b. If you counted out two beans, counted out two more, added them up, and got five, would that strange experience make you give up your belief that $2 + 2 = 4$?

c. Most, perhaps all, people believe that every event has a cause. Is that belief based upon experience? Try to think of argument for saying that it is not.

1. THE FORK: DAVID HUME

Earlier in this chapter we looked at Hume's skeptical views on the existence of an external world and on induction. In addition to pointing out the skeptical problems with our reasoning process, Hume also attempted to illuminate what good reasoning consists of. According to Hume, two—and only two—types of knowledge are possible: (1) reasoning about relations of ideas—such as is found in mathematics and logic—and (2) reasoning about matters of fact—things or events in the world. These two kinds of knowledge have been compared to two prongs of a fork, and in recent years this idea that knowledge must be divided into these two categories has been accordingly dubbed "Hume's fork." Hume draws this distinction near the outset of his *Enquiry Concerning Human Understanding* (1748).

FROM DAVID HUME, *Enquiry Concerning Human Understanding* (1748),
SECTIONS 4 AND 12

All the objects of human reason or enquiry may naturally be divided into two kinds, to wit, *relations of ideas* and *matters of act*. Of the first kind are the sciences of Geometry, Algebra, and Arithmetic; and in short, every affirmation which is either intuitively or demonstratively certain. *That the square of the hypotenuse is equal to the square of the two sides,* is a proposition which expresses a relation between these figures. *That three times five is equal to the half of thirty,* expresses a relation between these numbers. Propositions of this kind are discoverable by the mere operation of thought, without dependence on what is anywhere existent in the universe. Though there never were a circle or triangle in nature, the truths demonstrated by Euclid would forever retain their certainty and evidence.

Matters of fact, which are the second objects of human reason, are not ascertained in the same manner; nor is our evidence of their truth, however great, of a like nature with the foregoing. The contrary of every matter of fact is still possible; because it can never imply a contradiction, and is conceived by the mind with the same facility and distinctness, as if ever so conformable to reality. *That the sun will not rise tomorrow* is no less intelligible a proposition, and implies no more contradiction than the affirmation, *that it will rise.* We should in vain, therefore, attempt to demonstrate its falsehood. Were it demonstratively false, it would imply a contradiction, and could never be distinctly conceived by the mind.

47. What is the principal feature that distinguishes matters of fact from relations of ideas?

At the close of his *Enquiry,* Hume reiterates the rigid distinction between relations of ideas and matters of fact, and he explains why only relations of ideas produce certainty.

[Matters of fact] are evidently incapable of demonstration. Whatever *is* may *not be*. No negation of a fact can involve a contradiction. The non-existence of any being, without exception, is as clear and distinct an idea as its existence. The proposition, which affirms it not to be, however false, is no less conceivable and intelligible, than that which affirms it to be. The case is different with the sciences [involving relations of ideas], properly so called. Every proposition, which is not true, is there confused and unintelligible. That the cube root of 64 is equal to the half of 10, is a false proposition, and can never be distinctly conceived. But that Caesar, or the angel Gabriel, or any being never existed, may be a false proposition, but still is perfectly conceivable, and implies no contradiction.

The existence, therefore, of any being can only be proved by arguments from its cause or its effect; and these arguments are founded entirely on experience. If we reason *a priori,* any thing may appear able to produce any thing. The falling of a pebble may, for aught we know, extinguish the sun; or the wish of a man control the planets in their orbits. It is only experience, which teaches us the nature and bounds of cause and effect, and enables us to infer the existence of one object from that of another.

48. Compare "George Washington was not the first President" to "George Washington was not George Washington." Both of these are false. But only one of them can be known with certainty to be false. Which one and why?

Hume goes on to mention various kinds of legitimate knowledge that are grounded in either relations of ideas or matters of fact—such as natural science, political theory, history, and ethics. However, he rejects any remaining areas of study that include claims to having established truths about the world but that are not grounded in relations of ideas or matters of fact.

When we run over libraries, persuaded of these principles, what havoc must we make? If we take in our hand any volume; of divinity or school metaphysics, for instance; let us ask, *Does it contain any abstract reasoning concerning quantity or number?* No. *Does it contain any experimental reasoning concerning matter of fact and existence?* No. Commit it then to the flames: For it can contain nothing but sophistry and illusion.

49. What does Hume suggest that we do with books that aren't grounded in relations of ideas or matters of fact?

Thus Hume makes a sharp distinction between two kinds of knowledge. One kind is certain but includes no information about what the world is like. In that sense it is trivial, in the way that "all bachelors are unmarried" is trivial, even though certainly true. The other kind includes claims about what the world is like, but those claims can never be known to be true for certain, as Hume's skeptical arguments have purportedly shown. Everything that can reasonably be counted as knowledge must fall under one kind or the other. No third option is available.

2. ANALYTIC AND SYNTHETIC JUDGMENTS: IMMANUEL KANT

The German philosopher Immanuel Kant (1724–1804) wrote that he was awakened from his "dogmatic slumbers" by reading Hume. He believed that Hume had made a solid case for such skeptical claims as that we have no sufficient basis in experience for our causal beliefs, our beliefs in an enduring external world, and our beliefs in a substantial persisting self. However, Kant believed that we did in some sense have such knowledge. Therefore it must not arise from experience. How then should we account for it? In the following selections from his *Prolegomena to Any Future Metaphysics* (1783) Kant addresses this question by first establishing some terminology and conceptual distinctions.

IMMANUEL KANT (1724–1804)

German philosopher and author of the Critique of Pure Reason (1781).

Analytic Judgments. Kant distinguishes between two types of judgments: analytic and synthetic. Analytic judgments involve statements in which the predicate is contained in the subject, such as "All bachelors are unmarried men" and "triangles have three angles." These statements are true or false based on the definitions of the words themselves; they also do not provide any new information beyond what is already included in the subject term of the statement. Synthetic statements, by contrast, do not have the predicate contained in the subject. An example would be "the door is brown." As such, they are not true by definition; for example, the notion of "brown" is not included in the definition of "door." Furthermore, synthetic statements provide us with real information about objects—in this case, information that a particular object is brown.

FROM IMMANUEL KANT, *Prolegomena to Any Future Metaphysics* (1783), SECTIONS 2 AND 5

Of the Distinction between Analytic and Synthetic judgments in general. The peculiarity of its sources demands that metaphysical cognition must consist of nothing but *a priori* judgments. But whatever be their origin, or their logical form, there is a distinction in judgments, as to their content, according to which they are either merely explicative, adding nothing to the content of the cognition, or expansive, increasing the given cognition: the former may be called analytic, the latter synthetic, judgments.

Analytic judgments express nothing in the predicate but what has been already actually thought in the concept of the subject, though not so distinctly or with the same (full) consciousness. When I say: All bodies are extended, I have not amplified in the least my concept of body, but have only analyzed it, as extension was really thought to belong to that concept before the judgment was made, though it was not expressed, this judgment is therefore analytic. On the contrary, this judgment, All bodies have weight, contains in its predicate something not actually thought in the general concept of the body; it amplifies my knowledge by adding something to my concept, and must therefore be called synthetic.

The Common Principle of all Analytic Judgments is the Law of Contradiction. All analytic judgments depend wholly on the law of Contradiction, and are in their nature *a priori* cognitions, whether the concepts that supply them with matter be empirical or not. For the predicate of an affirmative analytic judgment is already contained in the concept of the subject, of which it cannot be denied without contradiction. In the same way its opposite is necessarily denied of the subject in an analytic, but negative, judgment, by the same law of contradiction. Such is the nature of the judgments: all bodies are extended, and no bodies are unextended (i.e., simple).

For this very reason all analytic judgments are *a priori* even when the concepts are empirical, as, for example, Gold is a yellow metal; for to know this I require no experience beyond my concept of gold as a yellow metal: it is, in fact, the very concept, and I need only analyze it, without looking beyond it elsewhere.

ASK YOURSELF

50. You may recall that Hume claimed that all statements about matters of fact can be denied without contradiction. Definitions, on his account, could *not* be denied without contradiction. Is Kant using the same criteria in order to determine which judgments are synthetic judgments?

51. Give one example of an analytic judgment.

Synthetic Judgments. Turning to synthetic judgments, Kant notes that the most obvious kind of synthetic judgments are empirical (*a posteriori*), such as "the door is brown," which we know through visual experience. However, in addition to empirical judgements, Kant argues that mathematical and metaphysical judgments are also synthetic.

Syntheic judgments require a different Principle from the Law of Contradiction. There are synthetic *a posteriori* judgments of empirical origin; but there are also others which are proved to be certain *a priori,* and which spring from pure Understanding and Reason. Yet they both agree in this, that they cannot possibly spring from the principle of analysis, viz., the law of contradiction, alone; they require a quite different principle, though, from whatever they may be deduced, they must be subject to the law of contradiction, which must never be violated, even though everything cannot be deduced from it. I shall first classify synthetic judgments.

1. *Empirical judgments* are always synthetic. For it would be absurd to base an analytic judgment on experience, as our concept suffices for the purpose without requiring any testimony from experience. . . .

2. *Mathematical judgments* are all synthetic. This fact seems hitherto to have altogether escaped the observation of those who have analyzed human reason; it even seems directly opposed to all their conjectures, though incontestably certain, and most important in its consequences. For as it was found that the conclusions of mathematicians all proceed according to the law of contradiction (as is demanded by all apodictic certainty), men persuaded themselves that the fundamental principles were known from the same law. This was a great mistake, for a synthetic proposition can indeed be comprehended according to the law of

contradiction, but only by presupposing another synthetic proposition from which it follows, but never in itself. . . .

It might at first be thought that the proposition 7 + 5 = 12 is a mere analytic judgment, following from the concept of the sum of seven and five, according to the law of contradiction. But on closer examination it appears that the concept of the sum of 7 + 5 contains merely their union in a single number, without its being at all thought what the particular number is that unites them. The concept of twelve is by no means thought by merely thinking of the combination of seven and five; and analyze this possible sum as we may, we shall not discover twelve in the concept. We must go beyond these concepts, by calling to our aid some concrete image, i.e., either our five fingers, or five points (as Segner has it in his Arithmetic), and we must add successively the units of the five, given in some concrete image, to the concept of seven. Hence our concept is really amplified by the proposition 7 + 5 = 12, and we add to the first a second, not thought in it. Arithmetical judgments are therefore synthetic, and the more plainly according as we take larger numbers; for in such cases it is clear that, however closely we analyze our concepts without calling visual images to our aid, we can never find the sum by such mere dissection.

ASK YOURSELF

52. Hume thought that mathematical judgments are "analytic" (though he did not use that term). Kant believes that they are synthetic. Illustrating his point with the proposition "7 + 5 = 12," what does he say about the relation between the predicate "12" and the subject "7 + 5"?

Metaphysical Synthetic *A Priori* Judgments. Like mathematical judgments, Kant believes that metaphysical judgments are also synthetic *a priori*. That is, they are non-empirical yet some of them provide us with genuine information. They are not all false, and they are not just trivially true, as are analytic judgments.

Metaphysical judgments, properly so called, are all synthetic. . . . Thus the judgment, that all the substance in things is permanent, is a synthetic and properly metaphysical judgment. . . .

The conclusion drawn in this section, then, is that metaphysics is properly concerned with synthetic propositions *a priori,* and these alone constitute its end . . . the generation of *a priori* cognition by concrete images as well as by concepts, in fine of synthetic propositions *a priori* in philosophical cognition, constitutes the essential subject of Metaphysics.

ASK YOURSELF

53. Give one of Kant's examples of a synthetic metaphysical judgment.

Kant argues that the success of metaphysics depends on our ability to show how synthetic *a priori* judgments are even possible. That is, we need to see how the mechanism of human reason provides us with non-empirical knowledge that is not trivial but has an application to the empirical world. Otherwise put, Kant wants to add a third prong to Hume's fork. He wants to do something that Hume insisted absolutely could not be done.

ASK YOURSELF

54. One prong of "Kant's fork" would consist of "analytic *a priori* judgments." Using Kant's terminology, list the other two prongs of "Kant's fork."

We have above learned the significant distinction between analytic and synthetic judgments. The possibility of analytic propositions was easily comprehended, being entirely founded on the law of Contradiction. The possibility of synthetic *a posteriori* judgments, of those which are gathered from experience, also requires no particular explanation; for experience is nothing but a continual synthesis of perceptions. There remain therefore only synthetic propositions *a priori,* of which the possibility must be sought or investigated, because they must depend upon principles other than the law of contradiction.

But here we need not first establish the possibility of such propositions so as to ask whether they are possible. For there are enough of them which indeed are of undoubted certainty, and as our present method is analytic, we shall start from the fact, that such synthetic but purely rational cognition actually exists; but we must now inquire into the reason of this possibility, and ask, *how* such cognition is possible, in order that we may from the principles of its possibility be enabled to determine the conditions of its use, its sphere and its limits. The proper problem upon which all depends, when expressed with scholastic precision, is therefore: *How* are *Synthetic Propositions a priori possible?* . . .

Metaphysics stands or falls with the solution of this problem: its very existence depends upon it.

To answer the crucial question of how synthetic *a priori* judgments are possible, Kant devises a very complex argument. In a nutshell, he shows that such synthetic *a priori* statements as "all events have a cause" (a statement Hume said we could not know to be true) *must* be true since if they were not, we would not be able to experience the world as we in fact do. Kant's arguments are not presented in this book, but they have been of great historical importance. They assume that the mind is not passive in experience, as Locke supposed, but is rather active. The mind's activity consists in imposing a kind of structure upon experience. If you look at the drawing in Searle's article on the intentionality of perception earlier in this chapter, you will see how some of our experience or perceptions depend upon what we bring to them, our "mental set" so to speak. It is impossible to experience anything without some such mental set. Kant operates with a similar notion but at a very high level of generality. Thus there is a universal "mind set" that structures experience in terms of cause–effect relations and in terms of other categories.

3. ONE DOGMA OF EMPIRICISM: WILLARD VAN ORMAN QUINE

Willard Van Orman Quine (1908–2001) became critical of some of the main features of the empiricist tradition. He was particularly anxious to avoid any philosophical "dogmas" that depend upon the notion of meaning, such as the analytic–synthetic distinction. His attack on that distinction also strikes at Kant, to the extent that Kant's views also depended upon such a distinction. In a famous article entitled "Two Dogmas of Empiricism," Quine attacked the two central assumptions made by empiricists. The first is the analytic–synthetic distinction. The second is the claim that all genuine factual knowledge must be traceable back to immediate experience. Thus, Quine attacks "Hume's fork" by breaking both prongs, rather than adding a third one as Kant did. Quine denies that there is any genuinely *a priori* knowledge. But neither is there *a posteriori* knowledge in the sense Hume supposed. However, Quine is not a skeptic. He believes scientific knowledge is possible but that it cannot be carved up into *a priori* and *a posteriori* parts.

FROM WILLARD VAN ORMAN QUINE, "Two Dogmas of Empiricism" (1951)

Modern empiricism has been conditioned in large part by two dogmas. One is a belief in some fundamental cleavage between truths which are analytic, or grounded in meanings independently of matters of fact and truths which are synthetic, or grounded in fact. The other dogma is reductionism: the belief that each meaningful statement is equivalent to some logical construct upon terms which refer to immediate experience. Both dogmas, I shall argue, are ill founded. One effect of abandoning them is, as we shall see, a blurring of the supposed boundary between speculative metaphysics and natural science. Another effect is a shift toward pragmatism.

The Analytic–Synthetic Distinction. Quine intends to dismantle this distinction, which played a crucial role in both rationalist and empiricist philosophy.

Kant's cleavage between analytic and synthetic truths was foreshadowed in Hume's distinction between relations of ideas and matters of fact, and in Leibniz's distinction between truths of reason and truths of fact. Leibniz spoke of the truths of reason as true in all possible worlds. Picturesqueness aside, this is to say that the truths of reason are those which could not possibly be false. In the same vein we hear analytic statements defined as statements whose denials are self-contradictory. But this definition has small explanatory value; for the notion of self-contradictoriness, in the quite broad sense needed for this definition of analyticity, stands in exactly the same need of clarification as does the notion of analyticity itself. The two notions are the two sides of a single dubious coin.

   Kant conceived of an analytic statement as one that attributes to its subject no more than is already conceptually contained in the subject. This formulation has two shortcomings: it limits itself to statements of subject-predicate form, and it appeals to a notion of containment which is left at a metaphorical level. But Kant's intent, evident more from the use he makes of the notion of analyticity than from his definition of it, can be restated thus: a statement is analytic when it is true by virtue of meanings and independently of fact. Pursuing this line, let us examine the concept of meaning which is presupposed.

Meaning and Naming Must Be Distinguished. Quine's strategy depends upon a distinction between the reference of terms and their meaning.

We must observe to begin with that meaning is not to be identified with naming or reference. Consider Frege's example of "Evening Star" and "Morning Star." Understood not merely as a recurrent evening apparition but as a body, the Evening Star is the planet Venus, and the Morning Star is the same. The two singular terms name the same thing. But the meanings must be treated as distinct, since the identity "Evening Star = Morning Star" is a statement of fact established by astronomical observation. If "Evening Star" and "Morning Star" were alike in meaning, the identity "Evening Star = Morning Star" would be analytic.

   . . . The distinction between meaning and naming is no less important at the level of abstract terms. The terms "9" and "the number of planets" name one and the same abstract entity but presumably must be regarded as unlike in meaning; for astronomical observation was needed, and not mere reflection on meanings, to determine the sameness of the entity in question.

"Bachelors are unmarried" is often proposed as an analytic statement—that is, a statement true by virtue of the meanings of "bachelor" and "unmarried." One can know such statements to be true just by thinking about the meanings of their terms. "It is raining," on the other hand, if it is true at all, is so not because of meanings but because of how the weather is as a matter of empirical fact. But Quine thinks the relevant notion of "meaning" is unexplained. Would a plausible explanation be that the meaning of a word is its reference, with the result that analytic statements are true because they contain terms having the same *reference?*

ASK YOURSELF

55. Meaning, Quine argues, is not a matter of reference since, to take but one example, "evening star" and "morning star" have the same reference, but obviously "the morning star is identical with the evening star" (both terms refer to Venus), though true, is not true by virtue of _____ and is thus obviously not analytic. In fact it was only discovered to be true long after people knew the "meaning" of its key expressions.

With general terms, or predicates [e.g., "Brown," "dog"], the situation is somewhat different but parallel. Whereas a singular term purports to name an entity, abstract or concrete, a general term does not; but a general term is true of an entity, or of each of many, or of none. The class of all entities of which a general term is true is called the extension of the term. Now paralleling the contrast between the meaning of a singular term and the entity named, we must distinguish equally between the meaning of a general term and its extension. The general terms "creature with a heart" and "creature with a kidney," e.g., are perhaps alike in extension but unlike in meaning.

ASK YOURSELF

56. To say that these two terms are alike in "extension" is to say that they are _____ of all and only the same _____.

It follows that meaning the same cannot be reduced to having the same extension; otherwise, "All creatures with a heart are creatures with a kidney" would be analytic, or true by definition, which it clearly is not.

Confusion of meaning with extension, in the case of general terms, is less common than confusion of meaning with naming in the case of singular terms. It is indeed a commonplace in philosophy to oppose intention (or meaning) to extension, or, in a variant vocabulary, connotation to denotation.

. . . For the theory of meaning the most conspicuous question is as to the nature of its objects: what sort of things are meanings? They are evidently intended to be ideas, somehow—mental ideas for some semanticists, Platonic ideas for others. Objects of either sort are so elusive, not to say debatable, that there seems little hope of erecting a fruitful science about them. It is not even clear, granted meanings, when we have two and when we have one; it is not clear when linguistic forms should be regarded as synonymous, or alike in meaning, and when they should not. If a standard of synonymy should be arrived at, we may reasonably expect that the appeal to meanings as entities will not have played a very useful part in the enterprise.

A felt need for meant entities may derive from an earlier failure to appreciate that meaning and reference are distinct. Once the theory of meaning is sharply separated from the theory of reference, it is a short step to recognizing as the business of the theory of meaning simply the synonymy of linguistic forms and the analyticity of statements; meanings themselves, as obscure intermediate entities, may well be abandoned. The description of analyticity as truth by virtue of meanings started us off in pursuit of a concept of meaning. But now we have abandoned the thought of any special realm of entities called meanings. So the problem of analyticity confronts us anew.

Statements which are analytic by general philosophical acclaim are not, indeed, far to seek. They fall into two classes. Those of the first class, which may be called logically true, are typified by:

1. No unmarried man is married.

The relevant feature of this example is that it is not merely true as it stands, but remains true under any and all reinterpretations of "man" and "married." If we suppose a prior inventory of logical particles, comprising "no," "un-" "if," "then," "and," etc., then in general a logical truth is a statement which is true and remains true under all reinterpretations of its components other than the logical particles.

ASK YOURSELF

57. A "reinterpretation" of the components of (1) might be "No unintelligent man is _____."

But there is also a second class of analytic statements, typified by:

2. No bachelor is married.

The characteristic of such a statement is that it can be turned into a logical truth by putting synonyms for synonyms; thus (2) can be turned into (1) by putting "unmarried man" for its synonym "bachelor." We still lack a proper characterization of this second class of analytic statements, and therewith of analyticity generally, inasmuch as we have had in the above description to lean on a notion of "synonymy" which is no less in need of clarification than analyticity itself.

Analytic statements are said to be true by definition. Does that explain anything? Only if we can make sense of the notion of synonymy.

The Notion of Synonymy. This notion is as obscure as the notion of meaning.

There are those who find it soothing to say that the analytic statements of the second class reduce to those of the first class, the logical truths, by definition; "bachelor," for example, is defined as "unmarried man." But how do we find that "bachelor" is defined as "unmarried man"? Who defined it thus, and when? Are we to appeal to the nearest dictionary, and accept the lexicographer's formulation as law? Clearly this would be to put the cart before the horse. The lexicographer is an empirical scientist, whose business is the recording of antecedent facts; and if he glosses "bachelor" as "unmarried man" it is because of his belief that there is a relation of synonymy between these forms, implicit in general or preferred usage prior to his own work. The notion of synonymy presupposed here has still to be clarified, presumably in terms relating to linguistic behavior. Certainly the "definition" which is the lexicographer's report of an observed synonymy cannot be taken as the ground of the synonymy.

. . . Just what it means to affirm synonymy, just what the interconnections may be which are necessary and sufficient in order that two linguistic forms be properly describable as synonymous, is far from clear; but, whatever these interconnections may be, ordinarily they are grounded in usage. Definitions reporting selected instances of synonymy come then as reports upon usage.

ASK YOURSELF

58. The lexicographer defines "bachelor" as "unmarried man" because he thinks there is a relation of _____ between them.

Quine goes on to consider variations on the idea that analytic truths are true by definition. All of them depend upon an unexplained notion of synonymy.

In formal and informal work alike, thus, we find that definition—except in the extreme case of the explicitly conventional introduction of new notation—hinges on prior relationships of synonymy. Recognizing then that the notation of definition does not hold the key to synonymy and analyticity, let us look further into synonymy and say no more of definition.

Perhaps two terms are synonymous if they are interchangeable. Then to say that "*all bachelors are unmarried male adults* is analytic" is simply to say that its terms ("bachelor" and "unmarried male adult") are interchangeable or can be substituted for one another in any sentence without changing the meaning.

Interchangeability Depends upon the Notion of Synonymy. This maneuver does not help, Quine claims, since we only know what terms are interchangeable if we know they are synonymous. And synonymy continues to be obscure.

A natural suggestion, deserving close examination, is that the synonymy of two linguistic forms consists simply in their interchangeability in all contexts without change of truth value; interchangeability, in Leibniz's phrase, salva veritate. Note that synonyms so conceived need not even be free from vagueness, as long as the vaguenesses match. . . .

The question remains whether interchangeability salva veritate (apart from occurrences within words) is a strong enough condition for synonymy, or whether, on the contrary, some non-synonymous expressions might be thus interchangeable. Now let us be clear that we are not concerned here with synonymy in the sense of complete identity in psychological associations or poetic quality; indeed no two expressions are synonymous in such a sense. We are concerned only with what may be called cognitive synonymy. Just what this is cannot be said without successfully finishing the present study.

ASK YOURSELF

59. If there are 9 planets going around the sun, then you might think that "9" would be interchangeable with "the number of the planets" salva veritate (i.e., preserving truth) in any sentence. But consider the following two sentences, and suppose the first one is true: (1) Bill knows that 9 is greater than 8. (2) Bill knows that the number of the planets is greater than 8. Notice that the only difference between them is that in (2) we substituted "the number of the planets" for "9" in statement (1). Explain how (2) might be false even though (1) is true. Does that show that "9" is not interchangeable with "the number of the planets" in all sentences?

Quine goes on to consider various explanations of interchangeability. The following seems to be the most promising.

Interchangeability salva veritate is meaningless until relativized to a language whose extent is specified in relevant respects. Suppose now we consider a language containing just the following materials. There is an indefinitely large stock of one- and many-place predicates mostly having to do with extralogical subject matter. The rest of the language is logical. The atomic sentences consist each of a predicate followed by one or more variables "x," "y," etc.; and the complex sentences are built up of atomic ones by truth functions ("not," "and," "or," etc.) and quantification. In effect such a language enjoys the benefits also of descriptions and class names and indeed singular terms generally, these being contextually definable in known ways.

The following would be an example of the sort of language Quine is describing: "There is at least one x such that x is brown, and x is clever." The truth of this sentence is a function of its parts, namely "there is at least one x (this is called a quantifier) such that x is brown" and "x is clever." ("brown" is a "one place predicate"). The logical term "and" is such that in this sentence both parts would have to be true for the whole sentence to be true. It is what logicians call a "conjunction," and conjunctions are always such that they are true only when both conjuncts are true.

Now a language of this type is extensional, in this sense: any two predicates which agree extensionally (that is, are true of the same objects) are interchangeable salva veritate. In an extensional language, therefore, interchangeability salva veritate is no assurance of cognitive synonymy of the desired type. That "bachelor" and "unmarried man" are interchangeable salva veritate in an extensional language assures us of no more than that ["all bachelors are unmarried"] is true. There is no assurance here that the extensional agreement of "bachelor" and "unmarried man" rests on meaning rather than merely on accidental matters of fact, as does extensional agreement of "creature with a heart" and "creature with a kidney."

ASK YOURSELF

60. Quine is claiming that since "creature with a heart" and "creature with a kidney" refer to all and only the same entities, and thus are "extensionally equivalent," then we cannot explain synonymy in terms of extensional _____. For it is obvious that these two expressions are not _____.

For most purposes extensional agreement is the nearest approximation to synonymy we need care about. But the fact remains that extensional agreement falls far short of cognitive synonymy of the type required for explaining analyticity in the manner of Section I. The type of cognitive synonymy required there is such as to equate the synonymy of "bachelor" and "unmarried man" with the analyticity of (3), not merely with the truth of (3).

So we must recognize that interchangeability salva veritate, if construed in relation to an extensional language, is not a sufficient condition of cognitive synonymy in the sense needed for deriving analyticity in the manner of Section I.

Quine goes on to consider whether an adequate account of "analytic" might be given for artificial or precisely defined languages. He concludes that such attempts to salvage analyticity also fail.

So—and this is the point—the famous distinction between analytic truths and synthetic truths has collapsed. This idea was a "dogma of empiricism" since it allowed people like Hume to account for the fact that some statements (for example, "$2 + 2 = 4$" or "all bachelors are unmarried") are supposedly known independently of experience, without falling back into rationalist accounts of knowledge. But Quine has argued we cannot maintain a distinction between what is known on the basis of experience and what is not. In fact, he argues, it cannot be maintained at all, in any way. Hume's fork does not exist. Neither does Kant's.

SUMMING UP *A PRIORI* KNOWLEDGE

Both empiricists and rationalists have noticed that there are some things we know, such as that $2 + 2 = 4$, which do not seem to depend upon or be derived from experience. Empiricists like Hume try to show that such knowledge is basically trivial, something like a matter of definition. Thus they can continue to assert that all significant knowledge is based on experience. Kant accepts at least part of the empiricist account, but he thought that *a priori* knowledge extended to nontrivial matters and that some *a priori* knowledge is not just a matter of grasping definitions. Such knowledge is "synthetic *a priori*." Knowledge that all bachelors are unmarried, however, is "analytic *a priori*" and is indeed trivial. Quine attacks the distinction between analytic and synthetic. It rests on confusions about meaning and reference. There is no clearly *a priori* knowledge, on his view. It does not follow, however, that all real knowledge is based on foundational sense data claims. If that is what is meant by *a posteriori* knowledge, then that idea is also confused, on his account.

CAN OF WORMS

Kant and Hume both deny that knowledge of God or direct knowledge of such things as the soul, the enduring self, or real causal connections in nature is possible. Their epistemological views thus lead to drastically reduced metaphysical schemes when we compare those views to some other philosophical views, or even to common sense views. Quine, on the other hand, is willing to accept just as much ontology as is required for science, and no more. His views on epistemology are directly linked to developments in the philosophy of language and to developments in logic in the twentieth century. Metaphysics, philosophy of science, philosophy of language, and logic are intertwined.

D. FOUNDATIONALISM AND COHERENCE

Much of modern epistemology has consisted of trying to find some sort of criteria for knowledge that would enable us to resist skepticism. In this section we consider two competing approaches to that project. Foundationalists in epistemology believe that knowledge claims must have secure foundations. What sort of foundations? We have already seen that Locke believes that knowledge can be founded upon experience. Thus if I really *know* that Napoleon was a general, I must be able to justify this claim. I do this either by referring to actual experiences of my own, such as seeing Napoleon leading troops, or by referring, through some chain of witnesses, to the actual experiences of others. Sense experience, then, is "foundational" for Locke. He was an *empiricist* foundationalist. One problem with Locke's view is that it is subject to skeptical challenge. Why should anyone trust sense experiences? We have seen why Sextus and Hume doubt that sense experience can provide a firm foundation for knowledge. Moreover the notion of "experience" may be more complicated than Locke realizes, as Searle and Kant argued. Experience, as Locke understood the notion, is just one possible foundation of knowledge. Descartes offered an alternative conception of foundationalism.

But coherentists have rejected the basic foundationalist assumption that knowledge requires certain privileged foundational statements that are known directly either through the senses or through rational intuition. Rather, knowledge requires "coherence" in a sense explained below.

QUESTIONS TO DISCUSS

a. Is your belief that there are such things as light waves based upon experience? Your own? Someone else's?

b. Sherlock Holmes put together pieces of evidence in somewhat the way one puts together pieces of a puzzle in order to get to a correct "picture" of a criminal. For example, one of the "pieces" might have been a necklace found at a murder scene. From such a find he might make inferences that would lead to further inferences, and so forth, until he concludes that the murderer is, say, the butler. Should he have made sure that he had unassailable evidence that what he found was indeed a necklace, or even a physical object, before he started the chain of inferences?

c. Suppose that Sherlock justified his claim that the necklace was evidence for something by showing how its presence at the murder scene fit together with other pieces of evidence. Does that sound to you like a good way to proceed?

1. FOUNDATIONALISM: RENÉ DESCARTES AND JOHN LOCKE

In the opening section of this chapter, we looked at Descartes' provisional attempt to show skepticism at its very best—most notably through the hypotheses that all is a dream, or that an evil genius might be deceiving us about everything we believe. Descartes' point is that sense experience offers a shoddy foundation for knowledge. In fact it collapses into skepticism. He continues, though, by proposing an alternative—and in his view more rational—foundation.

Extent of His Doubt. After engaging in his skeptical exercise, Descartes describes the extent of his doubt. Virtually every item of knowledge that he previously believed is subject to some kind of doubt.

Descartes   Logically-Challenged   Short Attention   Multiple Personality   The Little Descartes
                     Descartes   Span Descartes   Descartes   That Could

FROM RENÉ DESCARTES, *Meditations on the First Philosophy* (1641), MEDITATIONS 2 AND 3

The Meditation of yesterday filled my mind with so many doubts that it is no longer in my power to forget them. And yet I do not see in what manner I can resolve them. And, just as if I had all of a sudden fallen into very deep water, I am so baffled that I can neither make certain of setting my feet on the bottom, nor can I swim and so support myself on the surface. I will nevertheless make an effort and follow anew the same path as that on which I yesterday entered, that is, I will proceed by setting aside all that in which the least doubt could be supposed to exist, just as if I had discovered that it was absolutely false. And I will ever follow in this road until I have met with something which is certain, or at least, if I can do nothing else, until I have learned for certain that there is nothing in the world that is certain. Archimedes, in order that he might draw the terrestrial globe out of its place, and transport it elsewhere, demanded only that one point should be fixed and immovable. In the same way I will have the right to conceive high hopes if I am happy enough to discover one thing only which is certain and indubitable.

I suppose, then, that all the things that I see are false; I persuade myself that nothing has ever existed of all that my fallacious memory represents to me. I consider that I possess no senses; I imagine that body, figure, extension, movement and place are but the fictions of my mind. What, then, can be distinguished as true? Perhaps nothing at all, unless that there is nothing in the world that is certain.

ASK YOURSELF

61. Archimedes was an ancient Greek engineer who said "give me a fulcrum and a firm point, and I alone can move the earth." Finish this analogy: Archimedes' ability to move the world is to a firm and immovable point just as a true philosophical system (that is, "high hopes") is to _____.

62. What are the various things that Descartes doubts at this point in his quest?

But how can I know there is not something different from those things that I have just considered, of which one cannot have the slightest doubt? Is there not some God, or some other being by whatever name we call it, who puts these reflections into my mind? That is not necessary, for is it not possible that I am capable of producing them myself? I myself, am I not at least something? But I have already denied that I had senses and body. Yet I hesitate, for what follows from that? Am I so dependent on body and senses that I cannot exist without these? But I was persuaded that there was nothing in all the world, that there was no heaven, no earth, that there were no minds, nor any bodies: was I not then likewise persuaded that I did not exist? Not at all; of a surety I myself did exist since I persuaded myself of something. But there is some deceiver or other, very powerful and very cunning, who ever employs his ingenuity in deceiving me. Then without doubt I exist also if he deceives me, and let him deceive me as much as he will, he can never cause me to be nothing so long as I think that I am something. So that after having reflected well and carefully examined all things, we must come to the definite conclusion that this proposition: I am, I exist, is necessarily true each time that I pronounce it, or that I mentally conceive it.

ASK YOURSELF

ASK YOURSELF

63. The one thing Descartes recognizes that he can never doubt is the fact that he exists. Why could he not doubt it? Why could an evil demon not have deceived him about this fact?

In his *Discourse on Method,* Descartes summarizes the above line of reasoning in the famous phrase, "I think, therefore I am" (or in Latin, *"cogito ergo sum"*). Descartes borrowed this strategy from Augustine's attempt to refute skepticism in his own day. Augustine writes, "On none of these points do I fear the arguments of the skeptics of the Academy who say: what if you are deceived? For if I am deceived, I am. For he who does not exist cannot be deceived. And if I am deceived, by this same token I am" (*City of God,* 11:26).

Descartes now thinks that he has a foundation upon which he can build. Various commentators have contested whether he does indeed have such a foundation. Some have doubted whether we have any clear idea of the "I" in "I exist" and have claimed that Descartes could just as well have argued that "it thinks, therefore it exists," and it is very unclear just what that "it" might be. Others have argued that if only I exist, I would not be able to even state what is in my mind, such as that a doubt is in my mind. As Ludwig Wittgenstein argued, in order to state anything, I must know a language and, in order to know a language, I must live in a community of other people. But Descartes explicitly denies that I can know such things prior to knowing my own existence.

Some philosophers grant, perhaps just for the sake of argument, that Descartes has discovered a single secure truth, "I exist." Nevertheless, they criticize Descartes' attempt to build further truths on that one foundational truth. Here is an example of how he proceeds in his attempt to build more knowledge upon this foundational truth.

But in order that an idea should contain some one certain objective reality rather than another, it must without doubt derive it from some cause in which there is at least as much formal reality as this idea contains of objective reality. For if we imagine that something is found in an idea which is not found in the cause, it must then have been derived from nothing.

Descartes' discussion at this point depends upon a principle that seems obscure and doubtful to many, namely the principle that whatever caused any *x* (say, an idea in my mind of a stone) must have as much "formal reality" as the idea has "objective reality." The "objective reality" of the stone in my mind is those properties that I think in the stone, such as its hardness. So whatever caused that idea must either be itself hard or be in some other way capable of producing the idea of hardness. Perhaps the mind itself is capable of inventing from scratch, so to speak, such an idea. But, Descartes argues, not all ideas in the mind could have been invented by the mind. There is in my mind the idea of God, for instance.

ASK YOURSELF

64. What are some characteristics that might be included in the "objective" reality (as Descartes calls it) of my idea of God? That is, when I think of the concept "God" what properties or characteristics do I think such a being would have?

Hence there remains only the idea of God, concerning which we must consider whether it is something which cannot have proceeded from me myself. By the name God I understand a substance that is infinite [eternal, immutable], independent, all-knowing, all-powerful, and by which I myself and everything else, if anything else does exist, have been created. Now all these characteristics are such that the more diligently I attend to them, the less do they appear capable of proceeding from me alone; hence, from what has been already said, we must conclude that God necessarily exists.

Descartes now thinks that he can know God exists, on the basis of the proof just stated, which could be summarized as follows:

1. We have an idea of infinite perfection.
2. The idea we have of ourselves entails finitude and imperfection.
3. There must be as much reality in the cause of any idea as in the idea itself (the principle of cause and effect).
4. Therefore, the idea we have of infinite perfection originated not from ourselves but from a being with infinite perfection, and that being is God.

This "proof" depends upon assumptions that Descartes has not proven, such as the principle about causality stated above regarding "formal" and "objective" reality.

Descartes goes on to argue that God, being perfect, would not deceive us when we clearly and distinctly perceive that something is the case, such as that $2 + 2 = 4$ or that there is an object with quantitative, primary qualities causing our perception of, say, a piece of wax. The information we get from the senses is typically confused and unclear, but the mind is able to go beyond sense experience and distinctly conceive of a world containing material objects with primary qualities. If I am mistaken in that clear and distinct belief, or in clear and distinct mathematical beliefs, it could not be because I am confused, but only because God is deceiving me. But God, being morally perfect, is no deceiver.

Thus, Descartes ends up claiming that he knows not only that he exists, but also the truths of mathematics, that God exists, and that there exists an external world of the sort studied by physics. As it turns out, knowledge depends upon rational intuitions, such as the intuition that there must be as much reality in a cause as in its effects. In fact, despite his attempts to give knowledge a new foundation, Descartes still clung to principles that he has acquired from his education in scholastic philosophy. But his concern to find an indubitable foundation for knowledge cast a long shadow over the history of modern philosophy.

Lockean Foundationalism. As the selection from Locke given above shows, attempts have been made to base knowledge upon sense experience, despite the kinds of skeptical arguments brought against sense knowledge by Descartes in his Meditation I or by other skeptics. But Locke was seeking certainty also, and he attempted to draw a picture of knowledge as a structure built upon foundations of particular simple experiences, such as the experience of sourness, or the experience of my own thinking. Unfortunately, a great many of the things that we think we know, including some that seem quite certain, could not be built upon such a foundation. For example, many scientific claims are universal in form. Newton's gravitational law is an example. "All objects attract each other with a force directly proportional to their mass." This and other Newtonian claims are about all past objects, all present objects, and all future objects, including objects in the most remote galaxies. Probably the majority of the objects in all of these categories have never been observed by anyone at all. How could such claims have any status as knowledge if the basis for knowledge is sense experience? Yet such claims do have very eminent status. Moreover, Locke thinks that we must consciously seek to base our beliefs on experience, in his sense of the term. But most of our beliefs are not under our control in that way. We simply find ourselves believing a great many things.

ASK YOURSELF

65. What does Locke think knowledge is based upon?

Some contemporary philosophers have tried to develop alternative versions of foundationalism. Some versions are "fallibilist"; that is, they do not include the assumption that foundational claims must be absolutely certain—an assumption made by Descartes and probably Locke also. We will not explore these more recent formulations here. Suffice it to say that they certainly have not satisfied all philosophers.

If classical foundationalism, in both its empiricist and rationalist versions, is open to so many objections, perhaps it is a mistake to look for "foundations" in the first place. The word "foundations" suggests something like the foundation of a house, upon which the house itself rests. But perhaps the "house" of knowledge does not need foundations in order to consist of real knowledge. An alternative view is considered in the next selection.

2. KNOWLEDGE AND COHERENCE: JONATHAN DANCY

Jonathan Dancy is professor of philosophy at the University of Keele and the author of *Introduction to Contemporary Epistemology* (1985), from which the following discussion is taken.

What Is Coherence? Foundationalists suppose that the truth of the foundational propositions (basic propositions) directly or indirectly entails the truth of the propositions built on those foundations, but not vice versa. Thus if (A) "I am now having the perceptual experience of a table in front of me" is foundational, perhaps it entails (B) "there is a table in front

of me." That is, if (A) is true, (B) *must* be true (that is what "entail" means). But the reverse is not the case. (B) might well be true without (A) being true (suppose I am blind). The foundationalist might also say that A is *evidence* for, or confirms, or justifies, B. Indeed nearly anyone would say that. But B is certainly not evidence for A. This *asymmetry* is rejected by coherentists (a good example of an asymmetrical relation is "father of"; that is, if John is the father of Bill, then it *cannot* be the case that the same Bill is the father of that same John).

ASK YOURSELF

66. Give two illustrations of how the belief that (B) could be true even though the belief that (A) is false. If you suppose that the belief that (A) entails the belief that (B), then you have just shown that these two beliefs have an _____ relation to one another.

Coherentists argue, roughly, that I should consider those beliefs to be true that cohere best with my other beliefs. Suppose, for example, that I see with my own eyes someone jumping 20 feet into the air. I am likely to doubt that a human being can jump that high, even though I just "saw" it, simply because I have already formed a great many beliefs about how high humans can jump—and perhaps related beliefs about gravity, about the way certain tricks are done by magicians, and so forth. The belief that a human can actually jump 20 feet into the air, without assistance, from a standing position on the earth does not *cohere* with all those other beliefs. So I am likely to reject it and assume that my eyesight, or something or someone else, is playing tricks on me.

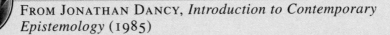

FROM JONATHAN DANCY, *Introduction to Contemporary Epistemology* (1985)

[W]e have begun to treat our beliefs as a kind of interrelated theory, and the problem has been how the beliefs are related. There are of course many aspects of this question which we have not examined, but we have found reason to reject one answer to it. This is the view that the relation is crucially asymmetrical; that there is an asymmetrical distinction between evidence and theory under which evidence confirms and disconfirms theory in a way in which theory cannot confirm or disconfirm evidence. Foundationalism offers such a structure in its assertion that the direction of justification is all one-way, and in its claim that there are some comparatively fixed points in the structure, the basic beliefs. The notion of inference from fixed points clearly embodies the relevant asymmetries. The notion of inference itself is asymmetrical. It is possible to infer B from A without being able to infer A from B.

The notion of coherence, on which a more completely holistic theory is based, is intended to be symmetrical. But to know whether that intention is successful we need to know more exactly what coherentists mean by "coherent."

For the purpose of better understanding the discussion that follows, consider this case: Suppose you are a detective investigating the murder of Mr. A. You come to have the following set of beliefs: (1) Mr. A was alive and well at 9 P.M. on June 10, 1990, but was pronounced dead by a doctor at 11 P.M. the same day. (2) Mr. A's throat was slit, and a knife with blood on it lay next to him. (3) That blood was type O positive, which was Mr. A's type. (4) There was blood on the carpet near Mr. A of type B negative. (5) The butler was reported to be out of town on June 10. (6). The butler has type B negative blood. (7) The butler did it (slit A's throat). Now ask yourself, is this set of beliefs, 1–7, coherent? To say the set is coherent must be, at the very least, to say that it is *consistent*. That is, it is not the case that if one or more is true, then one or more of the others *must* be false.

ASK YOURSELF

67. So, is the set 1–7 coherent? Explain

68. If we replaced (5) with "the butler was out of town on June 10" would the set be consistent? Explain.

However, coherence might mean more than mere consistency.

All coherentists agree that consistency is a necessary condition for coherence. Bradley added that a coherent set should be complete or comprehensive in some sense. (We shall see why soon.) But consistency and completeness were not enough; they did not capture the feeling that a coherent set stuck together or fitted together in a special way. To capture this, classical coherentists use the notion of entailment (*p* entails *q* iff, given *p*, *q must* be true), . . . But this account of coherence in terms of mutual entailment is disputed. . . . Indeed, can we make sense of the idea of a system within which each member entails all the rest?

In terms of our murder investigation example, it would seem bizarre to claim that 4, say, entails 5, or any of the others for that matter. Or vice versa.

Instead of answering this question directly, we can move towards it by considering an objection to any use of the notion of mutual entailment as the central element in a coherent set. That notion, as Blanshard uses it, is symmetrical enough. But entailment as traditionally understood is not a matter of degree. And this is important because coherentists want to give a sense to the notion that as one's belief-set grows, it improves (we hope); it becomes more coherent. And this is not just because it becomes more complete; completeness can hardly be a virtue in itself. And we cannot rely on the point that the relations of entailment only hold between members of a complete set, because this would not really capture the sense in which we aim, in expanding our belief-set, to make it more coherent. Since we are never likely to achieve a complete coherent set, the definition of coherence in terms of entailment has the consequence that nobody's beliefs are actually coherent at all.

So if we are to have a coherence theory of justification, we need to give a good sense to the idea that justification can grow.

An alternative account of coherence . . . defines a coherent set as one which is consistent, complete and mutually explanatory. The idea here will be that, as the set increases in size, we can hope that each member of it is better explained by the rest. Explanations can improve in quality; this accounts for the growth of justification. And the notion of mutual explanation is clearly symmetrical, in the required sense.

ASK YOURSELF

69. In terms of our murder investigation example, if I add to 1–7 a new belief, 8, that the man who reported that the butler was out of town on June 10 was conspiring to murder Mr. A, would the new set 1–8 be more mutually explanatory than the old?

Dancy goes on to argue that in fact the account of coherence in terms of mutual entailment, when properly understood, is consistent with the account in terms of mutual explanatoriness. He then turns to a related topic, namely, the theory of truth.

Before we turn to the coherence theory of justification we need first to consider the coherence theory of truth; the two are closely connected.

This theory holds that a proposition is true iff it is a member of a coherent set . . . the theory does purport to offer a definition of truth. It does not restrict itself to telling us what circumstances would justify us in taking a proposition to be true. It might do this by claiming that we are justified in believing that *p* is true to the extent that doing so would increase the coherence of our belief-set. The coherentist does make this claim; he does offer a *criterial* account of truth, a theory about what are the criteria for truth. But he also offers an account of what truth itself is, a *definitional* account. The two accounts are supposed to fit together, as we shall see.

So on Dancy's view, "*p* is true" equals by definition, "*p* belongs to a coherent set." He goes on to consider an objection to this definition. It is certainly possible for there to be more than one coherent complete set of statements. But there could not be more than one complete set of *true* statements, for if one set contains *all* the true statements, then any *different* set must contain at least one false statement. And if that is so, then you could not define truth in terms of belonging to a complete coherent set. This is called the *plurality objection* since it assumes there could be a plurality of coherent sets of beliefs. Dancy's main defense against the plurality objection is as follows:

The right defence against the plurality objection is offence. We should ask whether there is any other theory of truth, any other account of what truth is, which fares better. It emerges quickly that none of the standard theories of truth have the desired consequence that there can only be one set of truths. Certainly the traditional opponent of the coherence theory, [namely] the correspondence theory, faces the same difficulties. Correspondence theories try to erect an account of truth upon the undeniable remark that for a proposition to be true is for it to fit the facts. But as long as facts and true propositions are kept separate from each other, what is there to prevent there being two distinct sets of propositions which "fit the facts" equally well?

ASK YOURSELF

70. To revert to an example from Quine earlier in this chapter, the propositions "there are creatures with a heart here" and "there are creatures with a kidney here" will fit all and only the same _____ equally well. A set of propositions that contains one of these does not "correspond" to the facts any better than a set containing the other.

There is a general problem, also discussed by Quine, with the fact that different theories can be made to fit all the same facts.

But perhaps the plurality objection still has a point. After all, the coherentist must admit that the competing theories are all true (since they are all equally coherent), while the correspondence theorist can say that one is true and the others false. The correspondence theorist has this advantage because he says that there is something beyond and distinct from the competing theories, the world, which can make it the case that one is true and the rest false. So the coherentist cannot really give a good sense to the notion that the different theories compete or are incompatible, it seems. And this is a weakness not shared by his opponent.

The reply to this comes in two parts. First we can say that for the coherentist each theory is incompatible with every other because one cannot embrace two theories at once, on pain of loss of coherence. So from the point of view of someone with a theory, every other theory is false because it cannot be added to the true theory. And second, it is only from the point of view of the world, a point of view external to any theory, that the correspondence theorist has an advantage. Only those people who hold no theory at all but view all theories from outside can give a sense to the notion of incompatibility between theories beyond that which the coherentist has already given. But there is no such thing as a theory-free, external, viewpoint. So the coherentist can give an account of what it is for two coherent theories to be incompatible, and there is no further account which only the correspondence theorist can give.

For some arguments in favor of the claim that "there is no such thing as a theory-free external viewpoint," see the discussion of Kuhn later in this chapter.

The Coherence Theory of Justification. Dancy's coherence theory of truth complements his theory of justification.

This theory holds that a belief is justified to the extent to which the belief-set of which it is a member is coherent. Each belief is to be evaluated by appeal to the role it plays in the belief-set. If the coherence of the set would be increased by abandoning the belief and perhaps by replacing it by its opposite, the belief is not justified. If the set is more coherent with this belief as a member rather than with any alternative, the belief is justified. This notion of justification is relative to individual believers. The full account should be: if A's belief set is more coherent with the belief that p as a member than without it or with any alternative, A is (or would be) justified in believing that p.

ASK YOURSELF

71. In our example of the murder investigation, would the coherence of the original set be increased by abandoning any of 1–7? Which one seems not to fit too well?

Justification and Truth. Dancy explains that the coherentist notion of justification is intertwined with the coherentist notion of truth.

Coherentists stress as a virtue of their theory that truth and justification are according to them all of a piece. The coherence of a belief set goes to make its members justified; the coherence of a set of propositions, believed or not, goes to make its members true.

Suppose . . . we adopt a coherence theory of justification but reject the coherence theory of truth. (Perhaps we are impressed by the plurality objection.) We are left with a mystery. Surely our theory ought somehow to show why justification is worth having, why justified beliefs ought to be sought and adopted, and unjustified ones discarded. An obvious way of showing this is to show how or that justified beliefs are more likely to be true. If we take coherence as criterion both of truth and of justification, we have a good chance of being able to do this. The alternative is to suppose that justification is a matter of internal coherence, a question of fit between objects that are all of the same sort, while truth is a matter of the correspondence between propositions and objects of a different sort, facts or states of affairs. But then it would be difficult to find a reason for thinking that where the internal relation of justification is present, the external relation of truth is probably present too. So there is an enormous advantage in having theories of truth and justification that fit each other. The theory of truth ought to fit the epistemology and not be allowed to ride independent of it.

ASK YOURSELF

72. Dancy is claiming that having the most coherent set of beliefs would not count for much unless we had reason for supposing that that set was most likely the most _____ set.

Dancy goes on to discuss some advantages of coherentism over foundationalism. One advantage is that the coherentist account fits our actual practice better. Return to our detective example. There are various kinds of beliefs in the set. Belief 2 is very close to experience, a straightforward report of what was seen. Belief 3 is farther from experience. It involves theoretical notions that are tied to observation more loosely.

Suppose we have come to think something is wrong with our set. In an empiricist foundationalist view, the member we should be least likely to reject is belief 2 since it is so close to experience. But that will not and should not always be the case. We might actually be less likely to reject belief 3 than *any* of the others, partly because it is tied to a highly explanatory and coherent theory about blood.

ASK YOURSELF

73. If you knew at least one of 1–7 in our murder investigation example was false, but had no idea which one, which would you be most likely to throw out, and why?

Another advantage of coherentism, according to Dancy, is that it fits with the idea that knowledge is social. The coherentist can take that fact into account better than the foundationalist. Locke, for example, thinks that at the foundations of knowledge lie *individual* perceptual experiences. But it is arguable that we all rely heavily on parents, teachers, authors of books, researchers, and so on, in the acquisition of language, the development of concepts and ways of thinking, ways of perceiving, and a developed picture of what the world is like. If Searle is right, even our ability to *perceive* an apple as an apple is complex and assumes a previous background of interaction with others. Left on our own we would get nowhere.

These are . . . advantages which coherentists would claim for their theory. We now turn to consider the central attack on coherentism. This is the complaint that coherentism and empiricism are incompatible.

Coherentism and Empiricism. In the discussion that follows, a distinction is made between the "antecedent security" and the "consequent security" of a belief. The belief, based on visual experience that there is blood on the carpet, has high antecedent security. That is, it is not likely to turn out false even after many other beliefs are added. It seems likely to be true antecedent to, or before, any other beliefs are accepted. The belief that that blood is O negative has almost no antecedent security, since we only come to that belief after first acquiring many others, such as that certain tests were performed, they turned out a certain way, they fit within a theory about blood which explains many facts, and so forth. However, given the truth of those other beliefs, the belief that the blood is O negative could have a very high consequent security. We will be very certain about it consequent to, or after, those other beliefs are accepted.

ASK YOURSELF

74. How would you rate the belief that Mr. A died from loss of blood? Would that have high, medium, or low antecedent security?

The most fruitful coherentist approach can be found in the work of F. H. Bradley. Bradley is an empiricist, in this respect expressing himself as clearly as the most ardent could wish:

> I agree that we depend vitally on the sense-world, that our material comes from it, and that apart from it knowledge could not begin. To this world, I agree, we have forever to return, not only to gain new matter but to confirm and increase the old.

Here we see Bradley ascribing to the "data of perception" or the "sense-world" an asymmetrical role in the individual's epistemology. In fact the asymmetry is complex. It is partly genetic; mater*ial comes from* the sense-world, and without that world knowledge could not *begin*. And it has a continuing role, both in our need continually to return to previous "data of perception" and in our need to make sense of the continuing flow of new sensory life . . .

Bradley is willing to accept that the sense world plays a special role in epistemology, but he is unwilling to accept that that special role emerges in the sort of asymmetry which characterises foundationalism . . . :

> In order to begin my construction I take the foundation as absolute . . . But that my construction continues to rest on the beginnings of my knowledge is a conclusion which does not follow. For it is in another sense that my world rests upon the data of perception.

Bradley and Dancy hold that a lot of our knowledge does get started with sense experiences, just as the empiricist foundationalist claims. But the very empirical claims with which we begin (e.g., there is blood on the carpet) must have, in the long run, no more security or certainty attaching to them that do any other beliefs, if the coherentists are right. Ultimately, the test for acceptability even of such beliefs must be that they cohere well with our other beliefs.

[P]erhaps the problem is that different beliefs have different degrees of antecedent security, and that empiricists characteristically hold that sensory beliefs have *more* of it than others do. Can a coherentist make sense of this idea in his own terms? The problem seems to be that if one belief can be more secure than another in this way, this fact is independent of and prior to all considerations of coherence with other beliefs, and so reintroduces an asymmetry for which there can be no coherentist explanation.

The problem then is whether the coherentist *can* be an empiricist, not whether he *should* be one. And the empiricist is here distinguished by an attitude he takes towards his sensory beliefs; he demands more than another might before he is willing to reject them. But if this attitude is extrinsic to those beliefs themselves, and can without damaging distortion be seen as a further belief, it is a belief which the coherentist might share.

ASK YOURSELF

75. In addition to his empirical beliefs, an empiricist has a belief that is not itself empirical, namely, the following belief (called B1): "_____ beliefs are special, harder to refute, and should not be so quickly rejected as should other sorts of beliefs."

If that is so, then the coherentist who held that belief, namely B1, about the uniqueness of empirical beliefs, would do so because the rejection of any particular empirical belief, such as that there is blood on the carpet (call that one B2), would tend to clash with *that* belief, B1. But then the security of B2 would be consequent upon the security of B1, it would have no more antecedent security than any other belief, and coherence could still be what determines which beliefs are justified and true.

If this is right, pure coherentism is stronger than weak coherentism. If the weak coherentist is distinguished by his willingness to admit different degrees of antecedent security, his position is genuinely and unnecessarily weak.

The conclusion then is that coherentism is compatible with empiricism. Whether a coherentist *ought* to be an empiricist is a different question. . . . But the coherentist seems to have one promising avenue here. For him it is an empirical question whether at the end of the day a more coherent system will result from the adoption of the empiricist attitude to sensory beliefs—whether this form of empiricist stubbornness will eventually pay off. And this is the sort of way in which the coherentist *should* seek to justify empiricism.

Return to our detective example. Suppose that Mr. A's blood is not O positive after all. We would have to make some sort of adjustment in the original set of beliefs in order to make them cohere with this new "fact." Suppose further that we discover that the butler had always been intensely loyal to A. Further adjustments would be needed. It would seem difficult to reject belief 2, the claim that A's throat was slit, even though it now appears that the knife was not the instrument. Perhaps though the experience of seeing him on the floor with a cut across his throat was a hallucination. Or perhaps A was shaving with a barber's razor, had a spasm in his arm, and slit his own throat. Perhaps the razor was removed by someone in an attempt to frame the butler. And so forth. The general point is this. In the search for knowledge, we are continually making adjustments in our beliefs, in order to make them cohere with each other. We throw out some beliefs, modify some, keep some. If we are especially reluctant to throw out the most empirical ones, that could only be because we believe such beliefs are particularly secure. But *that* belief (the belief that empirical beliefs are particularly secure) is not intrinsically more secure than any other.

ASK YOURSELF

76. Think up some new fact that would throw belief 2 in our detective example into doubt.

3. THE RAFT VERSUS THE PYRAMID: ERNEST SOSA

Contemporary philosopher Ernest Sosa uses the metaphor of a pyramid to describe foundationalism. Classical foundationalists require that any proposition P that we are justified in claiming to know is either self-evident or certain in some other way, or, P is deducible from other propositions that are self-evident or otherwise certain. So either P stands on its own, or it is deducible from other propositions, which may in turn be deducible from others, and so forth, until we reach a self-evident or otherwise certain proposition. The resulting structure of beliefs can be represented as a pyramid. Any defect in our structure of beliefs will be due to a failure of some belief to meet one or both of the requirements just mentioned. If the foundations are bad, the whole structure will fall all at once.

An alternative is to picture knowledge as a raft. The image was suggested by the philosopher Otto Neurath. If a raft starts to leak while we are at sea, we cannot overhaul the whole raft. We must find a piece to replace the leaking plank. The new piece will of course have to fit in with the rest of the structure of the boat to do any good. This is a kind of metaphor for coherentism. If we reject any belief in our system of beliefs, the coherentist claims, we will want to replace it with one that coheres with the beliefs already in place. Otherwise our "knowledge boat" will sink. Each plank needs to fit with all the others if it is to function.

> ### ASK YOURSELF
>
> **77.** What theory of knowledge does the pyramid represent, and what theory of knowledge does the raft represent? Which of the two, do you think, portrays the enterprise of constructing a system of beliefs as most *risky?*

Sosa concludes his discussion of the controversy between these two approaches with the following summary, containing 11 parts (only eight of them are cited and discussed here).

> 2. *Knowledge and criteria.* Particularism is distinguished from Methodism: the first gives priority to particular examples of knowledge over general methods or criteria, whereas the second reverses that order. The Methodism of Descartes leads him to an elaborate dogmatism whereas that of Hume leads him to a very simple skepticism. The particularist is, of course, antiskeptical on principle.

Instead of looking for some general method (thus "Methodism") for distinguishing true from false beliefs, as Descartes, Locke, and Hume do, someone might simply start out with what appear to be particular clear cases of knowledge, such as that Napoleon was a general, it is evening now, or $2 + 2 = 4$, without attempting to find any common element or principle behind them.

> ### ASK YOURSELF
>
> **78.** What was Hume's *method* for determining which beliefs should be accepted and which rejected?

> 3. *Two metaphors: the raft and the pyramid.* For the foundationalist every piece of knowledge stands at the apex of a pyramid that rests on stable and secure foundations whose stability and security do not derive from the upper stories or sections. For the coherentist a body of knowledge is a free-floating raft every plank of which helps directly or indirectly

to keep all the others in place, and no plank of which would retain its status with no help from the others.

4. *A coherentist critique of foundatonalism.* No mental state can provide a foundation for empirical knowledge. For if such a state is propositional, then it is fallible and hence no secure foundation. But if it is not propositional, then how can it possibly serve as a foundation for belief? How can one infer or justify anything on the basis of a state that, having no propositional content, must be logically dumb? An analogy with ethics suggests a reason to reject this dilemma. Other reasons are also advanced and discussed.

Some mental states—for example, dizziness—have no propositional content. You can be in that state without having any concepts. Now recall the drawings in Searle's essay. When looking at the TOOT figure, do you see a word or a locomotive? One thing is sure, if you have no concept of a locomotive, you will not see a locomotive. So what you see is, so to speak, filtered by your concepts. Thus you do not have direct (nonfiltered) access to that reality. The idea can be extended to all knowledge involving concepts. None of it involves a direct grasp of reality. For that reason it is fallible—that is, could be mistaken. And if you could be mistaken about even the most basic empirical propositions, how could those propositions serve as a basis for knowledge? On the other hand, the notion that a mental state without propositional content could serve as the basis for knowledge, (which is always itself propositional) is mysterious.

A number of responses to this critique of foundationalism are possible. It is not clear that only infallible propositions can serve as the basis for knowledge. Nor is it clear that only propositions can justify propositions. Consider an analogy from ethics. Suppose I believe that I should refrain from breaking promises, because I think that generally breaking promises tends to produce more bad effects, more unhappiness overall, than does keeping them. What justifies my belief, if it is justified, will be the consequences of acting on it. And those consequences are not propositions. So not all beliefs are justified by propositions. Similarly, perhaps what justifies my belief that there is something red in front of me is a visual experience, of a nonpropositional kind, a "red-presenting" experience that I simply have, but do not put into concepts, so to speak.

5. *The regress argument.* In defending his position, the foundationalist often attempts to rule out the very possibility of an infinite regress of justification (which leads him to the necessity for a foundation). Some of his arguments to that end are examined.

Suppose I believe Vesuvius has erupted. Suppose I base this on having heard a news report stating that it did. Suppose I believe that news report because it came from a woman reporter I think is reliable. Suppose I think that reporter is reliable because in the past she has made claims, such as that the Ohio river is flooding, and I'm living by the Ohio and see it flooding. And suppose I trust my sight because it generally seems to be working well. Now, the foundationalist says, we cannot go on this way forever (have an infinite regress). Eventually we must get to something—for example, direct reports of the senses—which do not themselves depend upon any other beliefs. Those sense-report beliefs would then be foundational. Without some such basic beliefs, none of my beliefs would be justified, since I must be able to get to the *end* of a chain of justification for there to be real justification. However, Sosa argues that it might be possible to have a kind of foundationalism that does not rule out such infinite regresses.

Our discussion in this section has contrasted foundationalism with coherentism. But Sosa argues that coherentism is itself "formally" foundationalist.

7. *Two levels of foundationalism.* Substantive foundationalism is distinguished from formal foundationalism. . . . There turns out to be a surprising kinship between coherentism and substantive foundationalism, both of which aim at a formal foundationalism of the highest grade, at a theory of the greatest simplicity that explains how epistemic justification supervenes on non-epistemic factors.

The following illustration may help explain what is meant by "supervene." Terms like "good," or the properties they name, are "evaluative." To say that a knife is a good knife is to evaluate it positively. Now if two knives are identical with respect to such properties as sharpness, rigidity, durability (which are themselves nonevaluative properties), and so forth, then it would not make sense to say that one of those knives is good and the other is not. That is what it means to say that the property of goodness *supervenes* on other nonevaluative properties. Two knives can't differ with respect to goodness unless they differ with respect to those nonevaluative properties upon which goodness supervenes.

ASK YOURSELF

79. Why is sharpness a nonevaluative property? Ask yourself, is it generally the case that when I say of something that it is sharp, I am necessarily saying that there is either something good or bad about it? Might it sometimes be good, sometimes bad, sometimes neither?

Now, justification is evaluative. To say a belief is justified is to evaluate it positively. It appears that being justified is a property that supervenes upon other nonevaluative properties. In Descartes' view, a belief is justified if it is clear and distinct, or deducible directly or indirectly from one that is. In Locke's view, a belief is justified if it can be traced back to sense experience, or is deducible directly or indirectly from one that is. They are formally similar in that they both make justification a supervenient property. Moreover, both views propose a general theory of great simplicity which covers all justified beliefs. They tell us what the property is that makes *all* justified beliefs justified. Formally they are similar, though in substance they differ. They provide different accounts of what the nonevaluative properties are, upon which justification supervenes.

ASK YOURSELF

80. In Descartes' view, what are the nonevaluative properties upon which justification supervenes?

Formally, Sosa claims, coherentism is also foundationalist. For it too gives us a general theory about a nonevaluative property upon which justification supervenes. That property is coherence. A belief is justified if it has the property of cohering well with our other beliefs. Substantively coherentism differs from those views normally counted as foundationalist, but then those foundationalist views differ from each other substantively too.

8. *Doxastic ascent arguments.* The distinction between formal and substantive foundationalism provides an unusual viewpoint on some recent attacks against foundationalism. We consider doxastic ascent arguments as an example.

Coherentists sometimes argue against foundationalists in the following manner. A coherentist might say, "Take Locke as an example: Locke claims that the belief that, say, there is a table in front of me, is justified for me just in case it has the property of resting on experience, and he believes *that* because he believes that most of his beliefs that rest on sense experience are true, and that this belief in the table does rest on experience. But why should he believe that most of his beliefs that rest on sense experience are true? He must suppose that his senses operate properly, at the very least. But, what justifies the belief that one's senses are operating properly? One would need some further belief to justify that belief." We are now engaged in "doxastic ascent" ("*doxa*" is a Greek word meaning "belief"). What is to put a stop to this ascent? One belief piles up on top of another. Coherentists argue that foundationalists are not able to stop it. So foundationalism à la Locke falls apart because of this endless "ascent."

However, if coherentism is formally like foundationalism, then perhaps it will fall apart in a similar way. That is what Sosa claims. The coherentist holds that my belief, B, that there is a table in front of me is justified for me only if B coheres with my other beliefs. But I am justified in believing that only if I am justified in the belief, call it C, that most of my beliefs that cohere in that way are true, and that my belief in the table does cohere. But what justifies my believing C? Do I have to believe that C also coheres? What would justify that? Some further belief which also coheres?

> ### ASK YOURSELF
> **81.** Dancy argued that "most beliefs that cohere are true" is itself true *by definition*. If he is right, would that take some of the "bite" out of the preceding argument against this coherentist critique of foundationalism? Explain.

10. *The foundationalist's dilemma.* All foundationalism based on sense experience is subject to a fatal dilemma.

The dilemma goes something like this. We humans have visual experiences, including visual experiences of red. Such experiences give rise to the belief that something red is present. Suppose that there is a race of extraterrestrials who do not have visual experiences, but some other sort of experience we do not understand. Those experiences also give rise in them to certain beliefs. Assuming that these ways of arriving at beliefs are foundational for humans and the extraterrestrial race, how do we choose between them? Would we have any reason for thinking that the extraterrestrial way of forming beliefs is not as good as or better than ours, even though it is so different? In fact, this is already a problem *within* human perception. If we trust our visual experiences as sources of knowledge, should we also trust our tactile sense, which is so different, and sometimes even conflicts with visual experience? On the other hand, suppose such experiential beliefs are not foundational. Then perhaps both the human and extraterrestrial way of arriving at beliefs fall under some more general principles. But what would those principles be? Foundationalists have not given an answer.

> ### ASK YOURSELF
> **82.** Sextus Empiricus argued that since different animals perceive differently, we could never be sure which experiences get at "how the world really is." Does that argument sound anything like the fatal dilemma argument just described?

11. *Reliabilism.* An alternative to foundationalism of sense experience is sketched. [From Ernest Sosa, "The Raft and the Pyramid: Coherence Versus Foundations in the Theory of Knowledge"]

Given the problems Sosa has sketched with both coherentism and foundationalism, it might be wise to take a very different approach. First, consider a case from ethics, which will be discussed in the ethics section. On a "virtues" approach to ethics, what makes an action right is that it is the sort of action a virtuous person would likely perform. So even where an action leads to a bad result, it would still be right if it is the sort of action a virtuous person would perform. For such actions proceed from stable character traits (such as courage and truthfulness) that are generally the best, most valuable traits to have. Perhaps what is needed then is an approach to knowledge in terms of such intellectual virtues as fairmindedness, carefulness about sources, and so forth.

ASK YOURSELF

83. Carefulness about the sources of our beliefs is an intellectual virtue. It is a virtue lacking in those who treat sensationalist journalism as being on a par with encyclopedia articles. Try to think up two other examples of intellectual virtues and illustrate them.

SUMMING UP FOUNDATIONALISM VERSUS COHERENCE

"Mary is home." "How do you know?" "I just saw her in the kitchen." That is typical of how we defend or support many of our beliefs. My belief that Mary is home is founded upon, supported by, the claim that I just saw her at home. What more could anyone want? Much of the time we suppose that a basis or foundation in direct experience is sufficient to establish a belief as knowledge. With that basis I can claim to *know* that Mary is home. Such common-sense insights are behind empiricist foundationalism of the sort found in Locke. But not everything I know seems to be based upon direct experience in that way. In particular, there are truths that I seem to grasp immediately or through pure thought, without consulting the senses. Simple mathematical propositions seem to be like that, a fact stressed by Descartes. Perhaps more complex claims to knowledge can be based on such propositions.

There is, however, another way of seeking knowledge which does not treat *any* particular beliefs as foundational. Any belief, even such a "basic" belief as that I just saw Mary in the kitchen, might be challenged if that belief does not fit with, or cohere with, various other beliefs. Much of our quest for knowledge is something like detective work. This is often so in the exact sciences, as well as in daily life. The coherentist Dancy argues that claims to knowledge are justified only when they can be consistently fit into a larger system of beliefs.

CAN OF WORMS

Quine's discussion of the analytic/synthetic distinction depends upon various claims about meaning and reference. Quine's views on language could be employed by coherentists, since according to Quine we rule out claims to knowledge which put too much pressure on other beliefs in the "web of belief" which we have woven in coherentist fashion. Issues in the philosophy of language are themselves often intertwined with issues in the philosophy of mind. Epistemological disputes between coherentists and foundationalists are often entangled with disputes in the philosophy of language and in metaphysics.

E. PROBLEMS WITH JUSTIFIED BELIEF

The conflicts between foundationalism and coherentism have not been lessened by recent developments. But new difficulties have arisen. The notion of "justified belief" has itself begun to appear problematic in ways not noticed before. Moreover, many philosophers have begun to protest against the way in which disputes in epistemology have been conducted. "Particularism," which was mentioned above, is one such protest. Close attention to various senses of "justification" have also proved to be important, as have close analyses of intellectual vices and virtues.

**QUESTIONS
TO DISCUSS**

a. If you really do know something, *must* you always be able to show *how* you know it? If you cannot, does that show that it is not really knowledge after all? Illustrate your view, using an example.

b. Could it ever have been the case that a person who believed the earth to be flat was *justified* in believing that?

c. Suppose that you have a friend who is intellectually lazy. He believes things without bothering to do even a minimal checking of relevant facts. Does it seem likely to you that your friend really knows much, even in cases where what he believes is true?

d. Do you have a duty to check out all or most of your beliefs, in order to make sure they are true?

 1. **TRUE JUSTIFIED BELIEF IS NOT SUFFICIENT
FOR KNOWLEDGE: EDMUND GETTIER**

If it is true that I *know* P (where P is any proposition, say, "Napoleon was a general"), then it seems quite natural to think the following three things must be true:

1. I believe P (I believe Napoleon was a general).
2. P is true.
3. I am justified in believing P.

Statements 1–3 almost look like a *definition* of "knowledge." Knowledge simply is Justified True Belief. Call this the JTB analysis of knowledge. Anything that meets these three conditions is knowledge, and anything that is knowledge meets these three conditions.

> **ASK YOURSELF**
>
> **84.** The first two conditions seem obvious to most people today. But just believing something that is true is not knowledge. If you believed that the earth rotates on its axis because you had been told that it did by a scientifically ignorant witch doctor, would your belief amount to knowledge?

Some further condition beyond belief and truth is necessary, and the notion of being justified may seem to fill the bill.

In a short but famous article written in 1963, American philosopher Edmund Gettier challenged this "definition" by providing counterexamples—that is, cases where 1–3 obtained but nonetheless knowledge did not exist. Here is one of them:

Suppose that Smith and Jones have applied for a certain job. And suppose that Smith has strong evidence for the following conjunctive proposition:

(d) Jones is the man who will get the job, and Jones has ten coins in his pocket.

Smith's evidence for (d) might be that the president of the company assured him that Jones would in the end be selected, and that he, Smith, had counted the coins in Jones's pocket ten minutes ago. Proposition (d) entails:

(e) The man who will get the job has ten coins in his pocket.

Let us suppose that Smith sees the entailment from (d) to (e), and accepts (e) on the grounds of (d), for which he has strong evidence. In this case, Smith is clearly justified in believing that (e) is true.

But imagine, further, that unknown to Smith, he himself, not Jones, will get the job. And, also, unknown to Smith, he himself has ten coins in his pocket. Proposition (e) is then true, though proposition (d), from which Smith inferred (e), is false. In our example, then, all of the following are true: (i) (e) is true, (ii) Smith believes that (e) is true, and (iii) Smith is justified in believing that (e) is true. But it is equally clear that Smith does *not know* that (e) is true; for (e) is true in virtue of the number of coins in Smith's pocket, while Smith does not know how many coins are in Smith's pocket, and bases his belief in (e) on a count of the coins in Jones's pocket, whom he falsely believes to be the man who will get the job. [From Edmund Gettier, "Is Justified True Belief Knowledge?" (1963)]

This example may seem excessively contrived. However, it is possible to construct other examples, using the same strategy Gettier uses, which perhaps are more natural. Suppose, for example, Smith believes that his wife is in the living room because he got a clear look as he passed the door and is sure he saw her there. It happens that his wife has an identical twin sister, but he had good reason for thinking the sister was 1000 miles away. In fact, it *was* the twin that he saw, for she has just come to town on an emergency. So his looking at her and thinking it was his wife was a piece of epistemic bad luck. Now, offset this bad luck with good luck. His wife is in fact in the living room, though he did not see her there because she was in back of the sofa wiping up a spill. So, Smith believes his wife is in the living room, and he has good reason to believe that—that is, is justified in believing it—and it is true. He has a Justified True Belief. Yet it hardly seems like knowledge. That the belief is true is just a piece of epistemic luck. His belief is true *by accident*.

The significance of Gettier's counterexamples is this: The person who has knowledge of some proposition does *not* believe that proposition by accident. My *knowing* that "my wife is in the living room" cannot be simply a matter of accident.

Gettier's counterexamples to the analysis of knowledge as justified true belief (JTB) have not made philosophers give up that analysis completely. They may hedge their claim by saying that JTB is *nearly* sufficient for knowledge. At any rate, Gettier's counterexamples, as well as other factors, have caused many philosophers to rethink the notion of justification, and in some cases even to eliminate it from the analysis of knowledge, and to seek an alternative feature which, when added to true belief, would yield knowledge. This last strategy may seem extreme, but it is in fact precisely what the author of the next selection does.

2. JUSTIFICATION, INTERNALISM, AND WARRANT: ALVIN PLANTINGA

**ALVIN PLANTINGA
(B. 1932)**

American philosopher and defender of epistemological externalism.

Contemporary philosopher Alvin Plantinga believes that the notion of knowledge as justified true belief is confused and must be rejected. His position reflects a debate between "externalism" and "internalism." "Externalism" is, roughly, the view that it is possible for me to know something without knowing how I know it. Internalism is the view that I cannot really know something unless I can say how I know—such as "I know because I *saw* it." Plantinga is an externalist, and thus rejects the notion of justification as an essential ingredient in knowledge. In place of *justification,* he proposes the notion of *warrant.* The basic idea is something like this: What makes a belief of mine into knowledge is that it has the right kind of relationship to the world. To revert to an example mentioned in the earlier selection by Searle, if my belief that there is a yellow station wagon in front of me is being caused by a yellow station wagon in front of me, then that belief has the right kind of relation to the world. On the other hand, if there is no vehicle there and the belief is being caused by a hallucinogen, then that belief does not have the right kind of relation to the world. So even if I do not know what is causing the belief, as might be possible in the first case, I may still have knowledge. And if I do not know what is causing it, then it seems plausible to claim that I am not *justified* in what I believe. So justification is the wrong concept to use in discussing knowledge.

Justification and Duty. According to a view that Plantinga traces back to Locke and Descartes, a person is justified in her beliefs if she has done her "epistemic duty"—that is, has acquired those beliefs in a responsible way, has not been lazy, not accepted the testimony of people whom she has no reason to trust, and so forth. Moreover, if a person is justified in her beliefs when she has done her epistemic duty, she must know that she is justified and how she is justified. There is no sense to the idea that one has done one's duty but has no idea how one did it. So the conditions under which a person is justified in believing something must be accessible in some way. That accessibility is the main feature of internalism. Internalists hold that if I am justified in a belief, I should be able to determine by reflection, or in some fairly simple way, that I am justified. Thus, if a belief is self-evident, I should just by reflection be able to see that it is. If a belief is well grounded in evidence, I should be able to tell that it is and should understand how the evidence supports the belief.

ASK YOURSELF

85. Try to describe a case where you would be justified in believing that Napoleon was a cavalry officer even though that belief is false (he was in fact an artillery officer).

86. Does your example in the preceding question show that there is no regular connection between truth and justification?

The Connection Between Truth and Justification. What then is the connection between truth and justification? Plantinga quotes the philosopher William Alston, who has argued that a justified belief is one that has adequate grounds. In the passage below, Plantinga uses the term "deontological" (meaning what is obligatory or necessary) in reference to the view that we have an epistemic duty to acquire beliefs in a responsible way.

FROM ALVIN PLANTINGA, "Justification in the 20th Century" (1990)

So a justified belief is one that has adequate grounds. Alston adds that the justifying grounds in question must be accessible to the believer in question, thus honoring the classical connection between justification and internalism. In the classical case, as I have been arguing, there is a natural and inevitable connection between justification and accessibility, a connection rooted in the deontological conception of justification. Once one gives up the deontology, however, what is the reason or motivation for retaining the internalism? In support of the internalist requirement, Alston cites the fact that he finds

> widely shared and strong intuitions in favor of some kind of accessibility requirement for justification. We expect that if there is something that justifies my belief that *p*, I will be able to determine what it is. We find something incongruous, or conceptually impossible, in the notion of my being justified in believing that *p* while totally lacking any capacity to determine what is responsible for that justification.

Again, this makes perfect sense if we think of justification deontologically; and the reason he finds those widespread intuitions favoring an internalist requirement, I suggest, is a testimony to the hold the classical conception has upon us—but once we give up that deontology, what is the reason for the internalism? Is there any longer any reason for it? Cut off the deontology, and the internalism looks like an arbitrary appendage.

The Incoherence of the Received Tradition. Plantinga feels that the standard view of epistemology that we have inherited is flawed because of its improper reliance on various notions of justification.

I shall argue briefly that the 20th century received epistemological tradition with respect to justification is indeed mistaken and incoherent. The shape of this tradition is clear: it involves first the idea that justification is necessary and nearly sufficient for knowledge; second, the idea that justification is fundamentally a matter of responsibility, of fulfillment of epistemic duty; third, the idea that justification for a belief essentially involves its fitting the believer's evidence, and fourth, the internalist connection. More than one element here is deeply questionable. For example, there is the question whether our beliefs are sufficiently within our control for deontological justification to have the right kind of bearing on belief formation and maintenance.

ASK YOURSELF

87. Justification is fundamentally a matter of what?

88. If I have little or no voluntary control over what beliefs I have, could I really have "epistemic duties"?

Plantinga wants to replace the notion of justification with the notion of warrant. Warrant will be the thing which, when added to true belief, produces knowledge. We could, then, call this the WTB analysis of knowledge. And warrant, in his view, is *externalist*. That means that I can be warranted in a belief without knowing how I am warranted. It may be that a belief of mine was produced by a perfectly reliable belief forming mechanism (perceptual mechanisms, for instance) without my having any knowledge of that mechanism or how it produced my belief.

ASK YOURSELF

89. What does it mean to say that warrant is "externalist"?

But second, conceding the tradition all it might like by way of control over our beliefs, it is still clear that justification is neither necessary for warrant nor anywhere nearly sufficient for it. First, it is nowhere nearly sufficient. . . . Concede the dubious premise that there are intellectual duties of the sort Locke and Chisholm suggest; concede the control over our beliefs that go with that idea: it is still easy to see, I think, that a person can be doing her epistemic duty to the maximum and nevertheless (by way of the depredations of a brain lesion or the machinations of a Cartesian demon or Alpha Centaurian cognitive scientist) be such that her beliefs have little or no warrant.

ASK YOURSELF

90. If the Cartesian demon is deceiving me, then even when I am being as careful and responsible as possible in forming my beliefs—that is, doing my epistemic duty—it might be that none of my beliefs would be warranted. In that case could they all be false? Explain.

91. If the demon slips up and lets a true belief in now and then, would it be correct to say that I had *knowledge* in such cases?

So justification isn't sufficient for warrant. But it isn't necessary either. Suppose there is the sort of epistemic duty Chisholm suggests: a duty to try to bring it about that I attain and maintain the condition of epistemic excellence; and suppose I am dutiful, but a bit confused. I come nonculpably to believe that the Alpha-Centaurians thoroughly dislike the thought that I am perceiving something that is red; I also believe that they are monitoring my beliefs, and if I form the belief that I see something red, will bring it about that I have a set of beliefs most of which are absurdly false, thus depriving me of any chance for epistemic excellence. I then acquire an epistemic duty to try to withhold the beliefs I naturally form when I am appeared to redly: such beliefs as that I see a red hall, or a red fire engine, or whatever. I have the same epistemic inclinations everyone else has: when I am appeared to redly, I am powerfully inclined to believe that I see something that is red. By dint of heroic and unstinting effort, however, I am able to train myself to withhold the belief (on such occasions) that I see something red; of course it takes enormous effort and requires great willpower. On a given morning I go for a walk in London; I am appeared to redly several times (postboxes, traffic signals, redcoats practising for a reenactment of the American revolution); each time I successfully resist the belief that I see something red. . . . Finally I am appeared to redly in a particularly flagrant and insistent fashion by a large red London bus. "To hell with epistemic duty" I say, and relax blissfully into the belief that I am now perceiving something red. Then this would be a belief that was unjustified for me; in accepting it I would be going contrary to epistemic duty; yet could it not constitute knowledge?

To say that justification is necessary for warrant is to say that if I am warranted in believing *P*, then *P* is justified. Plantinga denies there is such a connection between warrant and justification.

92. Why, in Plantinga's example, would I *not* be justified in believing that there is a red object before me?

93. Why might I be warranted nonetheless?

94. What do the answers to the two previous questions show about the connection between justification and warrant?

According to the 20th century received tradition in Anglo-American epistemology—a tradition going back at least to Locke—justification is essentially deontological; it is also necessary and nearly sufficient for warrant. But this position is deeply incoherent: epistemic justification (taken in traditional deontological fashion) may be an important epistemic value or virtue, but it is neither necessary nor anywhere nearly sufficient for knowledge. Knowledge surely contains a normative element; but the normativity is not that of deontology. Perhaps this incoherence in the received tradition is the most important thing to see here: the tension between the idea that justification is a deontological matter, a matter of filling duties, being permitted or within one's rights, conforming to one's intellectual obligations, on the one hand, and, on the other, the idea that justification is necessary and sufficient (perhaps with a codicil to propitiate Gettier) for warrant. To put it another way, what we need to see clearly is the vast difference between justification and warrant. The lesson to be learned is that these two are not merely uneasy bedfellows—they are worlds apart.

Warrant and justification are worlds apart because, among other things, Plantinga's notion of warrant is externalist, as was explained in the introduction to this section. That is, a person can be warranted in believing *P* without knowing how they are warranted or even that they are. The notion of justification, on the other hand, is clearly internalist on his account. In the following essay a somewhat different version of externalism is critiqued and various epistemological positions are sketched.

3. NATURALIST EXTERNALISM VERSUS INTERNALISM: KEITH LEHRER

Keith Lehrer is professor of philosophy at the University of Arizona. The following selection is from his book *Theory of Knowledge* (1990). Lehrer argues against all forms of externalism, both reliabilism, which transforms properly *caused* beliefs into justification, and the more radical naturalism that repudiates justification as necessary for knowledge. But it is the justificatory type of externalism that Lehrer concentrates on. After identifying the strength of externalism as its ability to defeat the threat of skepticism, Lehrer sets forth two fundamental objections to externalism: (1) Possession of correct information is inadequate for knowledge, and (2) we may be justified in a belief even when it has not been caused (or sustained) by a reliable process. Note the idea of trustworthiness in Lehrer's account and the notion of reliability. "Reliabilism" is in fact a kind of externalism. It is the view that a belief will count as knowledge if it was produced by some reliable process—that is to say, a process that pretty reliably produces true beliefs.

Some Externalist Ideas and Their Problems

The fundamental doctrine of externalism is that what must be added to true belief to obtain knowledge is the appropriate connection between belief and truth. An earlier account presented by Goldman affirmed that the appropriate connection is causal. This is a very plausible sort of account of perceptual knowledge. The fact that I see something, the hand I hold before me, for example, causes me to believe that I see a hand. The fact that my seeing a hand causes me to believe I see a hand results, it is claimed, in my knowing that I see a hand. . . . It is not our conception of how we are related to a fact that yields knowledge but simply our being so related to it.

Suppose we are in my living room and then go to the kitchen. I ask you whether there was a red flowered couch in my living room. You do not recall looking at it or noticing its color, but you answer, correctly, that there was. Is that knowledge? You don't know how you know, but you are quite sure. Perhaps your belief was formed through reliable perceptual processes operating at a subconscious level.

ASK YOURSELF

95. Would the externalist call your belief knowledge in such a instance?

The early analysis, though providing a plausible account of perceptual knowledge, was a less plausible account of our knowledge of generalities, that men do not become pregnant, for example, or that neutrinos have a zero rest mass, or that there is no largest prime number. For here the nature of the required causal relationship between what is believed and the belief of it evades explication. That objection is, however, one of detail. Later analyses of others, and of Goldman himself, aim at preserving the thesis of externalism that some relationship of the belief to what makes it true yields knowledge, whether we have any idea of that relationship or not. . . . Goldman now claims that justified belief must be the result of a belief-forming process that reliably yields truth. Beliefs resulting from such a process are justified, he contends, while other externalists deny that justification is necessary for knowledge.

ASK YOURSELF

96. Would Plantinga be an externalist of the last sort just mentioned?

They all agree, however, that a belief resulting from a certain kind of process or relationship connecting belief with truth can yield knowledge without the sustenance or support of any other beliefs or system of beliefs.

Naturalized Epistemology. We have already mentioned that some philosophers have denied that inquiries into knowledge are best undertaken by philosophers. Perhaps knowledge is a phenomenon to be analyzed and understood by the *natural* sciences, such as psychology. In such a view, epistemology could be "naturalized."

Assuming that the required relationship is something like causation, externalist theories are *naturalistic*. What is a naturalistic theory? It is one in which all the terms used in the analysis are ones that describe phenomena of nature, such as causation, for example, or that can be reduced to such terms. Hume's theory of belief was naturalistic in this sense. He restricted his account of human knowledge to relations of causation, contiguity, and resemblance. It was, however, Quine who introduced the term *epistemology naturalized* and suggested that inquiry into the nature of human knowledge be restricted to accounts of how belief arises and is altered. Other philosophers have adopted the term to refer simply to all those accounts of knowledge couched in naturalistic vocabulary or reducible to such a vocabulary.

. . . One interesting aspect of some externalistic theories which naturalize epistemology is the way in which they attempt to avoid the problems of foundationalism. According to Dretske or Nozick, for example, there is no need either to justify beliefs or posit self-justified beliefs blindly because, contrary to the traditional analysis, the justification of beliefs is not required to convert true beliefs into knowledge. Beliefs or true beliefs having the appropriate sort of naturalistic external relationships to the facts are, as a result of such relationship, converted into knowledge without being justified. It is the way true beliefs are connected to the world that makes them knowledge rather than the way in which we might attempt to justify them. Notice how plausible this seems for perceptual beliefs. It is the way my belief that I see a bird is related to the facts, for example, when my seeing a bird causes the belief that I do, which accounts for my knowing that I see a bird, rather than some justification I have for that belief. What matters for knowledge is how the belief arises, not how I might reason on behalf of it. The traditional analysis says that knowledge is true belief coupled with the right sort of justification. One sort of externalist analysis says that knowledge is true belief coupled with the right sort of naturalistic relation. It is plausible to assume that the naturalistic relationship will be one concerning how the belief arises, in short, the natural history of the belief. Looked at in this way, the justification requirement can be eliminated altogether in favor of the right sort of historical account.

ASK YOURSELF

97. In terms of the example given in the preceding question, your belief that there is a red flowered couch in my living room will be knowledge just in case it was caused by what sorts of things or events?

Some Advantages of Externalism. Lehrer concedes that externalist views have advantages. In particular, they avoid skepticism.

It is helpful, as well, to notice how neatly this sort of theory deals with traditional and modern forms of skepticism. The skeptic, confronted with a commonsense perceptual claim, that I see a tree, for example, has traditionally raised some skeptical doubt, the Cartesian one, for example, that we might be deceived by an evil demon who supplies us with deceptive sensations which lead us to believe we see external objects when we do not see them at all. Or consider the case of a small object, a "braino,' implanted in our brain which, when operated by a computer, provides us with sensory states which are all produced by the computer influencing the brain rather than by the external objects we believe to exist. In neither case, affirms the skeptic, do I know I see a tree. The reply is simple. If my beliefs are, indeed, produced by the demon or by the braino, then they are false and I am ignorant. On the other hand, if the beliefs are true and produced in the appropriate way, then I do know.

To this the skeptic is wont to reply that I only know that I see a tree if I know that it is not the demon or the braino that produces my belief and, furthermore, to insist that I do not know this. Why do I not know that there is no demon or braino? I do not know so because my experience would be exactly the same if there were; that is what the demon and braino do, produce exactly the same experiences as I would have if I were to see a tree. I have no evidence whatever against these skeptical hypotheses and, therefore, the skeptic concludes, I do not know them to be false. The reply of the externalist is simple. I do not need to *know* that the skeptical hypotheses are false to know that I see a tree, though, of course, the skeptical hypotheses must *be* false. Otherwise, my belief that I see a tree will be false. All that is necessary is that my belief be true and that it arise in the appropriate way, that it have a suitable history, for knowledge to arise. If my belief is true and has arisen in the appropriate way, then I know that I see a tree, even if I do not know that the conflicting skeptical hypotheses are false. I might never have considered such skeptical machinations. Confronted with them, I might be astounded by them and find them so bizarre as not to be worthy of consideration.

ASK YOURSELF

98. What, according to naturalism as Lehrer describes it, is necessary in order for me to have knowledge that there is a tree in front of me?

Problems with the Naturalistic Relation. In spite of the advantages of naturalism, Lehrer argues, it does have its problems.

The advantages of naturalism are robust, but the theory must be true, not merely advantageous, to solve the problems with which we began. To ascertain whether the theory is true, we must have some account of the naturalistic relationship that is supposed to convert true belief into knowledge.

Lehrer discusses various refinements in naturalistic theories. The discussions tend to focus on perceptual knowledge, and provide plausible accounts of the kinds of naturalistic relations needed to turn true perceptual beliefs into knowledge. But these accounts are too restricted, he claims.

The foregoing analyses are, however, too restricted in scope to provide us with a general analysis of knowledge. There is more to knowledge than perceptual knowledge, and not all knowledge that *p* can be supposed to be caused by the fact that *p*. The most obvious example is general knowledge, my knowledge that all human beings die, for example. That fact includes the fact of death of as yet unborn humans which cannot now cause me to believe that all humans die or causally sustain that belief. Our knowledge that all neutrinos have zero rest mass is yet more difficult to account for on such a model, since no one has ever perceived a neutrino at rest. Assuming there to be mathematical knowledge, for example, that integers are infinite, the causal theory seems inappropriate. The integers appear to lie outside the temporal order and to be incapable of causing anything.

Lehrer considers various responses to this criticism, along with various refinements of externalist theories. Nonetheless, he thinks there are crushing objections to externalism.

Objections to Externalism: Information Without Knowledge. Lehrer argues that externalism will become implausible when we recognize the difference between knowing and merely recording or receiving information.

There is, however, a general objection to all externalist theories which is as simple to state as it is fundamental. . . . Any purely externalist account faces the fundamental objection that a person totally ignorant of the external factors connecting her belief with truth, might be ignorant of the truth of her belief as a result. All externalist theories share a common defect, to wit, that they provide accounts of the possession of information rather than of the attainment of knowledge. The appeal of such theories is their naturalistic character. They assimilate knowledge to other natural causal relationships between objects. Our attainment of knowledge is just one natural relationship between facts among all the rest. It is a relationship of causality, or nomological correlation, or frequency correlation, or counterfactual dependence. But this very attractive feature of such theories is their downfall. . . .

ASK YOURSELF

99. Thermometers receive and record information. Do they know anything?

The information a thermometer records is accurate if the changes in the thermometer are caused by or correlated with temperature changes in a lawful way. But does a thermometer *know* anything? Lehrer assumes the answer must be "no." However, someone might object that the only reason the thermometer does not know anything is that it cannot think. Leher argues that the reason it does not know goes deeper than that. Consider the following thought experiment.

Suppose a person, whom we shall name Mr. Truetemp, undergoes brain surgery by an experimental surgeon who invents a small device which is both a very accurate thermometer and a computational device capable of generating thoughts. The device, call it a tempucomp, is implanted in Truetemp's head so that the very tip of the device, no larger than the head of a pin, sits unnoticed on his scalp and acts as a sensor to transmit information about the temperature to the computational system in his brain. This device, in turn, sends a message to his brain causing him to think of the temperature recorded by the external sensor. Assume that the tempucomp is very reliable, and so his thoughts are correct temperature thoughts. All told, this is a reliable belief-forming process. Now imagine, finally, that he has no idea that the tempucomp has been inserted in his brain, is only slightly puzzled about why he thinks so obsessively about the temperature, but never checks a thermometer to determine whether these thoughts about the temperature are correct. He accepts them unreflectively, another effect of the tempucomp. Thus, he thinks and accepts that the temperature is 104 degrees. It is. Does he know that it is? Surely not. He has no idea whether he or his thoughts about the temperature are reliable. What he accepts, that the temperature is 104 degrees, is correct, but he does not know that his thought is correct. His thought that the temperature is 104 degrees is correct information, but he does not know this. Though he records the information because of the operations of the tempucomp, he is ignorant of the facts about the tempucomp and about his temperature telling reliability. Yet, the sort of causal, nomological, statistical, or counterfactual relationships required by externalism may all be present. Does he know that the temperature is 104 degrees when the thought occurs to him while strolling in Pima Canyon? He has no idea why the thought occurred to him or that such thoughts are almost always correct. He does not, consequently, know that the temperature is 104 degrees when that thought occurs to him.

The preceding example is not presented as a decisive objection against externalism and should not be taken as such. It is possible to place some constraint on relationships or processes converting belief to knowledge to exclude production by the tempucomp. The fundamental difficulty remains, however. It is that more than the possession of correct information is required for knowledge. One must have some way of knowing that the information is correct. Consider another example. Someone informs me that Professor Haller is in my office. Suppose I have no idea whether the person telling me this is trustworthy. Even if the information I receive is correct and 1 believe what I am told, I do not know that Haller is in my office, because I have no idea of whether the source of my information is trustworthy. The nomological, statistical, or counterfactual relationships or processes may be trustworthy, but I lack this information.

. . . To know that the information one possesses is correct, one requires background information about that information. One requires information about whether the received information is trustworthy or not, and lacking such information, one falls short of knowledge. . . . A necessary condition of knowledge is coherence with background information, with an acceptance system, informing us of the trustworthiness of the information we possess.

> ### ASK YOURSELF
>
> **100.** The preceding remarks amount to the claim that you cannot have knowledge without a _____ set of beliefs. There is thus an element of coherentism in Lehrer's account.

The Truth in Reliablism: The Absent-Minded Demon. Despite his rejection of externalism, Lehrer thinks it contains a valuable lesson. It reminds us that in order for any belief to amount to knowledge, it must indeed be the case that that belief was formed reliably. The following illustrates this point.

There is, however, an important lesson to be learned from reliabilism. It is that the sort of justification required for knowledge is not entirely an internal matter, either. On the contrary, the needed form of justification depends on the appropriate match between what one accepts about how one is related to the world and what is actually the case. To see this [suppose that] the demon, in a moment of cosmic absentmindedness, forgets for a moment to cloud our senses, with the result that we really perceive what we think we do. . . . I might perceive my hand for the first time and believe I see a hand, only to lose consciousness after this formidable event. Do I know that I see a hand in that brief moment? I believe I do, but, since such beliefs are almost all false, I am almost totally untrustworthy in such matters as is everybody else, though accepting myself to be worthy of trust. I am as much deceived about my trustworthiness in this case as I would be when confronted with a convincing liar who tells me almost all falsehoods about some party he attended except for one fact which, in a moment of absentmindedness, he accurately conveyed, namely, that he arrived before the host. If I accept all that he tells me and also that he is a trustworthy source of information about the event, I may be personally justified in accepting all that he says, but 1 do not know that the one truth he has conveyed is a truth. I do not know that he arrived before the host. The reason is that my assumption that my informant is trustworthy is in error, even if he has told me the truth in this one instance, and this error is sufficient to deprive me of the sort of justification I require for knowledge. This is the truth about justification contained in reliabilism.

ASK YOURSELF

101. The reliabilist claims that I have knowledge that *P* if and only if my belief that *P* is produced in a way that is reliable, in the sense that it is a way that almost always produces true beliefs, not false ones. Since beliefs produced by the demon, or the consistent and skilled liar, are not *generally* produced in a reliable way—that is, a way that makes for _____ beliefs—it follows that even when the demon or liar happens to produce a *true* belief in me, I do not have _____.

The truth contained in reliabilism is, however, concealed by an error. What a person originally believes as a result of prejudice may later be accepted on the basis of scientific evidence. Therefore, the reliabilist must be in error when he claims that it is what originates a belief that converts it into a justified belief and knowledge. This is, in effect, to confuse the *reason* a person has for believing something with the *cause* of his believing it. The confusion is such a common one that we might name it the *causal fallacy* . . . Often the evidence on which a justification is based does causally explain the existence of the belief . . . it may even be admitted that sometimes the belief is justified because of the way in which it is causally explained by the evidence. Nevertheless, it is also possible for a justified belief to be causally independent of the evidence that justifies it. Indeed, it may well be that the evidence in no way explains why the person holds the belief, even though her justification for the belief is based on the evidence. The evidence that justifies a person's belief may be evidence she acquired because she already held the belief, rather than the other way round. This is to be expected, since it is common sense to distinguish between the reasons that justify a belief and the causes that produce it. The causes of belief are various, and, though the reasons we have for a belief sometimes cause the belief to arise, the belief may also arise from some other cause.

ASK YOURSELF

102. The cause of my belief that it is hot outside (when in fact it is) might simply be that I dreamt that it was hot, but do not realize it was a dream. Give another example of a belief that is caused in a way that has nothing to do with its truth.

Having the reasons we do may justify the belief, however, even though they have no causal influence upon the belief at all.

An example will illustrate. It is easy to imagine the case of someone who comes to believe something for the wrong reason and, consequently, cannot be said to be justified in his belief, but who, as a result of his belief, uncovers some evidence that completely justifies his belief. Suppose that a man, Mr. Raco, is racially prejudiced and, as a result, believes that the members of some race are susceptible to some disease to which members of his [own] race are not susceptible. This belief, we may imagine, is an unshakable conviction. It is so strong a conviction that no evidence to the contrary would weaken his prejudiced conviction and no evidence in favor would strengthen it. Now imagine that Mr. Raco becomes a doctor and begins to study the disease in question. Imagine that he reads all that is known about the disease and discovers that the evidence, which is quite conclusive, confirms his conviction. The scientific evidence shows that only members of the race in question are susceptible to the disease. We may imagine as well that Mr. Raco has become a medical expert perfectly capable of understanding the canons of scientific evidence, though, unfortunately, he becomes no less prejudiced as a result of this. Nevertheless, he understands and appreciates the evidence as well as any medical expert and, as a result, has reason for his belief that justifies it. He has discovered that his conviction is confirmed by the scientific evidence. He knows that only members of the other race are susceptible to the disease in question. Yet, the reasons that justify him in this belief do not causally explain the belief. The belief is the result of prejudice, not reason, but it is confirmed by reason which provides the justification for the belief. Prejudice gives Mr. Raco conviction, but reason gives him justification.

ASK YOURSELF

103. To summarize: (1) What caused Raco's belief was _____. (2) What justified his belief was _____. (3) Therefore, it is important to have _____ beliefs, and to distinguish the _____ of a belief from what justifies it.

Lehrer thus concludes by rejecting externalism or reliablism. In his view I cannot be said to know something that I believe unless I can give reasons for thinking it is true. That idea is at the center of internalism. No matter how well produced my beliefs, no matter how truth-conducive the process that leads to them, I cannot be said to know unless I have access to that process and see that because of it my belief is justified. If I *can* do that, then, and only then, do I have knowledge. Lehrer's discussion has come around again to the topic of justification. Plantinga has argued that whether a belief is *justified* or not has nothing to do with whether it is *true*. Lehrer disagrees. Only justified beliefs can be knowledge.

ASK YOURSELF

104. Plantinga argues that justification, understood "deontologically" (i.e., as an epistemic *duty* to acquire beliefs in a responsible way) is not relevant to knowledge. Do you think Leher is using that same deontological concept of justification? That is, does he think that being justified is a matter of fulfilling certain intellectual obligations, such as the obligation to find evidence for one's beliefs?

105. How would you score the debate between internalists like Lehrer, and externalists like Plantinga or the naturalists Dretske and Nozick?

In the following selection the discussion continues, but from a somewhat different angle.

4. JUSTIFIED BELIEF AND INTELLECTUAL VIRTUES: LINDA ZAGZEBSKI

We have already encountered the notion of epistemic *duty* and its related term "deontology." Duty is an ethical concept. Thus the notion of being justified in a belief has often been understood in ethical terms. I am supposedly justified in a belief when I do my epistemic duty. These facts suggest a closer connection than we might at first suppose between ethics and epistemology. They also raise the following question: If epistemology must involve ethical notions, what sort of ethical notions should it involve and how are they to be understood? But many ethicists reject rigid duties as an adequate ethical model. For example, those ethicists who focus on character and virtues make the notion of duty secondary to character. Perhaps then it is also a mistake to focus on duty in thinking about knowledge. Perhaps we should focus on intellectual virtues and character rather than on performing epistemic duties. The following selections are from a book entitled *Virtues of the Mind* by contemporary philosopher Linda Zagzebski, who is attempting to make a case for such a focus. Focusing on intellectual virtues and vices may help us overcome the impasse between externalists and internalists, and it has, she argues, many other advantages.

Intellectual Virtues and Vices

FROM LINDA ZAGZEBSKI, *Virtues of the Mind* (1996)

Some of the most important questions we ask about our lives include "What should I think about?" and "What should I believe?" as well as "What should I want?" and "What should I do?" Furthermore, we criticize others for their beliefs and well as their actions, and we probably are even more inclined to criticize their beliefs than their feelings and desires. For example, a person who cannot help feeling envious but attempts to control such feelings is not criticized as much as someone who permits his envy to influence his beliefs on the morality of social and economic arrangements. The same point applies to beliefs formed, not out of undue influence by the passions, but by a more obviously "mental" error. So we blame a person who makes hasty generalizations or who ignores the testimony of reliable authority. Such criticism is much closer to *moral* criticism than the criticism of bad eyesight or poor blood circulation. When people call others shortsighted or pigheaded, their criticism is as much like moral criticism as when they call them offensive or obnoxious; in fact, what is obnoxious about a person can sometimes be limited to a certain pattern of thinking. The same point can be made, in differing degrees, of a variety of other names people are called for defects that are mostly cognitive: mulish, stiff-necked, pertinacious, recalcitrant, or obstinate, wrongheaded, vacuous, shallow, witless, dull, muddleheaded, thickskulled, or obtuse. Of course, the connotation of blame in the use of these terms may be partly conveyed by tone of voice, but their usage definitely differs from that of the purely nonmoral labels given to the brain damaged or congenitally mentally retarded. What's more, the association of praise and blame is explicitly extended to states of knowledge and ignorance when we use such expressions as "She should have known better."

It will take most of this book to demonstrate that epistemic evaluation is a form of moral evaluation, but I hope these few considerations explain in part the strong attraction to concepts and forms of argument from ethics in epistemological discourse, even in discourse on the nature of knowledge. . . . Epistemologists use ethical theory anyway. I suggest that it be done self-consciously and advisedly.

ASK YOURSELF

106. Patience is generally considered to be a moral virtue. That is, it is a good character trait, and impatience is a bad character trait. The teacher who spends a long time with slow students, trying to help them, exhibits patience. Patience could also be an *intellectual* virtue. Illustrate with an example.

107. Give some further examples of intellectual vices and virtues.

Ethical Models for Contemporary Epistemic Theories

A significant way in which contemporary epistemic theory parallels moral theory is that the locus of evaluation is the individual belief, just as the locus of evaluation in most modern ethics has been the individual act.

Modern ethicists have tended to focus on the rightness or wrongness of particular actions, such as the act of getting an abortion. Ethical debates have focused on attempts to find criteria for distinguishing right from wrong *acts*. Virtue ethics, on the other hand, focuses on *character*. A virtue ethicist might be more likely to ask, "What sort of character traits come into play when considering abortions?"

Zagzebski compares an emphasis on particular acts in ethics to an emphasis on particular beliefs in epistemology. She thinks both emphases are mostly mistaken or misleading.

ASK YOURSELF

108. Suppose Bob knows that the tides are caused by the gravitational attraction of the moon. In trying to understand what "knowing" amounts to, Zagzebski is suggesting that we should focus less on the particular way such a single belief would be justified or warranted, and focus more on the kinds of intellectual traits, or _____, which Bob has or lacks.

109. Suppose Bob is intellectually lazy. If we knew that about him, might we suspect that he does not really *know* about the moon–tide relation, even though what he believes about it is true? Why, or why not?

Zagzebski quotes Roderick Firth as a typical example of those who make individual beliefs the focus of analysis in epistemology.

"The ultimate task of a theory of knowledge is to answer the question, 'What is knowledge?' But to do this it is first necessary to answer the question, 'Under what conditions is a belief warranted?'" Firth calls this "the unavoidable first step," but in practice the first step is generally the major part of the theory. So whether the epistemologist is concerned with rational belief or with knowledge, the theory virtually always focuses on the belief and it makes the evaluation of belief conceptually basic.

Since contemporary epistemology is belief-based, it is no surprise that the type of moral theory from which these theories borrow moral concepts is almost always an act-based theory, either deontological or consequentialist. So we generally find that epistemologists refine their inquiry into one of two types of questions: (1) Does the belief violate any epistemic *rules* or any epistemic *duties?* Is it epistemically *permissible,* within one's epistemic *rights?* Theories of this sort take deontological moral theories as their normative model. (2) Was the belief formed by a reliable process for obtaining the truth? Theories of this sort are the forms of reliabilism, structurally parallel to consequentialism.

Consequentialism in ethics is the view that what makes a particular act right is the goal, in the sense of the foreseeable consequences, of that act. If the consequences are good, the act is right. Strictly speaking, it does not matter what the act itself is like, so long as it is aimed at the best foreseeable consequences overall.

In epistemology, reliabilists hold that the goal is to bring about true beliefs, or a balance of true over false beliefs. What matters for the reliabilist is the result, a true belief. It does not matter what the process is like that produces that result, so long as it does so reliably. So, consequentialism in ethics and reliabilism in epistemology are "structurally parallel."

110. Give an example of something you have done which you thought was right because of the good consequences it produced.

111. Suppose that you like to get drunk, and that whenever you do, certain vivid memories come back to you, and the memories are always accurate. For example, while staggering down the street you suddenly remember that Aunt Jane had red hair, and, in fact, she did. It seems that in your case alcohol reliably produces certain true beliefs. Should you be admired for having those beliefs? Should you be admired *as a knower?*

Advantages of Virtue Epistemology. Zagzebski goes on to argue that the moral concepts employed by contemporary epistemologists, such as "epistemic duty" or "epistemic obligation" are thin concepts, in the sense of having little content. Even in a moral context, these concepts tend to be thin. Just what does it mean to say "one is obligated to tell the truth?" Where does such an "obligation" come from? Does absolutely any person have that obligation, in any situation? The philosopher Gertrude Anscombe argued that such concepts become evacuated of content when, as in most contemporary philosophy, they are severed from the idea of a divine lawgiver who places obligations upon us. Virtue epistemology, on the other hand, operates with "thick" concepts in a sense explained below.

Now if Anscombe is right that legalistic moral language makes no sense without a divine lawgiver, such language in epistemology is even more peculiar. We can at least find practical reasons for continuing to judge acts and to render verdicts in the moral case, but it is hard to see the point of such a system in the evaluation of beliefs and cognitive activities. What purpose is served by putting Jones up before an epistemic tribunal for believing in UFOS? Is she to be declared epistemically guilty? What follows from *that?* This is not to deny that there is a point to the concept of epistemic duty, as we shall see at the end of Part II, and perhaps even of epistemic guilt. What is doubtful, however, is that these concepts are to be understood in the hard-hitting sense typically associated with legalistic language, with heavy social sanctions, punishments, and the like.

More convincing is Anscombe's point that the concepts of *right, wrong, obligation, and duty* lack content, as well as Williams's related point on the preferability of thick over thin moral concepts. In epistemic evaluation we also see this distinction between thick and thin concepts. The reaction of ordinary people to epistemic impropriety is not simply to say that a person's belief is unjustified but to direct evaluation toward the person himself and to call him "narrow-minded," "careless," "intellectually cowardly," "rash," "imperceptive," "prejudiced," "rigid," or "obtuse." People are accused of "jumping to conclusions," "ignoring relevant facts," "relying on untrustworthy authority," "lacking insight," being "unable to see the forest for the trees," and so on. Of course, the beliefs formed as the result of such defects are evaluated negatively, but any blanket term for this negative evaluation, such as "unjustified" or "irrational," fails to convey any other information than the negative evaluation alone and is therefore a thin concept in Williams' sense. Concepts such as the ones just named have a much richer content. They are not only normative terms, conveying a negative evaluation, but indicate the *way* in which the believer acted improperly. All of these terms are names either for intellectual vices or for categories of acts exhibiting intellectual vice.

ASK YOURSELF

112. Suppose Mary believes in UFOs. I complain that her belief is unjustified, and I'm right. Suppose, on the other hand, that I correctly complain that Mary typically relies on untrustworthy sources, which is an intellectual vice. Which complaint gives you the most, and the most definite, information about Mary? Explain.

The second set of reasons for preferring a virtue approach in ethics also applies to epistemology. There is no reason to think that being in an epistemically positive state is any more rule governed than being in a morally positive state. . . . Insight, for example, is an intellectual virtue that is not rule governed but differs significantly in the form it takes from one person to another and from one area of knowledge to another. Insight is necessary for another virtue, trust, which has an intellectual as well as a moral form. There is no algorithm for determining trustworthiness, even in principle. Not only does one need insight into the character of others to have trust in its virtuous form, but trust also involves certain affective qualities, and it is hard to see how these could be described procedurally. In addition, such intellectual virtues as adaptability of intellect, the ability to recognize the salient facts, sensitivity to detail, the ability to think up explanations of complex sets of data, and the ability to think up illuminating scientific hypotheses or interpretations of literary texts, as well as such virtues as intellectual care, perseverance, and discretion, are not strictly rule governed. In each case, the virtue involves an aspect of knowing-how that is partially learned by imitation and practice. John Henry Newman has a number of examples that support this view. In one, he discusses a medieval historian who asserts that the *Aeneid* could not be a thirteenth century forgery. The historian's conviction is built upon a lifetime of study of the differences between the classical and medieval minds. "We do not pretend to be able to draw the line between what the medieval intellect could or could not do; but we feel sure that at least it could not write the classics. An instinctive sense of this, and a faith in testimony, are the sufficient, but the undeveloped argument on which to ground our certitude."

ASK YOURSELF

113. Briefly, what is the second reason for preferring a virtues approach in epistemology?

The third advantage of aretaic [virtue] ethics also has a parallel in epistemic evaluation. Contemporary epistemology focuses on epistemic values that are impersonal: the value of possessing truth and the value of rationality and justified belief. Truth, like utility, is a good that does not depend upon the point of view of any given individual, and rationality and justifiability are typically understood in a way that also is impersonal. But there is one personal epistemic value so important that it is the one from which philosophy gets its name, and that is wisdom. Wisdom is a value that is at least difficult, probably impossible, to understand impersonally on the model of rationality. It is likely that wisdom, like friendship, takes a different form in each individual case, and it resists any analysis that does not make essential reference to the standpoint of the individual. This feature of wisdom is reflected in the fact that human knowledge is usually thought to increase over the ages, but few people would observe the same progress in human wisdom. This is presumably because there is no stock of wisdom possessed by the species comparable to the stock of knowledge. Each person has to begin at the beginning in developing wisdom, and the experience needed for wisdom requires a certain amount of time, whereas growth in knowledge can be accelerated by proper teaching of the most advanced knowledge of an age. A related reason for the difference is that much knowledge is propositional and can be learned a bit at a time, whereas wisdom unifies the whole of human experience and understanding. The unifying feature of wisdom explains another distinctive mark of wisdom, namely, that it cannot be misused, whereas knowledge surely *can* be misused. Wisdom not only unifies the knowledge of the wise person but unifies her desires and values as well. There is nothing incoherent or even surprising about a knowledgeable person who is immoral, but it is at least surprising, perhaps incoherent, to say that a wise person is immoral.

ASK YOURSELF

114. What are two things that distinguish wisdom from knowledge?

A further advantage of a virtues approach, Zagzebski argues, is that it can account for the value of what she calls "cognitive integration."

It is an intellectual virtue to be cognitively integrated, just as it is a moral virtue to be morally integrated. A person who is cognitively integrated has positive higher-order attitudes toward her own intellectual character and the quality of the beliefs and level of understanding that such a character produces. . . . To have a good intellectual character, it is not sufficient to simply pile up justified beliefs and judge that they are justified. A person who is cognitively integrated has epistemic values that determine such things as the proportion of one's time spent gathering evidence or considering arguments for and against an unpromising theory, as well as the epistemic worth of one belief over another and the way in which each belief fits into her overall belief structure and is conducive to understanding. Cognitive integration is partially constitutive of intellectual integrity, the virtue of having an intellect with an identity. I conclude that at least some intellectual virtues cannot be analyzed in terms of a relation to good (justified, warranted) beliefs. The virtue of intellectual integrity requires a virtue approach to at least *some aspects of epistemic evaluation.*

ASK YOURSELF

115. Most people sense that having a head stuffed with facts is not the highest intellectual state. What we do value is a person who understands how various facts hang together, knows how best to expand genuine understanding, and so forth. Does the case of Mr. Truetemp mentioned by Lehrer illustrate the same point?

This last point is related to a further advantage in a virtues epistemology—namely, its ability to take account of what might be called "cognitive power." Zagzebski borrows an example from the philosopher Charles Talieffero to make her point. Talieffero imagines two Gods, Christopher and Dennis, both of whom are all-knowing. That is, both of them know all truths. But Dennis knows them only because he trusts a reliable source, namely Christopher, who has supplied him with those truths. Christopher, on the other hand, arrived at those truths through his own cognitive powers, rather than relying on another being.

Compare, then, the human counterparts of Dennis and Christopher. Let us suppose that they both believe a large set of true propositions T. Assume that the differences in their other beliefs are insignificant since they believe the same number of true propositions and the same number of false propositions, and there is no difference in the importance of their respective beliefs. The only epistemic difference between them is that Christopher believes the propositions in T by the direct use of his own perceptual and cognitive powers, whereas Dennis believes them on the authority of Christopher. Let us assume also that Christopher is a perfectly reliable authority, so that Dennis's belief-forming process is just as truth conducive as Christopher's. According to reliabilism, the normative property of the beliefs of Dennis is equal to that of Christopher. On the assumption that this property is also the property that converts true belief into knowledge, Dennis and Christopher are equal in their knowledge of T. But intuitively Christopher is superior in knowledge to Dennis because he possesses greater cognitive power. But since he does not know more true propositions than Dennis does, his superiority in knowledge must involve superior quality.

Christopher's superiority might be explicated by a more detailed description of the case. Perhaps his superiority is due to the greater clarity or understanding that accompanies the acquisition of true beliefs by the exercise of one's own powers, but it might also be that we attach greater value to Christopher's mode of acquiring the truth quite apart from the extra value of such things as clarity and understanding. One thing that is bothersome about reliabilism, like what is bothersome about consequentialism, is the fact that on these theories self consciousness and the power of directing the activities of the self that self-consciousness allows are only incidentally related to the good under consideration. Just as a utility-calculating machine would be the ideal moral agent according to utilitarianism, a truth-producing machine would be the ideal epistemic agent according to reliabilism. The nature of the process leading to believing the truth and the extent of the agent's awareness of the process are only contingently related to the goal of knowledge, so something like the Oracle at Delphi (minus the riddles and with infallibility) would be epistemically ideal. Although I know of no actual argument against the acceptability of such a consequence, I find it unpalatable and imagine that others will too. It follows, then, that there are worries about reliabilism that parallel worries about utilitarianism. This gives us another reason to look for an alternative ethical model for epistemology.

I will conclude this section with one final advantage of a virtue theory that applies both to ethical and to epistemological evaluation. The basic evaluative concept in act-based ethics is that of the right act, where right means not wrong, or permissible. The focus of this type of ethics is on avoiding blameworthiness rather than on achieving moral praiseworthiness. Virtue ethics, in contrast, allows for a greater range of evaluative levels and gives due regard to the fact that our moral aim is not only to avoid the bottom level of the moral scale but to end up as high on the scale as possible. Similarly, the basic evaluative concept in belief-based epistemology is that of the justified belief, and again, to be justified is to do the minimum necessary to avoid the epistemic equivalent of blame; it is not to achieve a high level of epistemic worth. But presumably our epistemic aim is to reach as high a level of epistemic evaluation as we can. A virtue theory does justice to the full range of evaluative states, whereas an act-based ethics and a belief-based epistemology do not.

ASK YOURSELF

116. What, if anything, makes a "truth-producing machine" less admirable than a conscious agent who understands how to go about arriving at the truth?

117. In evaluating other people as thinkers, suppose that you do *not* tend to praise those who do best at avoiding error but do not do much else, and instead praise more those who, though they make mistakes now and then, are good at making startling discoveries or producing creative results. Would you then be in agreement with Zagzebski, or not?

A Further Advantage in a Virtues-Based Approach

Lately, contemporary epistemology has been criticized on a number of other grounds that would make a virtue approach promising. I will not go through these in any great detail but will merely call attention to them. For one thing, some philosophers have complained that contemporary epistemology is insufficiently attentive to the social aspects of cognitive activity, and this complaint is not limited to those outside mainstream epistemology, because Sosa and Goldman have made much the same point. It seems to me, though, that other things being equal, the social component in cognitive activity is handled more easily by the traditional concept of virtue than by either the concept of a reliable belief-forming mechanism (Goldman) or that of a reliable belief-forming faculty (Sosa). Mechanisms and faculties can be contextualized into a social framework only with quite a bit of artificiality, whereas a social context is intrinsic to the nature of a virtue as traditionally understood. On such accounts most virtues are traits that enable individuals to live well in communities. This is the position of Alasdair MacIntyre and is arguably the view of Aristotle. In addition, the way Aristotle understands the acquisition of virtue is fundamentally social since virtue is acquired primarily through imitation of those in one's society who already have it. Of course, this is no demonstration that the degree and kind of sociality to be found in the traditional concept of a virtue are sufficient to give epistemologists what is wanted in the social aspects of belief, but I suggest that at least some of the work of making the normative property of epistemic states more social is already done for us in the historical use of the concept of a virtue.

ASK YOURSELF

118. Is it Zagzebski's view that attention to the social context of knowledge is important?

Virtues approaches to ethics typically stress the idea that a virtue is not simply a disposition to act in certain ways—for example, courageously—but is also a tendency to feel and perceive in distinctive ways. For example, the courageous person actually *feels* less fear than the coward in certain situations. This fact might seem to suggest an important difference between the use of virtue concepts in ethics and their use in epistemology, for it might seem that having true justified, or warranted, beliefs, is not a matter of feeling at all. Feelings need to be left out in order for thinking to be clear and accurate. Real knowledge requires a "cool" disinterested intellect. Or does it? Zagzebski argues for a positive role for feelings and passions in knowledge acquisition, as well as for the idea that the intellectual virtues are needed to "tame" certain passions.

Feelings are involved in intellectual virtues, and intellectual virtues are involved in handling feelings, but their operation shows how blurry the distinction between intellectual and moral virtues really is. Intellectual prejudice, for example, is an intellectual vice, and the virtue that is its contrary is fair-mindedness, but clearly we think of prejudice as a moral failing and fairmindedness as a morally good quality. It is possible that the intellectual form of prejudice and the moral form are the same vice, and the same point could apply to other cases in which an intellectual trait has the same name as a moral trait, such as humility, autonomy, integrity, perseverance, courage, and trustworthiness. William James has said in "The Sentiment of Rationality" that faith is the same virtue in the intellectual realm as courage is in the moral realm: "Faith is the readiness to act in a cause the prosperous issue of which is not certified to us in advance. It is the same moral quality which we call courage in practical affairs; and there will be a very widespread tendency in men of vigorous nature to enjoy a certain amount of uncertainty in their philosophic creed, just as risk lends a zest to worldly activity." I will not take a stand here on whether a moral and an intellectual virtue can be the very same virtue. In any case, if there is a distinction between intellectual and moral virtue/vice, it cannot be on the grounds that the latter handles feelings and the former does not.

Not only is the proper handling of feelings involved in intellectual as well as moral virtues, but almost all moral virtues include an aspect of proper perceptual and cognitive activity. As I argued, virtue is a success concept. No one has the virtue of fairness or courage or compassion or generosity without generally being in cognitive contact with the aspect of reality handled by the respective virtue. Otherwise, one could not be reliably successful. We may make allowances for *some* mistakes in beliefs or perceptions in the possession of a moral virtue, but no one who regularly misperceives the situation or has mistaken beliefs about what should or should not be done in such cases can be said to possess the moral virtue that governs cases of that type. For example, anyone who regularly acts in a way that causes suffering to others can hardly be said to possess the virtue of compassion, no matter what his intentions and motivation. Similarly, a person who adopts policies in grading that clearly favor male over female students or vice versa cannot be said to possess the virtue of fairness, no matter how these policies look from his point of view. Being reasonably intelligent within a certain area of life is part of having almost any moral virtue.

ASK YOURSELF

119. Give an example of an intellectual virtue that involves managing feelings properly, say what the feelings are and what managing them properly would amount to.

Most traditional accounts of ethical virtue include the claim that the virtues cannot be taught, at least not in any very straightforward way. It would be more appropriate to say that they are "caught" from morally good people who provide a good example, which we may then try to imitate. On the other hand, intellectual virtues, like intellectual things generally, would, it has seemed to many, be teachable. Here again Zagzebski argues that there is no such difference between intellectual and moral virtues.

What can be taught are skills such as the codified part of logic. Moral skills, such as procedures for grading fairly or processes for aiding famine-ridden countries that will have the desired effect, can also be taught. What cannot be taught, or, at least, cannot be taught so easily, are intellectual virtues such as open-mindedness, the ability to think up an explanation for a complex set of data, or the ability to recognize reliable authority. These qualities are no more teachable than generosity or courage.

I propose that the stages of learning the intellectual virtues are exactly parallel to the stages of learning the moral virtues as described by Aristotle. They begin with the imitation of virtuous persons, [and] require practice which develops certain habits of feeling and acting. . . . One learns how to *believe* the way she should rather than the way she wants in a way parallel to her learning how to *act* the way she should rather than the way she wants. And just as ultimately she learns to want to act the way she should, ultimately she learns to want to believe the way she should. She learns such intellectual virtues as open-mindedness, the ability to recognize reliable authority, and the ability to think up good explanations for a complex set of data by imitating persons who have these qualities to an exemplary degree. In many cases she has to overcome contrary inclinations, or what might be called intellectual *akrasia* [weakness of will], and will have to go through a stage of developing intellectual self-control before she masters the virtue. In most cases the acquisition of an intellectual virtue involves training the feelings. For example, the ability to recognize reliable authority partly involves having trained feelings that permit one to be a reliable judge of the intellectual trustworthiness of another. The affective responses involved in the judgment that certain people are reliable or trustworthy are both a partial cause and a partial reason for the judgment of their reliability. Ultimately, she finds herself *wanting* to trust a person whom she knows she should trust and not wanting to trust the untrustworthy or unreliable.

ASK YOURSELF

120. Do you think of yourself as open-minded? If so, how do you think you got that way? If not, how do you think you might become more open-minded?

121. Do you have any tendency to trust unreliable authority? Or don't you know whether you do or not?

Thinking about intellectual vices may also help us to see the connection between moral and intellectual virtues.

[I]f we start with the vice, we can see the range of differences in intellectual character and how they correspond to the range of differences in moral character.

Some examples of intellectual vices are as follows: intellectual pride, negligence, idleness, cowardice, conformity, carelessness, rigidity, prejudice, wishful thinking, closed-mindedness, insensitivity to detail, obtuseness, and lack of thoroughness. There is probably also a vice contrary to intellectual perseverance, which involves giving up too soon and may be a form of intellectual laziness or proneness to discouragement. Some forms of self-deception may be a vice, but other forms may instead be a form of intellectual *akrasia* [lack of self-control].

A person who has intellectual vices may be unaware that she exhibits these vices on the occasions in which she does so. She may even mistake a vice for a virtue, just as in the case of moral vices. Aristotle thought that part of the process of acquiring virtue is learning where the mean is between two extremes. Some of the intellectual vices mentioned above may have contrary vices, where one is an excess and the other a deficiency, and the virtue is a mean between them. For example, there may be such a thing as intellectual rashness, the contrary of intellectual cowardice. In addition, it may be possible to be overly thorough, overly sensitive to detail, overly cautious, etc. Lorraine Code remarks, "One hesitates to attribute intellectual virtue to a voracious collector of facts, such as Sartre's self-taught man, or to an information gatherer of encyclopedic mind." These cases also show an intellectual excess of sorts, but they are probably not so much vices as a waste of intellectual-energy that could be put to better use.

ASK YOURSELF

122. Might it be intellectually rash to persist in a belief that is rejected by a great many authorities on the subject of that belief?

Zagzebski goes on to consider intellectual "vices" that appear to be a kind of pathological condition. She quotes from William James, who provides some clinical descriptions of people overcome by a "questioning mania," a pathological opposite of a tendency to believe without inquiry.

It follows from James's examples that there is a proper degree of doubt and the urge to inquire further. One must be neither too sanguine in one's convictions nor too obsessed with the desire to inquire further before reaching the state of settled belief. One must, in short, know when to stop, but also when to start and when to continue. The virtue that is the mean between the questioning mania and unjustified conviction has no simple name, as far as I know, but it is something like being both properly inquiring and properly doubtful. The learning of virtue consists in part of learning the extent of proper doubt and proper inquiry.

The acquisition of intellectual virtues involves a gradual process, from ignorance and moral incompetence, through a stage of knowing how to act but being too weak willed to act that way consistently, to self-control, and finally to the virtue, in which the praiseworthy behavior comes more or less naturally.

[An] example of intellectual *akrasia* [lack of self-control] would be knowing that the word of a certain person cannot be trusted but believing on his authority something that supports your own position. It frequently happens that people read newspaper articles that support their own political position but ignore the articles of those who may be more dependable and whom, furthermore, they *know* to be more dependable, or *would* know, if they were paying attention.

The stage after *akrasia* is intellectual self-control. At this stage a person has to stop herself from accepting inadequate evidence or poor testimony or lapsing into ways of speaking or reasoning of which she disapproves. But, unlike the previous stage, she does it successfully. Still, she lacks the virtue because she finds it difficult to weigh evidence properly or judge authority reliably or reason with care and according to the rules. Her behavior may be correct, but it is not grounded in a "firm and unchangeable character," as Aristotle characterizes the person who truly possesses virtue.

The final stage is the intellectual virtue. Examples include intellectual carefulness, perseverance, humility, vigor, flexibility, courage, and thoroughness, as well as open-mindedness, fairmindedness, insightfulness, and the virtues opposed to wishful thinking, obtuseness, and conformity. One of the most important virtues, I believe, is intellectual integrity.

ASK YOURSELF

123. Would it be possible to have one intellectual virtue, such as fairmindedness, without having many, or even all, of the others, such as courage? In answering this, try to imagine a situation where being fair-minded would get you into trouble of a sort that you fear.

Virtue theorists in ethics, such as Aristotle, argue that the various virtues are not reducible to rule following or some routine or algorithm, and that moreover they need to be governed and coordinated by a master virtue which is itself not rule governed. This feature of virtue ethics is often thought to be to its advantage. After all, the complexities and unpredictabilities of life require capacities for judgment of individual cases, subtle abilities to keep various inclinations in balance, and the like. No set of rules would suffice for such tasks.

Aristotle called the master capacity for judgment and discrimination *phronesis,* which means practical wisdom. Zagzebski argues that *phronesis* is also required for intellectual virtue.

Persons with practical wisdom learn how and when to trust certain feelings, and they develop habits of attitude and feeling that enable them to reliably make good judgments without being aware of following a procedure. There is a very strong element of inclination in most beliefs, even in the beliefs of those persons most intellectually practiced and aware. The difficult part is to train the inclinations themselves to reliably produce the desired end—in the case of intellectual activity, knowledge.

If the evidence proposed so far is not yet convincing, consider the way a good detective solves a mystery in the classic detective story. He will exhibit such virtues as the ability to recognize the salient facts, insightfulness, and the ability to think up explanations of complex sets of data . . . these virtues are no more rule governed than our previous examples. No specifiable procedures tell a person how to recognize the salient facts, how to get insight, or how to think up good explanations, much less how to use all three to get to a single end. All of these virtues operate together in the good detective. In the classic detective novel many other characters in the novel, as well as the reader, have access to the same data as the detective. They may also have good memories and have very good reasoning skills insofar as such skills can be taught. That is to say, they know the right procedures for valid deductive reasoning and may even know such things as the probability calculus and the looser rules of inductive logic. We may also suppose that they do not commit any of the so-called informal fallacies either. But they do not all have the ability to figure out the murderer's identity. A good detective story will explain how the detective came to his conclusion and should do so in a way that shows the reader that she could have figured it out herself if she had had the requisite intellectual traits. In some stories the detective claims that it is a matter of putting the evidence together in a certain order that permits him to "see" a pattern that points to a certain culprit, analogous to seeing where to put a piece in a jigsaw puzzle. Others stress the idea that solving a murder mystery is primarily a matter of psychological insight into human nature and the motives that lead people to murder. Still others stress the simplest explanation of the facts. In all these cases the detective's ability is something that is clearly not the following of a set of rules, at least not insofar as they can be known and taught. Of course, a person might be able to learn how to be a good detective by frequent and intense exposure to good detectives. The point is that they do not learn it by learning how to follow a procedure.

ASK YOURSELF

124. Mention three possible ways a good detective might operate.

A Definition of Knowledge. Zagzebski's discussion leads her, finally, to the following definition of an act of intellectual virtue, and then a definition of knowledge which incorporates the idea of intellectual virtue.

An act of intellectual virtue: A is an act that arises from the motivational component of A, is something a person with virtue A would (probably) do in the circumstances, is successful in achieving the end of the A motivation, and is such that the agent acquires a true belief (cognitive contact with reality) through these features of the act. I am interpreting cognitive contact with reality in a broad enough sense to include understanding and certainty.

I now propose that we define knowledge as follows:

Def. 1: Knowledge is a state of cognitive contact with reality arising out of acts of intellectual virtue. Alternatively,

Def. 2: Knowledge is a state of true belief arising out of acts of intellectual virtue.

Since the fact that a belief arises out of acts of intellectual virtue entails that it is true, the second definition can be formulated without redundancy as follows:

Def. 3: Knowledge is a state of belief arising out of acts of intellectual virtue.

The second definition follows the contemporary convention of defining knowledge as true belief plus something else, but its redundant element makes it misleading. The first definition may be preferable since it is noncommittal on such questions as the object of knowledge, the nature of truth, and the existence of propositions, which are not explored in this work. It also permits a broader interpretation of knowledge since knowledge may include cognitive contact with structures of reality other than the propositional.

Hilary Kornblith (1985) argues that Descartes has forced us to distinguish four distinct kinds of epistemic evaluation. We can evaluate either the nonvoluntary processes by which beliefs are formed or the voluntary acts that influence these processes, and then we can evaluate each of these from either an objective or a subjective perspective. Since the two questions asked from an objective perspective are not independent, Kornblith says we are left with three independent epistemic evaluations, and he proposes that an account of knowledge ought to incorporate all of them. "In particular, I want to suggest that knowledge requires: (1) belief which is arrived at in an objectively correct, that is, reliable, manner; (2) belief which is arrived at in a subjectively correct manner; and (3) belief which is the product of epistemically responsible action, that is, action regulated by a desire for true beliefs" (p. 273). The definition of knowledge proposed here satisfies Kornblith's three criteria.

ASK YOURSELF

125. If you have covered the readings on externalism/internalism, answer the following:

Does Kornblith's first requirement incorporate externalist notions? Does the second requirement incorporate internalist notions?

Zagzebski's definition of knowledge does in fact include a "reliabilist" component. Intellectual virtues are valued because they reliably produce a favorable balance of true beliefs in the person who has them. But reliabilists typically are externalists who claim that we can know, because of the operation of some reliable belief forming process, without knowing how we know. In contrast, it would be odd to suppose that the intellectually virtuous person does not know what it is about herself that tends to produce true beliefs. So Zagzebski's view is unlike reliabilist externalism, and it is more like internalism insofar as it requires that knowers have access to or be aware of what it is that reliably produces knowledge. It has some of the advantages of both internalism and externalism, she argues, without the disadvantages of either.

One problem with Zagzebski's definition of knowledge in terms of intellectual *virtue* is that it sometimes seems that intellectual *vices* might also reliably produce true beliefs. Here are a few examples that she cites. (1) A "nosey neighbor" might reliably acquire lots of true beliefs about her neighbors which she would not acquire if she were not nosey. But nosiness seems like a vice. (2) An excessively proud person, who refuses to take seriously challenges to his own beliefs, might just for that reason be more likely to have true beliefs, if in fact he is an intellectually powerful person who tends to get to the truth when he goes his own way. But intellectual pride looks like a vice, not a virtue. (3) Uncle Toby, a character in Laurence Sterne's *Tristram Shandy,* becomes obsessed with military architecture and related military matters. He neglects his health and piles up remarkably detailed (and useless) knowledge and cannot seem to stop pursuing these studies. He is a special case of a kind of person who fills his head with mountains of information. It is natural to think of this condition as a vice, a kind of *excess,* which in Aristotle's view is typical of vices. Nonetheless, Toby does acquire knowledge, and by reliable procedures. Cases like these seem to count against a theory such as Zagzebski's that associate reliable belief forming processes with virtue. She suggests two possible responses to these examples. The first response consists in denying that in such cases the individuals (the nosey neighbor, Toby) really have knowledge. Her preferred response, however, is to claim that these people do have knowledge, but also that they fit her definition of knowledge as a state of belief arising out of intellectual virtue. The following excerpt focuses on this second response.

First, it should be admitted that virtuous and vicious procedures can overlap. It would, in fact, be surprising if things were otherwise. Clearly, people can perform the same overt acts out of different motives, so it ought to be expected that they can also perform the same cognitive acts out of different motives. Some of these motives are praiseworthy; others are not. Some, in fact, may be blameworthy, and the examples just given may be in this category. So a nosey woman who snoops on her neighbor out of sexual envy will find out facts about her neighbor that are none of her business but that are facts nonetheless, and that she apparently knows. Similarly, some of the most successful minds are also the most prideful, and it definitely looks as if their discoveries are things they know. And the same goes for Tristram Shandy's charming Uncle Toby. I have already expressed reservations about claiming that Toby's intellectual acquisitiveness is a vice, but some readers may think so and still think that the result of this acquisitiveness is knowledge.

The notion of "mixed motives" is central to Zagzebski's treatment of this problem. The nosey neighbor may quite possibly be motivated to seek the truth about his neighbor. But he wants to know the truth in order to be able to gossip about his neighbor, or because he is jealous of him, or because of various other vicious motives. The motivation to discover the truth may lead him to use reliable processes in collecting information about his neighbor (though it is worth noting that the vicious motives might well interfere with his objectivity). That motivation is good. And it is a motivation typical of intellectual virtue. So the nosey neighbor really does possess some intellectual virtues, and the knowledge he acquires does result from the exercise of those virtues and thus fits the definition of knowledge as a state of belief arising out of intellectual virtues. However, the same acts that are motivated by the desire for truth are also motivated by vicious desires. They are cases of acts with mixed motives, and such acts are not unusual.

126. Briefly, why is the case of the nosey neighbor not necessarily a counterexample to Zagzebski's definition of knowledge? State the definition first.

Could we say that the believers in each of these cases satisfy my definition of knowledge after all? All of these believers are motivated to get the truth, but not because they place intrinsic value on truth. They are also motivated to be open-minded, careful, attentive, etc., so they have some particular intellectually virtuous motives. Their problem is that they also have another motive, an ulterior one, one that is deplorable—envy, pride, or the desire for fame. But the above definition of knowledge is loose enough that beliefs arising from vicious motives need not be precluded from being cases of knowing so long as they also arise from the desire for truth and other virtuous motives. The problem here is that we have cases of mixed motives.

127. The nosey person, the proud researcher, and Uncle Tobey thus do have intellectual virtues. We tend to think of them as not virtuous because they have _____ _____, some of which are indeed not virtuous.

128. Review this entire selection and cite at least two advantages claimed by Zagzebski for her approach to epistemology.

Zagzebski's account of knowledge manages to combine some externalist and some internalist insights and motives. It has several advantages over alternative accounts, some of which are listed above. One of these advantages is that it allots an important place to the social character of knowledge. That same theme becomes prominent in the following section. However, attention to the social character of knowledge carries with it a danger, the danger of cognitive relativism. An extreme cognitive relativist denies that knowing is *anything but* a product of social factors. She may also argue that the social factors themselves are such that there is no way to choose between competing accounts of knowledge arising from different social circumstances. This issue is central for the selections that follow.

SUMMING UP PROBLEMS WITH JUSTIFIED BELIEF

Suppose you know that *P*, where *P* is "Kangeroos are marsupials." If you know it, then obviously you believe it, and obviously it is true (you cannot "know" something false). But that is not enough. It might just be luck that what you believe is true. Something else is required. What is that something else? Many have thought that in addition to the truth of *P* and your believing *P*, what you need is justification for believing *P*. Whether the justification is empirical in nature, appeals to coherence criteria, or some other source, at any rate you must be justified in your belief in order to have knowledge. However, Gettier showed that some justified true beliefs are not knowledge. Perhaps then something else, rather than justification, is needed in order to turn true belief into knowledge. Plantinga has suggested "warrant," others have suggested some modified sense of "justification." Whatever term is used, a new divide has opened up between externalists and internalists. Externalists think that warrant or justification is the result of truth-conducive or reliable processes or grounds which the knower might sometimes be unaware of. Internalists, by contrast, continue to insist that I have knowledge only when I am able to say how I know, only when I have "access" so to speak, to whatever it is that makes my belief true.

The competing views both have intuitive appeal. Normally, if I ask you how you know *P*, I will not accept the answer "I just know." On the other hand, it is true that the processes that lead to true beliefs may be very complex and completely unfamiliar to most knowers. I do not myself have much knowledge of the perceptual mechanisms that operate to produce true perceptual beliefs. I do know that Napoleon was a general, but if someone asks me how I know, I will engage in hand waving; everyone knows that (although not everyone does), all the historians agree (although I definitely am not familiar with the views of *all* historians), and so forth. Perhaps what is needed then is a view that does some justice to at least some of our internalist *and* some of our externalist intuitions. Virtue epistemology has been put forth as something that can do that. Knowledge may be true belief arising out of acts of virtue. Intellectual virtues are traits that tend to produce true beliefs in the one who has them. Intellectual carefulness might be one. Even if the one who has intellectual virtues cannot give a good account of what a virtue is and has not tracked a virtue's operation in a particular case, the virtue may nonetheless have produced a true belief. So this approach does some justice to externalist intuitions. On the other hand, people who have virtues, whether ethical or intellectual, generally know that they have them and know that they are good things to have because of what they produce, namely good actions or true beliefs.

CAN OF WORMS

Externalist epistemology may be used to escape the constraints of foundationalism. Perhaps there are things I know even though I cannot cite grounds or show how I know them. Perhaps, for instance, I know that God exists, simply because my belief in God has been produced by a reliable belief producing mechanism, such as God's direct intervention in my thought processes. This approach in epistemology has in fact found applications in the philosophy of religion. But it could also be used to shore up naturalistic views of the world. Knowledge may be the result of the operation of natural processes that reliably produce true belief, although those processes may be largely unknown to a given knower, or even any knower. If externalists are right, what becomes of the notion of responsibility and duty with respect to knowledge? Epistemology does seem to overlap with ethics. It seems that it may sometimes be wrong or irresponsible to claim I know something when I lack the kind of certainty the old-fashioned foundationalists tried to supply. In fact the overlap or intertwining of ethics and epistemology is not limited to considerations of intellectual duty, as virtue epistemology shows. For the notion of a virtue can be understood independently of the notion of duty.

F. THE SOCIAL CONSTRUCTION OF KNOWLEDGE

The notion of "social construction" has become important recently in just about all academic domains, perhaps with the exception of mathematics. The basic idea is that how and what we think and believe, even when we are being most "objective," are the result of social factors, such as power relations or economic factors, rather than the result of bumping up against plain facts that constrain our thinking or belief systems.

a. Does how you think about the physical world reflect your particular background, or is it instead determined by scientific theories that you have learned and that are the same for all, regardless of background?

b. Do men and women have different "styles" of thinking? For example, do men tend to be more analytic, women more empathetic?

c. The science of psychology/psychotherapy once categorized homosexuals as abnormal. That has changed. Use this example in discussing the following question: Do changes in scientific theory result from ever closer approximations to the truth about nature, or do they merely reflect socially dominant values and perspectives?

 1.   ## SOCIAL FACTORS IN THE DEVELOPMENT OF KNOWLEDGE AND SCIENCE: THOMAS KUHN

In about the latter third of the twentieth century, some philosophers and historians of science began to question the "objectivity" of even the most exact sciences. In effect, they claimed that scientific knowledge was not "knowledge" as construed through most of the history of epistemology. But their reasons for these claims had nothing to do with the kind of skepticism about knowledge which we have encountered in Hume and others. One of the most influential of these thinkers was physicist Thomas Kuhn (1922–1996), whose interest in the history of science led him to author a seminal work entitled *The Structure of Scientific Revolutions* (1962, referred to as SSR in what follows).

Scientific and Political Revolutions. Kuhn argued that the most common accounts of scientific knowledge are flawed. Contrary to those accounts, there is no such thing as a single scientific method, and scientific knowledge is not, in the long run, cumulative. That is, later scientists do not necessarily build upon the work of earlier scientists. Rather, the history of science is a history of periods of work on specific issues in what he called "normal" science, punctuated by periods of revolution. Kuhn explicitly compares the revolutions in question to political revolutions (SSR 93). Within a given political system—for example, American representative democracy—differences arise and particular problems must be solved, such as the problem of what to do about medical care for indigent elderly people. The political system can contain disagreements about how to solve such problems up to a point. But if the disagreements become too sharp, the result may be a revolution, with a whole new political system, and that new political system may bring with it a new set of problems. Thus in some forms of a nondemocratic socialist state there would no longer be problems about what to do with elderly indigent people, but there would be problems with determining how best to plan the overall economy, which is a problem that does not even exist in American democracy.

Kuhn claims that something similar happens in the sciences. For example, within earth-centered (Ptolemaic) astronomy, specific problems arose about such matters as how to account for the apparent retrograde motion of the planets, given that the earth was fixed at the center of the "heavens." Once that assumption was abandoned, there was no longer a problem with planetary retrograde motions, but there was a new problem with finding an adequate or correct account of planetary orbits, a problem that did not and could not exist in the old astronomy.

ASK YOURSELF

129. Why could the problem of planetary orbits not even exist in the old astronomy?

In both political and scientific revolutions, all sorts of factors play a role. Changes in the balance of power, the intractability of certain problems, the development of new associations, and the dying off of older people wedded to a certain way of doing things may open the way for what Kuhn called a paradigm shift. The notion of a paradigm is fruitfully vague in Kuhn, but it includes such things as a new way of looking at things which brings with it new problems, the ignoring or irrelevance of old problems, new standards for what counts as a solution to a problem, new ways of educating young scientists involving the learning of cases that illustrate best the new paradigm, and even a new vocabulary or the investing of old terms with new meanings. The drawings in Searle's essay earlier in this chapter can be used to illustrate how "different ways of looking at things" can arise. Is the TOOT drawing *really* a drawing of a cart with wheels? Certainly one could not claim so simply on the basis of "experience" since someone with the "same" experience might not see it that way. Even in such a case, elements of a social background become important. For example, someone who does not know English will not see that drawing as the English word "TOOT," for obvious reasons.

Kuhn's account has been taken to show that scientific knowledge is largely or entirely "socially constructed." Scientific theories are not constrained by "how the world actually is" but rather by whatever happen to be the most socially entrenched ways of seeing the world, of educating scientists, of "doing" science. There is "no standard higher than the assent of the relevant community" (SSR 94) for determining scientific "truth." Kuhn even goes so far as to say that not only are paradigms constitutive of science, they are "constitutive of nature as well" (SSR 110). Moreover, Kuhn claims that paradigms are not truly commensurate. That means, in part, that we cannot say that one is better than another since they cannot be compared. Was it the case, in the early seventeenth century, that the old view that the earth is at the center was worse, more irrational, and less empirical than the new sun-centered view? It is difficult even to compare them. The old astronomers defined "earth" as "fixed body" so it would have been crazy for them to think of it as moving.

Initially, according to Kuhn, the new theories were no more empirical or capable of explaining more phenomena with fewer principles than were the old.

ASK YOURSELF

130. Does Kuhn think that the people who, in the seventeenth century, rejected the sun-centered hypothesis were "irrational" dogmatists who did not allot the proper place to experience in the development of knowledge?

In Kuhn's view, various social factors thus play a crucial role in determining what counts as scientific knowledge. Our scientific views are in some ways like our views about what makes a person beautiful. Clearly the latter views are "socially constructed." A woman's body that by present-day American standards is overweight and ugly might have been considered beautiful in seventeenth-century Europe. We cannot say that one of these views of beauty is right and the other wrong. They are simply different, they reflect different socially entrenched ways of looking at things. Likewise, the earth-centered and sun-centered theories of the "solar system" are just different. They are integral to socially entrenched ways of looking at things. Only a revolution could root out the set of habits associated with either one of these theories.

Kuhn's views seem very counterintuitive to most of us. But Kuhn would attribute that reaction to our ignorance of the actual history of science, a history that, he argues in detail, does not support the view of scientific knowledge as cumulative or as an endeavor that is always getting closer to the truth about how things "really are."

2. EPISTEMOLOGY AND THE SEX OF THE KNOWER: LORRAINE CODE

If Kuhn and others are even partly on the right track, then it will seem natural to begin looking for all sorts of social factors that influence the development of scientific theories and the ideas of knowledge that accompany them. The relevant social factors need not be confined to scientific communities. Can we safely suppose that more general social prejudices or habits exercise no influence upon science and upon the quest for knowledge in general? Thus feminists have claimed that sexist ways of looking at things have been powerful factors in the development of science and the views of knowledge that that development has supported. This is the view of Lorraine Code.

The Question. Code argues that typical analyses of knowledge in the modern era ignore or even systematically repress the question, "who is the knower?" Discussions of knowledge typically focus on the abstract formula "S knows that p," where "S" supposedly stands for any person.

FROM LORRAINE CODE, *What Can She Know: Feminist Theory and the Construction of Knowledge* (1991)

The question "Who is S?" is regarded neither as legitimate nor as relevant in these endeavors. As inquirers into the nature and conditions of human knowledge, epistemologists commonly work from the assumption that they need concern themselves only with knowledge claims that meet certain standards of *purity*. Questions about the circumstances of knowledge acquisition serve merely to clutter and confuse the issue with contingencies and other impurities. The question "Who is S?" is undoubtedly such a question. If it matters who S is, then it must follow that something peculiar to S's character or nature could bear on the validity of the knowledge she or he claims: that S's *identity* might count among the conditions that make that knowledge claim possible. For many philosophers, such a suggestion would undermine the cherished assumption that knowledge can—and should— be evaluated on its own merits. More seriously still, a proposal that it matters who the knower is looks suspiciously like a move in the direction of epistemological relativism. For many philosophers, an endorsement of relativism signals the end of knowledge and of epistemology.

ASK YOURSELF

131. Epistemological relativism is the view that knowledge is "relative to" individuals or cultures. Explain why raising the question "Who is the knower?" might seem to lead to relativism.

Broadly described, epistemological relativists hold that knowledge, truth, or even "reality" can be understood only in relation to particular sets of cultural or social circumstances, to a theoretical framework, a specifiable range of perspectives, a conceptual scheme, or a form of life. Conditions of justification, criteria of truth and falsity, and standards of rationality are likewise relative: there is no universal, unchanging framework or scheme for rational adjudication among competing knowledge claims.

Critics of relativism often argue that relativism entails incommensurability: that a relativist cannot evaluate knowledge claims comparatively. This argument is based on the contention that epistemological relativism entails conceptual relativism: that it contextualizes language just as it contextualizes knowledge, so that there remains no "common" or neutral linguistic framework for discussion, agreement, or disagreement. Other critics maintain that the very concept "knowledge" is rendered meaningless by relativism: that the only honest— and logical—move a relativist can make is once and for all to declare her or his skepticism. Where there are no universal standards, the argument goes, there can be no knowledge worthy of the name. . . . Now posing the question 'Who is S?'—that is, "Who is the knowing subject?" does indeed count as a move in the direction of relativism, and my intention in posing it is to suggest that the answer has epistemological import. But I shall invoke certain caveats to demonstrate that such a move is not the epistemological disaster that many theorists of knowledge believe it to be.

. . . There probably is no absolute authority, no practice of all practices or scheme of all schemes. Yet it does not follow that conceptual schemes, practices, and paradigms are radically idiosyncratic or purely subjective. Schemes, practices, and paradigms evolve out of communal projects of inquiry. To sustain viability and authority, they must demonstrate their adequacy in enabling people to negotiate the everyday world and to cope with the decisions, problems, and puzzles they encounter daily. From the claim that no single scheme has absolute explanatory power, it does not follow that all schemes are equally valid. Knowledge is qualitatively variable: some knowledge is *better* than other knowledge. Relativists are in a good position to take such qualitative variations into account and to analyze their implications.

ASK YOURSELF

132. In claiming that "some knowledge is better than other knowledge" Code is presumably not claiming that some knowledge is more *knowledge* than other knowledge. What then might she be claiming?

Even if these points are granted, though, it would be a mistake to believe that posing the "Who is S?" question indicates that the circumstances of the knower are all that counts in knowledge evaluation. The point is, rather, that understanding the circumstances of the knower makes possible a more *discerning* evaluation. The claim that certain of those circumstances are epistemologically significant—the sex of the knower, in this instance—by no means implies that they are definitive, capable of bearing the entire burden of justification and evaluation. This point requires special emphasis. Claiming epistemological significance for the sex of the knower might seem tantamount to a dismissal, to a contention that S made such a claim only because of his or her sex. Dismissals of this sort, both of women's knowledge and of their claims to be knowers in any sense of the word, are only too common throughout the history of western thought. But claiming that the circumstances of the knower are not epistemologically definitive is quite different from claiming that they are of no epistemological consequence. The position I take in this book is that the sex of the knower is one of a cluster of *subjective* factors (i.e., factors that pertain to the circumstances of cognitive agents) constitutive of received conceptions of knowledge and of what it means to be a knower. I maintain that subjectivity and the specificities of cognitive agency can and must be accorded central epistemological significance, yet that so doing does not commit an inquirer to outright subjectivism. Specificities count, and they require a place in epistemological evaluation, but they cannot tell the whole story.

ASK YOURSELF

133. Code claims that the sex (or other circumstances) of a knower is *not* _____.

Code goes on to argue that entrenched indifference to the question "Who is the knower?" is rooted in a conception of knowledge that in several respects derives from Descartes. Perhaps most notably, Descartes thinks of the knower as isolated (think of Descartes himself, who isolated himself in a remote cabin in order to try to think clearly about the foundations of knowledge). Code, like Dancy, Zagzebski, Kuhn, and others, wants to emphasize the social character of knowledge, the social setting within which knowledge claims are made. The sex of a knower is one feature of a social setting in the relevant sense. Post-cartesian epistemology, including empiricist varieties that stress the foundational nature of simple perceptual reports, appear to be completely indifferent to such social settings. In such individualist views, what matters is the perceptual report, not *who* makes the report.

Just what am I asking, then, with this question about the epistemological *significance* of the sex of the knower? First, I do not expect that the question will elicit the answer that the sex of the knower is pertinent among conditions for the existence of knowledge, in the sense that taking it into account will make it possible to avoid skepticism. Again, it is unlikely that information about the sex of the knower could count among criteria of evidence or means of justifying knowledge claims. Nor is it prima facie obvious that the sex of the knower will have a legitimate bearing on the qualitative judgments that could be made about certain claims to know. Comparative judgments of the following kind are not what I expect to elicit: that if the knower is female, her knowledge is likely to be better grounded; if the knower is male, his knowledge will likely be more coherent.

In proposing that the sex of the knower is epistemologically significant, I am claiming that the scope of epistemological inquiry has been too narrowly defined. My point is not to denigrate projects of establishing the best foundations possible or of developing workable criteria of coherence. I am proposing that even if it is not possible (or not *yet* possible) to establish an unassailable foundationalist or coherentist position, there are numerous questions to be asked about knowledge, whose answers matter to people who are concerned to know well. Among them are questions that bear not just on criteria of evidence, justification, and warrantability, but on the "nature" of cognitive agents: questions about their character; their material, historical, cultural circumstances; their interests in the inquiry at issue. These are questions about how credibility is established, about connections between knowledge and power, about the place of knowledge in ethical and aesthetic judgments, and about political agendas and the responsibilities of knowers. I am claiming that all of these questions are epistemologically significant.

ASK YOURSELF

134. Mention three things that Code is *not* claiming when she claims that the sex of the knower is significant.

Code discusses a number of views in which the sex of the knower is significant. Various thinkers have claimed that women are inherently inferior to men with respect to knowledge acquisition. She quotes Wilhelm von Humboldt, who claimed that "A sense of truth exists in [women] quite literally as a sense: . . . their nature also contains a lack or a failing of analytic capacity which draws a strict line of demarcation between ego and world; therefore, they will not come as close to the ultimate investigation of truth as man." On the other side, some feminist thinkers have made assumptions to the effect that women essentially have a particular "feminine" way of knowing and that that way of knowing may be superior. However, claims that either men or women naturally or essentially have some kind of cognitive superiority are suspect. The very notion of the "feminine" may itself be a "social construction" rather than a fact of nature.

Attempts to answer this question are complicated by the fact that sex/gender does not function uniformly and universally, even in Western societies. Its implications vary across class, race, age, ability, and numerous other interwoven specificities. A separated analysis of sex/gender, then, always risks abstraction and is limited in its scope by the abstracting process. Further, the question seems to imply that sex and gender are themselves constants, thus obscuring the processes of *their* sociocultural construction. Hence the formulation of adequately nuanced answers is problematic and necessarily partial.

Even brain studies that have been thought to show that women are more "right brained," men more "left brained" do not necessarily establish any essential differences in the way the sexes think.

[A]llegedly sex-specific differences are not observable in examinations of the structure of the brain itself, and in small children "both hemispheres appear to be equally proficient." At most, then, it would seem, the brain may come to control certain processes in sexually differentiated ways. Evidence suggests that the *brain develops* its powers through training and practice. Brains of creatures presented with a wide variety of tasks and stimuli develop strikingly greater performance capacities than brains of creatures kept in impoverished environments. As Ruth Bleier points out, "the biology of the brain itself is shaped by the individual's environment and experiences."

ASK YOURSELF

135. Why does examination of the structure of the brain not necessarily show any essential difference between men and women with respect to cognitive functioning?

Code is thus cautious about attempts to show that the sex of a knower is significant because of some *essential* differences between the way men and women think and acquire knowledge. That "essentialist" approach is appealing in some ways but also dangerous.

But these very traits are as problematic, both theoretically and practically, as they are attractive. It is not easy to separate their appeal from the fact that women—at least women of prosperous classes and privileged races—have been encouraged to cultivate them throughout so long a history of oppression and exploitation that they have become marks of acquiescence in powerlessness. Hence there is a persistent tension in feminist thought between a laudable wish to celebrate "feminine" values as tools for the creation of a better social order and a fear of endorsing those same values as instruments of women's continued oppression.

My recurring critique, throughout this book, of theoretical appeals to an *essential* femininity is one I engage in from a position sensitive to the pull of both sides in this tension. By "essentialism" I mean a belief in an essence, an inherent, natural, eternal female nature that manifests itself in such characteristics as gentleness, goodness, nurturance, and sensitivity. These are some of women's more positive attributes. Women are also represented, in essentialist thought, as naturally less intelligent, more dependent, less objective, more irrational, less competent, more scatterbrained than men: indeed, essential femaleness is commonly defined against a masculine standard of putatively human essence.

Essentialist attributions work both normatively and descriptively. Not only do they purport to describe how women essentially are, they are commonly enlisted in the perpetuation of women's (usually inferior) social status. Yet essentialist claims are highly contestable. Their diverse manifestations across class, race, and ethnicity attest to their having a sociocultural rather than a "natural" source. Their deployment as instruments for keeping women in their place means that caution is always required in appealing to them-even though they often appear to designate women's *strengths*. Claims about masculine essence need also to be treated with caution, though it is worth noting that they are less commonly used to oppress men.

ASK YOURSELF

136. Some have argued that the sex of a knower is epistemologically significant by claiming that women have certain essential traits (such as sensitivity) that might make them superior as knowers to men. Why does Code think this approach is risky?

How then *should* we approach the question? Code discusses the views of feminist philosopher Sandra Harding, who argues that empiricism in its Humean guise unconsciously portrays knowledge in a way that facilitates the exploitation of women. Harding's analysis does not involve any essentialist claims, but Code allows that Harding's account of Hume may be inaccurate. A similar analysis is cited from Moulton. It shares with Harding's argument the idea that in fact certain models of knowledge acquisition are marked by values that, as society is now structured, tend to favor men as knowers. Moreover, the values that are marked may get in the way of more fruitful approaches to knowledge in specific areas.

The influence of stereotypically sex-specific traits on conceptions of the proper way to do philosophy is instructively detailed in Janice Moulton's analysis of "The Adversary Method," as she perceptively names it. Moulton shows that a subtle conceptual "conflation of aggression and competence" has produced a paradigm for philosophical inquiry that is modeled on adversarial confrontation between opponents. This conflation depends, above all, on an association of aggression with such positive qualities as energy, power, and ambition: qualities that count as prerequisites for success in the white, middle-class, male professional world. Moulton questions the validity of this association in its conferral of normative status on styles of behavior stereotypically described as male. Yet what is most seriously wrong with the paradigm, she argues, is not so much its maleness as its constitutive role in the production of truncated philosophical problems, inquiries, and solutions.

The adversarial method is most effective, Moulton claims, in structuring isolated disagreements about specific theses and arguments. Hence it depends for its success on the artificial isolation of such claims and arguments from the contexts that occasion their articulation. Adversarial argument aims to show that an opponent is wrong, often by attacking conclusions implicit in, or potentially consequent on, his basic or alleged premises. Under the adversarial paradigm, the point is to confront the most extreme opposing position, with the object of showing that one's own position is defensible even against such stark opposition. Exploration, explanation, and understanding are lesser goals. The irony, Moulton claims, is that the adversarial paradigm produces bad reasoning, because it leads philosophers to adopt the mode of reasoning best suited to defeat an opponent-she uses "counterexample reasoning" to illustrate her point—as the paradigmatic model for reasoning as such. Diverse modes of reasoning which might be more appropriate to different circumstances, tend to be occluded, as does the possibility that a single problem might be amenable to more than one approach.

ASK YOURSELF

137. Zagzebski has claimed that one feature of "understanding" might be that a person with that virtue would hang on to a belief or theory despite counterexamples. Does her view have any similarity to Moulton's? Explain.

Like all paradigms, the adversarial method has a specific location in intellectual history. While it demarcates the kinds of puzzle a philosopher can legitimately consider, a recognition of its historical specificity shows that this is not how philosophy has always been done nor how it must, of necessity, be done. In according the method (interim) paradigm status, Moulton points to the historical contingency of its current hegemony. The fact that many feminist philosophers report a sense of dissonance between the supposed gender neutrality of the method and their own feminine gender puts the paradigm under serious strains. Such strains create the space and the possibilities for developing alternative methodological approaches. Whether the sex of the knower will be methodologically and/or epistemologically significant in such approaches must for now remain an open question.

ASK YOURSELF

138. Is their any parallel between Code's notion that philosophy can be and has been done in different ways and Kuhn's notion that science has been done in different ways or according to different paradigms? Explain.

Knowledge and Power. An important ingredient in the "construction of knowledge" is power relations. Sometimes ideas of what constitutes genuine knowledge tell us more about who is in power than about what the world is really like independent of all knowers. Here too there is a parallel with Kuhn, who claims that paradigm shifts are influenced by power relations within scientific communities.

The adversarial method is but one manifestation of a complex interweaving of power and knowledge which sustains the hegemony of mainstream epistemology. Like the empiricist theory of the mind, it presents a public demeanor of neutral inquiry, engaged in the disinterested pursuit of truth. Despite its evident interest in triumphing over opponents, it would be unreasonable to condemn this disinterest as merely a pose. There is no reason to believe that practitioners whose work is informed by these methodological assumptions have ruthlessly or tyrannically adopted a theoretical stance for the express purpose of engaging in projects that thwart the intellectual pursuit of women or of other marginalized philosophers. Could such a purpose be discerned, the task of revealing the epistemological significance of the sex of the knower would be easy. Critics could simply offer such practitioners a clear demonstration of the errors of their ways and hope that, with a presumption of goodwill on their part, they would abandon the path of error for that of truth and fairness.

Taking these practitioners at their word, acknowledging the sincerity of their convictions about their neutral, objective, impartial engagement in the pursuit of truth, reveals the intricacy of this task. Certain sets of problems, by virtue of their complexity or their intrinsic appeal, often become so engrossing for researchers that they override and occlude other contenders for attention. Reasons for this suppression are often subtle and not always specifically articulable. Nor is it clear that the exclusionary process is wholly conscious. A network of sociopolitical relationships and intellectual assumptions creates an invisible system of acceptance and rejection, discourse and silence, ascendancy and subjugation within and around disciplines. Implicit cultural presuppositions work with the personal idiosyncrasies of intellectual authorities to keep certain issues from placing high on research agendas. Critics have to learn how to notice their absence.

In "The Discourse on Language," Michel Foucault makes the astute observation that "within its own limits, every discipline recognizes true and false propositions, but it repulses a whole teratology of learning." The observation captures some of the subtleties involved in attempting to understand the often imperceptible workings of hegemonic, usually masculine power in mainstream philosophy. A discipline defines itself both by what it excludes (repulses) and by what it includes. But the self-definition process removes what is excluded (repulsed) from view so that it is not straightforwardly available for assessment, criticism, and analysis. Even in accepting mainstream avowals of neutral objectivity, critics have to learn to see what is repulsed by the disciplinarily imposed limits on methodology and areas of inquiry. The task is not easy. It is much easier to seek the flaws in existing structures and practices and to work at eradicating them than it is to learn to perceive what is not there to be perceived.

Feminist philosophy simply did not exist until philosophers learned to perceive the near-total absence of women in philosophical writings from the very beginning of Western philosophy, to stop assuming that "man" could be read as a generic term. Explicit denigrations of women, which became the focus of philosophical writing in the early years of the contemporary women's movement, were more readily perceptible. The authors of derogatory views about women in classical texts clearly needed power to be able to utter their pronouncements with impunity: a power they claimed from a "received" discourse that represented women's nature in such a way that women undoubtedly merited the negative judgments that Aristotle or Nietzsche made about them. Women are now in a position to recognize and refuse these overt manifestations of contempt.

The covert manifestations are more intransigent. Philosophers, when they have addressed the issue at all, have tended to group philosophy with science as the most gender-neutral of disciplines. But feminist critiques reveal that this alleged neutrality masks a bias in favor of institutionalizing stereotypical masculine values into the fabric of the discipline-its methods, norms, and contents. In so doing, it suppresses values, styles, problems, and concerns stereotypically associated with femininity. Thus, whether by chance or by design, it creates a hegemonic philosophical practice in which the sex of the knower is, indeed, epistemologically significant.

Michel Foucault, mentioned above, has been an important source for constructivist thinking. His stress on the role of power in the enterprise of acquiring knowledge has been very influential. Here is a possible example: A professor has claimed that he knows that there is no God. A student offers counterarguments, but the arguments are treated with contempt by the professor. Since the professor has power over the student, he is able to dismiss the student's arguments in a way that the student would not be able to dismiss his arguments. Moreover, the professor might claim that only by following a certain method can one arrive at knowledge, and that the student does not follow that method. For example, he might insist that the only real knowledge is the kind we get in the sciences and that there is no scientific evidence for belief in God. Since the professor has a good deal of backing (from colleagues, institutions, general cultural attitudes) for his claim that only science produces anything worth calling knowledge, he will appear to most people to have won the argument with the student. But has he really? Are there not other ways to know? Are their not whole domains of knowledge, such as ethical knowledge, in which science plays a minimal role? Is it at least possible that his version of the truth dominates because of his power and other power relations, rather than because it is indeed the truth?

ASK YOURSELF

139. Can you think of a case of a claim to knowledge which was in fact just part of an attempt to gain and maintain power? Invent one if necessary.

3. CONFUSIONS IN CONSTRUCTIVIST VIEWS: ALAN SOKAL

The contemporary physicist Alan Sokal argues that, while constructivist views contain valid points, nonetheless the ideas of Foucault and similar thinkers are either confused or get put to a confused use. In order to make his point, Sokal wrote an article in the style of postmodernist (constructivist) writers which was in fact a hoax, and it was published in an important journal devoted to post-modern and constructivist views. "Sokal's Hoax" has stirred quite a bit of controversy. His aim, however, was not simply to discredit the style of thinking which he satirized in his article. Rather he believes that constructivist views have bad political consequences.

Motives for the Sokal's Hoax. Sokal publicly admits the hoax and explains why he did it. In his explanation he uses such terms as "constructivist," "post-modern," "deconstruction," and "post-structuralist." These terms refer to related and overlapping movements and views, many of them French in origin, which have been particularly popular in departments of literature, sociology, and anthropology, as well as among various "left wing" intellectuals generally. These views have not received a lot of attention from scientists, but it is worth noting that Kuhn's ideas also overlap in many ways with these movements.

FROM ALAN SOKAL, "Transgressing the Boundaries: An Afterword" (1996)

Alas, the truth is out. My article, "Trangressing the Boundaries: Toward a Transformative Hermeneutics of Quantum Gravity," which appeared in the spring/summer 1996 issue of the cultural studies journal *Text*, is a parody. Clearly I owe the editors and readers of *Social Text* as well as the wider intellectual community, a nonparodic explanation of my motives and my true views. One of my goals here is to make a small contribution toward a dialogue on the Left between humanists and natural scientists, two cultures which, contrary to some optimistic pronouncements (mostly by the former group), are probably farther apart in mentality than at any time in the past fifty years.

Like the genre it is meant to satirize-myriad exemplars of which can be found in its reference list, my article is a melange of truths, halftruths, quarter-truths, falsehoods, non sequiturs, and syntactically correct sentences that have no meaning whatsoever. (Sadly, there are only a handful of the latter. I tried hard to produce them, but I found that, save for rare bursts of inspiration, I just didn't have the knack.) I also employed some other strategies that are well-established (albeit sometimes inadvertently) in the genre: appeals to authority in lieu of logic; speculative theories passed off as established science; strained and even absurd analogies; rhetoric that sounds good but whose meaning is ambiguous; and confusion between the technical and everyday sense of English words (for example: *linear, nonlinear, local, global, multidimensional, relative, frame of reference, field, anomaly, chaos, catastrophe, logic, irrational, imaginary, complex, real, equality, choice*).

I should emphasize that all works cited in my article are real, and all quotations are rigorously accurate; none are invented. Indeed, the most hilarious passages in my article were not written by me: they are direct quotes from the Masters.

But why did I do it? I confess that I'm an unabashed Old Leftist who never quite understood how deconstruction was supposed to help the working class. And I'm a stodgy old scientist who believes, naively, that there exists an external world, that there exist objective truths about that world, and that my job is to discover some of them. (If science were merely a negotiation of social conventions about what is agreed to be "true," why would I bother devoting a large fraction of my all-too-short life to it? I don't aspire to be the Emily Post of quantum field theory.)

But my main concern isn't to defend science from the barbarian hordes of lit crit. Rather, my concern is explicitly political: to combat a currently fashionable postmodernist/poststructuralist/social-constructivist discourse—and more generally a penchant for subjectivism which is, I believe, inimical to the values and future of the left. Alan Ryan said it well:

> It is, for instance, pretty suicidal for embattled minorities to embrace Michel Foucault, let alone Jacque Derrida. The minority view was always that power could be undermined by truth. . . . Once you read Foucault as saying that truth is simply an effect of power, you've had it.

ASK YOURSELF

140. Sokal and Ryan argue that embattled minorities (such as women) who claim that knowledge is simply a function of power deprive themselves of the one real tool they have in fighting oppression, namely, facts, real knowledge, good argument—in short, the truth. Do you agree that good argument can be used to fight oppression?

Likewise, Eric Hobsbawm has decried the rise of "postmodernist" intellectual fashions in Western universities, particularly in departments of literature and anthropology, which imply that all "facts" claiming objective existence are simply intellectual constructions. In short, that there is no clear difference between fact and fiction. But there is, and for historians, even for the most militantly antipositivist ones among us, the ability to distinguish between the two is absolutely fundamental. (Hobsbawm goes on to show how rigorous historical scholarship can refute the fictions propounded by reactionary nationalists in India, Israel, the

Balkans and elsewhere.). And as the ascerbic sociologist Stanislav Andreski noted long ago,

> So long as authority inspires awe, confusion and absurdity enhance conservative tenden-
> cies in society. Firstly, because clear and logical thinking leads to a cumulation of knowl-
> edge (of which the progress of the natural sciences provides the best example) and the
> advance of knowledge sooner or later undermines the traditional order. Confused thinking,
> on the other hand, leads nowhere in particular and can be indulged indefinitely without
> producing any impact upon the world.

Confusions in Constructivism

As an example of confused thinking, let's consider a chapter from Sandra Harding's *Whose
Science? Whose Knowledge?* entitled "Why 'Physics' Is a Bad Model for Physics." I select
this example both because of Harding's prestige in certain (but by no means all) feminist circles, and because her essay is, unlike much of this genre, very clearly written. Harding
wishes to answer the question, 'Are feminist criticisms of Western thought relevant to the
natural sciences?' She does so by raising, and then rebutting, six "false beliefs" about the nature of science. Some of her rebuttals are perfectly well taken; but they don't prove anything
like what she claims they do. That is because she conflates five quite distinct issues:

1. *Ontology.* What objects exist in the world? What statements about these objects
   are true?
2. *Epistemology.* How can human beings obtain knowledge of truths about the world?
   How can they assess the reliability of that knowledge?
3. *Sociology of knowledge.* To what extent are the truths known (or knowable) by humans in any given society influenced (or determined) by social, economic, political,
   cultural, and ideological factors? Same question for the false statements erroneously
   believed to be true.
4. *Individual ethics.* What types of research ought a scientist (or technologist) to undertake (or refuse to undertake)?
5. *Social ethics.* What types of research ought society to encourage, subsidize, or publicly fund (or alternatively to discourage, tax or forbid)?

ASK YOURSELF

141. Is Sokal denying that social, cultural and ideological factors have any
influence on the claims to knowledge made by scientists and others?

These questions are obviously related—e.g., if there are no objective truths about the world,
then there is not much point in asking how one can know those (nonexistent) truths. But they
are conceptually distinct.

For example, Harding (citing the work of Paul Forman) points out that American research in the 1940s and 50s on quantum electronics was motivated in large part by potential
military applications. True enough. Now, quantum mechanics made possible solid-state
physics, which in turn made possible quantum electronics (e.g., the transistor) which made
possible nearly all of modern technology (e.g., the computer). And the computer has had
applications that are beneficial to society (e.g., in allowing the postmodern cultural critic to
produce her articles more efficiently) as well as applications that are harmful (e.g., in allowing the U.S. military to kill human beings more efficiently).

ASK YOURSELF

142. Sokal is claiming that the research on quantum electronics can discover _____ truths about the world; the fact that that research can be used in applications that are _____ does not detract from the truth of those discoveries.

This raises a host of further social and individual ethical questions: Ought society to forbid or discourage certain applications of computers? Forbid or discourage research on computers per se? On quantum electronics? On solid-state physics? On quantum mechanics? Likewise for individual scientists and technologists. (Clearly, an affirmative answer to these questions becomes harder to justify as one goes down the list; but I do not want to declare any of these questions a priori illegitimate.) Likewise, sociological questions arise: To what extent is our knowledge of computer science, quantum electronics, solid-state physics and quantum mechanics—and our lack of knowledge about other scientific subjects, for example, the global climate—a result of public-policy choices favoring militarism? To what extent have the erroneous theories (if any) in computer science, quantum electronics, solid-state physics and quantum mechanics been the result (in whole or in part) of social, economic, political, cultural and ideological factors, in particular the culture of militarism? These are all serious issues which deserve careful investigation adhering to the highest standards of scientific and historical evidence. But they have no effect whatsoever on the underlying scientific questions: whether atoms (and silicon crystals, transistors, and computers) really do behave according to the laws of quantum mechanics (and solid-state physics, quantum electronics, and computer science). The militaristic orientation of American science has quite simply no bearing whatsoever on the ontological question, and only under a wildly implausible scenario could it have any bearing on the epistemological question (for instance, if the worldwide community of solid-state physicists, following what they believe to be the conventional standards of scientific evidence, were to hastily accept an erroneous theory of semiconductor behaviour because of their enthusiasm for the breakthrough in military technology that this theory would make possible).

In a selection earlier in this chapter, Keith Lehrer describes the case of Mr. Raco, who, because of his racism, holds that only a certain race gets a certain disease, and who then determines through accredited scientific procedures that indeed only that race gets that disease.

ASK YOURSELF

143. Lehrer is making the point that a person with biases can still know the truth, provided that certain procedures are followed. Is that similar to the point Sokal is making?

THINKING LOGICALLY

Consider the following argument:

1. Research funded by a cosmetic company on cosmetics is likely to be biased.
2. This particular research on the effects of eye shadow on the eyes was funded by a cosmetic company.
3. Therefore this research was biased.
4. Therefore its conclusions are false.

144. What kind of argument is this, deductive or inductive?

145. Do the premises of this argument provide strong, average, weak, or no support for the final conclusion (i.e., 4)? Explain.

146. What bearing, if any, does your critique of this argument have on social constructionist epistemology?

In a footnote, Sokal adds the following important points about a difference between the physical sciences and the social sciences.

The natural sciences have little to fear, at least in the short run, from postmodernist silliness; it is, above all, history and the social sciences and leftist politics that suffer when verbal game-playing displaces the rigorous analysis of social realities. Nevertheless, because of the limitations of my own expertise, my remarks here are restricted to the natural sciences (and indeed primarily to the physical sciences). While the basic epistemology of inquiry ought to be roughly the same for the natural and social sciences, I am of course perfectly aware that many special and difficult methodological issues arise in the social sciences from the fact that the objects of inquiry are human beings (including their subjective states of mind); that these objects of inquiry have intentions (including in some cases the concealment of evidence or the placement of deliberately self-serving evidence); that the evidence is expressed (usually) in human language whose meaning may be ambiguous; that the meaning of conceptual categories (e.g., childhood, masculinity, femininity, family, economics. etc.) changes over time; that the goal of historical inquiry is not just facts but interpretation, etc. So by no means do I claim that my comments about physics should apply directly to history and the social sciences—that would be absurd. To say that "physical reality is a social and linguistic construct" is just plain silly, but to say that "social reality is a social and linguistic construct" is virtually a tautology.

147. What are two differences between the exact sciences and the social sciences, according to Sokal.

SUMMING UP THE SOCIAL CONSTRUCTION OF KNOWLEDGE

Few things are more obvious than the fact that some knowledge claims are the result of prejudice, an "agenda" of some sort, or a limited perspective. But in recent years some thinkers have argued that *all* knowledge claims, or most of them, are infected by such factors. They point out that the very language that we use to articulate our thought may be infected by bias. If they are right, then it may be a short step to skepticism, the denial that we can have knowledge at all, or, at least, know that we have it. The view in question is "social constructionism," a view that typically stresses the operation of nonrational factors in the "construction" of knowledge. One has only to think a little about how one's beliefs may be affected by one's race, gender, economic status, or individual vices, such as greed or the desire for prestige, to realize how even socially approved claims to knowledge may be unjustified. Code, for example, tries to show how gender can influence our beliefs about how best to acquire knowledge. Kuhn argues that even in the "hard" sciences, social factors, such as peer approval, or community-approved ways of seeing the world, affect notions of what constitutes scientific knowledge. On the other hand, the findings of the hard sciences, or even such moral beliefs as that it is wrong to torture people for fun, certainly seem to many people to be objectively true. Such beliefs may in fact be arrived at by processes that deliberately screen for prejudice and other irrational factors, as Sokal has argued.

CAN OF WORMS

Metaphysical and moral realists hold that there is "a way things are" independently of how any person or group of persons happens to think. Realism in metaphysics and ethics may be challenged by constructionist strategies and insights. Taken far enough, those insights may actually lead to a kind of idealism or anti-realism, the view that there is no mind independent reality at all. Fundamental positions in metaphysics and ethics are at stake in recent epistemological controversies.

SUMMING UP THE CHAPTER

A little familiarity with the long history of disputes between rationalists, empiricists, skeptics, and various kinds of relativists should prompt some caution in thinking about what knowledge is and how we can and do get it. What is the role of "experience," and just what is meant by "experience"? Empiricists like Locke and Hume have insisted that experience is foundational for knowledge, though their accounts of experience are open to objections of the sort brought by Searle. But are "foundations" even needed? Perhaps I should judge the truth of any given belief in light of how well it coheres with my other beliefs. Against foundationalists, coherentists like Dancy have argued that coherence is the real test for knowledge. What is the role of tradition, inherited background, or gender in our conceptions of knowledge? Social constructionists, borrowing ideas from Kuhn, have sometimes claimed that our ideas of what knowledge is and when we have it are due largely or even entirely to such factors. Disputes have also broken out in recent years over the extent to which real knowledge requires that I must know *how* I know. Perhaps, as externalists like Plantinga or Goldman argue, I can have real knowledge provided that my beliefs are produced by some reliable, truth-conducive process—for example, through sense perception—or in some subconscious way, even though I may not know of or really understand how those processes work. Internalists, on the other hand, stress what at first may seem a more common-sense view, namely that I cannot claim to know something when I have no idea how I know it or whether I am justified in my claim to know.

It seems clear that claims to knowledge should not be made irresponsibly. Ethical considerations arise when we think about knowledge. But, what sort of ethical considerations? Virtue epistemologists like Zagzebski argue that our focus should be on intellectual virtues. Knowledge will result from acts of intellectual virtue. Carefulness, integrity, open-mindedness, patience, and other such virtues are necessary for knowledge and even as sufficient for it as anything could be. These questions and issues continue to provoke controversy. How the issues are resolved matters to us. For one thing, the progress of both the physical and social sciences, upon which much depends, requires a careful handling of epistemological issues.

These discussions also matter because we tend to think that our lives as knowers are ethically qualified in some way. What I believe may be the result of vices or virtues that I have. What I believe may be due to a failure to check my sources, or my calculations, carefully, or to organize my thinking logically. Such failures can sometimes be criminal. On the other hand, my beliefs may be a credit to me, insofar as they reveal good, or dutiful, intellectual character.

FINAL REACTIONS

Turn to the "First Reaction" questions at the outset of this chapter and answer them in terms of your present beliefs and feelings. Compare your present answers with the originals. Are there any important differences? If so, note what they are and indicate which readings may have influenced you.

FURTHER READINGS

GENERAL WORKS

Bernecker, Sven, and Dretske, Fred, eds., *Knowledge: Readings in Contemporary Epistemology* (New York: Oxford University Press, 2000).

Dancy, Jonathan, and Sosa, Ernest, eds., *A Companion to Epistemology* (Oxford: Blackwell, 1992).

Moser, Paul, and Vander Nat, Arnold, *Human Knowledge: Classical and Contemporary Approaches* (New York: Oxford University Press, 2003).

Pojman, Louis, ed., *The Theory of Knowledge—Classic and Contemporary Readings* (Belmont: Wadsworth Publishing, 2003).

Pojman, Louis, *What Can We Know?—An Introduction to the Theory of Knowledge* (Belmont, CA: Wadsworth Publishing, 2001).

Williams, Michael, *Problems of Knowledge: A Critical Introduction to Epistemology* (New York: Oxford University Press, 2001).

WORKS ON SPECIFIC TOPICS AND FIGURES

Chisholm, Roderick, *Theory of Knowledge* (Englewood Cliffs, NJ: Prentice-Hall, 1989).

Clifford, W. K. *Lectures and Essays* (London: Macmillan, 1879).

DeRose, Keith, and Warfield, Ted, eds., *Skepticism: A Contemporary Reader* (New York: Oxford University Press, 1999).

Feldman, Richard, "Reliabilism and Justification," *Monist* (1985), Vol. 68, pp. 159–174.

Grice, H. P., and Strawson P. F. "In Defense of a Dogma" *Philosophical Review* (1956), Vol. 65, pp. 141–158.

Kuhn, Thomas, *The Essential Tension* (Chicago: University of Chicago Press, 1971).

Longino, Helen, *Science and Social Knowledge* (Princeton, NJ: Princeton University Press, 1990).

Plantinga, Alvin, *Warrant and Proper Function* (Oxford: Oxford University Press, 1993).

CHAPTER 6

ETHICS

hree off-duty San Francisco police officers were celebrating at a bar following the promotion of one officer's father to deputy chief of police. During the celebration, they demanded that two other men at the bar hand over their steak fajitas. The men refused and a barroom brawl broke out. The police department attempted to block investigation of the episode, but, to their embarrassment, the cover-up was revealed. News stories such as this about unethical professional behavior are all too common. Financial investment companies cheat their clients. Con artists bilk unsuspecting senior citizens out of their life savings. When offenders are caught, they are typically thrown in jail. To raise moral consciousness, ethics advisory panels have been created within police departments, financial institutions, hospitals, and countless other organizations. These panels typically draw attention to and enforce moral standards that society has already endorsed. From a more philosophical perspective, though, there are basic questions about the nature of morality that lie beneath issues of enforcing morality. Most basic is the question of the *source* or *grounds* of morality. Some theorists maintain that morality is grounded in an unchanging spiritual realm; others hold that it is grounded in human convention, or even human physiology. Even if we can settle the issue about the grounds or source of morality, there remains another task, namely, determining how we are to conduct our lives morally. Suppose, for example, that morality is a cultural creation. That fact would not help us to see just what that morality consists in, how its precepts get applied in various situations, or what to do when those precepts conflict. Nor would that fact necessarily help us to see what social or personal conditions are required for people to actually become or be moral.

FIRST REACTIONS

a. Is there an unchanging standard of morality that applies to all people throughout the world?

b. Think about the last time you donated to charity. Was there anything selfish about your motivation?

c. Think about how you stand on some major ethical issue, such as abortion. Is your moral assessment based more on emotional reaction or on impartial reasoning?

d. People generally feel that men and women differ in important ways—for example, with respect to aggression and emotional sensitivity. Do you think that men and women also have differing conceptions of morality?

e. Think of a great moral leader, such as Gandhi, or an important moral influence on your life. Patience is probably one of the moral character traits that this person has. What are some other good character traits possessed by this person?

f. Many philosophers believe that there is an underlying rationale for all moral behavior. One commonly held view is that morality is grounded in respect for people; another is that morality is based on the greatest good for the greatest number of people. Which, if either, of these rationales strikes you as the best?

A. ARE MORAL VALUES OBJECTIVE?

Attitudes toward various kinds of sexual conduct vary from culture to culture. American and European societies are particularly permissive regarding homosexuality, premarital sex, and adultery. Other countries—most notably religiously conservative ones—not only condemn such behavior but even punish offenders with death. In 2000, an Afghani woman was stoned to death by the country's Taliban religious rulers after she was found guilty of committing adultery. So strict were that regime's attitudes about sexual promiscuity that any woman who was simply found in the company of a male stranger was guilty of a crime punishable by death. When we see such differing attitudes about moral issues such as adultery, it may make us wonder whether morality is just a matter of changing human conventions, or whether it is grounded in something more permanent.

QUESTIONS TO DISCUSS

a. Attitudes toward adultery differ to some extent from one culture or society to another. What are some other examples of differences in moral attitude or belief?

b. Can you think of any moral values that all societies endorse?

c. Suppose that moral values do vary radically from society to society. What, if anything, is troubling about that prospect?

Several distinct, yet interwoven, positions are at issue in controversy such as the one above about the Taliban treatment of women. At the risk of oversimplification, we might depict the two disputing sides as optimists and pessimists. The optimist believes that moral values are *objective* in the sense that they are based on some spiritual component of the universe, which is independent of human activity in the physical world or at any rate do not depend on what people actually think at any given time. The optimist believes further that moral values are *absolute*—or *eternal*—in that they don't change, and *universal* in that they apply to all people. One motivation behind this optimistic view is the feeling that morality is of great importance to human life, and must thus be insured against ever-shifting human whims.

The pessimist, by contrast, rejects the optimist's contentions. The pessimists are moral *skeptics* insofar as they deny the existence of an external spiritual realm or any other unchanging source of moral values. They are often moral *relativists* insofar as they believe that morality is a purely human creation—that is, morality is *relative* to particular styles of human activity. As relativists, they feel that morality either is the invention of each individual person or is the invention of different societies and cultures. Far from being absolute, says the pessimist, moral values frequently differ from person to person, or from society to society. Thus they do not apply universally to all people at all times. People and societies are bound only by their own unique values, and not those of other people and societies. One motivation behind this pessimistic view rests on a suspicion about the optimist's conceptions. Many pessimists incline to the view that all that truly exists is the physical world, so that there is no transcendent guarantee for moral beliefs. Moreover, when we observe human conduct, we will see that morality changes relative to the people or societies that we encounter.

1. MORALITY GROUNDED IN UNCHANGING SPIRITUAL FORMS: PLATO

**PLATO
(427–347 BCE)**
ancient Greek philosopher and author of the Republic.

The figure who best represents the views of the optimist is the ancient Greek philosopher Plato (427–347 BCE), who directly influenced other moral optimists for centuries to come. Plato seems to have developed his theory in reaction to pessimists with whom he was familiar, such as the sophist Protagoras (c. 490–c. 420 BCE).

Protagoras is best known for the remark that "man is the measure of all things," or, more correctly and completely translated, "A human being is the measure of all things; of the things that are, that they are, and of the things that are not, that they are not." There are two ways that we might interpret Protagoras's remark. First, to say that a human being is the measure of all things could be to say that each individual person is the measure or standard for what is true. Thus if something tastes sweet to me, then it *is* sweet (to me), and if the same thing tastes sour to you, then it *is* sour (to you). There does not seem to be any truth of the matter existing independently of the experience of individuals. Similarly, with moral issues Protagoras would say that all moral truths are relative to each individual. We can call this "individual moral relativism." Second, we might also interpret Protagoras as saying that humans in general, or human societies, are the measure of all things. For example, someone who argued that incest might be morally right in one society and morally wrong in another would be taking this second approach. The claim here would be that truth is "relative to" a given society, culture, group, or historical epoch. We can call this "cultural moral relativism." It is unclear exactly what Protagoras meant, but there is some evidence that he had the first interpretation in mind.

ASK YOURSELF

1. What are the two kinds of relativism mentioned above?

Plato's view on the subject is as contrary to Protagoras's relativism as we can imagine. Plato's dialogue, the *Republic,* is a detailed discussion of the moral value of justice. In this work, he draws a radical distinction between the physical world of appearances and the spiritual world of the forms that contain universal truths. According to Plato, things here on earth gain their true character by *participating* in—or being modeled after—the universal forms. Suppose, for example, that I want to figure out how much extra money I'll have at the end of the month once I've paid my bills. The solution is easy: I add up my monthly bills, subtract this amount from my paycheck, and that gives me the answer. What, though, gives me confidence in the mathematical principles upon which I base my calculation? According to Plato, mathematical principles are not things that humans simply invent. Instead, there are universal mathematical forms that exist in the spiritual realm, and all of our correct mathematical calculations are grounded in these forms. Morality works in a similar way. When people are charitable, benevolent, just, or good, they participate in the spiritual forms of charity, benevolence, justice, or goodness. Plato believes that it is very difficult to know the forms and model life on them. Throughout our lives we are immersed in the body and its appetites and opinions based on the senses, and we easily presume that there is nothing more to life. When we think about the moral value of justice, for example, we might be tempted to say that justice simply reflects the preferences of the people who are in power. After all, that's the way it very often appears. However, according to Plato, we must shut our eyes to how justice appears to be in the world around us, and, through a kind of mental insight, we must discover the true nature of justice as it is "in itself"; that is, we must achieve a clear view of the form of justice. The task is so difficult that we might need the help of an expert teacher—such as Plato's own teacher Socrates (469–399 BCE). We might also face strong resistance from people around us who have been captivated by the world of appearances. Plato makes this point in the most famous part of the *Republic,* namely, the allegory of the cave.

The Allegory of the Cave. Plato describes the struggle for knowledge and the form of the Good—the universal moral truth that is at the foundation of all good things. The key characters in Plato's dialogue here are Socrates—modeled after Plato's teacher, who here represents Plato's views—and Glaucon, a moral pessimist who believes that justice simply reduces to what people in power can get away with.

FROM PLATO, *Republic,* BOOK 7

SOCRATES   And now, I said, let me show in a figure how far our nature is enlightened or unenlightened: Consider human beings living in a underground den, which has a mouth open towards the light and reaching all along the den; here they have been from their childhood, and have their legs and necks chained so that they cannot move, and can only see before them, being prevented by the chains from turning round their heads. Above and behind them a fire is blazing at a distance, and between the fire and the prisoners there is a raised way; and you will see, if you look, a low wall built along the way, like the screen which marionette players have in front of them, over which they show the puppets.

GLAUCON   I see.

SOCRATES   And do you see, I said, men passing along the wall carrying all sorts of vessels, and statues and figures of animals made of wood and stone and various materials, which appear over the wall? Some of them are talking, others silent.

GLAUCON   You have shown me a strange image, and they are strange prisoners.

SOCRATES   Like ourselves, I replied; and they see only their own shadows, or the shadows of one another, which the fire throws on the opposite wall of the cave?

GLAUCON   True, he said; how could they see anything but the shadows if they were never allowed to move their heads?

SOCRATES   And of the objects which are being carried in like manner they would only see the shadows?

GLAUCON   Yes, he said.

SOCRATES   And if they were able to converse with one another, would they not suppose that they were naming what was actually before them?

GLAUCON   Very true.

SOCRATES   And suppose further that the prison had an echo which came from the other side, would they not be sure to fancy when one of the passers-by spoke that the voice which they heard came from the passing shadow?

GLAUCON   No question, he replied.

SOCRATES   To them, I said, the truth would be literally nothing but the shadows of the images.

GLAUCON   That is certain.

SOCRATES   And now look again, and see what will naturally follow if the prisoners are released and disabused of their error. At first, when any of them is liberated and compelled suddenly to stand up and turn his neck round and walk and look towards the light, he will suffer sharp pains; the glare will distress him, and he will be unable to see the realities of which in his former state he had seen the shadows. Next imagine someone saying to him, that what he saw before was an illusion, but that now, when he is approaching nearer to being and his eye is turned towards more real existence, he has a clearer vision—what will be his reply? And you may further imagine that his instructor is pointing to the objects as they pass and requiring him to name them, will he not be perplexed? Will he not fancy that the shadows which he formerly saw are truer than the objects which are now shown to him?

GLAUCON   Far truer.

SOCRATES   And if he is compelled to look straight at the light, will he not have a pain in his eyes which will make him turn away and take in the objects of vision which he can see, and which he will conceive to be in reality clearer than the things which are now being shown to him?

GLAUCON   True.

SOCRATES   And suppose once more, that he is reluctantly dragged up a steep and rugged ascent, and held fast until he's forced into the presence of the sun himself, is he not likely to be pained and irritated? When he approaches the light his eyes will be dazzled, and he will not be able to see anything at all of what are now called realities.

GLAUCON Not all in a moment, he said.

It is clear from the cave allegory that Plato thinks that acquisition of knowledge requires discipline and is painful. "No pain, no gain" is even more true in the realm of knowledge than it is in the realm of physical training and improvement. Plato thinks people contain the truth within their souls. But in his view, life in the body has made us forget what we know and led us to focus on what is perceptible and satisfies our bodily desires. It is very difficult to turn away from the body, and someone who prodded people into making that turn or conversion might not be too popular. Moreover, such a person might be thought a crackpot by some, since he claims that the familiar world is not fully real or worthy of our attention.

ASK YOURSELF

2. Give an example of a moral conviction, the discovery of which might result in the kind of intellectual pain that Plato describes.

SOCRATES He will require to grow accustomed to the sight of the upper world. And first he will see the shadows best, next the reflections of men and other objects in the water, and then the objects themselves; then he will gaze upon the light of the moon and the stars and the spangled heaven; and he will see the sky and the stars by night better than the sun or the light of the sun by day?

GLAUCON Certainly.

SOCRATES Last of all he will be able to see the sun, and not mere reflections of him in the water, but he will see him in his own proper place, and not in another; and he will contemplate him as he is.

GLAUCON Certainly.

SOCRATES He will then proceed to argue that this [the sun] is he who gives the season and the years, and is the guardian of all that is in the visible world, and in a certain way the cause of all things which he and his fellows have been accustomed to behold?

GLAUCON Clearly, he said, he would first see the sun and then reason about him.

SOCRATES And when he remembered his old habitation, and the wisdom of the den and his fellow-prisoners, do you not suppose that he would be happy with the change in himself, and pity them?

GLAUCON Certainly, he would.

SOCRATES And if they were in the habit of conferring honors among themselves on those who were quickest to observe the passing shadows and to remark which of them went before, and which followed after, and which were together, and who were therefore best able to draw conclusions as to the future, do you think that he would care for such honors and glories, or envy the possessors of them? Would he not say with Homer, "Better to be the poor servant of a poor master," and to endure anything, rather than think as they do and live after their manner?

GLAUCON Yes, he said, I think that he would rather suffer anything than entertain these false notions and live in this miserable manner.

SOCRATES　Imagine once more, I said, such an one coming suddenly out of the sun to be replaced in his old situation; would he not be certain to have his eyes full of darkness?

GLAUCON　To be sure, he said.

SOCRATES　And if there were a contest, and he had to compete in measuring the shadows with the prisoners who had never moved out of the den, while his sight was still weak, and before his eyes had become adjusted (and the time which would be needed to acquire this adjustment might be very considerable) would he not be ridiculous? Men would say of him that up he went and down he came without his eyes, and that it was better not even to think of ascending. And if any one tried to release another and lead him up to the light, let them only catch the offender, and they would put him to death.

GLAUCON　No question, he said.

SOCRATES　This entire allegory, I said, you may now append, dear Glaucon, to the previous argument; the prison-house is the world of sight, the light of the fire is the sun, and you will not misapprehend me if you interpret the journey upwards to be the ascent of the soul into the intellectual world according to my poor belief, which, at your desire, I have expressed, whether rightly or wrongly God knows.

But, whether true or false, my opinion is that in the world of knowledge the idea of good appears last of all, and is seen only with an effort; and, when seen, is also inferred to be the universal author of all things beautiful and right, parent of light and of the lord of light in this visible world, and the immediate source of reason and truth in the intellectual; and that this is the power upon which he who would act rationally, either in public or private life, must have his eye fixed.

ASK YOURSELF

3. The sun in Plato's allegory represents the form of the Good—that is, the ultimate standard of perfection in which every good thing participates. According to Plato, the good is the universal _____ of all things beautiful and right.

2. MORAL RELATIVISM: SEXTUS, MONTAIGNE, AND MACKIE

Plato represents the optimistic side of the dispute regarding the status of moral values. The pessimistic side—which espouses moral relativism—was articulated by several writers within a 2000-year-old philosophical tradition called "moral skepticism."

Relative Moral Practices: Sextus Empiricus. The earliest surviving systematic defense of moral relativism is from the writings of Greek skeptic Sextus Empiricus (second century CE). In the epistemology chapter earlier in this book, we've explored Sextus's conviction that we cannot gain knowledge of any subject, and the best way to achieve mental tranquility is to simply withhold our beliefs. This is so, Sextus argues, with moral knowledge as well as perceptual knowledge. According to Sextus, nothing is by nature good or evil, and moral notions are just a matter of personal and social preference. He makes his case by showing how both ordinary people and philosophers have differing opinions about what is good or bad.

Fire which heats by nature appears to all as heating, and snow which chills by nature appears to all as chilling, and all things which move by nature move equally all those who are, as they say, in a natural condition. But none of the so-called goods, as we shall show, moves all men as being good; therefore no natural good exists. And that none of the so-called goods moves all people alike is, they assert, an evident fact. . . . [Some ordinary folk] regard right bodily condition as good, others chambering, others gluttony, others drunkenness, others gambling, others greed, and others still worse things. . . . [Some philosophers] have accepted pleasure as a good, whereas some affirm that it is a downright evil, so that one professor of philosophy actually exclaimed, "I would sooner be mad than merry." If, then, things which move by nature move all people alike, while we are not all moved alike by the so-called goods, there is nothing good by nature. In fact it is impossible to believe either all the views now set forth, because of their conflicting character, or any one of them.

ASK YOURSELF

4. In the above, is Sextus defending individual moral relativism or cultural moral relativism?

Sextus continues by amassing examples of moral practices that seem to change from one society to another. His illustrations below regarding the relativity of sexual practices are particularly shocking:

Amongst us sodomy is regarded as shameful or rather illegal, but by the Germani, they say, it is not looked on as shameful but as a customary thing. . . . Having intercourse with a woman, too, in public, although deemed by us to be shameful, is not thought to be shameful by some of the Indians; at any rate they couple publicly with indifference, like the philosopher Crates, as the story goes. Moreover, prostitution is with us a shameful and disgraceful thing, but with many of the Egyptians it is highly esteemed; at least, they say that those men who have the greatest number of lovers wear an ornamental ankle ring as a token of their proud position. And with some of them the girls marry after collecting a dowry before marriage by means of prostitution. We see the Stoics declaring that it is not amiss to keep company with a prostitute or to live on the profits of prostitution. [From Sextus Empiricus, *Outlines of Pyrrhonism* (c. 200 CE), 3:23, 24]

ASK YOURSELF

5. In the above, is Sextus defending individual relativism or cultural relativism?

The Primacy of Custom: Montaigne. Moral relativism and the entire skeptical tradition declined in popularity during the middle ages, when philosophy was dominated by religious thought. God, it was believed, did not create a world with fluctuating moral values. Some religious philosophers modified the more optimistic theory of Plato, and others held that moral values are grounded in the will of God. In either case, medieval philosophers believed that morality was grounded in an objective spiritual realm, far beyond the changing whims of human beings. By the sixteenth century, however, a revival of interest in various Greco/Roman moral theories was underway, and the moral relativism of Sextus Empiricus was resurrected. One such disciple of Sextus was French essayist Michel Eyquem de Montaigne (1533–1592). The running theme of many of Montaigne's writings is the question "What do I know?" Montaigne's implied answer is, "not much of anything"—even regarding morality. In an essay entitled "Of Custom," Montaigne presents a long list of bizarre customs, many of which we may find morally disturbing.

**MICHEL EYQUEM
DE MONTAIGNE
(1533–1592)**

*French skeptical philosopher
and author of* Essays.

In one place, men feed upon human flesh. In another, it is reputed a holy duty for a man to kill his father at a certain age. Elsewhere, the fathers dispose of their children, while yet in their mothers' wombs, some to be preserved and carefully brought up, and others to be abandoned or made away. Elsewhere the old husbands lend their wives to young men; and in another place they are in common, without offence. In one place particularly, the women take it for a mark of honor to have as many gay fringed tassels at the bottom of their garment, as they have lain with several men.

For Montaigne, these are not simply interesting stories about people who have twisted conceptions of morality. Instead, they show how custom totally dominates our lives. If we think that somehow morality comes from a fixed natural order of things, then we are sorely mistaken: Morality rests on custom and nothing more.

To conclude, there is nothing, in my opinion, that she [i.e., custom] does not, or may not do; and, therefore, with very good reason it is, that Pindar calls her the queen, and empress of the world. He that was seen to beat his father, and reproved for so doing, made answer, that it was the custom of their family: that, in like manner his father had beaten his grandfather, his grandfather his great-grandfather, "and this," says he, pointing to his son, "when he comes to my age, shall beat me." The laws of conscience, which we pretend to be derived from nature, proceed from custom; everyone, having an inward veneration for the opinions and manners approved and received amongst his own people, cannot, without very great reluctance, depart from them, nor apply himself to them without applause. [From Michel Montaigne, *Essays* (1580), "Of Custom"]

ASK YOURSELF

6. According to Montaigne, from where do we pretend to get the laws of conscience, and where do they really come from?

Relativism and Moral Skepticism: Mackie. In more recent years, moral relativism has received support from many anthropologists as well as skeptical philosophers. Sextus and Montaigne did not travel to distant lands themselves or directly witness the strange customs that they relate. Instead, they relied on published accounts by explorers and sea merchants from their respective eras. During the nineteenth century, the fields of sociology and anthropology emerged—disciplines whose main task is to study diverse cultures and group behavior. As researchers explored and documented cultural practices from around the world, some drew the same conclusions that Sextus and Montaigne did, namely, that moral values are grounded in social custom and tradition, which appear differently in various cultures. Accordingly, many recent philosophers feel that the social sciences established cultural relativism as a descriptive fact about human societies. There remained, however, the philosophical difficulty of moving from (a) the apparent sociological *fact* that moral values are culturally varied to (b) the denial of an objectively grounded morality. Australian philosopher J. L. Mackie (1917–1981) takes on this task. A philosophical skeptic in the tradition of Sextus and Montaigne, Mackie staunchly rejects Plato's view that moral values are tied to objective universal truths that exist apart from human thought and culture. Human beings, Mackie argues, invent the notions of right and wrong. He calls his own position *moral skepticism,* and he believes that the descriptive fact of cultural relativism offers one of the strongest arguments for this view.

Mackie distinguishes between what he calls first-order and second-order ethical statements. First-order statements are claims about how we should behave—such as the claim that stealing is morally wrong. Second-order statements involve theories about the origin and objective status of moral values—such as Plato's view that morality is grounded in the realm of the forms. He concedes that the mere sociological fact of culturally varied moral practices is about neither first- nor second-order ethical claims:

> The argument from relativity has its premise in the well-known variation in moral codes from one society to another and from one period to another, and also the differences in moral beliefs between different groups and classes within a complex community. Such variation is in itself merely a truth of descriptive morality, a fact of anthropology which entails neither first-order nor second-order ethical views.

Nevertheless, Mackie argues, the sociological fact of culturally varied moral practices supports moral skepticism.

> [The fact of variation in moral practices] may indirectly support second-order subjectivism [i.e., moral skepticism]: radical differences between first-order moral judgments make it difficult to treat those judgments as apprehensions of objective truths. But it is not the mere occurrence of disagreements that tells against the objectivity of values. Disagreement on questions in history or biology or cosmology does not show that there are no objective issues in these fields for investigators to disagree about. But such scientific disagreement results from speculative inferences or explanatory hypotheses based on inadequate evidence, and it is hardly plausible to interpret moral disagreement in the same way. Disagreement about moral codes seems to reflect people's adherence to and participation in different ways of life. The causal connection seems to be mainly the other way round: it is that people approve of monogamy because they participate in a monogamous way of life rather than that they participate in a monogamous way of life because they approve of monogamy. [From John L. Mackie, *Ethics: Inventing Right and Wrong* (1977), 1.8]

ASK YOURSELF

7. According to Mackie, disagreements regarding morality are substantially different from disagreements in a field like biology. What do disagreement on questions in biology show?

8. According to Mackie, what do disagreements about moral codes reflect?

3. THE CASE AGAINST MORAL RELATIVISM: JAMES RACHELS

Critics of moral relativism have two main strategies when considering the apparent fact of culturally varied moral practices. First, one might deny that such variation says anything at all about the objective status of morality. Let's suppose that there are some societies in the world that practice incest. This does not mean that incest is morally permissible for those societies, or that the prohibition of incest is merely subjective. Instead, it may simply mean that societies that practice incest are morally degenerate in that respect. A second strategy adopted by critics of relativism is to question whether sociology has indeed established it as a "fact" that moral practices vary a great deal from one culture to another. Contemporary philosopher James Rachels examines these and other strategies. He begins his discussion by noting that cultural relativists make several different kinds of claims.

FROM JAMES RACHELS, *Elements of Moral Philosophy* (1999), CHAPTER 2

. . . Cultural Relativism, as it has been called, challenges our ordinary belief in the objectivity and universality of moral truth. It says, in effect, that there is no such thing as universal truth in ethics; there are only the various cultural codes, and nothing more. Moreover, our own code has no special status; it is merely one among many.

As we shall see, this basic idea is really a compound of several different thoughts. It is important to separate the various elements of the theory because, on analysis, some parts turn out to be correct, while others seem to be mistaken. As a beginning, we may distinguish the following claims, all of which have been made by cultural relativists:

1. Different societies have different moral codes.
2. There is no objective standard that can be used to judge one societal code better than another.
3. The moral code of our own society has no special status; it is merely one among many.
4. There is no "universal truth" in ethics; that is, there are no moral truths that hold for all peoples at all times.
5. The moral code of a society determines what is right within that society; that is, if the moral code of a society says that a certain action is right, then that action is right, at least within that society.
6. It is mere arrogance for us to try to judge the conduct of other peoples. We should adopt an attitude of tolerance toward the practices of other cultures.

ASK YOURSELF

9. Rachels gives six claims or ideas commonly expressed by cultural relativists, the first two are the most important. Statement number _____ is a claim about the ultimate foundation of moral values, and statement number _____ is a claim about sociological facts.

Although it may seem that these six propositions go naturally together, they are independent of one another, in the sense that some of them might be false even if others are true. In what follows, we will try to identify what is correct in Cultural Relativism, but we will also be concerned to expose what is mistaken about it.

The Cultural Differences Argument. Rachels next presents—then attacks—a standard argument for moral skepticism that is much like Mackie's.

Cultural Relativism is a theory about the nature of morality. At first blush it seems quite plausible. However, like all such theories, it may be evaluated by subjecting it to rational analysis; and when we analyze Cultural Relativism we find that it is not so plausible as it first appears to be.

The first thing we need to notice is that at the heart of Cultural Relativism there is a certain *form of argument*. The strategy used by cultural relativists is to argue from facts about the differences between cultural outlooks to a conclusion about the status of morality. Thus we are invited to accept this reasoning:

1. The Greeks believed it was wrong to eat the dead, whereas the Callatians believed it was right to eat the dead.
2. Therefore, eating the dead is neither objectively right nor objectively wrong. It is merely a matter of opinion, which varies from culture to culture.

Or, alternatively:

1. The Eskimos see nothing wrong with infanticide, whereas Americans believe infanticide is immoral.
2. Therefore, infanticide is neither objectively right nor objectively wrong. It is merely a matter of opinion, which varies from culture to culture.

ASK YOURSELF

10. Think of a moral practice that seems to be culturally relative, and present it in an argument similar to the above two.

Clearly, these arguments are variations of one fundamental idea. They are both special cases of a more general argument, which says:

1. Different cultures have different moral codes.
2. Therefore, there is no objective "truth" in morality. Right and wrong are only matters of opinion, and opinions vary from culture to culture.

We may call this the "Cultural Differences Argument." To many people, it is persuasive. But from a logical point of view, is it sound?

It is not sound. The trouble is that the conclusion does not follow from the premise—that is, even if the premise is true, the conclusion still might be false. The premise concerns what people *believe:* In some societies, people believe one thing; in other societies, people believe differently. The conclusions however, concerns *what really is the case*. The trouble is that this sort of conclusion does not follow logically from this sort of premise.

Consider again the example of the Greeks and Callatians. The Greeks believed it was wrong to eat the dead; the Callatians believed it was right. Does it follow, *from the mere fact that they disagreed,* that there is no objective truth in the matter? No, it does not follow; for it could be that the practice was objectively right (or wrong) and that one or the other of them was simply mistaken.

To make the point clearer, consider a different matter. In some societies, people believe the earth is flat. In other societies, such as our own, people believe the earth is (roughly) spherical. Does it follow, *from the mere fact that people disagree,* that there is no "objective truth" in geography? Of course not; we would never draw such a conclusion because we realize that, in their beliefs about the world, the members of some societies might simply be wrong. There is no reason to think that if the world is round everyone must know it. Similarly, there is no reason to think that if there is moral truth everyone must know it. The fundamental mistake in the Cultural Differences Argument is that it attempts to derive a substantive conclusion about a subject from the mere fact that people disagree about it.

This is a simple point of logic, and it is important not to misunderstand it. We are not saying (not yet, anyway) that the conclusion of the argument is false. It is still an open question whether the conclusion is true or false. The logical point is just that the conclusion does not *follow from* the premise. This is important, because in order to determine whether the conclusion is true, we need arguments in its support. Cultural Relativism proposes this argument, but unfortunately the argument turns out to be fallacious. So it proves nothing.

THINKING LOGICALLY

Rachels makes distinctions in the passage just cited which should be familiar to those who have studied the introductory section on logic. His conclusion is not that cultural relativism is false. It is rather that one of the main arguments for it is defective. The argument presented by the relativist may be deductively valid, however, despite Rachels' claim that the conclusion does not follow from the premise. The argument he is considering is the following:

1. People at different times and in different cultures disagree about moral claims. Therefore, there is no moral truth.

As it stands, it is true that the conclusion of this argument does not follow. But the argument is very likely an enthymeme. The missing premise would be 2, "When people disagree in this way that shows that there is no moral truth." From 1 and 2 the conclusion will follow. But of course defenders of moral absolutes would never grant 2, even if they granted 1.

One strategy employed by Rachels is an argument from analogy. Hardly anyone would accept the following argument:

1′. People at different times and in different cultures disagree about scientific facts (such as whether the world is round or flat).

2. When people disagree in this way, this shows that there is no scientific truth Therefore, there is no scientific truth.

Why then should anyone accept the first argument, which has the same form? Arguments from analogy are often very persuasive, and Rachels expects that we will answer that there is no reason to accept either argument. Both of them are silly, but we may not notice how silly the first one is until we compare it with the second. Both depend upon the idea that a "substantive conclusion" can be drawn from the fact that people disagree about something. A relativist will argue that in fact we can draw such conclusions where the disagreements are about moral matters. But Rachels would insist that *that* claim needs to be supported by argument, and the relativist fails to provide such support. Instead he merely points out that there is a disagreement.

The Consequences of Taking Cultural Relativism Seriously. Although Rachels believes that we should reject the cultural differences argument, he feels that it is important to note additional problems with cultural relativism. In particular, he notes some absurd consequences that result if we take the argument for cultural relativism seriously.

Even if the Cultural Differences Argument is invalid, Cultural Relativism might still be true. What would it be like if it were true?

In the passage quoted above, William Graham Sumner summarizes the essence of Cultural Relativism. He says that there is no measure of right and wrong other than the standards of one's society: "The notion of right is in the folkways. It is not outside of them, of independent origin, and brought to test them. In the folkways, whatever is, is right."

Suppose we took this seriously. What would be some of the consequences?

1. *We could no longer say that the customs of other societies are morally inferior to our own.* This, of course, is one of the main points stressed by Cultural Relativism. We would have to stop condemning other societies merely because they are "different." So long as we concentrate on certain examples, such as the funerary practices of the Greeks and Callatians, this may seem to be a sophisticated, enlightened attitude.

However, we would also be stopped from criticizing other, less benign practices. Suppose a society waged war on its neighbors for the purpose of taking slaves. Or suppose a society was violently anti-Semitic and its leaders set out to destroy the Jews. Cultural Relativism would preclude us from saying that either of these practices was wrong. We would not even be able to say that a society tolerant of Jews is *better* than the anti-Semitic society, for that would imply some sort of transcultural standard of comparison. The failure to condemn *these* practices does not seem enlightened; on the contrary, slavery and anti-Semitism seem wrong wherever they occur. Nevertheless, if we took Cultural Relativism seriously, we would have to regard these social practices as also immune from criticism.

ASK YOURSELF

11. One absurd consequence of cultural relativism is that we can no longer say that the customs of other societies are morally inferior to our own. Why is that an absurd consequence?

2. *We could decide whether actions are right or wrong just by consulting the standards of our society.* Cultural Relativism suggests a simple test for determining what is right and what is wrong: All one need do is ask whether the action is in accordance with the code of one's society. Suppose in 1975 a resident of South Africa was wondering whether his country's policy of *apartheid*—a rigidly racist system—was morally correct. All he has to do is ask whether this policy conformed to his society's moral code. If it did, there would have been nothing to worry about, at least from a moral point of view.

This implication of Cultural Relativism is disturbing because few of us think that our society's code is perfect; we can think of ways it might be improved. Yet Cultural Relativism would not only forbid us from criticizing the codes of other societies; it would stop us from criticizing our own. After all, if right and wrong are relative to culture, this must be true for our own culture just as much as for other cultures.

ASK YOURSELF

12. A second absurd consequence of cultural relativism is that we can decide whether actions are right or wrong just by consulting the standards of our society. Why is that an absurd consequence?

3. *The idea of moral progress is called into doubt.* Usually, we think that at least some social changes are for the better. (Although, of course, other changes may be for the worse.) Throughout most of Western history the place of women in society was narrowly circumscribed. They could not own property; they could not vote or hold political office; and generally they were under the almost absolute control of their husbands. Recently much of this has changed, and most people think of it as progress.

If Cultural Relativism is correct, can we legitimately think of this as progress? Progress means replacing a way of doing things with a better way. But by what standard do we judge the new ways as better? If the old ways were in accordance with the social standards of their time, then Cultural Relativism would say it is a mistake to judge them by the standards of a different time. Eighteenth-century society was, in effect, a different society from the one we have now. To say that we have made progress implies a judgment that present-day society is better, and that is just the sort of transcultural judgment that, according to Cultural Relativism, is impermissible.

Our idea of social reform will also have to be reconsidered. Reformers such as Martin Luther King, Jr., have sought to change their societies for the better. Within the constraints imposed by Cultural Relativism, there is one way this might be done. If a society is not living up to its own ideals, the reformer may be regarded as acting for the best: The ideals of the society are the standard by which we judge his or her proposals as worthwhile. But the "reformer" may not challenge the ideals themselves, for those ideals are by definition correct. According to Cultural Relativism, then, the idea of social reform makes sense only in this limited way.

These three consequences of Cultural Relativism have led many thinkers to reject it as implausible on its face. It does make sense, they say, to condemn some practices, such as slave and anti-Semitism, wherever they occur. It makes sense to think that our own society has made some moral progress, while admitting that it is still imperfect and in need of reform. Because Cultural Relativism says that these judgments make no sense, the argument goes, it cannot be right.

ASK YOURSELF

13. A third absurd consequence is that the idea of moral progress is called into doubt. How does our idea of a social reformer show the absurdity of this consequence?

Why There Is Less Disagreement than It Seems. Rachels continues his attack on cultural relativism by arguing that there are in reality fewer cultural differences than the skeptics claim. The problem is that skeptics dramatically overestimate the extent of the differences that do exist.

The original impetus for Cultural Relativism comes from the observation that cultures differ dramatically in their views of right and wrong. But just how much do they differ? It is true that there are differences. However, it is easy to overestimate the extent of those differences. Often, when we examine what seems to be a dramatic difference, we find that the cultures do not differ nearly as much as it appears.

Consider a culture in which people believe it is wrong to eat cows. This may even be a poor culture, in which there is not enough food; still, the cows are not to be touched. Such a society would appear to have values very different from our own. But does it? We have not yet asked why these people will not eat cows. Suppose it is because they believe that after death the souls of humans inhabit the bodies of animals, especially cows, so that a cow may be someone's grandmother. Now do we want to say that their values are different from ours? No; the difference lies elsewhere. The difference is in our belief systems, not in our values. We agree that we shouldn't eat Grandma; we simply disagree about whether the cow is (or could be) Grandma.

ASK YOURSELF

14. Rachels believes that relativists overestimate moral differences between various cultures. Explain how this overestimation arises in the case of Hindus not eating cows.

The point is that many factors work together to produce the customs of a society. The society's values are only one of them. Other matters, such as the religious and factual beliefs held by its members, and the physical circumstances in which they must live, are also important. We cannot conclude, then, merely because customs differ, that there is a disagreement about values. The difference in customs may be attributable to some other aspect of social life. Thus there may be less disagreement about values than there appears to be.

Consider again the Eskimos, who often kill perfectly normal infants, especially girls. We do not approve of such things; a parent who killed a baby in our society would be locked up. Thus there appears to be a great difference in the values of out two cultures. But suppose we ask why the Eskimos do this. The explanation is not that they have less affection for their children or less respect for human life. An Eskimo family will always protect its babies if conditions permit. But they live in a harsh environment, where food is in short supply. A fundamental postulate of Eskimo thought is: "Life is hard, and the margin of safety small." A family may want to nourish its babies but be unable to do so.

As in many "primitive" societies, Eskimo mothers will nurse their infants over a much longer period of time than mothers in our culture. The child will take nourishment from its mother's breast for four years, perhaps even longer. So even in the best of times there are limits to the number of infants that one mother can sustain. Moreover, the Eskimos are a nomadic people; unable to farm, they must move about in search of food. Infants must be carried, and a mother can carry only one baby in her parka as she travels and goes about her outdoor work. Other family members help whenever they can.

Infant girls are more readily disposed of because, first, in this society the males are the primary food providers—they are the hunters, according to the traditional division of labor—and it is obviously important to maintain a sufficient number of food providers. But there is an important second reason as well. Because the hunters suffer a high casualty rate, the adult men who die prematurely far outnumber the women who die early. Thus if male and female infants survived in equal numbers, the female adult population would greatly outnumber the male adult population. Examining the available statistics, one writer concluded that "were it not for female infanticide . . . there would be approximately one-and-a-half times as many females in the average Eskimo local group as there are food-producing males."

So among the Eskimos, infanticide does not signal a fundamentally different attitude toward children. Instead, it is a recognition that drastic measures are sometimes needed to ensure the family's survival. Even then, however, killing the baby is not the first option considered. Adoption is common; childless couples are especially happy to take a more fertile couple's "surplus." Killing is only the last resort. I emphasize this in order to show that the raw data of the anthropologists can be misleading; it can make the differences in values between cultures appear greater than they are. The Eskimos' values are not all that different from our values. It is only that life forces upon them choices that we do not have to make.

ASK YOURSELF

15. Explain the relativist's overestimation in the case of the Eskimos killing their infant children.

How All Cultures Have Some Values in Common. Rachels argues further against cultural relativism by noting that all societies actually have some common values.

It should not be surprising that, despite appearances, the Eskimos are protective of their children. How could it be otherwise? How could a group survive that did not value its young? It is easy to see that, in fact, all cultural groups must protect their infants:

1. Human infants are helpless and cannot survive if they are not given extensive care for a period of years.
2. Therefore, if a group did not care for its young, the young would not survive, and the older members of the group would not be replaced. After a while the group would die out.
3. Therefore, any cultural group that continues to exist must care for its young. Infants that are not cared for must be the exception rather than the rule.

Similar reasoning shows that other values must be more or less universal. Imagine what it would be like for a society to place no value at all on truth telling. When one person spoke to another, there would be no presumption at all that he was telling the truth for he could just as easily be speaking falsely. Within that society, there would be no reason to pay attention to what anyone says. (I ask you what time it is, and you say "four o'clock." But there is no presumption that you are speaking truly; you could just as easily have said the first thing that came into your head. So I have no reason to pay attention to your answer; in fact, there was no point in my asking you in the first place.) Communication would then be extremely difficult, if not impossible. And because complex societies cannot exist without communication among their members, society would become impossible. It follows that in any complex society there must be a presumption in favor of truthfulness. There may of course be exceptions to this rule: There may be situations in which it is thought to be permissible to lie. Nevertheless, these will be exceptions to a rule that is in force in the society.

Here is one further example of the same type. Could a society exist in which there was no prohibition on murder? What would this be like? Suppose people were free to kill other people at will, and no one thought there was anything wrong with it. In such a "society," no one could feel secure. Everyone would have to be constantly on guard. People who wanted to survive would have to avoid other people as much as possible. This would inevitably result in individuals trying to become as self-sufficient as possible—after all, associating with others would be dangerous. Society on any large scale would collapse. Of course, people might band together in smaller groups with others that they could trust not to harm them. But notice what this means: They would be forming smaller societies that did acknowledge a rule against murder. The prohibition of murder, then, is a necessary feature of all societies.

There is a general theoretical point here, namely, that *there are some moral rules that all societies will have in common, because those rules are necessary for society to exist.* The rules against lying and murder are two examples. And in fact, we do find these rules in force in all viable cultures. Cultures may differ in what they regard as legitimate exceptions to the rules, but this disagreement exists against a background of agreement on the larger issues. Therefore, it is a mistake to overestimate the amount of difference between cultures. Not every moral rule can vary from society to society. . . .

ASK YOURSELF

16. Why must these be common values to all societies?

SUMMING UP THE PROBLEM OF OBJECTIVE MORALITY

The issue of objective morality involves a dispute between two camps. Optimists believe that morality is objective, absolute, and universal. Plato, who best represents the optimists, held that morality is grounded in the eternal spiritual realm of the forms. Pessimists, on the other hand, tend to follow in the philosophical tradition of skepticism and deny the existence of an external spiritual realm of moral values or any other source of objective moral truth. They hold that morality is relative, that is, a purely human creation. Individual moral relativists believe that individual people create their own values, and cultural moral relativists believe that societies shape values. Champions of relativism include Sextus Empiricus, Montaigne, J. L. Mackie, and many social scientists. Rachels attacked cultural relativism on the grounds that moral attitudes around the world are not as varied as relativists have claimed. First, many apparent differences in moral values are due to differences in other beliefs such as scientific or religious beliefs. They are not actually differences in *moral* beliefs. Second, Rachels believes that all societies share some fundamental values, such as caring for children, prohibitions against lying, and prohibitions against stealing.

CAN OF WORMS

Theories about objective morality, such as Plato's view of the forms, immediately raise questions about the metaphysical makeup of the universe. Is the universe largely physical in nature, or is there some nonphysical spiritual element to it? Materialists who deny the existence of a spirit realm would reject Plato's view of the forms. Instead, they maintain that the values that we do have are the products of physical human beings operating in strictly natural environments. These issues bring us back to Chapters 3 and 4. Another theory of objective morality briefly mentioned in this chapter is the view that God willfully creates moral standards and imposes them on humans. This view is intertwined with issues in the philosophy of religion, particularly the existence of God and problems surrounding God's attribute of goodness. Critics of cultural relativism, such as James Rachels, raise questions about social science methodology: Do the data that sociologists report about moral values in different cultures accurately represent people's underlying moral convictions? What exactly follows about morality even if the data are accurate? More generally, how might we gain knowledge of people's true values in different cultures? These are questions connected with epistemology and logic.

B. CAN HUMAN CONDUCT BE SELFLESS?

Suppose that one chilly day while walking down a road you see a man in a nearby river struggling to stay afloat. Your own swimming skills are marginal, but you realize that if you don't attempt to rescue the man, he'll likely drown. You then wade in and successfully drag him to safety. You then think about why you took the risk. Did you do it out of the goodness of your heart, or was there some hidden selfish motive? On the one hand, you might consider that you were genuinely concerned about the man's well-being, and this outweighed the risk posed for yourself. On the other hand, you might consider that you knew your act would be heroic, and heroes receive great praise—often out of proportion to the risk that they assume. Questions like this about human selfishness dramatically impact how we view peoples' character as well as our views about the nature of moral goodness and obligations.

**QUESTIONS
TO DISCUSS**

a. Try thinking of an example of an action that is completely selfless. How might even that action be explained in terms of selfish motives?

b. Assume for the moment that every human action is selfishly motivated. Can we possibly expect people to show charity to others, or to love their neighbors as they do themselves?

c. Assume for the moment that some people were capable of truly selfless conduct. Would such people have an especially tough time surviving within a world of hostile and greedy people?

When examining this subject of selfless conduct, philosophers often distinguish between several related notions. First, there is the psychological question of whether human beings are at all capable of acting selflessly. The theory called "psychological egoism" maintains that human conduct is in fact selfishly motivated, and we cannot perform actions from any other motive. By contrast, "psychological altruism" is the theory that, while much of our conduct is selfishly motivated, human beings are at least occasionally capable of acting selflessly. Why, though, is this a moral issue, rather than simply a question for psychologists? The answer is that our moral responsibilities hinge to a large degree on what we are psychologically capable of doing. Philosophers make this point by insisting that "ought implies can." That is, I am morally obligated to do an action only if I am capable of performing that action. For example, I am not morally obligated to cure cancer or stop all wars; admirable though these goals may be, I personally am not capable of performing them, and so I cannot be morally obligated to perform them. Now consider psychological egoism's claim that all human conduct is selfishly motivated. If this is a true description of human nature, then I am not capable of a purely selfless action, and thus I cannot be morally required to act selflessly.

Related, then, to the theories of psychological egoism and psychological altruism are two ethical theories. "Ethical egoism" maintains that our moral obligation is to do actions that are self-serving. "Ethical altruism," by contrast, is the view that some of our principal moral obligations involve selfless behavior toward others. As the ethical views rise or fall based on the psychological ones, moral philosophers throughout history have wrestled at length with the theories of psychological egoism and psychological altruism. The foundational psychological issue will be the main focus of this section.

1. WHETHER HUMAN NATURE IS INHERENTLY GOOD OR EVIL: MENCIUS AND HSUN-TZU

Thoughts concerning egoism and altruism occur to us somewhat naturally, and so it should be no surprise that the issue is discussed in differing philosophical traditions from around the world. One of the more lively disputes took place among Confucian philosophers in China in the fourth and third centuries BCE. The specific issue under debate was whether human nature was inherently good or evil; but, in the course of the debate it is clear that selfishness is a central component in an evil person's character.

People Are Inherently Good: Mencius. Mencius—also called Mengzi—(390–305 BCE) lived a century or so after Confucius and, within the Confucian tradition, his writings are second in importance only to those of his great master. Mencius believed that human nature is inherently good. In the selection below, he debates the issue with the skeptical philosopher Kao-tzu (420–350 BCE), who holds that human nature is neither good nor evil, but can be fashioned in either direction through environmental influences.

FROM *The Mencius,* BOOK 6

KAO   Human nature is like a tree, and righteousness is like a wooden cup or a bowl. The fashioning of benevolence and righteousness out of a person's nature is like the making of cups and bowls from the tree.

MENCIUS   Without touching the nature of the tree, can you make it into cups and bowls? You must do violence and injury to the tree before you can make cups and bowls with it. If you must do violence and injury to the tree in order to make cups and bowls with it, on your principles you must in the same way do violence and injury to humanity in order to fashion from it benevolence and righteousness. Thus, your words would certainly lead all people on to consider benevolence and righteousness to be calamities.

KAO   Human nature is like water whirling around in a corner. Open a passage for it to the east, and it will flow to the east. Open a passage for it to the west, and it will flow to the west. Human nature is indifferent to good and evil, just as water is indifferent to the east and west.

MENCIUS   Water indeed will flow indifferently to the east or west, but will it flow indifferently up or down? The tendency of human nature to do good is like the tendency of water to flow downwards. All people have this tendency to good, just as all water flows downwards. Now, by striking water and causing it to leap up, you may make it go over your forehead, and, by damming and leading it, you may force it up a hill. But are such movements according to the nature of water? It is the force applied which causes them. When people are made to do what is not good, their nature is dealt with in this way.

ASK YOURSELF

17. Mencius believes that water naturally flows downward, but can be forced to leap up by striking it. What does the act of striking water represent in this analogy?

What precisely does it mean to say that human nature is inherently good? According to Mencius, this means that we naturally have specific emotions that direct us to follow moral principles.

KUNG-TU   The philosopher Kao says that human nature is neither good nor bad. Some say that human nature may be made to practice good and it may be made to practice evil . . . Others say that the nature of some is good, and the nature of others is bad. . . . And now you say that human nature is good. Are all those other views, then, wrong?

MENCIUS   From the feelings proper to it, human nature is constituted for the practice of what is good. This is what I mean in saying human nature is good. If people do what is not good, the blame cannot be placed on their natural powers. The feeling of commiseration belongs to all people. So do that of shame and dislike, and that of reverence and respect, and that of approving and disproving. The feeling of commiseration implies the principle of humanity. The feelings of shame and dislike imply the principle of righteousness. The feelings of reverence and respect imply the principle of social custom. The feelings of approving and disapproving imply the principle of knowledge. Humanity, righteousness, social custom, and knowledge are not infused into us from outside factors. We are certainly furnished with them. Any different view simply owes to an absence of reflection. Hence it is said, "Look and you will find them. Neglect and you will lose them." People differ from one another in regard to them: some have twice as much as others, some five times as much, and some to an incalculable amount. This is because they cannot fully carry out their natural powers. The *Book of Poetry* states that "In producing humankind, heaven gave people their various faculties and relations with their specific laws. These are the invariable rules of nature for everyone to hold; all love this admirable virtue." Confucius said, "The writer of this ode indeed knows the principle of our nature." We may thus see that every faculty and relation must have its law, and since there are invariable rules for all to hold, they consequently love this admirable virtue.

ASK YOURSELF

18. List the emotions that Mencius mentions, along with the moral principles that correspond to those emotions.

People Are Inherently Evil: Hsun-tzu. Even more skeptical than Kao-tzu, the Confucian philosopher Hsun-tzu (298–238 BCE) held the more extreme view that human nature is inherently bad—principally because of our selfish tendencies. Like Kao-tzu and Mencius, Hsun-tzu too recognized the importance of environmental influence in altering conduct. For Hsun-tzu, though, a positive environmental influence is necessary for morally good conduct, and we should not take this lightly if we hope to live in a civilized society.

FROM *The Hsun-tzu*, CHAPTER 17

Human nature is evil and the good that we show is artificial. Even at birth human nature includes the love of gain. Since we act according to our desires, conflict and robberies emerge. We will not find self-denial and altruism. Human nature includes envy and dislike, and as actions are in accordance with these, violence and injuries spring up, whereas loyalty and faith do not. Human nature includes the desires of the ears and the eyes, leading to the love of sounds and beauty. And as the actions are in accordance with these, lewdness and disorder spring up, whereas righteousness and social custom, with their various orderly displays, do not. It thus appears that following human nature and yielding to its feelings will surely create strife and theft. It will lead to violation of everyone's duties and disruption of all order, until we are in a state of savagery. We must have the influence of teachers and laws, and the guidance of social custom and righteousness. For, from these we get self-denial, altruism, and an observance of the well-ordered regulations of conduct, which results in a state of good government. From all this it is plain that human nature is evil; the good which it shows is artificial.

Consider some illustrations. A crooked stick must be submitted to the pressing-frame to soften and bond it, and then it becomes straight. A blunt knife must be submitted to the grindstone and whetstone, and then it becomes sharp. Similarly, human nature, being evil, must be submitted to teachers and laws, and then it becomes correct. It must be submitted to social custom and righteousness, and then it is capable of being governed. If people were without teachers and laws, our condition would be one of deviation and insecurity, and would be entirely wrong. If we were without social custom and righteousness, our condition would be one of rebellious disorder and we would reject all government. The sage kings of old understood that human nature was evil, in a state of hazardous deviation, improper, rebellious, disorderly, and resistant to governance. Accordingly, they set up the principles of righteousness and social custom, and framed laws and regulations. These efforts served to straighten and embellish our natural feelings. They correct them, tame them, change them and guide them. By this means we might proceed on a path of moral governance which is in agreement with reason. Now, the superior person is the one who is transformed by teachers and laws. He takes on the distinction of learning, and follows the path of social custom and righteousness. The inferior person is the one who follows his nature and its feelings, indulges its resentments, and walks contrary to social custom and righteousness. Looking at the subject in this way, we see clearly that human nature is evil, and the good that it shows is artificial.

ASK YOURSELF

19. According to Hsun-tzu, what are the main environmental influences that shape people toward moral goodness?

Hsun-tzu believes that the key to resolving the dispute over human nature is understanding precisely what it means for a quality to be natural or artificial. Mencius, he contends, dropped the ball here.

Mencius said, "Man has only to learn, and his nature appears to be good"; but I reply, It is not so. To say so shows that he had not attained to the knowledge of human nature, nor examined into the difference between what is natural in people and what is artificial. The natural is what the constitution spontaneously moves to: it does not need to be learned, it does not need to be followed hard after. Propriety and righteousness are what the sages have given birth to: it is by learning that people become capable of them, it is by hard practice that they achieve them. That which is in people—not needing to be learned and striven after—is what I call natural. That in people which is attained to by learning, and achieved by hard striving, is what I call artificial. This is the distinction between those two. By human nature, eyes are capable of seeing and ears are capable of hearing. But the power of seeing is inseparable from the eyes, and the power of hearing is inseparable from the ears. It is plain that the faculties of seeing and hearing do not need to be learned.

Mencius says, "The nature of man is good, but all lose and ruin their nature, and therefore it becomes bad." But I say that this representation is erroneous. People being born with their nature, when they thereafter depart from its simple constituent elements, must lose it. From this consideration we may see clearly that human nature is evil. What might be called the nature's being good, would be if there were no departing from its simplicity to beautify it, no departing from its elementary dispositions to sharpen it. Suppose that those simple elements no more needed beautifying, and the mind's thoughts no more needed to be turned to good, than the power of vision which is inseparable from the eyes, and the power of hearing which is inseparable from the ears, need to be learned. Then we might say that human nature is good, just as we say that eyes see and ears hear. It is human nature, when hungry, to desire to be filled; when cold, to desire to be warmed; when tired, to desire rest. These are the feelings and nature of people.

ASK YOURSELF

20. According to Hsun-tzu, what does it mean to say that a particular human tendency is *natural?*

Imagine, for example, that a person is hungry in the presence of an elder, but does not dare to sit before him. He instead yields to that elder; tired with labor, he nevertheless does not dare to ask for rest. Imagine similarly a son's yielding to his father and a younger brother to his elder; or, a son's laboring for his father and a younger brother for his elder. These examples illustrate conduct that is contrary to nature and against one's feelings. However, these actions are in accord with the course laid down for a filial son, and to the refined distinctions of propriety and righteousness. It appears, then, that if feelings and nature were in accord with each other, there would be no self-denial and yielding to others. Self-denial and yielding to others are simply contrary to the feelings and the nature. In this way we come to see how clear it is that human nature is evil, and the good which it shows is artificial.

One might ask, "If human nature is evil, what is the source of social custom and righteousness?" I reply, all social custom and righteousness are the artificial productions of the sages, and should not be thought of as growing out of human nature. It is just as when a potter makes a vessel from the clay. The vessel is the product of the workman's art, and should not be thought of as growing out of human nature. Or it is as when another workman cuts and hews a vessel out of wood; it is the product of his art, and is not to be considered as growing out of human nature. The sages pondered long in thought and gave themselves to practice, and so they succeeded in producing social custom and righteousness, and setting up laws and regulations. In this way social custom and righteousness, laws and regulations, are artificial products of the sages, and should not be seen as growing properly from human nature.

ASK YOURSELF

21. What, for Hsun-tzu, is the ultimate source of all social custom and righteousness?

2. THE SELFISH ORIGINS OF PITY AND CHARITY: THOMAS HOBBES

During the seventeenth and eighteenth centuries a debate about human nature raged in Europe that very much paralleled the earlier debate in China. This time, though, the issue rested squarely on whether human actions are selfishly motivated or whether we have benevolent motivations that enable us to act unselfishly. Discussion was sparked by British philosopher Thomas Hobbes (1588–1679), who championed psychological egoism. Educated at Oxford, Hobbes spent much of his life as a tutor. Amidst his teaching duties he traveled widely and wrote several political and philosophical works, the most famous of which is *The Leviathan* (1651). In many of his writings he adopts the view that people are fundamentally motivated by selfish inclinations. Hobbes does not systematically expound this view and his exact meaning is unclear. He occasionally expresses this view in statements such as this: "all society therefore is either for gain, or for glory; that is, not so much for love of our fellows, as for the love of ourselves" (*Citizen*, 1:2). We find a similar statement here: "of the voluntary acts of every man the object is some good to himself" (*Leviathan*, 14:8).

**THOMAS HOBBES
(1588–1679)**
English philosopher and author of Leviathan *(1651).*

Hobbes's most revealing discussion of human selfishness is his treatment of the feelings of pity and charity. We typically think that both pity and charity are selfless. For example, if I feel pity toward a person who is suffering, then I am unselfishly experiencing the suffering of that person. And, when motivated by pity, I will presumably help out the suffering person, without consideration for my own selfish inclinations. Against this common conception, Hobbes argues that there is in fact an underlying selfish motivation for pity:

> Pity is imagination or fiction of future calamity to ourselves proceeding from the sense of another man's calamity. But when it lights on such as we think have not deserved the same, the compassion is greater, because then there appears more probability that the same may happen to us: for, the evil that happens to an innocent man, may happen to every man. But when we see a man suffer for great crimes, which we cannot easily think will fall upon ourselves, the pity is the less. And therefore men are apt to pity those whom they love: for, whom they love, they think worthy of good, and therefore not worthy of calamity. Thence it is also, that men pity the vices of some persons at the first sight only, out of love to their aspect. The contrary of pity is hardness of heart, proceeding either from slowness of imagination, or some extreme great opinion of their own exemption from the like calamity, or from hatred of all or most men.

Similarly, we commonly think that if we have feelings of charity, we will help someone in need for that person's sake, and not for our own sake. Here, too, Hobbes finds a selfish motivation:

> There is yet another passion sometimes called love, but more properly good-will or charity. There can be no greater argument to a man, of his own power, than to find himself able not only to accomplish his own desires, but also to assist other men in theirs: and this is that conception wherein consists charity. In which, first, is contained that natural affection of parents to their children, which the Greeks call *storge,* as also, that affection wherewith men seek to assist those that adhere unto them. But the affection wherewith men many times bestow their benefits on strangers, is not to be called charity, but either contract, whereby they seek to purchase friendship; or fear, which makes them to purchase peace. [From Thomas Hobbes, *Human Nature* (1650), 9.17]

22. What, according to Hobbes, is the underlying selfish motivation for pity?

23. What, according to Hobbes, is the underlying selfish motivation for charity?

These brief hints in Hobbes's writings raise questions about what precisely Hobbes was saying. At times, Hobbes seemed to be saying this: *A person's voluntary actions are motivated only by that person's desires.* Philosophers today call this position "tautological egoism" and dismiss it as simply being true by definition. That is, we typically define "voluntary action" as actions that are motivated by our desires. Thus, we do little more than repeat ourselves when we say that voluntary actions are motivated by one's desires. A second point of confusion involves whether Hobbes and other egoists were advocating the more extreme position that *no actions toward either friends or strangers are benevolently motivated.* It is one thing for an egoist to say that we act selfishly toward strangers, but is it reasonable to say this about our actions toward close friends and family members? It seems here that many of our actions are indeed selfless. The most plausible version of psychological egoism seems to be a weaker claim that *some actions toward friends are benevolently motivated, but no actions toward strangers are benevolently motivated.* But even this weaker claim is liable to criticism. For there seem to be clear familiar cases in which some people act benevolently toward complete strangers.

ASK YOURSELF

24. Can you give an example of an action that certainly seems to be benevolent—that is, not motivated by selfish interests?

25. State both the strong and weak versions of psychological egoism

3. LOVE OF OTHERS NOT OPPOSED TO SELF-LOVE: JOSEPH BUTLER

In the decades after Hobbes, virtually every philosopher writing on morality felt compelled to take a stand on the issue of egoism and altruism. Joseph Butler (1692–1752) was a British clergyman and eventually a bishop. In the selection below from "Sermon 11" of Butler's *Fifteen Sermons,* he attacks egoism by showing that it is conceptually confused. This sermon, entitled "Upon the Love of Our Neighbor," is based upon Romans 13.9: "And if there be any other commandment, it is briefly comprehended in this saying, namely, You shall love your neighbor as yourself." Butler recognizes that people indeed act selfishly much of the time. He also recognized that acting benevolently often makes us happy. That does not imply, however, that a selfish desire to be happy motivates benevolent acts.

Against the Theory of Self-Love. Butler argues that the various common and theoretical defenses of egoism—such as those by Hobbes—are mistaken and confused.

JOSEPH BUTLER, *Fifteen Sermons* (1726), SERMON 11

Since there is generally thought to be some peculiar kind of contrariety between self-love and the love of our neighbor, between the pursuit of public and of private good, insomuch that when you are recommending one of these, you are supposed to be speaking against the other;

and from hence arises a secret prejudice against and frequently open scorn of all talk of public spirit and real goodwill to our fellow creatures; it will be necessary to inquire what respect benevolence has to self-love, and the pursuit of private interest to the pursuit of public; or whether there be anything of that peculiar inconsistency and contrariety between them, over and above what there is between self-love and other passions and particular affections, and their respective pursuits.

ASK YOURSELF

26. Butler is here alluding to a common view that if I am acting out of self-love, then I cannot be acting out of _____.

General Desires and Particular Affections. Butler's crucial point emerges in the following discussion where he argues that self-love is not a particular affection.

Every man has a general desire of his own happiness, and likewise a variety of particular affections, passions, and appetites to particular external objects. The former proceeds from or is self-love, and seems inseparable from all sensible creatures who can reflect upon themselves and their own interest or happiness, so as to have that interest an object to their minds; what is to be said of the latter is that they proceed from, or together make up, that particular nature according to which man is made. The object the former pursues is something internal—our own happiness, enjoyment, satisfaction, whether we have or have not a distinct particular perception what it is or wherein it consists; the objects of the latter are this or that particular external thing which the affections tend towards, and of which it has always a particular idea or perception. The principle we call "self-love" never seeks anything external for the sake of the thing, but only as a means of happiness or good; particular affections rest in the external things themselves. One belongs to man as a reasonable creature reflecting upon his own interest or happiness. The other, though quite distinct from reason, are as much a part of human nature.

ASK YOURSELF

27. Self-love, Butler says, is a _____ desire for happiness, and belongs to man as a _____ creature.

28. Particular affections, on the other hand, rest in _____ things and are distinct from _____.

29. Which of the following would be a "particular affection" on Butler's account: the love of tennis, the desire for revenge, the desire for a good life, the desire for a warm bath?

If, because every particular affection is a man's own, and the pleasure arising from its gratification his own pleasure, or pleasure to himself, such particular affection must be called self-love: according to this way of speaking no creature whatever can possibly act but merely from self-love, and every action and every affection whatever is to be resolved up into this one principle. But then this is not the language of mankind; or if it were, we should want words to express the difference between the principle of an action proceeding from cool consideration that it will be to my own advantage, and an action, suppose of revenge or of friendship, by which a man runs upon certain ruin to do evil or good to another.

> **ASK YOURSELF**
>
> **30.** The "language of mankind" makes a distinction between actions motivated by self-love and those done from some particular motive such as friendship or revenge. The idea that all actions proceed from self-love therefore ignores that distinction. What is the reason some people nonetheless claim that all actions proceed from self-love?

Happiness does not consist in self-love. The desire of happiness is no more the thing itself than the desire of riches is the possession or enjoyment of them. People may love themselves with the most entire and unbounded affection, and yet be extremely miserable. Neither can self-love anyway help them out, but by setting them on work to get rid of the causes of their misery, to gain or make use of those objects which are by nature adapted to afford satisfaction. Happiness or satisfaction consists only in the enjoyment of those objects which are by nature suited to our several particular appetites, passions, and affections. So that if self-love wholly engrosses us, and leaves no room for any other principle, there can be absolutely no such thing at all as happiness, or enjoyment of any kind whatever, since happiness consists in the gratification of particular passions, which supposes the having of them. Self-love then does not constitute *this* or *that* to be our interest or good; but, our interest or good being constituted by nature and supposed, self-love only puts us upon obtaining and securing it.

Acting out of self-love cannot be "gratifying a particular passion" since there is no such particular passion. Rather, if I want to love myself, I need to engage those particular passions I do have.

> **ASK YOURSELF**
>
> **31.** It follows that if one of my particular passions is tennis, then if I want to love myself I should arrange to play some _____. Loving myself could not consist in some particular thing above and beyond such things as playing tennis.

Butler has here touched upon what is sometimes called the "hedonistic paradox." A hedonist is a person who lives entirely for pleasure. The only thing she is *interested* in is pleasure. So if she plays tennis, she plays it not because she is interested in tennis but because she is interested in the pleasure she may get from playing. But of course, if she is not interested in tennis, she will not get any pleasure out of it! There is a practical side to this paradox: If you try too hard to enjoy something, you will not enjoy it much. This is true for all sorts of enjoyments.

Egoism and Happiness. Butler argues that egoism as usually understood actually conflicts with self-love, as we can see from the way it conflicts with happiness. Just as overfondness for a child may lead a parent to indulge that child in a way that will make it spoiled and eventually unhappy, so overfondness for oneself may have a similar effect.

Overfondness for a child is not generally thought to be for its advantage; and if there be any guess to be made from appearances, surely that character we call selfish is not the most promising for happiness. . . . Immoderate self-love does very ill consult its own interest; and how much soever a paradox it may appear, it is certainly true that even from self-love we should endeavor to get over all inordinate regard to and consideration of ourselves.

In other words, if you really want to love yourself, you should not "love yourself" too much. Pursuit of what immediately gratifies me can lead to much misery.

It might be argued, however, that even though self-love does not conflict with various particular affections (such as a love of tennis), it does nevertheless conflict with benevolence or love of neighbor. For benevolence is by definition an interest in the welfare of others, and benevolent people often act in sacrificial ways and give up some of their own interests or "particular affections" in order to benefit others. Butler considers, and rejects, this argument. He argues that there is no conflict between love of self and love of others.

Benevolence Is a Particular Affection. Butler argues that benevolence cannot, logically, conflict with self-love, since the former is itself one particular affection among others, whereas the latter is not a particular affection.

Self-love and interestedness was stated to consist in or be an affection to ourselves, a regard to our own private good; it is therefore distinct from benevolence, which is an affection to the good of our fellow creatures. But that benevolence is distinct from, that is, not the same thing with self-love, is no reason for its being looked upon with any peculiar suspicion; because every principle whatever, by means of which self-love is gratified, is distinct from it; and all things which are distinct from each other are equally so.

ASK YOURSELF

32. The fact that benevolence is distinct from self-love is no more reason for thinking it conflicts with self-love than is the fact that love of tennis is distinct from self-love is a reason for thinking that love of tennis conflicts with _____.

Egoists tend to argue that genuinely *disinterested* action is impossible and infer that genuine, as opposed to feigned, benevolence is impossible. Butler argues that benevolence is not more "disinterested" than any other particular affection.

All that is here insisted upon is that ambition, revenge, benevolence, all particular passions whatever, and the actions they produce, are equally interested or disinterested.

Thus it appears that there is no peculiar contrariety between self-love and benevolence, no greater competition between these than between any other particular affections and self-love.

If I am "interested" in being a rock star, that is a particular interest. Whether it contributes or detracts from self-love is an open question. I might fulfill that interest and still be a miserable person who treats himself very badly. On the other hand, if I have an "interest" in helping others, that is also a particular interest, and whether it leads to happiness or not is an open question. Butler remarks that there is a verbal dispute going on here. We can *call* ambition "interested" and the interest in helping others "disinterested" if we like, but logically the two are on a par.

ASK YOURSELF

33. Suppose that one of my "particular affections" (i.e., one of the things I enjoy) is helping other people have a good time. Does the fact that I increase their enjoyment in any way take away from mine?

Benevolence May Actually Increase Personal Happiness. Benevolence may lead to greater enjoyment of life, not, as the egoist supposes, less.

Does the benevolent man appear less easy with himself, from his love to his neighbor? Does he less relish his being? Is there any peculiar gloom seated on his face? Is his mind less open to entertainment, to any particular gratification? Nothing is more manifest than that being in good humor, which is benevolence while it lasts, is itself the temper of satisfaction and enjoyment.

ASK YOURSELF

34. Butler is saying that a benevolent person is even more likely to be _____ than a person who is "selfish," ambitious, and the like.

Butler speculates that the mistaken notion that benevolence is in conflict with self-love may arise from confusing happiness with property. If I give you some of my property (in the form of money, say), then I have less, and if property is happiness, then I have less happiness. But surely property and happiness are not identical, even though having wealth may conduce to happiness.

For if property and happiness are one and the same thing, as by increasing the property of another, you lessen your own property, so by promoting the happiness of another, you must lessen your own happiness. But whatever occasioned the mistake, I hope it has been fully proved to be one, as it has been proved that there is no peculiar rivalship or competition between self-love and benevolence; that as there may be a competition between these two, so there may also between any particular affection whatever and self-love; that every particular affection, benevolence among the rest, is subservient to self-love by being the instrument of private enjoyment; and that in one respect benevolence contributes more to private interest, that is, enjoyment or satisfaction, than any other of the particular common affections, as it is in a degree its own gratification.

ASK YOURSELF

35. In Butler's view could an act of genuine self-sacrifice for the sake of my neighbor bring me happiness?

4. ALTRUISM AND SOCIOBIOLOGY: EDWARD O. WILSON

The question of psychological egoism certainly seems to be of utmost ethical concern, and it might appear to be a matter of scientific fact that we should eventually be able to settle once and for all. In the twentieth century, though, some philosophers dismissed the question as a non-issue. Critics argued that the theory of psychological egoism simply cannot be either proven or disproven. All that the altruist can do is offer examples of conduct that seem to be truly altruistic—such as rescuing a stranger from a burning building. However, the egoist will be unconvinced by such examples and instead point out some hidden selfish motive that the rescuer possesses—such as the desire to become a hero. It's not just that the egoist will object to an example or two that seems to favor altruism; rather, the egoist is poised to reject *every* conceivable example. Psychological egoism, which begins as an empirical theory, thus degenerates into tautological egoism, as we've discussed earlier. The claim that all action is egoistic becomes theoretically *unfalsifiable,* and as such is not a truly factual claim. In recent decades, however, psychological egoism has regained some respectability as a factual issue worthy of scientific study, particularly from within the field of sociobiology.

"Sociobiology" is a term introduced by Edward O. Wilson in his 1975 book by that title. In a nutshell, the theory states that human social behavior emerged through human evolution. Humans who were genetically prone to behave in certain ways would survive, and those without that genetic predisposition would tend to die out. Since the days of Darwin, evolutionary theorists have struggled to discover the precise evolutionary mechanisms that produce new characteristics in an organism. Millions upon millions of subtle changes have taken place within the DNA of plants and animals over the millennia. But not all of these changes can be neatly explained by the simple evolutionary view that an individual organism will develop in a way that contributes to its own individual survival, and nothing more—a view sometimes called *individual* selection. Altruism is a case in point, and for that reason sociobiologists have given it special attention.

The starting point in these sociobiological discussions is the observation that humans—as well as many other animals—have an apparent tendency to help others at the expense of themselves. When I am charitable, for example, I give over some of my money or time to another person more needy than myself. How can such altruism be explained by individual selection? If I am genetically predisposed to help others, then "selfish" people will have advantages that may contribute to their longevity, thus enabling them to reproduce more "selfish" descendants. In particular, they will have the advantage of being able to exploit my altruistic tendencies. Since I have no similar advantage in relation to them, I am more likely to die young, for example, while saving some unrelated person's life. The long-run result will be that my line of altruistic descendants dies out.

ASK YOURSELF

36. Give an example of an altruistic action that you might perform, which could result in a selfish person taking advantage of you.

One solution to the problem of altruism—which Darwin himself suggested—is to differentiate between *individual* selection, as described above, and *kin* selection, by which an individual organism is predisposed to act in ways that improve the chances for survival of its family or tribe, and not just the survival of itself. Based on the notion of kin selection, I remain selfish regarding outsiders, but am altruistic when it comes to my family. But, Wilson sees a flaw in this solution, namely, that kin selection hampers global harmony:

> If human beings are to a large extent guided by programmed learning rules and canalized emotional development to favor their own relatives and tribe, only a limited amount of global harmony is possible. International cooperation will approach an upper limit, from which it will be knocked down by the perturbations of war and economic struggle, canceling each upward surge based on pure reason. The imperatives of blood and territory will be the passions to which reason is slave.

Wilson attempts to solve the riddle of altruism by distinguishing between different kinds of altruism. First, there is *hard-core* altruism, which is completely unselfish and is unaffected by the prospect of individual reward. Second, there is *soft-core* altruism, which is essentially selfish: Behavior programmed in such a way that people serve other people only when doing so serves their own survival in the long run. Wilson recognizes that humans may have some amount of hard-core altruism toward kin. However, he believes that the greatest balance of human altruism is soft-core and geared toward oneself. Most of our altruistic acts are based on elaborate and ever-changing calculations that we make about who is part of our in group at any particular point in time. Those "calculations" would themselves have to be the output of some complex evolutionary history:

> Human beings are consistent in their codes of honor but endlessly fickle with reference to whom their codes apply. The genius of human sociality is in fact the ease with which alliances are formed, broken, and reconstituted, always with strong emotional appeals to rules believed to be absolute. The important distinction is today, as it appears to have been since the Ice Age, between the ingroup and the outgroup, but the precise location of the dividing line is shifted back and forth with ease. Professional sports thrive on the durability of this basic phenomenon. For an hour or so the spectator can resolve his world into the elemental physical struggle between tribal surrogates. The athletes come from anywhere and are sold and traded on an almost yearly basis. The teams themselves are sold from city to city. But it does not matter; the fan identifies with an aggressive ingroup, admires teamwork, bravery, and sacrifice, and shares the exultation of victory. [From Edward O. Wilson, *On Human Nature* (1975), Chapter 7]

ASK YOURSELF

37. According to Wilson, human altruism is directed toward members of our ingroup. What does he say about the dividing line between our ingroup and outgroup?

The problem of altruism is one of the more vigorously debated issues in sociobiology, and Wilson is just one voice on the subject. There is considerable debate about the unit upon which environments operate: Is it the individual gene, or a sex-related group, or whole populations? And regardless of the level, the question whether a certain sort of behavior will arise and survive hinges upon questions about the varying effects of environments upon genetic change. Survival of certain genes might be relatively easy in one environment, but slightly more difficult in another. Thus disputes about altruism become stalled in theoretical disputes in the foundations of biology. Meanwhile, many philosophers look suspiciously at the whole project, seeing it as a case of *naturalism*—that is, the flawed view that ethical judgments are rooted in empirical facts, in this case biological facts. The next section examines this philosophical critique.

SUMMING UP THE PROBLEM OF SELFLESS HUMAN CONDUCT

The issue of selfless human conduct involves both a psychological and an ethical component. The psychological question concerns whether or not people are capable of behaving in a truly selfless manner. The ethical question concerns whether or not people are morally obligated to act selflessly. Altruists on both issues advocate selflessness, and egoists advocate selfishness—or self-interestedness. An early version of the debate took place in China. Mencius argued that people were inherently good, while his counterpart in the debate, Kao-tzu, argued that human nature could be molded toward either goodness or badness. Hsun-tzu argued even more skeptically that human nature is inherently evil, and people must be socially programmed to become good. In seventeenth century England, Thomas Hobbes argued that human conduct is fundamentally selfish, even in cases of acts of pity and charity, which we typically think are altruistic. Joseph Butler conceded that people in fact do at times act selfishly, and also that benevolent actions do bring us happiness. However, Butler argues that self-love is on a different logical level than love of others, so that there could not be a conflict between them. The mere fact that someone enjoys helping others in no way shows that the motivation for his act was selfish. Sociobiologists have tried to shed new light on the subject by considering mechanisms in human evolutionary develop-ment that may have shaped our apparent human tendency to act altruistically. Edward O. Wilson argued that most of our altruistic conduct is soft-core—that is, aimed to-ward oneself and not completely for the benefit of the receiver of our actions.

CAN OF WORMS

When I investigate whether I am capable of acting selflessly, I am already presum-ing that I understand how human actions in general occur. The problem of selfless-ness, then, is related to *action theory*—which explores more generally the causes of human action, such as brain states, intensions, beliefs, and volitions. Some of these notions have been explored in Chapter 4. Another issue lurking beneath the surface is that of free will. Egoists commit themselves to a kind of determinism: Our choices are constrained by our psychological makeup, which is the inevitable result of human evolutionary development. Determinism is discussed in Chapter 3. Issues relating to proofs of egoism—particularly whether it is theoretically falsifiable—are connected with the philosophy of science, which is part of epistemology.

C. REASON AND MORAL JUDGMENTS

An anti-abortion television commercial began with a close-up shot of a man's closed hand; he then slowly uncurled his fingers, revealing a tiny hand of an aborted fetus that he was holding. The aim of the commercial was to invoke feelings of revulsion toward abortion. Negative reaction to the commercial on the part of some of the public led to its being can-celed after its first airing. The abortion debate is a good example of the role that emotion often plays in moral assessments. At first we might think that the question of abortion can be resolved calmly by considering the best arguments on both sides of the dispute. However, tempers quickly flare, and participants on both sides often appeal to instinctive emotional reactions such as those that might be aroused by that television commercial. Although an extreme example, it does illustrate an important philosophical point: It is not entirely clear whether moral assessments are more closely connected with reason or emotion. Even when we reason very carefully about moral matters, at some level the issues engage our feelings. And, even if we think that our moral convictions are driven by our emotions, at some point we justify our convictions with rational arguments. Most moral philosophers recognize that morality taps both our reason and emotions. The issue up for debate, however, is which of the two is the principal source of moral assessments.

QUESTIONS TO DISCUSS

a. Imagine that two robots—capable of human reason but not human emotion—discussed the moral issue of abortion from opposite sides. Do you think the robots could reason their way to a mutually agreeable conclusion?

b. Imagine that two people—who could not reason very well but excelled in expressing their emotions—debated the abortion issue. Do you think they could resolve the issue to the satisfaction of each?

c. Suppose that your friend was mugged. What are the relevant facts in this situa-tion that would enable you to conclude that the mugger was morally bad?

1. CAN WE DERIVE OUGHT FROM IS? DAVID HUME AND JOHN SEARLE

The Is/Ought Problem: Hume. Scottish philosopher David Hume (1711–1776) believed that moral assessments are essentially emotional reactions. Our human reason, he contends, gives us raw data to work with, such as informing us of the fact that Smith donated to charity, or the fact that Jones held up someone at gunpoint. But this information, in and of itself, does not constitute a moral judgment. What we need is a special emotional reaction in the face of these facts. When informed that Smith donated to charity, I have a pleasing emotional reaction, and this emotion constitutes my moral approval. When informed that Jones held up someone at gunpoint, I have a painful emotional reaction, which constitutes my moral disapproval. Hume lays out the boundaries between reason and emotion here:

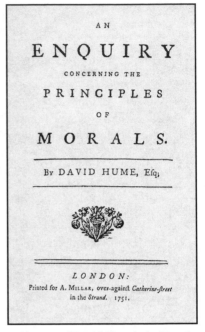

Title page of David Hume's An Enquiry Concerning the Principles of Morals *(1751), which Hume considered "incomparably the best" of his writings.*

> Thus, the distinct boundaries and offices of *reason* and of *taste* are easily ascertained. The former conveys the knowledge of truth and falsehood. The latter gives the sentiment of beauty and deformity, vice and virtue. The one discovers objects as they really stand in nature, without addition or diminution. The other has a productive faculty and (gilding or staining all natural objects with the colors borrowed from internal sentiment) raises in a manner a new creation. Reason, being cool and disengaged, is no motive to action, and directs only the impulse received from appetite or inclination, by showing us the means of attaining happiness or avoiding misery. Taste, as it gives pleasure or pain (and thereby constitutes happiness or misery) becomes a motive to action, and is the first spring or impulse to desire and volition. From circumstances and relations known or supposed, the former leads us to the discovery of the concealed and unknown. After all circumstances and relations are laid before us, the latter makes us feel from the whole a new sentiment of blame or approbation. The standard of the one, being founded on the nature of things, is eternal and inflexible, even by the will of the Supreme Being. The standard of the other, arising from the internal frame and constitution of animals, is ultimately derived from that Supreme will, which bestowed on each being its peculiar nature, and arranged the several classes and orders of existence. [From David Hume, *An Enquiry Concerning the Principles of Morals* (1751), Section 1]

ASK YOURSELF

38. According to Hume, are our actions motivated by reason or are they motivated by emotion?

Hume felt that moral philosophers of his time did not pay enough attention to the distinct roles of reason and emotion, most placing far too much weight on reason. Rationalist discussions of morality, he argued, typically begin with statements of fact, such as "Jones is starving," and then conclude with a statement of obligation, such as "We should help feed Jones." What is missing, according to Hume, is the emotional reaction, which constitutes the actual moral assessment. Thus, he contends, it is impossible to rationally deduce statements of obligation from statements of fact. This view of Hume's is encapsulated in the saying that, "*Ought* cannot be derived from *is*." He makes his point here:

> I cannot forbear adding to these reasonings an observation, which may, perhaps, be found of some importance. In every system of morality which I have hitherto met with, I have always remarked that the author proceeds for some time in the ordinary way of reasoning, and establishes the being of a God, or makes observations concerning human affairs. When of a sudden, I am surprised to find that, instead of the usual copulations of propositions, *is* and *is not,* I meet with no proposition that is not connected with an *ought* or an *ought not.* The change is imperceptible, but is, however, of the last [and greatest] consequence. For as this *ought* or *ought not* expresses some new relation or affirmation, it is necessary that it should be observed and explained. And at the same time, [it is necessary] that a reason should be given for (what seems altogether inconceivable) how this new relation can be a deduction from others, which are entirely different from it. But as authors do not commonly use this precaution, I shall presume to recommend it to the readers. And [I] am persuaded that this small attention would subvert all the vulgar [i.e., common] systems of morality, and let us see that the distinction of vice and virtue is not founded merely on the relations of objects nor is perceived by reason. [From David Hume, *Treatise of Human Nature* (1739), 3.1.1.]

ASK YOURSELF

39. What kind of facts, or "ordinary ways of reasoning," do moral rationalists typically start with?

Ought Derived from Institutional Facts: Searle. The is/ought problem is as much of a concern for contemporary philosophers as it was in Hume's day. Is it possible for us to rationally deduce statements of moral obligation from statements of mere fact? One of the more interesting solutions to this problem is by John Searle (b. 1932). In his essay "How to Derive 'Ought' from 'Is,'" he recasts the is/ought problem in contemporary language:

> It is often said that one cannot derive an "ought" from an "is." This thesis, which comes from a famous passage in Hume's *Treatise,* though not as clear as it might be, is at least clear in broad outline: there is a class of statements of fact which is logically distinct from a class of statements of value. No set of statements of fact by themselves entails any statement of value. Put in more contemporary terminology, no set of *descriptive* statements can entail an *evaluative* statement without the addition of at least one evaluative premise.

40. Give an example of a descriptive statement and an evaluative statement.

Searle agrees that typical descriptive statements of fact—such as the ball is round or the door is brown—cannot directly imply evaluative statements of obligation. However, he argues, there is a special set of facts—which he calls "institutional facts"—that can lead to statements of obligation:

> [S]tatements containing words such as "married," "promise," "home run," and "five dollars" state facts whose existence presupposes certain institutions: a man has five dollars, given the institution of money. Take away the institution and all he has is a rectangular bit of paper with green ink on it. A man hits a home run only given the institution of baseball; without the institution he only hits a sphere with a stick. Similarly, a man gets married or makes a promise only within the institutions of marriage and promising. Without them, all he does is utter words or make gestures. We might characterize such facts as institutional facts, and contrast them with noninstitutional, or brute, facts. . . . [From John Searle, "How to Derive Ought from Is" (1964)]

The *fact* that Bob hit a home run is a fact only within a set of rules and agreements. That fact logically implies other facts, for instance, that the team Bob is on gets an additional one (or more) points. Similarly, the fact that Bob made a promise to return a car is a fact only within a set of rules and agreements. Otherwise, it was just the mumbling of words. And that fact logically implies further facts, such as that Bob is obligated to return the car. The institution of promise keeping provides a good illustration of Searle's point. When we make promises, we step inside a framework of rules and expectations. To promise something implies that we *ought to do* something. Most simply, then, we can derive ought from is like this:

> Statement of institutional fact: Smith promised to return Bob's car.
> Ought statement: Smith is morally obligated to return Bob's car.

Searle's solution to the is/ought problem focuses on obvious institutional facts, such as promising. In this case, there is a particular verbal act by which we participate in the institution of promising, namely the utterance, under appropriate circumstances, of "I promise to do such and such." Aside from these more obvious institutions, there may be less obvious ones surrounding other kinds of moral behavior. This is so with the rules and expectations that we have about stealing. Here, the institutional fact might be something like this: "Society mandates that its members do not steal." This, then, would lead to the ought statement "Smith, who is a member of society, is morally obligated to not steal," given that Smith is indeed committed to membership in that society. Following Searle, we might be able to uncover institutional facts surrounding all of our basic moral obligations, such as prohibitions against lying, adultery, and murder.

41. What institutional facts might lead to the conclusion that we ought not commit murder?

2. EXPRESSING FEELINGS: ALFRED JULES AYER

One of the more extreme views regarding the relation of reason to morality was spelled out by British philosopher Alfred Jules Ayer (1910–1989). Following Hume, Ayer believes that moral assessments involve emotional reactions, and not rational judgments. However, Ayer goes a bit further in his rejection of reason's role, and the basis of this rejection rests in his account of the different ways that we use language.

Fact-Stating and Non-Fact-Stating Utterances. Sometimes when we speak, we state facts or describe something about the world, such as "The door in front of me is brown," and "George Washington was the first president of the United States." Not only can we describe objective facts like these, but we can also attempt to describe subjective psychological states of people, such as "Smith believes in Martians," "Jones has a headache," and "I disapprove of John's conduct." Philosophers have often held that moral assessments are descriptive or fact-stating utterances. Suppose that I make the statement "Stealing is wrong." A staunch moral objectivist like Plato might say that my statement "Stealing is wrong" is a descriptive utterance that means "Stealing is contrary to universal moral norms, grounded in the forms." A subjectivist, on the other hand, might say (thought it would be rather odd) that when I utter "Stealing is wrong" I am stating the fact that "I have feelings of disapproval regarding stealing." That is, I am stating a biographical fact about myself. There is a world of difference between the objectivist's and subjectivist's interpretation of my utterance. However, what they have in common is that my utterance, "Stealing is wrong," attempts to *describe* or *report* some fact about the world—whether it is a fact about objective moral forms or a fact about my subjective feelings.

In contrast to descriptive utterances such as the above, there are utterances that are not used to report facts but instead are used to do something else. For example, if I am at a football game I may shout "Hooray!" when my team gets a touchdown. My utterance here is not a factual description of anything—not even of my psychological state. My utterance, pure and simple, *expresses* my feelings. Similarly, when I say "What time is it?" I am not describing anything but instead am *asking* you to tell me the time. In neither case would it make sense to think of my utterance as either true or false. According to Ayer, moral utterances such as "Stealing is wrong" are not fact-stating utterances and are not used to describe anything. Instead, there are two distinct things that we do with our moral utterances: (1) We express our feelings or attitudes, and (2) we recommend that others adopt our attitude. These two components of his theory have since been dubbed emotivism and prescriptivism respectively.

ASK YOURSELF

42. Some utterances are used to report some fact about the world and are either _____ or _____. Other utterances are used to simply express a _____.

Emotivism and Prescriptivism. When rejecting the descriptive nature of moral statements, Ayer puts primary emphasis on the emotive function of our utterances:

> The presence of an ethical symbol in a proposition adds nothing to its factual content. Thus if I say to someone, "You acted wrongly in stealing that money," I am not stating anything more than if I had simply said, "You stole that money." In adding that this action is wrong I am not making any further statement about it. I am simply evincing my moral disapproval of it. It is as if I had said, "You stole that money," in a peculiar tone of horror, or written it with the addition of some special exclamation marks. The tone, or the exclamation marks, adds nothing to the literal meaning of the sentence. It merely serves to show that the expression of it is attended by certain feelings in the speaker.
>
> If now I generalize my previous statement and say, "Stealing money is wrong," I produce a sentence which has no factual meaning—that is, expresses no proposition which can be either true or false. It is as if I had written "Stealing money!!"—where the shape and

thickness of the exclamation marks show, by a suitable convention, that a special sort of moral disapproval is the feeling which is being expressed. It is clear that there is nothing said here which can be true or false.

ASK YOURSELF

43. According to Ayer, can moral utterances be true or false?

Turning to the prescriptive component, Ayer believes that moral utterances aim to spark similar feelings in others and prompt them to act in certain ways:

> It is worth mentioning that ethical terms do not serve only to express feeling. They are calculated also to arouse feeling, and so to stimulate action. Indeed some of them are used in such a way as to give the sentences in which they occur the effect of commands. Thus the sentence "It is your duty to tell the truth" may be regarded both as the expression of a certain sort of ethical feeling about truthfulness and as the expression of the command "Tell the truth." [From Alfred Jules Ayer, *Language, Truth and Logic* (1936), Chapter 6]

ASK YOURSELF

44. What is the prescriptive component of the statement "It is your duty to tell the truth"?

Ayer's view of emotivism and prescriptivism is controversial. It is one thing to say more modestly that *part* of the function of moral utterances is to express feelings and prompt action in others. In fact, it would be difficult to deny this when we see people debate issues such as abortion. However, Ayer makes a much more extreme claim by saying that the *only* function of our moral utterances is emotive and prescriptive. According to many of Ayer's critics, this is not only extreme, but wrong. When I make the statement "Stealing is wrong," it seems that I am describing some kind of fact—such as the psychological fact that I disapprove of stealing, or the sociological fact that society denounces stealing. Several philosophers after Ayer have developed more elaborate theories of emotivism and prescriptivism, particularly Charles Stevenson (1908–1979) and Richard Mervyn Hare (b. 1919). But, unlike Ayer, Stevenson and Hare find some room for a factually descriptive component of moral utterances. Morality, for them, thus involves both emotional and rational capacities.

3. MORALITY AND THE BEST REASONS: KURT BAIER

Although Stevenson and Hare attempt to find a middle ground on the issue of reason versus emotion, other philosophers believe that there is no place at all for emotion in moral assessments. When emotion does creep in, it tends to bias us. Impartiality is what we need when wrestling with moral issues, and human reason—rather than emotion—is the way to achieve this. How, though, does human reason operate in moral matters? According to Kurt Baier, morality begins with the question "What shall I do?", and our answer to this question involves weighing the best reasons in favor of a particular course of action. Although Baier advocates a reason-based approach to morality, he rejects the idea that we have special rational intuitions or insights—such as Plato's view that our reason grasps the moral forms. Instead, the process of moral reasoning is more like the way a judge weighs various facts when finding someone guilty or innocent.

The heart of morality, for Baier, is the implied question "What shall I do?", which he contends is a request for information. With the issue of stealing, for example, the basic question that I ask is "Should I steal this particular item?" By asking this question, I am in essence asking for reasons both for and against stealing. My task, then, is to consider the various pros and cons and decide which course of action is supported by the best reasons. The deliberation process has two main steps: surveying the facts and weighing the facts. As to the first step,

> The facts are surveyed with a view to determining those which are relevant reasons. I do this by bearing in mind my convictions about what constitute good reasons, my consideration-making beliefs, for example, that doing something would be enjoyable to me, or in my interest, or harmful to someone else, or against the law, or immoral, and so on. This primary deliberation may at any moment become an examination of the question whether my consideration-making beliefs are true.

ASK YOURSELF

45. What are some of the beliefs I have that impact my survey of the relevant facts?

As to the second step, we weigh the relevant facts based on rules of priority that society typically endorses. Society teaches us, for example, that long-range goals are better than short-range ones. To illustrate, suppose that I steal a thousand dollars from a convenience store, and that evening I spend the money extravagantly and live it up as I never did before. The next day, though, the police catch me. Although stealing may have given me some short-term benefit, it pales in comparison to the long-term disbenefit that I will experience after I'm caught.

> The second step in my deliberation consists in weighing those facts which my first step has revealed as relevant. It is not enough to know which reasons speak for and which against entering on a certain course of action; I must also know which are the strongest or best reasons. Here, too, I am helped by certain beliefs, the rules of priority which I take over from my social environment. It is generally agreed in our society that moral reasons are superior to reasons of self-interest, reasons of long-range interest superior to reasons of short-range interest, and reasons of self-interest superior to mere pleasure or pain.

ASK YOURSELF

46. What are some of the rules of priority that we commonly draw on when weighing morally relevant facts?

According to Baier, this two-step process of moral reasoning is not flawless, and errors can occur at either step. Our initial survey of facts will be flawed if we do not spot all of the relevant data. Our process of weighing facts may similarly be flawed if we fail to draw on all of the relevant rules. Baier thus warns that the moral conclusion we arrive at will only be *presumptively valid,* in anticipation of other relevant factors that might occur to us in the future.

> Every fact which is a pro sets up a presumption that I ought, and every fact which is a con sets up a presumption that I ought not, to do the thing in question. Any one of these presumptions can be rebutted or confirmed later *by the weighing* of the various pros and cons.

A given presumption is rebutted if some other reason or combination of reasons is found weightier than the one which has given rise to the original presumption. In other words, the fact that I have a reason for or against entering on the proposed line of action *does not entail* that I ought or ought not to enter on it—it merely "presumptively implies" it. That is to say, it must be taken to imply that I ought or ought not to enter on it unless, later on, in the weighing of considerations, I find some that are weightier than this one. In that case, the original presumptive implication has been rebutted. [From Kurt Baier, *The Moral Point of View* (1958), Chapter 3]

ASK YOURSELF

47. How might we "rebut" our original assessment of the right thing to do?

SUMMING UP THE PROBLEM OF REASON AND MORAL JUDGMENTS

Like the issue of selflessness, the question of the role of reason in morality has to do with the source of moral assessments within human thought. One extreme position is that morality involves our emotions, with no role for reason. A contrasting position, equally extreme, is that morality is purely a matter of rational judgment, with no role for emotions. Hume represents the first view and argues that moral assessments are nothing but emotional reactions. His view is represented in the statement that "ought cannot be derived from is"—that is, statements of fact can never lead to moral assessments. Contrary to Hume, Searle argues that if we begin with statements of institutional facts—facts about social rules and expectations—we can indeed arrive at statements of obligation. Following Hume, Ayer holds that moral assessments are emotional and not rational judgments. Ayer argues more particularly that moral judgments express feelings (emotivism) and are used to recommend that others adopt our attitudes (prescriptivism). Baier takes the reverse side of the dispute and argues that moral assessments are not emotional reactions but instead involve surveying the relevant facts and weighing those facts in order to arrive at the best reasons for acting one way rather than another.

CAN OF WORMS

The clash between reason and emotion in moral matters is connected with debates over mind and human nature, such as those discussed in earlier chapters. If mind, conceived of as a rational faculty, is basic to our nature, then emotions may be downplayed, as they were by Plato. Views that share this Platonic outlook tend to associate emotion with confusion and irrationality, even within the moral domain. Hume, Ayer, and other emotion-oriented philosophers have felt that moral feelings are not intrinsically "lower" and do in fact play an essential role in the moral life. To make their case, they often compare moral feelings with aesthetic feelings—emotions relating to our assessment of good and bad art. Thus the analysis of moral feeling can be connected with the philosophy of art. Moreover, claims about the various uses of language, for stating facts, expressing emotions, encouraging certain actions, and the like, have been important to debates within the philosophy of language, debates that have been particularly important in recent philosophy.

D. GENDER AND MORALITY

There is clear evidence that women smile more than men. What is less clear is why this is so, and, particularly, whether it is an inborn or culturally determined character trait. For example, women and men smile to the same degree when they are placed in similar occupational roles, which suggests that social conditioning is a factor. However, women smile more when there is social tension, perhaps as a means of restoring harmony, which might be an inborn capacity in women. We can ask a similar question about gender difference and morality. Men and women both have moral convictions and make moral assessments. However, do their views of morality differ, and, if so, is it because of genetics or social conditioning?

QUESTIONS TO DISCUSS

a. What are some of the common stereotypes about differences between men and women?

b. Does it seem as though men and women have differing moral conceptions about standard ethical issues such as lying, stealing, or donating to charity?

c. If women do have different conceptions of morality than men, on which issues might that difference be most evident?

The issue is about gender, and morality is complicated by unsettled questions about the nature of morality in general—for example, whether moral conduct is inherently selfish and whether moral assessments are rational or emotional. To this we add an additional puzzle about whether men and women have fundamentally different ways of thinking. One clinical psychologist expresses the difference as follows:

> Women on the other hand have four times as many brain cells (neurons) connecting the right and left side of their brain. This latter finding provides physical evidence that supports the observation that men rely easily and more heavily on their left brain to solve one problem one step at a time. Women have more efficient access to both sides of their brain and therefore greater use of their right brain. Women can focus on more than one problem at one time and frequently prefer to solve problems through multiple activities at a time. [Michael G. Conner, "Understanding the Difference Between Men and Women" (1999)]

If men and women do think differently, then we might expect differences to emerge in male and female assessments of moral matters.

1. RATIONAL MORALITY FOR MEN AND WOMEN: MARY WOLLSTONECRAFT

During the eighteenth century, many philosophers held that morality involves a rational ability, a typically masculine ability and thus not common among women. One of the first systematic voices against the prevailing notion was Mary Wollstonecraft (1759–1797). She lived at the right time, for in France at that time many women were involved in intellectual discussions about philosophical issues. But she was not born in the right place or social class. She was born in London in 1759, the second of seven children of an abusive father, and she had to educate herself and take responsibilities in her family at an early age. With the encouragement of friends, she began writing and published a first work in 1786. The last four years of her life were tumultuous. She conceived a child out of wedlock, married twice, and attempted suicide twice. Her second husband was the noted English writer

William Godwin, who wrote a memoir in tribute to her. She died in 1797 after giving birth to a second child, also named Mary, who married the poet Percy Bysshe Shelley and became famous as the author of the novel *Frankenstein*. Wollstonecraft's most lasting work is *A Vindication of the Rights of Women* (1792). The work reflects a strong confidence in human reason, which is particularly characteristic of enlightenment thought. Women, she argues, are bound to precisely the same rational moral standard that men are, and they are just as capable as men of employing those standards, contrary to some of the common prejudices of the time.

The Power of Women. Wollstonecraft argues that women may have power of a sort, but it is both a corrupt and corrupting power.

FROM MARY WOLLSTONECRAFT, *A Vindication of the Rights of Women* (1792)

It is impossible for any man, when the most favorable circumstances concur, to acquire sufficient knowledge and strength of mind to discharge the duties of a king, entrusted with uncontrolled power; how then must they be violated when his very elevation is an insuperable bar to the attainment of either wisdom or virtue; when all the feelings of a man are stifled by flattery, and reflection shut out by pleasure! Surely it is madness to make the fate of thousands depend on the caprice of a weak fellow creature, whose very station sinks him necessarily below the meanest of his subjects! But one power should not be thrown down to exalt another—for all power inebriates weak man; and its abuse proves that the more equality there is established among men, the more virtue and happiness will reign in society. But this and any similar maxim deduced from simple reason raises an outcry—the church or the state is in danger, if faith in the wisdom of antiquity is not implicit; and they who, roused by the sight of human calamity, dare to attack human authority are reviled as despisers of God and enemies of man.

ASK YOURSELF

48. What is it that makes a king deficient both in feeling and in thought (reflection)?

To account for, and excuse the tyranny of man, many ingenious arguments have been brought forward to prove that the two sexes, in the acquirement of virtue, ought to aim at attaining a very different character; or, to speak explicitly, women are not allowed to have sufficient strength of mind to acquire what really deserves the name of virtue. Yet it should seem, allowing them to have souls, that there is but one way appointed by Providence to lead mankind to either virtue or happiness. If then women are not a swarm of ephemeron triflers, why should they be kept in ignorance under the specious name of innocence? Men complain, and with reason, of the follies and caprices of our sex, when they do not keenly satirize our headstrong passions and groveling vices. Behold, I should answer, the natural effect of ignorance! The mind will ever be unstable that has only prejudices to rest on, and the current will run with destructive fury when there are no barriers to break its force. Women are told from their infancy, and taught by the example of their mothers, that a little knowledge of human weakness, justly termed cunning, softness of temper, outward obedience, and a scrupulous attention to a puerile kind of propriety, will obtain for them the protection of man; and should they be beautiful, every thing else is needless, for, at least, twenty years of their lives.

49. What are some of the bad qualities that Wollstonecraft claims are common among women, and what produced them?

The Educating Force of Society. According to Wollstonecraft, in order for there to be any worthwhile education for women, society must be transformed in its attitudes toward women. This is because the social order itself educates—and even more commonly mis-educates—people.

To prevent any misconstruction, I must add that I do not believe that a private education can work the wonders which some sanguine writers have attributed to it. Men and women must be educated, in a great degree, by the opinions and manners of the society they live in. In every age there has been a stream of popular opinion that has carried all before it, and given a family character, as it were, to the century. It may then fairly be inferred that, till society be differently constituted, much cannot be expected from education. It is, however, sufficient for my present purpose to assert that whatever effect circumstances have on the abilities, every being may become virtuous by the exercise of its own reason. . . . Consequently, the most perfect education, in my opinion, is such an exercise of the understanding as is best calculated to strengthen the body and form the heart. Or, in other words, to enable the individual to attain such habits of virtue as will render it independent. In fact, it is a farce to call any being virtuous whose virtues do not result from the exercise of its own reason. This was Rousseau's opinion respecting men: I extend it to women and confidently assert that they have been drawn out of their sphere by false refinement, and not by an endeavor to acquire masculine qualities. Still the regal homage which they receive is so intoxicating that till the manners of the times are changed, and formed on more reasonable principles, it may be impossible to convince them that the illegitimate power, which they obtain by degrading themselves, is a curse and that they must return to nature and equality, if they wish to secure the placid satisfaction that unsophisticated affections impart. But for this epoch we must wait—wait, perhaps, till kings and nobles, enlightened by reason, and, preferring the real dignity of man to childish state, throw off their gaudy hereditary trappings: and if then women do not resign the arbitrary power of beauty—they will prove that they have less mind than man.

50. The problem, in Wollstonecraft's view, is not that women lack power in the present social order, but that the power they do have is, like the power of _____, disconnected from true virtue and self-worth.

According to some, the kind of thinking or reasoning typical of women lacks systematic character, and it is defective for that reason. Wollstonecraft thinks that the characteristic ways in which women think is not the result of their being women but of their being mis-educated by a corrupt social order.

To do every thing in an orderly manner is a most important precept, which women, who, generally speaking, receive only a disorderly kind of education, seldom attend to with that degree of exactness that men, who from their infancy are broken into method, observe. This negligent kind of guesswork, for what other epithet can be used to point out the random exertions of a sort of instinctive common sense, never brought to the test of reason? prevents their generalizing matters of fact—so they do to-day what they did yesterday, merely because they did it yesterday. This contempt of the understanding in early life has more baneful consequences than is commonly supposed; for the little knowledge which women of strong minds attain is, from various circumstances, of a more desultory kind than the knowledge of men, and it is acquired more by sheer observations on real life than from comparing what has been individually observed with the results of experience generalized by speculation. Led by their dependent situation and domestic employments more into society, what they learn is rather by snatches; and as learning is with them, in general, only a secondary thing, they do not pursue any one branch with that persevering ardor necessary to give vigor to the faculties and clearness to the judgment.

ASK YOURSELF

51. What sort of knowledge is it which women of strong minds attain?

Some Men Are Mis-educated. Wollstonecraft concedes that women are preoccupied with manners, with artificial social graces, and with trivial social "niceness." However, she believes that this can also be found among a most "masculine" group of men.

As a proof that education gives this appearance of weakness to females, we may instance the example of military men, who are, like them, sent into the world before their minds have been stored with knowledge or fortified by principles. The consequences are similar; soldiers acquire a little superficial knowledge, snatched from the muddy current of conversation, and, from continually mixing with society, they gain what is termed a knowledge of the world; and this acquaintance with manners and customs has frequently been confounded with a knowledge of the human heart. But can the crude fruit of casual observation, never brought to the test of judgment, formed by comparing speculation and experience, deserve such a distinction? Soldiers, as well as women, practice the minor virtues with punctilious politeness. Where is then the sexual difference, when the education has been the same? All the difference that I can discern arises from the superior advantage of liberty, which enables the former to see more of life. It is wandering from my present subject, perhaps, to make a political remark; but, as it was produced naturally by the train of my reflections, I shall not pass it silently over. Standing armies can never consist of resolute, robust men; they maybe well disciplined machines, but they will seldom contain men under the influence of strong passions, or with very vigorous faculties. And as for any depth of understanding, I will venture to affirm that it is as rarely to be found in the army as amongst women; and the cause, I maintain, is the same. It may be further observed that officers are also particularly attentive to their persons, fond of dancing, crowded rooms, adventures, and ridicule. Like the fair sex, the business of their lives is gallantry. They were taught to please, and they only live to please. Yet they do not lose their rank in the distinction of sexes, for they are still reckoned superior to women, though in what their superiority consists, beyond what I have just mentioned, it is difficult to discover.

There is, Wollstonecraft believes, a particular motive for keeping women ignorant and obedient.

Strengthen the female mind by enlarging it, and there will be an end to blind obedience; but, as blind obedience is ever sought for by power, tyrants and sensualists are in the right when they endeavor to keep women in the dark, because the former only want slaves, and the latter a plaything.

Wollstonecraft, like many modern feminists, sees romantic love as an obstacle as much as a means to happiness.

To speak disrespectfully of love is, I know, high treason against sentiment and fine feelings; but I wish to speak the simple language of truth, and rather to address the head than the heart. To endeavor to reason love out of the world would be to out Quixote Cervantes and equally offend against common sense; but an endeavor to restrain this tumultuous passion, and to prove that it should not be allowed to dethrone superior powers, or to usurp the scepter which the understanding should ever coolly wield, appears less wild. . . . Love, from its very nature, must be transitory. To seek for a secret that would render it constant would be as wild a search as for the philosopher's stone, or the grand panacea; and the discovery would be equally useless, or rather pernicious to mankind. The most holy band of society is friendship. . . . Why must the female mind be tainted by coquettish arts to gratify the sensualist, and prevent love from subsiding into friendship, or compassionate tenderness, when there are not qualities on which friendship can be built? Let the honest heart show itself, and reason teach passion to submit to necessity; or, let the dignified pursuit of virtue and knowledge raise the mind above those emotions which rather embitter than sweeten the cup of life, when they are not restrained within due bounds.

ASK YOURSELF

52. Why should friendship be encouraged, rather than love?

Feminine "Gentleness." Wollstonecraft argues that supposedly feminine traits are the result of fear and repression; as such, they are not worth cultivating.

The Gentleness of manners, forbearance and long-suffering, are such amiable Godlike qualities that in sublime poetic strains the Deity has been invested with them; and, perhaps, no representation of his goodness so strongly fastens on the human affections as those that represent him abundant in mercy and willing to pardon. Gentleness, considered in this point of view, bears on its front all the characteristics of grandeur, combined with the winning graces of condescension; but what a different aspect it assumes when it is the submissive demeanor of dependence [i.e., when it is feminine genteelness], the support of weakness that loves, because it wants protection; and is forbearing, because it must silently endure injuries; smiling under the lash at which it dare not snarl. Abject as this picture appears, it is the portrait of an accomplished woman, according to the received opinion of female excellence, separated by specious reasoners from human excellence. Or, they (Rousseau, and Swedenborg) kindly restore the rib, and make one moral being of a man and woman; not forgetting to give her all the "submissive charms."

ASK YOURSELF

53. Why is the "gentleness" of women not worth keeping?

Proper Relations Between the Sexes. Wollstonecraft argues that neither gender should dominate. Rather, "reason" should rule.

I love man as my fellow; but his scepter, real, or usurped, extends not to me, unless the reason of an individual demands my homage; and even then the submission is to reason, and not to man. In fact, the conduct of an accountable being must be regulated by the operations of its own reason; or on what foundation rests the throne of God? It appears to me necessary to dwell on these obvious truths, because females have been insulated, as it were; and, while they have been stripped of the virtues that should clothe humanity, they have been decked with artificial graces that enable them to exercise a short-lived tyranny. Love, in their bosoms, taking place of every nobler passion, their sole ambition is to be fair, to raise emotion instead of inspiring respect; and this ignoble desire, like the servility in absolute monarchies, destroys all strength of character. Liberty is the mother of virtue, and if women be, by their very constitution, slaves, and not allowed to breathe the sharp invigorating air of freedom, they must ever languish like exotics, and be reckoned beautiful flaws in nature. As to the argument respecting the subjection in which the sex has ever been held, it retorts on man. The many have always been enthralled by the few; and monsters, who scarcely have shown any discernment of human excellence, have tyrannized over thousands of their fellow-creatures. Why have men of superior endowments submitted to such degradation? For, is it not universally acknowledged that kings, viewed collectively, have ever been inferior, in abilities and virtue, to the same number of men taken from the common mass of mankind—yet, have they not, and are they not still treated with a degree of reverence that is an insult to reason? China is not the only country where a living man has been made a God. Men have submitted to superior strength to enjoy with impunity the pleasure of the moment—women have only done the same, and therefore till it is proved that the courtier, who servilely resigns the birthright of a man, is not a moral agent, it cannot be demonstrated that woman is essentially inferior to man because she has always been subjugated. Brutal force has hitherto governed the world. . . . The divine right of husbands, like the divine right of kings, may, it is to be hoped, in this enlightened age, be contested without danger, and, though conviction may not silence many boisterous disputants, yet, when any prevailing prejudice is attacked, the wise will consider, and leave the narrow-minded to rail with thoughtless vehemence at innovation.

ASK YOURSELF

54. The preceding passage contains the following argument from analogy. Fill in the blanks.

    a. Hereditary kings are to their subjects as _____ are to _____.

    b. Kings do not deserve their power over their subjects due to any natural superiority they might have.

    c. Therefore, _____ do not deserve their power over _____.

The Mis-education of Women. In Wollstonecraft's view, the evil effects of unequal treatment of women can only be overcome by a complete overhaul of current customs. Specifically, the mis-education of women through social custom needs to be replaced by a real education, equal to male education, and even coeducational.

As for Rousseau's remarks, which have since been echoed by several writers, that they have naturally, that is from their birth, independent of education, a fondness for dolls, dressing, and talking—they are so puerile as not to merit a serious refutation. That a girl, condemned to sit for hours together listening to the idle chat of weak nurses, or to attend at her mother's toilet, will endeavor to join the conversation is, indeed, very natural; and that she will imitate her mother or aunts, and amuse herself by adorning her lifeless doll, as they do in dressing her, poor innocent babe! is undoubtedly a most natural consequence. For men of the greatest abilities have seldom had sufficient strength to rise above the surrounding atmosphere; and, if the page of genius have always been blurred by the prejudices of the age, some allowance should be made for a sex, who, like kings, always see things through a false medium. . . . It is time to effect a revolution in female manners—time to restore to them their lost dignity—and make them, as a part of the human species, labor by reforming themselves to reform the world. It is time to separate unchangeable morals from local manners. If men be demi-gods, why let us serve them! And if the dignity of the female soul be as disputable as that of animals—if their reason does not afford sufficient light to direct their conduct whilst unerring instinct is denied—they are surely of all creatures the most miserable! and, bent beneath the iron hand of destiny, must submit to be a fair defect in creation. But to justify the ways of Providence respecting them, by pointing out some irrefragable reason for thus making such a large portion of mankind accountable and not accountable, would puzzle the subtlest casuist. I have already animadverted on the bad habits which females acquire when they are shut up together; and, I think, that the observation may fairly be extended to the other sex, till the natural inference is drawn which I have had in view throughout—that to improve both sexes they ought, not only in private families, but in public schools, to be educated together.

> **ASK YOURSELF**
>
> **55.** There is disagreement among contemporary feminists as to the value of gender-segregation in education. What is Wollstonecraft's view?

Equality for Women, Marriage, Love, and Virtue. Marriage, Wollstonecraft says, would improve and sexual relations would be elevated to a more satisfactory level when women escape oppression, become occupied with something more than romance, and acquire real virtues.

If marriage be the cement of society, mankind should all be educated after the same model, or the intercourse of the sexes will never deserve the name of fellowship, nor will women ever fulfill the peculiar duties of their sex, till they become enlightened citizens, till they become free by being enabled to earn their own subsistence, independent of men; in the same manner, I mean, to prevent misconstruction, as one man is independent of another. Nay, marriage will never be held sacred till women, by being brought up with men, are prepared to be their companions rather than their mistresses; for the mean doublings of cunning will ever render them contemptible, whilst oppression renders them timid. So convinced am I of this truth, that I will venture to predict that virtue will never prevail in society till the virtues of both sexes are founded on reason; and, till the affections common to both are allowed to gain their due strength by the discharge of mutual duties. The best method, I believe, that can be adopted to correct a fondness for novels is to ridicule them: not indiscriminately, for then it would have little effect; but, if a judicious person, with some turn for humor, would read several to a young girl, and point out both by tones, and apt comparisons with pathetic incidents and heroic characters in history, how foolishly and ridiculously they caricatured human nature, just opinions might be substituted instead of romantic sentiments. In one respect, however, the majority of both sexes resemble and equally show a want of taste and modesty. Ignorant women, forced to be chaste to preserve their reputation, allow their imagination to revel in the unnatural and meretricious scenes sketched by the novel writers of the day, slighting as insipid the sober dignity and matron graces of history, whilst men carry the same vitiated taste into life, and fly for amusement to the wanton, from the unsophisticated charms.

ASK YOURSELF

56. It would appear that Wollstonecraft does not have in mind such novelists as her contemporary, Jane Austen. In her novels, Austen renders the life of women in the late eighteenth and early nineteenth centuries as individuals struggling for, and often achieving, genuine virtues, such as practical wisdom, self-control, courage, and constancy. Austen does not suppose that those struggles necessitate an overhaul of the social system. Has Wollstonecraft proved that what Austen thought possible is not possible?

Women are supposed to possess more sensibility, and even humanity, than men, and their strong attachments and instantaneous emotions of compassion are given as proofs; but the clinging affection of ignorance has seldom anything noble in it, and may mostly be resolved into selfishness, as well as the affection of children and brutes. I have known many weak women whose sensibility was entirely engrossed by their husbands; and as for their humanity, it was very faint indeed, or rather it was only a transient emotion of compassion. Humanity does not consist "in a squeamish ear," says an eminent orator. "It belongs to the mind as well as the nerves." But this kind of exclusive affection, though it degrades the individual, should not be brought forward as a proof of the inferiority of the sex, because it is the natural consequence of confined views: for even women of superior sense, having their attention turned to little employments, and private plans, rarely rise to heroism, unless when spurred on by love! and love, as an heroic passion, like genius, appears but once in an age. I therefore agree with the moralist who asserts, "that women have seldom so much generosity as men;" and that their narrow affections, to which justice and humanity are often sacrificed, render the sex apparently inferior, especially, as they are commonly inspired by men; but I contend that the heart would expand as the understanding gained strength, if women will lie fallow.

ASK YOURSELF

57. What are some of the customary female qualities that Wollstonecraft attacks?

Yet, true voluptuousness must proceed from the mind—for what can equal the sensations produced by mutual affection, supported by mutual respect? What are the cold, or feverish caresses of appetite, but sin embracing death, compared with the modest overflowings of a pure heart and exalted imagination? Yes, let me tell the libertine of fancy when he despises understanding in woman—that the mind, which he disregards, gives life to the enthusiastic affection from which rapture, short-lived as it is, alone can flow! And, that, without virtue, a sexual attachment must expire, like a tallow candle in the socket, creating intolerable disgust. To prove this, I need only observe that men who have wasted a great part of their lives with women, and with whom they have sought for pleasure with eager thirst, entertain the meanest opinion of the sex. Virtue, true refiner of joy!—if foolish men were to fright thee from earth, in order to give loose to all their appetites without a check—some sensual wight of taste would scale the heavens to invite thee back, to give a zest to pleasure! That women at present are by ignorance rendered foolish or vicious is, I think, not to be disputed; and, that the most salutary effects tending to improve mankind might be expected from a *revolution* in female manners appears, at least, with a face of probability, to rise out of the observation.

58. Wollstonecraft and many modern feminists agree on one fundamental point: Mere legal and public policy changes (such as extending the vote to women and opening all of the labor market to them) will not suffice to bring about the true emancipation of women. What then is required?

2. UNIQUELY FEMALE MORALITY: CAROL GILLIGAN

Wollstonecraft believed that traditional female ways of thinking were the result of mis-education and that women have exactly the same capacity for rationality as men. Her views here contrast with some modern feminists, who insist that some female ways of thinking—even those that Wollstonecraft denounces—are at least as good as, if not superior to, "male" ways. One such feminist writer is Carol Gilligan (b. 1936), professor of education at Harvard University. According to Gilligan, the most distinctive feature of female moral thinking is the focus on care within relationships. This contrasts sharply with the typical emphasis that men place on the moral rights and fairness or equality.

Care and Relationships. According to Gilligan, women both define and judge themselves in terms of their ability to care.

FROM CAROL GILLIGAN, *In a Different Voice* (1982)

[T]he assumption of responsibility for taking care lead women to attend to voices other than their own and to include in their judgment other points of view. Women's moral weakness, manifest in an apparent diffusion and confusion of judgment, is thus inseparable from women's moral strength, an overriding concern with relationships and responsibilities. The reluctance to judge may itself be indicative of the care and concern for others that infuse the psychology of women's development and are responsible for what is generally seen as prob-lematic in its nature.

Thus women not only define themselves in a context of human relationship but also judge themselves in terms of their ability to care. Women's place in man's life cycle has been that of nurturer, caretaker, and helpmate, the weaver of those networks of relationships on which she in turn relies. But while women have thus taken care of men, men have, in their theories of psychological development, as in their economic arrangements, tended to assume or devalue that care. When the focus on individuation and individual achievement extends into adulthood and maturity is equated with personal autonomy, concern with relationships appears as a weakness of women rather than as a human strength.

The discrepancy between womanhood and adulthood is nowhere more evident than in the studies on sex-role stereotypes reported by Broverman, Vogel, Broverman, Clarkson, and Rosenkrantz. The repeated finding of these studies is that the qualities deemed necessary for adulthood—the capacity for autonomous thinking, clear decision-making, and responsible action—are those associated with masculinity and considered undesirable as attributes of the feminine self. The stereotypes suggest a splitting of love and work that relegates expres-sive capacities to women while placing instrumental abilities in the masculine domain. Yet looked at from a different perspective, these stereotypes reflect a conception of adulthood that is itself out of balance, favoring the separateness of the individual self over connection to others, and leaning more toward an autonomous life of work than toward the interdepen-dence of love and care.

59. What is "out of balance" in the sex role stereotypes reported here?

The Male Bias in Moral Development Research. Some psychologists who have studied moral development have ignored women in their work, thus revealing a bias toward male moral ideals. This is particularly so with Lawrence Kohlberg (1927–1987), who proposed a theory that people go through a series of stages of moral development in the first two or three decades of their lives. Kohlberg presented his subjects with a series of moral dilemmas, such as whether it is permissible to steal food to feed one's starving family. He then noted the reasoning his subjects used in justifying their particular decisions. Kohlberg concluded that there are six levels of moral development which young people go through. In the first stage, starting at about age 10, people avoid breaking moral rules to avoid punishment. In the second stage, people follow moral rules only when it is to their advantage. In the third stage, starting about age 17, people try to live up to what is expected of them in small social groups, such as families. In the fourth stage, people fulfill the expectations of larger social groups, such as obeying laws that keep society together. In the fifth and sixth stages, starting at about age 24, people are guided by both absolute and relative moral principles; they follow these for altruistic reasons, though, and not because of what they might gain individually. According to Kohlberg, few people ever reach the highest stage.

The discovery now being celebrated by men in mid-life of the importance of intimacy, relationships, and care is something that women have known from the beginning. However, because that knowledge in women has been considered "intuitive" or "instinctive," a function of anatomy coupled with destiny, psychologists have neglected to describe its development. In my research, I have found that women's moral development centers on the elaboration of that knowledge and thus delineates a critical line of psychological development in the lives of both of the sexes. The subject of moral development not only provides the final illustration of the reiterative pattern in the observation and assessment of sex differences in the literature on human development, but also indicates more particularly why the nature and significance of women's development has been for so long obscured and shrouded in mystery.

The criticism that Freud makes of women's sense of justice, seeing it as compromised in its refusal of blind impartiality, reappears not only in the work of Piaget but also in that of Kohlberg. While in Piaget's account of the moral judgment of the child, girls are an aside, a curiosity to whom he devotes four brief entries in an index that omits "boys" altogether because "the child" is assumed to be male, in the research from which Kohlberg derives his theory, females simply do not exist. Kohlberg's six stages that describe the development of moral judgment from childhood to adulthood are based empirically on a study of eighty-four boys whose development Kohlberg has followed for a period of over twenty years. Although Kohlberg claims universality for his stage sequence, those groups not included in his original sample rarely reach his higher stages.

Prominent among those who thus appear to be deficient in moral development when measured by Kohlberg's scale are women, whose judgments seem to exemplify the third stage of his six-stage sequence. At this stage morality is conceived in interpersonal terms and goodness is equated with helping and pleasing others. This conception of goodness is considered by Kohlberg and Kramer to be functional in the lives of mature women insofar as their lives take place in the home. Kohlberg and Kramer imply that only if women enter the traditional arena of male activity will they recognize the inadequacy of this moral perspective and progress like men toward higher stages where relationships are subordinated to rules (stage four) and rules to universal principles of justice (stages five and six).

ASK YOURSELF

60. What are the characteristics of Kohlberg's stages 4, 5, and 6?

Yet herein lies a paradox, for the very traits that traditionally have defined the "goodness" of women, their care for and sensitivity to the needs of others, are those that mark them as deficient in moral development. In this version of moral development, however, the conception of maturity is derived from the study of men's lives and reflects the importance of individuation in their development. Piaget, challenging the common impression that a developmental theory is built like a pyramid from its base in infancy, points out that a conception of development instead hangs from its vertex of maturity, the point toward which progress is traced. Thus, a change in the definition of maturity does not simply alter the description of the highest stage but recasts the understanding of development, changing the entire account.

When one begins with the study of women and derives developmental constructs from their lives, the outline of a moral conception different from that described by Freud, Piaget, or Kohlberg begins to emerge and informs a different description of development. In this conception, the moral problem arises from conflicting responsibilities rather than from competing rights and requires for its resolution a mode of thinking that is contextual and narrative rather than formal and abstract. This conception of morality as concerned with the activity of care centers moral development around the understanding of responsibility and relationships, just as the conception of morality as fairness ties moral development to the understanding of rights and rules.

ASK YOURSELF

61. Briefly describe the two contrasting conceptions of morality mentioned.

This different construction of the moral problem by women may be seen as the critical reason for their failure to develop within the constraints of Kohlberg's system. Regarding all constructions of responsibility as evidence of a conventional moral understanding, Kohlberg defines the highest stages of moral development as deriving from a reflective understanding of human rights. That the morality of rights differs from the morality of responsibility in its emphasis on separation rather than connection, in its consideration of the individual rather than the relationship as primary, is illustrated by two responses to interview questions about the nature of morality. The first comes from a twenty-five-year-old man, one of the participants in Kohlberg's study:

> ["What does the word morality mean to you?"] Nobody in the world knows the answer. I think it is recognizing the right of the individual, the rights of other individuals, not interfering with those rights. Act as fairly as you would have them treat you. I think it is basically to preserve the human being's right to existence. I think that is the most important. Secondly, the human being's right to do as he pleases, again without interfering with somebody else's rights.
>
> [How have your views on morality changed since the last interview?] I think I am more aware of an individual's rights now. I used to be looking at it strictly from my point of view, just for me. Now I think I am more aware of what the individual has a right to.

62. The principal concerns of the man in this interview appear to be with
_____ and _____.

Kohlberg cites this man's response as illustrative of the principled conception of human rights that exemplifies his fifth and sixth stages. Commenting on the response, Kohlberg says, "Moving to a perspective outside of that of his society, he identifies morality with justice (fairness, rights, the Golden Rule), with recognition of the rights of others as these are defined naturally or intrinsically. The human being's right to do as he pleases without interfering with somebody else's rights is a formula defining rights prior to social legislation."

The second response comes from a woman who participated in the rights and responsibilities study. She also was twenty-five and, at the time, a third-year law student:

[Is there really some correct solution to moral problems, or is everybody's opinion equally right?] No, I don't think everybody's opinion is equally right. I think that in some situations there may be opinions that are equally valid, and one could conscientiously adopt one of several courses of action. But there are other situations in which I think there are right and wrong answers, that sort of inhere in the nature of existence, of all individuals here who need to live with each other to live. We need to depend on each other, and hopefully it is not only a physical need but a need of fulfillment in ourselves, that a person's life is enriched by cooperating with other people and striving to live in harmony with everybody else, and to that end, there are right and wrong, there are things which promote that end and that move away from it, and in that way it is possible to choose in certain cases among different courses of action that obviously promote or harm that goal.

63. What are the principal concerns of this woman?

[Is there a time in the past when you would have thought about these things differently?] Oh, yeah, I think that I went through a time when I thought that things were pretty relative, that I can't tell you what to do and you can't tell me what to do, because you've got your conscience and I've got mine.

["When was that?] When I was in high school. I guess that it just sort of dawned on me that my own ideas changed, and because my own judgment changed, I felt I couldn't judge another person's judgment. But now I think even when it is only the person himself who is going to be affected, I say it is wrong to the extent it doesn't cohere with what I know about human nature and what I know about you, and just from what I think is true about the operation of the universe, I could say I think you are making a mistake.

[What led you to change, do you think?] . . . just seeing more of life, just recognizing that there are an awful lot of things that are common among people. There are certain things that you come to learn promote a better life and better relationships and more personal fulfillment than other things that in general tend to do the opposite, and the things that promote these things, you would call morally right.

64. What are the criteria for rightness of action mentioned by this woman?

This response also represents a personal reconstruction of morality following a period of questioning and doubt, but the reconstruction of moral understanding is based not on the primacy and universality of individual rights, but rather on what she describes as a "very strong sense of being responsible to the world." Within this construction, the moral dilemma changes from how to exercise one's rights without interfering with the rights of others to how "to lead a moral life which includes obligations to myself and my family and people in general." The problem then becomes one of limiting responsibilities without abandoning moral concern. When asked to describe herself, this woman says that she values "having other people that I am tied to, and also having people that I am responsible to. I have a very strong sense of being responsible to the world, that I can't just live for my enjoyment, but just the fact of being in the world gives me an obligation to do what I can to make the world a better place to live in, no matter how small a scale that may be on." Thus while Kohlberg's subject worries about people interfering with each other's rights, this woman worries about "the possibility of omission, of your not helping others when you could help them."

ASK YOURSELF

65. Which is more important, not interfering with others or helping others in need?

66. Which would you rather have around you, someone who focuses on not interfering or someone who can be relied upon to help when trouble appears?

The issue that this woman raises is addressed by Jane Loevinger's fifth "autonomous" stage of ego development, where autonomy, placed in the context of relationships, is defined as modulating an excessive sense of responsibility through the recognition that other people have responsibility for their own destiny. The autonomous stage in Loevinger's account witnesses a relinquishing of moral dichotomies and their replacement with "a feeling for the complexity and multifaceted character of real people and real situations."

Whereas the rights conception of morality that informs Kohlberg's principled level (stages five and six) is geared to arriving at an objectively fair or just resolution to moral dilemmas upon which all rational persons could agree, the responsibility conception focuses instead on the limitations of any particular resolution and describes the conflicts that remain.

ASK YOURSELF

67. Describe a family conflict in which an objectively fair resolution would be possible, and say what it would be.

68. Describe a family conflict in which an objectively fair resolution would not be possible, and use Gilligan's account as an aid in developing suggestions on how to resolve the conflict.

Thus it becomes clear why a morality of rights and noninterference may appear frightening to women in its potential justification of indifference and unconcern. At the same time it becomes clear why, from a male perspective, a morality of responsibility appears inconclusive and diffuse, given its insistent contextual relativism. Women's moral judgments thus elucidate the pattern observed in the description of the developmental differences between the sexes, but they also provide an alternative conception of maturity by which these differences can be assessed and their implications traced. The psychology of women that has consistently been described as distinctive in its greater orientation toward relationships and interdependence implies a more contextual mode of judgment and a different moral understanding. Given the differences in women's conceptions of self and morality, women bring to the life cycle a different point of view and order human experience in terms of different priorities.

The myth of Demeter and Persephone, which McClelland cites as exemplifying the feminine attitude toward power, was associated with the Eleusinian Mysteries celebrated in ancient Greece for over two thousand years. As told in the Homeric Hymn to Demeter, the story of Persephone indicates the strengths of interdependence, building up resources and giving, that McClelland found in his research on power motivation to characterize the mature feminine style. Although, McClelland says, "it is fashionable to conclude that no one knows what went on in the Mysteries, it is known that they were probably the most important religious ceremonies, even partly on the historical record, which were organized by and for women, especially at the onset before men by means of the cult of Dionysos began to take them over." Thus McClelland regards the myth as "a special presentation of femine psychology." It is, as well, a life-cycle story par excellence.

Persephone, the daughter of Demeter, while playing in a meadow with her girlfriends, sees a beautiful narcissus which she runs to pick. As she does so, the earth opens and she is snatched away by Hades, who takes her to his underworld kingdom. Demeter, goddess of the earth, so mourns the loss of her daughter that she refuses to allow anything to grow. The crops that sustain life on earth shrivel up, killing men and animals alike, until Zeus takes pity on man's suffering and persuades his brother to return Persephone to her mother.

But before she leaves, Persephone eats some pomegranate seeds, which ensures that she will spend part of every year with Hades in the underworld. The elusive mystery of women's development lies in its recognition of the continuing importance of attachment in the human life cycle. Woman's place in man's life cycle is to protect this recognition while the developmental litany intones the celebration of separation, autonomy, individuation, and natural rights. The myth of Persephone speaks directly to the distortion in this view by reminding us that narcissism leads to death, that the fertility of the earth is in some mysterious way tied to the continuation of the mother–daughter relationship, and that the life cycle itself arises from an alternation between the world of women and that of men. Only when life-cycle theorists divide their attention and begin to live with women as they have lived with men will their vision encompass the experience of both sexes and their theories become correspondingly more fertile.

ASK YOURSELF

69. How does the myth of Demeter and Persephone illustrate the feminine approach to the resolution of conflict?

SUMMING UP THE ISSUE OF GENDER AND MORALITY

If there are at least some "natural" differences between men and women, a question arises about whether there are gender differences within morality. Many philosophers in the past believed that women were rationally inferior to men. Given that reason is fundamental to morality, it would follow that women would generally be less developed morally than men. Wollstonecraft disputed this view, arguing that women have the same rational abilities as men and, as rational creatures, have the same moral capacity. Women appear to be less rational, she argued, only because they've been mis-educated. Some recent psychological theories of moral development have been influenced by Kohlberg's contention that children and young adults pass through a series of stages in which their moral reasoning advances. Gilligan argued that Kohlberg's scheme reflects a heavy male bias, principally because of its assumption that morality involves rational assessment and abstract notions of justice. Instead, according to Gilligan, female moral thinking focuses on care within relationships, and some moralists would argue that care is more important than abstract conceptions of justice in genuinely moral development.

CAN OF WORMS

Central to the debate about gender differences in morality is whether society has forced social roles on women that are inferior to those of men. Even today in some parts of the world, women do not have the same educational advantages as men, are not allowed to compete for positions of social power, and, as Wollstonecraft charges, are brainwashed into behaving superficially. Like women, racial minorities have made similar charges regarding society's mistreatment of them. These concerns about gender and racial equality are taken up in both social and political philosophy. If we grant that women and other minorities even now are oppressed by their traditional social roles, how do we bring about change? It begins, some argue, by empowering minorities at every level of society, foremost, however, at the political and economic levels. This may require adopting affirmative action policies, which seek to give minorities a special competitive advantage in an effort to make up for disadvantages in the past. Affirmative action, however, is a hotly debated policy upon which social and political philosophers have expressed many views.

The debate about gender differences in morality also overlaps with the debate about the relative roles of reason and feeling in ethics. We have already seen something of how that debate has gone. Ethical views which stress the development of both reason and feeling, such as are discussed in the next section, are perhaps even more pertinent to an assessment of the kinds of claims Gilligan has made about female moral development.

It is also clear that assessments of gender differences depend in part upon theories of human nature and selfhood such as those discussed in Chapter 3.

E. VIRTUES

A woman from Texas ran over the manager of a McDonald's with her car because she wanted mayonnaise on her cheeseburger; she was sentenced to 10 years in prison for the offense. It is unlikely that her violent action came out of the blue. We might reasonably assume that she probably had poor anger management skills and routinely overreacted to trivial annoyances. Bad actions typically result from bad habits, or vices; and good actions typically result from good ones, or virtues.

QUESTIONS TO DISCUSS

a. Some law enforcement agencies have vice squads that focus on special types of crime, such as drugs, gambling, and prostitution. What is it about these specific crimes that make them vices?

b. Suppose that the mayor's office created a "virtue squad" that would reward people for being especially virtuous. What virtues might the squad focus on?

c. Virtues are good habits that have a distinctively moral value. Are there some good habits that would not count as *moral* virtues?

Up to this point we have considered various debates about the source of morality—whether it is invented by people, is driven by selfish inclinations, is an expression of mere feelings, and is the same for male and female alike. We turn now to a second set of issues, which involves how we are to conduct our lives morally. We are all familiar with a fundamental moral principle found in virtually all cultures: Behave toward others as you would want them to behave toward you. This principle—sometimes called the Golden Rule—is among the more effective and commonsensical recommendations for moral conduct. It tells us quite directly that I should not lie, steal, or kill since I would not want these things to be done to me. In spite of its intuitive appeal, the Golden Rule does not function very well as a systematic moral theory. One problem was pointed out by Augustine: "What if someone's lust is so great that he offers his wife to another and willingly allows him to commit adultery with her, and is eager to enjoy the same freedom with the other man's wife?" On parallel reasoning, it would be OK for me to sadistically torture someone if I would masochistically enjoy being tortured myself. The problem with the Golden Rule is that it assumes from the start that we have a decent conception of how we personally wish to be morally treated. But this initial conception of morality is precisely what moral philosophers want to explain. Over the centuries, ethicists have tried to devise systematic accounts of criteria for moral behavior or moral character. We will explore three of these in the remaining chapters.

The first is virtue theory which, most simply, is the view that morality must be understood in terms of the acquisition of certain character traits, or "virtues," which are themselves in some respects like habits. Examples of such virtues are courage, temperance, justice and wisdom. We become good people by acquiring virtues or good habits of conduct, and we become bad people when we acquire vices instead of virtues. One advantage of virtue ethics is that it easily accounts for common views that we have about moral motivation. Suppose, for example, that I visit a sick friend in the hospital and he asks why I showed up. It would sound silly if I said that I'm there because I'm following a dictate of reason or that I am maximizing general happiness. It would sound cold and uncaring if I said I was there because it was my duty. My friend would like to think that I visit because I have feelings of friendship, not just an obligation. He would like to think I am loyal and devoted. Friendship, loyalty, and devotion are all virtues, or character traits. Virtues are generally thought of as traits that enhance and ennoble the life of the person who has them, as well as the lives of others.

1. VIRTUE AND HAPPINESS: ARISTOTLE

The version of virtue theory that made the most lasting impression on the history of philosophy was worked out by the ancient Greek philosopher Aristotle (384–322 BCE). His *Nicomachean Ethics* is perhaps his most famous work and is still widely studied as a source for insights into virtue concepts and moral psychology.

The Highest Good for Humans. Aristotle's thinking about ethics stresses the idea of a good life, not just particular good actions.

FROM ARISTOTLE, *Nicomachean Ethics,* BOOKS 1 AND 2

Every art and every scientific inquiry, and similarly every action and purpose, may be said to aim at some good. Hence the good has been well defined as that at which all things aim. But it appears that there is a difference in the ends; for the ends are sometimes activities, and sometimes results beyond the mere activities. Also, where there are certain ends beyond the actions, the results are naturally superior to the activities.

70. Is there anything at all that you do that is *not* done for the sake of some "good"? If you think there is, name it here.

71. You might have heard a proverb that goes something like this: "There is nothing worse than getting all the way to the top and then discovering you are on the wrong ladder." This proverb is a way of saying that we need to think about the _____ of action, not just the means.

Aristotle claims that there is some ultimate goal that we all seek for its own sake. It will become evident as we proceed in what sense such an ultimate goal might be "one" or "single." Ethical reasoning is not like many other sorts of reasoning, such as that required for geometry or the construction of a watch. It does not have that kind of precision.

**ARISTOTLE
(384–322 BCE)**
Ancient Greek philosopher and author of Nicomachean Ethics.

But our statement of the case will be adequate, if it be made with all such clearness as the subject matter admits; for it would be wrong to expect the same degree of accuracy in all reasonings just as it would with respect to the products of the various crafts. Noble and just things, which are the subjects of investigation in political science, show so much variety and uncertainty that they are sometimes thought to have only a conventional, and not a natural, existence. There is the same sort of uncertainty in regard to good things, as it often happens that injuries result from them; thus people have been ruined by wealth, or again by courage. As our subjects then and our premises are of this nature, we must be content to indicate the truth roughly and in outline. . . .

72. Why does Aristotle think that it is not a bad thing that the subject matter of ethics is imprecise?

Aristotle takes everyday beliefs about the good life seriously. But he also is critical of some of them and sets out some objections to common views on what constitutes the good, or goods, at which our all our actions aim.

As every knowledge and moral purpose aspires to some good, what is in our view the good at which the political science aims, and what is the highest of all practical goods? As to its name, there is I may say, a general agreement. The masses and the cultured classes agree in calling it *happiness* (*eudaimonia*), and conceive that "to live well" or "to do well" is the same thing as "to be happy." But as to the *nature* of happiness, they do not agree, nor do the masses give the same account of it as the philosophers. The former describe it as something visible and palpable, e.g., pleasure, wealth or honour. People give various definitions of it, and often the same person gives different definitions at different times; for when a person has been ill, it is health, when he is poor, it is wealth.

This appears too superficial for our present purpose; for honor seems to depend more on the people who pay it rather than the upon the person to whom it is paid, and we have an intuitive feeling that the good is something that is proper to a man himself and cannot be easily taken away from him.

ASK YOURSELF

73. List the common conceptions of happiness mentioned so far.

Happiness and the Highest Good. Aristotle now attempts to reason his way toward an account of the good that can withstand the kinds of objections he has brought against some popular accounts. He agrees that happiness is the good, and he gives reasons for supposing it is.

We always desire happiness for its own sake and never as a means to something else, whereas we desire honour, pleasure, intellect, and every virtue, partly for their own sakes (for we should desire them independently of what might result from them) but partly also as being means to happiness, because we suppose they will prove the instruments of happiness. Nobody desires happiness, on the other hand, for the sake of these things, nor indeed as a means to anything else at all.

ASK YOURSELF

74. It is obvious that while we desire pleasures because we think they will make us _____, we do not desire _____ because we think it will bring pleasure.

We come to the same conclusion if we start from the consideration of self-sufficiency, if it may be assumed that the final good is self-sufficient. But when we speak of self-sufficiency, we do not mean that a person leads a solitary life all by himself, but that he has parents, children, wife, and friends, and fellow-citizens in general, as man is naturally a social being.

In other words, humans are political. A good life requires the "polis," that is, community. Family life, friendships, and other forms of relationship, such as churches and clubs, would be included in the "political" as Aristotle uses the term.

Perhaps, however, no one would ever disagree with the claim that happiness is the supreme good; what is wanted is to *define* its nature a little more clearly. The best way of arriving at such a definition will probably be to ascertain the function of Man.

Aristotle's view that there is a "function" common to all humans is central to his argument. Yet he seems aware that some people might find his idea odd. People can generally "function" in so many ways, fill so many roles, that it seems strange to suggest that there is *one* function that they all have. Even though we can ask a quarterback in football what his function is, it almost seems insulting to ask someone what his "function" is simply as a human being. A doorknob has a function. A human being does not. Or so it might seem.

What, then, can this function be? It is not life; for life is apparently something which man shares with the plants; and it is something peculiar to him that we are looking for. We must exclude therefore the life of nutrition. There is next what may be called the life of sensation.

But this too, is apparently shared by humans with horses, cattle, and all other animals. There remains what I may call the practical life of the rational part of human being. . . . The function of a human being then is the activity of soul in accordance with reason, or not independently of reason.

> ### ASK YOURSELF
>
> **75.** Aristotle determines the function of human beings by asking what is unique about people. Consider the following comparison. If you want to know what a good quarterback is, you will have to understand the unique _____ of a quarterback. If you think his _____ is to block tacklers, you will never know what a good quarterback is. Likewise, we must determine what characteristics distinguishes human beings from other beings in order to see what the function of human beings is. Aristotle thinks that _____ is the distinguishing trait.

Now the function of any x and of a *good* x will be the same (thus the function of a harpist and of a *good* harpist are the same, and likewise for all classes of things), This being so, *if* we (a) define the function of Man as a kind of life and (b) [define] this life as an activity of soul or a course of action in conformity with reason, and (c) if the function of a good man is to perform such activities well and finely and (d) if a function is performed well and finely when it is performed in accordance with its proper excellence (virtue, *arete*), *then* it follows that the good of human beings is an activity of soul [or a course of action] in accordance with [human beings'] proper excellence or virtue or if there are more virtues than one, in accordance with the best and most complete virtue. But it is necessary to add the words "in a complete life." For as one swallow or one day does not make a spring, so one day or a short time does not make a blessed or happy man.

The question is consequently raised whether happiness is something that can be learnt or acquired by habit or discipline of any other kind, or whether it comes by some divine dispensation or even by chance . . . if it is better that happiness should be produced in this way [by discipline] than by chance, it may reasonably be supposed that it is so produced, since everything is ordered in the best possible way in Nature and so too in art, and in causation generally and most of all in the highest kind of causation. But it would be altogether inconsistent to leave what is greatest and noblest to chance.

> ### ASK YOURSELF
>
> **76.** Try to think of a case where luck played a role in a person's becoming a good person, that is, a person who is "functioning well."

But the definition of happiness itself helps to clear up the question; for happiness has been defined as a certain kind of activity of the soul in accordance with virtue or excellence. Of the other goods, i.e., of goods besides those of the soul, some are necessary as antecedent conditions of happiness, others are in their nature co-operative and serviceable as instruments of happiness.

Aristotle is saying that if happiness consists of an activity, as he originally claimed, then it cannot be, or be the result of, something that simply "happens to you" like winning a lottery, but must rather be more like an achievement.

The Nature of Virtue. The notion of a virtue as Aristotle and the Greeks generally employed it is the notion of an excellence (some trait necessary for optimal functioning). So speed would be a virtue in a sprinter. What then are the moral virtues like? Aristotle argues that the unique function of humans is the use of reason. Reason, however, is complex. A rational being is one in whom reason is dominant. There are of course other aspects of the self, or soul, and in a virtuous person those aspects will not get out of hand but will partake of or obey reason.

All correction, rebuke and exhortation are a witness that the irrational part of the soul is in a sense subject to the influence of reason. But if we are to say that this part too possesses reason, then the part that possesses reason will have two divisions, one possessing reason absolutely and in itself, the other listening to it as a child listens to its father.

It seems natural to say of certain desires, or emotions, that they are rational or irrational. For example, the desire for pain, except in very unusual circumstances, would seem to be irrational. Fear of being in a crowd would seem to be irrational. Yet our desires and emotions do not belong to reason per se, on Aristotle's view, but they are capable of being organized or trained by reason. Aristotle turns to a more precise account of virtue and the means of acquiring it. Proper training is essential to the acquisition of virtue and a happy life.

Moral virtue . . . is the outcome of habit, and accordingly its name is derived by a slight deflection from habit. From this fact it is clear that no moral virtue is implanted in us by nature; a law of nature cannot be altered by habituation. Thus a stone naturally tends to fall downwards, and it cannot be habituated or trained to rise upwards, even if we were to [try to] habituate it by throwing it upwards ten thousand times. . . . It is neither by nature then nor in defiance of nature that virtues are implanted in us. Nature gives us the *capacity* of receiving them, and that capacity is perfected by *habit* . . . it is by doing just acts that we become just, by doing temperate acts that we become temperate, by doing courageous acts that we become courageous. It makes no small difference then how we are trained up from our youth; rather it is a serious, even an all-important matter.

ASK YOURSELF

77. Aristotle is saying that everyone has the capacity to be, say, courageous, but only those become courageous who get in the _____ of acting courageously, and only those get in the _____ who repeatedly act courageously.

Aristotle introduces the notion of a virtue as a kind of mean state, in which excess or deficiency is avoided.

The first point to be observed then is that in such matters as we are considering deficiency and excess are equally fatal. . . . A person who avoids and is afraid of everything and faces nothing becomes a coward; a person who is not afraid of anything but is ready to face everything becomes foolhardy. Similarly he who enjoys every pleasure and never abstains from any pleasure is licentious; he who eschews all pleasures like a boor is an insensible sort of person. For temperance and courage are destroyed by excess and deficiency but preserved by the mean state.

ASK YOURSELF

78. In Aristotle's account, virtues are mid-points between extremes. For example, courage is midway between being _____ and being _____.

Aristotle shows that virtues are traits that are connected in some way with our ability to manage pleasures and pains in a reasonable way.

For moral virtue is concerned with pleasures and pains. [This can be seen from the following fact]: It is pleasure which makes us do what is base, and pain which makes us abstain from doing what is noble. Hence the importance of having had a certain training from very early days, as Plato says, namely such a training as produces pleasure and pain at the right objects; for this is the true education.

ASK YOURSELF

79. Name an example of an emotion of yours that your parents or someone else has tried to "train."

Toward a Definition of Virtue. Virtue is a "state of the soul." Exactly what kind of state? Aristotle argues that virtues cannot be emotions since we do not blame or praise people for their emotions per se, in the way we blame or praise them for their vices or virtues. Nor, for the same reason, could they be merely capacities. They must be dispositions—that is, settled tendencies to act in certain ways in certain situations. But what specific kind of disposition? Remember, a good person is a happy person (and vice versa) since to be good is to be functioning well, and that is what happiness is. But functioning well, requires excellence. Moreover, we have already learned that excellence in human living requires the use of reason. Now Aristotle argues that reason, when employed in determining how to live, must take into account specific circumstances that can vary from person to person and time to time, in order to arrive at the "mean" or virtuous act.

By the mean considered relatively to ourselves I understand that which is neither too much nor too little; but this is not one thing, nor is it the same for everybody. It does not follow that if 10 pounds of meat be too much and 2 too little for a man to eat, a trainer will order him 6 pounds, as this may itself be too much or too little for the person who is to take it; it will be too little, e.g., for Milo [a very big Greek athlete], but too much for a beginner in gymnastics. In the same way an expert in any art seeks and chooses the mean, not the absolute mean, but the mean considered relatively to himself.

ASK YOURSELF

80. If you choose the mean relative to yourself, then assuming that you have the virtue of courage, would your choice whether, for example, to run away or stand firm when attacked by an armed enemy have to be the same if you were heavily armed or not?

81. Is a person who runs away from danger always a coward? Explain.

But virtue is concerned with emotions and actions, and here excess is an error and deficiency a fault, whereas the mean is successful and laudable, and success and merit are both characteristics of virtue. It appears then that virtue is a mean state, so far at least as it aims at the mean. . . . Again, error is many formed . . . while success is possible in only one way, which is why it is easy to fail and difficult to succeed, as it is easy to miss the mark and difficult to hit it. This is another reason why excess and deficiency are marks of vice, and observance of the mean a mark of virtue: Goodness is simple, badness is manifold.

Virtue then is a disposition with respect to choice, that is, the disposition to choose a mean that is relative to ourselves, the mean being determined by reasoned principle, that is, as a prudent man would determine it.

Aristotle's notion of "prudence" is the notion of practical wisdom, *phronesis,* and practical wisdom is indeed "practical," in the sense that it consists in discernment about matters that are uncertain and that can be approached in more than one way. Aristotle would sometimes be sympathetic to the remark "that is true in theory, but in practice it's another matter." His account of choice, which is detailed in Book III (not excerpted here), stresses the way in which reason and desire work together. "Choice" does not refer to a blind or arbitrary act of the will, nor to the output of desire or feeling alone, nor does it refer to something governed by a strict set of rules.

ASK YOURSELF

82. Present Aristotle's definition of virtue using the terms "disposition," "choice," "reasoned principle," and "prudence."

A Catalogue of the Virtues. Aristotle provides an outline of some of the main virtues and vices. We can imagine Aristotle pointing to a chart with three divisions: one for excesses, one for virtues, and one for defects.

But it is not enough to lay down this as a general rule; it is necessary to apply it to particular cases, as in reasonings upon actions generally, statements, although they are broader are less exact than particular statements. For all action refers to particulars, and it is essential that our theories should harmonize with the particular cases to which they apply.

We must take particular virtues then from the catalogue of virtues. In regard to feelings of fear and confidence, courage is a mean state. On the side of excess, he whose fearlessness is excessive has no name, as often happens, but he whose confidence is excessive is foolhardy, while he whose timidity is excessive and whose confidence is deficient is a coward.

In respect of pleasures and pains, although not indeed of all pleasures and pains, and to a less extent in respect of pains than of pleasures, the mean state is temperance, the excess is licentiousness. We never find people who are deficient in regard to pleasure; accordingly, such people again have not received a name, but we may call them insensible [dull, listless].

In respect of money there are other dispositions as well. There is the mean state which is magnificence; for the magnificent man, who is one who deals with large sums of money, differs from the liberal man who has to do only with small sums; and the excess corresponding to it is bad taste or vulgarity, the deficiency is meanness. These are different from the excess and deficiency of liberality; what the difference is will be explained hereafter.

When modern people hear the word "ethics," they think of questions such as whether it is ever right to tell a lie or to cheat, whether it is ever right to remove a respirator from a terminally ill person, and so forth. Many of us do not typically think about "character traits" when we hear the word "ethics." And, even if the notion of character is important to our ethical thinking, we would probably not include all the traits Aristotle is discussing here. For example, we might question whether it belongs to morality proper to discuss dispositions such as being a big spender on the one hand, or stingy on the other, as opposed to being "just right"—that is, knowing how to spend, buy presents, or throw a party with just the right degree of opulence. So, not only is Aristotle more concerned with character traits than with criteria for right actions, he is also concerned with character traits that we might not think of as having anything to do with ethics. But remember, he is raising the question, What is the best kind of life? or What is the ultimate goal of all our actions? and he has concluded that the answer is happiness. From that perspective, all sorts of character traits have a bearing on how happy we are, not just the "ethical" ones as we tend to think of "ethics." For example, how clever, or pleasant, or artistic a person is can obviously have a bearing on the quality of their life.

There are also mean states in the emotions and in the expression of the emotions. For although modesty is not a virtue, yet a modest person is praised as if he were virtuous; for here too one person is said to observe the mean and another to exceed it, as e.g. the bashful man who is never anything but modest, whereas a person who has insufficient modesty or no modesty at all is called shameless, and one who observes the mean modest.

Righteous indignation, again, is a mean state between envy and malice. They are all concerned with the pain and pleasure that we feel at the fortunes of our neighbors. A person who is righteously indignant is pained at the prosperity of the undeserving; but the envious person goes further and is pained at anybody's prosperity, and the malicious person is so far from being pained that he actually rejoices at misfortunes. We shall have another opportunity, however, of discussing these matters.

Notice that Aristotle's discussion of virtues and vices includes a discussion of the emotions or temperament. But of course such an emotion as envy tends to go with certain dispositions to act in certain ways. So Aristotle is claiming that the species of virtue is dispositions not only to act but to *feel* certain ways rather than others.

ASK YOURSELF

83. Give an example of how the existence of such feelings as envy or malice might be just as responsible for the miseries of life as what we call immoral actions.

Again, it is not easy to decide theoretically how far and to what extent a man may go before he becomes blamable, but neither is it easy to define theoretically anything else within the region of perception; such things fall under the head of particulars, and our judgment of them depends upon our perception.

Aristotle is claiming something here that is quite central to his way of thinking about ethics. He is saying that in order to achieve a good life, a life of virtue and happiness, we must have something like what we would now call "perceptiveness." We use this word to describe a sensitivity to particular persons and particular situations. It is part of what he calls "practical wisdom" and is essential to that "prudence" which figures into the definition of virtue.

84. Some people, in Aristotle's day and ever since, have thought that the best life is one of excess—eat, drink, and be merry. What would Aristotle say against such a view?

2. TRADITIONS AND VIRTUES: ALASDAIR MACINTYRE

One of the most articulate contemporary defenders of Aristotelian virtue theory is University of Notre Dame professor Alasdair MacIntyre (b. 1929). In his book *After Virtue* (1981), he argues that the dominant modern ethical theories rely on a largely incoherent tradition initially forged by Hume and others during the eighteenth and nineteenth centuries. The way out of this mess, he argues, is to look back to the virtue tradition founded by Aristotle. Doing that requires a recovery of the typical Aristotelian question, "What is the good for a human?" Unfortunately, there are numerous obstacles to any attempt to think about or discuss the virtues understood in this way.

The Virtues, the Unity of a Human Life, and Narrative. According to MacIntyre, the good for human life is the good for a whole life, not just for life next Monday. The virtues are what are needed to achieve such a "whole life" good. But there are social and philosophical obstacles to conceiving life "as a whole." One characteristic of our society is the notion that life consists of separate strongly demarcated stages, such as childhood, old age with its "special" problems, and so forth, and the notion of roles that break up the self, so that I am one person at work, another at home, another when out on the town. Moreover, the tendency among many contemporary philosophers to thinking atomistically about human action creates obstacles to thinking, as MacIntyre does, that actions make sense only in a context, particularly a narrative context. The kind of unity a life needs in order for the virtues to be possible is like the unity of stories, or of characters in stories.

FROM ALASDAIR MACINTYRE, *After Virtue* (1981)

The unity of a virtue in someone's life is intelligible only as a characteristic of a unitary life, a life that can be conceived and evaluated as a whole . . . so now, in defining the particular pre-modern concept of the virtues with which I have been preoccupied, it has become necessary to say something of the concomitant concept of selfhood, a concept of a self whose unity resides in the unity of a narrative which links birth to life to death as narrative beginning to middle to end.

It is a conceptual commonplace, both for philosophers and for ordinary agents, that one and the same segment of human behavior may be correctly characterized in a number of different ways. To the question "What is he doing?" the answers may with equal truth and appropriateness be "Digging," "Gardening," "Taking exercise," "Preparing for winter" or "Pleasing his wife." Some of these answers will characterize the agent's intentions, other unintended consequences of his actions, and of these unintended consequences some may be such that the agent is aware of them and others not.

ASK YOURSELF

85. Which of the five answers to "What is he doing?" mentioned above would most likely characterize an unintended consequence, in your judgment?

What is important to notice immediately is that any answer to the questions of how we are to understand or to explain a given segment of behavior will presuppose some prior answer to the question of how these different correct answers to the question "What is he doing?" are related to each other. For if someone's primary intention is to put the garden in order before the winter and it is only incidentally the case that in so doing he is taking exercise and pleasing his wife, we have one type of behavior to be explained; but if the agent's primary intention is to please his wife by taking exercise, we have quite another type of behavior to be explained and we will have to look in a different direction for understanding and explanation.

In the first place the episode has been situated in an annual cycle of domestic activity, and the behavior embodies an intention which presupposes a particular type of household-cum-garden setting with the peculiar narrative history of that setting in which this segment of behavior now becomes an episode. In the second instance the episode has been situated in the narrative history of a marriage, a very different, if related, social setting. We cannot, that is to say, characterize behavior independently of intentions, and we cannot characterize intentions independently of the settings which make those intentions intelligible both to agents themselves and to others.

For example, if your behavior includes regular class attendance, and you explain it in terms of your intention to get an "A," I will only understand this "intention" to the extent that I understand such things as what a university is, what a class is, how they are conducted, how work in them is evaluated, how university courses and success in them is related to the kinds of work available in a society, the kinds of responsibilities that must be met for personal and social existence, the kinds of institutional settings within which those responsibilities arise, and so forth.

In my earlier example the agent's activity may be part of the history both of the cycle of household activity and of his marriage, two histories which have happened to intersect. The household may have its own history stretching back through hundreds of years, as do the histories of some European farms, where the farm has had a life of its own, even though different families have in different periods inhabited it; and the marriage will certainly have its own history, a history which itself presupposes that a particular point has been reached in the history of the institution of marriage. If we are to relate some particular segment of behavior in any precise way to an agent's intentions and thus to the settings which that agent inhabits, we shall have to understand in a precise way how the variety of correct characterizations of the agent's behavior relate to each other first by identifying which characteristics refer us to an intention and which do not and then by classifying further the items in both categories.

Consider what the argument so far implies about the interrelationships of the intentional, the social and the historical. We identify a particular action only by invoking two kinds of context, implicitly if not explicitly. We place the agent's intentions, I have suggested, in causal and temporal order with reference to their role in his or her history; and we also place them with reference to their role in the history of the setting or settings to which they belong.

In doing this, in determining what causal efficacy the agent's intentions had in one or more directions, and how his short-term intentions succeeded or failed to be constitutive of long-term intentions, we ourselves write a further part of these histories. Narrative history of a certain kind turns out to be the basic and essential genre for the characterization of human action. . . .

ASK YOURSELF

86. Could the "actions" of a dog constitute a narrative history, in the sense expounded here by MacIntyre? Why or why not?

A central thesis then begins to emerge: man is in his actions and practice, as well as in his fictions, essentially a story-telling animal. . . . I can only answer the question "What am I to do?" if I can answer the prior question "Of what story or stories do I find myself a part?" We enter human society, that is, with one or more imputed characters—roles into which we have been drafted, and we have to learn what they are in order to be able to understand how others respond to us and how our responses to them are apt to be construed. It is through hearing stories about wicked stepmothers, lost children, good but misguided kings, wolves that suckle twin boys, youngest sons who receive no inheritance but must make their own way in the world and eldest sons who waste their inheritance on riotous living and go into exile to live with the swine, that children learn or mislearn both what a child and what a parent is, what the cast of characters may be in the drama into which they have been born and what the ways of the world are. Deprive children of stories and you leave them unscripted, anxious stutterers in their actions as in their words.

The twentieth century has been characterized as an "age of anxiety," and many cultural critics have complained about a lack of coherence in the lives of many people and in society itself. At the same time there has been a decline in the stock of shared stories that people know and use to understand what is valuable and worth doing. For example, stories about the nation's heroes such as George Washington that were once taught to nearly all children in grade school are perhaps less widely known, and certainly more widely debunked, than they once were.

ASK YOURSELF

87. Give an example of a shared story that has functioned importantly in your life—a family story, Bible story, national story, work of fiction.

Narratives and Quests. MacIntyre argues that human lives can be understood as attempts, successful or not, to achieve some ideal. The literary equivalent would be a narrated quest that describes people—and heroes—in the pursuit of a highest value goal.

It is now possible to return to the question from which this enquiry into the nature of human action and identity started: In what does the unity of an individual life consist? The answer is that its unity is the unity of a narrative embodied in a single life. To ask "What is the good for me?" is to ask how best I might live out that unity and bring it to completion. To ask "What is the good for man?" is to ask what all answers to the former question must have in common. But now it is important to emphasize that it is the systematic asking of these two questions and the attempt to answer them in deed as well as in word which provide the moral life with its unity. The unity of a human life is the unity of a narrative quest. Quests sometimes fail, are frustrated, abandoned or dissipated into distractions; and human lives may in all these ways also fail. But the only criteria for success or failure in a human life as a whole are the criteria of success or failure in a narrated or to-be-narrated quest. A quest for what?

ASK YOURSELF

88. Name three things that can happen on a quest that can cause it to fail.

It is in looking for a conception of the good which will enable us to order other goods, for a conception of the good which will enable us to extend our understanding of the purpose and content of the virtues, for a conception of the good which will enable us to understand the place of integrity and constancy in life, that we initially define the kind of life which is a quest for the good.

A life that is a quest for the good cannot just be a life in which I try to develop those traits necessary to be a better chess player, cook, or banker; these might be examples of "practices" or consist of various subpractices. Suppose I were all three. If I spent too much time on chess, the rest of my life might fall apart. I need to be able to order the various goods in my life, and doing that requires more than just having the traits and abilities necessary for chess or banking. A quest must be a search for a way to order a whole life, and thus the search for the good of a whole life.

ASK YOURSELF

89. Suppose that a person had all the skill necessary to cook, bank, and play chess. How might that person still lack "constancy"?

The Virtues and Community. My idea of the good, MacIntyre contends, cannot be independent of the particular social order of which I am a part.

For I am never able to seek for the good or exercise the virtues only qua individual . . . I am someone's son or daughter, someone else's cousin or uncle; I am a citizen of this or that city, a member of this or that guild or profession; I belong to this clan, that tribe, this nation. Hence what is good for me has to be the good for one who inhabits these roles. As such, I inherit from the past of my family, my city, my tribe, my nation, a variety of debts, inheritances, rightful expectations and obligations. These constitute the given of my life, my moral starting point. This is in part what gives my life its own moral particularity.

This thought is likely to appear alien and even surprising from the standpoint of modern individualism. From the standpoint of individualism I am what I myself choose to be . . . the young German who believes that being born after 1945 means that what Nazis did to Jews has no moral relevance to his relationship to his Jewish contemporaries [thinks that] the self is detachable from its social and historical roles and statuses. . . . The contrast with the narrative view of the self is clear. For the story of my life is always embedded in the story of those communities from which I derive my identity. I am born with a past; and to try to cut myself off from that past, in the individualist mode, is to deform my present relationships. The possession of an historical identity and the possession of a social identity coincide. Notice that rebellion against my identity is always one possible mode of expressing it.

ASK YOURSELF

90. Why will it not do for an American to say "I never owned any slaves"?

Notice also that the fact that the self has to find its moral identity in and through its member-ship in communities such as those of the family, the neighborhood, the city and the tribe does not entail that the self has to accept the moral limitations of the particularity of those forms of community. Without those moral particularities to begin from there would never be any-where to begin; but it is in moving forward from such particularity that the search for the good, for the universal, consists. Yet particularity can never be simply left behind or obliter-ated. The notion of escaping from it into a realm of entirely universal maxims which belong to man as such, whether in its eighteenth-century Kantian form or in the presentation of some modern analytical moral philosophies, is an illusion and an illusion.

What I am, therefore, is in key part what I inherit, a specific past that is present to some degree in my present. I find myself part of a history and that is generally to say, whether I like it or not, whether I recognize it or not, one of the bearers of a tradition. It was important when I characterized the concept of a practice to notice that practices always have histories and that at any given moment what a practice is depends on a mode of understanding it which has been transmitted often through many generations.

Consider, as examples, the practice of medicine or law or politics. All of these are what they are as a result of a long tradition and development.

And thus; insofar as the virtues sustain the relationships required for practices, they have to sustain relationships to the past-and to the future-as well as in the present. . . . Once again the narrative phenomenon of embedding is crucial: the history of a practice in our time is gener-ally and characteristically embedded in and made intelligible in terms of the larger and longer history of the tradition through which the practice in its present form was conveyed to us; the history of each of our own lives is generally and characteristically embedded in and made in-telligible in terms of the larger and longer histories of a number of traditions. I have to say "generally and characteristically" rather than "always," for traditions decay, disintegrate and disappear. What then sustains and strengthens traditions? What weakens and destroys them?

The answer in key part is: the exercise or the lack of exercise of the relevant virtues.

ASK YOURSELF

91. What virtues might be required for the practice of law?

The virtues find their point and purpose not only in sustaining those relationships necessary if the variety of goods internal to practices are to be achieved and not only in sustaining the form of an individual life in which that individual may seek out his or her good as the good of his or her whole life, but also in sustaining those traditions which provide both practices and individual lives with their necessary historical context. Lack of justice, lack of truthful-ness, lack of courage, lack of the relevant intellectual virtues—these corrupt traditions, just as they do those institutions and practices which derive their life from the traditions of which they are the contemporary embodiments. To recognize this is of course also to recognize the existence of an additional virtue, one whose importance is perhaps most obvious when it is least present, the virtue of having an adequate sense of the traditions to which one belongs or which confront one.

ASK YOURSELF

92. Is it possible, in MacIntyre's view, for a person to lead a good life without paying any attention to the history of their own family, religious and civic communities, or profession?

SUMMING UP THE ISSUE OF MORAL VIRTUES

The job of ethical theory, according to Aristotle, is to explain the type of life that is good for human beings, not just the type of actions that are good for us to perform. The good life is linked with happiness, and happiness, in turn, is linked with our human function as rational beings. More specifically, our happiness depends on our ability to rationally train our emotions and appetites; to this end, we will try, if we are well-advised, to develop good habits that are at a mean between two extremes. For example, when we have learned to properly or rationally handle fear when facing danger, we will have developed the virtue of courage, which is midway between cowardice and foolhardiness. Cultivating virtues requires the use of practical wisdom, a special sensitivity to particular persons and particular situations. MacIntyre, a contemporary advocate of virtue theory, argues that the proper development of virtues rests on a unified social tradition, which is similar in some ways to the unity that we find in stories. I must engage in a quest to organize my whole life, and not just one feature of it, and this quest must be within the context of a particular social order. A coherent social order of a certain kind is necessary to the formation of virtues in individuals.

CAN OF WORMS

A distinctive feature of Aristotle's theory is his contention that morality must be understood in terms of virtuous habits, and not in terms of good rules or good actions. Some contemporary philosophers have argued that, just as there are *moral* virtues, there are also *epistemological* virtues. Sometimes they overlap. That is, knowledge rests on acquiring good habits of perceiving and judging. For example, I develop good habits of judgment that incline me to question stories of alien abductions or Elvis sightings. I develop other habits that incline me to trust well-constructed scientific studies. This theory is explored in Chapter 5. MacIntyre's view stresses the importance of social traditions that define our characters and order our lives. Since we are by our nature attached to our communities, MacIntyre feels that the web of social relations which makes us what we are must be understood in order to understand the foundations of governments and the nature of their authority. MacIntyre's view is thus communitarian; it contrasts with liberalism, a political theory that stresses individual rights over against communal claims. The liberalism/communitarian debate has obvious relevance to MacIntyre's ethical views, and it is discussed in Chapter 7.

F. DUTIES

Suppose that one evening you look out your window and see someone stealing your car. Your first reaction would likely be to call the police in the hopes that the car thief would be caught and appropriately punished. The thief certainly acted wrongly. Virtue theorists would stress that his action was unjust and that injustice is a vice that destroys the goodness of individual and communal life. An alternative analysis focuses on the particular act itself rather than on the character of the person who committed it. The thief acted wrongly because he violated moral duties that all people are obligated to follow. The specific duty that he violated here was the duty to refrain from theft. In the Judeo-Christian tradition we are familiar with this duty in the form that is expressed in the Ten Commandments: "Thou shalt not steal!" Philosophers have latched onto this idea and developed a series of theories about the nature and scope of our moral duties. The basic presumption in many of these theories is that we know our moral duties through a kind of rational intuition or insight. Human reason *tells* us our principal obligations, and, because these are rational rules of conduct, they are universal and binding on all rational people. Some theorists believed that these principles are grounded in an external spiritual realm—such as Plato's realm of the forms. And, like mathematical principles, they are unchanging; God himself is obligated to follow them.

QUESTIONS TO DISCUSS

a. Many philosophers believe that human beings have instinctive notions of moral obligation—don't steal, don't kill, don't lie. Do you think that these notions are instinctive, learned, or some combination of the two?

b. Assuming that we have notions of moral obligation that are at least somewhat instinctive, roughly how many basic principles do we have—one, or ten, or one hundred?

c. Some philosophers feel that our notions of obligation are absolute in the sense that we are never justified in violating them. Can you think of some circumstance in which you might be morally justified in lying or stealing?

1. DUTIES TO GOD, ONESELF, AND OTHERS: SAMUEL PUFENDORF

One of the early champions of duty theory was German university professor Samuel Pufendorf (1632–1694), who influenced moral theorists for generations after him. Pufendorf developed an elaborate account of how basic moral duties are instilled in our nature by God and are the foundation of both moral behavior and civilized society. His chief work was the lengthy *On the Law of Nature and Nations* (1672), but in the following year he published a shorter and more lively account entitled *On the Duty of Man and Citizen According to Natural Law*. One of the more influential aspects of Pufendorf's theory was his division of all duties into three principal groups: those to God, to oneself, and to others. According to Pufendorf, God gives us a natural knowledge of moral laws, which come to consciousness in the normal course of child development.

FROM SAMUEL PUFENDORF, *The Duty of Man and Citizen* (1673), CHAPTERS 3–9

It is usually said that we have the knowledge of this [moral] law from nature itself. However, this is not to be taken to mean that plain and distinct notions concerning what is to be done or avoided were implanted in the minds of newborn people. Instead, nature is said to teach us, partly because the knowledge of this law may be attained by the help of the light of reason. It is also partly because the general and most useful points of it are so plain and clear that, at first sight, they force assent. In this way, they get such root in the minds of people,

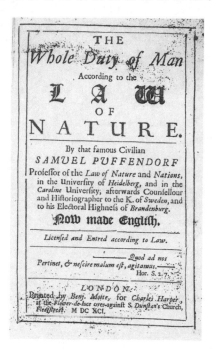

Title page of early English translation of Samuel Pufendorf's On the Duty of Man and Citizen *(1673).*

that nothing can eradicate them afterwards, let wicked people take ever so many pains to blunt the edge and numb themselves against the stings of their consciences. In this sense we find in holy scripture that this law is said to be "written in the hearts of people." Accordingly, from our childhood a sense of it was instilled into us together with other learning in the usual methods of education. Although we are not able to remember the precise time when they first took hold of our understandings and professed our minds, we can have no other opinion of our knowledge of this law except that it was native to our beings, or born together and at the same time with ourselves. The cause is the same with every person in learning his mother tongue.

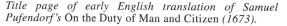

ASK YOURSELF

93. According to Pufendorf, in what sense does nature teach us moral laws?

Duties Toward God. Pufendorf argues that our naturally instilled moral notions involve three distinct sets of duties: those to God, those to oneself, and those to others. Our duties toward God, he contends, are of two general types. First, there are theoretical duties that impact the specific conception of God that we entertain. Specifically, we are duty bound to know that God exists and what kind of being he is. Second, there are practical duties that impact how we behave toward God, specifically worshiping him.

The duty of humans towards God, so far as it can be discovered by natural reason, encompasses these two duties. The first is that we have true notions concerning him, or know him properly. The second is that we conform our actions to his will, or obey him as we should. And, so, natural religion consists of two sorts of propositions, specifically, theoretical or speculative, and practical or active.

Among the [theoretical] *notions* that every person should have of God, the first of all is he firmly believes in God's existence. That is, that there is indeed some supreme and first being upon whom this universe depends. And this has been most plainly demonstrated by learned and wise men from the subordination of causes to one another, which must at last be found to have their origin in something that was before them all. It is also seen from the nature of motion, and from the consideration of this great machine, the world, and from similar arguments. . . . The second is that God is the creator of this universe. Since it is manifest from reason that none of these things could exist of themselves, it is absolutely necessary that they should have some supreme cause. This cause is the very same thing that we call God. . . .

The third is that God governs the whole world, and particularly humankind. This plainly appears from the admirable and constant order that we see in this universe. And it is to the same moral purpose whether someone denies that God is, or that he denies that God rules and regards the affairs of men. For either of these destroys all manner of religion. . . . The fourth is that no attribute can belong to God that implies any manner of imperfection. Given that God is the cause and source of all things, it would be absurd for anyone to think that that he could form a notion of any perfection which God does not fully possess. Lastly, it is utterly repugnant to the notion of divine perfection to say that there are more Gods than one. . . .

The propositions of *practical* natural religion partly concern the internal and partly the external worship of God. The internal worship of God consists of honoring him. Now, honor is a high opinion of another's power conjoined with goodness. And the human mind is obliged from a consideration of his power and goodness to fill itself with all that reverence towards him of which its nature is susceptible. . . . The external worship of God is chiefly shown in these instances. That we give thanks to God for so many good things received from him. That so far as is in our power, we copy God's will into our actions; that is, that we obey his commands. That we admire and celebrate his greatness. That we pour forth our prayers before him for the procuring of good and averting of evil. . . .

ASK YOURSELF

94. What are the three theoretical duties that we have toward God?

95. What are the internal and external duties to worship God?

Duties Toward Oneself. Next on Pufendorf's list are duties toward oneself. These also are split into two groups. First, we have duties directed toward our mental well-being, which involve developing our talents. We can't just sit around, squander our abilities, and leech off society. Second, we have duties directed toward our physical well-being, which means that we should not consciously do things that would harm our physical bodies, and, more importantly, we should not consciously end our lives by destroying our bodies.

Since human nature consists of two parts, a soul and a body, then the first gives us the part of a director, and the other that of an instrument or subordinate minister. So, our actions are all performed by the guidance of the mind, and by the assistance of the body. We are hence obliged to take care of both, but especially the former. And that part is, above all things, to be formed and accommodated to support an adequate part of social life, and to be instilled with a sense and love of duty and decency. Then we are to devote ourselves to learning that is somewhat proper to our capacity and our condition in the world. Otherwise, we will become a useless burden to the earth, cumbersome to ourselves, and troublesome to others. And in due time we are to make choice of some honest state of life. It should be agreeable to our natural inclinations, the abilities of our body and mind, extraction, or wealth. Or it should be according as the just authority of our parents, the commands of our superiors, occasion or necessity as required.

But since the soul is supported by and dependent on the body, it is necessary that the strength of the body be continued and confirmed by convenient nourishment and exercise. And it should not be weakened by any intemperate eating or drinking, nor deliberated by unseasonable and needless labors or otherwise. For this reason, gluttony, drunkenness, the immoderate use of women, and similar things are to be avoided. Unbridled and exorbitant passions not only frequently disturb human society, but they are very harmful even to the person himself. For this reason, we ought to try our utmost to suppress them and subject them to reason. And because many dangers may be escaped if we encounter them with courage, we reject all weakness of the mind, and to be firm against all of the terrible appearances that any event may set before us.

And yet because no person could give himself life, which must be considered the bountiful favor of God, it seems that man is by no means vested with such a power over his own life as that he may put an end to it when he pleases. Instead, he ought to tarry until he is called off by him who placed him in this station. There are some sorts of labor and over-straining in any occupation which may waste the strength of a man, so that old age and death many come on much sooner than if he had led an easy and painless life. However, since men both can and ought to be serviceable to one another, there is no doubt but that a man may choose that way of living—without breaking this law [against self-killing]—which may with some probability make his life the shorter, so that he may become more useful to mankind.

Also, frequently the lives of many will be lost unless some number of men expose themselves to a probability of losing their own on their behalf. In this case the lawful governor has power to lay an injunction on any private man under the most grievous penalties, not to decline by flight such danger of losing his life.

No, further, he may of his own accord provoke such danger, provided that there are not reasons more forcible to the contrary, and by adventuring in this way he has hopes to save the lives of others, and those others are such as are worthy of so dear a purchase. For it would be silly for any man to engage his life together with another to no purpose, or for a person of value to die for the preservation of a worthless scoundrel. But for any other cases, there seems nothing to be required by the laws of nature by which he should be persuaded to prefer another man's life before his own. All things rightly compared, every man is allowed to be most dear to himself. Some voluntarily put an end to their own lives, either for being tired with the many troubles which usually accompany this mortal state; or from an abhorrence of indignities and evils which yet would not make them scandalous to human society; or through fear of pains or torments (although by enduring them with fortitude they might become useful examples to others); or out of a vain ostentation of their fidelity and bravery. All these are to be certainly reputed as sinners against the law of nature. . . .

ASK YOURSELF

96. Although Pufendorf believes that suicide is wrong, what are some situations in which we may rightly expose ourselves to some risk of dying?

97. What are some bad reasons that people sometimes give for voluntarily putting an end to their lives?

Duties Toward Others. Turning finally to duties toward others, Pufendorf notes that some of these are *absolute* in that they are mandated for all people. Others, though, are *conditional* in that they are the result of contracts or agreements that specific people make with each other. Regarding absolute duties, there are three principal ones: (1) Don't intentionally harm others; (2) treat others as equals; and (3) improve the well-being of others through good deeds.

We come now to those duties that are to be practiced by one man towards another. Some of these proceed from that common obligation with it has pleased the creator to lay upon all men in general. Others have their origin in some certain human institutions or some particular invented or accidental state of men. The first of these are always to be practiced by every man towards all men. The latter obtain only among those who are in such peculiar condition or state. Hence the former may be called absolute, and the latter conditional.

Among those duties that we call absolute—or those of every man towards every man—the first is that that one do no wrong to another. And this is the fullest duty of all, involving all men as such. It is at the same time the easiest since it consists only in an omission of acting, unless when unreasonable desires and lusts are to be curbed. It is also the most necessary, because without it human society cannot be preserved. For I can live quietly with someone that does me no good, or with whom I have no manner of correspondence, provided that he do me no harm. In fact, this is all we desire from the greatest part of mankind, since only a few perform mutually good deeds offices with each other. But I can by no means live peaceably with him that wrongs me. Nature has instilled into every man such a warm love of himself and what is his own, that he cannot keep from using all means to repel those men who make any attempt upon one or the other.

This duty contains not only what we have by the bounty of nature (such as our laws, bodies, limbs, chastity, and liberty) but also whatever by any human institution or contract becomes our propriety. So, by this it is forbidden to take away, spoil, damage or withdraw in whole or in part from our use anything that we possess by a lawful title. From this all actions are thereby made crimes by which any wrong is done to others, such as murder, wounding, striking, plundering, theft, fraud, violence, whether practiced directly or indirectly, mediately or immediately, and the like.

Further, it follows that if any harm or damage were done to another, he who is truly chargeable as the author of the wrong ought to make reparations as much as he can. . . .

Human creatures are not only highly concerned about self-preservation, but they also have a nice estimation of themselves. To degrade someone's view of himself will frequently incite indignation in him as great as if harm were done to his body or property. In fact there seems to him to be somewhat of dignity in the title of "man." So, the last and most effective argument to curb the arrogance of insulting men is usually, "I am not a dog, but a man as well as yourself." Human nature, then, is the same in us all, and no man will or can cheerfully join in society with any by whom he is not at least to be esteemed equally as a man and as a partaker of the same common nature. It follows from this that that among those duties which men owe to each other, this has the second place: that every man respect and treat another as naturally equal to himself, or as one who is a man as well as he. . . . Now from this equality it follows that he who would make use of other men's labor for his own benefit ought to be ready to provide compensation. The same equality also shows what every man's behavior ought to be when his business is to distribute justice among others. That is, he should treat them as equals, and not give to one what he denies to another—unless there are reasons for doing so. For if he does otherwise, the person who is disfavored is at the same time slighted and wronged and loses some of the dignity that nature gives him. From this it follows that things that are in common are to be rightfully divided by equal parts among those who are equal. Where the thing will not admit of division, they who are equally concerned are to use it indifferently. . . .

The third duty of one man towards another that must be practiced for the sake of common society is this: that every man ought to promote the good of another as far as conveniently he may. Since all people are made by nature, as it were, akin to each other, it would be no great matter for us to not hurt or to not despise our fellows. But we also ought to do such good deeds to others, or mutually to communicate the same, so that common brotherly love may be kept up among men. . . .

ASK YOURSELF

98. According to Pufendorf, murder violates an absolute duty toward others. Which of the three key absolute duties does it violate?

Pufendorf turns next to conditional duties toward others, which are founded on special contracts or agreements that we make with others.

Leaving absolute duties and turning to conditional duties, we must make our passage, so to speak, through the medium of contracts. Since all duties (except those already mentioned) seem to presuppose some covenant either expressed or implied, we must next examine the nature of contracts, and what is to be observed by the parties involved.

Now it is plain that it was absolutely for people to enter into mutual contracts. For though the duties of humanity spread themselves near and far through all aspects of human life, still, that alone is not sufficient grounds upon which to establish all of the obligations that may be necessary to be made reciprocal between one and another. For all men are not endowed with so much good nature so that they will do good deeds to every man out of mere kindness. They do so only if they expect to have some specific expectation of receiving the like again. And very often it happens that the services that we would have to be done to us by other men are of that sort that we cannot with modesty desire then. . . . Therefore, to make sure that these mutual good deeds (which are the product of sociality) may be more freely and regularly exercised, it was necessary that men should agree among themselves concerning what was to be done on this side and on that, of which no man could have assured himself from the law of nature alone. Thus it was to be adjusted before hand what this man (acting in such a way toward his neighbor) was to expect in lieu of the same, and what he might lawfully demand. This is done by means of promises and contracts.

With respect to this general duty, there is an obligation of the law of nature that every man keep his word, or fulfill his promises and make good his contracts. For without this, a great part of that advantage would be lost, which otherwise might naturally accrue to mankind by a mutual communication of good offices and useful things.

ASK YOURSELF

99. What is the key conditional duty that we have toward others?

2. THE CATEGORICAL IMPERATIVE: IMMANUEL KANT

**IMMANUEL KANT
(1724–1804)**

German philosopher and author of the Groundwork of the Metaphysics of Morals (1785).

One of the great thinkers influenced by Pufendorf's duty theory was German philosophy professor Immanuel Kant (1724–1804). Kant agreed with Pufendorf that we know our moral duties by virtue of reason. He also held that we have duties to God, oneself, and others—although Kant considered duties toward God specifically a matter of religious obligation rather than moral obligation. Kant went a step further than Pufendorf, though, and argued that our various moral duties are founded on one general principle of duty—a principle that he called the "categorical imperative."

Morality Not Based on Virtue, Happiness, or Consequences. Kant begins with a general account of willful decisions. The function of the human will is to select one course of action from among several possible courses. Our specific willful decisions are influenced by several factors, such as laziness, immediate emotional gratification, or what is best in the long run. Kant argues that in moral matters the will is ideally influenced only by rational considerations, and not by subjective considerations such as one's emotions. This is because morality involves what is *necessary* for us to do; for example, you *must* keep your promises; only rational considerations, he argues, can produce necessity.

For Kant, the rational consideration that influences the will must be a *principle* of obligation, since only principles can provide purely rational grounds for action. Also, the principle must be a *command* (or imperative) since morality involves a command for us to perform a particular action. Finally, the principle cannot be one that appeals to the consequences of an action. For example, Kant would reject the view that I should donate to charity merely because it brings happiness to the person receiving the money. The only principle that fulfills these requirements is the categorical imperative. This dictates that we act in a way that we could will to be universal—applying to all people—irrespective of our individual needs and wants. He argues that it is the principle that would be adopted by a good will.

FROM IMMANUEL KANT, *Groundwork of the Metaphysics of Morals* (1785)

Nothing can possibly be conceived in the world, or even out of it, which can be called good, without qualification, except a good will. Intelligence, wit, judgment, and the other *talents* of the mind, however they may be named, or courage, resolution, perseverance, as qualities of temperament, are undoubtedly good and desirable in many respects; but these gifts of nature may also become extremely bad and mischievous if the will which is to make use of them, and which, therefore, constitutes what is called *character,* is not good. It is the same with the *gifts* of *fortune*. Power, riches, honor, even health, and the general well-being and contentment with one's condition, which is called *happiness,* inspire pride, and often presumption, if there is not a good will to correct the influence of these on the mind, and with this also to rectify the whole principle of acting and adapt it to its end. The sight of a being who is not adorned with a single feature of a pure and good will, enjoying unbroken prosperity, can never give pleasure to an impartial rational spectator. Thus a good will appears to constitute the indispensable condition even of being worthy of happiness.

There are even some qualities which are of service to this good will itself and may facilitate its action, yet which have no intrinsic unconditional value, but always presuppose a good will, and this qualifies the esteem that we justly have for them and does not permit us to regard them as absolutely good. Moderation in the affections and passions, self-control, and calm deliberation are not only good in many respects, but even seem to constitute part of the intrinsic worth of the person; but they are far from deserving to be called good without qualification, although they have been so unconditionally praised by the ancients. For without the principles of a good will, they may become extremely bad, and the coolness of a villain not only makes him far more dangerous, but also directly makes him more abominable in our eyes than he would have been without it.

ASK YOURSELF

100. According to Kant, why is morality not a matter of either (a) having certain character traits, like courage, or (b) producing good results or consequences through our actions?

A good will is good not because of what it performs or effects, not by its aptness for the attainment of some proposed end, but simply by virtue of the volition; that is, it is good in itself, and considered by itself is to be esteemed much higher than all that can be brought about by it in favor of any inclination, nay even of the sum total of all inclinations. Even if it should happen that, owing to special disfavor of fortune, or the niggardly provision of a stepmotherly nature, this will should wholly lack power to accomplish its purpose, if with its greatest efforts it should yet achieve nothing, and there should remain only the good will (not, to be sure, a mere wish, but the summoning of all means in our power), then, like a jewel, it would still shine by its own light, as a thing which has its whole value in itself. Its usefulness or fruitfulness can neither add nor take away anything from this value. It would be, as it were, only the setting to enable us to handle it the more conveniently in common commerce, or to attract to it the attention of those who are not yet connoisseurs, but not to recommend it to true connoisseurs, or to determine its value.

ASK YOURSELF

101. For Kant, the will is the only thing that can be called "good" without qualification. What is it about the will that makes it good?

Hypothetical Versus Categorical Imperatives. Kant distinguishes between types of imperatives. Imperatives in general are commands that dictate a particular course of action, such as "you shall clean your room." Hypothetical imperatives are commands that depend on my preference for a particular end, and they are stated in conditional form, such as, "If I want to lose weight, then I should eat less." In this case, the command to eat less hinges on my previous preference to lose weight. However, hypothetical imperatives are simply not moral imperatives since the command is based on subjective considerations that are not absolute. A categorical imperative, by contrast, is an absolute command, such as "you shall treat people with respect," which is not based on subjective considerations. Thus, the supreme principle of morality is a categorical imperative since it is not conditional upon one's preferences.

The conception of an objective principle, insofar as it is obligatory for a will, is called a command (of reason), and the formula of the command is called an imperative.

Now all *imperatives* command either *hypothetically* or *categorically.* The former represent the practical necessity of a possible action as means to something else that is willed (or at least which one might possibly will). The categorical imperative would be that which represented an action as necessary of itself without reference to another end, i.e., as objectively necessary.

Since every practical law represents a possible action as good and, on this account, for a subject who is practically determinable by reason, necessary, all imperatives are formulae determining an action which is necessary according to the principle of a will good in some respects. If now the action is good only as a means to *something else,* then the imperative is *hypothetical;* if it is conceived as good *in itself* and consequently as being necessarily the principle of a will which of itself conforms to reason, then it is *categorical.*

Thus the imperative declares what action possible by me would be good and presents the practical rule in relation to a will which does not forthwith perform an action simply because it is good, whether because the subject does not always know that it is good, or because, even if it know this, yet its maxims might be opposed to the objective principles of practical reason.

When I conceive a hypothetical imperative, in general I do not know beforehand what it will contain until I am given the condition. But when I conceive a categorical imperative, I know at once what it contains. For as the imperative contains besides the law only the necessity that the maxims shall conform to this law, while the law contains no conditions restricting it, there remains nothing but the general statement that the maxim of the action should conform to a universal law, and it is this conformity alone that the imperative properly represents as necessary.

ASK YOURSELF

102. According to Kant, what kind of imperative is good only as a means to something else?

Kant next presents the single categorical imperative of morality: Act only on that maxim by which you can at the same time will that it should become a universal law.

There is therefore but one categorical imperative, namely, this: Act only on that maxim whereby you can at the same time will that it should become a universal law.

Now if all imperatives of duty can be deduced from this one imperative as from their principle, then, although it should remain undecided what is called duty is not merely a vain notion, yet at least we shall be able to show what we understand by it and what this notion means.

Although there is only one categorical imperative, Kant argues that there can be four formulations of this principle:

- The Formula of the Law of Nature: "Act as if the maxim of your action were to become through your will a universal law of nature."
- The Formula of the End Itself: "Act in such a way that you always treat humanity, whether in your own person or in the person of any other, never simply as a means, but always at the same time as an end."
- The Formula of Autonomy: "So act that your will can regard itself at the same time as making universal law through its maxims."
- The Formula of the Kingdom of Ends: "So act as if you were through your maxims a law-making member of a kingdom of ends."

According to Kant, each of these four formulations will produce the same conclusion regarding the morality of any particular action. Thus, each of these formulas offers a step-by-step procedure for determining the morality of any particular action. We will consider only the first two of these formulations here. Kant presents this first formulation is the most fundamental one.

The Formula of the Law of Nature. The formula of the law of nature provides a test for determining the morality or rightness of any act. I must ask whether the maxim of my action, which is a statement describing what I intend to do and giving the motive for it, could be consistently willed as a law of nature. If it can be willed consistently, then the action is moral. If not, then it is immoral. To illustrate this formulation, Kant uses four examples that cover the range of morally significant situations that arise. These examples include committing suicide, making false promises, failing to develop one's abilities, and refusing to be charitable. In each case, the action is deemed immoral since a contradiction arises when trying to will the maxim as a law of nature.

Since the universality of the law according to which effects are produced constitutes what is properly called *nature* in the most general sense (as to form), that is the existence of things so far as it is determined by general laws, the imperative of duty may be expressed thus:

Act as if the maxim of your action were to become by your will a universal law of nature.

We will now enumerate a few duties, adopting the usual division of them into duties to ourselves and ourselves and to others, and into perfect and imperfect duties.

1. A man reduced to despair by a series of misfortunes feels wearied of life, but is still so far in possession of his reason that he can ask himself whether it would not be contrary to his duty to himself to take his own life. Now he inquires whether the maxim of his action could become a universal law of nature. His maxim is: "From self-love I adopt it as a principle to shorten my life when its longer duration is likely to bring more evil than satisfaction." It is asked then simply whether this principle founded on self-love can become a universal law of nature. Now we see at once that a system of nature of which it should be a law to destroy life by means of the very feeling whose special nature it is to impel to the improvement of life would contradict itself and, therefore, could not exist as a system of nature; hence that maxim cannot possibly exist as a universal law of nature and, consequently, would be wholly inconsistent with the supreme principle of all duty.

103. In Kant's first formulation of the categorical imperative (i.e., the formula of the law of nature), what is the specific contradiction that arises in the suicide example?

2. Another finds himself forced by necessity to borrow money. He knows that he will not be able to repay it, but sees also that nothing will be lent to him unless he promises stoutly to repay it in a definite time. He desires to make this promise, but he has still so much conscience as to ask himself: "Is it not unlawful and inconsistent with duty to get out of a difficulty in this way?" Suppose however that he resolves to do so: then the maxim of his action would be expressed thus: "When I think myself in want of money, I will borrow money and promise to repay it, although I know that I never can do so." Now this principle of self-love or of one's own advantage may perhaps be consistent with my whole future welfare; but the question now is, "Is it right?" I change then the suggestion of self-love into a universal law, and state the question thus: "How would it be if my maxim were a universal law?" Then I see at once that it could never hold as a universal law of nature, but would necessarily contradict itself. For supposing it to be a universal law that everyone when he thinks himself in a difficulty should be able to promise whatever he pleases, with the purpose of not keeping his promise, the promise itself would become impossible, as well as the end that one might have in view in it, since no one would consider that anything was promised to him, but would ridicule all such statements as vain pretenses.

104. What contradiction arises in the example of the deceitful borrower?

Let us consider this particular example in more detail. I need money. I formulate a "maxim," a description of a possible action, including the reasons for it, namely "in order to get needed money, make a lying promise." I ask whether the lying promise would work as a means to my end, namely, getting money. Suppose it would. Then my maxim passes the test of rationality posed by a hypothetical imperative. Next, I check this maxim against the categorical imperative. I ask, "could this maxim be a universal law of nature?" Well, suppose that everyone, as if by natural necessity, should lie when promising, or even lie when promising to repay money. In that case, clearly there would be no promising, or promising to pay back money. But in that case I could no longer will the maxim even as hypothetical. Lying would not be a viable means to the end I seek. So I cannot even consistently *imagine* a coherent world in which my maxim becomes a universal law, like a law of nature. Kant thinks that that is one mark of an immoral maxim. You can see from this example some of the connections between being rational and being moral which Kant wants to establish. Morality requires rational consistency. It does not require producing good consequences, however. The badness of making a lying promise does not consist in the fact that it produces bad consequences. It might well produce very nice consequences, even for the person lied to!

3. A third finds in himself a talent which with the help of some culture might make him a useful man in many respects. But he finds himself in comfortable circumstances and prefers to indulge in pleasure rather than to take pains in enlarging and improving his happy natural capacities. He asks, however, whether his maxim of neglect of his natural gifts, besides agreeing with his inclination to indulgence, agrees also with what is called duty. He

sees then that a system of nature could indeed subsist with such a universal law although men (like the South Sea islanders) should let their talents rest and resolve to devote their lives merely to idleness, amusement, and propagation of their species—in a word, to enjoyment; but he cannot possibly *will* that this should be a universal law of nature, or be implanted in us as such by a natural instinct. For, as a rational being, he necessarily wills that his faculties be developed, since they serve him and have been given him, for all sorts of possible purposes.

ASK YOURSELF

105. What contradiction arises from the example of neglecting one's talents?

4. A fourth, who is in prosperity, while he sees that others have to contend with great wretchedness and that he could help them, thinks: "What concern is it of mine? Let everyone be as happy as Heaven pleases, or as he can make himself; I will take nothing from him nor even envy him, only I do not wish to contribute anything to his welfare or to his assistance in distress!" Now no doubt if such a mode of thinking were a universal law, the human race might very well subsist and doubtless even better than in a state in which everyone talks of sympathy and good-will, or even takes care occasionally to put it into practice, but, on the other side, also cheats when he can, betrays the rights of men, or otherwise violates them. But although it is possible that a universal law of nature might exist in accordance with that maxim, it is impossible to *will* that such a principle should have the universal validity of a law of nature. For a will which resolved this would contradict itself, inasmuch as many cases might occur in which one would have need of the love and sympathy of others, and in which, by such a law of nature, sprung from his own will, he would deprive himself of all hope of the aid he desires.

ASK YOURSELF

106. What contradiction arises in the example of failing to be charitable?

Let us consider this example a little further too. In this case my maxim is something like this: "Ignore the needs of others, in order to avoid interference with my own plans." Suppose now that all people at all times should by a kind of natural necessity never help anyone else. Now, unlike the case of the lying promise, I can consistently *conceive* a world like that. But, could I consistently *will* it? Only if I cease to will that I should sometimes be helped. But there are a great many ends which I can rationally pursue only by means of the help of others. For example, if I accidentally get trapped with a broken arm under a fallen tree limb, I may need someone else to lift it and help me. In such a case I could not rationally pursue the end of continuing to live, without relying on others. So if I am a rational being, I shall will that others sometimes help me. But if I universalize my maxim ("don't help others"), I will be willing that I not be helped. So here there is clearly a contradiction in *willing*. I cannot, being the sort of vulnerable being I am, consistently will this maxim, while continuing to will the sorts of things I naturally do will (such as staying alive). So "ignore the needs of others" does not pass the test imposed by the categorical imperative. For that imperative says, "Act as if the maxim of your action were to become by your will a universal law of nature."

Notice that what makes refusing to help those in need wrong is not that failing to do so would bring bad consequences. Even if, in attempting to help someone, I produce a bad consequence, such as injury to them, it would still be to my credit that I tried to help, and it would still be the case that the kind of action I attempted *must* be attempted by anyone deserving to be called good. Note also that the moral law does not tell me how much help I should give others. It certainly does not tell me that I have a duty to maximize benefit for others.

The Formula of the End Itself. The formula of the end itself is more straightforward than the previous one: Always treat people as an end and never only as a means. There are two points to this principle. First, when performing an action we should treat people as beings that are intrinsically valuable. Second, we should not use people as a means to achieve some further benefit. People have intrinsic value, Kant argues, because of their ability to act freely. This gives humans a level of dignity that other humans must respect.

Supposing, however, that there were something *whose existence* has *in itself* an absolute worth, something which, being *an end in itself,* could be a source of definite laws; then in this and this alone would lie the source of a possible categorical imperative, i.e., a practical law.

Now I say: Man and generally any rational being *exists* as an end in himself, *not merely as a means* to be arbitrarily used by this or that will, but in all his actions, whether they concern himself or other rational beings, must be always regarded at the same time as an end. All objects of the inclinations have only a conditional worth, for if the inclinations and the wants founded on them did not exist, then their object would be without value. But the inclinations, themselves being sources of want, are so far from having an absolute worth for which they should be desired that on the contrary it must be the universal wish of every rational being to be wholly free from them. Thus the worth of any object which is *to be acquired* by our action is always conditional. Beings whose existence depends not on our will but on nature's, have nevertheless, if they are irrational beings, only a relative value as means, and are therefore called *things;* rational beings, on the contrary, are called *persons,* because their very nature points them out as ends in themselves, that is as something which must not be used merely as means, and so far therefore restricts freedom of action (and is an object of respect). These, therefore, are not merely subjective ends whose existence has a worth *for us* as an effect of our action, *but objective ends,* that is, things whose existence is an end in itself; an end moreover for which no other can be substituted, which they should subserve *merely* as means, for otherwise nothing whatever would possess *absolute worth;* but if all worth were conditioned and therefore contingent, then there would be no supreme practical principle of reason whatever.

ASK YOURSELF

107. What is Kant's distinction between things and persons?

If then there is a supreme practical principle or, in respect of the human will, a categorical imperative, it must be one which, being drawn from the conception of that which is necessarily an end for everyone because it is *an end in itself,* constitutes an *objective* principle of will, and can therefore serve as a universal practical law. The foundation of this principle is: *rational nature exists as an end in itself.* Man necessarily conceives his own existence as being so; so far then this is a *subjective* principle of human actions. But every other rational being regards its existence similarly, just on the same rational principle that holds for me: so that it is at the same time an objective principle, from which as a supreme practical law all laws of the will must be capable of being deduced. Accordingly the practical imperative will be as follows:

> So act as to treat humanity, whether in your own person or in that of any other, in every case as an end, never as means only.

We will now inquire whether this can be practically carried out.

Examples. Using the same examples already given, Kant continues by showing how this formulation of the categorical imperative also confirms our basic duties.

To abide by the previous examples:

Firstly, under the head of necessary duty to oneself: He who contemplates suicide should ask himself whether his action can be consistent with the idea of humanity *as an end in itself.* If he destroys himself in order to escape from painful circumstances, he uses a person merely as *a mean* to maintain a tolerable condition up to the end of life. But a man is not a thing, that is to say, something which can be used merely as means, but must in all his actions be always considered as an end in himself. I cannot, therefore, dispose in any way of a man in my own person so as to mutilate him, to damage or kill him. (It belongs to ethics proper to define this principle more precisely, so as to avoid all misunderstanding, e.g., as to the amputation of the limbs in order to preserve myself, as to exposing my life to danger with a view to preserve it, etc. This question is therefore omitted here.)

ASK YOURSELF

108. With Kant's second formulation of the categorical imperative (i.e., the formula of the end itself), why is suicide wrong?

Secondly, as regards necessary duties, or those of strict obligation, towards others: He who is thinking of making a lying promise to others will see at once that he would be using another man *merely as a mean,* without the latter containing at the same time the end in himself. For he whom I propose by such a promise to use for my own purposes cannot possibly assent to my mode of acting towards him and, therefore, cannot himself contain the end of this action. This violation of the principle of humanity in other men is more obvious if we take in examples of attacks on the freedom and property of others. For then it is clear that he who transgresses the rights of men intends to use the person of others merely as a means, without considering that as rational beings they ought always to be esteemed also as ends, that is, as beings who must be capable of containing in themselves the end of the very same action.

ASK YOURSELF

109. Why would it be wrong to make a deceitful promise?

3. *PRIMA FACIE* DUTIES: WILLIAM D. ROSS

Suppose that you borrow a gun from your neighbor under the condition that you return it when he needs it. A few days later he knocks on your door, visibly distressed and muttering something about being unfairly fired by his boss. He then asks for the gun. What should you do? It seems that you're trapped between two basic duties. On the one hand, you have a duty to make good on your promise to return the weapon. On the other hand, you have a duty to avoid endangering the lives of others. This is a typical example of what philosophers call a "moral dilemma." In real life we have a way of resolving many moral dilemmas with little difficulty. In this case, for example, we simply shouldn't return the gun. Since at least part of our moral life involves handling moral dilemmas, we would expect moral theories to give us some guidance. Unfortunately, many classic theories are silent on the issue. We learn from Pufendorf that we have a duty to others to keep our agreements and another duty to others to avoid harming people. He doesn't tell us, however, which duty prevails if they come into conflict. Similarly, we learn from Kant that we violate the categorical imperative when breaking promises and when harming others, but the categorical imperative doesn't help us prioritize our options. British philosopher William David Ross (1877–1971) addressed this issue in his account of duty theory.

The Nature and Number of Our Duties. Like earlier duty theorists, Ross believes that understanding our duties is an intuitive process, and part of this moral intuition involves determining which of two duties is the strongest in a particular situation. He clarifies this intuitive process by distinguishing between *prima facie* duties and actual duties. The term *prima facie* is Latin for first appearance, and it is an expression borrowed from the legal profession; we presume some contention to be *prima facie* true unless it is disproved by a fact to the contrary. In the context of moral obligations, Ross holds that *prima facie* duties are those that we presume to have—such as keeping promises—unless they are outweighed by a stronger duty—such as the duty to avoid endangering the lives of others. Once we pinpoint the stronger duty, that then becomes our *actual* duty, and the weaker one thereby becomes no duty at all.

FROM WILLIAM DAVID ROSS, *The Right and the Good* (1930), CHAPTER 2

When I am in a situation, as perhaps I always am, in which more than one of these *prima facie* duties is incumbent on me, what I have to do is to study the situation as fully as I can until I form the considered opinion (it is never more) that in the circumstances one of them is more incumbent than any other; then I am bound to think that to do this *prima facie* duty is my duty *sans phrase* [or actual duty] in the situation.

I suggest "prima facie duty" or "conditional duty" way of referring to the characteristic (quite distinct from that of being a duty proper) which an act has, in virtue of being of a certain kind (e.g. the keeping of a promise), of being an act which would be a duty proper if it were not at the same time of another kind which is morally significant. Whether an act is a duty proper or actual duty depends on all the morally significant kinds it is an instance of The phrase *"Prima facie* duty" must be apologized for, since (1) it suggests that what we are speaking of is a certain kind of duty, whereas it is in fact not a duty, but something related in a special way to duty. Strictly speaking, we want not a phrase in which duty is qualified by an adjective, but a separate noun. (2) *"Prima facie"* suggests that one is speaking only of an appearance which a moral situation presents at first sight, and which may turn out to be illusory; whereas what I am speaking of is an objective fact involved in the nature of the situation, or more strictly in an element of its nature, though not, as duty proper does, arising from its *whole* nature. I can, however, think of no term which fully meets the case. "Claim" has been suggested by Professor Prichard. The word "claim" has the advantage of being quite a familiar one in this connection, and it seems to cover much of the ground. It would be quite natural to say, "a person to whom I have made a promise has a claim on me," and also, "a person whose distress I could relieve (at the cost of breaking the promise) has a claim on me." But (1) while "claim" is appropriate from *their* point of view, we want a word to express the corresponding fact from the agent's point of view—the fact of his being, subject to claims that can be made against him; and ordinary language provides us with no such correlative to "claim." And (2) (what is more important) "claim" seems inevitably to suggest two persons, one of whom might make a claim on the other; and while this covers the ground of social duty, it is inappropriate in the case of that important part of duty which is the duty of cultivating a certain kind of character in oneself. It would be artificial, I think, and at any rate metaphorical, to say that one's character has a claim on oneself.

ASK YOURSELF

110. Technically speaking, according to Ross, *prima facie* duties are not duties at all but merely suggest the appearance of duty "which may turn out to be _____."

Unlike Kant, who believes that our moral obligations are grounded in a single rule of duty, Ross argues that there are several foundational duties—six in total. In this regard, Ross's account of duties is closer to Pufendorf's. In fact, most of the duties that Ross describes have some counterpart in Pufendorf's list.

There is nothing arbitrary about these *prima facie* duties. Each rests on a definite circumstance which cannot seriously be held to be without moral significance. Of *prima facie* duties I suggest, without claiming completeness or finality for it, the following division.

(1) Some duties rest on previous acts of my own. These duties seem to include two kinds: (a) Those resting on a promise or what may fairly be called an implicit promise, such as the implicit undertaking not to tell lies which seems to be implied in the act of entering into conversation (at any rate by civilized men), or of writing books that purport to be history and not fiction. These may be called the duties of fidelity. (b) Those resting on a previous wrongful act. These may be called the duties of reparation. (2) Some rest on previous acts of other men, i.e. services done by them to me. These may be loosely described as the duties of "gratitude." (3) Some rest on the fact or possibility of a distribution of pleasure or happiness (or of the means thereto) which is not in accordance with the merit of the persons concerned; in such cases there arises a duty to upset or prevent such a distribution. These are the duties of justice. (4) Some rest on the mere fact that there are other beings in the world whose condition we can make better in respect of virtue, or of intelligence, or of pleasure. These are the duties of beneficence. (5) Some rest on the fact that we can improve our own condition in respect of virtue or of intelligence. These are the duties of self-improvement. (6) I think that we should distinguish from (4) the duties that may be summed up under the title of "not injuring others." No doubt to injure others is incidentally to fail to do them good; but it seems to me clear that non-maleficence is apprehended as a duty distinct from that of beneficence, and as a duty of a more stringent character. It will be noticed that this alone among the types of duty has been stated in a negative way. An attempt might no doubt be made to state this duty, like the others, in a positive way. It might be said that it is really the duty to prevent ourselves from acting either from an inclination to harm others or from an inclination to seek our own

pleasure, in doing which we should incidentally harm them. But on reflection it seems clear that the primary duty here is the duty not to harm others, this being a duty whether or not we have an inclination that if followed would lead to our harming them; and that when we have such an inclination the primary duty not to harm others gives rise to a consequential duty to resist the inclination. The recognition of this duty of non-maleficence is the first step on the way to the recognition of the duty of beneficence; and that accounts for the prominence of the commands "thou shalt not kill," "thou shalt not commit adultery," "thou shalt not steal," "thou shalt not bear false witness" in so early a code as the Decalogue. But even when we have come to recognize the duty of beneficence, it appears to me that the duty of non-maleficence is recognized as a distinct one and as *prima facie* more binding. We should not in general consider it justifiable to kill one person in order to keep another alive, or to steal from one in order to give alms to another.

ASK YOURSELF

111. Consider the example of a moral dilemma discussed above regarding your distressed neighbor who wants you to return his gun. What are the two *prima facie* duties involved here?

Rationally Apprehending Our Duty. We noted that a distinctive feature of duty theory is the contention that we naturally know our principal duties through a rational intuition. Ross argues that our apprehension of duties involves two distinct intuitions. The first involves our initial apprehension of the six principal *prima facie* duties, which, he contends, is self-evident. Like previous duty theorists, he believes that we intuitively apprehend these in the same way that we do mathematical principles.

Something should be said of the relation between our apprehension of the *prima facie* rightness of certain types of act and our mental attitude towards particular acts. It is proper to use the word "apprehension" in the former case and not in the latter. That an act, *qua* fulfilling a promise, or *qua* effecting a just distribution of good, or *qua* returning services rendered, or qua promoting the good of others, or *qua* promoting the virtue or insight of the agent, is *prima facie* right, is self-evident; not in the sense that it is evident from the beginning of our lives, or as soon as we attend to the proposition for the first time, but in the sense that when we have reached sufficient mental maturity and have given sufficient attention to the proposition it is evident without any need of proof, or of evidence beyond itself. It is self-evident just as a mathematical axiom, or the validity of a form of inference, is evident. The moral order expressed in these propositions is just as much part of the fundamental nature of the universe (and, we may add, of any possible universe in which there were moral agents at all) as is the spatial or numerical structure expressed in the axioms of geometry or arithmetic. In our confidence that these propositions are true there is involved the same trust in our reason that is involved in our confidence in mathematics; and we should have no justification for trusting it in the latter sphere and distrusting it in the former. In both cases we are dealing with propositions that cannot be proved, but that just as certainly need no proof. . . .

ASK YOURSELF

112. Ross believes that there is a moral order underlying our duties that is "part of the fundamental nature of the universe." Is Ross's position more like Plato's or more like Sextus Empiricus's—as discussed at the outset of this chapter?

The second intuition involves our ability to resolve moral dilemmas and determine which of two competing duties is our actual one. This intuition, however, does not rise to the level of self-evident certainty; instead, it is only a matter of probability, like our ability to judge aesthetic beauty.

Our judgements about our actual duty in concrete situations have none of the certainty that attaches to our recognition of the general principles of duty. A statement is certain, i.e. is an expression of knowledge, only in one or other of two cases: when it is either self-evident, or a valid conclusion from self-evident premises. And our judgments about our particular duties have neither of these characters. (1) They are not self-evident. Where a possible act is seen to have two characteristics, in virtue of one of which it is *prima facie* right, and in virtue of the other *prima facie* wrong, we are (I think) well aware that we are not certain whether we ought or ought not to do it; that whether we do it or not, we are taking a moral risk. We come in the long run, after consideration, to think one duty more pressing than the other, but we do not feel certain that it is so. And though we do not always recognize that a possible act has two such characteristics, and though there *may* be cases in which it has not, we are never certain that any particular possible act has not, and therefore never certain that it is right, nor certain that it is wrong. For, to go no further in the analysis, it is enough to point out that any particular act will in all probability in the course of time contribute to the bringing about of good or of evil for many human beings, and thus have a *prima facie* rightness or wrongness of which we know nothing. (2) Again, our judgments about our particular duties are not logical conclusions from self-evident premises. The only possible premises would be the general principles stating their *prima facie* rightness or wrongness *qua* having the different characteristics they do have; and even if we could (as we cannot) apprehend the extent to which an act will tend on the one hand, for example, to bring about advantages for our benefactors, and on the other hand to bring about disadvantages for fellow men who are not our benefactors, there is no principle by which we can draw the conclusion that it is on the whole right or on the whole wrong. In this respect the judgment as to the rightness of a particular act is just like the judgment as to the beauty of a particular natural object or work of art. A poem is, for instance, in respect of certain qualities beautiful and in respect of certain others not beautiful; and our judgment as to the degree of beauty it possesses on the whole is never reached by logical reasoning from the apprehension of its particular beauties or particular defects. Both in this and in the moral case we have more or less probable opinions which are not logically justified conclusions from the general principles that are recognized as self-evident.

> **ASK YOURSELF**
>
> **113.** For Ross, the rational ability to apprehend our actual duty in a moral dilemma is similar to our judgment about whether a poem is or is not beautiful. According to Ross, do we make such judgments using logical reasoning?

4. DUTIES TOWARD ANIMALS: KANT AND REGAN

One New Year's Eve, an 18-year-old boy sprayed the family parakeet with hairspray and then set it on fire. Many laws today protect the interests of animals and, in this case, the boy was arrested on animal cruelty charges and faced a penalty of up to two years in prison.

What, morally speaking, justifies such a stiff penalty? Duty theorists have addressed this issue but have come up with different answers. The heart of the debate is a distinction between direct duties and indirect duties. For example, I have a direct duty to avoid slandering you because of the harm that I would directly cause you by doing so. On the other hand, I have only an indirect duty to avoid slandering your deceased grandfather. My obligation cannot be connected with your grandfather himself since he is no longer alive; my obligation, instead, is based on the harm that I would cause you and his other surviving relatives. Kant argued that duties toward animals are only indirect: Animals themselves are not entitled to direct obligations since they are irrational and are at best only items of property. The duties that we owe animals, such as the parakeet in the above story, are based only on how our treatment of them affects human beings and not on any pain that the animal itself might experience. Animal behavior, according to Kant, exhibits some similarities with human behavior, and by being cruel to animals we desensitize ourselves to human decency, so that gives another reason for not being cruel to them.

> [S]o far as animals are concerned, we have no direct duties. Animals are not self-conscious and are there merely as a means to an end. That end is man. We can ask, "Why do animals exist?" But to ask, "Why does man exist?" is a meaningless question. Our duties towards animals are merely indirect duties towards humanity. Animal nature has analogies to human nature, and by doing our duties to animals in respect of manifestations which correspond to manifestations of human nature, we indirectly do our duty towards humanity. Thus, if a dog has served his master long and faithfully, his service, on the analogy of human service, deserves reward, and when the dog has grown too old to serve, his master ought to keep him until he dies. Such action helps to support us in our duties towards human beings, where they are bounden duties.
>
> If then any acts of animals are analogous to human acts and spring from the same principles, we have duties towards the animals because thus we cultivate the corresponding duties towards human beings. If a man shoots his dog because the animal is no longer capable of service, he does not fail in his duty to the dog, for the dog cannot judge, but his act is inhuman and damages in himself that humanity which it is his duty to show towards mankind. If he is not to stifle his human feelings, he must practice kindness towards animals, for he who is cruel to animals becomes hard also in his dealings with men. [From Immanuel Kant, "Duties Towards Animals" (1775)]

ASK YOURSELF

114. How, according to Kant, does cruelty to animals damage a person's humanity?

Contemporary philosopher Tom Regan believes that views such as Kant's are horribly misguided. It presumes that animals are not conscious creatures and thus not capable of experiencing pain.

> Such views may be called indirect duty views. By way of illustration: suppose your neighbor kicks your dog. Then your neighbor has done something wrong. But not to your dog. The wrong that has been done is a wrong to you. After all, it is wrong to upset people, and your neighbor's kicking your dog upsets you. So you are the one who is wronged, not your dog. . . . How could someone try to justify such a view? Someone might say that your dog doesn't feel anything and so isn't hurt by your neighbor's kick, doesn't care about the pain since none is felt, is as unaware of anything as is your windshield. Someone might say this,

but no rational person will, since, among other considerations, such a view will commit anyone who holds it to the position that no human being feels pain either—that human beings also don't care about what happens to them. [From Tom Regan, "The Case for Animal Rights" (1985)]

ASK YOURSELF

115. According to Regan, why must we dismiss the view that animals are incapable of feeling pain?

According to Regan, we have direct duties to many animals for the same reasons that we have direct duties toward humans; that is, humans and many animals have psychological capacities, such as having preferences, beliefs, feelings, recollections, and expectations. These are features that give any creature a direct moral standing.

SUMMING UP THE ISSUE OF MORAL DUTY

Philosophers and theologians have commonly felt that human beings are endowed with intuitive—or instinctive—notions of moral obligation. In the seventeenth century, Pufendorf systematized this view by dividing all duties between those to God, oneself, and others. Kant agreed that we have rationally intuitive notions of moral obligation, but argued that they arose from a single rational moral principle that he called the "categorical imperative." Unlike hypothetical imperatives—nonmoral obligations that arise from personal preferences—the categorical imperative is absolute and rules out appeals to people's desires and other inclinations. Kant believes that there is only one categorical imperative, but that it can be expressed in four different ways. One version, the Formula of the Law of Nature, is "Act as if the maxim of your action were to become through your will a universal law of nature." The Formula of the End Itself is "Act in such a way that you always treat humanity, whether in your own person or in the person of any other, never simply as a means, but always at the same time as an end." The rationale underlying this principle is respect: Human beings have a special dignity because of their ability to act freely on principles, and we must respect this in all people. Like Pufendorf and Kant, Ross believed that we have intuitive notions of duty, but he felt that more needs to be said about how to handle conflicting obligations. We might, for example, be in a situation in which telling the truth causes great harm to someone. According to Ross, we have six fundamental duties that are *prima facie* valid; when two come into conflict, the stronger duty becomes our actual obligation, and the weaker one becomes no duty at all. Duty theorists have varying rationales for the ethical treatment of animals. Kant argued that we have only an indirect obligation toward animals based on how cruel treatment weakens our sense of humanity. Regan argued that our obligation is direct because animals indeed experience pain and are capable of other mental states that give them moral status.

CAN OF WORMS

A central assumption behind duty theory is that we have intuitive conceptions of moral obligation. This involves an epistemological claim that rationalists and empiricists battled over since the seventeenth century—namely the claim that we have innate ideas. Rationalists have tended to endorse both innate ideas and duty theory.

Rejecting these notions, empiricists argued that all knowledge—including knowledge of moral obligation—rest on emotional and sensory experiences. The same dilemmas regarding innate ideas emerge when considering intuitive duties: What are the exact principles that we know innately? How do we explain the fact that not everyone has the same notions? Can we better account for these principles empirically without depending on the elusive notions of "innateness" and "intuition"? It is evident then that duty theory is tangled up from the start with epistemological disputes.

G. PLEASURE AND CONSEQUENCES

Let's look again at an example that we used earlier: You look out your window one evening and to your extreme chagrin, see someone steal your car. The virtue theorist may account for such a reaction by trying to show how stealing, which is a species of injustice and thus a vice, is destructive of what is good in individuals and societies. According to duty theory, the thief is immoral for failing to follow basic foundational moral duties that we know intuitively—specifically, the duty not to steal. There is yet a third basic approach to assessing the thief's behavior and our reaction to it: The action is morally wrong because it results in more unhappiness than happiness.

QUESTIONS TO DISCUSS

a. Many philosophers have argued that pleasure is our ultimate aim in life. Can you think of something you desire that is not connected with any kind of pleasure?

b. List all of the negative and positive consequences that might result from a crime such as a successful bank robbery, and determine whether the negative consequences outweigh the positive ones.

c. Human pleasures are often categorized into two groups, namely lower pleasures, such as those experienced when eating a good meal, and higher pleasures, such as those experienced when playing a challenging game of chess. Can you think of some pleasures that seem to be both lower and higher at the same time?

Philosophers today call this general strategy "consequentialism" insofar as moral rightness is grounded solely in the foreseeable consequences of our conduct—not in intuitively grasped duties. Like theories of virtue and duty, consequentialism has a long tradition in the history of philosophy with three distinct versions standing out. First, there is a theory now called "ethical egoism" that holds that an action is morally right if the foreseeable consequences of that action are more favorable than unfavorable *only to the agent* performing the action. Second there is the theory of "ethical altruism," namely, that an action is morally right if the foreseeable consequences of that action are overall more favorable than unfavorable *to everyone except the agent*. Finally, there is "utilitarianism": An action is morally right if the foreseeable consequences of that action are more favorable than unfavorable *to everyone* who might be affected by that action. The differences between these three theories is simply a matter of whose interests count: only mine, only people other than myself, or everyone who is affected.

1. HEDONISTIC ETHICAL EGOISM: EPICURUS

An early writer who influenced the development of consequentialism was the ancient Greek philosopher Epicurus (341–270 BCE), who founded the philosophical school of Epicureanism. Two features of his ethical theory stand out. First, Epicurus believed that experiences of pleasure and pain were foundational for ethics. This component of Epicurus's theory is called "hedonism"—based on the Greek word *hedone,* meaning "pleasure." Second, Epicurus appears to have advocated a kind of egoism. The principal pleasures and pains that count are those experienced by the person performing the action, and not those of affected people. The combination of these two features made Epicurus's theory controversial, both in his own day and for centuries to come. This is because Epicurus appears to be telling us to maximize pleasure in life—eat, drink, and be merry—and forget about anything else. That's not a particularly admirable foundation for a moral theory! However, Epicurus does not advocate self-indulgence. Epicurus recognized that there was a point of diminishing returns in our pursuit of pleasure: If we indulge too much, we bring on pain, such as the pain of a bloated stomach from overeating or a hangover from overdrinking. Moderation is the key to happiness. Epicurus felt that it was more important to reduce pains in our lives than it was to heap on pleasures. The ideal life for Epicurus, then, was far from that of the drunken party-goer.

Pleasure and Pain. According to Epicurus, pleasure is the goal that nature has ordained for us. It is also the standard by which we judge everything good. However, we need to be cautious in pursuing pleasures. Specifically, we should seek a pleasure only when it pains us if we don't have it.

FROM EPICURUS, *Letter to Menoecius*

We should keep bearing in mind that the future is neither wholly ours nor wholly not ours, so that we neither entirely expect its sure occurrence, nor give up hope as though it were entirely beyond reach.

We must consider that some desires are inborn, some vain, and of those inborn some are necessary and others inborn only. Of those which are necessary some are necessary for *eudaimonia* [i.e., happiness], some for bodily repose, others for life itself. Now undisturbed contemplation of these matters enables us to bring back all choice and avoidance into the service of bodily health and *ataraxia* [mental repose], for such is the goal of the blessed life. Thanks to these we perform all our actions, so as to feel neither distress nor fright. Once this is the case for us, the tempest of the soul is dispersed so that the living being does not have to proceed as though lacking something nor seek something different by which he might fulfill the good of body and soul. For we have need of pleasure when we feel distress at its absence, but when we are not distressed we are no longer addicted to pleasure. Accordingly we count pleasure as the originating principle and the goal of the blessed life. For we recognize pleasure as the first and fitting good, for from it proceeds all choice and avoidance, and we return to it as the feeling-standard by which we judge every good.

ASK YOURSELF

116. Give an example of a pleasure that we should forego, since the absence of that pleasure would cause us no pain.

Even though we should pursue pleasure and reduce pain, we should not actively pursue every pleasure nor actively avoid every pain. Sometimes, we improve the overall balance of pleasure by accepting some pains, such as those that might result from a trip to the dentist. Furthermore, the fewer desires we have, the more easily we can be pleased.

But since pleasure is the first and natural good, for this very reason we do not choose every pleasure, but pass over many where great discomfort for us follows from them. And we consider many pains to be better than pleasure, since a greater pleasure comes to us after enduring distress for a long time. Every pleasure is good by natural kinship to us, yet not all are to be chosen, even as all distress is bad, yet not all is of such a nature as to be avoided. By calculating the advantages and disadvantages, one will look to make a judgment on all these things. For sometimes we treat the good as bad, and conversely the bad as good. Therefore habituation to plain things rather than luxuries produces complete health, and makes a person fit for the exigencies of life and disposes us better when approaching luxuries after long intervals [without them], and prepares us to be without fear in the face of contingency.

We consider self-sufficiency a great good not because we always prefer having few things, but so that, where we lack plenty, we may use what little we have in the genuine conviction that those enjoy the sweetest luxuries who need them least, and that all that is natural is easily obtained, while vain things are difficult to attain. So, when all the pain of need is removed, plain flavors bring us pleasure equal to that of gourmet dining. Bread and water give the highest pleasure when set before one who needs them.

When therefore we declare pleasure to be the goal, we do not refer to the pleasures of profligates and those at ease in enjoyments, as some think who are ignorant and disagree or scarcely get the point, but rather we refer to the absence of bodily pain and mental disturbance. For it is not continuous drinking and reveling or indulgences in boys and women, nor fish and all the rest born by a rich table, which produce a pleasant life, but rather sober reasoning, searching out the grounds of all choice and avoidance, and extirpating opinion, from which the greatest disturbance of the soul proceeds.

ASK YOURSELF

117. Since pleasure is "our first and native good," it might seem that we should eat, drink, and be merry and really live it up. Why would Epicurus disagree?

2. UTILITARIAN CALCULUS: JEREMY BENTHAM

Jeremy Bentham (1748–1832) was an important moral and political philosopher of the late eighteenth and early nineteenth centuries. He studied law, but never practiced it; instead he devoted much of his life to writing on issues of legal reform. Influenced by early discussions of moral theory, particularly Hume's, he developed one of the first systematic expositions of the utilitarian moral theory. According to Bentham, the pleasing or painful consequences of actions are the only relevant factor in assessing their moral worth. The most unique aspect of his theory is his method for precisely quantifying pleasures and pains, better known as the utilitarian calculus. The complete range of pleasing and painful consequences of actions, he believes, can be quantified according to specific criteria. Like Epicurus, Bentham advocated the hedonistic view that pleasure is our ultimate goal in life, and moral conduct is that which brings about a greater balance of pleasure over pain. However, Bentham departed from Epicurus's egoism and argued that we must consider the pleasurable and painful consequences of all people who are affected, not just ourselves.

FROM JEREMY BENTHAM, *Principles of Morals and Legislation* (1789), CHAPTERS 1 AND 4

1.1. Nature has placed humankind under the governance of two sovereign masters, *pain* and *pleasure*. It is for them alone to point out what we ought to do, as well as to determine what we shall do. On the one hand the standard of right and wrong, on the other the chain of causes and effects, are fastened to their throne. They govern us in all we do, in all we say, in all we think: every effort we can make to throw off our subjection, will serve but to demonstrate and confirm it. In words a man may pretend to abjure their empire: but in reality he will remain subject to it all the while. The *principle of utility* recognizes this subjection, and assumes it for the foundation of that system, the object of which is to rear the fabric of felicity by the hands of reason and of law. Systems which attempt to question it, deal in sounds instead of sense, in caprice instead of reason, in darkness instead of light.

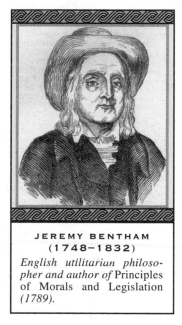

JEREMY BENTHAM (1748–1832)
English utilitarian philosopher and author of Principles of Morals and Legislation *(1789).*

1.3. By utility is meant that property in any object, whereby it tends to produce benefit, advantage, pleasure, good, or happiness (all this in the present case comes to the same thing), or (what comes again to the same thing) to prevent the happening of mischief, pain, evil, or unhappiness to the party whose interest is considered: if that party be the community in general, then the happiness of the community: if a particular individual, then the happiness of that individual.

1.4. The interest of the community is one of the most general expressions that can occur in the phraseology of morals: no wonder that the meaning of it is often lost. When it has meaning, it is this. The community is a fictitious *body,* composed of the individual persons who are considered as constituting as it were its *members.* The interest of the community then is, what?—the sum of the interests of the several members who compose it.

1.5. It is in vain to talk of the interest of the community, without understanding what is the interest of the individual. A thing is said to promote the interest, or to be *for* the interest, of an individual, when it tends to add to the sum total of his pleasures: or, what comes to the same thing, to diminish the sum total of his pains.

1.6. An action then may be said to be conformable to the principle of utility, or, for shortness sake, to utility (meaning with respect to the community at large), when the tendency it has to augment the happiness of the community is greater than any it has to diminish it.

1.7. A measure of government (which is but a particular kind of action, performed by a particular person or persons) may be said to be conformable to or dictated by the principle of utility, when in like manner the tendency which it has to augment the happiness of the community is greater than any which it has to diminish it.

118. State in one sentence what Bentham means by the principle of utility.

Bentham argued that we need to perform a numerical calculation for each morally significant action under consideration. For example, if a thief steals my car, we can supposedly determine the wrongness of that action by balancing the pleasures and pains that result from it. Specifically, by stealing my car the thief may have caused more pain for my family and me than can be outweighed by the pleasure gained for himself. The thief will also have created a certain amount of pain for himself as he attempts to dodge the police and is, perhaps, caught. The pleasure that he gains, by contrast, may be minimal and short-lived. Bentham explains that seven specific factors are involved when calculating the total amounts of pleasure and pain resulting from any action.

4.1. Pleasures then, and the avoidance of pains, are the ends which the legislator has in view: it behoves him therefore to understand their *value*. Pleasures and pains are the *instruments* he has to work with: it behoves him therefore to understand their force, which is again, in other words, their value.

4.2. To a person considered *by himself,* the value of a pleasure or pain considered *by itself,* will be greater or less, according to the four following circumstances: (1) its *intensity;* (2) its *duration;* (3) its *certainty* or *uncertainty;* (4) its *propinquity* or *remoteness.*

4.3. These are the circumstances which are to be considered in estimating a pleasure or a pain considered each of the m by itself. But when the value of any pleasure or pain is considered for the purpose of estimating the tendency of any *act* by which it is produced, there are two other circumstances to be taken into the account; these are: (5) its *fecundity,* or the chance it has of being followed by sensations of the *same* kind—that is, pleasures if it be a pleasure, pains if it be a pain; (6) its *purity,* or the chance it has of *not* being followed by sensations of the *opposite* kind—that is, pains if it be a pleasure, pleasures if it be a pain.

These two last, however, are in strictness scarcely to be deemed properties of the pleasure or the pain itself; they are not, therefore, in strictness to be taken into the account of the value of that pleasure or that pain. They are in strictness to be deemed properties only of the act, or other event, by which such pleasure or pain has been produced; and accordingly are only to be taken into the account of the tendency of such act or such event.

4.4. To a *number* of persons, with reference to each of whom the value of a pleasure or a pain is considered, it will be greater or less, according to seven circumstances: to wit, the six preceding ones; *viz.* (1) its *intensity;* (2) its *duration;* (3) its *certainty* or *uncertainty;* (4) its *propinquity* or *remoteness;* (5) its *fecundity;* (6) its *purity.* And one other; to wit: (7) its *extent;* that is, the number of persons to whom it extends; or (in other words) who are affected by it.

119. Suppose that a thief steals my car. On a scale of 1–10, give numerical values to factors 1–5 regarding the pleasure that the thief would experience.

120. Factor 6 in Bentham's calculus involves any pain that the thief might experience from stealing the car (Bentham states that each pain would have to be separately evaluated based on criteria 1–5). What kind of pain might the thief experience from his conduct?

3. UTILITARIANISM AND HIGHER PLEASURES: JOHN STUART MILL

John Stuart Mill (1806–1873) was a brilliant child, whose father started him in the study of Greek at age three and Latin at eight. He was a member of parliament from 1865 to 1868 and wrote on a variety of philosophical and political subjects. By Mill's time, utilitarianism was a comparatively popular moral theory, due largely to the writings of the earlier British utilitarian philosophers, particularly Bentham and William Paley. In 1861 he published a short defense of utilitarianism, which quickly became the principal articulation of that theory. Mill does not claim originality for his theory and, in fact, maintains that he is articulating many of the views of Epicurus and Bentham.

Inductive Versus Intuitive School of Ethics. Mill argues that moral theories are divided between two distinct approaches: the intuitive and inductive schools—that is, duty theories

Simultaneously, both Socrates and the pig
realized that they were standing in a mud pit.

and consequentialist theories. By Mill's day, Pufendorf's duty theory was overshadowed by Kant's and, from Mill's perspective, duty theorists and consequentialists both agreed that there is a single and highest moral principle. They only disagreed about whether we have knowledge of that principle intuitively (without appeal to experience) or inductively (through experience and observation).

FROM JOHN STUART MILL, *Utilitarianism* (1861), CHAPTERS 1 AND 2

The intuitive, no less than what may be termed the inductive, school of ethics, insists on the necessity of general laws. They both agree that the morality of an individual action is not a question of direct perception, but of the application of a law to an individual case. They recognize also, to a great extent, the same moral laws, but differ as to their evidence, and the source from which they derive their authority. According to the one opinion, the principles of morals are evident *a priori;* requiring nothing to command assent, except that the meaning of the terms be understood. According to the other doctrine, right and wrong, as well as truth and falsehood, are questions of observation and experience. But both hold equally, that morality must be deduced from principles; and the intuitive school affirm, as strongly as the inductive, that there is a science of morals. Yet they seldom attempt to make out a list of the *a priori* principles which are to serve as the premises of the science; still more rarely do they make any effort to reduce those various principles to one first principle, or common ground of obligation. They either assume the ordinary precepts of morals as of *a priori* authority, or they lay down as the common groundwork of those maxims some generality much less obviously authoritative than the maxims themselves, and which has never succeeded in gaining popular acceptance. Yet, to support their pretensions, there ought either to be some one fundamental principle or law at the root of all morality; or, if there be several, there should be a determinate order of precedence among them; and the one principle, or the rule for deciding between the various principles when they conflict, ought to be self-evident.

ASK YOURSELF

122. What are some of the problems that Mill finds with intuitionist theories of duty?

Against the intuitive school, Mill criticizes Kant's categorical imperative noting that it is essentially the same as utilitarianism since it involves calculating the good or bad consequences of an action to determine its morality.

It is not my present purpose to criticize these thinkers; but I cannot help referring, for illustration, to a systematic treatise by one of the most illustrious of them—the "Metaphysics of Ethics," by Kant. This remarkable man, whose system of thought will long remain one of the landmarks in the history of philosophical speculation, does the treatise in question, lay down an universal first principle as the origin and ground of moral obligation. It is this: "So act, that the rule on which thou actest would admit of being adopted as a law by all rational beings." But, when he begins to deduce from this precept any of the actual duties of morality, he fails, almost grotesquely, to show that there would be any contradiction, any logical (not to say physical) impossibility, in the adoption by all rational beings of the most outrageously immoral rules of conduct. All he shows is that the *consequences* of their universal adoption would be such as no one would choose to incur.

On the present occasion, I shall, without further discussion of the other theories, attempt to contribute something towards the understanding and appreciation of the Utilitarian or Happiness theory, and towards such proof as it is susceptible of.

ASK YOURSELF

123. According to Kant's categorical imperative, wrong actions are those that cannot be willed universally without contradiction. Contrary to Kant, what, for Mill, is the only thing that the categorical imperative shows about wrong actions?

Having rejected the theory of intuitive duty and, specifically, Kant's categorical imperative, Mill defends the inductive utilitarian approach.

The creed which accepts, as the foundation of morals, Utility, or the Greatest Happiness Principle, holds that actions are right in proportion as they tend to promote happiness, wrong as they tend to produce the reverse of happiness. By happiness is intended pleasure and the absence of pain; by unhappiness, pain and the privation of pleasure. To give a clear view of the moral standard set up by the theory, much more requires to be said; in particular, what things it includes in the ideas of pain and pleasure, and to what extent this is left an open question. But these supplementary explanations do not affect the theory of life on which this theory of morality is grounded—namely, that pleasure, and freedom from pain, are the only things desirable as ends; and that all desirable things (which are as numerous in the utilitarian as in any other scheme) are desirable either for the pleasure inherent in themselves, or as means to the promotion of pleasure and the prevention of pain.

Higher and Lower Pleasures. Mill departed from Bentham by emphasizing an important difference between types of pleasures. On the one hand, there are lower bodily pleasures that to a large degree humans share with the animal world, such as the pleasures of good food and other physical gratifications. On the other hand, there are higher intellectual pleasures that are unique to humans, such as pleasures associated with literature, art, music, philosophy, science, and other areas of mental cultivation. According to Mill, utilitarianism isn't simply a quest for maximizing any pleasure; although we should not denounce lower pleasures, our principal aim should be to maximize the higher intellectual ones.

Now, such a theory of life excites in many minds, and among them in some of the most estimable in feeling and purpose, inveterate dislike. To suppose that life has (as they express it) no higher end than pleasure—no better and nobler object of desire and pursuit—they designate as utterly mean and groveling; as a doctrine worthy only of swine, to whom the followers of Epicurus were, at a very early period, contemptuously likened; and modern holders of the doctrine are occasionally made the subject of equally polite comparisons by its German, French, and English assailants.

When thus attacked, the Epicureans have always answered, that it is not they, but their accusers, who represent human nature in a degrading light, since the accusation supposes human beings to be capable of no pleasures except those of which swine are capable. If this supposition were true, the charge could not be gainsaid, but would then be no longer an imputation; for, if the sources of pleasure were precisely the same to human beings and to swine, the rule of life which is good enough for the one would be wood enough for the other. The comparison of the Epicurean life to that of beasts is felt as degrading, precisely because a beast's pleasures do not satisfy a human being's conceptions of happiness. Human beings have faculties more elevated than the animal appetites; and, when once made conscious of them, do not regard any thing as happiness which does not include their gratification. I do not, indeed, consider the Epicureans to have been by any means faultless in drawing out their scheme of consequences from the utilitarian principle. To do this in any sufficient manner, many Stoic as well as Christian elements require to be included.

ASK YOURSELF

124. How have Epicureans responded to the accusation that they propose a doctrine worthy only of swine?

But there is no known Epicurean theory of life which does not assign to the pleasures of the intellect, of the feelings and imagination, and of the moral sentiments, a much higher value as pleasures than to those of mere sensation. It must be admitted, however, that utilitarian writers in general have placed the superiority of mental over bodily pleasures chiefly in the greater permanency, safety, uncostliness, etc., of the former—that is, in their circumstantial advantages rather than in their intrinsic nature. And, on all these points, utilitarians have fully proved their case; but they might have taken the other, and, as it may be called, higher ground, with entire consistency. It is quite compatible with the principle of utility to recognize the fact, that some *kinds* of pleasure are more desirable and more valuable than others. It would be absurd that while, in estimating all other things, quality is considered as well as quantity, the estimation of pleasures should be supposed to depend on quantity alone.

ASK YOURSELF

125. What does the Epicurean theory of life include?

If I am asked what I mean by difference of quality in pleasures, or what makes one pleasure more valuable than another, merely as a pleasure, except its being greater in amount, there is but one possible answer. Of two pleasures, if there be one to which all or almost all who have experience of both give a decided preference, irrespective of any feeling of moral obligation to prefer it, that is the more desirable pleasure. If one of the two is, by those who are competently acquainted with both, placed so far above the other that they prefer it, even though knowing it to be attended with a greater amount of discontent, and would not resign it for any quantity of the other pleasure which their nature is capable of, we are justified in ascribing to the preferred enjoyment a superiority in quality, so far outweighing quantity, as to render it, in comparison, of small account.

ASK YOURSELF

126. Do you think Mill's test for distinguishing higher from lower pleasures would work? Try to imagine some objections to it.

127. Give some examples of higher and lower pleasures.

Higher Pleasures and the Sense of Dignity. According to Mill, people choose higher pleasures over the lower ones because they have a sense of dignity.

Now, it is an unquestionable fact that those who are equally acquainted with and equally capable of appreciating and enjoying both do give a most marked preference to the manner of existence which employs their higher faculties, Few human creatures would consent to be changed into any of the lower animals, for a promise of the fullest allowance of a beast's pleasures: no intelligent human being would consent to be a fool, no instructed person would be an ignoramus, no person of feeling and conscience would be selfish and base, even though they should be persuaded that the fool, the dunce, or the rascal is better satisfied with his lot than they are with theirs. They would not resign what they possess more than he for the most complete satisfaction of the desires which they have in common with him. If they ever fancy they would, it is only in cases of unhappiness so extreme that, to escape from it, they would exchange their lot for almost any other, however undesirable in their own eyes. A being of higher faculties requires more to make him happy, is capable probably of more acute suffering, and certainly accessible to it at more points, than one of an inferior type; but, in spite of these liabilities, he can never really wish to sink into what he feels to be a lower grade of existence. We may give what explanation we please of this unwillingness; we may attribute it to pride, a name which is given indiscriminately to some of the most and to some of the least estimable feelings of which mankind are capable; we may refer it to the love of liberty and personal independence—an appeal to which was with the Stoics one of the most effective means for the inculcation of it; to the love of power, or to the love of excitement, both of which do really enter into and contribute to it: but its most appropriate appellation is a sense of dignity, which all human beings possess in one form or other, and in some, though by no means in exact, proportion to their higher faculties, and which is so essential a part of the happiness of those in whom it is strong, that nothing which conflicts with it could be, otherwise than momentarily, an object of desire to them.

ASK YOURSELF

128. What are some of the common explanations for why we chose higher pleasures?

Whoever supposes that this preference takes place at a sacrifice of happiness; that the superior being, in any thing like equal circumstances, is not happier than the inferior confounds the two very different ideas of happiness and content. It is indisputable, that the being whose capacities of enjoyment are low has the greatest chance of having them fully satisfied; and a highly endowed being will always feel that any happiness which he can look for, as the world is constituted, is imperfect. But he can learn to bear its imperfections, if they are at all bearable; and they will not make him envy the being who is indeed unconscious of the imperfections, but only because he feels not at all the good which those imperfections qualify. It is better to be a human being dissatisfied, than a pig satisfied; better to be Socrates dissatisfied, than a fool satisfied. And if the fool or the pig are of a different opinion, it is because they only know their own side of the question. The other party to the comparison knows both sides.

ASK YOURSELF

129. Mill states that it is better to be Socrates dissatisfied than a fool satisfied. What does he mean?

Why People Reject Higher Pleasures. Mill continues explaining why many people reject higher pleasures for lower ones.

It may be objected that many who are capable of the higher pleasures, occasionally, under the influence of temptation, postpone them to the lower. But this is quite compatible with a full appreciation of the intrinsic superiority of the higher. Men often, from infirmity of character, make their election for the nearer good, though they know it to be the less valuable, and this no less when the choice is between two bodily pleasures than when it is between bodily and mental. They pursue sensual indulgences to the injury of health, though perfectly aware that health is the greater good. It may be further objected that many who begin with youthful enthusiasm for every thing noble, as they advance in years sink into indolence and selfishness. But I do not believe that those who undergo this very common change voluntarily choose the lower description of pleasures in preference to the higher. I believe that before they devote themselves exclusively to the one, they have already become incapable of the other. Capacity for the nobler feelings is in most natures a very tender plant, easily killed, not only by hostile influences, but by mere want of sustenance; and, in the majority of young persons, it speedily dies away if the occupations to which their position in life has devoted them, and the society into which it has thrown them, are not favorable to keeping that higher capacity in exercise. Men lose their high aspirations as they lose their intellectual tastes, because they have not time or opportunity for indulging them; and they addict themselves to inferior pleasures, not because they deliberately prefer them, but because they are either the only ones to which they have access, or the only ones which they are any longer capable of enjoying. It may be questioned whether any one who has remained equally susceptible to both classes of pleasures ever knowingly and calmly preferred the lower; though many in all ages have broken down in an ineffectual attempt to combine both.

ASK YOURSELF

130. What are some reasons why people often choose lower pleasures over higher ones?

From this verdict of the only competent judges, I apprehend there can be no appeal. On a question, which is the best worth having of two pleasures, or which of two modes of existence is the most grateful to the feelings, apart from its moral attributes and from its consequences, the judgment of those who are qualified by knowledge of both, or, if they differ, that of the majority among them, must be admitted as final. And there needs be the less hesitation to accept this judgment respecting the quality of pleasures, since there is no other tribunal to be referred to even on the question of quantity. What means are there of determining which is the acutest of two pains, or the intensest of two pleasurable sensations, except the general suffrage of those who are familiar with both? Neither pains nor pleasures are homogeneous, and pain is always heterogeneous with pleasure. What is there to decide whether a particular pleasure is worth purchasing at the cost of a particular pain, except the feelings and judgment of the experienced? When, therefore, those feelings and judgment declare the pleasures derived from the higher faculties to be preferable *in kind,* apart from the question of intensity, to those of which the animal nature, disjoined from the higher faculties, is susceptible, they are entitled on this subject to the same regard.

According to Mill, an essential feature of utilitarianism is the fact that we judge an action according to the general happiness it produces, rather than merely the agent's private happiness.

I have dwelt on this point, as being a necessary part of a perfectly just conception of Utility or Happiness, considered as the directive rule of human conduct. But it is by no means an indispensable condition to the acceptance of the utilitarian standard; for that standard is not the agent's own greatest happiness, but the greatest amount of happiness altogether: and, if it may possibly be doubted whether a noble character is always the happier for its nobleness, there can be no doubt that it makes other people happier, and that the world in general is immensely a gainer by it. Utilitarianism, therefore, could only attain its end by the general cultivation of nobleness of character, even if each individual were only benefited by the nobleness of others, and his own, so far as happiness is concerned, were a sheer deduction from the benefit. But the bare enunciation of such an absurdity as this last renders refutation superfluous.

ASK YOURSELF

131. What is the only way that utilitarianism could achieve its aim of advancing general happiness over private happiness?

According to the Greatest Happiness Principle, as above explained, the ultimate end, with reference to and for the sake of which all other things are desirable (whether we are considering our own good or that of other people), is an existence exempt as far as possible from pain, and as rich as possible in enjoyments, both in point of quantity and quality; the test of quality, and the rule for measuring it against quantity, being the preference felt by those, who in their opportunities of experience, to which must be added their habits of self-consciousness and self-observation, are best furnished with the means of comparison. This, being, according to the utilitarian opinion, the end of human action, is necessarily also the standard of morality: which may accordingly be defined, the rules and precepts for human conduct, by the observance of which an existence such as has been described might be, to the greatest extent possible, secured to all mankind; and not to them only, but, so far as the nature of things admits, to the whole sentient creation.

ASK YOURSELF

132. Mill again notes that there is a test for determining the qualitative value of a pleasure (as opposed to its quantitative value). What is that test?

Rejection of Virtue Theory. Mill continues by arguing that the principle of utility involves an assessment solely of an action's consequences and not the motives or character traits of the agent performing the action. In this regard, he rejects classical virtue theory. Mill speculates about what an advocate of virtue theory might say about untilitarianism.

It is often affirmed that utilitarianism renders men cold and unsympathizing; that it chills their moral feelings towards individuals; that it makes them regard only the dry and hard consideration of the consequences of actions, not taking into their moral estimate the qualities from which those actions emanate. If the assertion means that they do not allow their judgment respecting the rightness or wrongness of an action to be influenced by their opinion of the qualities of the person who does it, this is a complaint, not against utilitarianism, but against having any standard of morality at all: for certainly no known ethical standard decides an action to be good or bad because it is done by a good or a bad man; still less because done by an amiable, a brave, or a benevolent man, or the contrary. These considerations are relevant, not to the estimation of actions, but of persons; and there is nothing in the utilitarian theory inconsistent with the fact, that there are other things which interest us in persons besides the rightness and wrongness of their actions. The Stoics indeed, with the paradoxical misuse of language which was part of their system, and by which they strove to raise themselves above all concern about any thing but virtue, were fond of saying, that he who has that, has every thing; that he, and only he, is rich, is beautiful, is a king. But no claim of this description is made for the virtuous man by the utilitarian doctrine. Utilitarians are quite aware that there are other desirable possessions and qualities besides virtue, and are perfectly willing to allow to all of them their full worth. They are also aware that a right action does not necessarily indicate a virtuous character; and that actions which are blamable often proceed from qualities entitled to praise. When this is apparent in any particular case, it modifies their estimation, not certainly of the act, but of the agent. I grant that they are, notwithstanding, of opinion that, in the long run, the best proof of a good character is good actions; and resolutely refuse to consider any mental disposition as good, of which the predominant tendency is to produce bad conduct. This makes them unpopular with many people: but it is an unpopularity which they must share with every one who regards the distinction between right and wrong in a serious light; and the reproach is not one which a conscientious utilitarian need be anxious to repel.

ASK YOURSELF

133. Mill claims that actions that are blamable could arise from a good character trait. Try to think up an example. Then recount what Mill would say about such a case.

If no more be meant by the objection than that many utilitarians look on the morality of actions, as measured by the utilitarian standards, with too exclusive a regard, and do not lay sufficient stress upon the other beauties of character which go towards making a human being lovable or admirable, this may be admitted. Utilitarians who have cultivated their moral feelings, but not their sympathies nor their artistic perceptions, do fall into this mistake; and so do all other moralists under the same conditions. What can be said in excuse for other moralists is equally available for them; namely, that, if there is to be any error, it is better that it should be on that side. As a matter of fact, we may affirm that among utilitarians, as among adherents of other systems, there is every imaginable degree of rigidity and of laxity in the application of their standard: some are even puritanically rigorous, while others are as indulgent as can possibly be desired by sinner or by sentimentalist. But, on the whole, a doctrine which brings prominently forward the interest that mankind have in the repression and prevention of conduct which violates the moral law, is likely to be inferior to no other in turning the sanctions of opinion against such violations. It is true, the question, What does violate the moral law? is one on which those who recognize different standards of morality are likely now and then to differ. But difference of opinion on moral questions was not first introduced into the world by utilitarianism; while that doctrine does supply, if not always an easy, at all events a tangible and intelligible, mode of deciding such differences.

134. Virtue theorists may criticize utilitarianism because it does not take into account the motives behind peoples actions, but instead focuses only on the consequences of those actions. What is Mill's response to this?

Rule Utilitarianism. One unique aspect of Mill's theory, we've seen, is its emphasis on higher pleasures. A second unique part of his theory is that he advocates a position that philosophers today call "rule utilitarianism." Bentham suggested an approach that has been dubbed "act utilitarianism" since he advocates tallying the consequences of each *act* that we perform. Mill, by contrast, believes that we should not always tally the consequences of specific actions. Instead, he states that we assess the rightness of particular actions by seeing if they violate some accepted moral rule. This policy, he believes, is legitimated by the fact that moral rules constitute a summary of what the human race has learned about which actions tend to promote overall happiness. For example, Mill would say that a car thief's action was immoral since he broke a major social prohibition against stealing. That social prohibition against stealing is a valid moral rule since societies with that rule are presumably better off than societies that lack such a rule. In the discussion below, Mill introduces this notion of rule utilitarianism in reaction to a criticism: Utilitarianism is a useless theory since we simply don't have time to calculate all the relevant consequences of an action. In response, Mill argues that we need not weigh the consequences of each action we perform. Instead we may sometimes simply follow well-established moral rules.

Again: defenders of Utility often find themselves called upon to reply to such objections as this—that there is not time, previous to action, for calculating and weighing the effects of any line of conduct on the general happiness. This is exactly as if any one were to say that it is impossible to guide our conduct by Christianity, because there is not time, on every occasion on which any thing has to be done, to read through the Old and New Testaments. The answer to the objection is that there has been ample time; namely, the whole past duration of the human species. During all that time, mankind have been learning by experience the tendencies of actions, on which experience all the prudence as well as all the morality of life are dependent. People talk as if the commencement of this course of experience had hitherto been put off, and as if, at the moment when some man feels tempted to meddle with the property or life of another, he had to begin considering for the first time whether murder and theft are injurious to human happiness. Even then, I do not think that he would find the question very puzzling; but, at all events, the matter is now done to his hand. It is truly a whimsical supposition that, if mankind were agreed in considering utility to be the test of morality, they would remain without any agreement as to what *is* useful, and would take no measures for having their notions on the subject taught to the young, and enforced by law and opinion.

135. Mill contends that we shouldn't calculate the consequences of each of our actions but should, instead, consult a type of record showing the results of types of actions. Where do we find that record?

There is no difficulty in proving any ethical standard whatever to work ill, if we suppose universal idiocy to be conjoined with it; but, on any hypothesis short of that, mankind must by this time have acquired positive beliefs as to the effects of some actions on their happiness; and the beliefs which have thus come down are the rules of morality for the multitude, and for the philosopher, until he has succeeded in finding better. That philosophers might easily do this, even now, on many subjects; that the received code of ethics is by no means of divine right; and that mankind have still much to learn as to the effects of actions on the general happiness—I admit, or, rather, earnestly maintain. The corollaries from the principle of utility, like the precepts of every practical art, admit of indefinite improvement; and, in a progressive state of the human mind, their improvement is perpetually doing on. But to consider the rules of morality as improvable is one thing; to pass over the intermediate generalizations entirely, and endeavor to test each individual action directly by the first principle, is another. It is a strange notion that the acknowledgment of a first principle is inconsistent with the admission of secondary ones.

Mill continues by arguing that we should appeal directly to the principle of utility itself only when we face a moral dilemma. Suppose, for example, that the principle of charity dictates that I should feed a starving neighbor, and the principle of self-preservation dictates that I should feed myself. If I do not have enough food to do both, then I should determine whether general happiness would be better served by feeding my neighbor or feeding myself.

If utility is the ultimate source of moral obligations, utility may be invoked to decide between them when their demands are incompatible. Though the application of the standard may be difficult, it is better than none at all: while in other systems, the moral laws all claiming independent authority, there is no common umpire entitled to interfere between them; their claims to precedence one over another rest on little better than sophistry; and unless determined, as they generally are, by the unacknowledged influence of considerations of utility, afford a free scope for the action of personal desires and partialities. We must remember that only in these cases of conflict between secondary principles is it requisite that first principles should be appealed to. There is no case of moral obligation in which some secondary principle is not involved; and, if only one, there can seldom be any real doubt which one it is, iii the mind of any person by whom the principle itself is recognized.

ASK YOURSELF

136. According to Mill, what are the only circumstances under which we should directly evaluate the morality of an action by the principle of utility?

SUMMING UP HEDONISM AND CONSEQUENTIALISM

Consequentialism is the view that morality is grounded solely in the consequences of our conduct—not in virtues or duties. The theory was inspired in some respects by Epicurus, who believed that pursuit of a life in which there is a favorable balance of pleasure over pain should be our ultimate aim in life. In the eighteenth century, this developed into the theory of utilitarianism—the idea that morality is based on the greatest good for the greatest number of people. Bentham developed the notion of a utilitarian calculus, which involves numerical quantification of the pleasures and pains that all people affected by an given action experience as a consequence of that action. Mill criticized Bentham's idea of a numerical calculus and denied that pleasures can always be quantified. He argued that there are higher intellectual pleasures that are qualitatively preferable to lower bodily pleasures. Mill also parted with Bentham on the issue of whether utilitarians should be assessing the consequences of actions or the consequences of rules. Bentham held to a view now called "act utilitarianism," which maintains that we should calculate the consequences of each action that we perform. Mill adopted a view now called "rule utilitarianism," according to which we consider the consequences of rules that society adopts, rather than the consequences of individual actions, when deciding how to act. According to Mill, we should ordinarily follow established social rules, since they are founded upon a history of experience respecting the beneficial or harmful tendencies of types of actions. Only when those rules conflict with each other should we calculate consequences for particular actions.

**CAN OF
WORMS**

Utilitarianism is strongly connected with political philosophy. Bentham's utilitarian theory was meant as a guide for legislators engaged in social reforms. Rather than being influenced by blind tradition or some misguided political theory, Bentham felt that utilitarianism offered a clear, scientific set of criteria for directing law-making decisions. In fact, Bentham's theory sparked a nineteenth-century political movement called the *philosophical radicals* that staunchly defended Utilitarianism as a tool for legislators. Even today, in Congressional and Parliamentary debates we hear members wrestle with whether a proposed bill serves the greater good of society—an implicit recognition of the validity of utilitarian reasoning with respect to at least some issues.

Utilitarians also tend to be empiricists, who believe that moral knowledge is possible and believe that that knowledge is grounded in experience—specifically, experiences of pleasure and pain. Utilitarianism is thus tangled up with a controversial position in epistemology.

SUMMING UP THE CHAPTER

Philosophical ethics has usually consisted in attempts to pin down the sources or grounds of morality, and to establish general standards for moral conduct. Some philosophers have argued that the grounds can be found in objective, absolute, and universal standards, such as the Platonic forms. Moral relativists, on the other hand, have argued that moral values are merely human creations and usually vary from community to community. Other questions about the source or grounds of morality are more psychological in nature. We might ask whether people are psychologically capable of performing selfless actions; altruists say that we are, and egoists say that we aren't. We might ask whether moral assessments are, psychologically speaking, rational judgments or expressions of feelings. We also might ask whether there are uniquely male and female ways of approaching moral issues that are grounded in basic psychological differences between men and women.

There are three particularly influential general moral or ethical theories. First, championed by Aristotle is the view that the central ethical concept is that of virtue. We become good people and achieve happiness by developing virtues and avoiding vices. MacIntyre argued further that virtues depend upon established social traditions. Second, duty theory, as articulated by Pufendorf, maintains that morality is grounded in foundational rules of obligation intuited by reason. Kant argued that all particular duties are derived from a single principle, the categorical imperative—a command issuing from human reason mandating that we act respectfully toward people. Ross rejected the idea of a single principle of duty and instead suggested that we have six presumptively valid duties (i.e., *prima facie* duties).

Third, a consequentialist tradition inspired in part by Epicurus maintains that morality is grounded in the consequences of our actions—particularly their pleasing versus painful consequences. Bentham proposed the idea of a utilitarian calculus that would enable the numerical quantification of the pleasures and pains of all those affected by actions that we perform. Mill rejected the idea of a numerical calculus and argued that some pleasures, such as the pleasures of intellectual inquiry, are qualitatively higher than others, and that we should seek to maximize the higher pleasures. He also argued that societal rules usually represent the experience of the human race respecting which types of actions conduce to the greatest overall happiness, and should be followed when they do not conflict with one another.

**FINAL
REACTIONS**

a. In the opening section on objective morality, Sextus Empiricus, Montaigne, and Mackie all endorse cultural moral relativism—the view that human societies create our moral standards. How might Plato, an advocate of objective morality, respond to these relativists?

b. Wollstonecraft argued that morality is a rational enterprise that men and women are equally capable of engaging in. Gilligan, by contrast, argued that there are distinctly male and female conceptions of morality that are based on distinctly male and female ways of thinking. Can you think of a middle-ground position with which Wollstonecraft and Gilligan might agree?

c. Hume argued that moral assessments are emotional reactions, and not rational judgments. How would Kant respond to Hume?

d. The selection from Mill's *Utilitarianism* opens with a criticism of Kant's Categorical Imperative. How might Kant respond to Mill's attack?

e. The selection from Mill's *Utilitarianism* contains a criticism of virtue theory. How might Aristotle or MacIntyre respond to Mill's attack?

f. Take one morally significant action, such as a bank robbery, and run it through the seven criteria of Bentham's utilitarian calculus. Is Bentham's calculus a plausible way of determining the rightness or wrongness of that action?

FURTHER READINGS

GENERAL WORKS

Fieser, James, *Metaethics, Normative Ethics, and Applied Ethics: Historical and Contemporary Readings* (Belmont, CA: Wadsworth Publishing, 2000).

Fieser, James, *Moral Philosophy Through the Ages* (New York: McGraw-Hill, 2001).

Olen, Jeffrey, and Barry, Vincent E., *Applying Ethics* (Belmont, CA: Wadsworth Publishing, 2002).

Pojman, Louis, *Ethics: Discovering Right and Wrong* (Belmont, CA: Wadsworth Publishing, 2001).

Pojman, Louis, *Moral Philosophy: A Reader* (Indianapolis, IN: Hackett Publishing Company, 2003).

Singer, Peter, ed., *A Companion to Ethics* (Oxford: Blackwell, 1991).

WORKS ON SPECIFIC TOPICS AND FIGURES

Brandt, Richard B., *Morality, Utilitarianism, and Rights* (New York: Cambridge University Press, 1992).

Crisp, R., and Slote, M., *Virtue Ethics* (Oxford: Oxford University Press, 1997).

Harman, Gilbert, and Thomson, Judith Jarvis, *Moral Objectivity* (Oxford: Blackwell, 1996).

Nagel, Thomas, *The Last Word* (New York: Oxford University Press, 1997).

Schneewind, John B., *The Invention of Autonomy* (Cambridge: Cambridge University Press, 1998).

Sullivan, Roger J., *An Introduction to Kant's Ethics* (Cambridge: Cambridge University Press, 1994).

Williams, Bernard, *Ethics and the Limits of Philosophy,* Cambridge, MA: Harvard University Press, 1985).

CHAPTER 7

POLITICAL PHILOSOPHY

I n the spring of 2003, the United States military entered the Iraqi capital city of Baghdad, removing the oppressive political regime of dictator Saddam Hussein. As Saddam's government crumbled, the people of Baghdad responded quite dramatically. Many crowded the streets cheering the American troops as liberators. Others went on a looting rampage; ironically, one of the more famous stolen items was the 3800-year-old Code of Hammurabi, which set the law for ancient Babylon. Disputes erupted about how the country should be rebuilt—whether it should be a religious Islamic state or a secular one, whether its resources should be privately or publicly owned, and whether the country itself was capable of sustaining a democratic form of government. The debates surrounding the rebuilding of Iraq were a grand exercise in political philosophy, which is defined as the study of the nature and justification of political institutions.

FIRST REACTIONS

a. When governments fall, lawlessness often breaks out, such as the looting that took place in Baghdad. Is it possible to restore order without setting up a new government?

b. Where do governments get the authority to exercise control over society?

528

c. One task of governments is to keep the peace. What beyond this should governments do?

d. Can you think of circumstances in which political leaders should not be restricted by normal codes of moral conduct?

e. Governments by their very nature restrict our freedom. Can you think of some activities that governments unjustly restrict?

f. What are some situations in which you would feel morally entitled to disobey the government?

Governments are in some ways like living organisms, with a beginning and end to their lives. Philosophical issues arise at each stage throughout a government's lifespan, so we can first inquire into what—if anything—justifies the initial creation of governments. Once governments are instituted, we then may investigate whether they focus on the interests of citizens individually or on the collective good of the community. As leaders emerge, we can consider what kind of moral standard we can hold our leaders to. As governments create laws that restrict our activities, we can ask what sort of limits there should be to government coercion. And if the government pushes things too far, we may ask whether disobedience to the law or even revolt is justified. These are the main issues treated in this chapter.

A. ANARCHISM

Throughout the world, when the government of a country is overthrown, it is invariably replaced with a new and hopefully better one. The American colonies, for example, threw off British rule and instituted a new and independent government. Diverse theories of political philosophy typically share an important presumption: The existence of governments is justified and their authority is legitimate. Most ordinary citizens feel this way too. If left on our own without governmental oversight, society as we know it would collapse and we'd all end up battling it out for survival. However, some political philosophers have argued that the existence of governments is completely unjustified. This is the position called "anarchism," which literally means no rule. The term "anarchy," as we often use it, conjures up notions of chaos, confusion, or disorder. But this is far from its meaning in political philosophy, where it refers to the idea of a peaceful society without the existence of governments.

QUESTIONS TO DISCUSS

a. What are some major abuses by governments that might incline you to think that we should abolish political institutions entirely?

b. Are people capable of getting along well enough with each other so that governments would be unnecessary?

c. If we did abolish all governments, what other institutions might rise up in their place?

Systematic defenses of anarchy have three key themes. First, there is some explanation of why governments are illegitimate—such as that they rob us of our freedom or they create more misery than happiness. Second, there is some description of what a truly anarchical society would be like—such as one directed by natural benevolence and common interests.

Third, there is some explanation of how to achieve anarchy. Moderate anarchists accept the idea of provisional governments, which would ultimately dissolve and make way for a society free of political authority. More radical anarchists, though, feel that revolutionary activity is needed to wipe out the disease of government completely and permit people to be free once and for all.

1. GOVERNMENTS CONTRARY TO THE WAY OF NATURE: CHUANG-TZU

Although systematic expressions of anarchism appeared only within the last few hundred years, we find anarchist notions in the philosophical school of Taoism, which originated in China 2500 years ago. At the time, China was embroiled in bitter social conflict, with regular bloody feuds occurring between local warlords. Taoism offered a solution to China's civil unrest: People should resist rigidly organized governmental institutions and instead follow the *Tao*—that is, the "way" or "path." To follow the *Tao* means that our actions should be effortless, in harmony with things around us, spontaneous, and uncontrived. In a word, we should flow with what is natural and avoid what is artificial. The political message of Taoism, then, is to steer clear of political systems that require structure and conformity, and instead let people act naturally. This intuition appears vividly in the Taoist classic *Chuang-tzu*, which tradition ascribes to a Taoist teacher by that name. The *Chuang-tzu* work stands out for its lively literary technique of story telling. The story below describes how craftspeople disfigure nature by forcing an artificial structure on things. The first horse-tamer did this with horses; the first potter did this with clay, the first carpenter did this with wood.

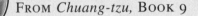

FROM *Chuang-tzu*, BOOK 9

With their hoofs horses can tread on ice and snow, and with their hair withstand the wind and cold; they feed on the grass and drink water; they prance with their legs and leap. This is the true nature of horses. Even if grand towers and large dormitories were made for them, they would prefer not to use them. One day Poh Loh [i.e., the original mythical tamer of horses] said, "I know well how to manage horses," Accordingly, he clipped them, pared their hoofs, haltered their heads, bridled them and shackled their legs, and confined them in stables and corrals. [With this treatment] two or three in every ten of them died. Still, he subjected them to hunger and thirst; he galloped them and raced them, and made them prance in regular order. In front of the horses were the evils of the bit and ornamented breast bands, and behind were the terrors of the whip and switch. With this treatment more than half of them died.

The [original mythical] potter said, "I know well how to deal with clay. I can mold it into circles as exact as if made by the compass, and into squares as exact as if formed by the measuring square." The [original mythical] carpenter said, "I know well how to deal with wood. I can make it bent if I use curve, and I can make it straight if I use a plumb-line." But does the nature of clay and wood require the application of the compass and square, of a curve and line? And yet age after age people have praised Poh Loh saying, "He knew well how to manage horses," and also the [original mythical] potter and carpenter, saying, "They knew well how to deal with clay and wood." This is the same error committed by those who govern the world.

1. What are some of the ways that artisans impose their design on their materials?

Chuang-tzu is probably not suggesting that people should never domesticate animals, make pots, or fashion things out of wood. Rather, he is attempting to illustrate a general point: Bad things happen when we force our own design on the natural order of things. Similarly, the ruler should not impose a rigid structure on society. Chuang-tzu continues by describing how people lived in accord with nature before societies imposed rules and structures.

According to my idea, those who know how to properly govern humankind would not act so. People had their regular and constant nature. They originally wove and made themselves clothes; they tilled the ground and for food. These are common to humanity. They all agreed on this, and did not form themselves into separate classes. In this way they were constituted and left to their natural tendencies. Therefore in the age of perfect virtue people walked along quietly, steadily looking forward. At that time, on the hills there were no footpaths or excavated passages. On the lakes there were no boats or dams. All creatures lived in groups, and the places of their settlement were made close to one another. Birds and beasts multiplied to flocks and herds. The grass and trees grew luxuriant and long. In this condition the birds and beasts could be led about without feeling constrained. One could climb up to the nest of the raven and peep into it. Yes, in the age of perfect virtue, people lived in common with birds and beasts, and were on equal terms with all creatures, forming one family. How could they have distinctions between superior and inferior people? As they were all without knowledge, they did not leave their condition of natural virtue. Equally free from evil desires, they were in the state of natural integrity. In that state of natural integrity, the nature of the people was what it ought to be.

2. In the ideal natural state of things, why would we not form distinctions between superior and inferior people?

We typically think that we keep society at peace when we advocate moral duties and attempt to instill these notions in the minds of all people. According to Chuang-tzu, however, this actually has the effect of fracturing society because it keeps us from following the natural harmonious course of things.

But when sages appeared, tripping people up with charity and constraining people with the duty to one's neighbor, then people universally began to be perplexed. The sages went to excess in performing music and fussed over the practice of ceremonies. Then people began to be separated from each other. If raw materials were not cut and hacked, who could have made a sacrificial vase from them? If natural jade was not broken, who could have made the handles for the ceremonial drinking cups? If the Tao was not abandoned, who could have introduced charity and duty to one's neighbor? If they did not depart from the natural instincts, how could ceremonies and music have come into use? If the five colors were not confused, who would practice decoration? If the five notes were not confused, who would adopt the six pitched-pipes? The cutting and hacking of the raw materials to form vessels was the crime of the artisans. The injury done to the Tao in order to practice charity and duty to one's neighbor was the error of the sages.

ASK YOURSELF

3. What kind of social customs lead to the division of a country?

Who is at fault for this social fragmentation? Chuang-tzu places it squarely on the shoulders of the sages—that is, philosophers, teachers, and politicians—who devise their own artificial schemes of order. Under these conditions, the function of governments is to enforce these unnatural rules.

Horses, when living in the open country, eat the grass and drink water. When pleased, they intertwine their necks and rub one another. When enraged, they turn back to back and kick one another. This is all that they know to do. But if we put a yoke on their necks with metal plates on their foreheads, then they know to look mean, to curve their necks to bite, to rush viciously, trying to get the bit out of their mouths, and to snatch the reins [from their driver]. This knowledge of the horse and its ability thus to act depraved is the crime of Poh Loh. In the time of Ho Hsu people did nothing in particular when at rest. They went nowhere in particular when out walking. They ate food and were glad. They slapped their stomachs to express their satisfaction. This was all the ability that they possessed. When the sages appeared, they worried people with ceremonies and music; they instituted governments, they dangled charity and duty to one's neighbor in order to comfort their minds. Then people developed a taste for knowledge and struggled with each other in their pursuit of gain, and there was no stopping them. This was the error of those sages.

ASK YOURSELF

4. What kind of life does Chuang-tzu recommend?

Technically speaking, Chuang-tzu is not a full-fledged anarchist since he accepts that there should be some kind of government. However, to the extent that governments exist at all, they should be very minimal and even invisible. Another Taoist classic, the *Tao Te Ching,* states that "the sage manages affairs without doing anything, and conveys his instructions without the use of speech." Thus, the ruler's task is to allow people to act naturally, and this is a very passive job description.

2. AN ARGUMENT FOR ANARCHY: ERRICO MALATESTA

One of the great twentieth-century advocates of anarchism was Errico Malatesta (1853–1932), who spent much of his life as a political activist. Born in Italy, he continually fled from one European country to another, escaping arrest for his anti-government demonstrations and writings. His brief pamphlet *Anarchy,* published during one of his stays in London, graphically expresses the main philosophical themes of anarchism. He argues that people wrongly assume that we need governments to overcome personal antagonism toward each other. We then sacrifice our liberties to governmental authorities, which then brutally oppress us. The alternative to government, Malatesta believes, is organized cooperation without governmental oversight.

Typical Justifications of Governmental Authority. Malatesta believes that the very notion of government is based on a metaphysical illusion. We arrive at an abstract concept of government, and then we assume that this abstract thing has real properties.

FROM ERRICO MALATESTA, *Anarchy* (1891)

We have said that anarchy is society without government. But is the suppression of government possible, desirable, or wise? Let us see.

What is the government? There is a disease of the human mind, called the metaphysical tendency, that causes man, after he has by a logical process abstracted the quality from an object, to be subject to a kind of hallucination that makes him take the abstraction for the real thing. This metaphysical tendency, in spite of the blows of positive science, has still strong root in the minds of the majority of our contemporary fellowmen. It has such influence that many consider government an actual entity, with certain given attributes of reason, justice, equity, independent of the people who compose the government. . . .

ASK YOURSELF

5. What are the real properties that we ascribe to our abstract conception of government?

For us, the government is the aggregate of the governors, and the governors—kings, presidents, ministers, members of parliament, and what not—are those who have the power to make laws regulating the relations between men, and to force obedience to these laws. They are those who decide upon and claim the taxes, enforce military service, judge and punish transgressors of the laws. They subject men to regulations, and supervise and sanction private contracts. They monopolize certain branches of production and public services, or, if they wish, all production and public service. They promote or hinder the exchange of goods. They make war or peace with governments of other countries. They concede or withhold free trade and many things else. In short, the governors are those who have the power, in a greater or lesser degree, to make use of the collective force of society, that is, of the physical, intellectual, and economic force of all, to oblige each to their (the governors') wish. And this power constitutes, in our opinion, the very principle of government and authority.

ASK YOURSELF

6. What, according to Malatesta, are the kinds of powers that governments exercise over us?

The principal assumption justifying governmental authority is that people are naturally antagonistic to each other, and we need governments to mediate our private conflicts. Malatesta argues, however, that when we hand this task over to governing officials, we also give up our liberty.

But what reason is there for the existence of government?

Why abdicate one's own liberty, one's own initiative in favor of other individuals? Why give them the power to be the masters, with or against the wish of each, to dispose of the forces of all in their own way? Are the governors such exceptionally gifted men as to enable them, with some show of reason, to represent the masses and act in the interests of all men better than all men would be able to act for themselves? Are they so infallible and incorruptible that one can confide to them, with any semblance of prudence, the fate of each and all, trusting to their knowledge and goodness? . . .

Many and various are the theories by which men have sought to justify the existence of government. All, however, are founded, confessedly or not, on the assumption that the individuals of a society have contrary interests, and that an external superior power is necessary to oblige some to respect the interests of others, by prescribing and imposing a rule of conduct, according to which each may obtain the maximum of satisfaction with the minimum of sacrifice. If, say the theorists of the authoritarian school, the interests, tendencies, and desires of an individual are in opposition to those of another individual, or perhaps all society, who will have the right and the power to oblige the one to respect the interests of the other or others? Who will be able to prevent the individual citizen from offending the general will? The liberty of each, they say, has for its limit the liberty of others. But who will establish those limits, and who will cause them to be respected? The natural antagonism of interests and passions creates the necessity for government and justifies authority. Authority intervenes as moderator of the social strife and defines the limits of the rights and duties of each.

This is the theory; but to be sound the theory should be based upon an explanation of facts. We know well how in social economy theories are too often invented to justify facts, that is, to defend privilege and cause it to be accepted tranquilly by those who are its victims. Let us here look at the facts themselves.

> **ASK YOURSELF**
>
> **7.** All justifications of government, according to Malatesta, are based on the assumption that people are naturally antagonistic. Think of an example of antagonism between individuals that seems to require governmental mediation.

What Is Wrong with Governments? A common theme in anarchist literature is that governments should be abolished since they are ineffective, and society could be much better advanced through nongovernmental arrangements. Malatesta argues that there are two principal problems with governments: They brutally oppress people, and they decrease society's production by restricting initiative to a few people.

In all the course of history, as in the present epoch, government is either brutal, violent, arbitrary domination of the few over the many, or it is an instrument devised to secure domination and privilege to those who, by force, or cunning, or inheritance, have taken to themselves all the means of life, first and foremost the soil, whereby they hold the people in servitude, making them work for their advantage.

Governments oppress mankind in two ways, either directly, by brute force, that is physical violence, or indirectly, by depriving them of the means of subsistence and thus reducing them to helplessness. Political power originated in the first method; economic privilege arose from the second. Governments can also oppress man by acting on his emotional nature, and in this way constitute religious authority. There is no reason for the propagation of religious superstitions but that they defend and consolidate political and economic privileges. . . .

8. What are the two ways that governments oppress people?

Thus, in the contest of centuries between liberty and authority, or, in other words, between social equality and social castes, the question at issue has not really been the relations between society and the individual, or the increase of individual independence at the cost of social control, or vice versa. Rather it has had to do with preventing any one individual from oppressing the others; with giving to everyone the same rights and the same means of action. It has had to do with substituting the initiative of all, which must naturally result in the advantage of all, for the initiative of the few, which necessarily results in the suppression of all the others. It is always, in short, the question of putting an end to the domination and exploitation of man by man in such a way that all are interested in the common welfare, and that the individual force of each, instead of oppressing, combating, or suppressing others, will find the possibility of complete development, and everyone will seek to associate with others for the greater advantage of all.

From what we have said, it follows that the existence of a government, even upon the hypothesis that the ideal government of authoritarian socialists were possible, far from producing an increase of productive force, would immensely diminish it, because the government would restrict initiative to the few. It would give these few the right to do all things, without being able, of course, to endow them with the knowledge or understanding of all things.

In fact, if you divest legislation and all the operations of government of what is intended to protect the privileged, and what represents the wishes of the privileged classes alone, nothing remains but the aggregate of individual governors. "The State," says Sismondi, "is always a conservative power which authorizes, regulates, and organizes the conquests of progress (and history testifies that it applies them to the profit of its own and the other privileged classes) but never does it inaugurate them. New ideas always originate from beneath, are conceived in the foundations of society, and then, when divulged, they become opinion and grow. But they must always meet on their path, and combat the constituted powers of tradition, custom, privilege and error."

9. Why, according to Malatesta, does governmental authority decrease society's productive force?

The Alternative to Government. What, however, is the alternative to government? Malatesta argues that in many facets of our lives we operate quite well without assistance from government. Some things we can do privately. But other components of our lives may often require cooperation with those around us—for example, the provision of such things as roads, water, and electricity. Even these, though, are best handled through voluntary associations of individual people, rather than through government. Malatesta resists the contention that capitalism is the principal force that drives people to cooperate. Instead, cooperation is best motivated by the love of humanity, the desire for knowledge, and the passion for amusement. These motivations, he believes, result in less strife. All large-scale collective undertakings require some division of labor, but we do not need governments to force those divisions upon people.

In order to understand how society could exist without a government, it is sufficient to turn our attention for a short space to what actually goes on in our present society. We shall see that in reality the most important functions are fulfilled even nowadays outside the intervention of government. Also that government only interferes to exploit the masses, or defend the privileged, or, lastly, to sanction, most unnecessarily, all that has been done without its aid, often in spite of and opposition to it. Men work, exchange, study, travel, follow as they choose the current rules of morality or hygiene; they profit by the progress of science and art, have numberless mutual interests without ever feeling the need of ant one to direct them how to conduct themselves in regard to these matters. On the contrary, it is just those things in which no governmental interference that prosper best and give rise to the least contention, being unconsciously adapted to the wish of all in the way found most useful and agreeable.

Nor is government more necessary for large undertakings, or for those public services which require the constant cooperation of many people of different conditions and countries. Thousands of these undertakings are even now the work of voluntarily formed associations. And these are, by the acknowledgment of everyone, the undertakings that succeed the best. We do not refer to the associations of capitalists, organized by means of exploitation, although even they show capabilities and powers of free association, which may extended until it embraces all the people of all lands and includes the widest and most varying interests. We speak rather of those associations inspired by the love of humanity, or by the passion for knowledge, or even simply by the desire for amusement and love of applause, as these represent better such groupings as will exist in a society where, private property and internal strife between men being abolished, each will find his interests compatible with the interest of everyone else and his greatest satisfaction in doing good and pleasing others. Scientific societies and congresses, international lifeboat and Red Cross associations, laborers' unions, peace societies, volunteers who hasten to the rescue at times of great public calamity, are all examples, among thousands, of that power of the spirit of association which always shows itself when a need arises or an enthusiasm takes hold, and the means do not fail. That voluntary associations do not cover the world and do not embrace every branch of material and moral activity is the fault of the obstacles placed in their way by governments, of the antagonisms created by the possession of private property, and of the impotence and degradation to which the monopolizing of wealth on the part of the few reduces the majority of mankind.

ASK YOURSELF

10. Give some of Malatesta's examples of successful cooperative projects that we have today that are not supervised by the government.

3. THE CONFLICT BETWEEN AUTHORITY AND AUTONOMY: ROBERT PAUL WOLFF

A key intuition behind anarchism resides in a notion of human freedom as the ability to exercise choice without unjustified constraints from governments. American philosopher and renowned Kant scholar Robert Paul Wolff explains the conflict between human freedom and governmental authority. In the chapter on ethics earlier in this book, we presented Immanuel Kant's view that human beings have dignity precisely because of their freedom to make choices. Kant argues that we are at our best when choosing to follow reason, which guides us to do the morally right thing. Nevertheless, whether our choices are good or bad ones, we are entitled to respect because of our unique ability to create our own worlds amidst the array of options that we face. Freedom, Kant thinks, is crucial to our human identity. Wolff agrees with Kant on the importance of rational choice and human autonomy—that is, self-rule. According to Wolff, moral responsibility arises from both our capacity to make free choices and our ability to reason. For example, insane people lack moral responsibility because they have no free choice, and children lack moral responsibility because their reasoning is only partially developed. Human autonomy, then, is our ability to make free rational choices, and as Kant suggested, we should value this more than virtually anything else. A problem arises, though, when we consider that the principal role of government is to restrict our autonomy. It doesn't matter if such restrictions are imposed on us in the name of keeping the peace. All governmental authority is fundamentally in conflict with human autonomy. Preserving human autonomy, then, means rejecting governmental authority.

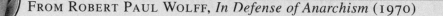

From Robert Paul Wolff, *In Defense of Anarchism* (1970)

The defining mark of the state is authority, the right to rule. The primary obligation of man is autonomy, the refusal to be ruled. It would seem, then, that there can be no resolution of the conflict between the autonomy of the individual and the putative authority of the state. Insofar as a man fulfills his obligation to make himself the author of his decisions, he will resist the state's claim to have authority over him. That is to say, he will deny that he has a duty to obey the laws of the state *simply because they are the laws.* In that sense, it would seem that anarchism is the only political doctrine consistent with the virtue of autonomy.

ASK YOURSELF

11. According to Wolff, how does the anarchist view his duty to obey the laws?

Wolff is not advocating the extreme anarchist position that governmental institutions should be toppled. In fact, he concedes that the anarchist may have no prospect of eradicating governments. Nevertheless, the anarchist would still hold that governmental authority is illegitimate.

Now, of course, an anarchist may grant the necessity of complying with the law under certain circumstances or for the time being. He may even doubt that there is any real prospect of eliminating the state as a human institution. But he will never view the commands of the state as *legitimate,* as having a binding moral force. In a sense, we might characterize the anarchist as a man without a country, for despite the ties which bind him to the land of his childhood, he stands in precisely the same moral relationship to "his" government as he does to the government of any other country in which he might happen to be staying for a time.

We thus may have no choice but to live under the governmental rule of any country in which we happen to reside. But isn't there any genuine sense of bonding we may have with our homeland government? Wolff thinks not.

When I take a vacation in Great Britain, I obey its laws, both because of prudential self-interest and because of the obvious moral considerations concerning the value of order, the general good consequences of preserving a system of property, and so forth. On my return to the United States, I have a sense of reentering my country, and if I think about the matter at all, I imagine myself to stand in a different and more intimate relation to American laws. They have been promulgated by my government, and I therefore have a special obligation to obey them. But the anarchist tells me that my feeling is purely sentimental and has no objective moral basis. All authority is equally illegitimate, although of course not therefore equally worthy or unworthy of support, and my obedience to American laws, if I am to be morally autonomous, must proceed from the same considerations which determine me abroad.

ASK YOURSELF

12. What does the anarchist tell me about any special obligation I might feel toward the government of my native land?

SUMMING UP THE ISSUE OF ANARCHISM

Anarchism is the theory that the existence of governments is completely unjustified. The idea of anarchism found early expression in the Taoist work attributed to Chuang-tzu, who argues that society invariably disfigures nature by forcing an artificial structure on things. Political leaders, he argues, harm natural social harmony by imposing rigid rules on people—even moral rules which are supposedly for society's benefit. Italian anarchist Errico Malatesta contends that governments do far more harm than good. In the name of preserving peace, they viciously subjugate us and reduce society's production. The tasks that governments assume, he argues, can be better handled either individually or through voluntary associations. Following Kant's view of freedom, Robert Paul Wolff argues that human autonomy is vital to our human identity. Governments, however, are in the job of limiting our autonomy; so, to preserve our freedom we must deny the legitimacy of governmental authority.

CAN OF WORMS

A central question underlying anarchist theory is whether people are naturally capable of cooperating with each other, without governments forcing us to behave. This overlaps with a fundamental question in ethical theory, namely whether people are inherently selfish or whether we are naturally capable of acting for the betterment of others irrespective of our own benefit. The more altruistic we are, the less we might need governmental crutches to keep the peace. Wolff's defense of anarchism rests on an important assumption: People have free wills that enable us to shape our own futures. Chapter 3 addresses the debate between free will and determinism. If determinism is true—and we are not free in any meaningful sense—then Wolff's argument for anarchism falls flat.

B. Sources of Political Authority

Anarchism is a minority view, and most people accept the legitimacy of some form of government. But where do governments get their legitimacy? The answer is far from clear. We're born into social environments that already contain political structures, and we quickly accept these institutions as facts of life. It often takes some kind of crisis—such as political oppression or a revolution—before we seriously investigate the sources of political authority.

Seventeenth-century Europe was a period of great political upheaval, and philosophers of the time responded by providing many of the classic statements concerning the foundations of political authority. We will look at three views here: natural law theory, social contract theory, and natural rights theory.

QUESTIONS TO DISCUSS

a. Many religiously minded people believe that true governmental authority rests in the will of God. Do you see any shortcoming in such a view?

b. The United States Constitution holds that true governmental authority rests in the will of the people. Do you see any shortcoming in such a view?

c. Imagine that you are a cave dweller and you cut a deal with your neighbors: you won't harm them if they don't harm you. Would that arrangement work?

1. NATURAL LAW: SAMUEL PUFENDORF

The theory of natural law is the view that foundational laws of social order are fixed features of the universe, which all people can discover through reason. Strictly speaking, according to natural law theorists, there is only one highest principle of natural law—such as "we ought to be sociable." Additional moral rules and civil laws are derived from this, such as "we ought not murder." These additional rules carry the force of natural law to the degree that they are necessary for the fulfillment of the highest obligation. Classic natural law theorists differ as to whether the highest natural law is created by God or exists independently of God in some eternal spiritual realm. In any case, theorists contend that the basic principles of natural law are unchanging and universal. This, they believe, distinguishes natural law from human-created laws, such as "drive only on the right-hand side of the road." An early systematic presentation of natural law theory was by the medieval philosopher Thomas Aquinas (1225–1274), whose views are still revered among Roman Catholic philosophers today. In Protestant European countries, however, one of the principal advocates of natural law theory was German philosopher Samuel Pufendorf (1632–1694). In Chapter 6 we noted that Pufendorf devised an influential theory of moral duties to God, oneself, and others. According to Pufendorf, moral duty and political authority are both grounded in natural law.

Sociability, the Fundamental Law of Nature. Pufendorf begins his analysis of natural law by considering the fact that individual human beings are vulnerable and must live in society to survive. God, as our creator, wills that we should be sociable, and this becomes the highest natural law. Our moral duties arise from this mandate; in turn, these duties lead to civil and international laws.

FROM SAMUEL PUFENDORF, *The Duty of Man and Citizen* (1673), 1.3 AND 2.5

People are animals that are very desirous of their own preservation. We are liable to many wants, unable to support ourselves without the help of others of our kind, and yet wonderfully fit in society to promote a common good. But then we are malicious, insolent, and easily provoked, and not less prone to do harm to our fell humans than we are cable of executing it.

From this it must be inferred that to attain our self-preservation, it is absolutely necessary that we be sociable. That is, we should join with those of our kind, and also conduct ourselves towards them so that they many have no justifiable cause to do us harm, but instead to promote and secure for us all our interests.

The rules then of this fellowship are called the laws of nature and are the laws of human society, by which people are directed how to make themselves useful members of it, and without which it falls to pieces.

From what has been said, it appears that this is a *fundamental law of nature:* to the extent that we can, every person ought to preserve and promote society, that is, the welfare of humankind. He who designs the end cannot but be supposed to also design those means without which the end cannot be obtained. It follows from this that all actions commanded by the law of nature which tend generally and are absolutely necessary to the preservation of this society. This is just as, on the contrary, those that disturb and dissolve it are forbidden by the same. All other precepts are to be accounted as only subsumptions or consequences of this universal law. The evidence of this is made out by the natural light which is engrafted in humankind.

ASK YOURSELF

13. What is the fundamental law of nature for Pufendorf?

Laws of Nature Mandated by God. To attain the status of "laws," Pufendorf believes that moral and political rules must be both authored by God and commanded by him. "Law" implies a lawgiver. These laws certainly have a human utility—or usefulness—but the authority of these laws goes beyond utility and rests in God. The sense of religion that humans have, he argues, confirms that God is the source of the natural law.

These [moral and political] rules do plainly contain that which is for the general good. But so that these rules may obtain the force of *laws*, it must necessarily be presupposed that there is a God who governs all things by his providence, and that he has commanded us mortals to observe these dictates of our reason as laws, proclaimed by him to us by the powerful mediation of that light which is born with us. Otherwise we might perhaps pay some obedience to them when we consider their utility (or usefulness), similar to how we observe the directions of physicians in regard to our health. But this would not have us view them as "laws," to the composition of which it is necessary to suppose a *superior,* and that such a superior as has actually undertaken the government of the other.

It is demonstrated as follows that God is the author of the Law of Nature (considering humankind only in its present state, without inquiring whether the first condition of us morals were different from this, nor how the change was brought about). Our nature is so framed that humankind cannot be preserved without a sociable life. And it is also plain that the mind of humans is capable understanding of all those notions which are subservient to this purpose. And, finally, it is also clear that people, like other creatures, not only owe their origin to God, but that God governs them (let their condition be as it will) by the wisdom of his providence. Hence it follows that it must be supposed to be the will of God that humans should make use of those faculties with which he is peculiarly endowed beyond the animals to the preservation of his own nature. Consequently, the life of humans should be different from the lawless life of the irrational creatures. Since this cannot otherwise be achieved except through observing the natural law, it must be understood that there is from God an obligation laid upon humans to pay obedience to it. This law is not a means invented by human intelligence or imposed by the will of humans, nor is capable of being changed by their humors [i.e., physical constitution] and inclinations. Instead, it is expressly ordained by God himself in order accomplish this end. For he that obliges us to pursue such an end must be thought to oblige us to make use of those means which are necessary to the attainment of it. And that the social life is positively commanded by God to us, we find proof in the fact that in no other animal do we find any sense of religion or fear of a Deity. This does not seem to fall within the understanding of the ungovernable animal, and yet it has the power to excite in the minds of people (not altogether corrupt) the most delicate sense. This sense convinces them that by sinning against this natural law they offend him who is lord of the soul of humans, and who is to be feared even where we are secure of any punishment from our fellow creatures.

ASK YOURSELF

14. Suppose that we could physiologically change human nature so that, from birth, we could live independently, apart from any society. For Pufendorf, what bearing would this have on the content of natural law?

Governments Ordained by God. Pufendorf argues that only a community of a considerable number of people will offer effective protection against harm from others, especially from those outside the community. The people in the community must form an initial covenant indicating who is included, and they cannot break this covenant when it suits their private advantage. After that, they must construct a constitution that establishes a ruling government. This is because, Pufendorf argues, the wills of people in this community are best united in one person, or one assembly. The function of the government is to promote safety, and citizens are under the authority of this government. Such governments are indeed willed by God. God ordains natural law, and he is the source of legitimacy for civil governments insofar as they are the only way of creating a safe environment within which we can follow natural law.

What we have said concerning the origin of civil societies in no way contradicts the fact that civil government is truly said to be from God. For it is his will that the practices of people should be ordered according to the laws of nature. Yet, given the multiplication of humankind, human life would become so horrid and confused that hardly any room would be left for natural law to exert its authority. Since the exercise of natural law would be greatly improved by instituting civil societies, and since he who commands the end must be supposed to command likewise the means necessary to the said end, we conclude the following. God also by the mediation of the dictates of reason is to be understood previously to have willed that humankind (when they were multiplied) should construct and constitute civil societies that are, as it were, animated with supreme authority. The degrees of this he explicitly approve of in divine law, ratifying their divine institution by particular laws, and declaring that God himself takes them into his special care and protection.

ASK YOURSELF

15. How does God endorse the laws of civil governments?

2. THE SOCIAL CONTRACT: THOMAS HOBBES

**THOMAS HOBBES
(1588–1679)**

English political philosopher and author of Leviathan *(1651).*

In Plato's dialogue the Republic, one of the characters argues that the laws of justice are created in a compact between people who instinctively exploit one another. Since no one likes to be exploited, each person agrees not to exploit others on the condition that others do not exploit him. This is the central idea of social contract theory—also called contractarianism. British philosopher Thomas Hobbes (1588–1679) presents the definitive statement of social contract theory in his book *Leviathan* (1651). The starting point for Hobbes's moral theory is the psychological position that humans are essentially machines that are motivated by self-interest. In Chapter 6 we examined Hobbes's argument that every action we perform, no matter how charitable or benevolent, is done for reasons that are ultimately self-serving. For example, when I donate to charity, I am actually taking delight in demonstrating my powers over other people. In its most extreme form, this view of human nature has since been termed psychological egoism. Hobbes believes that any account of human action, including morality, must be consistent with the fact that we are all self-serving. Hobbes speculates about how selfish people would behave in a state of nature, prior to the formation of any government.

The State of Nature: Equality, Quarrel, and War. Hobbes begins by noting that humans are essentially equal, both mentally and physically, insofar as even the weakest person has the strength to kill the strongest.

FROM THOMAS HOBBES, *Leviathan* (1651), CHAPTERS 13–15

Nature has made men so equal in the faculties of body and mind, as that though there be found one man sometimes manifestly stronger in body or of quicker mind than another, yet when all is reckoned together, the difference between man and man is not so considerable as that one man can thereupon claim to himself any benefit to which another may not pretend as well as he. For as to the strength of body, the weakest has strength enough to kill the strongest, either by secret machination or by confederacy with others that are in the same danger with himself.

As to the faculties of the mind . . . I find yet a greater equality among men than that of strength. For prudence is but experience, which equal time equally bestows on all men in those things they equally apply themselves to. That which may perhaps make such equality incredible, is but a vain conceit of one's own wisdom which almost all men think they have in a greater degree than the vulgar, that is, than all men but themselves and a few others whom by fame, or for concurring with themselves, they approve. For such is the nature of men, that howsoever they may acknowledge many others to be more witty, or more eloquent, or more learned, yet they will hardly believe there be many so wise as themselves; for they see their own wit at hand, and other men's at a distance. But this proves that men are in that point equal, rather than unequal. For there is not ordinarily a greater sign of the equal distribution of anything, than that every man is contented with his share.

Title page of Thomas Hobbes's Leviathan
(1651).

ASK YOURSELF

16. How is it that people are equal in body?

17. How is it that people are equal in mind?

Hobbes continues by noting how situations in nature make us naturally prone to quarrel. There are three natural causes of quarrel: competition for limited supplies of material possessions, distrust of one another, and "glory," insofar as people remain hostile to preserve their powerful reputation.

From this equality of ability arises equality of hope in the attaining of our ends. And therefore if any two men desire the same thing, which nevertheless they cannot both enjoy, they become enemies. And in the way to their end (which is principally their own conservation, and sometimes their own delectation only), [they] endeavor to destroy or subdue one another. And from hence it comes to pass that where an invader has no more to fear than another man's single power, if one plants, sows, builds, or possesses a convenient seat, others may probably be expected to come prepared with forces united, to dispossess and deprive him, not only of the fruit of his labor, but also of his life or liberty. And the invader again is in the like danger of another.

And from this diffidence [or distrust] of one another, there is no way for any man to secure himself so reasonably as [through] anticipation. That is, by force or wiles, to master the persons of all men he can, so long till he sees no other power great enough to endanger him. And this is no more than his own conservation requires, and is generally allowed. Also because there be some, that taking pleasure in contemplating their own power in the acts of conquest (which they pursue farther than their security requires); if others, that otherwise would be glad to be at ease within modest bounds, should not by invasion increase their power, they would not be able [for a] long time (by standing only on their defense) to subsist. And by consequence, such augmentation of dominion over men, being necessary to a man's conservation, it ought to be allowed him.

Again, men have no pleasure (but on the contrary a great deal of grief) in keeping company where there is no power able to over-awe them all. For every man looks that his companion should value him at the same rate he sets upon himself. And upon all signs of contempt or undervaluing, [he] naturally endeavors, as far as he dares . . . to extort a greater value from his contemners [or scorners] by damage, and from others by example.

So that in the nature of man, we find three principle causes of quarrel. First, competition; secondly, diffidence [or distrust]; thirdly, glory. The first makes men invade for gain, the second for safety, and the third for reputation. The first uses violence to make themselves masters of other men's persons, wives, children, and cattle; the second to defend them; the third for trifles, [such] as a word, a smile, a different opinion, and any other sign of undervalue, either direct in their persons, or by reflection in their kindred, their friends, their nation, their profession, or their name.

ASK YOURSELF
18. What is "glory" and how is glory a factor in perpetuating quarrel?

Because of the natural causes of quarrel, Hobbes argues, the natural condition of humans is a state of perpetual war of all against all, where no morality exists, and everyone lives in constant fear.

Hereby it is manifest that during the time men live without a common power to keep them all in awe, they are in that condition which is called war; and such a war as is of every man against every man. For *war* consists not in battle only, or the act of fighting, but [also] in a tract of time, wherein the will to contend by battle is sufficiently known; and therefore the notion of *time* is to be considered in the nature of war, as it is in the nature of weather. For as the nature of foul weather lies not in a shower or two of rain, but in an inclination thereto of many days together; so the nature of war consists not in actual fighting, but in the known disposition thereto, during all the time there is no assurance to the contrary. All other time is *peace*.

Whatever therefore is consequent to a time of war, where every man is enemy to every man, the same is consequent to the time wherein men live without other security, than what their own strength and their own invention shall furnish them withal. In such condition, there is no place for industry, because the fruit thereof is uncertain; and consequently no culture of the earth, no navigation, nor use of the commodities that may be imported by sea; no commodious building, no instruments of moving and removing such things as require much force; no knowledge of the face of the earth, no account of time, no arts, no letters, no society; and which is worst of all, continual fear and danger of violent death; and the life of man, solitary, poor, nasty, brutish, and short.

ASK YOURSELF
19. Explain why in the state of nature there would be no industry, agriculture, imports, or building.

Proof of the State of Nature. Hobbes next offers proofs that the state of nature would be as brutal as he describes.

It may seem strange to some man, that has not well weighed these things, that nature should thus dissociate, and render men apt to invade and destroy one another. And he may therefore (not trusting to this inference made from the passions) desire perhaps to have the same confirmed by experience. Let him therefore consider with himself [that], when taking a journey, he arms himself and seeks to go well accompanied. When going to sleep, he locks his doors. When even in his house, he locks his chests, and this when he knows there be laws and public officers armed, to revenge all injuries [which] shall be done [to] him. [Consider] what opinion he has of his fellow subjects when he rides armed; of his fellow citizens when he locks his doors; and of his children and servants when he locks his chests. Does he not there as much accuse mankind by his actions as I do by my words? But neither of us accuse man's nature in it. The desires, and other passions of man, are in themselves no sin. No more are the actions, that proceed from those passions, till they know a law that forbids them; which till laws be made they cannot know, nor can any law be made till they have agreed upon the person that shall make it.

ASK YOURSELF

20. What are some activities in our daily lives that suggest that Hobbes is correct in his account of the state of nature?

It may perhaps be thought [that] there was never such a time nor condition of war as this, and I believe it was never generally so over all the world. But there are many places where they live so now. For the savage people in many places of *America* (except the government of small families the concord whereof depends on natural lust) have no government at all and live at this day in that brutish manner, as I said before. However, it may be perceived what manner of life there would be, where there were no common power to fear; [and] by what manner of life, which men that have formerly lived under a peaceful government, . . . [would] degenerate into in a civil war.

But though there had never been anytime wherein particular men were in a condition of war one against another; yet in all times, kings and persons of sovereign authority (because of their independence) are in continual jealousies and in the state and posture of gladiators, having their weapons pointing and their eyes fixed on one another. That is, their forts, garrisons, and guns [are fixed] upon the frontiers of their kingdoms, and continual spies [are fixed] upon their neighbors, which is a posture of war. But because they uphold thereby the industry of their subjects, there does not follow from it that misery which accompanies the liberty of particular men.

ASK YOURSELF

21. According to Hobbes, in countries that have yet to be civilized, how do people treat each other?

To this war of every man against every man, this also is consequent, that nothing can be unjust. The notions of right and wrong, justice and injustice have there no place. Where there is no common power, there is no law; where no law, no injustice. Force and fraud are in war the two cardinal virtues. Justice and injustice are none of the [instinctive] faculties, neither of the body nor mind. If they were, they might be in a man that were alone in the world, as well as his senses and passions. They are qualities that relate to men in society, not in solitude. It is consequent also to the same condition, that there be no propriety, no dominion, no *mine* and *thine* distinct; but only that to be every man's that he can get, and for so long as he can keep it. And thus much for the ill condition which man by mere nature is actually placed in; though with a possibility to come out of it consisting partly in the passions [and] partly in his reason.

ASK YOURSELF

22. What is the status of morality in the state of nature?

Further on, Hobbes notes that humans have three motivations for ending this state of war: the fear of death, the desire to have an adequate living, and the hope to attain this through one's labor. Nevertheless, until the state of war ends, each person has a right to everything, including another person's life.

First Law of Nature. Hobbes next explores the process by which we get out of the state of nature. The first step involves making contracts with others to secure peace. In articulating this peace-securing process, he draws on the language of the natural law tradition of his time, according to which all particular moral principles derive from immutable principles of reason. Since these moral mandates are fixed in nature, they are thus called "laws of nature." By using the terminology of natural law theory, Hobbes is suggesting that, from human self-interest and social agreement alone, one can derive the same kinds of laws that more traditional natural law theorists believed were immutably fixed in nature. Throughout his discussion of morality, Hobbes continually redefines traditional moral terms (such as right, liberty, contract, and justice) in ways which reflect his account of self-interest and social agreement.

The *passions* that incline men to peace are fear of death, desire of such things as are necessary to commodious living, and a hope by their industry to obtain them. And *reason* suggests convenient articles of peace, upon which men may be drawn to agreement. These articles are they which otherwise are called the laws of nature, whereof I shall speak more particularly in the two following Chapters.

The *right of nature,* which writers commonly call *jus naturale,* is the liberty each man has to use his own power as he will himself, for the preservation of his own nature (that is to say, of his own life, and consequently of doing anything which, in his own judgment and reason, he shall conceive to be the aptest means thereunto).

By *liberty* is understood, according to the proper signification of the word, the absence of external impediments; which impediments may often take away part of a man's power to do what he would, but cannot hinder him from using the power left him, according as his judgment and reason shall dictate to him.

A *Law of Nature* (*lex naturalis*) is a precept, or general rule, found out by reason, by which a man is forbidden to do that which is destructive of his life, or takes away the means of preserving the same; and to omit that by which he thinks it may be best preserved. For though they that speak of this subject use to confound *jus,* and *lex, right* and *law;* yet they ought to be distinguished. Because, *right* consists in the liberty to do or to forbear, whereas *law* determines and binds to one of them, so that law and right differ as much as obligation and liberty, which in one and the same matter are inconsistent.

ASK YOURSELF

23. For traditional natural law theorists, a law of nature is an unchangeable truth that establishes proper conduct. How does Hobbes define "law of nature"?

Hobbes continues by listing specific laws of nature, all of which aim at preserving a person's life. He derives his laws of nature deductively, modeled after the type of reasoning used in geometry. That is, from a set of general principles, more specific principles are logically derived. Hobbes's general principles so far are (1) that people pursue only their own self-interest, (2) the equality of people, (3) the causes of quarrel, (4) the natural condition of war, and (5) the motivations for peace. From these he derives at least 15 specific laws. The first three are the most important since they establish the overall framework for putting an end to the state of nature. Since we desire to get out of the state of nature, and thereby preserve our lives, we should therefore seek peace. This for Hobbes is the first law of nature.

And because the condition of man (as has been declared in the precedent chapter) is a condition of war of everyone against everyone, in which case everyone is governed by his own reason (and there is nothing he can make use of that may not be a help to him in preserving his life against his enemies), it follows that in such a condition, every man has a right to everything, even to one another's body. And therefore, as long as this natural right of every man to everything endures, there can be no security to any man (how strong or wise soever he be) of living out the time which nature ordinarily allows men to live. And consequently it is a precept, or general rule of reason, *That every man ought to endeavor peace as far as he has hope of obtaining it; and when he cannot obtain it, that he may seek and use all helps and advantages of war;* the first branch of which rule contains the first and fundamental Law of Nature, which is, *To seek peace and follow it;* the second, the sum of the right of nature, which is, *By all means we can, to defend ourselves.*

ASK YOURSELF

24. What do we have rights to in the state of nature?

Second Law of Nature. The reasonableness of seeking peace, indicated by the first law, immediately suggests a second law of nature, which is that we mutually divest ourselves of certain rights (such as the right to take another person's life) so as to achieve peace. The mutual transferring of these rights is called a contract and is the basis of the notion of moral obligation. For example, I agree to give up my right to steal from you, if you give up your right to steal from me. We have then transferred these rights to each other and thereby become obligated to not steal from each other. From selfish reasons alone, we are both motivated to mutually transfer these and other rights, since this will end the dreaded state of war between us.

From this fundamental Law of Nature, by which men are commanded to endeavor peace, is derived this second Law, *That a man be willing, when others are so too (as far-forth as for peace and defense of himself he shall think it necessary), to lay down this right to all things; and be contented with so much liberty against other men, as he would allow other men against himself.* For so long as every man holds this right of doing anything he likes, [then] so long are all men in the condition of war. But if other men will not lay down their right as well as he, then there is no reason for anyone to divest himself of his. For that were to expose himself to prey (which no man is bound to) rather than to dispose himself to peace. This is that law or the gospel: *Whatever you require that others should do to you, that do you to them.* And that law of all men: *Do not do to others what you would not want done to yourself.*

To *lay down* a man's *right* to anything, is to *divest* himself of the *liberty* of hindering another of the benefit of his own right to the same. For he that renounces or passes away his right, gives not to any other man a right which he had not before. Because, there is nothing to which every man had not [a] right by nature; but [a person] only stands out of his way, that he may enjoy his own original right, without hindrance from him, [though] not [necessarily] without hindrance from another [person]. So that the effect which redounds [or accrues] to one man by another man's defect of right, is but so much diminution of impediments to the use of his own right original.

> **ASK YOURSELF**
>
> **25.** According to Hobbes's second law of nature, what rights do we divest ourselves of in the peace process?

The second law of nature consists of a contract between the agreeing parties. Hobbes takes this notion of contract somewhat literally, and he describes at length the validity of certain contracts. For example, contracts made in the state of nature are not generally binding, for, if I fear that you will violate your part of the bargain, then no true agreement can be reached. No contracts can be made with animals since animals cannot understand an agreement. Most significantly, I cannot contract to give up my right to self-defense since self-preservation is my sole motive for entering into any contract.

Third Law of Nature. Simply making contracts will not in and of itself secure peace. We also need to keep the contracts we make, and this is Hobbes's third law of nature.

From that Law of Nature, by which we are obliged to transfer to another such rights as being retained hinder the peace of mankind, there follows a third, which is this: *That men perform their covenants made,* without which, covenants are in vain, and but empty words. And the right of all men to all things remaining, we are still in the condition of war.

And in this Law of Nature consists the fountain and original of *justice*. For where no covenant has preceded, there has no right been transferred, and every man has right to everything, and consequently no action can be unjust. But when a covenant is made, then to break it is *unjust*. And the definition of *injustice* is no other than *the not performance of covenant.* And whatever is not unjust, is just.

Hobbes notes a fundamental problem underlying all contracts: As selfish people, each of us will have an incentive to violate a contract when it serves our best interests. For example, it is in the mutual best interests of Jones and me to agree to not steal from each other. However, it is also in my best interest to break this contract and steal from Jones if I can get away with it. And, what complicates matters more, Jones is also aware of this fact. So, it seems that no contract can ever get off the ground. This problem can only be solved, according to Hobbes, by giving unlimited power to a political sovereign who will punish us if we violate our contracts. Again, it is for purely selfish reasons—that is, in order to end the state of nature—that I agree to set up a policing power that will punish me if I violate a contract.

But because covenants of mutual trust [are invalid] where there is a fear of not performance on either part . . . , though the original of justice be the making of covenants; yet injustice actually there can be none, till the cause of such fear be taken away, which while men are in the natural condition of war, cannot be done. Therefore before the names of *just* and *unjust* can have place, there must be some coercive power to compel men equally to the performance of their covenants, by the terror of some punishment greater than the benefit they expect by the breach of their covenant. And [this coercive power serves] to make good that propriety, which by mutual contract men acquire, in recompense of the universal right they abandon. And such power there is none before the erection of a commonwealth. And this is also to be gathered out of the ordinary definition of justice in the schools: for they say that *Justice is the constant will of giving to every man is own.* And therefore where there is no *own,* that is, no propriety, there is no injustice. And where there is no coercive power erected (that is, where there is no commonwealth), there nothing is unjust. So that the nature of justice consists in [the] keeping of valid covenants. But the validity of covenants begins not but with the constitution of a civil power, sufficient to compel men to keep them. And then it is also that propriety begins.

The fool has said in his heart, there is no such thing as justice . . . [and that] to make or not make, keep or not keep covenants [is] not against reason when it conduces to one's benefit. . . . This specious reasoning is nevertheless false. . . . [H]e that breaks his covenant, and consequently declares that he thinks he may with reason do so, cannot be received into any society that unite themselves for peace and defense, but by the error of them that receive him. Nor [can he] be retained in it when he is received, without seeing the danger of the error, which errors a person cannot reasonably reckon upon as the means of his security. And therefore if he be left or cast out of society, he perishes. And if he lives in society, it is by the errors of other people which he could not foresee, nor reckon upon, and consequently against the reason of his preservation. . . . Justice, therefore (that is to say keeping of covenant), is a rule of reason by which we are forbidden to do anything destructive to our life, and consequently a law of nature. . . .

ASK YOURSELF

26. Suppose that I think I can still beat the system by entering into a social contract with no real intention of keeping the contracts that I make. What is Hobbes response to this tactic?

As noted, Hobbes's first three laws of nature establish the overall framework for putting an end to the state of nature. The remaining laws give content to the earlier ones by describing more precisely the kinds of contracts that will preserve peace. For example, the fourth law is to show gratitude toward those who comply with contracts; otherwise, people will regret that they complied when someone is ungrateful. Similarly, the fifth law is that we should be accommodating to the interests of society. For, if we quarrel over every minor issue, then this will interrupt the peace process. Briefly, here are the remaining laws: (6) Cautiously pardon those who commit past offenses; (7) recognize that the purpose of punishment is to correct the offender, not "an eye for an eye" retribution; (8) avoid direct or indirect signs of hatred or contempt of another; (9) avoid pride; (10) retain only those rights that you would acknowledge in others; (11) be impartial; (12) share in common that which cannot be divided, such as rivers; (13) assign by lot those items which cannot be divided or enjoyed in common; (14) allow mediators of peace safe conduct; (15) resolve disputes through an arbitrator.

Hobbes explains that there are other possible laws that are less important, such as those against drunkenness, which tends to the destruction of particular people.

Concluding Comments About the Laws of Nature. At the close of his account of the laws of nature, Hobbes states that morality consists entirely of these laws, which are arrived at through social contract.

The Laws of Nature are immutable and eternal. For injustice, ingratitude, arrogance, pride, iniquity, acception of persons, and the rest, can never be made lawful. For it can never be that war shall preserve life, and peace destroy it.

The laws, because they oblige only to a desire and [an] endeavor (I mean an unfeigned and constant endeavor) are easy to be observed. For in that they require nothing but [an] endeavor, he that endeavors their performance, fulfills them. And he that fulfills the law is just.

And the science of them is the true and only moral philosophy. For moral philosophy is nothing else but the science of what is *good* and *evil* in the conservation and society of mankind. *Good* and *evil* are names that signify our appetites and aversions, which in different tempers, customs, and doctrines of men, are different. And diverse men differ not only in their judgment on the senses of what is pleasant and unpleasant to the taste, smell, hearing, touch, and sight, but also of what is conformable or disagreeable to reason in the actions of common life. Nay, the same man in diverse times differs from himself, and one time praises (that is, calls good) what another time he dispraises and calls evil, from whence arise disputes controversies, and at last war. And therefore so long a man is in the condition of mere nature (which is a condition of war) as private appetite is the measure of good and evil.

ASK YOURSELF

27. In what sense are the laws of nature "immutable"?

Contrary to Aristotle's theory of the virtuous mean, Hobbes adds that moral virtues are relevant to ethical theory only insofar as they promote peace. Outside of this function, virtues have no moral significance.

And consequently all men agree on this, that peace is good, and therefore also the way or means of peace (which, as I have shown before, are *justice, gratitude, modesty, equity, mercy,* and the rest of the laws of nature) are good. That is to say, *moral virtues* [are good], and their contrary *vices* evil. Now the science of virtue and vice is moral philosophy, and therefore the true doctrine of the Laws of Nature is the true moral philosophy. But the writers of moral philosophy, though they acknowledge the same virtues and vices (yet not seeing wherein consisted their goodness, [and] not [seeing] that they come to be praised, as the means of peaceable, sociable, and comfortable living), place them in a mediocrity of passions. [Thus, they treat virtue] as if, not the cause but the *degree* of daring made fortitude—or, not the cause but the *quantity* of a gift made liberality.

3. NATURAL RIGHTS: JOHN LOCKE

In Chapter 5 we've seen that British philosopher John Locke (1632–1704) was a leading expounder of empiricism—the view that human knowledge rests on experience, rather than innate rational concepts. Locke is equally renowned, though, for his political philosophy, expounded in the two-part *Two Treatises of Government* (1689–1690). Locke was heavily influenced by both Pufendorf's theory of natural law and Hobbes's account of social contract. In a nutshell, he argues in his *Treatise* that in the state of nature all people are created free and equal, and no person is by nature sovereign over others. Given our natural equality in the state of nature, it is a law of nature that no one should harm another person's life, health, liberty, or possessions. For Locke, these are our natural rights, given to us by God. Violations of this law put us in a state of war and deserve punishment, including death. Conflicts in the state of nature are remedied by entering into a contract creating a civil society empowered to judge people and to defend natural rights. Governments may ultimately be dissolved if they violate the social contract.

Against the Divine Right of Kings. Locke's *Treatise* was written in reaction to a short work by British philosopher Robert Filmer (1588–1653) entitled *Patriarcha, or the Natural Power of Kings* (1680), which defends the absolute authority of monarchs over subjects. Specifically, Filmer argues that kings have absolute rights over citizens in the way that fathers have natural rights over their children, and they inherit that authority from the patriarchal authority of Adam. Locke's first task in the *Treatise* is to refute Filmer's biblical arguments by objecting to Filmer's initial contention that Adam had natural rights over his children. Even if God did give him such rights, Locke argues, it is not clear how these rights would be passed down to other generations.

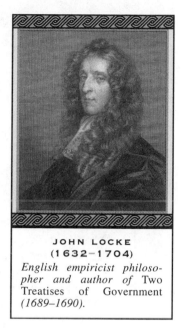

JOHN LOCKE (1632–1704)
English empiricist philosopher and author of Two Treatises of Government *(1689–1690).*

FROM JOHN LOCKE, *Two Treatises of Government* (1689–1690), CHAPTERS 1–5, 8

1. It having been shewn in the foregoing discourse, (1) That Adam had not, either by natural right of fatherhood, or by positive donation from God, any such authority over his children, or dominion over the world, as is pretended. (2) That if he had, his heirs, yet, had no right to it. (3) That if his heirs had, there being no law of nature nor positive law of God that determines which is the right heir in all cases that may arise, the right of succession, and consequently of bearing rule, could not have been certainly determined. (4) That if even that had been determined, yet the knowledge of which is the eldest line of *Adam*'s posterity, being so long since utterly lost, that in the races of mankind and families of the world, there remains not to one above another, the least pretence to be the eldest house, and to have the right of inheritance.

All these premises having, as I think, been clearly made out, it is impossible that the rulers now on earth should make any benefit, or derive any the least shadow of authority from that, which is held to be the fountain of all power, *Adam's private dominion and paternal jurisdiction;* so that he that will not give just occasion to think that all government in the world is the product only of force and violence, and that men live together by no other rules but that of beasts, where the strongest carries it, and so lay a foundation for perpetual disorder and mischief, tumult, sedition and rebellion (things that the followers of that hypothesis so loudly cry out against), must of necessity find out another rise of government, another original of political power, and another way of designing and knowing the persons that have it, than what Sir *Robert Filmer* has taught us.

Locke argues that there are different kinds of power, and political power is the right of making laws to regulate property and defend the country and also to enforce the laws. His focus here is on political power.

2. To this purpose, I think it may not be amiss to set down what I take to be political power; that the power of a magistrate over a subject may be distinguished from that of a father over his children, a master over his servant, a husband over his wife, and a lord over his slave. All which distinct powers happening sometimes together in the same man, if he be considered under these different relations, it may help us to distinguish these powers one from wealth, a father of a family, and a captain of a galley.

3. Political power, then, I take to be a right of making laws with penalties of death, and consequently all less penalties, for the regulating and preserving of property, and of employing the force of the community, in the execution of such laws, and in the defence of the common-wealth from foreign injury; and all this only for the public good.

ASK YOURSELF

28. What are the differing types of power that Locke notes?

The State of Nature and Its Laws. For Locke, the state of nature is a pre-political, yet moral, society where humans are equal and bound by divinely commanded natural law.

4. To understand political power right, and derive it from its original, we must consider what state all men are naturally in, and that is, a *state of perfect freedom* to order their actions, and dispose of their possessions and persons, as they think fit, within the bounds of the law of nature, without asking leave, or depending upon the will of any other man.

A *state* also of *equality,* wherein all the power and jurisdiction is reciprocal, no one having more than another; there being nothing more evident, than that creatures of the same species and rank, promiscuously born to all the same advantages of nature, and the use of the same faculties, should also be equal one amongst another without subordination or subjection, unless the lord and master of them all should, by any manifest declaration of his will, set one above another, and confer on him, by an evident and clear appointment, an undoubted right to dominion and sovereignty.

ASK YOURSELF

29. In what ways are we equal in the state of nature?

In view of our condition of natural equality, Locke says, reason informs us of the fundamental principle law of nature: We ought not harm others with respect to life, health, liberty, or possessions. These, then, constitute our fundamental rights in the state of nature. Although we have these freedoms, we do not have the right to kill ourselves since human lives are the property of God. Notice the complete contrast with Hobbes's view.

6. But though this be a *state of liberty,* yet it is not a *state of license:* though man in that state have an uncontrollable liberty to dispose of his person or possessions, yet he has not liberty to destroy himself, or so much as any creature in his possession, but where some nobler use than its bare preservation calls for it. The *state of nature* has a law of nature to govern it, which obliges every one: and reason, which is that law, teaches all mankind, who will but consult it, that being all equal and independent, no one ought to harm another in his life, health, liberty, or possessions: for men being all the workmanship of one omnipotent, and infinitely wise maker; all the servants of one sovereign master, sent into the world by his order, and about his business; they are his property, whose workmanship they are, made to last during his, not one another's pleasure: and being furnished with like faculties, sharing all in one community of nature, there cannot be supposed any such *subordination* among us, that may authorize us to destroy one another, as if we were made for one another's uses, as the inferior ranks of creatures are for our's. Everyone, as he is *bound to preserve himself,* and not to quit his station willfully, so by the like reason, when his own preservation comes not in competition, ought he, as much as he can, to preserve the rest of mankind, and may not, unless it be to do justice on an offender, take away, or impair the life, or what tends to the preservation of the life, the liberty, health, limb, or goods of another.

ASK YOURSELF

30. According to Locke, we are mandated to preserve our own lives. Assuming that our own survival is not in competition with others, what then is our duty?

Locke continues by noting that, in the state of nature, each person has the authority to punish those who break the law of nature. Punishment, for Locke, is justified only on the basis of reparation and restraint, not on the basis of anger.

7. And that all men may be restrained from invading others rights, and from doing hurt to one another, and the law of nature be observed, which willeth the peace and *preservation of all mankind,* the *execution* of the law of nature is, in that state, put into every man's hands, whereby every one has a right to punish the transgressors of that law to such a degree, as may hinder its violation: for the *law of nature* would, as all other laws that concern men in this world 'be in vain, if there were no body that in the state of nature had a *power to execute* that law, and thereby preserve the innocent and restrain offenders. And if any one in the state of nature may punish another for any evil he has done, every one may do so: for in that *state of perfect equality,* where naturally there is no superiority or jurisdiction of one over another, what any may do in prosecution of that law, every one must needs have a right to do.

8. And thus, in the state of nature, *one man comes by a power over another;* but yet no absolute or arbitrary power, to use a criminal, when he has got him in his hands, according to the passionate heats, or boundless extravagancy of his own will; but only to retribute to him, so far as calm reason and conscience dictate, what is proportionate to his transgression, which is so much as may serve for *reparation and restraint:* for these two are the only reasons, why one man may lawfully do harm to another, which is that we call *punishment.* In transgressing the law of nature, the offender declares himself to live by another rule than that of *reason* and common equity, which is that measure God has set to the actions of men, for their mutual security; and so he becomes dangerous to mankind, the tye, which is to secure them from injury and violence, being slighted and broken by him. Which being a trespass against the whole species, and the peace and safety of it, provided for by the law of nature, every man upon this

score, by the right he hath to preserve mankind in general, may restrain, or where it is necessary, destroy things noxious to them, and so may bring such evil on any one, who hath transgressed that law, as may make him repent the doing of it, and thereby deter him, and by his example others, from doing the like mischief. And in the case, and upon this ground, *every man hath a right to punish the offender, and be executioner of the law of nature.*

ASK YOURSELF

31. What is the basis of our right to punish offenders?

The State of War. Just as innocent victims in the state of nature can punish offenders of natural law, so too are the innocent justified in waging war against those who threaten their safety. This includes a justification to kill, even when the perpetrator doesn't present an obvious threat to life.

16. The *state of war* is a state of enmity and destruction: and therefore declaring by word or action, not a passionate and hasty, but a sedate settled design upon another man's life, *puts him in a state of war* with him against whom he has declared such an intention, and so has exposed his life to the other's power to be taken away by him, or any one that joins with him in his defence, and espouses his quarrel; it being reasonable and just, I should have a right to destroy that which threatens me with destruction: for, *by the fundamental law of nature, man being to be preserved* as much as possible, when all cannot be preserved, the safety of the innocent is to be preferred: and one may destroy a man who makes war upon him, or has discovered an enmity to his being, for the same reason that he may kill a *wolf* or a *lion;* because such men are not under the ties of the commonlaw of reason, have no other rule, but that of force and violence, and so may be treated as beasts of prey, those dangerous and noxious creatures, that will be sure to destroy him whenever he falls into their power.

ASK YOURSELF

32. Why are potential attackers on the same level as animals and thus allowed to be killed?

17. And hence it is, that he who attempts to get another man into his absolute power, does thereby *put himself into a state of war* with him; it being to be understood as a declaration of a design upon his life: for I have reason to conclude, that he who would get me into his power without my consent, would use me as he pleased when he had got me there, and destroy me too when he had a fancy to it; for no body can desire to *have me in his absolute power,* unless it be to compel me by force to that which is against the right of my freedom, i.e., make me a slave. To be free from such force is the only security of my preservation; and reason bids me look on him, as an enemy to my preservation, who would take away that *freedom* which is the fence to it; so that he who makes an attempt to enslave me, thereby puts himself into a state of war with me. He that, in the state of nature, *would take away the freedom* that belongs to any one in that state, must necessarily be supposed to have a design to take away everything else that, *freedom* being the foundation of all the rest; as he that in the state of society would take away the *freedom* belonging to those of that society or commonwealth, must be supposed to design to take away from them every thing else, and so be looked on as in a *state of war.*

18. This makes it lawful for a man to *kill a thief,* who has not in the least hurt him, nor declared any design upon his life, any farther than, by the use of force, so to get him in his power, as to take away his money, or what he pleases, from him; because using force, where he has no right, to get me into his power, let his pretence be what it will, I have no reason to suppose, that he, who would *take away my liberty,* would not, when he had me in his power, take away every thing else. And therefore it is lawful for me to treat him as one who has put *himself into a state of war* with me, i.e., kill him if I can; for to that hazard does he justly expose himself, whoever introduces a state of war, and is aggressor in it.

ASK YOURSELF

33. Why am I justified in killing a thief even when he doesn't present an obvious threat to my life?

Distinction Between the State of Nature and State of War. Locke clarifies his distinction between the state of nature and state of war, which, he believes, some philosophers confuse. Both are pre-political conditions. However, in the state of nature we live peacefully as rational beings, whereas in the state of war we protect ourselves against aggressors.

19. And here we have the plain *difference between the state of nature and the state of war,* which however some men have confounded, are as far distant, as a state of peace, good will, mutual assistance and preservation, and a state of enmity, malice, violence and mutual destruction, are one from another. Men living together according to reason, without a common superior on earth, with authority to judge between them, is *properly the state of nature.* But force, or a declared design of force, upon the person of another, where there is no common superior on earth to appeal to for relief, *is the state of war:* and it is the want of such an appeal gives a man the right of war even against an aggressor, though he be in society and a fellow subject. Thus a *thief,* whom I cannot harm, but by appeal to the law, for having stolen all that I am worth, I may kill, when he sets on me to rob me but of my horse or coat; because the law, which was made for my preservation, where it cannot interpose to secure my life from present force, which, if lost, is capable of no reparation, permits me my own defense, and the right of war, a liberty to kill the aggressor, because the aggressor allows not time to appeal to our common judge, nor the decision of the law, for remedy in a case where the mischief may be irreparable. *Want of a common judge with authority, puts all men in a state of nature: force without right, upon a man's person, makes a state of war,* both where there is, and is not, a common judge.

ASK YOURSELF

34. How does Locke define "state of nature" and "state of war" respectively?

Locke also implies that a state of war emerges when someone harms us and a corrupt political system prevents adequate redress.

20. But when the actual force is over, the *state of war* ceases between those that are in society, and are equally on both sides subjected to the fair determination of the law; because then there lies open the remedy of appeal for the past injury, and to prevent future harm: but where no such appeal is, as in the state of nature, for want of positive laws, and judges with authority to appeal to, *the state of war once begun, continues,* with a right to the innocent

party to destroy the other whenever he can, until the aggressor offers peace, and desires reconciliation on such terms as may repair any wrongs he has already done, and secure the innocent for the future; nay, where an appeal to the law, and constituted judges, lies open, but the remedy is denied by a manifest perverting of justice, and a barefaced wresting of the laws to protect or indemnify the violence or injuries of some men, or party of men, *there* it is hard to imagine any thing but a *state of war:* for wherever violence is used, and injury done, though by hands appointed to administer justice, it is still violence and injury, however colored with the name, pretences, or forms of law, the end whereof being to protect and redress the innocent, by an unbiased application of it, to all who are under it; wherever that is not *bona fide* done, *war is made* upon the sufferers, who having no appeal on earth to right them, they are left to the only remedy in such cases, an appeal to heaven.

21. To avoid this state of war (wherein there is no appeal but to heaven, and wherein every the least difference is apt to end, where there is no authority to decide between the contenders) is one great *reason of men's putting themselves into society,* and quitting the state of nature: for where there is an authority, a power on earth, from which relief can be had by appeal, there the continuance of the state of war is excluded, and the controversy is decided by that power. . . .

ASK YOURSELF

34. What is the principle way of avoiding the state of war?

Mixing Our Labor with What Is Held in Common. Like other natural rights, each of us individually has a right to property, which other people are not permitted to violate. If people do steal from us, they forfeit their own rights and may be justly punished. But how does property ownership come about in the first place? Initially, Locke argues, everything in the world belongs to all humans in common. However, when we mix our labor with an object held in common, it then becomes our own. For example, I might walk through a wild forest and see a tree that someone else has not yet claimed. I can then chop the tree down, carve it into a boat, and thereby claim ownership of that boat.

27. Though the earth, and all inferior creatures, be common to all men, yet every man has a *property* in his own *person*: this no body has any right to but himself. The *labor* of his body, and the *work* of his hands, we may say, are properly his. Whatsoever then he removes out of the state that nature hath provided, and left it in, he hath mixed his *labor* with, and joined to it something that is his own, and thereby makes it his *property*. It being by him removed from the common state nature hath placed it in, it hath by this *labor* something annexed to it, that excludes the common right of other men: for this *labor* being the unquestionable property of the laborer, no man but he can have a right to what that is once joined to, at least where there is enough, and as good, left in common for others.

28. He that is nourished by the acorns he picked up under an oak, or the apples he gathered from the trees in the wood, has certainly appropriated them to himself. No body can deny but the nourishment is his. I ask then, when did they begin to be his? when he digested? or when he eat? or when he boiled? or when he brought them home? or when he picked them up? and it is plain, if the first gathering made them not his, nothing else could. That *labor* put a distinction between them and common: that added something to them more than nature, the common mother of all, had done; and so they became his private right. And will any one say, he had no right to those acorns or apples, he thus appropriated, because he had not the

consent of all mankind to make them his? Was it a robbery thus to assume to himself what belonged to all in common? If such a consent as that was necessary, man had starved, notwithstanding the plenty God had given him. We see in *commons,* which remain so by compact, that it is the taking any part of what is common, and removing it out of the state na- ture leaves it in, which *begins the property;* without which the common is of no use. And the taking of this or that part, does not depend on the express consent of all the commoners. Thus the grass my horse has bit; the turfs my servant has cut; and the ore I have digged in any place, where I have a right to them in common with others, become my *property,* without the assignation or consent of any body. The *labor* that was mine, removing them out of that common state they were in, hath *fixed* my *property* in them.

ASK YOURSELF

35. According to Locke, why don't we need permission from humanity at large to mix our labor with some common object?

Locke anticipates the objection that if we gain property by mixing our labor with common goods, then we will be greedy and acquire everything we can. This, then, will harm others. Locke's response is that God has provided virtually unlimited natural resources and we may acquire what we can without harming others.

31. It will perhaps be objected to this, that if gathering the acorns, or other fruits of the earth, etc. makes a right to them, then anyone may *engross* as much as he will. To which I an- swer, Not so. The same law of nature, that does by this means give us property, does also *bound* that *property* too. *God has given us all things richly,* 1 Tim. vi. 12, is the voice of rea- son confirmed by inspiration. But how far has he given it us? To enjoy. As much as any one can make use of to any advantage of life before it spoils, so much he may by his labor fix a property in: whatever is beyond this, is more than his share, and belongs to others. Nothing was made by God for man to spoil or destroy. And thus, considering the plenty of natural provisions there was a long time in the world, and the few spenders; and to how small a part of that provision the industry of one man could extend itself, and engross it to the prejudice of others; especially keeping within the *bounds,* set by reason, of what might serve for his *use;* there could be then little room for quarrels or contentions about property so established.

Acquiring Land. Locke believes that the basic formula for obtaining property applies to ac- quiring land as well as artifacts like boats. Again, we do not have to get permission from humankind at large when we acquire unclaimed common land, which, he contends, is in virtually unlimited supply.

32. But the *chief matter of property* being now not the fruits of the earth, and the beasts that subsist on it, but the *earth itself;* as that which takes in and carries with it all the rest; I think it is plain, that *property* in that too is acquired as the former. As much land as a man tills, plants, improves, cultivates, and can use the product of, so much is his property. He by his labor does, as it were, enclose it from the common. Nor will it invalidate his right, to say every body else has an equal title to it; and therefore he cannot appropriate, he cannot enclose, without the consent of all his fellow-commoners, all mankind. God, when he gave the world in common to all mankind, commanded man also to labor, and the penury of his condition required it of him. God and his reason commanded him to subdue the earth, i.e.

improve it for the benefit of life, and therein lay out something upon it that was his own, his labor. He that in obedience to this command of God, subdued, tilled and sowed any part of it, thereby annexed to it something that was his *property,* which another had no title to, nor could without injury take from him.

ASK YOURSELF

36. In Genesis, God commanded that humans should subdue the earth. According to Locke, what happens when we do this?

33. Nor was this *appropriation* of any parcel of *land,* by improving it, any prejudice to any other man, since there was still enough, and as good left; and more than the yet unprovided could use. So that, in effect, there was never the less left for others because of his enclosure for himself: for he that leaves as much as another can make use of, does as good as take nothing at all. No body could think himself injured by the drinking of another man, though he took a good draught, who had a whole river of the same water left him to quench his thirst: and the case of land and water, where there is enough of both, is perfectly the same.

ASK YOURSELF

37. To what does Locke compare the virtually unlimited availability of land?

Locke concedes that most land in agricultural or industrialized communities—such as most of Europe—is already spoken for. The process of land acquisition is sped up in areas where money or some common currency is in use. However, he contends that there are vast amounts of land elsewhere that are as yet unclaimed, specifically in America.

45. Thus labor, in the beginning, *gave a right of property,* wherever any one was pleased to employ it upon what was common, which remained a long while the far greater part, and is yet more than mankind makes use of. Men, at first, for the most part, contented themselves with what unassisted nature offered to their necessities: and though afterwards, in some parts of the world (where the increase of people and stock, with the *use of money,* had made land scarce, and so of some value), the several *communities* settled the bounds of their distinct territories, and by laws within themselves regulated the properties of the private men of their society, and so, by *compact* and agreement, *settled the property* which labor and industry began; and the leagues that have been made between several states and kingdoms, either expressly or tacitly disowning all claim and right to the land in the others possession, have, by common consent, given up their pretences to their natural common right, which originally they had to those countries, and so have, by *positive agreement, settled a property* amongst themselves, in distinct parts and parcels of the earth; yet there are still great tracts of ground to be found, which (the inhabitants thereof not having joined with the rest of mankind, in the consent of the use of their common money) *lie waste,* and are more than the people who dwell on it do, or can make use of, and so still lie in common; though this can scarce happen amongst that part of mankind that have consented to the use of money.

ASK YOURSELF

38. For Locke, the inhabitants of uncultivated areas such as America have no property rights. Why?

Some aspects of Locke's theory of property are clearly out of date—specifically the contention that there is an unlimited supply of unclaimed land, which will meet the demands of all people who wish to acquire some. That certainly is not the case today, and probably wasn't so even in Locke's time. What appeared to Locke as uncultivated land in America and other foreign places was in fact tribal territory of native peoples. The absence of specific social conventions—such as fences, written property deeds, and tilled soil—led Locke to believe that the land was not in use by the local people, whom he viewed as savages. Many feel now that colonizing this land was wide-scale theft. Nevertheless, there are central components to Locke's theory that are foundational to many political theories and capitalist economic systems today. Specifically, private property is an individual right protected by governments, and the acquisition of new private property is intimately linked with our labor. But Locke's view of property did not go unchallenged. In a pamphlet titled "What Is Property?" French anarchist Pierre Joseph Proudhon (1809–1865) argued that private property was totally unjustifiable. He writes, "neither labor, nor occupation, nor law, can create property; . . . it is an effect without a cause." Property, he believes, is theft since invariably some people end up owning major resources, and other people own none. Proudhon felt that people should instead share resources, rather than claim them individually. The most important critique of private property came from the pen of Karl Marx (1818–1883), whom we've discussed in Chapter 3. Unlike Proudhon, who thought that property should be *shared* by people, Marx felt that it should be *owned* by people collectively. The capitalist and socialist traditions set by Locke and Marx, respectively, had the effect of politically dividing countries around the world for much of the twentieth century.

The Beginning of Political Societies. For Locke, the first societies were small families, which later became extended families with servants. As both Hobbes and Pufendorf argued, larger communities form for the benefit of mutual protection. When this occurs, people forego a certain amount of liberty in exchange for protection. Decisions are made on the basis of the will of the majority, which are typically made by representative assemblies. Such assemblies, then, have the authority to mandate decisions on behalf of the whole.

95. Men being, as has been said, by nature, all free, equal, and independent, no one can be put out of this estate, and subjected to the political power of another, without his own *consent*. The only way whereby any one divests himself of his natural liberty, and *puts on the bonds of civil society,* is by agreeing with other men to join and unite into a community for their comfortable, safe, and peaceable living one amongst another, in a secure enjoyment of their properties, and a greater security against any, that are not of it. This any number of men may do, because it injures not the freedom of the rest; they are left as they were in the liberty of the state of nature. When any number of men have so *consented to make one community* or government, they are thereby presently incorporated, and make *one body politic,* wherein the *majority* have a right to act and conclude the rest.

96. For when any number of men have, by the consent of every individual, made a *community,* they have thereby made that *community* one body, with a power to act as one body, which is only by the will and determination of the *majority:* for that which acts any community, being only the consent of the individuals of it, and it being necessary to that which is one body to move one way; it is necessary the body should move that way whither the greater force carries it, which is the *consent of the majority:* or else it is impossible it should act or continue one body, *one community,* which the consent of every individual that united into it,

agreed that it should; and so every one is bound by that consent to be concluded by the *majority*. And therefore we see, that in assemblies, empowered to act by positive laws, where no number is set by that positive law which empowers them, the act of the majority passes for the act of the whole, and of course determines, as having, by the law of nature and reason, the power of the whole.

ASK YOURSELF

39. According to Locke, what determines the direction in which the entire community moves?

The Constraints of the Original Compact. Locke argues that it is unreasonable to expect unanimous agreement on decisions within a community; consequently, we must follow the will of the majority. If we did otherwise, the original compact would mean nothing. This compact to follow the will of the majority is the only basis of a lawful government.

97. And thus every man, by consenting with others to make one body politic under one government, puts himself under an obligation, to every one of that society, to submit to the determination of the majority, and to be concluded by it; or else this *original compact,* whereby he with others incorporates into *one society*, would signify nothing, and be no compact, if he be left free, and under no other ties than he was in before in the state of nature. For what appearance would there be of any compact? What new engagement if he were no farther tied by any decrees of the society, than he himself thought fit, and did actually consent to? This would be still as great a liberty, as he himself had before his compact, or any one else in the state of nature hath, who may submit himself, and consent to any acts of it if he thinks fit.

98. For if *the consent of the majority* shall not, in reason, be received as the act of the whole, and conclude every individual; nothing but the consent of every individual can make any thing to be the *act of the whole:* but such a consent is next to impossible ever to be had, if we consider the infirmities of health, and avocations of business, which in a number, though much less than that of a common-wealth, will necessarily keep many away from the public assembly. To which if we add the variety of opinions, and contrariety of interests, which unavoidably happen in all collections of men, the coming into society upon such terms would be only like *Cato's* coming into *the* theatre, only to go out again. Such a constitution as this would make the mighty Leviathan of a shorter duration, than the feeblest creatures, and not let it outlast the day it was born in: which cannot be supposed, till we can think, that rational creatures should desire and constitute societies only to be dissolved: for where the majority cannot conclude the rest, there they cannot act as one body, and consequently will be immediately dissolved again.

99. Whosoever therefore out of a state of nature unite into a *community,* must be understood to give up all the power, necessary to the ends for which they unite into society, to the *majority* of the community, unless they expressly agreed in any number greater than the majority. And this is done by barely agreeing to *unite into one political society,* which is *all the compact that* is, or needs be, between the individuals, that enter into, or make up a *commonwealth.* And thus that, which begins and actually constitutes any political society, is nothing but the consent of any number of freemen capable of a majority to unite and incorporate into such a society. And this is that, and that only, which did, or could give *beginning* to any *lawful government* in the world.

ASK YOURSELF

40. For Locke, what would happen to a community (or "mighty Leviathan") if we waited for a unanimous decision among community members?

SUMMING UP THE ISSUE OF THE SOURCES OF POLITICAL AUTHORITY

During the seventeenth century, philosophers formulated several theories of political authority, which have impacted views of the subject down to present times. According to Pufendorf, moral duty and political authority are both grounded in natural law. The main principle of natural law, as authored and mandated by God, is that we should be sociable. We construct civil governments as a means of having a suitable environment in which we can follow natural law. Hobbes defended social contract theory, which is the view that, to secure our survival, we mutually agree to set aside our hostilities and establish a government to assure that we abide by our agreements. Without this agreement, we will be in a constant state of war, each of us selfishly battling it out in competition for a limited supply of necessities. For Hobbes, the transition from a state of war to a state of peace is facilitated by following laws of nature. The three most important laws are, first, to seek peace as a means of self-preservation, second, to mutually divest ourselves of hostile rights, and, third, to keep the agreements that we make. Locke defended a view of natural rights: God has invested all people with fundamental rights to life, health, liberty, and possessions. We retain our right to life unless we forfeit it by violating the rights of others. We create private property when we mix our labor with an object held in common. We form larger communities for the benefit of mutual protection, but in exchange for this we give up some of our liberty.

CAN OF WORMS

Hobbes's account of social contract theory rests on some form of psychological egoism—the contention that human beings are fundamentally selfish. However, psychological egoism, which we discussed in Chapter 6, is controversial and at odds with the competing theory that people are capable of performing at least some selfless actions. Locke's theory of rights is related to the moral theory of duty: For each right I claim, there is a corresponding duty that others have to respect my rights. Moreover, Locke, like Pufendorf, believes that we are "endowed by our creator" with some natural rights. So there is a religious dimension to their political theories.

C. LIBERALISM AND COMMUNITARIANISM

Ants have a unique social structure insofar as the focus of all their activity is the good of the colony. Each particular ant's function is defined in terms of how it connects with the larger group, and individual ants will routinely sacrifice their lives in the interests of the unit. By contrast, many fish seem to follow the motto "every fish for himself." Even when they swim in schools, there is no division of labor for the betterment of the group, and they are not likely to sacrifice their lives on behalf of others. At times human beings seem community oriented, like ants, and at other times individual oriented, like fish. The question on the table, though, is whether governments should be fundamentally community oriented or individual oriented.

a. What are some features of human society that are community oriented?

b. What are some features of human society that are individual oriented?

c. Most people feel that the government is entitled to tax us to pay for police and military protection. What other types of things might governments justly tax us for?

Many political theories in recent centuries have been largely individual oriented. In particular, the theories of Pufendorf, Hobbes, and Locke influenced a conception of government called "liberalism." Liberalism is a notoriously slippery notion, but the principal ingredient is that human freedoms are precious and governments should protect, rather than threaten, liberty. To the extent that governments do infringe on our liberties, there must be some strong justification. Liberal traditions stemming from Locke emphasize a collection of rights that all people possess, such as the right to life, liberty, and the pursuit of happiness, and, notably, the right to own private property. We've seen that Locke specifically argued that I have the right to accumulate private property, and one task of the government is to protect this right. Insofar as private property is foundational to liberal political theories, much of the battle surrounding liberalism has focused on just that issue.

In this section we will look at three perspectives on liberalism. The first is John Rawls's notion of liberty as grounded in fairness—a view that permits serious governmental restrictions on an individual's accumulation of property for the betterment of others. Second is the theory of libertarianism as articulated by Robert Nozick, who, contrary to Rawls, holds that governments cannot take away my property to help those less fortunate than myself. Third is the theory of communitarianism, which questions the central presumption underlying liberalism: that people can have any real identity independently of the wider communities to which they belong. Communitarian advocate Michael J. Sandel argues that, insofar as people are truly bound by a sense of community, the focus of government should be that community and not individual liberty.

1. JUSTICE IN THE ORIGINAL POSITION: JOHN RAWLS

One of the foremost discussions of political philosophy in recent years is *A Theory of Justice* (1971) by Harvard University philosophy professor John Rawls (b. 1921). Like Hobbes and Locke, Rawls attempts to justify the existence of governments through the notion of the social contract. However, unlike Hobbes who presumes that individual selfishness guides the terms of the contract, Rawls envisions a contractual arrangement in which people are impartial. He explains that, in what he calls the "original position," a group of rational and impartial people will establish mutually beneficial principles of justice as the foundation for regulating all rights, duties, power, and wealth. These people are not trying to start a new social system, but are seeking to establish a mutually beneficial guideline that will reform and regulate all rights and duties within their system. In establishing this foundational guideline, it is necessary to consider what principles we would pick behind a *veil of ignorance*. That is, we must imagine ourselves to be ignorant about our actual position in society with respect to such matters as how much property we have, how physically sound we might be, and the like. This ensures impartiality in our foundational principles, since we will not pick a principle that will favor any particular group or ignore the needs of the disadvantaged. Rawls argues that the foundational guideline arrived at in this way will consist of two rules of justice: one that ensures equal rights and duties for all, and a second that regulates power and wealth.

The Original Position and the Veil of Ignorance. Rawls assumes that societies rest upon an implicit "contract" that exists among its members. The contract will justify or legitimate basic rules of justice acceptable to the people concerned.

FROM JOHN RAWLS, *A Theory of Justice* (1971)

My aim is to present a conception of justice which generalizes and carries to a higher level of abstraction the familiar theory of the social contract as found, say, in Locke, Rousseau, and Kant. In order to do this we are not to think of the original contract as one to enter a particular society or to set up a particular form of government. Rather, the guiding idea is that the principles of justice for the basic structure of society are the object of the original agreement. They are the principles that free and rational persons concerned to further their own interests would accept in an initial position of equality as defining the fundamental terms of their association. These principles are to regulate all further agreements; they specify the kinds of social cooperation that can be entered into and the forms of government that can be established. This way of regarding the principles of justice I shall call justice as fairness.

ASK YOURSELF

41. The principles of justice are ones that _____, and _____ persons who want to further their own interests would agree to in an initial position of _____.

Thus we are to imagine that those who engage in social cooperation choose together, in one joint act, the principles which are to assign basic rights and duties and to determine the division of social benefits. Men are to decide in advance how they are to regulate their claims against one another and what is to be the foundation charter of their society. Just as each person must decide by rational reflection what constitutes his good, that is, the system of ends which it is rational for him to pursue, so a group of persons must decide once and for all what is to count among them as just and unjust. The choice which rational men would make in this hypothetical situation of equal liberty, assuming for the present that this choice problem has a solution, determines the principles of justice.

In justice as fairness the original position of equality corresponds to the state of nature in the traditional theory of the social contract. This original position is not, of course, thought of as an actual historical state of affairs, much less as a primitive condition of culture. It is understood as a purely hypothetical situation characterized so as to lead to a certain conception of justice. Among the essential features of this situation is that no one knows his place in society, his class position or social status, nor does any one know his fortune in the distribution of natural assets and abilities, his intelligence, strength, and the like. I shall even assume that the parties do not know their conceptions of the good or their special psychological propensities.

ASK YOURSELF

42. Name three things people do not know in the original position.

The negotiations that take place in the original position are done by participants whom we assume to be behind the veil of ignorance—that is, unaware of their actual standing in society.

The principles of justice are chosen behind a veil of ignorance. This ensures that no one is advantaged or disadvantaged in the choice of principles by the outcome of natural chance or the contingency of social circumstances. Since all are similarly situated and no one is able to design principles to favor his particular condition, the principles of justice are the result of a fair agreement or bargain. For given the circumstances of the original position, the symmetry of everyone's relations to each other, this initial situation is fair between individuals as moral persons, that is, as rational beings with their own ends and capable, I shall assume, of a sense of justice. The original position is, one might say, the appropriate initial status quo, and thus the fundamental agreements reached in it are fair.

ASK YOURSELF

43. The "veil of ignorance" ensures that no one is _____ or _____.

When the principles of justice are arrived at behind the veil of ignorance, they will be fair and will subsequently be used as guidelines for more specific political rules, such as specific constitutional rules.

This explains the propriety of the name "justice as fairness": it conveys the idea that the principles of justice are agreed to in an initial situation that is fair. The name does not mean that the concepts of justice and fairness are the same, any more than the phrase "poetry as metaphor" means that the concepts of poetry and metaphor are the same.

   Justice as fairness begins, as I have said, with one of the most general of all choices which persons might make together, namely, with the choice of the first principles of a conception of justice which is to regulate all subsequent criticism and reform of institutions. Then, having chosen a conception of justice, we can suppose that they are to choose a constitution and a legislature to enact laws, and so on, all in accordance with the principles of justice initially agreed upon. Our social situation is just if it is such that by this sequence of hypothetical agreements we would have contracted into the general system of rules which defines it.

   . . . It may be observed, however, that once the principles of justice are thought of as arising from an original agreement in a situation of equality, it is an open question whether the principle of utility would be acknowledged. Offhand it hardly seems likely that persons who view themselves as equals, entitled to press their claims upon one another, would agree to a principle which may require lesser life prospects for some simply for the sake of a greater sum of advantages enjoyed by others. Since each desires to protect his interests, his capacity to advance his conception of the good, no one has a reason to acquiesce in an enduring loss for himself in order to bring about a great net balance of satisfaction. In the absence of strong and lasting benevolent impulses, a rational man would not accept a basic structure merely because it maximized the algebraic sum of advantages irrespective of its permanent effects on his own basic rights and interests. Thus it seems that the principle of utility is incompatible with the conception of social cooperation among equals for mutual advantage. It appears to be inconsistent with the idea of reciprocity implicit in the notion of a well-ordered society. Or, at any rate, so I shall argue.

44. What is the principle that Rawls is rejecting, and why does he reject it?

Since the negotiations concerning justice will take place fairly behind the veil of ignorance, the principles of justice arrived at will express this fairness. Rawls argues that participants in the negotiations will arrive at two distinct principles of justice. He states the specific principles later on, but before doing so he emphasizes how they are fair. First, contrary to utilitiarian theories of justice, the principles do not permit exploiting people for the sake of the greater good. Second, the principles will not unfairly give preference to people who have special advantages, such as the children of rich and powerful parents, or those with exceptional intelligence or physical strength.

I shall maintain instead that the persons in the initial situation would choose two rather different principles: the first requires equality in the assignment of basic rights and duties, while the second holds that social and economic inequalities, for example inequalities of wealth and authority, are just only if they result in compensating benefits for everyone, and in particular for the least advantaged members of society. These principles rule out justifying institutions on the grounds that the hardships of some are offset by a greater good in the aggregate. It may be expedient but it is not just that some should have less in order that others may prosper. But there is no injustice in the greater benefits earned by a few provided that the situation of persons not so fortunate is thereby improved. The intuitive idea is that since everyone's well-being depends upon a scheme of cooperation without which no one could have a satisfactory life, the division of advantages should be such as to draw forth the willing cooperation of everyone taking part in it, including those less well situated. Yet this can be expected only if reasonable terms are proposed. The two principles mentioned seem to be a fair agreement on the basis of which those better endowed, or more fortunate in their social position, neither of which we can be said to deserve, could expect the willing cooperation of others when some workable scheme is a necessary condition of the welfare of all. Once we decide to look for a conception of justice that nullifies the accidents of natural endowment and the contingencies of social circumstance as counters in quest for political and economic advantage, we are led to these principles. They express the result of leaving aside those aspects of the social world that seem arbitrary from a moral point of view. . . .

45. Give an example of an "accident of natural endowment" and an example of a "contingency of social circumstance."

. . . The idea here is simply to make vivid to ourselves the restrictions that it seems reasonable to impose on arguments for principles of justice, and therefore on these principles themselves. Thus it seems reasonable and generally acceptable that no one should be advantaged or disadvantaged by natural fortune or social circumstances in the choice of principles. It also seems widely agreed that it should be impossible to tailor principles to the circumstances of one's own case. We should insure further that particular inclinations and aspirations, and persons' conceptions of their good, do not affect the principles adopted. The aim is to rule out those principles that it would be rational to propose for acceptance, however little the chance of success, only if one knew certain things that are irrelevant from the standpoint of justice.

For example, if a man knew that he was wealthy, he might find it rational to advance the principle that various taxes for welfare measures be counted unjust; if he knew that he was poor, he would most likely propose the contrary principle. To represent the desired restrictions one imagines a situation in which everyone is deprived of this sort of information. One excludes the knowledge of those contingencies which sets men at odds and allows them to be guided by their prejudices. In this manner the veil of ignorance is arrived at in a natural way. . . .

ASK YOURSELF

46. What are Rawls's examples of information that would make a person biased in his choice of laws?

The Two Principles of Justice. Rawls now articulates the two principles themselves, the first of which guarantees equal rights and duties for everyone, and the second of which regulates the amount of power or wealth any person can hold.

I shall now state in a provisional form the two principles of justice that I believe would be chosen in the original position. In this section I wish to make only the most general comments, and therefore the first formulation of these principles is tentative. As we go on I shall run through several formulations and approximate step by step the final statement to be given much later. I believe that doing this allows the exposition to proceed in a natural way.

The first statement of the two principles reads as follows.

First: each person is to have an equal right to the most extensive basic liberty compatible with a similar liberty for others.

Second: social and economic inequalities are to be arranged so that they are both (a) reasonably expected to be to everyone's advantage and (b) attached to positions and offices open to all.

There are two ambiguous phrases in the second principle, namely "everyone's advantage" and "open to all." . . .

By way of general comment, these principles primarily apply, as I have said, to the basic structure of society. They are to govern the assignment of rights and duties and to regulate the distribution of social and economic advantages. As their formulation suggests, these principles presuppose that the social structure can be divided into two more or less distinct parts, the first principle applying to the one, the second to the other. They distinguish between those aspects of the social system that define and secure the equal liberties of citizenship and those that specify and establish social and economic inequalities. The basic liberties of citizens are, roughly speaking, political liberty (the right to vote and to be eligible for public office) together with freedom of speech and assembly; liberty of conscience and freedom of thought; freedom of the person along with the right to hold (personal) property; and freedom from arbitrary arrest and seizure as defined by the concept of the rule of law. These liberties are all required to be equal by the first principle, since citizens of a just society are to have the same basic rights.

The second principle applies, in the first approximation, to the distribution of income and wealth and to the design of organizations that make use of differences in authority and responsibility, or chains of command. While the distribution of wealth and income need not be equal, it must be to everyone's advantage, and at the same time, positions of authority and offices of command must be accessible to all. One applies the second principle by holding positions open, and then, subject to this constraint, arranges social and economic inequalities so that everyone benefits.

These principles are to be arranged in a serial order with the first principle prior to the second. This ordering means that a departure from the institutions of equal liberty required by the first principle cannot be justified by, or compensated for, by greater social and economic advantages. The distribution of wealth and income, and the hierarchies of authority, must be consistent with both the liberties of equal citizenship and equality of opportunity.

It is clear that these principles are rather specific in their content, and their acceptance rests on certain assumptions that I must eventually try to explain and justify. A theory of justice depends upon a theory of society in ways that will become evident as we proceed. For the present, it should be observed that the two principles (and this holds for all formulations) are a special case of a more general conception of justice that can be expressed as follows.

> All social values—liberty and opportunity, income and wealth, and the bases of self-respect—are to be distributed equally unless an unequal distribution of any, or all, of these values is to everyone's advantage.

Injustice, then, is simply inequalities that are not to the benefit of all. Of course, this conception is extremely vague and requires interpretation.

ASK YOURSELF

47. What are some of the rights generated by the first principle of justice?

Redistributing Wealth. Rawls's first principle maintains that people have an equal right to the widest possible liberty compatible with the liberty of others, and it is this claim that places him squarely in the liberal tradition of Locke. Thus, most liberals would find little problem with this first principle. The second principle of justice, however, is more problematic, particularly clause (a), which is called the "difference principle": Social and economic inequalities are to be arranged in ways that are reasonably expected to be to everyone's advantage. This allows for a redistribution of wealth—lowering that of the rich and raising that of the poor. How exactly should this redistribution take place? Rawls suggests that we begin with a tentative arrangement in which everyone gets equal shares. We can then allow for some people to have more, and others less, but only if such arrangements benefit everyone. For example, we might find it appropriate to allow the CEO of a company to receive a salary of $10 million a year if everyone benefits from the existence of that kind of business enterprise. For example, in that situation, I might get a better paying job than I would otherwise, due to the entrepreneurial skills of that CEO, and I might have better consumer goods than I would otherwise. However, that arrangement is justified by the difference principle only if *everyone* in the society would be better off than they would under some alternative arrangement, such as one in which the CEO gets $5 million.

As a first step, suppose that the basic structure of society distributes certain primary goods, that is, things that every rational man is presumed to want. These goods normally have a use whatever a person's rational plan of life. For simplicity, assume that the chief primary goods at the disposition of society are rights and liberties, powers and opportunities, income and wealth. These are the social primary goods. Other primary goods such as health and vigor, intelligence and imagination, are natural goods; although their possession is influenced by the basic structure, they are not so directly under its control. Imagine, then, a hypothetical initial arrangement in which all the social primary goods are equally distributed: everyone has similar rights and duties, and income and wealth are evenly shared. This state of affairs provides a benchmark for judging improvements. If certain inequalities of wealth and organizational powers would make everyone better off than in this hypothetical starting situation, then they accord with the general conception.

Now it is possible, at least theoretically, that by giving up some of their fundamental liberties men are sufficiently compensated by the resulting social and economic gains. The general conception of justice imposes no restrictions on what sort of inequalities are permissible; it only requires that everyone's position be improved. . . .

Now the second principle insists that each person benefit from permissible inequalities in the basic structure. This means that it must be reasonable for each relevant representative man defined by this structure, when he views it as a going concern, to prefer his prospects with the inequality to his prospects without it. One is not allowed to justify differences in income or organizational powers on the ground that the disadvantages of those in one position are outweighed by the greater advantages of those in another. Much less can infringements of liberty be counterbalanced in this way. Applied to the basic structure, the principle of utility would have us maximize the sum of expectations of representative men (weighted by the number of persons they represent, on the classical view); and this would permit us to compensate for the losses of some by the gains of others. Instead, the two principles require that everyone benefit from economic and social inequalities.

ASK YOURSELF

48. Try to think of an inequality in income that would be to everyone's advantage. Ask yourself whether there are certain socially necessary tasks that no one would be willing to do under strict equality of income.

2. LIBERTARIANISM: ROBERT NOZICK

Three years after the appearance of Rawls's *Theory of Justice,* a book by Harvard University philosophy professor Robert Nozick was published, entitled *Anarchy, State, and Utopia* (1974). The work was quickly embraced as a conservative answer to Rawls, and since then it has been difficult to discuss Rawls without similarly considering Nozick's attack. Nozick defends a version of political libertarianism—also called "classic liberalism." Although libertarians disagree on several fine points, a theme that they have in common is a distrust of government. This is particularly so regarding governments that try to control people's lives and institute welfare programs that take the wealth of the rich and redistribute it to the poor. Nozick argues that only a minimal state is justified—one which protects people's rights by punishing rights-violators, but does not infringe on our liberties. Rawls's view on the redistribution of wealth, he believes, is unjustified.

Justification of the Minimal State. Nozick believes that only a minimal state is justified, and anything beyond that will trample on people's rights. But why have any government at all? Insofar as governments are inherently restrictive, it would seem that die-hard libertarians would really be anarchists and oppose all forms of government. Nozick, though, believes that there is a natural justification for the existence of a minimal state. In the state of nature, each person is entitled to protect themselves against others. To make the job easier, protective agencies would arise—similar to private security companies—which would protect clients' rights and punish violators. Smaller ones would join together creating a dominant protective agency, which eventually would evolve into minimal states. Nozick feels that each step in the development from private protection to minimal state is both justified and practically inevitable. The first major advance beyond private attempts at self-defense is the development of mutual protection associations. Each member would voluntarily come to the defense of others in the association since they would see that there is strength in numbers.

FROM ROBERT NOZICK, *Anarchy, State, and Utopia* (1974)

In a state of nature an individual may himself enforce his rights, defend himself, exact compensation, and punish (or at least try his best to do so). Others may join with him in his defense, at his call. They may join with him to repulse an attacker or to go after an aggressor because they are public spirited, or because they are his friends, or because he has helped them in the past, or because they wish him to help them in the future, or in exchange for something. Groups of individuals may form mutual-protection associations: all will answer the call of any member for defense or for the enforcement of his rights. In union there is strength. Two inconveniences attend such simple mutual protection associations: (1) everyone is always on call to serve a protective function (and how shall it be decided who shall answer the call for those protective functions that do not require the services of all members?); and (2) any member may call out his associates by saying his rights are being, or have been, violated. Protective associations will not want to be at the beck and call of their cantankerous or paranoid members, not to mention those of their members who might attempt, under the guise of self-defense, to use the association to violate the rights of others. Difficulties will also arise if two different members of the same association are in dispute, each calling upon his fellow members to come to his aid.

ASK YOURSELF

49. What are some of the initial problems that mutual protection associations face?

To streamline the protection process, mutual protection associations would develop procedures for handling conflicts with members of other protection associations.

A mutual-protection association might attempt to deal with conflict among its own members by a policy of nonintervention. But this policy would bring discord within the association and might lead to the formation of subgroups who might fight among themselves and thus cause the breakup of the association. This policy would also encourage potential aggressors to join as many mutual-protection associations as possible in order to gain immunity from retaliatory or defensive action, thus placing a great burden on the adequacy of the initial screening procedure of the association. Thus protective associations (almost all of those that will survive which people will join) will not follow a policy of nonintervention; they will use some procedure to determine how to act when some members claim that other members have violated their rights. Many arbitrary procedures can be imagined (for example, act on the side of that member who complains first), but most persons will want to join associations that follow some procedure to find out which claimant is correct. When a member of the association is in conflict with nonmembers, the association also will want to determine in some fashion who is in the right, if only to avoid constant and costly involvement in each member's quarrels, whether just or unjust. The inconvenience of everyone's being on call, whatever their activity at the moment or inclinations or comparative advantage, can be handled in the usual manner by division of labor and exchange. Some people will be *hired* to perform protective functions, and some entrepreneurs will go into the business of selling protective services. Different sorts of protective policies would be offered, at different prices, for those who may desire more extensive or elaborate protection. . . .

ASK YOURSELF

50. Nozick believes that mutual protection *associations* will give rise to mutual protection *agencies*. What is the difference between the two?

Once we become clients of mutual protection agencies, the agencies would limit our right to individual retaliation.

Will protective agencies *require* that their clients renounce exercising their right of private retaliation if they have been wronged by nonclients of the agency? Such retaliation may well lead to counter-retaliation by another agency or individual, and a protective agency would not wish *at that late stage* to get drawn into the messy affair by having to defend its client against the counter-retaliation. Protective agencies would refuse to protect against counter-retaliation unless they had first given permission for the retaliation. . . .

Initially, several different protective associations or companies will offer their services in the same geographical area. What will occur when there is a conflict between clients of different agencies? Things are relatively simple if the agencies reach the same decision about the disposition of the case. (Though each might want to exact the penalty.) But what happens if they reach different decisions as to the merits of the case, and one agency attempts to protect its client while the other is attempting to punish him or make him pay compensation? . . .

ASK YOURSELF

51. Why would mutual protection agencies limit our right to individual retaliation?

Conflicts between different agencies will give rise to a common system that judges between competing claims. Ultimately, a dominant protection agency would emerge.

Out of anarchy, pressed by spontaneous groupings, mutual-protection associations, division of labor, market pressures, economies of scale, and rational self-interest, there arises something very much resembling a minimal state or a group of geographically distinct minimal states. Why is this market different from all other markets? Why would a virtual monopoly arise in this market without the government intervention that elsewhere creates and maintains it? The worth of the product purchased, protection against others, is *relative:* it depends upon how strong the others are. Yet unlike other goods that are comparatively evaluated, maximal competing protective services cannot coexist; the nature of the service brings different agencies not only into competition for customers' patronage, but also into violent conflict with each other. Also, since the worth of the less than maximal product declines disproportionately with the number who purchase the maximal product, customers will not stably settle for the lesser good, and competing companies are caught in a declining spiral. . . .

ASK YOURSELF

ASK YOURSELF

52. Nozick believes that a natural monopoly would emerge among various protection agencies, thereby producing a dominant one. Why would customers gravitate toward larger agencies, thus driving smaller ones out of business?

The dominant protective agencies become what Nozick calls ultra-minimal states. Membership is voluntary, and not all members need to join. Nevertheless, the agency constitutes a minimal state because it monopolizes coercive force in a geographical area and offers protection to most people.

Distributive Justice and Entitlement. Nozick feels that we cannot justify the existence of governments more elaborate than minimal states. That is, we can see how governments gain the right to protect and punish, but it is a different matter when governments attempt to take away some of our property to pay for welfare programs. The issue is that of *distributive justice,* which concerns the just allocation of resources.

The minimal state is the most extensive state that can be justified. Any state more extensive violates people's rights. Yet many persons have put forth reasons purporting to justify a more extensive state. It is impossible within the compass of this book to examine all the reasons that have been put forth. Therefore, I shall focus upon those generally acknowledged to be most weighty and influential, to see precisely wherein they fail. . . .

The term "distributive justice" is not a neutral one. Hearing the term "distribution," most people presume that some thing or mechanism uses some principle or criterion to give out a supply of things. Into this process of distributing shares some error may have crept. So it is an open question, at least, whether redistribution should take place; whether we should do again what has already been done once, though poorly. . . . We shall speak of people's holdings; a principle of justice in holdings describes (part of) what justice tells us (requires) about holdings. I shall state first what I take to be the correct view about justice in holdings, and then turn to the discussion of alternate views.

ASK YOURSELF

53. Why is the very term "distributive justice" not a neutral one?

Nozick believes that the only theory of justice that is consistent with the notion of a minimal state is that of *entitlement.* For Nozick, this involves (a) initially acquiring property by just means—such as mixing our labor with a commonly held object, as Locke suggests, and (b) voluntarily transferring that property to another person by just means—such as a gift or sales contract.

Entitlement Theory. The subject of justice in holdings consists of three major topics. The first is the *original acquisition of holdings,* the appropriation of unheld things. This includes the issues of how unheld things may come to be held, the process, or processes, by which unheld things may come to be held, the things that may come to be held by these processes, the extent of what comes to be held by a particular process, and so on. We shall refer to the complicated truth about this topic, which we shall not formulate here, as the principle of justice in acquisition. The second topic concerns the *transfer of holdings* from one person to another. By what processes may a person transfer holdings to another? How may a person acquire a holding from another who holds it? Under this topic come general descriptions of voluntary exchange, and gift and (on the other hand) fraud, as well as reference to particular conventional details fixed upon in a given society. The complicated truth about this subject (with placeholders for conventional details) we shall call the principle of justice in transfer. (And we shall suppose it also includes principles governing how a person may divest himself of a holding, passing it into an unheld state.) If the world were wholly just, the following inductive definition would exhaustively cover the subject of justice in holdings.

1. A person who acquires a holding in accordance with the principle of justice in acquisition is entitled to that holding.

2. A person who acquires a holding in accordance with the principle of justice in transfer, from someone else entitled to the holding, is entitled to the holding.

3. No one is entitled to a holding except by (repeated) applications of 1 and 2.

The complete principle of distributive justice would say simply that a distribution is just if everyone is entitled to the holdings they possess under the distribution. . . .

ASK YOURSELF

54. The principle of "justice in _____" involves how we come to own things that were not previously held by anyone. The principle of "justice in _____" involves how we assign our property to others.

According to Nozick, any other way of distributing wealth will interfere with our rights. Suppose, for example, that the government imposes taxes on me for the purpose of improving the welfare of poor people. This amounts to forced labor since I will be working for the benefit of others without any choice or reward.

Historical Principles and End-Result Principles. Entitlement theory, according to Nozick, follows a *historical* principle of wealth distribution since it has us look at the history of how people acquired some property—that is, was it justly acquired or justly transferred. This, he believes, is the only valid way of looking at the issue. Other theories of justice tend to ignore the history of ownership and only examine the current distribution of ownership as it appears here and now in the *current-time-slice*. Governmental welfare programs focus on the current-time-slice since they look at how much money people have right now, and they take from the wealthier in order to improve the lot of the poorer.

The general outlines of the entitlement theory illuminate the nature and defects of other conceptions of distributive justice. The entitlement theory of justice in distribution is *historical;* whether a distribution is just depends upon how it came about. In contrast, *current-time-slice principles* of justice hold that the Justice of a distribution is determined by how things are distributed (who has what) as judged by some *structural* principle(s) of just distribution. A utilitarian who judges between any two distributions by seeing which has the greater sum of utility and, if the sums tie, applies some fixed equality criterion to choose the more equal distribution, would hold a current time-slice principle of justice. As would someone who had a fixed schedule of trade-offs between the sum of happiness and equality. According to a current time-slice principle, all that needs to be looked at, in judging the justice of a distribution, is who ends up with what; in comparing any two distributions one need look only at the matrix presenting the distributions. No further information need be fed into a principle of justice. It is a consequence of such principles of justice that any two structurally identical distributions are equally just. (Two distributions are structurally identical if they present the same profile, but perhaps have different persons occupying the particular slots. My having ten and your having five, and my having five and your having ten are structurally identical distributions.) Welfare economics is the theory of current time-slice principles of justice. The subject is conceived as operating on matrices representing only current information about distribution. This, as well as some of the usual conditions (for example, the choice of distribution is invariant under relabeling of columns), guarantees that welfare economics will be a current-time-slice theory, with all of its inadequacies.

ASK YOURSELF

55. Utilitarian theories seek to distribute wealth in a way that serves the greatest good for the greatest number of people. Do utilitarian theories follow the principle of historical entitlement or do they only take account of the *current-time-slice?*

Nozick rejects current-time-slice principles of wealth distribution, and he feels that most people see difficulties with that notion too. Another way of understanding the problem with current-time-slice theories is to see that they focus on some *end result,* rather than historical entitlement. The end result might be the elimination of poverty, a more equal distribution of wealth, or a better society on the whole. Regardless of the specific end result aimed at, however, such views ignore how a person's wealth was originally acquired.

Most persons do not accept current-time-slice principles as constituting the whole story about distributive shares. They think it relevant in assessing the justice of a situation to consider not only the distribution it embodies, but also how that distribution came about. If some persons are in prison for murder or war crimes, we do not say that to assess the justice of the distribution in the society we must look only at what this person has, and that person has, and that person has, . . . at the current time. We think it relevant to ask whether someone did something so that he *deserved* to be punished, deserved to have a lower share. Most will agree to the relevance of further information with regard to punishments and penalties. Consider also desired things. One traditional socialist view is that workers are entitled to the product and full fruits of their labor; they have earned it; a distribution is unjust if it does not give the workers what they are entitled to. Such entitlements are based upon some past history. . . .

We construe the position we discuss too narrowly by speaking of *current*-time-slice principles. Nothing is changed if structural principles operate upon a time sequence of current-time-slice profiles and, for example, give someone more now to counterbalance the less he has had earlier. A utilitarian or an egalitarian or any mixture of the two over time will inherit the difficulties of his more myopic comrades. He is not helped by the fact that *some of* the information others consider relevant in assessing a distribution is reflected, unrecoverably, in past matrices. Henceforth, we shall refer to such unhistorical principles of distributive justice, including the current-time-slice principles, as *end-result principles or end-state principles.*

In contrast to end-result principles of justice, *historical principles* of justice hold that past circumstances or actions of people can create differential entitlements or differential deserts to things. An injustice can be worked by moving from one distribution to another structurally identical one, for the second, in profile the same, may violate people's entitlements or deserts; it may not fit the actual history.

ASK YOURSELF

56. Nozick feels that it is more accurate to speak of current-time-slice principles as _____ principles.

The Original Position and End-Result Principles. Nozick devotes much attention to Rawls's notion of distributive justice. We've seen that, on Rawls's view, we consider questions of justice in the original position, where we assume ignorance of our actual standing in society. The notion of distributive justice that we arrive at in the original position is the difference principle: social and economic inequalities are to be arranged so that they are reasonably expected to be to everyone's advantage. Nozick feels that Rawls's view of distributive justice runs contrary to our accepted views of historical entitlement. True entitlement assumes that the past history of the property owner is central to the legitimacy of his claim to ownership. The veil of ignorance, though, strips us of any knowledge of our history, and, thus, the principles of distributive justice that we arrive at will rest on end-result principles.

If things fell from heaven like manna, and no one had any special entitlement to any portion of it, and no manna would fall unless all agreed to a particular distribution, and somehow the quantity varied depending on the distribution, then it is plausible to claim that persons placed so that they couldn't make threats, or hold out for specially large shares, would agree to the difference principle rule of distribution. But is *this* the appropriate model for thinking about how the things people produce are to be distributed? Why think the same results should obtain for situations where there *are* differential entitlements as for situations where there are not?

A procedure that founds principles of distributive justice on what rational persons who know nothing about themselves or their histories would agree to *guarantees that end-state principles of justice will be taken as fundamental.* Perhaps some historical principles of justice are derivable from end-state principles, as the utilitarian tries to derive individual rights, prohibitions on punishing the innocent, and so forth, from *his* end-state principle; perhaps such arguments can be constructed even for the entitlement principle. But no historical principle, it seems, could be agreed to in the first instance by the participants in Rawls' original position. For people meeting together behind a veil of ignorance to decide who gets what, knowing nothing about any special entitlements people may have, will treat anything to be distributed as manna from heaven. . . . The nature of the decision problem facing persons deciding upon principles in an original position behind a veil of ignorance limits them to end-state principles of distribution. . . .

[L]et us add that as Rawls states the root idea underlying the veil of ignorance, that feature which is the most prominent in excluding agreement to an entitlement conception, it is to prevent someone from tailoring principles to his own advantage, from designing principles to favor his particular condition. But not only does the veil of ignorance do this; it ensures that no shadow of entitlement considerations will enter the rational calculations of ignorant, nonmoral individuals constrained to decide in a situation reflecting some formal conditions of morality. Perhaps, in a Rawls-like construction, some condition weaker than the veil of ignorance could serve to exclude the special tailoring of principles, or perhaps some other "structural-looking" feature of the choice situation could be formulated to mirror entitlement considerations. But as it stands there is no reflection of entitlement considerations in any form in the situation of those in the original position; these considerations do not enter even to be overridden or outweighed or otherwise put aside. Since no glimmer of entitlement principles is built into the structure of the situation of persons in the original position, there is no way these principles could be selected; and Rawls' construction is incapable in principle of yielding them. This is not to say, of course, that the entitlement principle (or "the principle of natural liberty") couldn't be *written* on the list of principles to be considered by those in the original position. Rawls doesn't do even this, perhaps because it is so transparently clear that there would be no point in including it to be considered *there*.

ASK YOURSELF

57. Nozick argues that, behind the veil of ignorance, people will not even be in a position to consider an historical entitlement principle of wealth distribution. Why would entitlement not be a consideration behind the veil of ignorance?

3. COMMUNITARIANISM: MICHAEL J. SANDEL

In spite of the great differences between Rawls's and Nozick's views of distributive justice, they nevertheless share a strong commitment to the notion that government is grounded in the liberties of individuals. People wish to advance their liberties and seek out governmental arrangements that best do this. Rawl's egalitarian liberalism presumes *individualism*—that is, the liberties of individual people are basic to political arrangements. Rawls specifically argued that a central job of governments is to establish and fairly arrange the liberties and economic resources that individual people require in their freely chosen lives. Several recent political philosophers—known as communitarians—have lashed out against individualism and liberalism in general, and Rawls's liberalism in particular. According to communitarianism, the interests of collective units are basic to political arrangements. One advocate of communitarianism is Alasdair MacIntyre, whose views we examined in Chapter 6. For MacIntyre, people are by nature attached to their communities, and the good that each of us seeks as individuals involves the community. Liberalism distorts human nature insofar as it depicts people as isolated from their traditions and larger social contexts.

MacIntyre directed his attack very broadly at the entire lineup of liberal thinkers from Hobbes and Locke onwards. Another communitarian defender, Michael J. Sandel, took aim specifically at Rawls. Sandel asks us to consider three distinct concepts of community. The first is a purely instrumental notion along the lines of what Hobbes advances: We'd rather not have anything to do with community, but we're forced to in order to best pursue our private goals. The second is Rawls's conception of community: People have some shared final ends, and cooperation toward these goals is good in itself. Both of these views, Sandel argues, are individualistic.

> The instrumental account is individualistic in that the subjects of co-operation are assumed to be governed by self-interested motivations alone, and the good of community consists solely in the advantages individuals derive from co-operating in pursuit of their egoistic ends. Rawls' account is individualistic in the sense of assuming the antecedent individuation of the subjects of cooperation, whose actual motivations may include benevolent aims as well as selfish ones. As a result, the good of community for Rawls consists not only in the direct benefits of social co-operation but also in the quality of motivations and ties of sentiment that may attend this cooperation and be enhanced in the process. Where community on the first [instrumentalist] account is wholly *external* to the aims and interests of the individuals who comprise it, community on Rawls' view is partly *internal* to the subjects, in that it reaches the feelings and sentiments of those engaged in a cooperative scheme. In contrast to the instrumental conception of a community, we might describe Rawls' account as the sentimental conception.

For Sandel, Rawls has a "sentimental" conception of community; that is, individuals receive emotional gratification when they cooperate with others.

58. Illustrate Rawls's sentimental conception of community by describing a situation in which someone might feel emotionally gratified when acting benevolently toward others.

Sandel feels that both the instrumental and sentimental conceptions of community miss the boat. Community cannot be reduced to mere self-interest or personal emotional gratification. Instead, we must see that community actually constitutes part of our identity:

[T]o say that the members of a society are bound by a sense of community is not simply to say that a great many of them profess communitarian sentiments and pursue communitarian aims, but rather that they conceive their identity—the subject and not just the object of their feelings and aspirations—as defined to some extent by the community of which they are a part. For them, community describes not just what they *have* as fellow citizens but also what they *are,* not a relationship they choose (as in a voluntary association) but an attachment they discover, not merely an attribute but a constituent of their identity. In contrast to the instrumental and sentimental conceptions of community, we might describe this strong view as the constitutive conception. [From Michael J. Sandel, *Liberalism and the Limits of Justice* (1982)]

59. What are some features of Sandel's "constitutive conception" of community?

SUMMING UP THE ISSUE OF LIBERALISM AND COMMUNITARIANISM

A recent debate among political philosophers involves whether governments and societies should be community-oriented or individual-oriented. The theory of liberalism, inspired largely by John Locke, is strongly geared toward individual people: governments should protect our individual liberties, rather than threaten them. Writing within this tradition, Rawls argued that liberty should be grounded in the notion of fairness. We create a fair set of guidelines by stepping behind a veil of ignorance—ignoring our actual economic position within society. The guidelines we arrive at will guarantee equal rights and duties for all, and also regulate wealth in a way that would benefit both rich and poor. This view permits governments to restrict an individual's accumulation of property for the betterment of others. Also writing within the Lockean tradition of liberalism, Nozick argued that the role of governments should be very minimal, being restricted to protecting our rights, particularly our property rights. The only just mechanism for distributing wealth is entitlement: initially acquiring property justly and voluntarily transferring it by just means. In this view, governments cannot take away our private property against our wills, even for noble tasks such as helping the less fortunate. In contrast to the individual-oriented stance of liberalism, Sandel advocates communitarianism, which places primary value on the wider communities to which individuals belong. In this view, governments should be directed toward the advancement of community well-being, and not toward individual liberty as a value conceived independently of our nature as communal beings.

CAN OF WORMS

For different reasons, Rawls and Nozick both oppose the utilitiarian view that governments aim to serve the greatest good for the greatest number of people. In attacking this view, Rawls and Nozick raise questions about the fairness of utilitarianism as an ethical theory as well as a political theory. The issue of communitarianism raises fundamental questions about our human identities. In Chapter 3 we discussed a variety of theories that bolster the conviction that people are intimately connected with their larger environment. Marx argued that humans are essentially social beings that exist within communities, and capitalist economic structures strip us of this. Classical Hindu and Taoist philosophies connect human identity with a larger cosmic reality, suggesting that notions of individual identity are at best misguided and at worst illusions. Naess argued that we must see ourselves as connected with our larger ecological surroundings. Various forms of communitarianism question the concept of the "individual," which seems to function almost unconsciously in liberal and libertarian theories.

D. VIRTUOUS LEADERSHIP

We routinely hear about politicians accepting bribes, lying to the public, being involved in sex scandals, and, more generally, being incapable of standing up for what is right. When gross moral corruption is exposed, political careers quickly come to an end. We entrust leaders with the most important social tasks, and our confidence in them is often irreparably broken when we spot immoral behavior. Our officials should not only be effective administrators, but be moral leaders as well. There is, though, another side to the issue. Different factions of society place conflicting demands on our political leaders. One group favors nationalized health care, another wants it privatized. One group wants abortion outlawed; another wants it permitted. One group favors the death penalty; another is against it. Aside from internal disputes like these among citizens, surrounding countries engage in power struggles that often entangle one's own country—forcing complex alliances with foreign rulers. Part of political survival is a degree of craftiness when dealing with volatile issues. It seems unrealistic, then, to expect our leaders to be openly honest or completely free from the influence of special interests. One task of political philosophy is to understand the nature of virtuous leadership; should we expect our politicians to be perfectly virtuous or more like scheming snakes whose only virtue is craftiness?

QUESTIONS TO DISCUSS

a. Although former U.S. President Bill Clinton had a notorious reputation for marital infidelity, many Americans felt that this didn't necessarily make him a bad leader. Is marital fidelity an important virtue for political leadership?

b. Political leaders are often caught lying. Are there situations in which lying might be a sign of strong leadership?

c. Politicians, like athletes, are often looked up to as role models who influence the behavior of others. Even if politicians are morally upstanding, does this mean that their good behavior will be emulated by others?

1. VIRTUOUS LEADERS AT THE ROOT OF GOOD GOVERNMENT: CONFUCIANISM

**CONFUCIUS
(551–479 BCE)**

Founder of the Confucian religion.

The concept of a morally upright ruler is something that we find in political writings throughout the world. In the Confucian tradition, virtuous leadership isn't just an added bonus to society, but it is in fact essential for the stability of the entire country. Confucius stated specifically that "He who exercises government by means of his virtue may be compared to the north polar star, which keeps its place and all the stars turn toward it." How, though, does virtuous leadership have such a sweeping effect on society? This question is addressed in a brief Confucian classic from the third-century BCE called *The Great Learning*. The anonymous author of this work suggests that there is a trickle-down effect with virtuous leadership. The top ruler becomes virtuous through a proper knowledge of the world. Once his personal life is properly cultivated, he will pass this on to his family and then to his entire country.

FROM *The Great Learning*

The path of learning to be great consists of exhibiting clear character, loving people, and resting in the highest good. If we know the point in which we are to rest, we can determine the object of pursuit. When we determine that, we can attain a calmness, and from that will follow tranquility. In tranquility we can carefully deliberate, and that deliberation will be followed by the attainment of the desired end.

Things have their roots and their branches. Affairs have their beginnings and ends. To know what is first and what is last will lead us near the path of learning to be great.

The ancients who wished to exhibit their clear character to the world first brought order to their states. Wishing to order their states, they first regulated their families. Wishing to regulate their families, they first cultivated their personal lives. Wishing to cultivate their personal lives, they first corrected their minds. Wishing to correct their minds, they first sought to be sincere in their thoughts. Wishing to be sincere in their thoughts, they first extended their knowledge. Such extension of knowledge rests in investigating things.

Things being investigated, knowledge became complete. Their knowledge being complete, their thoughts were sincere. Their thoughts being sincere, their minds were then corrected. Their minds being corrected, their personal lives were cultivated. Their personal lives being cultivated, their families were regulated. Their families being regulated, their states were rightly governed. Their states being rightly governed, the whole kingdom was made tranquil and happy.

From the son of heaven down to the common people on earth, all must consider the cultivation of one's personal life as the root of everything else. When the root is neglected, what springs from it will not be well ordered. No one has ever taken slight care of greatly important things, and no one has greatly cared for slightly important things.

ASK YOURSELF

60. The discussion above rests on the metaphor of a tree. What does the root represent, and what do the branches represent?

61. The first step in the above discussion is for the ruler to investigate things, and the final step is a well-ordered state. List the in-between steps.

2. THE PHILOSOPHER KING: PLATO

In Western civilization, the philosopher who best articulates the view of the morally upright leader is Plato. In his dialogue the Republic, he offers a vision of the perfect ruler: the *philosopher king*. According to Plato, everyone has his or her own station in society and we all should excel in our specialized tasks—whether we're farmers, craftspeople, soldiers, or administrators. The ruler's task is to oversee all of these functions, and to do so he must be committed to truth and moral virtue. The selection below is part of a dialogue between the character Socrates, who represents Plato's views, and the character Glaucon, whom Socrates is trying to convince.

Lovers of Truth. Socrates argues that some people are born followers and others leaders. Leaders must be philosophers in the sense that they love wisdom and have a special ability to judge what is good. To that end, they must be lovers of absolute, eternal, and unchanging truth, and not lovers of mere opinion.

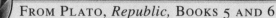

FROM PLATO, *Republic*, BOOKS 5 AND 6

SOCRATES Until philosophers are kings, or the kings and princes of this world have the spirit and power of philosophy, and political greatness and wisdom meet in one, and those commoner natures who pursue either to the exclusion of the other are compelled to stand aside, cities will never have rest from their evils—no, nor the human race, as I believe—and then only will this our State have a possibility of life and behold the light of day. . . . There will be discovered to be some natures who ought to study philosophy and to be leaders in the State; and others who are not born to be philosophers, and are meant to be followers rather than leaders. . . .

And may we not say of the philosopher that he is a lover, not of a part of wisdom only, but of the whole?

GLAUCON Yes, of the whole.

SOCRATES And he who dislikes learning, especially in youth, when he has no power of judging what is good and what is not, such a one we maintain not to be a philosopher or a lover of knowledge, just as he who refuses his food is not hungry, and may be said to have a bad appetite and not a good one?

GLAUCON Very true, he said.

SOCRATES Whereas he who has a taste for every sort of knowledge and who is curious to learn and is never satisfied, may be justly termed a philosopher? Am I not right?

GLAUCON If curiosity makes a philosopher, you will find many a strange being will have a title to the name. All the lovers of sights have a delight in learning, and must therefore be included. Musical amateurs, too, are a folk strangely out of place among philosophers, for they are the last persons in the world who would come to anything like a philosophical discussion, if they could help, while they run about at the Dionysiac festivals as if they had let out their ears to hear every chorus; whether the performance is in town or country—that makes no difference—they are there. Now are we to maintain that all these and any who have similar tastes, as well as the professors of quite minor arts, are philosophers?

SOCRATES Certainly not, I replied; they are only an imitation.

GLAUCON He said: Who then are the true philosophers?

SOCRATES Those, I said, who are lovers of the vision of truth. . . .

ASK YOURSELF

62. According to Socrates, philosophers must display curiosity about every sort of knowledge. Glaucon, though, notes that many somewhat inferior people have a delight in learning, such as those obsessed with music. Socrates, in response, says that these are not true philosophers. What are they instead?

Lovers of truth, Socrates argues, will not be swayed by the mere appearances of things but instead will be able to see truth in its absolute and unchanging form. He illustrates this with the knowledge of beauty, contrasting the views of the multitude that are grounded in opinion, and the views of the philosopher that are grounded in the eternal realm of forms.

SOCRATES   Thus then we seem to have discovered that the many ideas which the multitude entertain about the beautiful and about all other things are tossing about in some region which is halfway between pure being and pure not-being?

GLAUCON   We have.

SOCRATES   Yes; and we had before agreed that anything of this kind which we might find was to be described as matter of opinion, and not as matter of knowledge; being the intermediate flux which is caught and detained by the intermediate faculty.

GLAUCON   Quite true.

SOCRATES   Then those who see the many beautiful, and who yet neither see absolute beauty, nor can follow any guide who points the way thither; who see the many just, and not absolute justice, and the like—such persons may be said to have opinion but not knowledge?

GLAUCON   That is certain.

SOCRATES   But those who see the absolute and eternal and immutable may be said to know, and not to have opinion only?

GLAUCON   Neither can that be denied.

ASK YOURSELF

63. The philosopher has true knowledge, but the multitude has mere opinion. What are some features of opinion?

Virtues of the Philosopher King.   Aside from having a love of unchanging truth, philosophers must acquire and display a range of moral virtues.

SOCRATES   Another criterion of the philosophical nature has also to be considered.

GLAUCON   What is that?

SOCRATES   There should be no secret corner of illiberality; nothing can be more antagonistic than meanness to a soul which is ever longing after the whole of things both divine and human.

GLAUCON   Most true, he replied.

SOCRATES   Then how can he who has magnificence of mind and is the spectator of all time and all existence, think much of human life?

GLAUCON   He cannot.

SOCRATES   Or can such a one account death fearful?

GLAUCON   No, indeed.

SOCRATES   Then the cowardly and mean nature has no part in true philosophy?

GLAUCON   Certainly not.

SOCRATES   Or again: can he who is harmoniously constituted, who is not covetous or mean, or a boaster, or a coward—can he, I say, ever be unjust or hard in his dealings?

GLAUCON   Impossible.

SOCRATES   Then you will soon observe whether a man is just and gentle, or rude and unsociable; these are the signs which distinguish even in youth the philosophical nature from the unphilosophical.

GLAUCON　True.

SOCRATES　There is another point which should be remarked.

GLAUCON　What point?

SOCRATES　Whether he has or has not a pleasure in learning; for no one will love that which gives him pain, and in which after much toil he makes little progress.

GLAUCON　Certainly not.

SOCRATES　And again, if he is forgetful and retains nothing of what he learns, will he not be an empty vessel?

GLAUCON　That is certain.

SOCRATES　Laboring in vain, he must end in hating himself and his fruitless occupation?

GLAUCON　Yes.

SOCRATES　Then a soul which forgets cannot be ranked among genuine philosophic natures; we must insist that the philosopher should have a good memory?

GLAUCON　Certainly.

SOCRATES　And once more, the inharmonious and unseemly nature can only tend to disproportion?

GLAUCON　Undoubtedly.

SOCRATES　And do you consider truth to be akin to proportion or to disproportion?

GLAUCON　To proportion.

SOCRATES　Then, besides other qualities, we must try to find a naturally wellproportioned and gracious mind, which will move spontaneously toward the true being of everything.

GLAUCON　Certainly.

SOCRATES　Well, and do not all these qualities, which we have been enumerating, go together, and are they not, in a manner, necessary to a soul, which is to have a full and perfect participation of being?

GLAUCON　They are absolutely necessary, he replied.

SOCRATES　And must not that be a blameless study which he only can pursue who has the gift of a good memory, and is quick to learn—noble, gracious, the friend of truth, justice, courage, temperance, who are his kindred?

GLAUCON　The god of jealousy himself, he said, could find no fault with such a study.

SOCRATES　And to men like him, I said, when perfected by years and education, and to these only you will intrust the State.

ASK YOURSELF

64. According to Socrates, what are the key moral virtues that the philosopher king must possess?

3.　POLITICAL SURVIVAL: NICCOLÒ MACHIAVELLI

Plato's conception of the philosopher king loomed large over European political philosophy for some time, offering an ideal of moral perfection that every ruler should strive to attain. Almost 2000 years later, however, Renaissance philosopher Niccolò Machiavelli

(1469–1527) presented a quite different view of the successful leader's moral character. His famous treatise, *The Prince,* is an expression of *realpolitik*—that is, governmental policy based on retaining power rather than pursuing moral ideals. Machiavelli was born in Florence, Italy, at a time when the country was in political upheaval. Italy was divided between four dominant city-states, and each of these was continually at the mercy of stronger foreign governments in Europe. Since 1434 the wealthy Medici family ruled Florence. Their rule was temporarily interrupted by a reform movement, begun in 1494, in which the young Machiavelli became an important diplomat. When the Medici family regained power in 1512 with the help of Spanish troops, Machiavelli was tortured and removed from public life. For the next 10 years he devoted his time to writing history, political philosophy, and even plays. He ultimately gained favor with the Medici family and was called back to public duty for the last two years of his life. Machiavelli wrote *The Prince* in 1513, but it remained unpublished until

NICCOLÒ MACHIAVELLI (1469–1527)

Italian political philosopher and author of The Prince *(1532).*

1532, after his death. The work immediately provoked controversy and was soon condemned by Pope Clement VIII. Its main theme is that princes should retain absolute control of their territories, and they should use any means of accomplishing this end, including deceit. In several sections Machiavelli praises Caesar Borgia, a Spanish aristocrat who became a notorious and much despised tyrant of the Romagna region of northern Italy. During Machiavelli's early years as a diplomat, he was in contact with Borgia and witnessed Borgia's rule first hand. Some readers initially saw *The Prince* as a satire on absolute rulers such as Borgia, which showed the repugnance of arbitrary power—thereby implying the importance of liberty. However, this interpretation fell apart when, in 1810, a letter by Machiavelli was discovered in which he reveals that he wrote *The Prince* to endear himself to the ruling Medici family in Florence. To liberate Italy from the influence of foreign governments, Machiavelli explains, strong indigenous governments are important even if they are absolutist.

Alleged Qualities of a Good Monarch. Machiavelli makes clear his intention to describe the truth about surviving as a monarch, rather than recommending lofty moral ideals.

FROM NICCOLÒ MACHIAVELLI, *The Prince,* CHAPTERS 15–19

It remains now to see what should be the rules of conduct for a prince towards subject and friends. And as I know that many have written on this point, I expect I will be considered presumptuous in mentioning it again, especially since my discussion will depart from the methods of other people. But, since it is my intention to write something which will be useful to those who grasp it, it appears to me more appropriate to follow up with the real truth of a matter rather than the imagination of it. For many describe republics and monarchies which in fact have never been known or seen. This is because how one actually lives is so far removed from how one *ought* to live. Thus, he who neglects what *is* done for what *ought* to be done, more quickly causes his destruction rather than his preservation. For a person who wishes to act entirely according to his declarations of virtue soon meets with an array of evils which destroy him.

ASK YOURSELF

65. For Machiavelli, what happens to a monarch who is guided only by "what ought to be done" (i.e., lofty moral ideals)?

Machiavelli continues describing those virtues that, on face value, we think a ruler should possess. He concludes that some "virtues" will lead to a ruler's destruction, whereas some "vices" allow him to survive.

Thus, if a prince wishes to keep his position, it is necessary that he knows how to do wrong, and to make use of it or not according to necessity. Therefore, let us set aside imaginary things concerning a prince, and discuss those which are real. Accordingly, I say that when all people are spoken of (and especially princes since they are more visible) they are distinguished based on specific qualities which bring them either blame or praise. Because of this one person is said to be generous, another miserly, using a Tuscan term (because an avaricious person in our language is still he who desires to own things through theft, whereas we call one miserly who deprives himself too much of the use of what he owns). One is reputed to be generous, another greedy; one cruel, one compassionate; one dishonest, another honest; one weak and cowardly, another bold and brave; one friendly, another arrogant; one lustful, another chaste; one sincere, another cunning; one hard, another easy; one solemn, another frivolous; one religious, another unbelieving, and the like. And I know that everyone will acknowledge that it would be most admirable for a prince to exhibit all the above qualities that are considered good. But these good qualities can neither be entirely possessed nor observed, since human conditions do not permit it. It is then necessary for a prince to be sufficiently careful so that he may know how to avoid the negative effects of those vices which would make him lose his state. If possible, he must also take care to keep himself from those which would not lose him it; and if this is not possible, he may give himself to them with less hesitation. And again, he need not worry about subjecting himself to criticism for those vices which, if he lacked, would make saving his state difficult. For considering everything carefully, we see that something which looks like virtue would lead to his destruction if followed; alternatively, something else, which looks like vice, will bring him security and prosperity if followed.

ASK YOURSELF

66. What are the virtues that we commonly praise in people but that might lead to the downfall of a prince?

Concerning Generosity and Stinginess. We commonly think that it is best for a ruler to have a reputation of being generous. However, if his generosity is done in secret, no one will know about it and he will be thought to be greedy. If it is done openly, then he risks going broke to maintain his reputation. He will then extort more money from his subjects and thus be hated. For Machiavelli, it is best for a prince to have a reputation for being stingy.

Starting then with the first of the above-named characteristics, [suppose] I say that it is best if one is thought to be generous. However, generosity injures you when exercised in a way that does not bring you the reputation for it. For if one exercises it honestly, as it should be exercised, people will not know about it, and you will not avoid the criticism of its opposite. Therefore, [it seems that] if anyone wishes to maintain a reputation of generosity among people, one should not avoid the attribute of lavishness. However, by doing so a prince will consume all his property in such acts and, if he wishes to keep the reputation of generosity, he will unjustly burden his people, and tax them, and do everything he can to get money. This will soon make him despised by is subjects, and becoming poor he will be little valued by anyone. Thus, having offended many and rewarded few with his generosity, he is affected by every trouble and threaten by every danger. Recognizing this himself, and wishing to draw back from it, he runs immediately into criticism for being miserly.

ASK YOURSELF

67. What unfortunate chain of events occurs if a prince wants to openly maintain a reputation of being generous?

Therefore, a prince is not able to visibly exercise this virtue of generosity, except at great cost. If he is wise, then, he should not worry about having a reputation of being stingy. For in time he will be considered generous when people see that, with his economizing, his income is sufficient to defend himself against all attacks, and he is able to engage in enterprises without burdening his people. In this way he shows generosity towards the numberless people from whom he does not take, and stinginess only towards the few people to whom he does not give.

We have not seen great things done in our time except by those who have been considered stingy. The rest have failed. Pope Julius the Second was assisted in reaching the papacy by a reputation for generosity, yet he did not try afterwards to keep it up when he made war on the King of France. And he made many wars without imposing any extraordinary tax on his subjects, for he supplied his additional expenses out of his long thriftiness. The present King of Spain would not have undertaken or succeeded in so many efforts if he had a generous reputation. Thus, a prince should not worry about having a reputation for being stingy, provided that does not have to rob his subjects, that he can defend himself, that he does not become poor and abject, that he is not forced to become greedy. For it is one of those vices which will enable him to govern.

ASK YOURSELF

68. How can a prince eventually gain a reputation for showing generosity, even though he is stingy?

Machiavelli anticipates examples one might give of generous monarchs who have been successful. He concludes that generosity should only be shown to soldiers with goods taken from a pillaged enemy city.

Suppose someone says that Caesar obtained his empire though generosity, and many others have reached the highest positions by having been generous, and by being considered so. To this I answer that either you are currently a prince, or are in the process of becoming one. In the first case this generosity is dangerous, in the second it is very necessary to be considered generous. And Caesar was one of those who wished to become pre-eminent in Rome. But if he had survived after becoming so, and had not moderated his expenses, he would have destroyed his government. Suppose someone replies that there have been many princes who have done great things with armies, and yet have been considered very generous. To this I reply that either a prince spends that which is his own or his subjects', or else that of others. In the first case he should be sparing, and in the second case he should not neglect any opportunity for generosity. And to the prince who advances with his army, supporting it by pillage, destruction, and extortion, handling that which belongs to others, this generosity is necessary, otherwise he would not be followed by soldiers. You can be a willing giver of that which is neither yours nor your subjects' (as Cyrus, Caesar, and Alexander were) because it does not take away your reputation if you squander that of others, but adds to it. It is only squandering your own that injures you.

ASK YOURSELF

69. Machiavelli concedes that a prince should be generous with his soldiers when pillaging a conquered city. Why?

And there is nothing that dissipates so rapidly as generosity. For even while you exercise it, you lose the power to do so, and become either poor or despised. Alternatively, in avoiding poverty you become greedy and hated. Above everything else, a prince should guard himself against being despised and hated, and generosity leads you to both. Therefore it is wiser to have a reputation for stinginess which brings reproach without hatred, than to be compelled through seeking a reputation for generosity to incur a reputation for greed which results in disapproval with hatred.

Concerning Severity and Mercy. Machiavelli argues that it is better to be severe when punishing people than to be merciful. Severity through death sentences affects only a few, but it deters crimes that affect many.

Turning now to the other qualities mentioned above, [suppose] I say that every prince should desire to be considered merciful and not cruel. Nevertheless he should try not to misuse this mercy. Cesare Borgia was considered cruel. In spite of his cruelty, he reconciled the Romagna, unified it, and restored it to peace and loyalty. And if this is properly considered, we will see that he was much more merciful than the Florentine people, who, to avoid a reputation for cruelty, permitted Pistoia [a city in northern Italy] to be destroyed. Therefore, so long as a prince keeps his subjects united and loyal, he should not mind the criticism of cruelty. With a few examples of cruelty he will be more merciful than princes who, through too much mercy, allow disorders to arise, from which result murders or robberies. For these typically injure the whole people, whereas those executions which originate with a prince harm the individual only.

And of all princes, it is impossible for a new prince to avoid the accusation of cruelty, since new states are full of dangers. Hence Virgil, through the mouth of Dido, excuses the inhumanity of her reign because of its newness, saying,

Against my will, my fate,
A throne unsettled, and an infant state,
Bid me defend my realms with all my powers,
And guard with these severities my shores.

ASK YOURSELF

70. Why must princes of new kingdoms be particularly severe in punishment?

Nevertheless he should be slow to believe and to act. He should also not display fear, but act calmly with thought and humanity so that too much confidence does not make him incautious and too much distrust make him intolerable.

Better to Be Feared than Loved. Machiavelli argues that it is better for rulers to be feared than to be loved. However, the prince should avoid being hated, which he can easily accomplish by not confiscating the property of his subjects.

From this issue another question arises: is it be better to be loved than feared, or feared than loved? It may be answered that one should wish to be both, but, because it is difficult to unite them in one person, is much safer to be feared than loved, when one of the two must be dispensed with. For we can generally say of people that they are ungrateful, fickle, deceitful, cowardly, and selfish. But as long as you benefit them, they are yours entirely. They will offer you their blood, property, life and children (as I noted above) when the need is far off. But when the need approaches, they turn against you. And the prince is ruined who relies only on their promises and has neglected other precautions. This is because friendships that are obtained by payments, and not by greatness or nobility of mind, may indeed be *earned*, but they are not *secured,* and in time of need cannot be counted on. And people have less scruple in offending someone who is beloved rather than someone who is feared. For love is preserved by the link of obligation which, because of the corruption of people, is broken at every opportunity for their advantage. But fear preserves you by a fear of punishment which never fails.

ASK YOURSELF

71. Why is it better to be feared than to be loved?

Nevertheless a prince should create fear in such a way that, if he does not win love, he avoids hatred. For, he can survive very well being feared so long as he is not hated. And he will not be hated as long as he abstains from the property of his citizens and subjects and from their women. But when it is necessary for him to take someone's life, he must do it on proper justification and for clear cause. Above all, though, he must keep his hands off the property of others, because people more quickly forget the death of their father than the loss of their inheritance. Besides, excuses about for taking away property. For he who begins to live by robbery will always find excuses for seizing others' possessions. But reasons for taking life, on the contrary, are more difficult to find and sooner lapse. When a prince is with his army and in control of a large number of soldiers, then it is absolutely necessary for him to disregard the reputation of cruelty, for without it he would never keep his army united or willing to follow their duties.

ASK YOURSELF

72. Machiavelli says that "people more quickly forget the death of their father than the loss of their inheritance." What is his point?

The Severity of Hannibal. Machiavelli illustrates his point with the story of Hannibal (the third-century CE general from Carthage), who was severe yet militarily successful. Scipio, by contrast, was humane but a failure militarily.

Among the wonderful deeds of Hannibal, one is particularly noteworty. Hannibal led an enormous army, composed of various races of people, to fight in foreign lands and whether in his bad or in his good fortune, no conflict arose either among the soldiers or against the prince. This arose from nothing other than his inhuman cruelty, which, with his boundless courage, made him revered and frightening in the sight of his soldiers. But without that cruelty, his other virtues would not be sufficient to produce this effect. And shortsighted writers admire his deeds from one point of view, yet from another condemn the principal cause of them. To prove that his other virtues would not have been sufficient for him, we may consider the case of Scipio, that most excellent person both within his own times and withing the memory of humankind. Nevertheless, his army rebelled against him in Spain. This arose from nothing but his too great tolerance, which gave his soldiers more license than is consistent with military discipline. For this he was condemned in the Senate by Fabius Maximus, and called the corrupter of the Roman army. The Locrians were destroyed by an officer of Scipio, yet they were not avenged by him, nor was the insult of the legate punished, owing entirely to his easy nature. Insomuch that someone in the Senate, wishing to excuse him, said there were many people who knew much better how not to err than to correct the errors of others. This disposition, if he had been continued in the command, would have destroyed in time the fame and glory of Scipio; but, he being under the control of the Senate, this injurious characteristic not only concealed itself, but contributed to his glory.

Returning to the question of being feared or loved, I come to the conclusion that, people loving according to their own will and fearing according to that of the prince, a wise prince should establish himself on that which is in his own control and not in that of others; he must endeavor only to avoid hatred, as is noted.

ASK YOURSELF

73. According to Machiavelli, what was the key to Hannibal's success and the cause of Scipio's failure?

Honesty: Emulate Both the Fox and the Lion. In perhaps the most controversial part of *The Prince,* Machiavelli argues that the prince should know how to be deceitful when it suits his purpose. In this way, the prince should have the qualities of both the fox and the lion when it comes to ruling by force—as opposed to ruling by reason.

Everyone admits how good it is in a prince be honest, and to live with integrity and not with deceit. Nevertheless our experience has been that those princes who have done great things have had little regard for honesty, and have known how to circumvent the intellect of people by deceit, and in the end have overcome those who have relied on their word. You must know that there are two ways of contesting, the one by the law, the other by force. The first method is proper to humans, the second to beasts. But because the first is frequently not sufficient, it is necessary to have recourse to the second. Therefore it is essential for a prince to understand how to make use of both the beast and the human. This has been figuratively taught to princes by ancient writers. It is described how Achilles and many other past princes were given to Chiron, the Centaur, to nurse and be raised in his discipline. The meaning of this story is that, just as they had for a teacher one who was half beast and half human, so it is necessary for a prince to know how to make use of both natures, and that one without the other cannot survive. Since a prince is therefore compelled to consciously adopt the persona of beast, he should choose both the fox and the lion. This is because the lion cannot defend himself against snares, and the fox cannot defend himself against wolves. Thus, it is necessary to be a fox to discover the snares, and a lion to terrify the wolves. Those who rely simply on the lion do not understand what they are about. Accordingly, a wise ruler cannot nor should he be honest when such observance may be turned against him, and when the reasons that caused him to pledge it no longer exist. If people were entirely good, this precept would not hold. But because they are bad, and will not be honest with you, you too are not bound to observe it with them. Nor will a prince ever be lacking good reasons to excuse this nonobservance. Endless modern examples of this could be given, showing how many treaties and engagements have been made void and ineffective because of the dishonesty of princes. And he who has known best how to employ the fox has succeeded best.

ASK YOURSELF

74. To be successful rulers, what two animal personas should rulers adopt and why?

Appearance of Virtue. Machiavelli contends that when a ruler needs to be deceitful, he must not appear that way. Indeed rulers must always at least appear to have five virtues in particular: mercy, honesty, humaneness, uprightness, and religiousness.

But it is necessary to know well how to disguise this characteristic, and to be a great pretender and deceiver. People are so simple and so subject to present needs, that anyone who seeks to deceive will always find someone who will allow himself to be deceived. There is one recent example which I cannot pass over in silence. Alexander VI did nothing but deceive people, nor ever thought of doing otherwise, and he always found victims. For there never was a person who had greater ability in asserting, or who with greater oaths would affirm something, yet would observe it less. Nevertheless his deceits always succeeded according to his wishes, because he well understood this side of humankind.

Therefore it is unnecessary for a prince to have all the virtuous qualities I have enumerated. But it is very necessary for him to appear to have them. And I will dare to say this also, that to have them and always to observe them is injurious, and that to appear to have them is useful. Thus one should appear merciful, honest, humane, religious, upright, and also be that way. But your mind should framed so that if you are required not to be so, you may be able and know how to change to the opposite.

ASK YOURSELF

75. What virtues should the prince appear to have (although in reality doing the opposite where circumstances dictate)?

And you have to understand that a prince, especially a new one, cannot follow all those things for which people are respected. For, in order to maintain the state, he is often forced to act contrary to honesty, friendship, humanity, and religion. Therefore it is necessary for him to have a mind ready to turn itself with the winds and changes of fortune force it. Yet, as I have said above, he should not diverge from the good if he can avoid doing so, but, if compelled to go against the good, he should know how to set about it.

For this reason a prince should take care that he never lets anything slip from his lips that is not overflowing with the above-named five qualities, so that he may appear to those who see and hear him altogether merciful, honest, humane, upright, and religious. There is nothing more necessary to appear to have than this last quality. For, people generally judge more by the eye than by the hand, and everybody is capable of seeing you, and few can come in touch with you. Everyone sees what you appear to be, few really know what you are, and those few dare not oppose themselves to the opinion of the many, who have the majesty of the state to defend them. And in the actions of all people, and especially of princes which it is not prudent to challenge, one judges by the result.

ASK YOURSELF

76. How is it that people typically judge our religious attitudes?

For that reason, let a prince aim at conquering and keeping his state, and the means of attaining it will always be considered honest, and he will be praised by everybody. This is because the common people are always taken by what a thing seems to be and by what comes of it. And in the world there are only common people. For the few who are not common people find a place in the world only when the many have no ground on which to.

One prince of the present time, whom it is not best to name [i.e., Maximilian I, Holy Roman Emperor], never preaches anything else but peace and honesty, and to both he is most hostile, and either, if he had kept it, would have deprived him many times of reputation and kingdom.

Avoiding Being Despised and Hated. According to Machiavelli, the prince must avoid doing things that will cause him to be hated. This is accomplished by not confiscating property and by not appearing greedy or wishy-washy.

Now, concerning the characteristics of which mention is made above, I have spoken of the more important ones. The others I wish to discuss briefly under this generality, that the prince must consider, as has been in part said before, how to avoid those things that will make him hated or contemptible. And as often as he succeeds he will have fulfilled his part, and he won't need to fear any danger in other condemnations.

To be greedy, as I have said, makes him hated above everything, and he must abstain from violating both his subjects' property and women. And when neither their property nor honor is touched, the majority of people live content, and he has only to contend with the ambition of a few, whom he can curb with ease in many ways.

It makes him contemptible to be considered fickle, frivolous, weak, mean-spirited, irresolute, from all of which a prince should guard himself as from a rock. In his actions he should try to show greatness, courage, gravity, and fortitude. In his private dealings with his subjects, let him show that his judgments are irrevocable, and maintain himself in such reputation that no one can hope either to deceive him or to get round him.

That prince is highly respected who conveys this impression of himself, and he who is highly respected is not easily conspired against. For, provided it is well known that he is an excellent person and revered by his people, he can only be attacked with difficulty. For this reason a prince should have two fears, one from within, on account of his subjects, the other from without, on account of external powers. From the latter he is defended by being well armed and having good allies, and if he is well armed he will have good friends, and affairs will always remain quiet within when they are quiet without, unless they should have been already disturbed by conspiracy; and even should affairs outside be disturbed, if he has carried out his preparations and has lived as I have said, as long as he does not despair, he will resist every attack, as I said Nabis the Spartan did.

77. What is the best way for the prince to defend himself against outside attack?

The Best Way to Avoid Being Overthrown. For Machiavelli, the best way to avoid being overthrown is to avoid being hated.

> But concerning his subjects, when affairs outside are disturbed he has only to fear that they will conspire secretly, from which a prince can easily secure himself by avoiding being hated and despised, and by keeping the people satisfied with him, which it is most necessary for him to accomplish, as I said above at length. And one of the most effective remedies that a prince can have against conspiracies is not to be hated and despised by the people. For those who conspire against a prince always expects to please people by his removal. But when the conspirator can only look forward to offending people, he will not have the courage to take such a course, for the difficulties that confront a conspirator are infinite. And as experience shows, many have been the conspiracies, but few have been successful. This is because he who conspires cannot act alone, nor can he take a companion except from those whom he believes to be malcontents, and as soon as you have opened your mind to a malcontent you have given him the material with which to content himself, for by denouncing you he can look for every advantage; so that, seeing the gain from this course to be assured, and seeing the other to be doubtful and full of dangers, he must be a very rare friend, or a thoroughly obstinate enemy of the prince, to keep faith with you.
>
> And, to reduce the matter into a small compass, I say that, on the side of the conspirator, there is nothing but fear, jealousy, and prospect of punishment to terrify him. But on the side of the prince there is the majesty of the monarchy, the laws, the protection of friends and the state to defend him. Adding to all these things the popular goodwill, it is impossible that anyone should be so rash as to conspire. For whereas in general the conspirator has to fear *before* the execution of his plot, in this case he has also to fear the what will occur *after* his crime. Because of this he has the people for an enemy, and thus cannot hope for any escape.

78. Why are few conspiracies successful when a monarch is well liked by the masses?

SUMMING UP THE ISSUE OF VIRTUOUS LEADERSHIP

We expect moral integrity from our political leaders, but the question remains whether some amount of dishonesty is necessary for political survival. According to classical Confucian philosophy, political rulers are models that impact the moral conduct of the entire country. Rulers begin by obtaining knowledge of the world and cultivating their own lives. They then pass virtuous character onto their families and then to the whole country. Plato argued that all tasks within society are governed by the philosopher king, who devotes his life to the pursuit of ultimate truth and moral virtue. In contrast to both of these views, Machiavelli argued that rulers should use any means of retaining power, including conduct traditionally thought to be vicious, such as stinginess, fierceness, and deceitfulness. Although rulers must always appear to be virtuous in the eyes of their subjects, their true conduct must be aimed at survival, not virtue.

**CAN OF
WORMS**

The question of virtuous leadership connects with a fundamental issue of ethics, namely, whether there is an unchanging standard of morality that applies to all people, or whether morality is a human invention. Plato believed that there indeed exists an objective standard that all people, including kings, must discover. Machiavelli, on the other hand, felt that leaders could ignore ordinary standards of morality and adopt any set of values that facilitates political survival. Thus Machiavelli makes certain assumptions about the domain of morality and the universality of ethical principles.

E. LIMITS OF POLITICAL COERCION

From almost the moment we're born, people boss us around. Our parents mold our behavior under threat of punishment. Our school teachers direct us to perform academic tasks, again under threat of punishment. As we get older we see that governments force us to follow the laws, yet again under threat of punishment. We can justify at least some coercion of children in the name of child-rearing. But once we're adults, what justification is there for governments ordering us about almost as though we were still children? It's not just that we feel bothered when governments encroach on our private space. Rather, the kind of coercion that governments impose on us might rise to the level of enslavement. For the sake of argument, let's grant that governments are justly empowered to exercise authority over us to preserve the peace, to protect citizens' rights, to bring about a better society, or for some similar reason. This does not mean that governments can do whatever they want. They can't, for example, hang us by our thumbs and horsewhip us for skipping church on Sunday. As powerful as governments are, there are at least *some* restrictions to their coercive authority. Political philosophers examine the possible grounds and limits of governmental coercion.

**QUESTIONS
TO DISCUSS**

a. The majority of people in the United States today believe that capital punishment is justified. What would be an argument against capital punishment?

b. Should the government restrict the use of recreational drugs such as marijuana?

c. Racist groups such as the Ku Klux Klan burn crosses as a means of intimidating black Americans. Should racist groups be allowed to burn crosses as a matter of free speech?

There are six common justifications behind governmental restrictions. First is the *harm principle,* which aims to prevent us from harming other citizens. If I assault, rob, or harm you in some similar way, the government can justly step in and restrain me. A second justification for coercion is the *offense principle,* which seeks to prevent us from offending other people. We don't ordinarily let people run around naked downtown, or let couples get too hot and heavy when publicly showing affection toward each other. This is also the justification behind laws restricting obscene photographs or literature. Third, there is the principal of *legal paternalism,* according to which people should be prevented from harming themselves. Governments restrict us from many self-destructive activities, such as playing exceptionally dangerous sports or taking harmful recreational drugs. Fourth, the principle of *legal moralism* expresses the conviction that sinful or immoral conduct should be prohibited. Examples of such conduct might include making blasphemous statements or engaging in certain kinds of sexual activities—even in private among consenting adults. Fifth, the principle of *extreme paternalism* involves coercing individuals in ways that benefit themselves—such as forcing them to become more educated and cultured. Sixth, the *welfare principle* aims to have us act in ways that benefit others by, for example, devoting tax money to provide food or housing for the poor.

Although governments typically coerce us for all six of these reasons, some of these justifications are more questionable than others. For example, most people would agree that government should restrict our conduct when it harms others—although what counts as "harm" may be up for debate. By contrast, there is much opposition to the principle of legal moralism, specifically concerning laws regarding sexual activities between consenting adults. Thus, not all six of the above justifications are necessarily good ones, and governments may be overstepping their bounds when they rely on some of them. In this section, we will look at three discussions concerning the limits of governmental coercion. The first, by Cesare Beccaria, examines the type of punishment that governments can justifiably impose on offenders. The second, by John Stuart Mill, considers whether any grounds for coercion are justifiable beyond the harm principle. The third, by Joel Feinberg, explores the validity of governmental restrictions aimed at preventing us from offending other people.

1. THE LIMITED PURPOSE OF PUNISHMENT: CESARE BECCARIA

Behind all governmental coercion is the threat of punishment, and throughout history political institutions have imposed the most dreadful sentences on offenders. Perhaps no other work had such a rapid and widespread impact on reforming the penal systems of Europe as Cesare Beccaria's *On Crimes and Punishments* (1764). Beccaria (1738–1794) was born the eldest son in an aristocratic family and educated at a Jesuit school. In his mid-twenties he joined an intellectual organization called "the academy of fists," which focused on reforming the criminal justice system. Through this group Beccaria became acquainted with French and British political philosophers of his day and composed *On Crimes and Punishments* at the urging of a friend. Almost immediately, the work was translated into French and English and went through several editions. Philosophers of the time hailed it, and several European emperors vowed to follow it. Beccaria's work relentlessly protests against torture to obtain confessions, secret accusations, the arbitrary discretionary power of judges, the inconsistency and inequality of sentencing, using personal connections to get a lighter sentence, and the use of capital punishment for both minor and major offenses. Beccaria develops his position by appealing to two key philosophical theories: social contract and utility. He argues that punishment is justified only to defend the social contract and to ensure that everyone will be motivated to abide by it. He also argued, in utilitarian fashion, that the method of punishment selected should be that which serves the greatest public good.

The Intent of Punishments. Contemporary political philosophers distinguish between two principal theories of justifying punishment. First, the *retributive* approach maintains that punishment is deserved and should be equal to the harm done, either literally an eye for an eye, or more figuratively in a way that allows for alternative forms of compensation. The retributive approach tends to be retaliatory and vengeance-oriented. The second approach is *utilitarian.* It maintains that punishment should increase the total amount of happiness in the world. This often involves punishment as a means of reforming the criminal, incapacitating him from repeating his crime, and deterring others. Beccaria clearly takes a utilitarian stance. For Beccaria, the purpose of punishment is to create a better society, not revenge. Punishment serves to deter others from committing crimes, as well as to prevent the criminal from repeating his crime.

FROM CESARE BECCARIA, *On Crimes and Punishment* (1764), CHAPTERS 12, 19, 27, 28

From the foregoing considerations it is evident that the intent of punishments is not to torment a sentient being, nor to undo a crime already committed. Is it possible that torments and useless cruelty, the instrument of furious fanaticism or of impotency of tyrants, can be authorized by a political body? Instead of being influenced by passion, such institutions should be the cool moderator of the passions of individuals. Can the groans of a tortured wretch bring back the time past, or reverse the crime he has committed?

The end of punishment, therefore, is no other than to prevent the criminal from doing further injury to society, and to prevent others from committing the same offense. Such punishments, therefore, and such a mode of inflicting them ought to be chosen in a way that will make the strongest and most lasting impressions on the minds of others, with the least torment to the body of the criminal.

ASK YOURSELF

79. What should the main factor be in determining the type of punishment?

Advantages of Immediate Punishment. Beccaria argues that punishment should be swift since this has the greatest deterrence value.

The more immediately after the commission of a crime a punishment is inflicted, the more just and useful it will be. It will be more just because it spares the criminal the cruel and superfluous torment of uncertainty, which increases in proportion to the strength of his imagination and the sense of weakness. It will also be more just because the removal of liberty, being a punishment, should be inflicted before condemnation only for as short a time as possible. Imprisonment, then, is only the means of securing the accused person until he is tried, condemned, or acquitted, and should not only be of a short duration, but it should be accompanied with as little severity as possible. The time of imprisonment should be determined by the necessary preparation for the trial, along with the right of priority for the oldest prisoners. The confinement should not be stricter than is required to prevent his escape or his concealing the evidence of his crime, and the trial should be conducted with all possible speed. Can there be more a cruel contrast than between the habitual idleness of a judge, and the painful anxiety of the accused? Or, the comforts and pleasures of an insensible magistrate, and the filth and misery of prison? In general as I have observed above, the degree of the punishment and the consequences of a crime, should be contrived so that it has the greatest possible effect on others, with the least possible pain to the delinquent. If there is any society in which this is not a fundamental principle, it is an unlawful society. For, humankind by their union, originally intended to subject themselves to the fewest evils possible.

80. What is the justification for confining a person before his trial?

Association of Ideas. Beccaria defends his view about the swiftness of punishment by appealing to the theory of the association of ideas—developed most notably by David Hume and David Hartley. According to associationists, if we know the rules by which the mind connects together two different ideas—such as the ideas of crime and punishment—then we can strengthen their association. For Beccaria when a punishment quickly follows a crime, then the two ideas of "crime" and "punishment" will be more quickly associated in a person's mind. Also, the link between a crime and a punishment is stronger if the punishment is somehow related to the crime.

An immediate punishment is more useful because the smaller the interval or time between the punishment and the crime, the stronger and more lasting will be the association of the two ideas of *crime* and *punishment*. Accordingly, one is considered as the cause, and the other as the unavoidable and necessary effect. It is demonstrated that the association of ideas is the cement which unites the fabric of the human intellect, without which pleasure and pain would be insignificant mental sensations. The common people (that is, all people who have no general ideas or universal principles) act in view of the most immediate and familiar associations. However, our more remote and complex ideas present themselves to only to the minds of people who are passionately attached to a single object. This is also so of people with greater intellects who have acquired a habit of quickly comparing together a number of objects and forming a conclusion. The result is that the action in consequence becomes less dangerous and uncertain by this means.

It is then of the greatest importance that the punishment should follow the crime as immediately as possible. This is so if we hope that, in the unrefined minds of the multitude, the seducing picture of the advantage arising from the crime should instantly awake the attendant idea of punishment. Delaying the punishment serves only to separate these two ideas; and thus affects the minds of spectator rather as being a terrible fight, than the necessary consequence of crime; the horror of which should contribute to heighten the idea of punishment.

81. For Beccaria, what happens when we delay a punishment?

There is another excellent method of strengthening this important connection between the ideas of crime and punishment. And this is to make the punishment as analogous as possible to the nature of the crime in order that the punishment may lead the mind to consider the crime in a different point of view from that in which it was placed by the flattering idea of promised advantages.

Crimes of less importance are commonly punished either in the obscurity of a prison, or the criminal is *transported* and enslaved by a distant society which he never offended. This makes him an absolutely useless example considering how far he is from the place where the crime was committed. People do not, in general, commit great crimes deliberately, but rather in a sudden burst of passion. And they commonly look on the punishment due to a great crime as remote and improbable. Therefore, the public punishment of small crimes will make a greater impression; and by deterring people from the smaller, we will effectively prevent the greater.

Against Severe Punishments. Given the fact that the swiftness of punishment has the greatest impact on deterring others, Beccaria argues that there is no justification for severe punishments.

The course of my ideas has carried me away from my subject, to the elucidation of which I now return. Crimes are more effectively prevented by the *certainty* of the punishment, rather than the *severity*. Hence, to become useful virtues, the necessary caution of a magistrate and the necessary inflexibility of a judge need to be joined with mild legislation. The certainty of a small punishment will make a stronger impression than will the fear of one more severe, if attended with the hopes of escaping. For it is the nature of humankind to be terrified at the approach of the smallest inevitable evil, while hope (the best gift of heaven) has the power of dispelling the apprehension of a greater. This is especially if supported by examples of rescue, which weakness or avarice too frequently afford.

If punishments are very severe, people are naturally led to the perpetration of other crimes to avoid the punishment due to the first. The countries and times most notorious for severity of punishments were always those in which the most bloody and inhuman actions and the most atrocious crimes were committed. For the hand of the legislator and the assassin were directed by the same spirit of ferocity. On the throne, this attitude dictated ironclad laws for slaves and savages. In private it motivated people to sacrifice one tyrant, to make room for another.

People Adjust to Increases of Severity. According to Beccaria, in time we will naturally grow accustomed to increases in severity of punishment, and, thus, the initial increase in severity will lose its effect.

In proportion as punishments become more cruel, the minds of people grow hardened and insensible; this is just as a fluid rises to the same height with that which surrounds it. And because of the continual force of the passions, in a period of a hundred years, the *wheel* terrifies no more than the *prison* did before. For a punishment to be effective, all that is needed is that the *evil* it brings about should exceed the *good* expected from the crime. Included in the calculation should be the certainty of the punishment, and the loss of the expected advantage. All severity beyond this is superfluous, and therefore tyrannical.

People regulate their conduct by the repeated impressions of evils they know, and not by those with which they are unacquainted. For example, let us suppose that there are two nations. In one the greatest punishment is *perpetual slavery,* and in the other it is *the wheel*. I say that both will inspire the same degree of terror. Further, there can be no reasons for increasing the punishments of the first, which are not equally valid for augmenting those of the second, thus creating more lasting and more creative modes of tormenting, and so on to the most exquisite refinements of a science too well known to tyrants.

Beccaria argues that there are limits both to how much torment we can endure, and also how much we can inflict.

There are yet two other consequences of cruel punishments, which counter-act the purpose of their institution (which was to prevent crimes). The *first* arises from the impossibility of establishing an exact proportion between the crime and punishment. For though creative cruelty has greatly multiplied the variety of torments, yet the human frame can suffer only to a certain degree, beyond which it is impossible to proceed, regardless of how great was the initial crime. The *second* consequence is, exemption from penalty. Human nature is limited no less in evil than in good. Excessive cruelty can only be temporary since it is impossible for it to be supported by a permanent system of legislation. For if the laws are too cruel, they must be altered otherwise anarchy will follow.

Who would not shudder with horror when reading in history about the barbarous and useless torments that were coolly invented and executed by people who were called sages? Who does not tremble at the thought of thousands of wretches forced desperately to return to a state of nature because of what the laws caused or tolerated (insofar as the laws favor the few and outrage the many). Or at people accused of impossible crimes, fabricated from ignorance and superstition. Or at people guilty only of having been faithful to their own principles. Who, I say, can without horror, think of them being torn to pieces with slow and studied barbarity, by people endowed with the same passions and the same feelings? A delightful spectacle to a fanatic multitude!

ASK YOURSELF

85. What are some examples of cruelty which Beccaria believes most people would not inflict on others?

We Don't Give Up Our Right to Life. Beccaria presents one of the first sustained critiques of the use of capital punishment. Briefly, his position is that capital punishment is not necessary to deter, and long-term imprisonment is a more powerful deterrent since execution is transient. Beccaria begins by describing the connection between the social contract and our right to life. Locke argued that people forfeit their right to life when they initiate a state of war with other people. Beccaria disagrees. Following Hobbes, Beccaria believes that, in the social contract, we negotiate away only the minimal number of rights necessary to bring about peace. Thus, people hold onto their right to life, and they do not hand this over to the public good.

The useless profusion of punishments, which has never made people better, induces me to inquire whether punishment by *death* is really just or useful in a well-governed state. What *right,* I ask, do people have to cut the throats of their fellow-creatures? Certainly not the right on which the sovereignty and laws are founded. The laws, as I have said before, are only the sum of the smallest portions of the private liberty of each individual, and represent the general will which is the aggregate of that of each individual. Did anyone ever give to others the right of taking away his life? Each person gives only the smallest portion of his liberty over to the good of the public. Is it possible that this small portion contains the greatest good of all, namely, that person's life? If this were so, how can it be reconciled to the maxim which tells us that a person has no right to kill himself? Certainly he must have this if he could give it away to another.

ASK YOURSELF

86. As noted, philosophers such as Locke believe that we can forfeit our right to life. For Beccaria, this is inconsistent with another position also held by Locke and others. What is that second position?

Capital Punishment Does Not Deter. Given the fact that capital punishment cannot be justified by Locke's reasoning, Beccaria argues that the only other justification is that it is either necessary or useful for public good. He contests both of these claims.

But the punishment of death is not authorized by any right. For I have demonstrated that no such right exists. It is therefore a war of a whole nation against a citizen, whose destruction they consider as necessary, or useful to the general good. But if I can further demonstrate that it is neither necessary nor useful, I shall have gained the cause of humanity.

The death of a citizen cannot be necessary, except in one case. This is when he is deprived of his liberty and yet still has enough power and connections to endanger the security of the nation; that is, when his existence may produce a dangerous revolution in the established form of government. But even in this case, it is only necessary when a nation is on the verge of recovering or losing its liberty, or, in times of absolute anarchy, when the disorders themselves hold the place of laws. But this is not so in a reign of peace, or in a form of government approved by the united wishes of the nation, or in a state well fortified from enemies without, and supported by strength within (and, even more effectively, by popular opinion), or where all power is lodged in the hands of the true sovereign, or where riches can purchase pleasures and not authority. In these there can be no necessity for taking away the life of a subject.

ASK YOURSELF

87. What is the only circumstance in which capital punishment may be necessary?

For Beccaria, history shows that capital punishment fails to deter determined criminals. What we know about human nature also suggests that it has minimal deterrence value. A steady example over a long period of time is more effective in creating moral habits than is a single shocking example of an execution.

Consider if the experience of all ages is not sufficient to prove that the punishment of death has never prevented determined people from injuring society; if the example of the Romans; if twenty years reign of Elizabeth, empress of Russia, in which she gave the fathers of their country an example more illustrious than many conquests bought with blood. If, I say, all this is not sufficient to persuade humankind, who always suspect the voice of reason and who chose rather to be led by authority, then let us consult human nature in proof of my assertion.

It is not the intenseness of the pain that has the greatest effect on the mind, but its continuance. For our sensibility is more easily and more powerfully affected by weak but repeated impressions than by a violent, but momentary, impulse. The power of habit is universal over every sentient being. It is by habit that we learn to speak, to walk, and to satisfy our necessities. So too the ideas of morality are stamped on our minds by repeated impressions. The death of a criminal is a terrible but momentary spectacle, and therefore a less effective method of deterring others than the continued example of a person deprived of his liberty and condemned (as a beast of burden) to repair by his labor the injury he has done to society. "If I commit such a crime," says the spectator to himself, "I shall be reduced to that miserable condition for the rest of my life." This is a much more powerful preventive than the fear of death, which people always behold in distant obscurity.

ASK YOURSELF

88. According to Beccaria, what kind of punishment is more effective than the death penalty?

The terrors of death make so slight an impression that it does not have enough force to withstand our natural human forgetfulness, even in the most essential things and when assisted by the passions. Violent impressions surprise us, but their effect is momentary. They are fit to produce those revolutions which instantly transform a common person into a Lacedemonian or a Persian. But in a free and quiet government such impressions should be frequent rather than strong.

To the masses, the execution of a criminal is entertainment, and in some it excites compassion mixed with indignation. Both of these sentiments fill the mind with a greater terror than the needed terror which the laws try to inspire. But in the contemplation of continued suffering, terror is the only (or at least the predominant) sensation. The severity of a punishment should be just sufficient to excite compassion in the spectators, as it is intended more for them than for the criminal.

Advantages of Perpetual Slavery. Beccaria argues that perpetual slavery is a more effective deterrent than capital punishment. Since we should choose the least severe punishment that accomplishes our purpose (i.e., deterrence), then perpetual slavery is the preferred type of punishment for the worst crimes. From the spectator's perspective, observing perpetual slavery will have a more lasting impression than capital punishment. Perpetual slavery will also seem more terrible to spectators than to the criminals who are being punished.

For a punishment to be just, it should have only that degree of severity that is sufficient to deter others. Now there is no person, with the least reflection, who would jeopardize the total and continual loss of his liberty for the sake of the greatest advantages he could possibly obtain resulting from a crime. Consequently, perpetual slavery contains all that is necessary to deter the most hardened and determined, as much as the punishment of death. In fact, I say it has more. There are many who can look upon death with courage and steadfastness. Some approach it through fanaticism, and others through vanity that attends us even to the grave. Others approach it from a desperate resolution either to get rid of their misery, or cease to live. But fanaticism and vanity abandon the criminal in slavery, in chains and fetters, in an iron cage. And despair seems rather the beginning than the end of their misery. By collecting itself and uniting all its force the mind can momentarily repel the attack of grief. But its strongest efforts are insufficient to resist perpetual wretchedness.

ASK YOURSELF

89. For Beccaria, many of us can face death stoically. However, how do we face the prospect of perpetual slavery?

In all nations where death is used as a punishment, every example supposes a new crime committed. However, in perpetual slavery, every criminal affords a frequent and lasting example. And if it is necessary for people to frequently be witnesses of the power of the laws, then criminals should frequently be put to death. But this supposes a frequency of crimes and for that reason this punishment will cease to have its effect, and thus it becomes useful and useless at the same time.

Suppose you say that perpetual slavery is as painful a punishment as death, and therefore as cruel. I answer that if all the miserable moments in the life of a slave were collected into one point, it would be a more cruel punishment than any other. But these are scattered through his whole life, whereas the pain of death exerts all its force in a moment. There is also another advantage in the punishment of slavery, which is, that it is more terrible to the spectator than to the sufferer himself. For the spectator considers the sum of all his wretched moments, whereas the sufferer, by the misery of the present, is prevented from thinking of the future. All evils are increased by the imagination, and the sufferer finds resources and consolations, of which the spectators are ignorant (judge by their own sensibility of what passes in a mind, by habit grown callous to misfortune).

ASK YOURSELF

90. What is Beccaria's response to someone who says that perpetual slavery is as cruel as the death penalty?

Beccaria explains the psychology of the criminal who wishes to return to the state of nature in view of the gross inequity between the rich and the poor. Again, perpetual slavery is the best deterrence against this motivation.

Let us, for a moment, note the reasoning of a thief or assassin, who is deterred from violating the laws by the gibbet or the wheel. (I am aware that developing the feelings of one's own heart is an art which education only can teach; nevertheless, although a villain may not be able to give a clear account of his principles, they still influence his conduct.) He reasons as follows: "What are these laws that I am obligated to respect which make so great a difference between me and a rich man? He refuses me the pocket change I ask of him, and excuses himself by instructing me to have recourse to labor, with which he is unacquainted. Who made these laws? The rich and the great, who never stooped to visit the miserable huts of the poor; who have never seen a poor person dividing a piece of moldy bread, surrounded by the cries of his starving children and the tears of his wife. Let us break those ties that are fatal to the greatest part of humankind, and only useful to a few indolent tyrants. Let us attack injustice at its source. I will return to my natural state of independence. I will live free and happy on the fruits of my courage and industry. A day of pain and repentance many come, but it will be short. And for an hour of grief I will enjoy years of pleasure and liberty. As king of a small number of people who are as determined as myself, I will correct the mistakes of fortune, and I will see those tyrants grow pale and tremble at the sight of him, whom with insulting pride, they would not even rank with their dogs and horses."

Religion then presents itself to the mind of this lawless villain by promising him almost a certainty of eternal happiness upon the easy terms of repentance. This contributes much to lessen the horror of the last scene of the tragedy.

Consider now the villain who foresees that he will pass many years, even his whole life, in pain and slavery. He will be a slave to those laws by which he was protected, in sight of his fellow citizens with whom he lives in freedom and society. He thus makes a useful comparison between those evils, the uncertainty of his success, and the shortness of the time in which he shall enjoy the fruits of his crime. The example of those wretches continually before his eyes makes a much greater impression on him than a punishment, which, instead of correcting, makes him more hardened.

ASK YOURSELF

91. What are some of the features of perpetual slavery which Beccaria recommends?

Harmful Effects of the Death Penalty. Beccaria continues by arguing that the death penalty in fact has bad effects on society since it reduces our sensitivity to human suffering. Potential criminals see it as one more method of perpetuating tyranny.

The punishment of death is harmful to society from the example of cruelty it presents. If the passions, or the necessity of war, have taught people to shed the blood of their fellow-creatures, the laws, which are intended to moderate the savagery of humankind, should not increase it by examples of cruelty, which is even more horrible since punishment is usually attended with formal ceremony. Is it not absurd that the laws, which detest and punish homicide, should, in order to prevent murder, publicly commit murder themselves? What are the true and most useful laws? Those compacts and conditions which all would propose and observe in those moments when private interest is silent, or combined with that of the public. What are the natural feelings of every person concerning the punishment of death? We may read them in the contempt and indignation with which everyone looks on the executioner, who is nevertheless an innocent executor of the public will. In this light, the executioner is a good citizen, who contributes to the advantage of society and is the instrument of the general security within, just as good soldiers are without. What then is the origin of this contradiction? Why is this sentiment of humankind permanent, even though contrary to reason? It is that in a secret corner of the mind in which the original impressions of nature are still preserved, people discover a sentiment which tells them that their lives are not lawfully in the power of anyone, except only that *necessity* which with its iron scepter rules the universe.

What must people [i.e., potential criminals] think when they see wise magistrates and grave ministers of justice, with indifference and tranquillity, dragging a criminal to death? Or consider, while a wretch trembles with agony expecting the fatal stroke, the judge who has condemned him, with the coldest insensibility, and perhaps with no small gratification from the exertion of his authority, quits his tribunal to enjoy the comforts and pleasures of life? They will say, "Ah! Those cruel formalities of justice are a cloak to tyranny. They are a secret language, a solemn veil, intended to conceal the sword by which we are sacrificed to the insatiable idol of despotism. Murder, which they would represent to us as an horrible crime, we see practiced by them without repugnance, or remorse. Let us follow their example. A violent death appeared terrible in their descriptions, but we see that it is the affair of a moment. It will be still less terrible to him, who not expecting it, escapes almost all the pain." Such is the fatal, though absurd reasoning of people who are disposed to commit crimes, on whom the abuse of religion has more influence than religion itself.

ASK YOURSELF

92. What are people's natural feelings toward the executioner?

Beccaria argues that, although capital punishment is practiced in most countries, it is still an error that in time will become rare. He urges rulers to adopt his stance against capital punishment, and he predicts that this will give them lasting fame as peacemakers.

If it is objected that almost all nations in all ages have punished certain crimes with death, I answer that the force of these examples disappears when opposed to truth, against which it is vain to offer further recommendation. The history of humankind is an immense sea of errors in which a few obscure truths may here and there be found.

Consider that human sacrifices have also been common in almost all nations. That some societies only, either few in number, or for a very short time, abstained from the punishment of death, is in fact favorable to my argument. For such is the fate of great truths that their duration is only as a flash of lightning in the long and dark night of error. The happy time is not yet arrived when truth will be the portion of the majority (as falsehood was previously).

I am aware that the voice of one philosopher is too weak to be heard when surrounded by the uproar of a multitude, blindly influenced by custom. But there is a small number of sages, scattered around the earth, who will echo my views from the bottom of their hearts. And if these truths should happily force their way to the thrones of princes, let it be known to them that they come attended with the secret wishes of all humankind. And tell the sovereign who patronizes them with a gracious reception that his name will outshine the glory of conquerors, and that equal fame will elevate his peaceful trophies above those of a Titus, an Antoninus or a Trajan.

How happy humankind would be if laws were now first formed, especially since we see benevolent monarchs on the thrones of Europe. They are friends to the virtues of peace and to the arts and sciences; they are fathers of their people and, though crowned, remain citizens. The increase of their authority augments the happiness of their subjects by destroying that transitional despotism which intercepts the prayers of the people to the throne. If these humane princes have allowed the old laws to continue, it is undoubtedly because they are deterred by the numberless obstacles, which oppose the subversion of errors established by the sanction of many ages. Accordingly, every wise citizen will wish for the increase of their authority.

ASK YOURSELF

93. What is Beccaria's description of the ruler who he hopes will adopt his views?

2. PRESERVING INDIVIDUAL LIBERTY: JOHN STUART MILL

In Chapter 6 we examined the utilitarian theory of British philosopher John Stuart Mill (1806–1873). According to Mill, right actions are those that we foresee will bring about the most favorable balance of pleasure over pain for those affected by those actions. Mill felt that utility was not just the standard for morality, but the foundational standard for governments as well. The existence of governments is justified on utilitarian grounds, since their presence brings about more pleasure than would otherwise be the case. Furthermore, the decisions that governments make should be guided by how much benefit a particular policy will have for society. Mill felt very strongly, though, that there was a limit to how far governments can justifiably interfere in our private lives. In fact, Mill takes one of the more extremely liberal stands on the issue of governmental coercion: Governmental restrictions on our liberty are justified only when our actions harm other people. That is, of the six liberty-limiting principles that we listed earlier, only the harm principle is valid. He defends this position in his book *On Liberty* (1859).

The Tyranny of the Majority. Mill argues that majority opinion may tyrannize over minorities by other means than the law.

FROM JOHN STUART MILL, *On Liberty* (1859), CHAPTERS 1 AND 2

Like other tyrannies, the tyranny of the majority was at first, and is still vulgarly, held in dread, chiefly as operating through the acts of the public authorities. But reflecting persons perceived that when society is itself the tyrant—society collectively over the separate individuals who compose it—its means of tyrannizing are not restricted to the acts which it may do by the hands of its political functionaries. Society can and does execute its own mandates: and if it issues wrong mandates instead of right, or any mandates at all in things with which it ought not to meddle, it practices a social tyranny more formidable than many kinds of political oppression, since, though not usually upheld by such extreme penalties, it leaves fewer means of escape, penetrating much more deeply into the details of life and enslaving the soul itself. Protection, therefore, against the tyranny of the magistrate is not enough: there needs protection also against the tyranny of the prevailing opinion and feeling; against the tendency of society to impose, by other means than civil penalties, its own ideas and practices as rules of conduct on those who dissent from them. . . .

JOHN STUART MILL (1806–1873)

English utilitarian philosopher and author of On Liberty *(1859).*

ASK YOURSELF

94. What might be an example of the kind of "tyranny" Mill is speaking of here?

What Should Be the Limits to Individual Independence? Most people recognize that there must be some limits placed on the behavior of individuals in a society. But how do we determine what those limits should be? Mill considers some possible criteria.

There is a limit to individual independence: and to find that limit, and maintain it against encroachment, is as indispensable to a good condition of human affairs, as protection against political despotism. But though this proposition is not likely to be contested in general terms, the practical question, where to place the limit—how to make the fitting adjustment between individual independence and social control—is a subject on which nearly everything remains to be done. All that makes existence valuable to anyone depends on the enforcement of restraints upon the actions of other people. Some rules of conduct, therefore, must be imposed, by law in the first place, and by opinion on many things which are not fit subjects for the operation of law. What these rules should be is the principal question in human affairs; but if we except a few of the most obvious cases, it is one of those which least progress has been made in resolving. No two ages, and scarcely any two countries, have decided it alike; and the decision of one age or country is a wonder to another. Yet the people of any given age and country no more suspect any difficulty in it than if it were a subject on which mankind had always been agreed. The rules which obtain among themselves appear to them self-evident and self-justifying. This all but universal illusion is one of the examples of the magical influence of custom, which is not only, as the proverb says, a second nature, but is continually mistaken for the first. The effect of custom in preventing any misgiving respecting the rules of conduct which mankind impose on one another is all the more complete because the subject is one on which it is not generally considered necessary that reasons should be given, either by one person to others or by each to himself. People are accustomed to believe, and have been encouraged in the belief by some who aspire to the character of philosophers, that their feelings, on subjects of this nature, are better than reasons, and render reasons unnecessary. The practical principle which guides them to their opinions on the regulation of human conduct is the feeling in each person's mind that everybody should be required to act as he, and those with whom he sympathizes, would like them to act. No one, indeed, acknowledges to himself that his standard of judgment is his own liking; but an opinion on a point of conduct, not supported by reasons, can only count as one person's preference; and if the reasons, when given, are a mere appeal to a similar preference felt by other people, it is still only many people's liking instead of one. To an ordinary man, however, his own preference, thus supported, is not only a perfectly satisfactory reason, but the only one he generally has for any of his notions of morality, taste, or propriety, which are not expressly written in his religious creed; and his chief guide in the interpretation even of that. Men's opinions, accordingly, on what is laudable or blamable are affected by all the multifarious causes which influence their wishes in regard to the conduct of others, and which are as numerous as those which determine their wishes on any other subject. Sometimes their reason—at other times their prejudices or superstitions: often their social affections, not seldom their antisocial ones, their envy or jealousy, their arrogance or contemptuousness: but most commonly their desires or fears for themselves—their legitimate or illegitimate self-interest.

ASK YOURSELF

95. In Mill's view, what are some of the things that have served as criteria for determining what restrictions should be placed on individuals in a society?

Wherever there is an ascendant class, a large portion of the morality of the country emanates from its class interests and its feelings of class superiority. The morality between Spartans and Helots, between planters and negroes, between princes and subjects, between nobles and roturiers, between men and women, has been for the most part the creation of these class interests and feelings: and the sentiments thus generated react in turn upon the moral feelings of the members of the ascendant class, in their relations among themselves. Where, on the other hand, a class, formerly ascendant, has lost its ascendancy, or where its ascendancy is unpopular, the prevailing moral sentiments frequently bear the impress of an impatient dislike of superiority.

Another grand determining principle of the rules of conduct, both in act and forbearance, which have been enforced by law or opinion, has been the servility of mankind towards the supposed preferences or aversions of their temporal masters or of their gods. This servility, though essentially selfish, is not hypocrisy; it gives rise to perfectly genuine sentiments of abhorrence; it made men burn magicians and heretics.

ASK YOURSELF

96. What might be an example of morality emanating from "class interests"? Use one of Mill's examples.

97. Why do you suppose Mill thinks "servility" toward God is essentially selfish?

Among so many baser influences, the general and obvious interests of society have of course had a share, and a large one, in the direction of the moral sentiments: less, however, as a matter of reason, and on their own account, than as a consequence of the sympathies and antipathies which grew out of them: and sympathies and antipathies which had little or nothing to do with the interests of society, have made themselves felt in the establishment of moralities with quite as great force. The likings and dislikings of society, or of some powerful portion of it, are thus the main thing which has practically determined the rules laid down for general observance, under the penalties of law or opinion. And in general, those who have been in advance of society in thought and feeling, have left this condition of things unassailed in principle, however they may have come into conflict with it in some of its details. They have occupied themselves rather in inquiring what things society ought to like or dislike, than in questioning whether its likings or dislikings should be a law to individuals. They preferred the sympathies and antipathies which grew out of them: and sympathies and antipathies which had little or nothing to do with the interests of society, have made themselves felt in the establishment of moralities with quite as great force. The likings and dislikings of society, or of some powerful portion of it, are thus the main thing which has practically determined the rules laid down for general observance, under the penalties of law or opinion. And in general, those who have been in advance of society in thought and feeling, have left this condition of things unassailed in principle, however they may have come into conflict with it in some of its details. They have occupied themselves rather in inquiring what things society ought to like or dislike, than in questioning whether its likings or dislikings should be a law to individuals. They preferred endeavoring to alter the feelings of mankind on the particular points on which they were themselves heretical, rather than make common cause in defence of freedom, with heretics generally. . . .

ASK YOURSELF

98. Instead of trying to change the likes and dislikes of society, Mill claims, we should realize that what society _____ or _____ is no basis for _____.

The only freedom which deserves the name is that of pursuing our own good in our own way, so long as we do not attempt to deprive others of theirs, or impede their efforts to obtain it. Each is the proper guardian of his own health, whether bodily, or mental and spiritual. Mankind are greater gainers by suffering each other to live as seems good to themselves, than by compelling each to live as seems good to the rest. Though this doctrine is anything but new, and, to some persons, may have the air of a truism, there is no doctrine which stands more directly opposed to the general tendency of existing opinion and practice.

99. Does it follow from these remarks that there should be no Food and Drug Administration or other government agencies that watch out for the health of citizens? Explain.

The Harm Principle. Mill argues that there must be some principled way of deciding how much interference with individual liberty is appropriate. The principle he advocates is stated first here.

There is . . . no recognized principle by which the propriety or impropriety of government interference is customarily tested. People decide according to their personal preferences. Some, whenever they see any good to be done, or evil to be remedied, would willingly instigate the government to undertake the business; while others prefer to bear almost any amount of social evil, rather than add one to the departments of human interests amenable to governmental control. And men range themselves on one or the other side in any particular case, according to this general direction of their sentiments; or according to the degree of interest which they feel in the particular thing which it is proposed that the government should do, or according to the belief they entertain that the government would, or would not, do it in the manner they prefer; but very rarely on account of any opinion to which they consistently adhere, as to what things are fit to be done by a government. And it seems to me that in consequence of this absence of rule or principle, one side is at present as of wrong as the other; the interference of government is, with about equal frequency, improperly invoked and improperly condemned. The object of this essay is to assert one very simple principle, as entitled to govern absolutely the dealings of society with the individual in the way of compulsion and control, whether the means used be physical force in the form of legal penalties, or the moral coercion of public opinion. That principle is, that the sole end for which mankind are warranted, individually or collectively, in interfering with the liberty of action of any of their number, is self-protection. That the only purpose for which power can be rightfully exercised over any member of a civilized community, against his will, is to prevent harm to others.

100. State in your own words Mill's principle.

His own good, either physical or moral, is not a sufficient warrant. He cannot rightfully be compelled to do or forbear because it will be better for him to do so, because it will make him happier, because, in the opinions of others, to do so would be wise, or even right. These are good reasons for remonstrating with him, or reasoning with him, or persuading him, or entreating him, but not for compelling him, or visiting him with any evil in case he do otherwise. To justify that, the conduct from which it is desired to deter him must be calculated to produce evil to some one else. The only part of the conduct of any one, for which he is amenable to society, is that which concerns others. In the part which merely concerns himself, his independence is, of right, absolute. Over himself, over his own body and mind, the individual is sovereign.

101. Give an example of some behavior that does not concern anyone but the author of that behavior.

The Basis for Freedom of the Press. According to Mill, it is important that we have wide-ranging liberties with respect to the expression of opinion, as well as with respect to other actions. Freedom to think unpopular views and freedom to express them is important for the discovery of truth. It is also crucial, he believes, to protect us from oppressive governments.

The time, it is to be hoped, is gone by, when any defense would be necessary of the "liberty of the press" as one of the securities against corrupt or tyrannical government. No argument, we may suppose, can now be needed, against permitting a legislature or an executive, not identified in interest with the people, to prescribe opinions to them, and determine what doctrines or what arguments they shall be allowed to hear. This aspect of the question, besides, has been so triumphantly enforced by preceding writers, that it needs not be specially insisted on in this place. Though the law of England, on the subject of the press, is as servile to this day as it was in the time of the Tudors, there is little danger of its being actually put in force against political discussion, except during some temporary panic, when fear of insurrection drives ministers and judges from their propriety; and, speaking generally, it is not, in constitutional countries, to be apprehended, that the government, whether completely responsible to the people or not, will often attempt to control the expression of opinion, except when in doing so it makes itself the organ of the general intolerance of the public. Let us suppose, therefore, that the government is entirely at one with the people, and never thinks of exerting any power of coercion unless in agreement with what it conceives to be their voice. But I deny the right of the people to exercise such coercion, either by themselves or by their government. The power itself is illegitimate. The best government has no more title to it than the worst. It is as noxious, or more noxious, when exerted in accordance with public opinion, than when in opposition to it. If all mankind minus one were of one opinion, and only one person were of the contrary opinion, mankind would be no more justified in silencing that one person, than he, if he had the power, would be justified in silencing mankind. Were an opinion a personal possession of no value except to the owner; if to be obstructed in the enjoyment of it were simply a private injury, it would make some difference whether the injury was inflicted only on a few persons or on many. But the peculiar evil of silencing the expression of an opinion is that it is robbing the human race; posterity as well as the existing generation; those who dissent from the opinion, still more than those who hold it. If the opinion is right, they are deprived of the opportunity of exchanging error for truth: if wrong, they lose what is almost as great a benefit, the clearer perception and livelier impression of truth. . . .

ASK YOURSELF

102. What is especially bad about "silencing the expression of an opinion"?

Offensive Conduct. Mill thinks that he has produced a principle that will allow an appropriate amount of interference with individual liberty. For instance, the government is entitled to prevent me, by police force, from assaulting another citizen. Nearly everyone would agree that this much interference is necessary. But of course there are many kinds of "harm." For example, there have been laws against slander in many communities, even though no physical harm is involved. Would Mill's principle allow such laws? He does not make precise distinctions between physical and mental harm, but he seems to have a somewhat narrow interpretation of "harm." That is, he would not favor governmental restrictions on actions that simply disgust others. He makes this point with respect to conduct that people find repugnant on religious grounds.

The majority of Spaniards consider it a gross impiety, offensive in the highest degree to the Supreme Being, to worship him in any other manner than the Roman Catholic; and no other public worship is lawful on Spanish soil. The people of all Southern Europe look upon a married clergy as not only irreligious, but unchaste, indecent, gross, disgusting. What do Protestants think of these perfectly sincere feelings, and of the attempt to enforce them against non-Catholics? Yet, if mankind are justified in interfering with each other's liberty in things which do not concern the interests of others, on what principle is it possible consistently to exclude these cases? or who can blame people for desiring to suppress what they regard as a scandal in the sight of God and man?

No stronger case can be shown for prohibiting anything which is regarded as a personal immorality, than is made out for suppressing these practices in the eyes of those who regard them as impieties; and unless we are willing to adopt the logic of persecutors, and to say that we may persecute others because we are right, and that they must not persecute us because they are wrong, we must beware of admitting a principle of which we should resent as a gross injustice the application to ourselves.

ASK YOURSELF

103. What types of conduct among believers of other religions do some religious believers find disgusting?

Bringing the issue closer to home, Mill points out the kind of restrictions that Puritanical thinking has imposed within Great Britain itself. According to Mill, if we yield to the restrictions imposed by one religious group in the name of morality or decency, the door will be open to restrictions imposed by any religious group that might acquire power.

The preceding instances may be objected to, although unreasonably, as drawn from contingencies impossible among us: opinion, in this country, not being likely to enforce abstinence from meats, or to interfere with people for worshipping, and for either marrying or not marrying, according to their creed or inclination. The next example, however, shall be taken from an interference with liberty which we have by no means passed all danger of. Wherever the Puritans have been sufficiently powerful, as in New England, and in Great Britain at the time of the Commonwealth, they have endeavored, with considerable success, to put down all public, and nearly all private, amusements: especially music, dancing, public games, or other assemblages for purposes of diversion, and the theatre. There are still in this country large bodies of persons by whose notions of morality and religion these recreations are condemned; and those persons belonging chiefly to the middle class, who are the ascendant power in the present social and political condition of the kingdom, it is by no means impossible that persons of these sentiments may at some time or other command a majority in Parliament. How will the remaining portion of the community like to have the amusements that shall be permitted to them regulated by the religious and moral sentiments of the stricter Calvinists and Methodists? Would they not, with considerable peremptoriness, desire these intrusively pious members of society to mind their own business? This is precisely what should be said to every government and every public, who have the pretension that no person shall enjoy any pleasure which they think wrong. But if the principle of the pretension be admitted, no one can reasonably object to its being acted on in the sense of the majority, or other preponderating power in the country; and all persons must be ready to conform to the idea of a Christian commonwealth, as understood by the early settlers in New England, if a religious profession similar to theirs should ever succeed in regaining its lost ground, as religions supposed to be declining have so often been known to do.

3. OFFENSE TO OTHERS: JOEL FEINBERG

Mill's principle of harm is one of the more extreme positions that one can take on the issue of governmental coercion. Other political philosophers, though, feel that governmental restraint is justified in more situations than those that simply involve harming others. In his book *Offense to Others,* University of Arizona philosophy professor Joel Feinberg argues that governments can justifiably prevent us from engaging in seriously offensive behavior. Not every offensive action that people perform rises to this level of gravity, and he believes it is important to uncover the features that distinguish the serious from the trivial. He opens this work by contrasting the notion of offense with that of harm, and setting forth the offense principle that he defends.

FROM JOEL FEINBERG, *Offense to Others* (1985), CHAPTERS 7–9

Passing annoyance, disappointment, disgust, embarrassment, and various other disliked conditions such as fear, anxiety, and minor ("harmless") aches and pains are not in themselves necessarily harmful. Consequently, no matter how the harm principle is mediated, it will not certify as legitimate those interferences with the liberty of some citizens that are made for the sole purpose of preventing such unpleasant states in others. For convenience I will use the word "offense" to cover the whole miscellany of universally disliked mental states and not merely that species of the wider genus that are offensive in a strict and proper sense. If the law is justified, then, in using its coercive methods to protect people from mere offense, it must be by virtue of a separate and distinct legitimizing principle, which we can label "the offense principle" and formulate as follows: *It is always a good reason in support of a proposed criminal prohibition that it would probably be an effective way of preventing serious offense (as opposed to injury or harm) to persons other than the actor, and that it is probably a necessary means to that end* (i.e., there is probably no other means that is equally effective at no greater cost to other values). The principle asserts, in effect, that the prevention of offensive conduct is properly the state's business.

Examples of Offensive Conduct. Feinberg feels that the best way to understand the nature and scope of offensive conduct is to consider possible scenarios that range from mildly bothersome to severely disturbing. The more we try to imagine ourselves in these situations, he argues, the more we will understand why at least some of these behaviors should be restricted by the government. Be warned: Some of his illustrations are not for the squeamish!

There is a limit to the power of abstract reasoning to settle questions of moral legitimacy. The question raised by this chapter is whether there are any human experiences that are harmless in themselves yet so unpleasant that we can rightly demand legal protection from them even at the cost of other persons' liberties. The best way to deal with that question at the start is to engage our imaginations in the inquiry, consider hypothetically the most offensive experiences we can imagine, and then sort them into groups in an effort to isolate the kernel of the offense in each category. Accordingly, this section will consist of a number of vividly sketched imaginary tales, and the reader is asked to project himself into each story and determine as best he can what his reaction would be. In each story the reader should think of himself as a passenger on a normally crowded public bus on his way to work or to some important appointment in circumstances such that if he is forced to leave the bus prematurely, he will not only have to pay another fare to get where he is going, but he will probably be late, to his own disadvantage. If he is not exactly a captive on the bus, then, he would nevertheless be greatly inconvenienced if he had to leave the bus before it reached his destination. In each story, another passenger, or group of passengers, gets on the bus, and proceeds to cause, by their characteristics or their conduct, great offense to you. The stories form six clusters corresponding to the kind of offense caused.

A. Affronts to the Senses

Story 1. A passenger who obviously hasn't bathed in more than a month sits down next to you. He reeks of a barely tolerable stench. There is hardly room to stand elsewhere on the bus and all other seats are occupied.

Story 2. A passenger wearing a shirt of violently clashing orange and crimson sits down directly in your forward line of vision. You must keep your eyes down to avoid looking at him.

Story 3. A passenger sits down next to you, pulls a slate tablet from his brief case, and proceeds to scratch his finger' nails loudly across the slate, sending a chill up your spine and making your teeth clench. You politely ask him to stop, but he refuses.

Story 4. A passenger elsewhere in the bus turns on a portable radio to maximum volume. The sounds it emits are mostly screeches, whistles, and static, but occasionally some electronically amplified rock and roll music blares through.

ASK YOURSELF

106. Feinberg's first category of offensive behavior focuses on basic senses. Which of these examples do you think is the least offensive and why?

B. Disgust and Revulsion

Story 5. This is much like story 1 except that the malodorous passenger in the neighboring seat continually scratches, drools, coughs, farts, and belches.

Story 6. A group of passengers enters the bus and shares a seating compartment with you. They spread a tablecloth over their laps and proceed to eat a picnic lunch that consists of live insects, fish heads, and pickled sex organs of lamb, veal, and pork, smothered in garlic and onions. Their table manners leave almost everything to be desired.

Story 7. Things get worse and worse. The itinerant picnickers practice gluttony in the ancient Roman manner, gorging until satiation and then vomiting on to their table cloth.

Their practice, however, is a novel departure from the ancient custom in that they eat their own and one another's vomit along with the remaining food.

Story 8. A coprophagic sequel to story 7.

Story 9. At some point during the trip the passenger at one's side quite openly and nonchalantly changes her sanitary napkin and drops the old one into the aisle.

ASK YOURSELF

107. Which, if any, of the offenses on this second list do you think should be legally prohibited?

C. Shock to Moral, Religious, or Patriotic Sensibilities

Story 10. A group of mourners carrying a coffin enter the bus and share a seating compartment with you. Although they are all dressed in black their demeanor is by no means funereal. In fact they seem more angry than sorrowful, and refer to the deceased as "the old bastard," and "the bloody corpse." At one point they rip open the coffin with hammers and proceed to smash the corpse's face with a series of hard hammer blows.

Story 11. A strapping youth enters the bus and takes a seat directly in your line of vision. He is wearing a T-shirt with a cartoon across his chest of Christ on the cross. Underneath the picture appear the words "Hang in there, baby!"

Story 12. After taking the seat next to you a passenger produces a bundle wrapped in a large American flag. The bundle contains, among other things, his lunch, which he proceeds to eat. Then he spits into the star-spangled corner of the flag and uses it first to clean his mouth and then to blow his nose. Then he uses the main striped part of the flag to shine his shoes.

ASK YOURSELF

108. Think of your own example of a behavior that would shock moral, religious, or patriotic sensibilities.

D. Shame, Embarrassment (Including Vicarious Embarrassment), and Anxiety

Story 13. The passenger who takes the seat directly across from you is entirely naked. In one version of the story, he or she is the same sex as you; on the other version of the story, he or she is the opposite sex.

Story 14. The passenger in the previous story proceeds to masturbate quietly in his or her seat.

Story 15. A man and woman, more or less fully clothed to start, take two seats directly in front of you, and then begin to kiss, hug, pet, and fondle one another to the accompaniment of loud sighs and groans of pleasure. They continue these activities throughout the trip.

Story 16. The couple of the previous story, shortly before the bus reaches their destination, engage in acts of mutual masturbation, with quite audible instructions to each other and other sound effects.

Story 17. A variant of the previous story which climaxes in an act of coitus, somewhat acrobatically performed as required by the crowded circumstances.

Story 18. The seat directly in front of you is occupied by a youth (of either sex) wearing a T-shirt with a lurid picture of a copulating couple across his or her chest.

Story 19. A variant of the previous story in which the couple depicted is recognizable (in virtue of conventional representations) as Jesus and Mary.

Story 20. The couple in stories 15–17 perform a variety of sadomasochistic sex acts with appropriate verbal communications ("Oh, that hurts so sweet! Hit me again! Scratch me! Publicly humiliate me!").

Story 21. The two seats in front of you are occupied by male homosexuals. They flirt and tease at first, then kiss and hug, and finally perform mutual fellatio to climax.

Story 22. This time the homosexuals are both female and they perform cunnilingus.

Story 23. A passenger with a dog takes an aisle seat at your side. He or she keeps the dog calm at first by petting it in a familiar and normal way, but then petting gives way to hugging, and gradually goes beyond the merely affectionate to the unmistakably erotic, culminating finally with oral contact with the canine genitals.

ASK YOURSELF

109. Are there any behaviors on this list that you think should be legally permitted?

E. Annoyance, Boredom, Frustration

Story 24. A neighboring passenger keeps a portable radio at a reasonably low volume, and the sounds it emits are by no means offensive to the senses. Nor is the content of the program offensive to the sensibilities. It is, however, a low quality "talk show" which you find intensely boring, and there is no possible way for you to disengage your attention.

Story 25. The two seats to your left are occupied by two persons who put on a boring "talk show" of their own. There is no way you can avoid hearing every animated word of their inane conversation, no way your mind can roam to its own thoughts, problems, and reveries.

Story 26. The passenger at your side is a friendly bloke, garrulous and officious. You quickly tire of his conversation and beg leave to read your newspaper, but he persists in his chatter despite repeated requests to desist. The bus is crowded and there are no other empty seats.

F. Fear, Resentment, Humiliation, Anger (from Empty Threats, Insults, Mockery, Flaunting, or Taunting)

Story 27. A passenger seated next to you reaches into a military kit and pulls out a "hand grenade" (actually only a realistic toy), and fondles and juggles it throughout the trip to the accompaniment of menacing leers and snorts. Then he pulls out a (rubber) knife and "stabs" himself and others repeatedly to peals of maniacal laughter. He turns out to be harmless enough. His whole intent was to put others in apprehension of harm.

Story 28. A passenger sits next to you wearing a black arm band with a large white swastika on it.

Story 29. A passenger enters the bus straight from a dispersed street rally. He carries a banner with a large and abusive caricature of the Pope and an anti-Catholic slogan. (You are a loyal and pious Catholic.)

Story 30. Variants of the above. The banner displays a picture of a black according to some standard offensive stereotype (Step 'n' Fetchit, Uncle Tom, etc.) with an insulting caption, or a picture of a sneering, sniveling, hook-nosed Fagin or Shylock, with a scurrilous anti-Jewish caption, or a similar offensive denunciation or lampooning of groups called "Spicks," "Dagos," "Polacks," etc.

Story 31. Still another variant. A counter-demonstrator leaves a feminist rally to enter the bus. He carries a banner with an offensive caricature of a female and the message, in large red letters: "Keep the bitches barefoot and pregnant."

110. Which of stories 24–31 is the least offensive to you, and which is the most offensive?

Difference Between Offensive Nuisances and Profound Offense. Not all of the offenses above are of the same seriousness. The more tame ones Feinberg calls nuisances, and he suggests that four factors distinguish these from the more serious ones.

1. *The magnitude of the offense,* which is a function of its intensity, duration, and extent.
   a. *Intensity.* The more intense a typical offense taken at the type of conduct in question, the more serious is an actual instance of such an offense.
   b. *Duration.* The more durable a typical offense taken at the type of conduct in question, the more serious is an actual instance of such offense.
   c. *Extent.* The more widespread the susceptibility to a given kind of offense, the more serious is a given instance of that kind of offense.
2. *The standard of reasonable avoidability.* The more difficult it is to avoid a given offense without serious inconvenience to oneself the more serious is that offense.
3. *The Volenti maxim.* Offended states that were voluntarily incurred, or the risk of which was voluntarily assumed by the person who experienced them, are not to count as "offenses" at all in the application of a legislative "offense principle."
4. *The discounting of abnormal susceptibilities.* (This can be thought of as a kind of corollary of 1.) Insofar as offended states occur because of a person's abnormal susceptibility to offense, their seriousness is to be discounted in the application of a legislative "offense principle."

111. According to the fourth factor above, offensive conduct that bothers only a minority with exceptional susceptibility to that offense should be discounted. What might be an example of this?

In view of the above four factors, several distinguishing features of merely offensive nuisances emerge.

These experiences are, first of all, relatively trivial or shallow, not only compared to harms but also compared to some other mental states, for example those that result from offense to higher-order sensibilities. Second, the wrong in mere offensive nuisance coincides with the perceptual experience that is imposed on the victim and its caused aftereffects, and is inseparable from those experiences. Without the direct perception of the offending conduct, there would be no offense, even if the person learned secondhand that the offending conduct would occur or had occurred. It is experiencing the conduct, not merely knowing about it, that offends. In respect to a mere offensive nuisance, its *esse est percipii* (its being consists in its being perceived). Third, the offense in ordinary offensive nuisance is experienced in all cases as at least partly personal, and in most cases as wholly personal. The offended party thinks of himself as the wronged victim of the conduct that causes him to have certain unpleasant and inescapable states of mind. Being disgusted, revolted, shocked, frightened, angered, bored, embarrassed, shamed, or made anxious are like being hurt in that one has a grievance in one's own name, on one's own behalf, against the offender for making one undergo the experience. And if one had not been present, one could have had no such complaint. Fourth, it is generally characteristic of the wrong in mere offensive nuisances that it derives from an affront to one's senses, or to one's lower order sensibilities. One does not think of the offending conduct as the sort that would be wrong (in contravention of one's own standards) wherever it might occur, but wrong only because it occurs here and now, thus victimizing its reluctant witnesses. In language suggested by Kurt Baier, the conduct affronts our sensibility without necessarily violating any of our standards of sensibility or propriety. It can therefore "offend our senses" (or lower-order sensibilities) without offending us. Fifth and finally, in ordinary offensive nuisances the offending behavior is thought wrong (and hence resented, and hence an "offense" in the strict and narrow sense) because it produces unpleasant states in the captive witnesses, not the other way around. It does not produce unpleasant states because it is thought wrong on independent grounds.

ASK YOURSELF

112. Feinberg's first group of stories presented earlier involve affronts to our senses. Do these qualify as mere offensive nuisances?

In contrast with the five distinguishing features of offensive nuisances, there are five features of profound offense. It is only the more serious offenses, Feinberg argues, that justify governmental coercion.

The characteristics of profound offense contrast with those of the ordinary nuisances in all five respects. First, they have an inexpressibly different felt "tone," best approximated by saying that they are deep, profound, shattering, serious, even more likely to cause harm by their obsessiveness to those who experience them. That is why the word "nuisance," with its unavoidable suggestions of triviality, is inadequate. Second, even when one does not perceive the offending conduct directly, one can be offended "at the very idea" of that sort of thing happening even in private. A nude person on the public bus may be an offense in my sight, but I am not offended at the very idea of that person being nude in the privacy of his or her own rooms, which is to say that my offense is not of the profound kind. Some of the examples of disgusting conduct (mere offensive nuisance) may seem different in this respect. I am disgusted by the sight of the bus passengers eating vomit, and at first it might seem that I am almost as offended by the very thought of them doing so in the privacy of their own dining rooms. But in fact my offense at what is not present seems to grow only as I succeed in forming a precise image—visual, auditory, and olfactory—in my imagination, in which case it is not that a standard of propriety is violated by the very idea of certain conduct; rather an offense is produced by my own energetic image-making. I am the party in that case who produces an offensive experience in myself, and I can have a grievance only against myself. It is as if by intense concentration I form a precise image of the bus passenger naked in his or her own bedroom, focus all of my attention on it, and then complain that that person "profoundly offends" me by his or her habitual unwitnessed nudity. My offense at the very idea of certain conduct is not profound because I would be offended by that conduct if I were to witness it; rather it is profound because I am offended by its taking place at all whether I witness it or not. On the other hand, if it were possible for a person to have the strange basic moral conviction that even private nudity is sinful because (say) it is an embarrassment to God," then the offense such a person feels at others being naked in their own homes every night would indeed be of the "profound" variety.

Third, in the case of profound offense, even when the evil is in the perceiving, something offends us and not merely our senses or lower order sensibilities. Our reaction is not like that of the man in the proverbial tale who, unable to bear the sight of a lady standing in the bus, always averted his eyes (rather than offer his seat) when confronted with the prospect. Profound offense cannot be avoided by averting one's eyes. Fourth, because profound offense results from an affront to the standards of propriety that determine one's higher-order sensibilities, it offends because it is believed wrong, not the other way round. It is not believed to be wrong simply and entirely because it causes offense.

Finally, profound offenses in all cases are experienced as at least partly impersonal, and in most cases as entirely impersonal. The offended party does not think of himself as the victim in unwitnessed flag defacings, corpse mutilations, religious icon desecrations, or abortions, and he does not therefore feel aggrieved (wronged) on his own behalf. The peeping-Tom and racial insult cases are, of course, exceptions to this. Here we should say that there is a merging of the two kinds of offense. The victim's outrage is profound because it is caused by a shocking affront to his or her deepest moral sensibilities, but he or she also happens to be the violated or threatened victim of the affronting behavior. In contrast, in the flag, icon, dead body, and abortion cases, there is no person at all in whose name to voice a complaint, except the profoundly offended party, and the only thing he could complain about in his own behalf is his offended state of mind. But that is not what he is offended at.

Feinberg believes that profound offense—which is fundamentally impersonal—should remain impersonal, and offended parties weaken their case when attempting to make it simply an issue of how they personally are offended.

Still, in the confusion of strong feelings of different kinds, people are likely to mistake what it is they are indignant about. Mill reminds us that there are many who consider as an injury to themselves any conduct which they have a distaste for [witnessed or not], and resent it as an outrage to their feelings. . . ." These people might be those whose profound offense at the reported private conduct of others is taken on behalf of an impersonal principle, or sacred symbol, or the like. Then coming to resent their own unpleasant state of mind as a nuisance (even though its character as felt annoyance was originally an insignificant component in what was experienced), they refocus their grievance, putting themselves in the forefront as "injured" parties. When they take this further step, however, their grievance originally impersonal but now voiced in their own behalf loses almost all its moral force. Mill's response to them is devastating:

> . . . a religious bigot, when charged with disregarding the religious feelings of others, has been known to retort that they disregard his feelings by persisting in their abominable worship or creed. But there is no parity between the feeling of a person for his own opinion and

the feeling of another who is offended at his holding it, no more than between the desire of a thief to take a purse and the desire of the right owner to keep it. And a person's taste is as much his own peculiar concern as his opinion or his purse.

Takers of profound offense at unwitnessed conduct are better advised to rest their claim for "protection" on impersonal grounds.

ASK YOURSELF

115. According to Feinberg, when we personalize our negative reaction to a serious offense, we thereby reduce the issue to a battle over personal preferences. Do you agree that personalizing our reactions *always* has this effect?

SUMMING UP THE ISSUE OF THE LIMITS OF POLITICAL COERCION

A defining characteristic of all political institutions is the ability to use coercive force against citizens. Coercion is commonly justified on six main grounds: the harm principle, the offense principle, legal paternalism, legal moralism, extreme paternalism, and the welfare principle. Punishment, the ultimate expression of political coercion, is commonly defended on two grounds. The first is retributive, that punishment is deserved and should be equal to the harm done, and the second is utilitarian, that punishment should increase the total amount of happiness in the world. Beccaria defended the utilitarian view, arguing that punishment should aim at creating a better society by deterring others and preventing the criminal from repeating his crime. Capital punishment, he believed, does not deter and even has harmful effects on society. Mill believed that the harm principle is the only justification for governmental coercion—that is, governments may restrict our liberties only when our actions harm other people. Even if my conduct offends other people and harms me personally, Mill argues, governments cannot rightly prohibit my action. Contrary to Mill, Feinberg argues that governments can justifiably prevent us from engaging in behavior that seriously offends others, although they can't when our actions are only trivially offensive.

CAN OF WORMS

The issue of political coercion is connected with a controversy discussed earlier in this chapter—that between liberalism and communitarianism. Liberalism emphasizes the rights and freedoms of individual people and maintains that governments cannot ordinarily limit our freedoms. Liberalism, then, is inclined toward Mill's position regarding minimal governmental interference in our lives. Communitarianism, by contrast, de-emphasizes individual freedoms and instead emphasizes our role in the larger community. To the degree that the community has a major stake in our individual conduct, governments may justly intervene on many grounds beyond the harm principle—such as to avoid public offense, or to enhance the welfare of others. Like the issue of liberalism versus communitarianism, the issue of coercion connects to differing concepts of the human self, and whether our individual lives are intimately intertwined with a larger reality. The discussions of self-hood and identity in, for example, MacIntyre or Marx are very much connected with questions about community, the good life, and government's role as enforcer of communal standards of all sorts.

F. CIVIL OBEDIENCE, DISOBEDIENCE, AND REVOLUTION

We'd like to think that the laws of our community are decent ones, founded on some concept of fairness, and not excessively coercive. That, though, is not always the case. Laws in many countries around the world discriminate against their citizens on the basis of race, gender, or religion. Other laws permit the roundup and incarceration of their government's critics without fair procedures. Still other laws permit the exploitation of children in labor. Less dramatically, even in the world's most developed countries, citizens frequently complain about excessive taxation, overly coercive police tactics, or restrictions on some private recreational activities. Imagine that you lived in a country where the law permitted the police to arrest and interrogate you on no other grounds than the color of your skin. Imagine that the laws also prohibited you from voicing any opposition to these prejudicial policies. Would you grin and bear it? Would you go against the system?

QUESTIONS TO DISCUSS

a. Can you think of some laws (either real laws or imaginary ones) that you would willingly violate on moral grounds?

b. Are there any moral or political beliefs which are so important to you that you would actively protest against governmental laws or policies which violated those beliefs?

c. What kinds of governmental misconduct do you think would justify the launching of a full-scale revolution?

These are questions concerning civil obedience and disobedience, and wrestling with them brings us to the heart of political philosophy's subject matter. If we believe that our obligation is to comply with unjust laws, then we must explain how political institutions get that kind of absolute authority over us. If on the other hand we feel justified in opposing such laws, then we must explain the authority that we as individuals have to undermine and potentially destroy political systems. The notion of "civil disobedience" as we use the term today is restricted to nonviolent infringements of the law that aim to prompt change in some law or policy and thereby improve society. In the United States, for example, black Americans violated segregation laws by attempting to attend white-only schools. The person engaged in civil disobedience must also be willing to accept punishment for the violation. Civil disobedience is a comparatively moderate kind of rebellious behavior. A step up from this is an attempted *coup d'état,* a forcible change of a regime or political system initiated by some organized group within a society. Then there is a *rebellion,* which opposes one element of a political system. A step up from that is an all-out *revolution,* which seeks to completely transform a political system. Each of these challenges to political authority require distinct justifications, and we will look at some of them here.

1. OBEDIENCE TO THE STATE: PLATO

One of the great works of political philosophy is the *Crito* by Plato—which describes the death of his teacher Socrates, who at age 70 was tried and executed for atheism and corrupting the youth. Many leaders in the city of Athens felt that Socrates' freewheeling method of philosophical inquiry badly influenced younger Athenians and risked undermining the government. Socrates' attitude toward civil obedience is paradoxical. On the one

**SOCRATES
(469–399 BCE)**
Ancient Greek philosopher.

hand, he appears to be a model of civil disobedience to the degree that he was a vocal social critic and bluntly spoke the truth, in spite of the unpopularity of his views. On the other hand, the *Crito* presents Socrates as an advocate of civil obedience insofar as he insists that he must follow the laws of Athens and comply with the judgment brought against him by the court, rather than escape. As the dialogue opens, we find Socrates in prison the day before his execution. In a last-ditch effort to save Socrates' life, his student Crito tries to convince Socrates to escape.

Only the Good and Just Life Is Worth Having. Crito begins by giving Socrates several reasons why he should escape, and in essence argues that he and other friends of Socrates will be scorned by "the many" if they allow their friend and teacher to be executed. But Socrates insists that none of that is important. All that matters is that one act justly.

FROM PLATO, *Crito*

SOCRATES   And will life be worth having, if that higher part of man be depraved, which is improved by justice and deteriorated by injustice? Do we suppose that principle, whatever it may be in man, which has to do with justice and injustice, to be inferior to the body?

CRITO   Certainly not.

SOCRATES   More honored, then?

CRITO   Far more honored.

SOCRATES   Then, my friend, we must not regard what the many say of us: but what he, the one man who has understanding of just and unjust, will say, and what the truth will say. And therefore you begin in error when you suggest that we should regard the opinion of the many about just and unjust, good and evil, honorable and dishonorable. Well, someone will say, "But the many can kill us."

ASK YOURSELF

116. Why according to Socrates should we not listen to the opinions of the many regarding justice?

CRITO   Yes, Socrates; that will clearly be the answer.

SOCRATES   That is true; but still I find with surprise that the old argument is, as I conceive, unshaken as ever. And I should like to know whether I may say the same of another proposition—that not life, but a good life, is to be chiefly valued?

CRITO   Yes, that also remains.

Socratic Civil Obedience

SOCRATES   And a good life is equivalent to a just and honorable one—that holds also?

CRITO   Yes, that holds.

SOCRATES   From these premises I proceed to argue the question whether I ought or ought not to try to escape without the consent of the Athenians: and if I am clearly right in escaping, then I will make the attempt; but if not, I will abstain. The other considerations which you mention, of money and loss of character, and the duty of educating children, are, I fear, only the doctrines of the multitude, who would be as ready to call people to life, if they were able, as they are to put them to death—and with as little reason. But now, since the argument has thus far prevailed, the only question which remains to be considered is, whether we shall do rightly either in escaping or in suffering others to aid in our escape and paying them in money and thanks, or whether we shall not do rightly; and if the latter, then death or any other calamity which may ensue on my remaining here must not be allowed to enter into the calculation.

CRITO   I think that you are right, Socrates; how then shall we proceed?

SOCRATES   Let us consider the matter together, and do you either refute me if you can, and I will be convinced; or else cease, my dear friend, from repeating to me that I ought to escape against the wishes of the Athenians: for I am extremely desirous to be persuaded by you, but not against my own better judgment. And now please to consider my first position, and do your best to answer me.

CRITO   I will do my best.

ASK YOURSELF

117. What argument does Socrates give against Crito's proposal that he escape?

It is implied in this dialogue that Socrates and Crito have had a continuing discussion on wrongdoing. Their conclusion was that wrong actions are never justified by good consequences. By reemphasizing this conclusion, Socrates makes clear that what is at issue in his escaping is whether it is *right* for him to escape, and not whether his remaining would result in bad consequences.

SOCRATES   Are we to say that we are never intentionally to do wrong, or that in one way we ought and in another way we ought not to do wrong, or is doing wrong always evil and dishonorable, as I was just now saying, and as has been already acknowledged by us? Are all our former admissions which were made within a few days to be thrown away? And have we, at our age, been earnestly discoursing with one another all our life long only to discover that we are no better than children? Or are we to rest assured, in spite of the opinion of the many, and in spite of consequences whether better or worse, of the truth of what was then said, that injustice is always an evil and dishonor to him who acts unjustly? Shall we affirm that?

CRITO   Yes.

SOCRATES   Then we must do no wrong?

CRITO   Certainly not.

SOCRATES   Nor when injured injure in return, as the many imagine; for we must injure no one at all?

CRITO   Clearly not.

SOCRATES   Again, Crito, may we do evil?

CRITO   Surely not, Socrates.

SOCRATES   And what of doing evil in return for evil, which is the morality of the many— is that just or not?

CRITO   Not just.

SOCRATES   For doing evil to another is the same as injuring him?

CRITO   Very true.

SOCRATES   Then we ought not to retaliate or render evil for evil to anyone, whatever evil we may have suffered from him. But I would have you consider, Crito, whether you really mean what you are saying. For this opinion has never been held, and never will be held, by any considerable number of persons; and those who are agreed and those who are not agreed upon this point have no common ground, and can only despise one another, when they see how widely they differ. Tell me, then, whether you agree with and assent to my first principle, that neither injury nor retaliation nor warding off evil by evil is ever right. And shall that be the premise of our agreement? Or do you decline and dissent from this? For this has been of old and is still my opinion; but, if you are of another opinion, let me hear what you have to say. If, however, you remain of the same mind as formerly, I will proceed to the next step.

CRITO   You may proceed, for I have not changed my mind.

SOCRATES   Then I will proceed to the next step, which may be put in the form of a question: Ought a man to do what he admits to be right, or ought he to betray the right?

CRITO   He ought to do what he thinks right.

SOCRATES   But if this is true, what is the application? In leaving the prison against the will of the Athenians, do I wrong any? or rather do I not wrong those whom I ought least to wrong? Do I not desert the principles which were acknowledged by us to be just? What do you say?

CRITO   I cannot tell, Socrates, for I do not know.

ASK YOURSELF

118. In the above exchange between Crito and Socrates, what is Socrates' argument for his claim that one should not render evil for evil?

Gratitude and Civil Obedience. In an imaginary conversation Socrates has with the Laws, Socrates gives a number of reasons for obeying the decision of the court. Two of his reasons are general moral arguments for civil obedience, the first of which is a debt of gratitude argument.

SOCRATES   Then consider the matter in this way: Imagine that I am about to play truant (you may call the proceeding by any name which you like), and the laws and the government come and interrogate me: "Tell us, Socrates," they say; "what are you about? are you going by an act of yours to overturn us—the laws and the whole State, as far as in you lies? Do you imagine that a State can subsist and not be overthrown, in which the decisions of law have no power, but are set aside and overthrown by individuals?" What will be our answer, Crito, to these and the like words? Anyone, and especially a clever rhetorician, will have a good deal to urge about the evil of setting aside the law which requires a sentence to be carried out; and we might reply, "Yes; but the State has injured us and given an unjust sentence." Suppose I say that?

CRITO   Very good, Socrates.

SOCRATES   "And was that our agreement with you?" the law would say, "or were you to abide by the sentence of the State?" And if I were to express astonishment at their saying this, the law would probably add: "Answer, Socrates, instead of opening your eyes: you are in the habit of asking and answering questions. Tell us what complaint you have to make against us which justifies you in attempting to destroy us and the State? In the first place did we not bring you into existence? Your father married your mother by our aid and gave birth to you. Say whether you have any objection to urge against those of us who regulate marriage?" None, I should reply. "Or against those of us who regulate the system of nurture and education of children in which you were trained? Were not the laws, who have the charge of this, right in commanding your father to train you in music and gymnastic?" Right, I should reply. "Well, then, since you were brought into the world and nurtured and educated by us, can you deny in the first place that you are our child and slave, as your fathers were before you? And if this is true you are not on equal terms with us; nor can you think that you have a right to do to us what we are doing to you. Would you have any right to strike or revile or do any other evil to a father or to your master, if you had one, when you have been struck or reviled by him, or received some other evil at his hands?—you would not say this? And because we think right to destroy you, do you think that you have any right to destroy us in return, and your country as far as in you lies? And will you, O professor of true virtue, say that you are justified in this? Has a philosopher like you failed to discover that our country is more to be valued and higher and holier far than mother or father or any ancestor, and more to be regarded in the eyes of the gods and of men of understanding? also to be soothed, and gently and reverently entreated when angry, even more than a father, and if not persuaded, obeyed? And when we are punished by her, whether with imprisonment or stripes, the punishment is to be endured in silence; and if she leads us to wounds or death in battle, thither we follow as is right; neither may anyone yield or retreat or leave his rank, but whether in battle or in a court of law, or in any other place, he must do what his city and his country order him; or he must change their view of what is just: and if he may do no violence to his father or mother, much less may he do violence to his country." What answer shall we make to this, Crito? Do the laws speak truly, or do they not?

CRITO   I think that they do.

The debt of gratitude argument states that Socrates owes the city of Athens a debt of gratitude, and should obey the city's decisions. The argument is based on an analogy between parental rearing and civil rearing: (a) Athens has been like a parent to Socrates insofar as Athens has raised him and seen to his education; (b) Socrates owes his real parents a debt of gratitude and should thus obey them. (c) Therefore, Socrates owes Athens a debt of gratitude and should obey its laws.

ASK YOURSELF

119. State the "gratitude" argument in your own words.

The Social Contract and Civil Obedience. The second argument is based on a social contract that Socrates has made with Athens.

SOCRATES   Then the laws will say: "Consider, Socrates, if this is true, that in your present attempt you are going to do us wrong. For, after having brought you into the world, and nurtured and educated you, and given you and every other citizen a share in every good that we had to give, we further proclaim and give the right to every Athenian, that if he does not like us when he has come of age and has seen the ways of the city, and made our acquaintance, he may go where he pleases and take his goods with him; and none of us laws will forbid him or interfere with him. Any of you who does not like us and the city, and who wants to go to a colony or to any other city, may go where he likes, and take his goods with him. But he who has experience of the manner in which we order justice and administer the State, and still remains, has entered into an implied contract that he will do as we command him. And he who disobeys us is, as we maintain, thrice wrong: first, because in disobeying us he is disobeying his parents; secondly, because we are the authors of his education; thirdly, because he has made an agreement with us that he will duly obey our commands; and he neither obeys them nor convinces us that our commands are wrong; and we do not rudely impose them, but give him the alternative of obeying or convincing us; that is what we offer and he does neither. These are the sort of accusations to which, as we were saying, you, Socrates, will be exposed if you accomplish your intentions; you, above all other Athenians." Suppose I ask, why is this? they will justly retort upon me that I above all other men have acknowledged the agreement. "There is clear proof," they will say, "Socrates, that we and the city were not displeasing to you. Of all Athenians you have been the most constant resident in the city, which, as you never leave, you may be supposed to love. For you never went out of the city either to see the games, except once when you went to the Isthmus, or to any other place unless when you were on military service; nor did you travel as other men do. Nor had you any curiosity to know other States or their laws: your affections did not go beyond us and our State; we were your especial favorites, and you acquiesced in our government of you; and this is the State in which you gave birth to your children, which is a proof of your satisfaction. Moreover, you might, if you had liked, have fixed the penalty at banishment in the course of the trial—the State which refuses to let you go now would have let you go then. But you pretended that you preferred death to exile, and that you were not grieved at death. And now you have forgotten these fine sentiments, and pay no respect to us, the laws, of whom you are the destroyer; and are doing what only a miserable slave would do, running away and turning your back upon the compacts and agreements which you made as a citizen. And first of all answer this very question: Are we right in saying that you agreed to be governed according to us in deed, and not in word only? Is that true or not?" How shall we answer that, Crito? Must we not agree?

CRITO   There is no help, Socrates.

SOCRATES   Then will they not say: "You, Socrates, are breaking the covenants and agreements which you made with us at your leisure, not in any haste or under any compulsion or deception, but having had seventy years to think of them, during which time you were at liberty to leave the city, if we were not to your mind, or if our covenants appeared to you to be unfair. You had your choice, and might have gone either to Lacedaemon or Crete, which you often praise for their good government, or to some other Hellenic or foreign State. Whereas you, above all other Athenians, seemed to be so fond of the State, or, in other words, of us her laws (for who would like a State that has no laws?), that you never stirred out of her: the halt, the blind, the maimed, were not more stationary in her than you were. And now you run away and forsake your agreements. Not so, Socrates, if you will take our advice; do not make yourself ridiculous by escaping out of the city.

The social contract argument is this: (a) If one chooses to take up residence in a particular area, then one is thereby agreeing to obey the laws and decisions of the lawmakers; (b) Socrates chose to reside in Athens; (c) Therefore, Socrates has agreed to follow the decisions of the lawmakers (regarding his execution).

ASK YOURSELF

120. State the "contract" argument in your own words.

Additional Arguments for Compliance. In addition to the above two moral arguments for obedience to the laws in general, the Laws (personified here) give five or so pragmatic arguments for why Socrates should obey the specific decisions of the court regarding his execution.

SOCRATES   "For just consider, if you transgress and err in this sort of way, what good will you do, either to yourself or to your friends? That your friends will be driven into exile and deprived of citizenship, or will lose their property, is tolerably certain; and you yourself, if you fly to one of the neighboring cities, as, for example, Thebes or Megara, both of which are well-governed cities, will come to them as an enemy, Socrates, and their government will be against you, and all patriotic citizens will cast an evil eye upon you as a subverter of the laws, and you will confirm in the minds of the judges the justice of their own condemnation of you. For he who is a corrupter of the laws is more than likely to be corrupter of the young and foolish portion of humankind. Will you then flee from well-ordered cities and virtuous men? and is existence worth having on these terms? Or will you go to them without shame, and talk to them, Socrates? And what will you say to them? What you say here about virtue and justice and institutions and laws being the best things among men? Would that be decent of you? Surely not. But if you go away from well-governed States to Crito's friends in Thessaly, where there is great disorder and license, they will be charmed to have the tale of your escape from prison, set off with ludicrous particulars of the manner in which you were wrapped in a goatskin or some other disguise, and metamorphosed as the fashion of runaways is—that is very likely; but will there be no one to remind you that in your old age you violated the most sacred laws from a miserable desire of a little more life? Perhaps not, if you keep them in a good temper; but if they are out of temper you will hear many degrading things; you will live, but how?—as the flatterer of all men, and the servant of all men; and doing what?—eating and drinking in Thessaly, having gone abroad in order that you may get a dinner. And where will be your fine sentiments about justice and virtue then? Say that you wish to live for the sake of your children, that you may bring them up and educate them—will you take them into Thessaly and deprive them of Athenian citizenship? Is that the benefit which you would confer upon them? Or are you under the impression that they will be better cared for and educated here if you are still alive, although absent from them; for that your friends will take care of them? Do you fancy that if you are an inhabitant of Thessaly they will take care of them, and if you are an inhabitant of the other world they will not take care of them? Nay; but if they who call themselves friends are truly friends, they surely will.

"Listen, then, Socrates, to us who have brought you up. Think not of life and children first, and of justice afterwards, but of justice first, that you may be justified before the princes of the world below. For neither will you nor any that belong to you be happier or holier or juster in this life, or happier in another, if you do as Crito bids. Now you depart in innocence, a sufferer and not a doer of evil; a victim, not of the laws, but of men. But if you go forth, returning evil for evil, and injury for injury, breaking the covenants and agreements which you have made with us, and wronging those whom you ought least to wrong, that is to say, yourself, your friends, your country, and us, we shall be angry with you while you live, and our brethren, the laws in the world below, will receive you as an enemy; for they will know that you have done your best to destroy us. Listen, then, to us and not to Crito."

SOCRATES   This is the voice which I seem to hear murmuring in my ears, like the sound of the flute in the ears of the mystic; that voice, I say, is humming in my ears, and prevents me from hearing any other. And I know that anything more which you will say will be in vain. Yet speak, if you have anything to say.

CRITO   I have nothing to say, Socrates.

SOCRATES   Then let me follow the intimations of the will of God.

ASK YOURSELF

121. In the above two paragraphs, what are the various pragmatic reasons that the Laws give for why Socrates should not try to escape?

2.   CIVIL DISOBEDIENCE: MARTIN LUTHER KING

The Civil Rights movement in the United States during the 1960s involved dramatic acts of civil disobedience. The gross unjustness of racist policies throughout the country—but especially in Southern states—prompted thousands of African Americans to engage in nonviolent protest. Racial segregation, which prohibited African Americans from frequenting "white-only" establishments, such as restaurants, hotels, and schools, was the key issue. The turning point in the campaign against desegregation occurred in the spring of 1963 with a major public demonstration in Birmingham, Alabama. The event drew national attention when city policemen released dogs and turned fire hoses on participants. The famed civil rights leader Martin Luther King, Jr. (1929–1968), was jailed for his role in the demonstration—along with many of his supporters, including several hundred children. He spent eleven days in jail, during which time he wrote a letter of response to eight fellow clergymen who criticized his tactics. King's "Letter from Birmingham Jail" is not only a great political document in U.S. history, but also a clear philosophical treatise on the subject of nonviolent demonstrations and civil disobedience. The essence of his message is that nonviolent civil disobedience is justified when lawful attempts at ending unjust policies have failed, and the oppressed group is left with no other alternative to bring about change. Nonviolent protest, he argues, creates tension within an oppressive community and forces the issue. "It seeks so to dramatize the issue so that it can no longer be ignored." King looks to Socrates' life activity as a model for tension-producing civil disobedience:

FROM MARTIN LUTHER KING, JR., "Letter from Birmingham Jail" (1963)

Just as Socrates felt that it was necessary to create a tension in the mind so that individuals could rise from the bondage of myths and half-truths to the unfettered realm of creative analysis and objective appraisal, we must see the need of having nonviolent gadflies to create the kind of tension in society that will help men to rise from the dark depths of prejudice and racism to the majestic heights of understanding and brotherhood. So the purpose of the direct action is to create a situation so crisis-packed that it will inevitably open the door to negotiation.

King argues that academic freedom is a reality today because Socrates practiced civil disobedience.

The issue of civil disobedience, according to King, rests on a distinction between just and unjust laws:

One may well ask: "How can you advocate breaking some laws and obeying others?" The answer is found in the fact that there are two types of laws: There are just and there are unjust laws. I would agree with Saint Augustine that "An unjust law is no law at all." Now, what is the difference between the two? How does one determine when a law is just or unjust? A just law is a man-made code that squares with the moral law or the law of God. An unjust law is a code that is out of harmony with the moral law. To put it in the terms of Saint Thomas Aquinas, an unjust law is a human law that is not rooted in eternal and natural law. Any law that uplifts human personality is just. Any law that degrades human personality is unjust.

ASK YOURSELF

122. What is Augustine's view about unjust laws?

123. According to Aquinas, what is the difference between just and unjust laws?

The principal danger of civil disobedience—no matter how peaceful—is that it undermines the authority of political institutions and risks throwing a society into anarchy. King recognizes this risk and says that the solution is for the protestor to retain a sense of respect for the law even during demonstrations:

In no sense do I advocate evading or defying the law as the rabid segregationist would do. This would lead to anarchy. One who breaks an unjust law must do it openly, lovingly . . . and with a willingness to accept the penalty. I submit that an individual who breaks a law that conscience tells him is unjust, and willingly accepts the penalty by staying in jail to arouse the conscience of the community over its injustice, is in reality expressing the very highest respect for law.

3.   A Defense of Revolution: John Locke

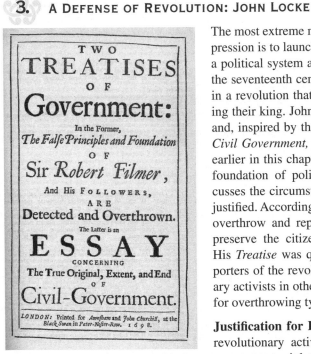

Title page of John Locke's Two Treatises of Government (1689–1690).

The most extreme measure in opposing political oppression is to launch an all out revolution to destroy a political system and replace it with a new one. In the seventeenth century, Great Britain was engaged in a revolution that involved removing and executing their king. John Locke supported the revolution and, inspired by those events, wrote his *Treatise of Civil Government,* portions of which we examined earlier in this chapter. In addition to explaining the foundation of political authority, Locke also discusses the circumstances under which revolution is justified. According to Locke, citizens are entitled to overthrow and replace a government that fails to preserve the citizen's fundamental natural rights. His *Treatise* was quickly embraced by fellow supporters of the revolution in Britain, and revolutionary activists in other countries saw it as a handbook for overthrowing tyrannical governments.

Justification for Revolution. Locke believes that revolutionary activity is fully justified when the government violates laws and threatens the life, liberty, and property of the individual. According to Locke, governments come into power for the purpose of preserving our basic rights, and when they fail to keep their part of the agreement, the people may remove the offending government and set up a better one. One way of dissolving a government is through a voluntary and peaceful disbanding of the government itself. The second involves violent resistance or insurrection—short of all-out civil war.

FROM JOHN LOCKE, *Two Treatises of Government* (1689–1690)

212. Besides this over-turning from without, *governments are dissolved from within. First,* when the *legislative* is *altered.* . . .

221. There is therefore, secondly, another way whereby *governments are dissolved,* and that is, when the legislative, or the prince, either of them, act contrary to their trust. *First,* the *legislative acts against the trust* reposed in them, when they endeavor to invade the property of the subject, and to make themselves, or any part of the community, masters, or arbitrary disposers of the lives, liberties, or fortunes of the people.

222. The reason why men enter into society, is the preservation of their property; and the end why they chuse and authorize a legislative, is, that there may be laws made, and rules set, as guards and fences to the properties of all the members of the society, to limit the power, and moderate the dominion, of every part and member of the society: for since it can never be supposed to be the will of the society, that the legislative should have a power to destroy that which every one designs to secure, by entering into society, and for which the people submitted themselves to legislators of their own making; whenever the *legislators endeavor to take away, and destroy the property of the people,* or to reduce them to slavery under arbitrary power, they put themselves into a state of war with the people, who are thereupon absolved from any farther obedience, and are left to the common refuge, which God hath provided for all men, against force and violence. Whensoever therefore the legislative shall transgress this fundamental rule of society; and either by ambition, fear, folly or corruption, *endeavor to grasp* themselves, *or put into the hands of any other, an absolute power* over the lives, liberties, and estates of the people; by this breach of trust they *forfeit the power* the people had put into their hands for quite contrary ends, and it devolves to the people, who have a right to resume their original liberty, and, by the establishment of a new legislative (such as they shall think fit), provide for their own safety and security, which is the end for which they are in society. What I have said here, concerning the legislative in general, holds true also concerning the *supreme executor,* who having a double trust put in him, both to have a part in the legislative, and the supreme execution of the law, acts against both, when he goes about to set up his own arbitrary will as the law of the society. He *acts* also *contrary to his trust,* when he either employs the force, treasure, and offices of the society, to corrupt the representatives, and gain them to his purposes; or openly pre-engages the *electors,* and prescribes to their choice, such, whom he has, by solicitations, threats, promises, or otherwise, won to his designs; and employs them to bring in such, who have promised before-hand what to vote, and what to enact. . . .

ASK YOURSELF

125. In what ways might the executive branch of the government violate the public trust and thereby justify a revolution?

Justification for Civil War. Locke anticipates several criticisms of his justification for revolution. Perhaps people will always be dissatisfied with a government and thus continually overthrow and replace it. In that situation no effective government could ever be formed. Locke replies that people grow content with their systems and would not likely do this. The critic may also contend that such permissiveness regarding insurrections may lead to all-out civil war, and this is not justified. Locke responds by defending the individual's right even to engage in civil war.

228. But if they, who say it *lays a foundation for rebellion,* mean that it may occasion civil wars, or intestine broils, to tell the people they are absolved from obedience when illegal attempts are made upon their liberties or properties, and may oppose the unlawful violence of those who were their magistrates, when they invade their properties contrary to the trust put in them; and that therefore this doctrine is not to be allowed, being so destructive to the peace of the world: they may as well say, upon the same ground, that honest men may not oppose robbers or pirates, because this may occasion disorder or bloodshed. If any *mischief* come in such cases, it is not *to be charged* upon him who defends his own right, but *on him*

that *invades* his neighbors. If the innocent honest man must quietly quit all he has, for peace sake, to him who will lay violent hands upon it, I desire it may be considered, what a kind of peace there will be in the world, which consists only in violence and rapine; and which is to be maintained only for the benefit of robbers and oppressors. Who would not think it an admirable peace betwixt the mighty and the mean, when the lamb, without resistance, yielded his throat to be torn by the imperious wolf?

ASK YOURSELF

126. For Locke, who is at fault for the harm that comes from civil war?

Locke had a profound impact on eighteenth-century political reformers, most notably Thomas Jefferson, and we can clearly see the influence of Locke's ideas in the opening of the Declaration of Independence:

> We hold these Truths to be self-evident, that all Men are created equal, that they are endowed by their Creator with certain unalienable Rights, that among these are Life, Liberty, and the Pursuit of Happiness—That to secure these Rights, Governments are instituted among Men, deriving their just Powers from the Consent of the Governed, that whenever any Form of Government becomes destructive of these Ends, it is the Right of the People to alter or to abolish it, and to institute new Government, laying its Foundation on such Principles, and organizing its Powers in such Form, as to them shall seem most likely to effect their Safety and Happiness.

We also see Locke's influence in the 1789 "Declaration of the Rights of Man" adopted by the French assembly during the French Revolution:

> Men are born and remain free and equal in rights . . . [and the] aim of all political association is the conservation of the natural and imprescriptable rights of man . . . [including] liberty, property, security, and resistance to oppression.

ASK YOURSELF

127. Which words or phrases in the Declaration of Independence imply the notion of a social contract?

SUMMING UP THE ISSUE OF CIVIL OBEDIENCE, DISOBEDIENCE, AND REVOLUTION

When governments are incompetent or immoral, citizens often respond in a variety of confrontational ways. One of the more moderate responses is civil disobedience, which involves violating the law in a nonviolent manner for the purpose of changing some law. A more extreme measure would be to start a revolution to overthrow the entire political system. In either case, discontented people break the law, and this requires some justification. Plato argues against civil disobedience on two grounds. First, he maintains that there is a strong analogy between the obligation that we owe our parents and the obligation that we owe our government since both have raised us. Second, he argues that if we choose to reside in a particular area, then we thereby agree to follow the laws of the area. In contrast with Plato's arguments, King contended that nonviolent civil disobedience is justified when lawful attempts at ending unjust policies have failed. Locke argued that all out revolution is justified when the government violates laws and threatens the life, liberty, and property of citizens. Even if this results in widespread bloodshed, Locke argues, the fault rests with the government and not with the revolutionaries.

CAN OF WORMS

Issues of civil disobedience and revolution rest directly on the question of how governments obtain their authority to begin with. Earlier in this chapter we looked at three theories: natural law, social contract, and natural rights. Proponents of these theories differed with respect to the issue of civil disobedience or revolution. Hobbes, for example, argued that the governments that we establish through the social contract must be absolute; otherwise, governments could not effectively keep the peace. Thus, according to Hobbes, citizens are not entitled to topple their rulers, and he bases this claim in a certain conception of natural law that also informs his general ethical views. Locke, by contrast, argued that the preservation of our natural rights is of the highest importance, and governments can be overthrown when they fail to do this. He based this view on a conception of natural law that grounded it in the will of God. It is also clear that the arguments employed by Martin Luther King, Jr., depend upon an acceptance of the sorts of natural law theory discussed and critiqued in the chapter on ethics in this volume. The arguments of both Locke and King depend in turn upon some of the arguments and considerations that figure crucially in philosophical discussions of religion (Chapter I).

SUMMING UP THE CHAPTER

Political philosophy is the study of the nature and justification of political institutions. An initial philosophical question about governments is whether they are even necessary. Anarchism is the theory that the existence of governments is completely unjustified; they rob us of our rights and incompetently perform social tasks that could be better supervised through private cooperation. If we assume that governments are justified, however, a question immediately arises about where they get their authority. Many contemporary theories of governmental authority rest on three specific theories developed in the seventeenth century. Pufendorf argued that God mandates as a natural law that we should be sociable, and governments are a means of maintaining sociability. Hobbes argued that to ensure peace, we devise a social contract with others and set up governments to ensure that we abide by our agreements. Locke argued that governments are needed to preserve our natural rights to life, health, liberty, and possessions. Once governments are instituted, we can then ask whether they should focus on the interests of citizens individually, or the collective good of the community. Liberalism is the view that governments should preserve the rights of the individual. Communitarianism is the view that governments should be directed toward the advancement of community well-being. One view of liberalism, offered by John Rawls, is that our liberties should be based on fairness, and to arrive at fair social guidelines, we negotiate from behind a veil of ignorance regarding our actual economic status. The resulting guidelines would permit governments to restrict an individual's property for the betterment of others. Another view of liberalism, by Robert Nozick, is that governments should be very minimal and function mainly to protect our rights. In this view, wealth is based on entitlement, and governments cannot take away our property for the benefit of others.

As we examine the conduct of our leaders, we may ask what kind of moral standard we can hold them to. Confucius and Plato felt that rulers should follow the highest moral norms, while Machiavelli held that a ruler may need to be deceitful in order to survive. By their very nature, governments are coercive institutions and establish laws that restrict our activities. We may ask what the limits to their coercion are. Punishment itself, Beccaria argued, is justified only as a means toward creating a better society, and not as a way of retaliating or getting revenge. Mill argued that governments can restrict our actions only to prevent us from harming others. Feinberg argued that governments can also restrict seriously offensive behavior. If a government overextends its authority, we may next ask if we can disobey the laws, or even revolt. Plato argued that we should obey laws that we object to, while King argued that in especially grievous situations we can nonviolently disobey laws as a means of protest. Locke argued that revolution is justified when governments fail to protect our fundamental rights.

FINAL REACTIONS

a. Hobbes argued that people are inherently selfish and confrontational, and governments are needed to keep people at peace with each other. How would an anarchist philosopher such as Malatesta respond to Hobbes?

b. Chuang-tzu, Hobbes, and Locke have competing conceptions of the state of nature. Which conception seems most correct to you, and what are some flaws in the competing conceptions?

c. Nozick believes that the only just way of distributing wealth is through entitlement: people are entitled to property acquired by just means and/or to property voluntarily transferred to them by people who hold it justly. What would Rawls say is wrong with this theory?

d. Plato believed that rulers should always be guided by truth and moral virtue. Machiavelli argued that political leaders may need to be deceitful in order to survive. Which if either of these views is correct, and why?

e. Mill argued that the government may justly restrict behavior of individuals only to prevent harm to others. Feinberg argued that the government may also restrict our actions if they are seriously offensive. Which of these two views seems most correct to you and why?

f. King argued that we may nonviolently disobey unjust laws. How would Plato respond to this? How would you respond?

FURTHER READINGS

GENERAL WORKS

Barcalow, Emmett, *Justice, Equality, and Rights* (Belmont, CA: Wadsworth Publishing, 2004).

Goodin, R., and Pettit, P., eds., *A Companion to Contemporary Political Philosophy* (Oxford: Blackwell, 1993).

Kymlicka, Will, *Contemporary Political Philosophy* (New York: Oxford University Press, 1999).

Pojman, Louis, ed., *Political Philosophy: Classic and Contemporary Readings* (New York: McGraw-Hill, 2002).

Pojman, Louis, *Global Political Philosophy* (New York: McGraw-Hill, 2003).

Rosen, Michael, and Wolff, Jonathan, eds., *Political Thought* (New York: Oxford University Press, 1999).

Wolff, Jonathan, *An Introduction to Political Philosophy* (Oxford: Oxford University Press, 1996).

WORKS ON SPECIFIC TOPICS AND FIGURES

Annas, Julia, *An Introduction to Plato's Republic* (Oxford: Clarendon Press, 1981).

Ashcraft, R., *Locke's Two Treatises of Government* (London: Unwin & Hyman, 1987).

Crowder, G. *Classical Anarchism: The Political Thought of Godwin, Proudhon, Bakunin, and Kropotkin,* Oxford: Oxford University Press (1991).

Gray, J., *Mill on Liberty: A Defence* (London: Routledge, 1996).

Kraus, Jody S., *The Limits of Hobbesian Contractarianism* (Cambridge: Cambridge University Press, 1993).

Kukathas, Chandran, *Rawls: A Theory of Justice and Its Critics* (Stanford: Stanford University Press, 1990).

Nino, Carlos Santiago, *The Ethics of Human Rights* (Oxford: Clarendon Press, 1991).

GLOSSARY

a posteriori: known on the basis of, or after ("posterior" to), experience. Contrasted with *a priori.*

a priori: known to be true independently of, or "prior" to, experience.

act utilitarianism: a version of utilitarianism associated with Bentham that advocates tallying the positive and negative consequences of each act that we perform. Acts that have the most favorable balance of positive consequences are moral acts. Contrasts with rule utilitarianism.

agency theory: the view that human beings sometimes cause their own actions independently of prior causes.

AI: Artificial Intelligence. Interdisciplinary study of computational systems, such as computers or robots, which have or simulate various human mentalistic traits, such as cognition and perception.

alienation: a notion associated particularly with Karl Marx, who claimed that workers under capitalism are alienated from themselves, their work, and other people.

anarchism: literally "no rule"; the view that no governments have legitimate authority over people.

Anselm (1033–1109): medieval Christian philosopher who developed what is now called the ontological argument for God's existence.

anthropomorphize (anthropomorphism): to attribute human traits to nonhumans without sufficient justification. A child who seriously attributes thoughts to her doll is anthropomorphizing.

Aquinas, Thomas (1225–1274): medieval philosopher who proposed five proofs for God's existence and developed the definitive medieval account of natural law theory.

argument: a set of statements, some of which, the premise or premises, are supposed to support others, the conclusion or conclusions.

Aristotle (384–322 BCE): ancient Greek philosopher who emphasized the notion of a thing's purpose (*telos*) and who treated ethics in terms of the development of virtues.

Atman-Brahman: the notion of the Self-God in Brahmanic and Vedanta Hinduism which maintains that our true inner self is identical to the all-pervasive God.

Atomism: ancient Greek view championed by Leucippus and Democritus according to which the world is composed entirely of indivisible particles called atoms.

Behaviorism: the view that mental attributes, such as thoughts, beliefs, fears, and the like, can be reduced to, or eliminated in favor of, behavior or behavioral dispositions. Behaviorists deny that there is a metaphysically distinct "mental" realm.

Bentham, Jeremy (1748–1832): British political philosopher whose classic statement of utilitarianism involves calculating units of pleasure resulting from actions.

best reasons ethics: the moral theory associated with Stephen Toulmin and Kurt Baier that the morally right course of action is simply the one that is supported by the best reasons.

Bhagavad Gita: literally, "song of God," short philosophical dialogue within the Hindu *Mahabharata* epic which discusses the Atman-Brahman and ways of achieving liberation.

Buddha: literally, "englightened one," Buddhist term which variously refers to Gautama Siddhartha, or any enlightened person.

Buddhism: religion founded in India by Gautama Siddhartha (563–483 BCE) that stresses the four noble truths; Buddhism's main two main divisions are the Theravada and Mahayana schools.

Butler, Joseph (1692–1752): British philosopher who opposed Hobbes's theory of selfishness and argued instead that human actions are sometimes motivated by benevolent concerns.

categorical imperative: a central principle in Kant's moral theory, namely, "Act only on that maxim by which you can at the same time will that it should become a universal law."

Chuang-tzu (369–286 BCE): Taoist philosopher attributed with composing the first portion of the text entitled the *Chuang-tzu,* which describes the notions of the Tao, non-action, non-mind, transformation, and freedom artificial social constraints.

civil disobedience: nonviolent infringements of the law that aim to prompt change in some law or policy and thereby improve society.

cogito ergo sum: "I think therefore I am," a central philosophical claim associated with Descartes' philosophy.

communitarianism: political theory that questions a central presumption underlying liberalism, namely that people can exist and be understood independently of the wider communities to which they belong.

compatibilism: also called "soft determinism," the theory that free will is compatible with determinism.

conclusion: see *argument.*

conditioning: the process by which the likelihood of a given behavior being repeated is increased or decreased.

Confucianism: religious and philosophical system of China based on the teachings of Confucius which emphasizes social values such as filial obedience, custom, and governing by way of example.

Confucius (551–479 BCE): Latinized name for Kung Fu-tzu, Chinese founder of Confucianism whose sayings are preserved in the *Analects.*

d'Holbach, Paul-Henri Thiry, Baron (1723–1789): French philosopher whose *System of Nature* (1770) defends hard determinism.

Democritus (fifth century BCE): ancient Greek philosopher who held that the world is composed of indivisible particles.

Descartes, René (1596–1650): rationalist philosopher who developed a method of scientific investigation and argued that all knowledge is derived from the truth of one's existence.

determinism: the theory that everything that happens, including human actions, is determined by prior conditions; determinism appears to be incompatible with free will.

distributive justice: justice in allocation of benefits and burdens within a social order.

dualism: a metaphysical position opposed to monism. There are two main types of ultimate reality, usually, matter and spirit, or body and mind.

duty theory: a moral theory originally arising out of the natural law tradition according to which we judge moral conduct in reference to an intuitive list of duties, typically duties to God, oneself, and others.

ecological self, deep ecology: the view promoted by some environmentalists that humans must think of themselves simply as part of a larger "eco-system" rather than masters of the world who are free to manipulate it as they please.

emotivism: the theory that moral utterances are principally performative and express our feelings; this theory is associated with prescriptivism.

empiricism: the view that knowledge is gained primarily or entirely through the five senses.

Empiricism, British: seventeenth- and eighteenth-century philosophical movement associated with Locke, Berkeley, and Hume that denies innate ideas and emphasizes knowledge through experience and inductive reasoning.

enthymeme: an argument with missing premises or conclusions; see *argument*.

Epicureanism: ancient Greek school founded by Epicurus, who emphasized achieving happiness by minimizing pain and pursuing pleasure.

Epicurus (341–270 BCE): ancient Greek philosopher and founder of Epicureanism.

epistemology: the part of philosophical inquiry that focuses on the nature, the possibility, and the sources of knowledge.

externalism: the view, in epistemology, that it is possible for someone to know something without be able to say how they know. One version is *reliabilism* (q.v.).

femininist ethics: approaches to ethics that stress the experiences of women. In some versions, the claim is made that moral theory should focus on appropriately caring for others in each unique circumstance, rather than on general and abstract moral principles.

fideism: the view that religious knowledge is obtained through faith alone, and not through reason.

folk psychology: the psychological theory employed by ordinary people in explaining their own behavior and the behavior of others. If you *desired* food and you ate the hamburger offered to you, you must have *believed* that it was food. This natural explanation mentions needs, desires, and beliefs, which are typical concepts of folk psychology.

forms, theory of: Plato's theory that the most real and knowable objects exist in a realm "apart" from the physical world which contains archetypes of ordinary objects.

formula of the end itself: a version of the categorical imperative in Kant's theory maintaining that we should treat persons as ends in themselves, and never as means to an end.

formula of the law of nature: a version of the categorical imperative in Kant's theory, namely, "Act as if the maxim of your action were to become through your will a universal law of nature."

functionalism: the view that mental concepts, such as "belief" or "desire," are names for functional characteristics of people or other organisms. A robot and a human, though constructed of very different kinds of stuff, could both believe there is a red apple here, provided that they function in the same way in relation to it.

Great Learning: short philosophical section from the Confucian *Book of Rites* which states that a ruler's virtuous conduct will be transferred down the social hierarchy to the people.

harm principle: the view that governmental coercion is justified only when it seeks to prevent people from harming others.

hedonism: a moral theory associated with Epicurus and the utilitarians based on the idea that pleasure is or figures into the criterion of moral goodness.

hedonistic utilitarianism: the utilitarian theory associated with Bentham and Mill that we should maximize total pleasure; this is in contrast with ideal and preference utilitarianism.

higher pleasures: a notion associated with Mill's utilitarianism. He held that higher intellectual pleasures are qualitatively superior to lower bodily pleasures.

Hindu: general term designating the religion of India and its various movements including Vedic Hinduism, Brahmanism, and Bhakti Hinduism.

Hobbes, Thomas (1588–1679): British philosopher who argued the egoistic position that human actions are largely motivated by self-interest.

holism (holistic): a term referring to "wholes." For example, if understanding is holistic, that would mean that it requires seeing all the parts of a problem (solution) in the light of the whole problem (solution). Another example: to live holistically might mean to live with a sense for one's connections to a larger whole (nature, God).

Hsun-tzu (298–238 BCE): early skeptical Confucian philosopher who argued that humans are by nature selfish.

Hume, David (1711–1776): Scottish skeptical philosopher and British empiricist who argued that causal connections are grounded in mental habits and morality is a matter of feeling and not rational judgment.

hypothetical imperatives: in Kant's theory, hypothetical imperatives are conditional obligations of the form "*If* you want some thing, then you must perform some act to get it"; this is in contrast with the categorical imperative.

idealism: the metaphysical theory (opposed to materialism) that reality exists in the minds of spirits or is mind-like.

immediacy: experience unmediated by thought or reasoning.

inductive argument: an argument in which the premises provide less than conclusive evidence for the conclusion. Inductive arguments vary from very strong to very weak.

intentionality: a term designating the fact that mental phenomenon are "about" something. A thought, for example, must always have a content or be about something.

internalism: the view, in epistemology, that when someone knows something, they must be able to say how they know it. Contrasted with *externalism* (q.v.).

is/ought problem: a problem described by David Hume which arises in the attempt to derive statements of obligation (e.g., you ought to tell the truth) from statements of fact (e.g., truth telling usually pays off). Hume denied that there could be such derivations.

James, William (1842–1910): American philosopher of the school of Pragmatism who emphasized belief in God on pragmatic grounds.

Kant, Immanuel (1724–1804): German philosopher who argued that human knowledge is grounded in mental categories, and that morality consists in following the categorical imperative.

Kierkegaard, Søren (1813–1855): Danish philosopher who poetically portrayed various ways of living (aesthetic, ethical, religious) in order to stimulate genuine decisions about life.

Krishna: Legendary Hindu figure in the Bhagavad Gita who is said to be a human incarnation of the god Vishnu.

liberalism: political theory associated especially with John Locke. Individual freedoms are of primary importance, and governments exist primarily to protect individual rights.

libertarianism: the view that governmental power should be limited to a few basic functions, such as protection from assault, and should not be employed to promote abstract notions of equality and distributive justice.

Locke, John (1632–1704): British philosopher of the empiricist tradition who denied innate ideas and argued that knowledge comes from experience.

Machiavelli, Niccolò (1469–1527): Italian philosopher whose book *The Prince* (1532) recommends that rulers should pursue what is expedient and even be deceitful in order to remain in power.

Marx, Karl (1818–1883): German political philosopher and founder of communism who argued that all of culture is entirely determined by economic factors.

materialism: the monistic metaphysical theory, opposed to idealism, that all reality is physical in nature.

mean, doctrine of the: Aristotle's view that virtues lie at a mean between two more extreme vices. For example, courage is a mean between cowardice and rashness.

meaning: the notion of meaning is complex. Words have meanings. Sentences are sometimes said to have meanings. A rough distinction can be made between the *reference* of a term and its meaning or sense or connotation. The reference of "dog" in a given use might be a specific dog, whereas the "meaning" (sense) of the term is "thing that has four legs, barks, etc."

Mencius (390–305 BCE): Confucian writer who argued that human nature is essentially good.

metaphysics: the part of philosophical inquiry that attempts to answer such questions as "What is real?" and "What are the ultimate, irreducible constituents of reality?"

Mill, John Stuart (1806–1873): British philosopher in the empiricist tradition who advocated utilitarianism and emphasized the difference between higher and lower pleasures.

minimal state: political theory associated with libertarianism. Only minimal governments are justified and their main function is to protect citizens from attack by other people or countries.

monism: the metaphysical position that there is only one reality, or one kind of underlying reality.

moral objectivism: the theory that morality has an objective foundation that is independent of human approval; this theory is in opposition to moral relativism and anti-realism.

moral relativism: the general moral theory that moral values are *human* inventions, and that these inventions can vary in arbitrary ways; varieties include both individual relativism and cultural relativism.

moral rights: a term in rights theory referring to rights that apply universally to all humans and are not merely creations of governments; moral rights are contrasted with legal rights.

moral skepticism: the theory that there are no known objective moral values.

mysticism (mystical): in the history of religion, the idea that one can achieve a kind of union with God or come to a more or less direct knowledge of God through special experiences that follow upon meditation or other disciplines.

Naess, Arne: Norwegian philosopher and advocate of deep ecology, the view that the true self is intertwined with the larger natural world around us.

natural law theory: the theory that God endorses specific moral standards and fixes them in human nature, and which humans can discover through rational intuition.

Nietzsche, Friedrich (1844–1900): German philosopher who argued that we should replace traditional values with new values of the new ideal Superhuman (*Übermensch*).

no self (*anatta*): Buddhist doctrine that we have no unified and individual self, but only a fluctuating series of material and conscious states (*skandhas*). No self is one of the Three Marks of Existence (*ti-lakkhana*) in Buddhism.

offense principle: the view that governmental coercion is justified in order to prevent people from seriously offending others.

ontology (adj. ontological): the study of being or of what exists most fundamentally. If you believe that God exists, then God is included in your ontology.

original position: a device in John Rawls's moral theory designed to show that impartiality is essential to a correct notion of justice.

Paley, William (1743–1805): a British philosopher who defended the design argument for God's existence.

pantheism: the view that God is identical to nature or history as a whole; versions of this view are associated with Xenophanes, Parmenides, Plotinus, Spinoza, and Hegel.

parallelism: the view that mental events and physical events run in a parallel series, so that, for example, a wound to the flesh will always occur along with a painful, rather than a pleasant, sensation, even though there is no causal connected between the wound and the pain. A view developed by Leibniz in particular.

Pascal, Blaise (1623–1662): French religious philosopher of the fideist tradition who proposed that we wager in favor of belief in God when reason cannot determine whether or not there is a God.

Period of 100 Philosophers: period of philosophical creativity in reaction to China's warring states period (403–221 BCE), later classed into six schools: Confucianism, Taoism, Mohism, Yin and Yang School, Logicians, and Legalism.

philosopher-king: theory in Plato's *Republic* that rulers should be philosophers in the sense that they are committed to truth and moral virtue.

Plato (427–347 BCE): ancient Greek philosopher who argued for the theory of the forms, the immortality of the soul, and the grounding of justice in eternal invariant norms.

pluralism: metaphysical position, opposed to monism, according to which ultimate reality is constituted by more than one thing or kind of thing.

practical wisdom: in Aristotle's ethics the indispensable master virtue which is required for the right use of any other virtue such as courage or patience.

premise: see *argument.*

prescriptivism: the theory that moral utterances are principally performative and prescribe behavior; this theory is associated with emotivism.

***prima facie* duty:** a term introduced in the duty theory of W. D. Ross which refers to duties that appear to be binding, unless outweighed by a stronger duty.

Protagoras (*c.* 490–*c.* 420 BCE): ancient Greek Sophist who is remembered for the statement that "man is the measure of all things," a statement taken to express relativism.

psychological egoism: the theory sometimes attributed to Hobbes that humans are motivated exclusively by selfish inclinations.

Pufendorf, Samuel (1632–1694): German natural law philosopher who presents a systematic theory of natural law and moral duties to God, oneself, and others.

Pyrrhonism: ancient Greece skeptical school founded by Pyrrho. Extreme skepticism.

Questions of King Milinda (*Milindapanha*): Important Theravada Buddhist philosophical text written about 100 CE in the Pali language; the issues discussed include the self, karma, and reincarnation.

Quine, Willard Van Orman (b. 1908): American philosopher and logician who insisted that the natural sciences give us the best knowledge we can hope for, and scientific knowledge itself is always subject to revision.

rationalism: the philosophical view that knowledge is acquired through reason, without the aid of the senses.

rationalism, continental: seventeenth-century philosophical movement begun by Descartes that emphasizes innate ideas and the use of deductive reasoning.

Rawls, John (b. 1921): contemporary American moral philosopher who, inspired by social contract theory, argued that just rules are those that all would agree upon in a hypothetical "original position."

realism: generally, the idea that our thinking is or should be constrained or limited by how things are independently of our thinking. Realism in epistemology and ethics thus assumes that knowledge, or correct moral belief, consists in getting in touch with objective realities of some kind. Constrasted with anti-realism and social constructionism.

reductionism: roughly, the notion that a given domain (of objects, concepts and so forth) can be reduced to some other domain. For example, in some views, nations can be "reduced to" individual citizens. That is, a nation is nothing more than a collection of individual citizens. A notion especially important in the sciences and the philosophy of mind.

reference: see *meaning*.

Reid, Thomas (1710–1796): Scottish philosopher of the common-sense tradition who defended free will and common-sense moral and metaphysical realism.

relativism: the view that there is no absolute truth that is independent of particular people or particular cultures at particular times and places.

reliabilism: the view, in epistemology, that what turns a true belief into knowledge is that the belief was produced by some reliable belief forming mechanism, that is, one which always or usually does produce true beliefs. Reliabilism generally assumes an externalist view, since the reliable belief forming mechanism does not need to be known to the knower in question. See *externalism*.

rights theory: a moral theory arising out of the natural law tradition according to which we have basic rights that are not creations of governments, including natural, human, and moral rights.

rule utilitarianism: a version of utilitarianism that advocates acting according to rules insofar as the adoption of such rules benefits the greater good; this is in contrast with act utilitarianism.

Russell, Bertrand (1872–1970): British philosopher in the linguistic and analytical tradition who argued that mystical religious states are delusional and untrustworthy.

scientific method: formalized procedures by which we gain scientific knowledge; proposed accounts can be found in Bacon, Descartes, Newton, and other early scientists.

Scientific Revolution: intellectual movement started in the renaissance, which rejected Aristotle and emphasized experimental scientific methods.

semantics: the study of meaning. Words have shapes when written and sounds when spoken, but they also have meaning. The notion of meaning is surprisingly difficult and may seem mysterious. Philosophers have been working on semantics for thousands of years.

Sextus Empiricus (fl. 200 CE): Greek philosopher of the Pyrrhonian skeptical tradition who offered ten modes of skepticism.

skepticism: philosophical position that questions the ability to attain various kinds of knowledge.

Skepticism, ancient Greek: school of thought in ancient Greece founded by Pyrrho.

social constructionism: the idea that knowledge is constructed in the service of ideologies and prejudices of various kinds. A species of anti-realism. Opposed to realism.

social contract theory: the moral theory first developed by Thomas Hobbes. In order to preserve our lives, we mutually agree or contract to set aside our hostilities and live in peace.

sociobiology: the theory that human social behavior emerged through natural selection.

Socrates (469–399 BCE): ancient Greek moral philosopher and teacher of Plato, famous for his profession of ignorance, his irony, his moral earnestness, and his dialectical method of questioning people.

solipsism: the idea that it is impossible to know anything other than the contents of one's own mind. One cannot know that other people, or an external world generally, exist.

state of nature: a pre-political environment described by Hobbes and other social contract theorists, which fosters conflicts and thus inclines us to form a contract to live in peace.

substance: in Aristotle, a thing that exists on its own, not simply as part of another thing. The term is also used to refer to a substrate, the underlying stuff of a thing.

Tao Te Ching: literally, "The Way and Its Power"; oldest and most important text in Taoism, which emphasizes living according to the Tao, the virtuous power (*te*) we attain from the Tao, the return of everything to Tao, and the principles of non-action, non-mind.

Taoism: Chinese movement originating in the warring states period that advocates following the Tao and living in harmony with nature; "Philosophical Taoism" and "Religious Taoism" are its two principal approaches.

teleology: an explanation of some event or thing in terms of goals or purposes or aims or functions.

universals: general terms that apply to more than one thing, such as "dog" or "black."

Upanishads: 108 philosophical texts of Brahmanic Hinduism composed between 800 BCE and 500 BCE which emphasize the notion of the Atman-Brahman.

utilitarian calculus: a notion associated with Bentham's utilitarianism that we can quantitatively calculate units of pleasure that result from our actions.

utilitarianism: the ethical theory associated with John Stuart Mill that morally right actions are those that promote or tend to produce the best overall consequences.

valid deductive argument: an argument in which, if the premises are true, the conclusion must be true. The conclusion is proved by the premises.

veil of ignorance: a notion in John Rawls's moral theory according to which we become ignorant of our social status while devising rules of justice in the original position.

verificationism: the idea that the meaning of a sentence is given by its method of verification. Anticipated in Hume's notion that a belief or idea that cannot be traced back to experience is meaningless.

virtue theory: moral theory that focuses on the development of good character traits, or virtues, rather than on rules for solving moral dilemmas.

Wittgenstein, Ludwig (1889–1951): Austrian philosopher who argued that meaning is grounded in language games or social practice, rather than in some kind of mental state.

Wollstonecraft, Mary (1759–1797): British philosopher whose *Vindication of the Rights of Woman* (1792) presents the view that morality is a function of reason, to which women as well as men have access, provided they receive equal educations.

yoga: Hindu meditative practices; the formal school of Yoga developed in the middle ages contains seven subschools: Jnana Yoga (knowledge), Karma Yoga (action), Bhakti Yoga (devotion), Mantra Yoga (sounds), Laya Yoga (dissolution), Hatha Yoga (postures, breathing), and Raja Yoga (meditation).

WORKS CITED

Below is a list of works cited in their order of their appearance throughout this book. Information is also provided for easily accessible editions of these works, which may not necessarily be the ones used by the authors.

CHAPTER 1. INTRODUCING THE BOOK

Matthews, Gareth, *Dialogues with Children* (Cambridge, MA: Harvard University Press, 1984).

CHAPTER 2. THE PHILOSOPHY OF RELIGION

Tari, Mel, *Like a Mighty Wind* (Carol Stream, IL: Creation House, 1971).

Hume, David, *An Enquiry Concerning Human Understanding* (1748). The standard edition by Tom L. Beauchamp (Oxford: Clarendon Press, 2000).

Briggs, John, *The Nature of Religious Zeal* (London: T. Payne, 1775).

Marx, Karl, *Toward a Critique of Hegel's Philosophy of Right* (1843). A recent translation is in Karl Marx, *Early Writings,* L. Colletti, ed. (Harmondsworth: Penguin, 1975).

Marx, Karl, *Economic and Philosophical Manuscripts* (1844). A recent translation is by Martin Mulligan (Moscow: Progress Publishers, 1959).

Nietzsche, Friedrich, *The Joyful Wisdom* (1882). A recent translation is by Walter Kaufmann, *The Gay Science* (New York: Vintage, 1974).

Dostoevsky, Fyodor, *The Brothers Karamazov* (1879). A recent translation is by C. Garnett (New York: Modern Library, 1950).

Mackie, John L., "Evil and Omnipotence," *Mind* (1955), Vol. 64, pp. 200–212. Reprinted by permission of Oxford University Press.

Rowe, William L., *Philosophy of Religion,* third edition (Belmont, CA: Wadsworth Publishing Company, 2001).

Hick, John, "An Irenaean Theodicy," in *Encountering Evil: Live Options in Theodicy*, Stephen Davis, ed. (Edinburgh: T. & T. Clark, 1981), pp. 39–52.

Al-Ghazali, *The Deliverer from Evil* (1108). A recent translation is by R. J. McCarthy, *Freedom and Fulfillment* (Boston: Twayne, 1980).

Tennyson, Alfred Lord, *Alfred Lord Tennyson: A Memoir* (London: Macmillan, 1897).

Bhagavad Gita. A recent translation is by Juan Mascaró (London: Penguin, 1962).

Patanjali, *Yoga Sutra*. A recent translation is in S. Radhakrishnan and C. A. Moore, *A Sourcebook of Indian Philosophy* (Princeton, NJ: Princeton University Press, 1957).

James, William, *The Varieties of Religious Experience* (1902). A critical edition of this work is edited by John E. Smith (Cambridge, MA: Harvard University Press, 1985).

Russell, Bertrand, *Religion and Science* (London: Oxford University Press, 1935). Reprinted by permission of Oxford University Press.

Broad, C. D., *Religion, Philosophy and Psychical Research* (London: Routledge & Kegan Paul, 1953).

Swinburne, Richard, *The Existence of God* (New York: Oxford University Press, 1979). Reprinted by permission of Oxford University Press.

Adams, Douglas, *The Hitchhiker's Guide to the Galaxy* (New York: Harmony Books, 1979).

Anselm, *Prosologian* (1077). A recent translation is by J. Hopkins, *A New Interpretive Translation of St. Anselm's Monologion and Proslogion* (Minneapolis: Banning, 1986).

Gaunilo, *On Behalf of the Fool*. Included in Hopkins's *A New Interpretative Translation of St. Anselm's Monologion and Proslogion* (as above).

Anselm, "Reply to Gaunilo." Included in Hopkins's *A New Interpretative Translation of St. Anselm's Monologion and Proslogion* (as above).

Aquinas, Thomas, *Summa Theologica* (1266). A recent translation is the 23-volume *Summa Theologiae: Latin Text and Translation* (Blackfriars; New York, McGraw-Hill, 1963).

Kant, Immanuel, *The Critique of Pure Reason* (1781). A recent translation is by P. Gruyer and A. W. Wood (Cambridge: Cambridge University Press, 1998).

Aquinas, Thomas, *Summa Theologica* (1266), as above.

Clarke, Samuel, *A Demonstration of the Being and Attributes of God* (1705), included in *The Works of Samuel Clarke* (London: John & Paul Knapton, 1738).

Hume, David, *Dialogues Concerning Natural Religion* (1779). A good edition is by Norman Kemp Smith, ed. (Oxford: Clarendon Press, 1935).

Aquinas, Thomas, *Summa Theologica* (1266), as above.

Hume, David, *Dialogues Concerning Natural Religion* (1779), as above.

Paley, William, *Natural Theology* (1802). A recent abridged edition of this is *Natural Theology; Selections* (Indianapolis: Bobbs-Merrill, 1963).

Darwin, Charles, *Life and Letters of Charles Darwin* (London: John Murray, 1887).

Darwin, Charles, *Variation of Animals and Plants under Domestication* (London: John Murray, 1868).

Collins, Robin, "The Fine-Tuning Design Argument: A Scientific Argument for the Existence of God." In *Reason for the Hope Within*. Michael Murray, ed. (Grand Rapids, MI: Eerdmans, 1999).

Pascal, Blaise, *Thoughts* (1670). A recent edition of this is *Pascal's Pensées*, translated by A. J. Krailsheimer (Harmondsworth: Penguin Books, 1966).

James, William, *The Will to Believe* (1897). A critical edition of this work is edited by Frederick Burkhardt (Cambridge, MA: Harvard University Press, 1979).

Oswald, James, *An Appeal to Common Sense in Behalf of Religion* (1766). A recent edition of this is in Volume 1 of *Scottish Common Sense Philosophy*, James Fieser, ed. (Bristol: Thoemmes Press, 2000).

Plantinga, Alvin, "Is Belief in God Properly Basic," *Nous* (1981), Vol. 15, pp. 41–51.

Van Hook, Jay, "Knowledge, Belief, and Reformed Epistemology," *The Reformed Journal* (1981), pp. 12–17.

CHAPTER 3. HUMAN NATURE AND THE SELF

Thiry, Paul Henri, Baron d'Holbach, *System of Nature* (1770). A recent translation is by Henry D. Robinson (Manchester: Clinamen Press, 2000).

Hume, David, *An Enquiry Concerning Human Understanding* (1748). The standard edition is edited by Tom L. Beauchamp (Oxford: Clarendon Press, 2000).

Reid, Thomas, *Essays on the Active Powers of the Human Mind* (1788). Included in *The Works of Thomas Reid* (Bristol: Thoemmes Press, 1994).

Taylor, Richard, *Metaphysics* (Englewood Cliffs, NJ, Prentice-Hall, 1963). Reprinted by permission of Pearson Education, Inc., Upper Saddle River, NJ.

Questions of King Milinda (c. 100 CE). A recent translation is by I. B. Horner (Oxford: Pali Text Society, 1990).

Frankfurt, Harry, "Freedom of the Will and the Concept of a Person, *The Journal of Philosophy* (1971), Vol. LXVII, p. 1. Reprinted by permission.

Hume, David, *Treatise of Human Nature* (1739–1740). The standard edition is by David Fate Norton, Mary J. Norton (Oxford: Clarendon Press, 2000).

Penelhum, Terence, *Religion and Rationality* (New York, Random House, 1971). Reprinted by permission of the publisher.

Kierkegaard, Søren, *The Sickness Unto Death* (1849). A recent translation is by H. V. Hong and E. H. Hong, *The Sickness Unto Death* (Princeton, NJ: Princeton University Press, 1980).

Marx, Karl, *Economic and Philosophical Manuscripts* (1844). A recent translation is by Martin Mulligan (Progress Publishers, Moscow: Progress Publishers, 1959).

Nietzsche, Friedrich, *The Joyful Wisdom* (1882). A recent translation is by Walter Kaufmann, *The Gay Science* (New York: Vintage, 1974).

Nietzsche, Friedrich, *Thus Spake Zarathustra* (1883–1885). A recent translation is by Walter Kaufmann in *The Portable Nietzsche* (New York: Viking, 1954).

Martin Heidegger, *Being and Time* (1927). A standard translation is by John MacQuarrie and Edward Robinson (New York: Harper and Row, 1962). Reprinted by permission of HarperCollins.

Upanishads (c. fifth century BCE). A recent translation is by P. Olivelle (Oxford: Oxford University Press, 1996).

Chuang-tzu, *Chuang-tzu* (fourth century BCE). A recent translation is by Burton Watson, *The Complete Works of Chuang-tzu* (New York: Columbia University Press, 1968).

Naess, Arne, "Self Realization: An Ecological Approach to Being in the World" *Trumpeter* 4 (1987). Reprinted by permission of the Trumpeter.

Darwin, Charles, *The Descent of Man* (1871). A recent reprint edition is *The Descent of Man* (Buffalo: Prometheus Books, 1997).

CHAPTER 4. SOULS, MINDS, BODIES, AND MACHINES

Democritus, fragments (fifth century BCE). Fragments translated by Jonathan Barnes in *Early Greek Philosophy* (Harmondsworth: Penguin, 1987).

Lucretius, *On the Nature of Things* (c. 55 BCE). A recent translation is by J. Godwin (London: Penguin, 1994).

Plato, *Phaedo* (fourth century BCE). A recent edition is by C. J. Rowe (Cambridge: Cambridge University Press, 1995).

Plato, *Phaedus* (fourth century BCE). A recent translation is by A. Nehamas and P. Woodruff (Indianapolis, IN: Hackett Publishing, 1995).

Aristotle, *On the Soul* (fourth century BCE). A recent translation is included in Jonathan Barnes, ed., *The Complete Works of Aristotle* (Princeton, NJ: Princeton University Press, 1984).

Descartes, René, *Meditations* (1641). A recent translation by J. Cottingham is in *The Philosophical Writings of Descartes* (Cambridge: Cambridge University Press, 1984).

Descartes, René, *The Passions of the Soul* (1649). A recent translation by J. Cottingham is in *The Philosophical Writings of Descartes* (Cambridge: Cambridge University Press, 1984).

Conway, Anne, *Principles of the Most Ancient and Modern Philosophy* (1690). A recent translation from the original Latin edition is by A. Condert and T. Corse (Cambridge: Cambridge University Press, 1996).

Upanishads (c. fifth century CE). A recent translation is by P. Olivelle (Oxford: Oxford University Press, 1996).

Sankara, *Commentary on the Vedanta Sutra* (eighth century CE). A recent translation is by Swami Gambhirananda (Calcutta: Advaita Ashrama, 1965).

Ramanuja, *Commentary on the Vedanta Sutra* (eleventh century CE). A recent translation is by S. S. Raghavachar (Mysore: Sri Ramakrishna Ashram, 1968).

Spinoza, Benedict, *Ethics* (1677). A recent translation is by Edwin Curley (Princeton, NJ: Princeton University Press, 1985).

Leibniz, Gottfried Willhelm, *Monadology* (1721). A recent translation is by R. Ariew and D. Garber in *Leibniz: Philosophical Essays* (Indianapolis: Hackett Publishing Company, 1989).

Ryle, Gilbert, *The Concept of Mind* (London: Hutchinson 1949).

Smart, J. J. C., "Sensations and Brain Processes," *Philosophical Review* (1958), Vol. 68, pp. 141–156.

Churchland, Paul, *Matter and Consciousness* (Cambridge, MA: The MIT Press, 1988).

Fodor, Jerry, *Psychological Explanation* (New York: Random House, 1968). Reprinted by permission of the publisher.

Brentano, Franz, *Psychology from an Empirical Standpoint* (1874). A recent translation is by A. C. Rancurello (London, Routledge, 1969).

Dennett, Daniel, "Three Kinds of Intentional Psychology," in *Reduction, Time, and Reality,* Richard Healey ed. (New York: Cambridge University Press, 1981). Reprinted by permission of the publisher.

Huxley, Thomas, *Methods and Results: Essays* (London: Macmillan, 1893).

Wittgenstein, Ludwig, *Philosophical Investigations* (1953). The standard translation is by G. E. M. Anscombe, Oxford: Blackwell (1953).

Ziff, Paul, "The Feelings of Robots," *Analysis* (1959), Vol. 19, pp. 64–68.

Searle, John, "Minds, Brains and Programs" *The Behavioral and Brain Sciences* (1980), Vol. 3, pp. 417–424. Reprinted by permission of Cambridge University Press.

Lycan, William G., "The Functionalist Reply," *Behavioral and Brain Sciences* (1980), Vol. 3, pp. 434–435. Reprinted by permission of Cambridge University Press.

Haugeland, John, "Understanding Natural Languages," *The Journal of Philosophy* (1979), Vol. 76, pp. 619–632. Reprinted by permission.

CHAPTER 5. EPISTEMOLOGY

Sextus Empiricus, *Outlines of Pyrrhonism* (c. 200 CE). A recent translation is by J. Annas and J. Barnes (Cambridge: Cambridge University Press, 1994).

Descartes, René, *Meditations on the First Philosophy* (1641). A recent translation by J. Cottingham is in *The Philosophical Writings of Descartes* (Cambridge: Cambridge University Press, 1984).

Hume, David, *Treatise of Human Nature* (1739–1740). The standard edition is by David Fate Norton, Mary J. Norton (Oxford: Clarendon Press, 2000).

Hume, David, *An Enquiry Concerning Human Understanding* (1748). The standard edition is edited by Tom L. Beauchamp (Oxford: Clarendon Press, 2000).

Strawson, Peter, *Introduction to Logical Theory* (New York: John Wiley and Sons, 1952).

Plato, *Phaedo* (fourth century BCE). A recent edition is by C. J. Rowe (Cambridge: Cambridge University Press).

Locke, John, *Essay Concerning Human Understanding* (1689). The standard edition is by P. H. Nidditch (Oxford: Oxford University Press, 1975).

Searle, John, *Intentionality* (Cambridge: Cambridge University Press, 1983). Reprinted by permission of Cambridge University Press.

Hume, David, *An Enquiry Concerning Human Understanding* (1748). As above.

Kant, Immanuel, *Prolegomena to Any Future Metaphysics* (1783). A recent translation is by G. Hatfield (Cambridge: Cambridge University Press, 1997).

Quine, Willard Van Orman, "Two Dogmas of Empiricism" (1951). A revised version is in Quine's *From a Logical Point of View* (Cambridge: Harvard University Press, 1961). Reprinted by permission from *Philosophical Review* 60 (1951).

Descartes, René, *Meditations on the First Philosophy* (1641). As above.

Dancy, Jonathan, *Introduction to Contemporary Epistemology* (Oxford: Blackwell, 1985). Reprinted by permission.

Sosa, Ernst. "The Raft and the Pyramid: Coherence Versus Foundations in the Theory of Knowledge." *Midwest Studies in Philosophy,* Vol. 5: *Studies in Epistemology* (Minneapolis: University of Minnesota Press, 1980), pp. 3–25.

Gettier, Edmund, "Is Justified True Belief Knowledge?" *Analysis* (1963), Vol. 23, pp. 121–123.

Plantinga, Alvin. "Justification in the 20th Century," *Philosophy and Phenomenological Research* (1990), Vol. 50: Supplement, pp. 45–71. Reprinted by permission of the publisher.

Lehrer, Keith, *Theory of Knowledge* (Boulder: Westview Press, 1990). Reprinted by permission of Westview Press, a member of Perseus Books, L.L.C.

Zagzebski, Linda, *Virtues of the Mind* (New York: Cambridge University Press, 1996). Reprinted with the permission of Cambridge University Press.

Kuhn, Thomas, *The Structure of Scientific Revolutions* (Chicago: University of Chicago Press, 1962).

Code, Lorraine, *What Can She Know: Feminist Theory and the Construction of Knowledge* (Ithaca, NY: Cornell University Press, 1991). Used by permission of the publisher, Cornell University Press.

Sokal, Alan, "Transgressing the Boundaries: "*Philosophy and Literature* (1996), Vol. 20, pp. 338–346. Reprinted by permission of the publisher.

CHAPTER 6. ETHICS

Plato, *The Republic* (fourth century BCE). A recent translation is by G. M. A. Grube, revised by C. D. C. Reeve (Indianapolis: Hackett Publishing Company, 1992).

Sextus Empiricus, *Outlines of Pyrrhonism* (c. 200 CE). A recent translation is by J. Annas and J. Barnes, *Outlines of Scepticism* (Cambridge: Cambridge University Press, 1994).

Montaigne, Michel, *Essays* (1580). A recent translation, by D. M. Frame, is included in *The Complete Works of Montaigne* (Stanford, CA: Stanford University Press, 1957).

Mackie, John L., *Ethics: Inventing Right and Wrong* (New York: Penguin Books, 1977).

Rachels, James, *Elements of Moral Philosophy,* third edition (New York: McGraw-Hill, 1999). Reprinted by permission of the publisher.

Mencius, *The Mencius* (fourth century BCE). A recent translation is by D. C. Lau (New York: Penguin Books, 1970).

Hsun-tzu, *The Hsun-tzu* (third century BCE). A recent translation is by J. Knoblock, *Xunzi: A Translation and Study of the Complete Works* (Stanford, CA: Stanford University Press, 1988–1994).

Hobbes, Thomas, *Citizen* (1642). A recent translation is by Richard Tuck, Michael Silverthorne (Cambridge: Cambridge University Press, 1998).

Hobbes, Thomas, *Leviathan* (1651). A recent edition is by Edwin Curly (Indianapolis: Hackett Publishing Company, 1994).

Hobbes, Thomas, *Human Nature* (1650). Included in *The Elements of Law Natural and Politic,* F. Tonnies, ed. (London: Simpkin & Marshall, 1889).

Butler, Joseph, *Fifteen Sermons* (1726). A recent edition of the central sermons is *Five Sermons* (Indianapolis: Hackett Publishing Company, 1983).

Wilson, Edward O., *Sociobiology. The New Synthesis* (Cambridge, MA: Harvard University Press, 1975).

Wilson, Edward O., *On Human Nature* (Cambridge, MA: Harvard University Press, 1978).

Hume, David, *An Enquiry Concerning the Principles of Morals* (1751). The standard edition is by Tom L. Beauchamp (Oxford: Clarendon Press, 1998).

Hume, David, *Treatise of Human Nature* (1739–1740). The standard edition is by David Fate Norton, Mary J. Norton (Oxford: Clarendon Press, 2000).

Searle, John, "How to Derive Ought from Is," *Philosophical Review* (1964), Vol. 73, pp. 43–58.

Ayer, Alfred Jules, *Language, Truth and Logic* (1936). A recent edition is *Language, Truth and Logic* (New York: Dover Publications, 1952).

Baier, Kurt, *The Moral Point of View* (Ithaca, NY: Cornell University Press, 1958).

Conner, Michael G., "Understanding the Difference Between Men and Women," 1999, www.oregoncounseling.org

Wollstonecraft, Mary, *A Vindication of the Rights of Women* (1792). The standard edition is by J. Todd and M. Butler (London: William Pickering, 1989).

Gilligan, Carol, *In a Different Voice* (Cambridge, MA: Harvard University Press, 1982). Reprinted by permission of the publisher.

Kohlberg, Lawrence, *Essays on Moral Development,* New York: Harper & Row, 1981).

Aristotle, *Nichomachean Ethics.* A recent translation is by Terence Irwin (Indianapolis: Hackett Publishing Company, 2000).

MacIntyre, Alasdair, *After Virtue* (1981). A second revised edition is (Notre Dame: Notre Dame University Press, 1984). Used by permission of the publisher.

Pufendorf, Samuel, *The Duty of Man and Citizen* (1673). A recent translation is by Michael Silverthorne (Cambridge: Cambridge University Press, 1991).

Kant, Immanuel, *Groundwork of the Metaphysics of Morals* (1785). A recent translation is by Mary Gregor (Cambridge: Cambridge University Press, 1998).

Ross, William David, *The Right and the Good* (Oxford: Clarendon Press, 1930). Reprinted by permission of the publisher.

Kant, Immanuel, "Duties Towards Animals" in *Lectures on Ethics* (1775–1794). A recent translation is by Peter Heath (Cambridge: Cambridge University Press, 1997).

Regan, Tom, "The Case for Animal Rights" in *In Defense of Animals,* Peter Singer, ed. (Oxford: Basil Blackwell, 1985), pp. 13–26.

Epicurus, *Letter to Menoecius,* included in Diogenes Laertius's *Lives of the Philosophers.* A recent translation of this is R. D. Hicks and H. S. Long (Cambridge, MA: Harvard University Press, 1972).

Bentham, Jeremy, *Principles of Morals and Legislation* (1789). The standard edition is by J. H. Burns (Oxford: Clarendon Press, 1996).

Mill, John Stuart, *Utilitarianism* (1861). The standard edition is included in J. M. Robson, ed., *Essays on Ethics, Religion and Society* (Toronto: University of Toronto Press, 1969).

CHAPTER 7. POLITICAL PHILOSOPHY

Chuang-tzu, *The Chuan-tzu* (fourth century BCE). A recent translation is by Burton Watson, *The Complete Works of Chuang-tzu* (New York: Columbia University Press, 1968).

Malatesta, Errico, *Anarchy* (1891). A recent translation is by Vernon Richards (London: Freedom Press, 1974).

Wolff, Robert Paul, *In Defense of Anarchism* (New York: Harper Torchbooks, 1970).

Pufendorf, Samuel, *The Duty of Man and Citizen* (1673). A recent translation is by Michael Silverthorne (Cambridge: Cambridge University Press, 1991).

Hobbes, Thomas, *Leviathan* (1651). A recent edition is by Edwin Curly (Indianapolis, IN: Hackett Publishing Company, 1994).

Locke, John, *Two Treatises of Government* (1689–1690). The standard edition of this work is by Peter Laslett (Cambridge: Cambridge University Press, 1967).

Rawls, John, *A Theory of Justice* (Cambridge, MA: Harvard University Press, 1971). Reprinted by permission of the publisher.

Nozick, Robert, *Anarchy, State, and Utopia* (Oxford: Blackwell, 1974). Reprinted by permission.

MacIntyre, Alasdair, *After Virtue* (1981). A second revised edition is *After Virtue* (Notre Dame, IN: Notre Dame University Press, 1984).

Sandel, Michael J., *Liberalism and the Limits of Justice* (Cambridge: Cambridge University Press, 1982).

Confucius, *Analects* (fifth century BCE). A recent translation is by D. C. Lau (Hong Kong: Chinese University Press, 1992).

Confucius, The Great Learning (third century BCE). A recent translation is in Wing-tsit Chan's *A Source Book in Chinese Philosophy* (Princeton, NJ: Princeton University Press. 1963).

Plato, *Republic* (fourth century BCE). A recent translation is by G. M. A. Grube, revised by C. D. C. Reeve (Indianapolis, IN: Hackett Publishing Company, 1992).

Machiavelli, Niccolò, *The Prince* (1532). A recent translation of this is by L. Ricci (New York: Modern Library, 1950).

Beccaria, Cesare, *On Crimes and Punishments* (1764). A recent translation is by Richard Bellamy (Cambridge: Cambridge University Press, 1995).

Mill, John Stuart, *On Liberty* (1859). The standard edition is included in J. M. Robson, ed., *Essays on Ethics, Religion and Society* (Toronto: University of Toronto Press, 1969).

Feinberg, Joel, *Offense to Others* (New York: Oxford University Press, 1985). Used by permission of Oxford University Press, Inc.

Plato, *Crito* (fourth century BCE). A recent translation is by G. M. A. Grube and John M. Cooper (Indianapolis: Hackett Publishing Company, 2000).

King, Martin Luther, "Letter from Birmingham Jail" (1963). This letter is included in many recent anthologies.

Locke, John, *Two Treatises of Government* (1689–1690). As above.

ILLUSTRATION ACKNOWLEDGMENTS

Portraits of classic philosophers appear courtesy of Thoemmes/Continuum Press.
Photographs of Robin Collins, Alvin Plantinga, and John Searle appear courtesy of those authors.
Cartoons appear courtesy of Steven Campbell.
Chapter 3: Buddha head detail. Photo: Jeremy Hoarc/Life File/Getty Images.
Chapter 3: Taoist temple. Photo: Flora Torrance/Life File/Getty Images.
Chapter 7: Statue of Confucius. Photo: Jack Hollingsworth/Getty Images.

INDEX